INTERACTIVE COMPUTER GRAPHICS

A TOP-DOWN APPROACH WITH SHADER-BASED OPENGL®

6th Edition

INTERACTIVE COMPUTER GRAPHICS
A TOP-DOWN APPROACH WITH SHADER-BASED OPENGL®

6th Edition

EDWARD ANGEL

University of New Mexico

•

DAVE SHREINER

ARM, Inc.

International Edition contributions by

SOUMEN MUKHERJEE

RCC Institute of Information Technology

•

ARUP KUMAR BHATTACHARJEE

RCC Institute of Information Technology

Boston   Columbus   Indianapolis   New York   San Francisco   Upper Saddle River
Amsterdam   Cape Town   Dubai   London   Madrid   Milan   Munich   Paris   Montreal   Toronto
Delhi   Mexico City   Sao Paulo   Sydney   Hong Kong   Seoul   Singapore   Taipei   Tokyo

Editorial Director: Marcia Horton
Editor-in-Chief: Michael Hirsch
Acquisitions Editor: Matt Goldstein
Editorial Assistant: Chelsea Bell
Vice President, Marketing: Patrice Jones
Marketing Manager: Yezan Alayan
Marketing Coordinator: Kathryn Ferranti
Vice President, Production: Vince O'Brien
Managing Editor: Jeff Holcomb
Senior Production Project Manager: Marilyn Lloyd
Publisher, International Edition: Angshuman Chakraborty
Acquisitions Editor, International Edition: Arunabha Deb
Publishing Assistant, International Edition: Shokhi Shah
Senior Operations Supervisor: Alan Fischer
Operations Specialist: Lisa McDowell
Text Designer: Beth Paquin
Cover Designer: Central Covers
Cover Art: Hue Walker, Fulldome Project, University of New Mexico
Media Editor: Daniel Sandin
Media Project Manager: Wanda Rockwell
Full-Service Project Management: Coventry Composition
Cover and Insert Printer: Lehigh-Phoenix Color

Pearson Education Limited
Edinburgh Gate
Harlow
Essex CM20 2JE
England

and Associated Companies throughout the world

Visit us on the World Wide Web at: www.pearsoninternationaleditions.com

© Pearson Education Limited 2012

ISBN 10: 0-273-75226-X
ISBN 13: 978-0-273-75226-4

British Library Cataloguing-in-Publication Data
A catalogue record for this book is available from the British Library

10 9 8 7 6 5 4 3 2 1

Typeset in Minion by Coventry Composition, using ZzTEX
Printed and bound by Edwards Brothers in The United States of America

The publisher's policy is to use paper manufactured from sustainable forests.

CONTENTS

PREFACE

NEW TO THE SIXTH EDITION

- Use of modern Shader-Based OpenGL throughout

- No use of OpenGL functions deprecated with OpenGL 3.1

- Increased detail on implementing transformations and viewing in both application code and shaders

- Consistency with OpenGL ES 2.0 and WebGL

- Use of C++ instead of C

- Addition of vector and matrix classes to create application code compatible with the OpenGL Shading Language (GLSL)

- Discussion of per-vertex and per-fragment lighting

- Addition of polygon and Delaunay triangularization

- Introduction to volume rendering

- All code examples redone to be compatible with OpenGL 3.1

- New co-author, Dave Shreiner, author of the *OpenGL Programming Guide*

This book is an introduction to computer graphics, with an emphasis on applications programming. The first edition, which was published in 1997, was somewhat revolutionary in using a standard graphics library and a top-down approach. Over the succeeding 13 years and five editions, this approach has been adopted by most introductory classes in computer graphics and by virtually all the competing textbooks.

The major changes in graphics hardware over the past few years have led to major changes in graphics software. For its first fifteen years, new OpenGL versions were released with new versions always guaranteeing backward compatibility. The ability to reuse code as the underlying software was upgraded was an important virtue, both for developers of applications and for instructors of graphics classes. OpenGL 3.0 announced major changes, one of the key ones being that, starting with OpenGL 3.1, many of the most common functions would be deprecated. This radical departure from previous versions reflects changes needed to make use of the capabilities of the latest programmable graphics units (GPUs). These changes are also part of OpenGL ES 2.0, which is being used to develop applications on mobile devices such as cell phones and tablets, and WebGL, which is supported on most of the latest browsers.

As the authors of the previous five editions of this textbook (EA) and of the *OpenGL Programming Guide* and *OpenGL ES 2.0 Programming Guide* (DS), we were confronted with a dilemma as to how to react to these changes. We had been writing books and teaching introductory OpenGL courses at SIGGRAPH for many years. We found that almost no one in the academic community, or application programmers outside the high-end game world, knew about these changes, and those of our colleagues who did know about them did not think we could teach these concepts at the beginning level. That was a challenge we couldn't resist. We started by teaching a half-day short course at SIGGRAPH, which convinced us that we could teach someone without previous graphics programming experience how to write a nontrivial shader-based OpenGL application program with just a little more work than with earlier versions of OpenGL.

As we developed this edition, we discovered some other reasons that convinced us that this approach is not only possible but even better for students learning computer graphics. Only a short while ago, we touted the advantages OpenGL gave us by being available for Windows, Linux, and Mac OS X so we could teach a course in which students could work in the environment they preferred. With OpenGL ES and WebGL they can now develop applications for their cell phones or Web browsers. We believe that this will excite both students and instructors about computer graphics and open up many new educational and commercial opportunities.

We feel that of even greater importance to the learning experience is the removal of most defaults and the fixed function pipeline in these new versions of OpenGL. At first glance, this removal may seem like it would make teaching a first course much harder. Maybe a little harder; but we contend much better. The tendency of most students was to rely on these functions and not pay too much attention to what the textbook and instructor were trying to teach them. Why bother when they could use built-in functions that did perspective viewing or lighting? Now that those functions are gone and students have to write their own shaders to do these jobs, they have to start by understanding the underlying principles and mathematics.

A Top-Down Approach

These recent advances and the success of the first five editions continue to reinforce our belief in a top-down, programming-oriented approach to introductory computer graphics. Although many computer science and engineering departments now support more than one course in computer graphics, most students will take only a single course. Such a course is placed in the curriculum after students have already studied programming, data structures, algorithms, software engineering, and basic mathematics. A class in computer graphics allows the instructor to build on these topics in a way that can be both informative and fun. We want these students to be programming three-dimensional applications as soon as possible. Low-level algorithms, such as those that draw lines or fill polygons, can be dealt with later, after students are creating graphics.

John Kemeny, a pioneer in computer education, used a familiar automobile analogy: You don't have to know what's under the hood to be literate, but unless you know how to program, you'll be sitting in the back seat instead of driving. That same analogy applies to the way we teach computer graphics. One approach—the algorithmic approach—is to teach everything about what makes a car function: the engine, the transmission, the combustion process. A second approach—the survey approach—is to hire a chauffeur, sit back, and see the world as a spectator. The third approach—the programming approach that we have adopted here—is to teach you how to drive and how to take yourself wherever you want to go. As the old auto-rental commercial used to say, "Let us put *you* in the driver's seat."

Programming with OpenGL and C++

When Ed began teaching computer graphics over 25 years ago, the greatest impediment to implementing a programming-oriented course, and to writing a textbook for that course, was the lack of a widely accepted graphics library or application programmer's interface (API). Difficulties included high cost, limited availability, lack of generality, and high complexity. The development of OpenGL resolved most of the difficulties many of us had experienced with other APIs (such as GKS and PHIGS) and with the alternative of using home-brewed software. OpenGL today is supported on all platforms. It is bundled with Microsoft Windows and Mac OS X. Drivers are available for virtually all graphics cards. There is also an OpenGL API called Mesa that is included with most Linux distributions.

A graphics class teaches far more than the use of a particular API, but a good API makes it easier to teach key graphics topics, including three-dimensional graphics, lighting and shading, client–server graphics, modeling, and implementation algorithms. We believe that OpenGL's extensive capabilities and well-defined architecture lead to a stronger foundation for teaching both theoretical and practical aspects of the field and for teaching advanced concepts, including texture mapping, compositing, and programmable shaders.

Ed switched his classes to OpenGL about 15 years ago, and the results astounded him. By the middle of the semester, *every* student was able to write a moderately complex three-dimensional program that required understanding of three-dimensional viewing and event-driven input. In previous years of teaching computer graphics, he had never come even close to this result. That class led to the first edition of this book.

This book is a textbook on computer graphics; it is not an OpenGL manual. Consequently, it does not cover all aspects of the OpenGL API but rather explains only what is necessary for mastering this book's contents. It presents OpenGL at a level that should permit users of other APIs to have little difficulty with the material.

Unlike previous editions, this one uses C++ rather than C as the dominant programming language. The reason has to do with the OpenGL Shading Language (GLSL) used to write shaders, the programs that control the GPU. GLSL is a C-like language with atomic data types that include vectors and matrices, and overloaded basic operators to manipulate them. All the modern versions of OpenGL require every application to provide two shaders; hence students need to use these features, which are supported in C++. By using just this part of C++ (simple classes, constructors, overloaded operators), we can implement fundamental graphics concepts, such as transformations and lighting, in either the application or in a shader with virtually identical code. In addition, using the simple matrix and vector classes that are provided on the book's Web site leads to much clearer, shorter code. Students who have started with Java or C should have little trouble with the code in the book.

Intended Audience

This book is suitable for advanced undergraduates and first-year graduate students in computer science and engineering and for students in other disciplines who have good programming skills. The book also will be useful to many professionals. Between us, we have taught well over 100 short courses for professionals; our experiences with these nontraditional students have had a great influence on what we have chosen to include in the book.

Prerequisites for the book are good programming skills in C++, Java, or C; an understanding of basic data structures (linked lists, trees); and a rudimentary knowledge of linear algebra and trigonometry. We have found that the mathematical backgrounds of computer science students, whether undergraduates or graduates, vary considerably. Hence, we have chosen to integrate into the text much of the linear algebra and geometry that is required for fundamental computer graphics.

Organization of the Book

The book is organized as follows. Chapter 1 provides an overview of the field and introduces image formation by optical devices; thus, we start with three-dimensional concepts immediately. Chapter 2 introduces programming using OpenGL. Although the first example program that we develop—each chapter has one or more complete programming examples—is two-dimensional, it is embedded in a three-dimensional setting and leads to a three-dimensional extension. We also introduce interactive graphics and develop event-driven graphics programs. Chapters 3 and 4 concentrate on three-dimensional concepts: Chapter 3 is concerned with defining and manipulating three-dimensional objects, whereas Chapter 4 is concerned with viewing them. Chapter 5 introduces light–material interactions and shading. These chapters should be covered in order and can be taught in about 10 weeks of a 15-week semester.

The next six chapters can be read in almost any order. All six are somewhat open ended and can be covered at a survey level, or individual topics can be pursued in depth. Chapter 6 surveys rasterization. It gives one or two major algorithms for each of the basic steps, including clipping, line generation, and polygon fill. Chapter 7 introduces many of the new discrete capabilities that are now supported in graphics hardware and by OpenGL. All these techniques involve working with various buffers. It concludes with a short discussion of aliasing problems in computer graphics. Chapters 6 and 7 conclude the discussion of the standard viewing pipeline used by all interactive graphics systems.

Chapter 8 contains a number of topics that fit loosely under the heading of hierarchical modeling. The topics range from building models that encapsulate the relationships between the parts of a model, to high-level approaches to graphics over the Internet. It includes an introduction to scene graphs and Open Scene Graph. Chapter 9 introduces a number of procedural methods, including particle systems, fractals, and procedural noise. Curves and surfaces, including subdivision surfaces, are discussed in Chapter 10. Chapter 11 surveys alternate approaches to rendering. It includes expanded discussions of ray tracing and radiosity, and an introduction to image-based rendering and parallel rendering.

Programs, primarily from the first part of the book, are included in Appendix A. They are also available online (see Support Materials). Appendices B and C contain a review of the background mathematics. Appendix D contains a synopsis of the OpenGL functions used in the book.

Changes from the Fifth Edition

The reaction of readers to the first five editions of this book was overwhelmingly positive, especially to the use of OpenGL and the top-down approach. Although each edition added material to keep up with what was going on in the field, the fifth edition made a major change by introducing programmable shaders and the OpenGL Shading Language. This material was somewhat optional because the existing versions of OpenGL were backward compatible. Most instructors chose to focus on the first six chapters and didn't get to programmable shaders.

As we pointed out at the beginning of this preface, with modern OpenGL, every application must provide shaders. Most of the basic functions from earlier versions, including those that specified geometry, transformations, and lighting parameters, have been deprecated. Consequently, programmable shaders and GLSL need to be introduced in Chapter 2. Many of the examples produce the same output as in previous editions but the code is very different.

We decided to incorporate the core material on interactivity in Chapter 2 and eliminate the separate chapter on input and interactivity. Thus, Chapter 2 became a little longer, but compared to previous editions, we feel that the added material on programmable shaders will only slightly delay the assignment of a first programming exercise.

Programmable shaders give the application programmer a choice of where to carry out most of the core graphics functionality. We have reorganized some of the material so as to be able to show the options together for a particular topic. For example, carrying out the lighting calculation in the application, in a vertex shader, and in a fragment shader are all in Chapter 5.

Given the positive feedback we've received on the core material from Chapters 1–6 in previous editions, we've tried to keep the changes to those chapters (now Chapters 1–5) to a minimum. We still see Chapters 1–5 as the core of any introductory course in computer graphics. Chapters 6–11 can be used in almost any order, either as a survey in a one-semester course or as the basis of a two-semester sequence.

Support Materials

The support for the book is on the Web, both through the author's Web site www.cs .unm.edu/~angel and www.pearsoninternationaleditions.com/angel. Support material that is available to all readers of this book includes

- Sources of information on OpenGL
- Instructions on how to get started with OpenGL on the most popular systems
- Additional material on writing more robust OpenGL applications
- Program code
- Solutions to selected exercises
- PowerPoint lectures
- Figures from the book

Additional support materials, including solutions to all the nonprogramming exercises, are available only to instructors adopting this textbook for classroom use at www.pearsoninternationaleditions.com/angel. Please contact your school's Addison-Wesley representative for information on obtaining access to this material.

Acknowledgments

Ed has been fortunate over the past few years to have worked with wonderful students at UNM. They were the first to get him interested in OpenGL, and he has learned much from them. They include Hue (Bumgarner-Kirby) Walker, Ye Cong, Pat Crossno, Tommie Daniel, Chris Davis, Lisa Desjarlais, Kim Edlund, Lee Ann Fisk, Maria Gallegos, Brian Jones, Christopher Jordan, Max Hazelrigg, Sheryl Hurley, Thomas Keller, Ge Li, Pat McCormick, Al McPherson, Ken Moreland, Martin Muller, David Munich, Jim Pinkerton, Jim Prewett, Dave Rogers, Hal Smyer, Takeshi Hakamata, Dave Vick, Brian Wylie, and Jin Xiong. Many of the examples in the color plates were created by these students.

The first edition of this book was written during Ed's sabbatical; various parts were written in five different countries. The task would not have been accomplished without the help of a number of people and institutions that made their facilities available to him. He is greatly indebted to Jonas Montilva and Chris Birkbeck of the Universidad de los Andes (Venezuela), to Rodrigo Gallegos and Aristides Novoa of the Universidad Tecnologica Equinoccial (Ecuador), to Long Wen Chang of the National Tsing Hua University (Taiwan), and to Kin Hong Wong and Pheng Ann Heng of the Chinese University of Hong Kong. Ramiro Jordan of ISTEC and the University of New Mexico made possible many of these visits. John Brayer and Jason Stewart at the University of New Mexico and Helen Goldstein at Addison-Wesley somehow managed to get a variety of items to him wherever he happened to be. His Web site contains a description of his adventures writing the first edition.

David Kirk and Mark Kilgard at NVIDIA were kind enough to provide cards for testing many of the algorithms. A number of other people provided significant help. He thanks Ben Bederson, Gonzalo Cartagenova, Tom Caudell, Kathi Collins, Kathleen Danielson, Roger Ehrich, Robert Geist, Chuck Hansen, Mark Henne, Bernard Moret, Dick Nordhaus, Helena Saona, Dave Shreiner, Vicki Shreiner, Gwen Sylvan, and Mason Woo. Mark Kilgard, Brian Paul, and Nate Robins are owed a great debt by the OpenGL community for creating software that enables OpenGL code to be developed over a variety of platforms.

At the University of New Mexico, the Art, Research, Technology, and Science Laboratory (ARTS Lab) and the Center for High Performance Computing have provided support for many of Ed's projects. The Computer Science Department, the Arts Technology Center in the College of Fine Arts, the National Science Foundation, Sandia National Laboratories, and Los Alamos National Laboratory have supported many of Ed's students and research projects that led to parts of this book. David Beining formerly with the Lodestar Astronomy Center and now at the ARTS Lab has provided tremendous support for the Fulldome Project. Sheryl Hurley, Christopher Jordan, Laurel Ladwig, Jon Strawn and Hue (Bumgarner-Kirby) Walker provided some of the images in the color plates through Fulldome projects. Hue Walker has done the wonderful covers for the previous three editions and her images are the basis of the cover for this edition.

Dave would like to first thank Ed for asking him to participate in this project. We've exchanged ideas on OpenGL and how to teach it for many years, and it's exciting to advance those concepts to new audiences. Dave would first like to thank his colleagues who worked at Silicon Graphics Computer Systems and who created OpenGL, and the OpenGL Working Group of the Khronos Group who continue to evolve the API. As Ed mentioned, SIGGRAPH has featured prominently in the development of these materials, and is definitely owed a debt of gratitude for providing access to enthusiastic test subjects for exploring our ideas.

Reviewers of the manuscript drafts provided a variety of viewpoints on what we should include and what level of presentation we should use. These reviewers for previous editions include Gur Saran Adhar (University of North Carolina at Wilmington), Mario Agrular (Jacksonville State University), Michael Anderson (University of Hartford), C. S. Bauer (University of Central Florida), Marty Barrett (East Tennessee State University), Kabekode V. Bhat (The Pennsylvania State University), Eric Brown, Robert P. Burton (Brigham Young University), Sam Buss (University of California, San Diego), Kai H. Chang (Auburn University), Ron DiNapoli (Cornell University), Eric Alan Durant (Milwaukee School of Engineering), David S. Ebert (Purdue University), Richard R. Eckert (Binghamton University), Jianchao (Jack) Han (California State University, Dominguez Hills), Chenyi Hu (University of Central Arkansas), Mark Kilgard (NVIDIA Corporation), Lisa B. Lancor (Southern Connecticut State University), Chung Lee (CA Polytechnic University, Pomona), John L. Lowther (Michigan Technological University), R. Marshall (Boston University and Bridgewater State College), Hugh C. Masterman (University of Massachusetts, Lowell), Bruce A. Maxwell (Swathmore College), James R. Miller (University of Kansas), Rodrigo Obando (Columbus State University), Andrea Salgian (The College of New Jersey), Lori L. Scarlatos (Brooklyn College, CUNY), Han-Wei Shen (The Ohio State University), Oliver Staadt (University of California, Davis), Stephen L. Stepoway (Southern Methodist University), Bill Toll (Taylor University), Michael

Wainer (Southern Illinois University, Carbondale), Yang Wang (Southern Methodist State University), Steve Warren (Kansas State University), Mike Way (Florida Southern College), George Wolberg (City College of New York), Xiaoyu Zhang (California State University San Marcos), Ye Zhao (Kent State University). and Ying Zhu (Georgia State University). Although the final decisions may not reflect their views—which often differed considerably from one another—each reviewer forced us to reflect on every page of the manuscript.

The reviewers for this edition were particularly supportive. They include Norman I. Badler (University of Pennsylvania), Mike Bailey(Oregon State University), Bedrich Benes (Purdue University), Isabelle Bichindaritz (University of Washington, Tacoma), Cory D. Boatright, (University of Pennsylvania), Eric Brown, James Cremer (University of Iowa), John David N. Dionisio (Loyola Marymount University), W Randolph Franklin (Rensselaer Polytechnic Institute), Natacha Gueorguieva, (City University of New York/College of Staten Island), George Kamberov (Stevens Institute of Technology), Hugh Masterman (University of Massachusetts, Lowell), Tim McGraw (West Virginia University), Jon A. Preston (Southern Polytechnic State University), and Bill Toll (Taylor University). They were asked to review material that was not in their own courses and if adapted would change their courses significantly. Each one recognized the importance of our approach and indicated a willingness to adopt it.

We would also like to acknowledge the entire production team at Addison-Wesley. Ed's editors, Peter Gordon, Maite Suarez-Rivas, and Matt Goldstein, have been a pleasure to work with through six editions of this book and the OpenGL primer. Through six editions, Paul Anagnostopoulos at Windfall Software has always been more than helpful in assisting with TeX problems. Ed is especially grateful to Lyn Dupré. If the readers could see the original draft of the first edition, they would understand the wonders that Lyn does with a manuscript.

Ed wants to particularly recognize his wife, Rose Mary Molnar, who did the figures for his first graphics book, many of which form the basis for the figures in this book. Probably only other authors can fully appreciate the effort that goes into the book production process and the many contributions and sacrifices our partners make to that effort. The dedication to the book is a sincere but inadequate recognition of all of Rose Mary's contributions to Ed's work.

Dave would like to recognize the support and encouragement of Vicki, his wife, without whom creating works like this would never occur. Not only does she provide warmth and companionship, but also provides invaluable feedback on our presentation and materials. She's been a valuable, unrecognized partner in all of Dave's OpenGL endeavors.

Ed Angel
Dave Shreiner

INTERACTIVE COMPUTER GRAPHICS

A TOP-DOWN APPROACH WITH SHADER-BASED OPENGL®

6th Edition

CHAPTER 1

GRAPHICS SYSTEMS AND MODELS

It would be difficult to overstate the importance of computer and communication technologies in our lives. Activities as wide-ranging as film making, publishing, banking, and education have undergone revolutionary changes as these technologies alter the ways in which we conduct our daily activities. The combination of computers, networks, and the complex human visual system, through computer graphics, has been instrumental in these advances and has led to new ways of displaying information, seeing virtual worlds, and communicating with both other people and machines.

Computer graphics is concerned with all aspects of producing pictures or images using a computer. The field began humbly 50 years ago, with the display of a few lines on a **cathode-ray tube (CRT)**; now, we can generate images by computer that are indistinguishable from photographs of real objects. We routinely train pilots with simulated airplanes, generating graphical displays of a virtual environment in real time. Feature-length movies made entirely by computer have been successful, both critically and financially.

In this chapter, we start our journey with a short discussion of applications of computer graphics. Then we overview graphics systems and imaging. Throughout this book, our approach stresses the relationships between computer graphics and image formation by familiar methods, such as drawing by hand and photography. We will see that these relationships can help us to design application programs, graphics libraries, and architectures for graphics systems.

In this book, we introduce a particular graphics software system, **OpenGL**, which has become a widely accepted standard for developing graphics applications. Fortunately, OpenGL is easy to learn, and it possesses most of the characteristics of other popular graphics systems. Our approach is top-down. We want you to start writing, as quickly as possible, application programs that will generate graphical output. After you begin writing simple programs, we shall discuss how the underlying graphics library and the hardware are implemented. This chapter should give a sufficient overview for you to proceed to writing programs.

1.1   APPLICATIONS OF COMPUTER GRAPHICS

The development of computer graphics has been driven both by the needs of the user community and by advances in hardware and software. The applications of computer graphics are many and varied; we can, however, divide them into four major areas:

1. Display of information
2. Design
3. Simulation and animation
4. User interfaces

Although many applications span two or more of these areas, the development of the field was based on separate work in each.

1.1.1 Display of Information

Classical graphics techniques arose as a medium to convey information among people. Although spoken and written languages serve a similar purpose, the human visual system is unrivaled both as a processor of data and as a pattern recognizer. More than 4000 years ago, the Babylonians displayed floor plans of buildings on stones. More than 2000 years ago, the Greeks were able to convey their architectural ideas graphically, even though the related mathematics was not developed until the Renaissance. Today, the same type of information is generated by architects, mechanical designers, and draftspeople using computer-based drafting systems.

For centuries, cartographers have developed maps to display celestial and geographical information. Such maps were crucial to navigators as these people explored the ends of the earth; maps are no less important today in fields such as geographic information systems. Now, maps can be developed and manipulated in real time over the Internet.

Over the past 100 years, workers in the field of statistics have explored techniques for generating plots that aid the viewer in determining the information in a set of data. Now, we have computer plotting packages that provide a variety of plotting techniques and color tools that can handle multiple large data sets. Nevertheless, it is still the human's ability to recognize visual patterns that ultimately allows us to interpret the information contained in the data. The field of information visualization is becoming increasingly more important as we have to deal with understanding complex phenomena from problems in bioinformatics to detecting security threats.

Medical imaging poses interesting and important data-analysis problems. Modern imaging technologies—such as computed tomography (CT), magnetic resonance imaging (MRI), ultrasound, and positron-emission tomography (PET)—generate three-dimensional data that must be subjected to algorithmic manipulation to provide useful information. Color Plate 20 shows an image of a person's head in which the skin is displayed as transparent and the internal structures are displayed as opaque. Although the data were collected by a medical imaging system, computer graphics produced the image that shows the structures.

Supercomputers now allow researchers in many areas to solve previously intractable problems. The field of scientific visualization provides graphical tools that help these researchers to interpret the vast quantity of data that they generate. In fields such as fluid flow, molecular biology, and mathematics, images generated by conversion of data to geometric entities that can be displayed have yielded new insights into complex processes. For example, Color Plate 19 shows fluid dynamics in the mantle of the earth. The system used a mathematical model to generate the data. We present various visualization techniques as examples throughout the rest of the text.

1.1.2 Design

Professions such as engineering and architecture are concerned with design. Starting with a set of specifications, engineers and architects seek a cost-effective and esthetic solution that satisfies the specifications. Design is an iterative process. Rarely in the real world is a problem specified such that there is a unique optimal solution. Design problems are either *overdetermined*, such that they possess no solution that satisfies all the criteria, much less an optimal solution, or *underdetermined*, such that they have multiple solutions that satisfy the design criteria. Thus, the designer works in an iterative manner. She generates a possible design, tests it, and then uses the results as the basis for exploring other solutions.

The power of the paradigm of humans interacting with images on the screen of a CRT was recognized by Ivan Sutherland over 40 years ago. Today, the use of interactive graphical tools in computer-aided design (CAD) pervades fields such as architecture and the design of mechanical parts and of very-large-scale integrated (VLSI) circuits. In many such applications, the graphics are used in a number of distinct ways. For example, in a VLSI design, the graphics provide an interactive interface between the user and the design package, usually by means of such tools as menus and icons. In addition, after the user produces a possible design, other tools analyze the design and display the analysis graphically. Color Plates 9 and 10 show two views of the same architectural design. Both images were generated with the same CAD system. They demonstrate the importance of having the tools available to generate different images of the same objects at different stages of the design process.

1.1.3 Simulation and Animation

Once graphics systems evolved to be capable of generating sophisticated images in real time, engineers and researchers began to use them as simulators. One of the most important uses has been in the training of pilots. Graphical flight simulators have proved both to increase safety and to reduce training expenses. The use of special VLSI chips has led to a generation of arcade games as sophisticated as flight simulators. Games and educational software for home computers are almost as impressive.

The success of flight simulators led to the use of computer graphics for animation in the television, motion-picture, and advertising industries. Entire animated movies can now be made by computer at a cost less than that of movies made with traditional hand-animation techniques. The use of computer graphics with hand animation allows the creation of technical and artistic effects that are not possible with either alone. Whereas computer animations have a distinct look, we can also generate photorealistic images by computer. Images that we see on television, in movies, and in magazines often are so realistic that we cannot distinguish computer-generated or computer-altered images from photographs. In Chapter 5 we discuss many of the lighting effects used to produce computer animations. Color Plates 23 and 16 show realistic lighting effects that were created by artists and computer scientists using animation software. Although these images were created for commercial animations, interactive software to create such effects is widely available, Color Plate 14 shows some of the steps used to create an animation. The images in Color Plates 15 and 16 also are realistic renderings.

The field of virtual reality (VR) has opened up many new horizons. A human viewer can be equipped with a display headset that allows her to see separate images with her right eye and her left eye so that she has the effect of stereoscopic vision. In addition, her body location and position, possibly including her head and finger positions, are tracked by the computer. She may have other interactive devices available, including force-sensing gloves and sound. She can then act as part of a computer-generated scene, limited only by the image-generation ability of the computer. For example, a surgical intern might be trained to do an operation in this way, or an astronaut might be trained to work in a weightless environment. Color Plate 22 shows one frame of a VR simulation of a simulated patient used for remote training of medical personnel.

Simulation and virtual reality have come together in many exciting ways in the film industry. Recently, stereo (3D) movies have become both profitable and highly acclaimed by audiences. Special effects created using computer graphics are part of virtually all movies, as are more mundane uses of computer graphics such as removal of artifacts from scenes. Simulations of physics are used to create visual effects ranging from fluid flow to crowd dynamics.

1.1.4 User Interfaces

Our interaction with computers has become dominated by a visual paradigm that includes windows, icons, menus, and a pointing device, such as a mouse. From a user's perspective, windowing systems such as the X Window System, Microsoft Windows, and the Macintosh Operating System differ only in details. More recently, millions of people have become users of the Internet. Their access is through graphical network browsers, such as Firefox, Chrome, Safari, and Internet Explorer, that use these same interface tools. We have become so accustomed to this style of interface that we often forget that what we are doing is working with computer graphics.

Although we are familiar with the style of graphical user interface used on most workstations,[1] advances in computer graphics have made possible other forms of in-

---

1. Although personal computers and workstations evolved by somewhat different paths, at present, there is virtually no fundamental difference between them. Hence, we shall use the terms *personal computer* and *workstation* synonymously.

terfaces. Color Plate 13 shows the interface used with a high-level modeling package. It demonstrates the variety both of the tools available in such packages and of the interactive devices the user can employ in modeling geometric objects.

1.2 A GRAPHICS SYSTEM

A computer graphics system is a computer system; as such, it must have all the components of a general-purpose computer system. Let us start with the high-level view of a graphics system, as shown in the block diagram in Figure 1.1. There are six major elements in our system:

1. Input devices
2. Central Processing Unit
3. Graphics Processing Unit
4. Memory
5. Frame buffer
6. Output devices

This model is general enough to include workstations and personal computers, interactive game systems, mobile phones, GPS systems, and sophisticated image-generation systems. Although most of the components are present in a standard computer, it is the way each element is specialized for computer graphics that characterizes this diagram as a portrait of a graphics system.

1.2.1 Pixels and the Frame Buffer

Virtually all modern graphics systems are raster based. The image we see on the output device is an array—the **raster**—of picture elements, or **pixels**, produced by the graphics system. As we can see from Figure 1.2, each pixel corresponds to a location,

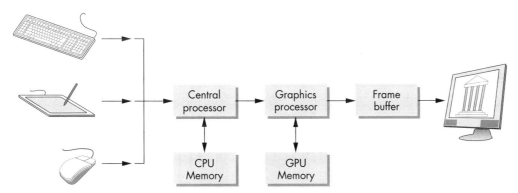

FIGURE 1.1   A graphics system.

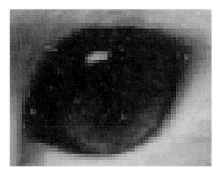

FIGURE 1.2   Pixels. (a) Image of Yeti the cat. (b) Detail of area around one eye showing individual pixels.

or small area, in the image. Collectively, the pixels are stored in a part of memory called the **frame buffer**. The frame buffer can be viewed as the core element of a graphics system. Its **resolution**—the number of pixels in the frame buffer—determines the detail that you can see in the image. The **depth**, or **precision**, of the frame buffer, defined as the number of bits that are used for each pixel, determines properties such as how many colors can be represented on a given system. For example, a 1-bit-deep frame buffer allows only two colors, whereas an 8-bit-deep frame buffer allows 2^8 (256) colors. In **full-color** systems, there are 24 (or more) bits per pixel. Such systems can display sufficient colors to represent most images realistically. They are also called **true-color** systems, or **RGB-color** systems, because individual groups of bits in each pixel are assigned to each of the three primary colors—red, green, and blue—used in most displays. **High dynamic range** (HDR) systems use 12 or more bits for each color component. Until recently, frame buffers stored colors in integer formats. Recent frame buffers use floating point and thus support HDR colors more easily.

In a very simple system, the frame buffer holds only the colored pixels that are displayed on the screen. In most systems, the frame buffer holds far more information, such as depth information needed for creating images from three-dimensional data. In these systems, the frame buffer comprises multiple buffers, one or more of which are **color buffers** that hold the colored pixels that are displayed. For now, we can use the terms *frame buffer* and *color buffer* synonymously without confusion.

1.2.2 The CPU and the GPU

In a simple system, there may be only one processor, the **central processing unit** (**CPU**) of the system, which must do both the normal processing and the graphical processing. The main graphical function of the processor is to take specifications of graphical primitives (such as lines, circles, and polygons) generated by application programs and to assign values to the pixels in the frame buffer that best represent these entities. For example, a triangle is specified by its three vertices, but to display its outline by the three line segments connecting the vertices, the graphics system must generate a set of pixels that appear as line segments to the viewer. The conversion of geometric entities to pixel colors and locations in the frame buffer is known as **rasterization**, or **scan conversion**. In early graphics systems, the frame buffer was part of the standard memory that could be directly addressed by the CPU. Today, virtually all graphics systems are characterized by special-purpose **graphics processing units** (**GPUs**), custom-tailored to carry out specific graphics functions. The GPU can be either on the mother board of the system or on a graphics card. The frame buffer is accessed through the graphics processing unit and usually is on the same circuit board as the GPU.

GPUs have evolved to where they are as complex or even more complex than CPUs. They are characterized by both special-purpose modules geared toward graphical operations and a high degree of parallelism—recent GPUs contain over 100 processing units, each of which is user programmable. GPUs are so powerful that they can often be used as mini supercomputers for general purpose computing. We will discuss GPU architectures in more detail in Section 1.7.

1.2.3 Output Devices

Until recently, the dominant type of display (or **monitor**) was the **cathode-ray tube** (**CRT**). A simplified picture of a CRT is shown in Figure 1.3. When electrons strike the phosphor coating on the tube, light is emitted. The direction of the beam is controlled by two pairs of deflection plates. The output of the computer is converted, by digital-to-analog converters, to voltages across the x and y deflection plates. Light appears on the surface of the CRT when a sufficiently intense beam of electrons is directed at the phosphor.

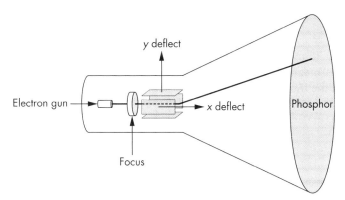

FIGURE 1.3   The cathode-ray tube (CRT).

If the voltages steering the beam change at a constant rate, the beam will trace a straight line, visible to a viewer. Such a device is known as the **random-scan**, **calligraphic**, or **vector** CRT, because the beam can be moved directly from any position to any other position. If intensity of the beam is turned off, the beam can be moved to a new position without changing any visible display. This configuration was the basis of early graphics systems that predated the present raster technology.

A typical CRT will emit light for only a short time—usually, a few milliseconds—after the phosphor is excited by the electron beam. For a human to see a steady, flicker-free image on most CRT displays, the same path must be retraced, or **refreshed**, by the beam at a sufficiently high rate, the **refresh rate**. In older systems, the refresh rate is determined by the frequency of the power system, 60 cycles per second or 60 Hertz (Hz) in the United States and 50 Hz in much of the rest of the world. Modern displays are no longer coupled to these low frequencies and operate at rates up to about 85 Hz.

In a raster system, the graphics system takes pixels from the frame buffer and displays them as points on the surface of the display in one of two fundamental ways. In a **noninterlaced** system, the pixels are displayed row by row, or scan line by scan line, at the refresh rate. In an **interlaced** display, odd rows and even rows are refreshed alternately. Interlaced displays are used in commercial television. In an interlaced display operating at 60 Hz, the screen is redrawn in its entirety only 30 times per second, although the visual system is tricked into thinking the refresh rate is 60 Hz rather than 30 Hz. Viewers located near the screen, however, can tell the difference between the interlaced and noninterlaced displays. Noninterlaced displays are becoming more widespread, even though these displays process pixels at twice the rate of the interlaced display.

Color CRTs have three different colored phosphors (red, green, and blue), arranged in small groups. One common style arranges the phosphors in triangular groups called **triads**, each triad consisting of three phosphors, one of each primary. Most color CRTs have three electron beams, corresponding to the three types of phosphors. In the shadow-mask CRT (Figure 1.4), a metal screen with small holes—the **shadow mask**—ensures that an electron beam excites only phosphors of the proper color.

Although CRTs are still common display devices, they are rapidly being replaced by flat-screen technologies. Flat-panel monitors are inherently raster based. Although there are multiple technologies available, including light-emitting diodes (LEDs), liquid-crystal displays (LCDs), and plasma panels, all use a two-dimensional grid to address individual light-emitting elements. Figure 1.5 shows a generic flat-panel monitor. The two outside plates each contain parallel grids of wires that are oriented perpendicular to each other. By sending electrical signals to the proper wire in each grid, the electrical field at a location, determined by the intersection of two wires, can be made strong enough to control the corresponding element in the middle plate. The middle plate in an LED panel contains light-emitting diodes that can be turned on and off by the electrical signals sent to the grid. In an LCD display, the electrical field controls the polarization of the liquid crystals in the middle panel, thus turning on and off the light passing through the panel. A plasma panel uses the voltages on

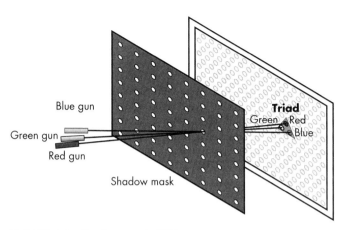

FIGURE 1.4   Shadow-mask CRT.

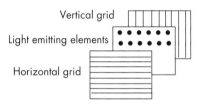

FIGURE 1.5   Generic flat-panel display.

the grids to energize gases embedded between the glass panels holding the grids. The energized gas becomes a glowing plasma.

Most projection systems are also raster devices. These systems use a variety of technologies, including CRTs and digital light projection (DLP). From a user perspective, they act as standard monitors with similar resolutions and precisions. Hard-copy devices, such as printers and plotters, are also raster based but cannot be refreshed.

1.2.4 Input Devices

Most graphics systems provide a keyboard and at least one other input device. The most common input devices are the mouse, the joystick, and the data tablet. Each provides positional information to the system, and each usually is equipped with one or more buttons to provide signals to the processor. Often called **pointing devices**, these devices allow a user to indicate a particular location on the display.

Modern systems, such as game consoles, provide a much richer set of input devices, with new devices appearing almost weekly. In addition, there are devices which provide three- (and more) dimensional input. Consequently, we want to provide a flexible model for incorporating the input from such devices into our graphics programs.

We can think about input devices in two distinct ways. The obvious one is to look at them as physical devices, such as a keyboard or a mouse, and to discuss how they work. Certainly, we need to know something about the physical properties of our input devices, so such a discussion is necessary if we are to obtain a full understanding of input. However, from the perspective of an application programmer, we should not need to know the details of a particular physical device to write an application program. Rather, we prefer to treat input devices as *logical* devices whose properties are specified in terms of what they do from the perspective of the application program. A **logical device** is characterized by its high-level interface with the user program rather than by its physical characteristics. Logical devices are familiar to all writers of high-level programs. For example, data input and output in C are done through functions such as `printf`, `scanf`, `getchar`, and `putchar`, whose arguments use the standard C data types, and through input (`cin`) and output (`cout`) streams in C++. When we output a string using `printf`, the physical device on which the output appears could be a printer, a terminal, or a disk file. This output could even be the input to another program. The details of the format required by the destination device are of minor concern to the writer of the application program.

In computer graphics, the use of logical devices is slightly more complex because the forms that input can take are more varied than the strings of bits or characters to which we are usually restricted in nongraphical applications. For example, we can use the mouse—a physical device—either to select a location on the screen of our CRT or to indicate which item in a menu we wish to select. In the first case, an x, y pair (in some coordinate system) is returned to the user program; in the second, the application program may receive an integer as the identifier of an entry in the menu. The separation of physical from logical devices allows us to use the same physical devices in multiple markedly different logical ways. It also allows the same program to work, without modification, if the mouse is replaced by another physical device, such as a data tablet or trackball.

1.2.5 Physical Input Devices

From the physical perspective, each input device has properties that make it more suitable for certain tasks than for others. We take the view used in most of the workstation literature that there are two primary types of physical devices: pointing devices and keyboard devices. The **pointing device** allows the user to indicate a position on the screen and almost always incorporates one or more buttons to allow the user to send signals or interrupts to the computer. The **keyboard device** is almost always a physical keyboard but can be generalized to include any device that returns character codes. We use the American Standard Code for Information Interchange (ASCII) in our examples. ASCII assigns a single unsigned byte to each character. Nothing we do restricts us to this particular choice, other than that ASCII is the prevailing code used. Note, however, that other codes, especially those used for Internet applications, use multiple bytes for each character, thus allowing for a much richer set of supported characters.

The mouse (Figure 1.6) and trackball (Figure 1.7) are similar in use and often in construction as well. A typical mechanical mouse when turned over looks like a trackball. In both devices, the motion of the ball is converted to signals sent back to the computer by pairs of encoders inside the device that are turned by the motion of the ball. The encoders measure motion in two orthogonal directions.

There are many variants of these devices. Some use optical detectors rather than mechanical detectors to measure motion. Small trackballs are popular with portable computers because they can be incorporated directly into the keyboard. There are also various pressure-sensitive devices used in keyboards that perform similar functions to the mouse and trackball but that do not move; their encoders measure the pressure exerted on a small knob that often is located between two keys in the middle of the keyboard.

We can view the output of the mouse or trackball as two independent values provided by the device. These values can be considered as positions and converted—either within the graphics system or by the user program—to a two-dimensional location in a convenient coordinate system. If it is configured in this manner, we can use the device to position a marker (cursor) automatically on the display; however, we rarely use these devices in this direct manner.

It is not necessary that the output of the mouse or trackball encoders be interpreted as a position. Instead, either the device driver or a user program can interpret the information from the encoder as two independent velocities. The computer can then integrate these values to obtain a two-dimensional position. Thus, as a mouse moves across a surface, the integrals of the velocities yield x, y values that can be converted to indicate the position for a cursor on the screen, as shown in Figure 1.8. By interpreting the distance traveled by the ball as a velocity, we can use the device as a variable-sensitivity input device. Small deviations from rest cause slow or small changes; large deviations cause rapid large changes. With either device, if the ball does not rotate, then there is no change in the integrals and a cursor tracking the position of the mouse will not move. In this mode, these devices are **relative-positioning** devices because changes in the position of the ball yield a position in the user program; the absolute location of the ball (or the mouse) is not used by the application program.

Relative positioning, as provided by a mouse or trackball, is not always desirable. In particular, these devices are not suitable for an operation such as tracing a diagram. If, while the user is attempting to follow a curve on the screen with a mouse, she lifts and moves the mouse, the absolute position on the curve being traced is lost.

FIGURE 1.6   Mouse.

FIGURE 1.7   Trackball.

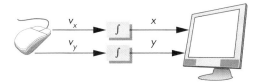

FIGURE 1.8   Cursor positioning.

FIGURE 1.9   Data tablet.

FIGURE 1.10   Joystick.

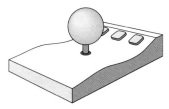

FIGURE 1.11   Spaceball.

Data tablets provide absolute positioning. A typical data tablet (Figure 1.9) has rows and columns of wires embedded under its surface. The position of the stylus is determined through electromagnetic interactions between signals traveling through the wires and sensors in the stylus. Touch-sensitive transparent screens that can be placed over the face of a CRT have many of the same properties as the data tablet. Small, rectangular, pressure-sensitive touchpads are embedded in the keyboards of many portable computers. These touchpads can be configured as either relative- or absolute-positioning devices.

One other device, the **joystick** (Figure 1.10), is particularly worthy of mention. The motion of the stick in two orthogonal directions is encoded, interpreted as two velocities, and integrated to identify a screen location. The integration implies that if the stick is left in its resting position, there is no change in the cursor position and that the farther the stick is moved from its resting position, the faster the screen location changes. Thus, the joystick is a variable-sensitivity device. The other advantage of the joystick is that the device can be constructed with mechanical elements, such as springs and dampers, that give resistance to a user who is pushing the stick. Such a mechanical feel, which is not possible with the other devices, makes the joystick well suited for applications such as flight simulators and games.

For three-dimensional graphics, we might prefer to use three-dimensional input devices. Although various such devices are available, none have yet won the widespread acceptance of the popular two-dimensional input devices. A **spaceball** looks like a joystick with a ball on the end of the stick (Figure 1.11); however, the stick does not move. Rather, pressure sensors in the ball measure the forces applied by the user. The spaceball can measure not only the three direct forces (up–down, front–back, left–right) but also three independent twists. The device measures six independent values and thus has six **degrees of freedom**. Such an input device could be used, for example, both to position and to orient a camera.

The Nintendo Wiimote provides three-dimensional position and orientation of a hand-held device by sending infrared light to the device, which then sends back what it measures wirelessly to the host computer.

Other three-dimensional devices, such as laser-based structured-lighting systems and laser-ranging systems, measure three-dimensional positions. Numerous tracking systems used in virtual reality applications sense the position of the user. Virtual reality and robotics applications often need more degrees of freedom than the 2 to 6 provided by the devices that we have described. Devices such as data gloves can sense motion of various parts of the human body, thus providing many additional input signals.

1.2.6 Logical Devices

We can now return to looking at input from inside the application program—that is, from the logical point of view. Two major characteristics describe the logical behavior of an input device: (1) the measurements that the device returns to the user program and (2) the time when the device returns those measurements.

The logical **string** device is the same as the use of character input through `scanf` or `cin`. A physical keyboard will return a string of characters to an application program; the same string might be provided from a file or the user may see a keyboard displayed on the output and use the pointing device to generate the string of characters. Logically, all three methods are examples of a string device, and application code for using such input can be the same regardless of which physical device is used.

The physical pointing device can be used in a variety of logical ways. As a **locator** it can provide a position to the application in either a device-independent coordinate system, such as world coordinates, as in OpenGL, or in screen coordinates, which the application can then transform to another coordinate system. A logical **pick** device returns the identifier of an object on the display to the application program. It is usually implemented with the same physical device as a locator but has a separate software interface to the user program.

A **widget** is a graphical interactive device, provided by either the window system or a toolkit. Typical widgets include menus, scrollbars, and graphical buttons. Most widgets are implemented as special types of windows. Widgets can be used to provide additional types of logical devices. For example, a menu provides one of a number of **choices** as may a row of graphical buttons. A logical **valuator** provides analog input to the user program, usually through a widget such as a slidebar, although the same logical input could be provided by a user typing numbers into a physical keyboard.

1.2.7 Input Modes

Besides the variety of types of input that characterize computer graphics, how the input is provided to the application is more varied than with simple C and C++ programs that use only a keyboard. The manner by which physical and logical input devices provide input to an application program can be described in terms of two entities: a measure process and a device trigger. The **measure** of a device is what the device returns to the user program. The **trigger** of a device is a physical input on the device with which the user can signal the computer. For example, the measure of a keyboard contains a string, and the trigger can be the Return or Enter key. For a locator, the measure includes the position, and the associated trigger can be a button on the pointing device.

We can obtain the measure of a device in three distinct modes. Each mode is defined by the relationship between the measure process and the trigger. Once the measure process is started, the measure is taken and placed in a buffer, even though the contents of the buffer may not yet be available to the program. For example, the position of a mouse is tracked continuously by the underlying window system, regardless of whether the application program needs mouse input.

In **request mode**, the measure of the device is not returned to the program until the device is triggered. This input mode is standard in nongraphical applications. For example, if a typical C program requires character input, we use a function such as `scanf`. When the program needs the input, it halts when it encounters the `scanf` statement and waits while we type characters at our terminal. We can backspace to correct our typing, and we can take as long as we like. The data are placed in a keyboard buffer, whose contents are returned to our program only after a particular key, such as the Enter key (the trigger), is depressed. For a logical device, such as a locator, we can move our pointing device to the desired location and then trigger the device with its button; the trigger will cause the location to be returned to the application program.

Sample-mode input is immediate. As soon as the function call in the application program is encountered, the measure is returned. In sample mode, the user must have positioned the pointing device or entered data using the keyboard before the function call, because the measure is extracted immediately from the buffer.

One characteristic of both request- and sample-mode input in APIs that support them is that the user must identify which device is to provide the input. Consequently, we ignore any other information that becomes available from any input device other than the one specified. Both request and sample modes are useful for situations where the program guides the user, but they are not useful in applications where the user controls the flow of the program. For example, a flight simulator or computer game might have multiple input devices—such as a joystick, dials, buttons, and switches—most of which can be used at any time. Writing programs to control the simulator with only sample- and request-mode input is nearly impossible, because we do not know what devices the pilot will use at any point in the simulation. More generally, sample- and request-mode input are not sufficient for handling the variety of possible human–computer interactions that arise in a modern computing environment.

Our third mode, **event mode**, can handle these other interactions. Suppose that we are in an environment with multiple input devices, each with its own trigger and each running a measure process. Each time that a device is triggered, an **event** is generated. The device measure, including the identifier for the device, is placed in an **event queue**. This process of placing events in the event queue is completely independent of what the application program does with these events. One way that the application program can work with events is shown in Figure 1.12. The user program can examine the front event in the queue or, if the queue is empty, can wait for an event to occur. If there is an event in the queue, the program can look at the event's type and then decide what to do.

Another approach is to associate a function called a **callback** with a specific type of event. From the perspective of the window system, the operating system queries or polls the event queue regularly and executes the callbacks corresponding to events in the queue. We take this approach because it is the one currently used with the major window systems and has proved effective in client–server environments.

FIGURE 1.12   Event-mode model.

1.3 IMAGES: PHYSICAL AND SYNTHETIC

For many years, the pedagogical approach to teaching computer graphics started with how to construct raster images of simple two-dimensional geometric entities (for example, points, line segments, and polygons) in the frame buffer. Next, most textbooks discussed how to define two- and three-dimensional mathematical objects in the computer and image them with the set of two-dimensional rasterized primitives.

This approach worked well for creating simple images of simple objects. In modern systems, however, we want to exploit the capabilities of the software and hardware to create realistic images of computer-generated three-dimensional objects—a task that involves many aspects of image formation, such as lighting, shading, and properties of materials. Because such functionality is supported directly by most present computer graphics systems, we prefer to set the stage for creating these images here, rather than to expand a limited model later.

Computer-generated images are synthetic or artificial, in the sense that the objects being imaged do not exist physically. In this chapter, we argue that the preferred method to form computer-generated images is similar to traditional imaging methods, such as cameras and the human visual system. Hence, before we discuss the mechanics of writing programs to generate images, we discuss the way images are formed by optical systems. We construct a model of the image-formation process that we can then use to understand and develop computer-generated imaging systems.

In this chapter, we make minimal use of mathematics. We want to establish a paradigm for creating images and to present a computer architecture for implementing that paradigm. Details are presented in subsequent chapters, where we shall derive the relevant equations.

1.3.1 Objects and Viewers

We live in a world of three-dimensional objects. The development of many branches of mathematics, including geometry and trigonometry, was in response to the desire to systematize conceptually simple ideas, such as the measurement of size of objects and distance between objects. Often, we seek to represent our understanding of such spatial relationships with pictures or images, such as maps, paintings, and photographs. Likewise, the development of many physical devices—including cameras, microscopes, and telescopes—was tied to the desire to visualize spatial relationships among objects. Hence, there always has been a fundamental link between the physics and the mathematics of image formation—one that we can exploit in our development of computer image formation.

Two basic entities must be part of any image-formation process, be it mathematical or physical: *object* and *viewer*. The object exists in space independent of any image-formation process and of any viewer. In computer graphics, where we deal with synthetic objects, we form objects by specifying the positions in space of various geometric primitives, such as points, lines, and polygons. In most graphics systems, a set of locations in space, or of **vertices**, is sufficient to define, or approximate, most

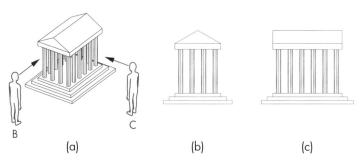

FIGURE 1.13 Image seen by three different viewers. (a) A's view. (b) B's view. (c) C's view.

objects. For example, a line can be specified by two vertices; a polygon can be specified by an ordered list of vertices; and a sphere can be specified by two vertices that specify its center and any point on its circumference. One of the main functions of a CAD system is to provide an interface that makes it easy for a user to build a synthetic model of the world. In Chapter 2, we show how OpenGL allows us to build simple objects; in Chapter 8, we learn to define objects in a manner that incorporates relationships among objects.

Every imaging system must provide a means of forming images from objects. To form an image, we must have someone or something that is viewing our objects, be it a human, a camera, or a digitizer. It is the **viewer** that forms the image of our objects. In the human visual system, the image is formed on the back of the eye. In a camera, the image is formed in the film plane. It is easy to confuse images and objects. We usually see an object from our single perspective and forget that other viewers, located in other places, will see the same object differently. Figure 1.13(a) shows two viewers observing the same building. This image is what is seen by an observer A who is far enough away from the building to see both the building and the two other viewers, B and C. From A's perspective, B and C appear as objects, just as the building does. Figures 1.13(b) and (c) show the images seen by B and C, respectively. All three images contain the same building, but the image of the building is different in all three.

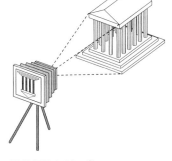

FIGURE 1.14 Camera system.

Figure 1.14 shows a camera system viewing a building. Here we can observe that both the object and the viewer exist in a three-dimensional world. However, the image that they define—what we find on the projection plane—is two-dimensional. The process by which the specification of the object is combined with the specification of the viewer to produce a two-dimensional image is the essence of image formation, and we shall study it in detail.

1.3.2 Light and Images

The preceding description of image formation is far from complete. For example, we have yet to mention light. If there were no light sources, the objects would be dark,

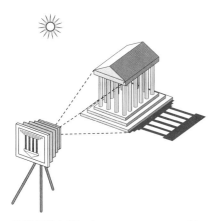

FIGURE 1.15   A camera system with an object and a light source.

and there would be nothing visible in our image. Nor have we indicated how color enters the picture or what the effects of the surface properties of the objects are.

Taking a more physical approach, we can start with the arrangement in Figure 1.15, which shows a simple physical imaging system. Again, we see a physical object and a viewer (the camera); now, however, there is a light source in the scene. Light from the source strikes various surfaces of the object, and a portion of the reflected light enters the camera through the lens. The details of the interaction between light and the surfaces of the object determine how much light enters the camera.

Light is a form of electromagnetic radiation. Taking the classical view, we look at electromagnetic energy travels as waves[2] that can be characterized by either their wavelengths or their frequencies.[3] The electromagnetic spectrum (Figure 1.16) includes radio waves, infrared (heat), and a portion that causes a response in our visual systems. This **visible spectrum**, which has wavelengths in the range of 350 to 780 nanometers (nm), is called (visible) **light**. A given light source has a color determined by the energy that it emits at various wavelengths. Wavelengths in the middle of the range, around 520 nm, are seen as green; those near 450 nm are seen as blue; and those near 650 nm are seen as red. Just as with a rainbow, light at wavelengths between red and green, we see as yellow, and wavelengths shorter than blue generate violet light.

Light sources can emit light either as a set of discrete frequencies or continuously. A laser, for example, emits light at a single frequency, whereas an incandescent lamp emits energy over a range of frequencies. Fortunately, in computer graphics, except for recognizing that distinct frequencies are visible as distinct colors, we rarely need to deal with the physical properties of light.

---

2. In Chaper 11, we will introduce photon mapping that is based on light being emitted in discrete packets.

3. The relationship between frequency (f) and wavelength (λ) is $f\lambda = c$, where c is the speed of light.

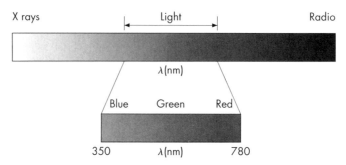

FIGURE 1.16   The electromagnetic spectrum.

Instead, we can follow a more traditional path that is correct when we are operating with sufficiently high light levels and at a scale where the wave nature of light is not a significant factor. **Geometric optics** models light sources as emitters of light energy, each of which have a fixed intensity. Modeled geometrically, light travels in straight lines, from the sources to those objects with which it interacts. An ideal **point source** emits energy from a single location at one or more frequencies equally in all directions. More complex sources, such as a light bulb, can be characterized as emitting light over an area and by emitting more light in one direction than another. A particular source is characterized by the intensity of light that it emits at each frequency and by that light's directionality. We consider only point sources for now. More complex sources often can be approximated by a number of carefully placed point sources. Modeling of light sources is discussed in Chapter 5.

1.3.3 Imaging Models

There are multiple approaches to how we can form images from a set of objects, the light-reflecting properties of these objects, and the properties of the light sources in the scene. In this section, we introduce two physical approaches. Although these approaches are not suitable for the real-time graphics that we ultimately want, they will give us some insight into how we can build a useful imaging architecture. We return to these approaches in Chapter 11.

We can start building an imaging model by following light from a source. Consider the scene in Figure 1.17; it is illuminated by a single point source. We include the viewer in the figure because we are interested in the light that reaches her eye. The viewer can also be a camera, as shown in Figure 1.18. A **ray** is a semi-infinite line that emanates from a point and travels to infinity in a particular direction. Because light travels in straight lines, we can think in terms of rays of light emanating in all directions from our point source. A portion of these infinite rays contributes to the image on the film plane of our camera. For example, if the source is visible from the camera, some of the rays go directly from the source through the lens of the camera and strike the film plane. Most rays, however, go off to infinity, neither entering the camera directly nor striking any of the objects. These rays contribute nothing to the

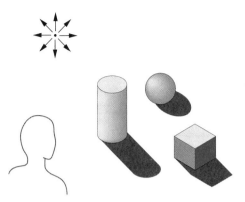

FIGURE 1.17   Scene with a single point light source.

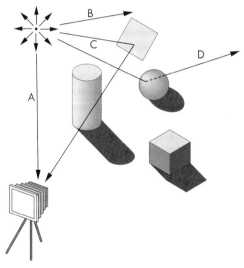

FIGURE 1.18   Ray interactions. Ray A enters camera directly. Ray B goes off to infinity. Ray C is reflected by a mirror. Ray D goes through a transparent sphere.

image, although they may be seen by some other viewer. The remaining rays strike and illuminate objects. These rays can interact with the objects' surfaces in a variety of ways. For example, if the surface is a mirror, a reflected ray might—depending on the orientation of the surface—enter the lens of the camera and contribute to the image. Other surfaces scatter light in all directions. If the surface is transparent, the light ray from the source can pass through it and may interact with other objects, enter the camera, or travel to infinity without striking another surface. Figure 1.18 shows some of the possibilities.

Ray tracing and **photon mapping** are image-formation techniques that are based on these ideas and that can form the basis for producing computer-generated images. We can use the ray-tracing idea to simulate physical effects as complex as we wish, as long as we are willing to carry out the requisite computing. Although tracing rays can provide a close approximation to the physical world, it is usually not well suited for real-time computation.

Other physical approaches to image formation are based on conservation of energy. The most important in computer graphics is **radiosity**. This method works best for surfaces that scatter the incoming light equally in all directions. Even in this case, radiosity requires more computation than can be done in real time. We defer discussion of these techniques until Chapter 11.

1.4   IMAGING SYSTEMS

We now introduce two imaging systems: the pinhole camera and the human visual system. The pinhole camera is a simple example of an imaging system that will enable us to understand the functioning of cameras and of other optical imagers. We emulate it to build a model of image formation. The human visual system is extremely complex but still obeys the physical principles of other optical imaging systems. We introduce it not only as an example of an imaging system but also because understanding its properties will help us to exploit the capabilities of computer-graphics systems.

1.4.1 The Pinhole Camera

The pinhole camera in Figure 1.19 provides an example of image formation that we can understand with a simple geometric model. A **pinhole camera** is a box with a small hole in the center of one side of the box; the film is placed inside the box on the side opposite the pinhole. Suppose that we orient our camera along the z-axis, with the pinhole at the origin of our coordinate system. We assume that the hole is

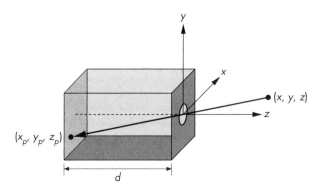

FIGURE 1.19   Pinhole camera.

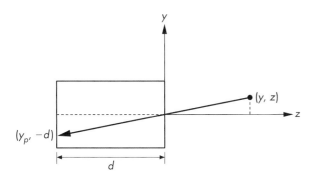

FIGURE 1.20 Side view of pinhole camera.

so small that only a single ray of light, emanating from a point, can enter it. The film plane is located a distance d from the pinhole. A side view (Figure 1.20) allows us to calculate where the image of the point (x, y, z) is on the film plane $z = -d$. Using the fact that the two triangles in Figure 1.20 are similar, we find that the y coordinate of the image is at y_p, where

$$y_p = -\frac{y}{z/d}.$$

A similar calculation, using a top view, yields

$$x_p = -\frac{x}{z/d}.$$

The point $(x_p, y_p, -d)$ is called the **projection** of the point (x, y, z). In our idealized model, the color on the film plane at this point will be the color of the point (x, y, z). The **field**, or **angle, of view** of our camera is the angle made by the largest object that our camera can image on its film plane. We can calculate the field of view with the aid of Figure 1.21.[4] If h is the height of the camera, the angle of view θ is

$$\theta = 2 \tan^{-1} \frac{h}{2d}.$$

The ideal pinhole camera has an infinite **depth of field**: Every point within its field of view is in focus. Every point in its field of view projects to a point on the back of the camera. The pinhole camera has two disadvantages. First, because the pinhole is so small—it admits only a single ray from a point source—almost no light enters the camera. Second, the camera cannot be adjusted to have a different angle of view.

---

4. If we consider the problem in three, rather than two, dimensions, then the diagonal length of the film will substitute for h.

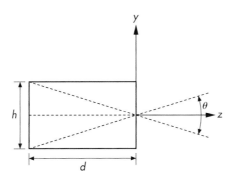

FIGURE 1.21   Angle of view.

The jump to more sophisticated cameras and to other imaging systems that have lenses is a small one. By replacing the pinhole with a lens, we solve the two problems of the pinhole camera. First, the lens gathers more light than can pass through the pinhole. The larger the aperture of the lens, the more light the lens can collect. Second, by picking a lens with the proper focal length—a selection equivalent to choosing d for the pinhole camera—we can achieve any desired angle of view (up to 180 degrees). Lenses, however, do not have an infinite depth of field: Not all distances from the lens are in focus.

For our purposes, in this chapter we can work with a pinhole camera whose focal length is the distance d from the front of the camera to the film plane. Like the pinhole camera, computer graphics produces images in which all objects are in focus.

1.4.2 The Human Visual System

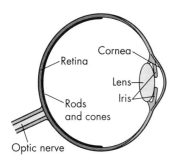

FIGURE 1.22   The human visual system.

Our extremely complex visual system has all the components of a physical imaging system, such as a camera or a microscope. The major components of the visual system are shown in Figure 1.22. Light enters the eye through the lens and cornea, a transparent structure that protects the eye. The iris opens and closes to adjust the amount of light entering the eye. The lens forms an image on a two-dimensional structure called the **retina** at the back of the eye. The rods and cones (so named because of their appearance when magnified) are light sensors and are located on the retina. They are excited by electromagnetic energy in the range of 350 to 780 nm.

The rods are low-level-light sensors that account for our night vision and are not color sensitive; the cones are responsible for our color vision. The sizes of the rods and cones, coupled with the optical properties of the lens and cornea, determine the **resolution** of our visual systems, or our **visual acuity**. Resolution is a measure of what size objects we can see. More technically, it is a measure of how close we can place two points and still recognize that there are two distinct points.

The sensors in the human eye do not react uniformly to light energy at different wavelengths. There are three types of cones and a single type of rod. Whereas intensity is a physical measure of light energy, **brightness** is a measure of how intense we perceive the light emitted from an object to be. The human visual system does not have the same response to a monochromatic (single-frequency) red light as to a monochromatic green light. If these two lights were to emit the same energy, they would appear to us to have different brightness, because of the unequal response of the cones to red and green light. We are most sensitive to green light, and least sensitive to red and blue.

Brightness is an overall measure of how we react to the intensity of light. Human color-vision capabilities are due to the different sensitivities of the three types of cones. The major consequence of having three types of cones is that instead of having to work with all visible wavelengths individually, we can use three standard primaries to approximate any color that we can perceive. Consequently, most image-production systems, including film and video, work with just three basic, or **primary**, colors. We discuss color in depth in Chapter 2.

The initial processing of light in the human visual system is based on the same principles used by most optical systems. However, the human visual system has a back end much more complex than that of a camera or telescope. The optic nerves are connected to the rods and cones in an extremely complex arrangement that has many of the characteristics of a sophisticated signal processor. The final processing is done in a part of the brain called the visual cortex, where high-level functions, such as object recognition, are carried out. We shall omit any discussion of high-level processing; instead, we can think simply in terms of an image that is conveyed from the rods and cones to the brain.

1.5 THE SYNTHETIC-CAMERA MODEL

Our models of optical imaging systems lead directly to the conceptual foundation for modern three-dimensional computer graphics. We look at creating a computer-generated image as being similar to forming an image using an optical system. This paradigm has become known as the **synthetic-camera model**. Consider the imaging system shown in Figure 1.23. We again see objects and a viewer. In this case, the viewer is a bellows camera.[5] The image is formed on the film plane at the back of the camera. So that we can emulate this process to create artificial images, we need to identify a few basic principles.

First, the specification of the objects is independent of the specification of the viewer. Hence, we should expect that, within a graphics library, there will be separate functions for specifying the objects and the viewer.

Second, we can compute the image using simple geometric calculations, just as we did with the pinhole camera. Consider the side view of the camera and a simple object in Figure 1.24. The view in part (a) of the figure is similar to that of the

5. In a bellows camera, the front plane of the camera, where the lens is located, and the back of the camera, the film plane, are connected by flexible sides. Thus, we can move the back of the camera independently of the front of the camera, introducing additional flexibility in the image-formation process. We use this flexibility in Chapter 4.

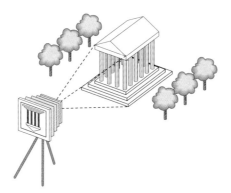

FIGURE 1.23   Imaging system.

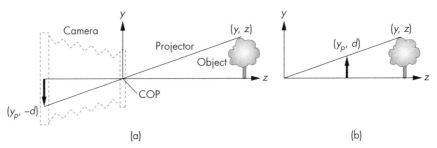

FIGURE 1.24   Equivalent views of image formation. (a) Image formed on the back of the camera. (b) Image plane moved in front of the camera.

pinhole camera. Note that the image of the object is flipped relative to the object. Whereas with a real camera we would simply flip the film to regain the original orientation of the object, with our synthetic camera we can avoid the flipping by a simple trick. We draw another plane in front of the lens (Figure 1.24(b)) and work in three dimensions, as shown in Figure 1.25. We find the image of a point on the object on the virtual image plane by drawing a line, called a **projector**, from the point to the center of the lens, or the **center of projection** (**COP**). Note that all projectors are rays emanating from the center of projection. In our synthetic camera, the virtual image plane that we have moved in front of the lens is called the **projection plane**. The image of the point is located where the projector passes through the projection plane. In Chapter 4, we discuss this process in detail and derive the relevant mathematical formulas.

We must also consider the limited size of the image. As we saw, not all objects can be imaged onto the pinhole camera's film plane. The angle of view expresses this limitation. In the synthetic camera, we can move this limitation to the front by placing a **clipping rectangle**, or **clipping window**, in the projection plane (Figure 1.26). This rectangle acts as a window, through which a viewer, located at the center of pro-

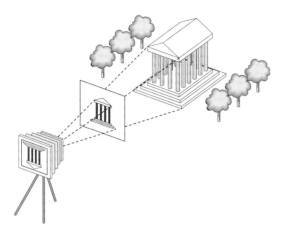

FIGURE 1.25   Imaging with the synthetic camera.

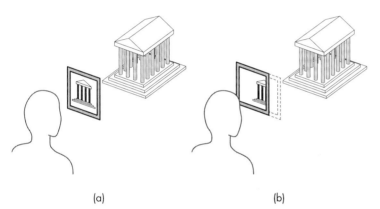

(a)   (b)

FIGURE 1.26   Clipping. (a) Window in initial position. (b) Window shifted.

jection, sees the world. Given the location of the center of projection, the location and orientation of the projection plane, and the size of the clipping rectangle, we can determine which objects will appear in the image.

1.6   THE PROGRAMMER'S INTERFACE

There are numerous ways that a user can interact with a graphics system. With completely self-contained packages, such as those used in the CAD community, a user develops images through interactions with the display using input devices, such as a mouse and a keyboard. In a typical application, such as the painting program in Figure 1.27, the user sees menus and icons that represent possible actions. By clicking

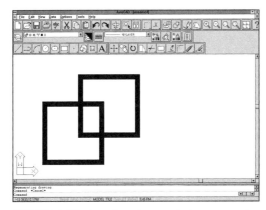

FIGURE 1.27   Interface for a painting program.

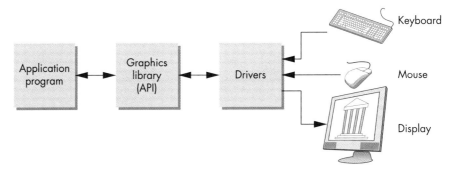

FIGURE 1.28   Application programmer's model of graphics system.

on these items, the user guides the software and produces images without having to write programs.

Of course, someone has to develop the code for these applications, and many of us, despite the sophistication of commercial products, still have to write our own graphics application programs (and even enjoy doing so).

The interface between an application program and a graphics system can be specified through a set of functions that resides in a graphics library. These specifications are called the **application programming interface (API)**. The application programmer's model of the system is shown in Figure 1.28. The application programmer sees only the API and is thus shielded from the details of both the hardware and the software implementation of the graphics library. The software **drivers** are responsible for interpreting the output of the API and converting these data to a form that is understood by the particular hardware. From the perspective of the writer of an application program, the functions available through the API should match the conceptual model that the user wishes to employ to specify images.

1.6.1 The Pen-Plotter Model

Historically, most early graphics systems were two-dimensional systems. The conceptual model that they used is now referred to as the *pen-plotter model*, referencing the output device that was available on these systems. A **pen plotter** (Figure 1.29) produces images by moving a pen held by a gantry, a structure that can move the pen in two orthogonal directions across the paper. The plotter can raise and lower the pen as required to create the desired image. Pen plotters are still in use; they are well suited for drawing large diagrams, such as blueprints. Various APIs—such as LOGO and PostScript—have their origins in this model. Although they differ from one another, they have a common view of the process of creating an image as being similar to the process of drawing on a pad of paper. The user works on a two-dimensional surface of some size. She moves a pen around on this surface, leaving an image on the paper.

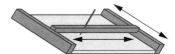

FIGURE 1.29   Pen plotter.

We can describe such a graphics system with two drawing functions:

```
moveto(x,y);
lineto(x,y);
```

Execution of the `moveto` function moves the pen to the location (x, y) on the paper without leaving a mark. The `lineto` function moves the pen to (x, y) and draws a line from the old to the new location of the pen. Once we add a few initialization and termination procedures, as well as the ability to change pens to alter the drawing color or line thickness, we have a simple—but complete—graphics system. Here is a fragment of a simple program in such a system:

```
moveto(0, 0);
lineto(1, 0);
lineto(1, 1);
lineto(0, 1);
lineto(0, 0);
```

This fragment would generate the output in Figure 1.30(a). If we added the code

```
moveto(0, 1);
lineto(0.5, 1.866);
lineto(1.5, 1.866);
lineto(1.5, 0.866);
lineto(1, 0);
moveto(1, 1);
lineto(1.5, 1.866);
```

we would have the image of a cube formed by an oblique projection, as is shown in Figure 1.30(b).

For certain applications, such as page layout in the printing industry, systems built on this model work well. For example, the PostScript page-description language, a sophisticated extension of these ideas, is a standard for controlling typesetters and printers.

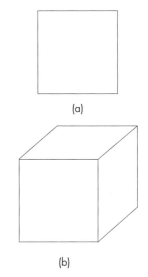

FIGURE 1.30   Output of pen-plotter program for (a) a square, and (b) a projection of a cube.

An alternate raster-based, but still limiting, two-dimensional model relies on writing pixels directly into a frame buffer. Such a system could be based on a single function of the form

```
write_pixel(x, y, color);
```

where `x`,`y` is the location of the pixel in the frame buffer and `color` gives the color to be written there. Such models are well suited to writing the algorithms for rasterization and processing of digital images.

We are much more interested, however, in the three-dimensional world. The pen-plotter model does not extend well to three-dimensional graphics systems. For example, if we wish to use the pen-plotter model to produce the image of a three-dimensional object on our two-dimensional pad, either by hand or by computer, then we have to figure out where on the page to place two-dimensional points corresponding to points on our three-dimensional object. These two-dimensional points are, as we saw in Section 1.5, the projections of points in three-dimensional space. The mathematical process of determining projections is an application of trigonometry. We develop the mathematics of projection in Chapter 4; understanding projection is crucial to understanding three-dimensional graphics. We prefer, however, to use an API that allows users to work directly in the domain of their problems and to use computers to carry out the details of the projection process automatically, without the users having to make any trigonometric calculations within the application program. That approach should be a boon to users who have difficulty learning to draw various projections on a drafting board or sketching objects in perspective. More important, users can rely on hardware and software implementations of projections within the implementation of the API that are far more efficient than any possible implementation of projections within their programs would be.

1.6.2 Three-Dimensional APIs

The synthetic-camera model is the basis for a number of popular APIs, including OpenGL and Direct3D. If we are to follow the synthetic-camera model, we need functions in the API to specify the following:

- Objects
- A viewer
- Light sources
- Material properties

Objects are usually defined by sets of vertices. For simple geometric objects—such as line segments, rectangles, and polygons—there is a simple relationship between a list of **vertices**, or positions in space, and the object. For more complex objects, there may be multiple ways of defining the object from a set of vertices. A circle, for example, can be defined by three points on its circumference, or by its center and one point on the circumference.

Most APIs provide similar sets of primitive objects for the user. These primitives are usually those that can be displayed rapidly on the hardware. The usual sets include points, line segments, polygons, and sometimes text. OpenGL programs define primitives through lists of vertices. The following code fragment specifies three vertices:

```
float vertices[3][3];

vertices[0][0] = 0.0;  /* vertex A */
vertices[1][0] = 0.0;
vertices[2][0] = 0.0;
vertices[0][1] = 0.0;  /* vertex B */
vertices[1][1] = 1.0;
vertices[2][1] = 0.0;
vertices[0][2] = 0.0;  /* vertex C */
vertices[1][2] = 0.0;
vertices[2][2] = 1.0;
```

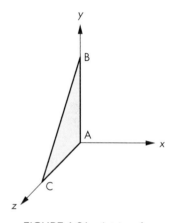

FIGURE 1.31   A triangle.

In OpenGL, we could either send this array to the GPU each time that we want it to be displayed or store it on the GPU for later display. Note that these three vertices only give three locations in a three-dimensional space and do not specify the geometric entity that they define. The locations could describe a triangle, as in Figure 1.31, or we could use them to specify two line segments using the first two locations to specify the first segment and the second and third locations to specify the second segment. We could also use the three points to display three pixels at locations in the frame buffer corresponding to the three vertices. We make this choice on our application by setting a parameter corresponding to the geometric entity we would like these locations to specify. For example, in OpenGL we would use GL_TRIANGLES, GL_LINE_STRIP, or GL_POINTS for the three possibilities we just described. Although we are not yet ready to describe all the details of how we accomplish this task, we can note that regardless of which geometric entity we wish our vertices to specify, we are specifying the geometry and leaving it to the graphics system to determine which pixels to color in the frame buffer.

Some APIs let the user work directly in the frame buffer by providing functions that read and write pixels. Additionally, some APIs provide curves and surfaces as primitives; often, however, these types are approximated by a series of simpler primitives within the application program. OpenGL provides access to the frame buffer.

We can define a viewer or camera in a variety of ways. Available APIs differ both in how much flexibility they provide in camera selection and in how many different methods they allow. If we look at the camera in Figure 1.32, we can identify four types of necessary specifications:

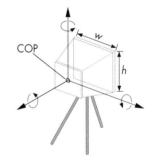

FIGURE 1.32   Camera specification.

1. **Position**   The camera location usually is given by the position of the center of the lens, which is the center of projection (COP).

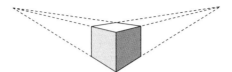

FIGURE 1.33   Two-point perspective of a cube.

2. **Orientation**   Once we have positioned the camera, we can place a camera coordinate system with its origin at the center of projection. We can then rotate the camera independently around the three axes of this system.

3. **Focal length**   The focal length of the lens determines the size of the image on the film plane or, equivalently, the portion of the world the camera sees.

4. **Film plane**   The back of the camera has a height and a width. On the bellows camera, and in some APIs, the orientation of the back of the camera can be adjusted independently of the orientation of the lens.

These specifications can be satisfied in various ways. One way to develop the specifications for the camera location and orientation uses a series of coordinate-system transformations. These transformations convert object positions represented in a coordinate system that specifies object vertices to object positions in a coordinate system centered at the COP. This approach is useful, both for doing implementation and for getting the full set of views that a flexible camera can provide. We use this approach extensively, starting in Chapter 4.

Having many parameters to adjust, however, can also make it difficult to get a desired image. Part of the problem lies with the synthetic-camera model. Classical viewing techniques, such as are used in architecture, stress the *relationship* between the object and the viewer, rather than the *independence* that the synthetic-camera model emphasizes. Thus, the classical two-point perspective of a cube in Figure 1.33 is a *two-point* perspective because of a particular relationship between the viewer and the planes of the cube (see Exercise 1.7). Although the OpenGL API allows us to set transformations with complete freedom, it also provides helpful extra functions. For example, consider the two function calls

```
LookAt(cop, at, up);
Perspective(field_of_view, aspect_ratio, near, far);
```

The first function call points the camera from the center of projection toward a desired point (the *at* point), with a specified *up* direction for the camera. The second selects a lens for a perspective view (the *field of view*) and how much of the world that the camera should image (the *aspect ratio* and the *near* and *far* distances). However, none of the APIs built on the synthetic-camera model provide functions for directly specifying a desired relationship between the camera and an object.

Light sources are defined by their location, strength, color, and directionality. APIs provide a set of functions to specify these parameters for each source. Material properties are characteristics, or attributes, of the objects, and such properties are specified through a series of function calls at the time that each object is defined. Both light sources and material properties depend on the models of light–material interactions supported by the API. We discuss such models in Chapter 5.

1.6.3 A Sequence of Images

In Chapter 2, we begin our detailed discussion of the OpenGL API that we will use throughout this book. The images defined by your OpenGL programs will be formed automatically by the hardware and software implementation of the image-formation process.

Here we look at a sequence of images that shows what we can create using the OpenGL API. We present these images as an increasingly more complex series of renderings of the same objects. The sequence not only loosely follows the order in which we present related topics but also reflects how graphics systems have developed over the past 30 years.

Color Plate 1 shows an image of an artist's creation of a sunlike object. Color Plate 2 shows the object rendered using only line segments. Although the object consists of many parts, and although the programmer may have used sophisticated data structures to model each part and the relationships among the parts, the rendered object shows only the outlines of the parts. This type of image is known as a **wireframe** image because we can see only the edges of surfaces: Such an image would be produced if the objects were constructed with stiff wires that formed a frame with no solid material between the edges. Before raster-graphics systems became available, wireframe images were the only type of computer-generated images that we could produce.

In Color Plate 3, the same object has been rendered with flat polygons. Certain surfaces are not visible, because there is a solid surface between them and the viewer; these surfaces have been removed by a hidden-surface-removal (HSR) algorithm. Most raster systems can fill the interior of polygons with a solid color in approximately the same time that they can render a wireframe image. Although the objects are three-dimensional, each surface is displayed in a single color, and the image fails to show the three-dimensional shapes of the objects. Early raster systems could produce images of this form.

In Chapters 2 and 3, we show you how to generate images composed of simple geometric objects—points, line segments, and polygons. In Chapters 3 and 4, you will learn how to transform objects in three dimensions and how to obtain a desired three-dimensional view of a model, with hidden surfaces removed.

Color Plate 4 illustrates smooth shading of the polygons that approximate the object; it shows that the object is three-dimensional and gives the appearance of a smooth surface. We develop shading models that are supported by OpenGL in Chapter 5. These shading models are also supported in the hardware of most recent workstations; generating the shaded image on one of these systems takes approximately the same amount of time as does generating a wireframe image.

Color Plate 5 shows a more sophisticated wireframe model constructed using NURBS surfaces, which we introduce in Chapter 10. Such surfaces give the application programmer great flexibility in the design process but are ultimately rendered using line segments and polygons.

In Color Plates 6 and 7, we add surface texture to our object; texture is one of the effects that we discuss in Chapter 6. All recent graphics processors support texture mapping in hardware, so rendering of a texture-mapped image requires little additional time. In Color Plate 6, we use a technique called *bump mapping* that gives the appearance of a rough surface even though we render the same flat polygons as in the other examples. Color Plate 7 shows an *environment map* applied to the surface of the object, which gives the surface the appearance of a mirror. These techniques will be discussed in detail in Chapter 7.

Color Plate 8 shows a small area of the rendering of the object using an environment map. The image on the left shows the jagged artifacts known as aliasing errors that are due to the discrete nature of the frame buffer. The image on the right has been rendered using a smoothing or antialiasing method that we shall study in Chapters 5 and 6.

Not only do these images show what is possible with available hardware and a good API, but they are also simple to generate, as we shall see in subsequent chapters. In addition, just as the images show incremental changes in the renderings, the programs are incrementally different from one another.

1.6.4 The Modeling–Rendering Paradigm

In many situations—especially in CAD applications and in the development of complex images, such as for movies—we can separate the modeling of the scene from the production of the image, or the **rendering** of the scene. Hence, we can look at image formation as the two-step process shown in Figure 1.34. Although the tasks are the same as those we have been discussing, this block diagram suggests that we might implement the modeler and the renderer with different software and hardware. For example, consider the production of a single frame in an animation. We first want to design and position our objects. This step is highly interactive, and we do not need to work with detailed images of the objects. Consequently, we prefer to carry out this step on an interactive workstation with good graphics hardware. Once we have designed the scene, we want to render it, adding light sources, material properties, and a variety of other detailed effects, to form a production-quality image. This step requires a tremendous amount of computation, so we might prefer to use a

FIGURE 1.34   The modeling–rendering pipeline.

render farm, a cluster of computers configured for numerical computing. Not only is the optimal hardware different in the modeling and rendering steps, but the software that we use also may be different.

The interface between the modeler and renderer can be as simple as a file produced by the modeler that describes the objects and that contains additional information important only to the renderer, such as light sources, viewer location, and material properties. Pixar's RenderMan Interface follows this approach and uses a file format that allows modelers to pass models to the renderer in text format. One of the other advantages of this approach is that it allows us to develop modelers that, although they use the same renderer, are custom-tailored to particular applications. Likewise, different renderers can take as input the same interface file. It is even possible, at least in principle, to dispense with the modeler completely and to use a standard text editor to generate an interface file. For any but the simplest scenes, however, users cannot edit lists of information for a renderer. Rather, they use interactive modeling software. Because we must have at least a simple image of our objects to interact with a modeler, most modelers use the synthetic-camera model to produce these images in real time.

This paradigm has become popular as a method for generating computer games and images over the Internet. Models, including the geometric objects, lights, cameras, and material properties, are placed in a data structure called a **scene graph** that is passed to a renderer or game engine. We shall examine scene graphs in Chapter 8.

1.7 GRAPHICS ARCHITECTURES

On one side of the API is the application program. On the other is some combination of hardware and software that implements the functionality of the API. Researchers have taken various approaches to developing architectures to support graphics APIs.

Early graphics systems used general-purpose computers with the standard von Neumann architecture. Such computers are characterized by a single processing unit that processes a single instruction at a time. A simple model of these early graphics systems is shown in Figure 1.35. The display in these systems was based on a calligraphic CRT display that included the necessary circuitry to generate a line segment connecting two points. The job of the host computer was to run the application program and to compute the endpoints of the line segments in the image (in units of the display). This information had to be sent to the display at a rate high enough to avoid

FIGURE 1.35   Early graphics system.

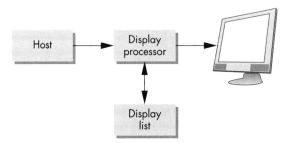

FIGURE 1.36   Display-processor architecture.

flicker on the display. In the early days of computer graphics, computers were so slow that refreshing even simple images, containing a few hundred line segments, would burden an expensive computer.

1.7.1 Display Processors

The earliest attempts to build special-purpose graphics systems were concerned primarily with relieving the general-purpose computer from the task of refreshing the display continuously. These **display processors** had conventional architectures (Figure 1.36) but included instructions to display primitives on the CRT. The main advantage of the display processor was that the instructions to generate the image could be assembled once in the host and sent to the display processor, where they were stored in the display processor's own memory as a **display list**, or **display file**. The display processor would then execute repetitively the program in the display list, at a rate sufficient to avoid flicker, independently of the host, thus freeing the host for other tasks. This architecture has become closely associated with the client–server architectures that are used in most systems.

1.7.2 Pipeline Architectures

The major advances in graphics architectures parallel closely the advances in workstations. In both cases, the ability to create special-purpose VLSI chips was the key enabling technology development. In addition, the availability of inexpensive solid-state memory led to the universality of raster displays. For computer-graphics applications, the most important use of custom VLSI circuits has been in creating **pipeline** architectures.

The concept of pipelining is illustrated in Figure 1.37 for a simple arithmetic calculation. In our pipeline, there is an adder and a multiplier. If we use this configuration to compute $a + (b * c)$, the calculation takes one multiplication and one addition—the same amount of work required if we use a single processor to carry out both operations. However, suppose that we have to carry out the same computation with many values of a, b, and c. Now, the multiplier can pass on the results of its calculation to the adder and can start its next multiplication while the adder carries out the second step of the calculation on the first set of data. Hence, whereas it takes

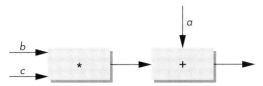

FIGURE 1.37   Arithmetic pipeline.

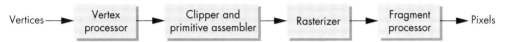

FIGURE 1.38   Geometric pipeline.

the same amount of time to calculate the results for any one set of data, when we are working on two sets of data at one time, our total time for calculation is shortened markedly. Here the rate at which data flows through the system, the **throughput** of the system, has been doubled. Note that as we add more boxes to a pipeline, it takes more time for a single datum to pass through the system. This time is called the **latency** of the system; we must balance it against increased throughput in evaluating the performance of a pipeline.

We can construct pipelines for more complex arithmetic calculations that will afford even greater increases in throughput. Of course, there is no point in building a pipeline unless we will do the same operation on many data sets. But that is just what we do in computer graphics, where large sets of vertices and pixels must be processed in the same manner.

1.7.3 The Graphics Pipeline

We start with a set of objects. Each object comprises a set of graphical primitives. Each primitive comprises a set of vertices. We can think of the collection of primitive types and vertices as defining the **geometry** of the scene. In a complex scene, there may be thousands—even millions—of vertices that define the objects. We must process all these vertices in a similar manner to form an image in the frame buffer. If we think in terms of processing the geometry of our objects to obtain an image, we can employ the block diagram in Figure 1.38, which shows the four major steps in the imaging process:

1. Vertex processing
2. Clipping and primitive assembly
3. Rasterization
4. Fragment processing

In subsequent chapters, we discuss the details of these steps. Here we are content to overview these steps and show that they can be pipelined.

1.7.4 Vertex Processing

In the first block of our pipeline, each vertex is processed independently. The two major functions of this block are to carry out coordinate transformations and to compute a color for each vertex.

Many of the steps in the imaging process can be viewed as transformations between representations of objects in different coordinate systems. For example, in our discussion of the synthetic camera, we observed that a major part of viewing is to convert to a representation of objects from the system in which they were defined to a representation in terms of the coordinate system of the camera. A further example of a transformation arises when we finally put our images onto the output device. The internal representation of objects—whether in the camera coordinate system or perhaps in a system used by the graphics software—eventually must be represented in terms of the coordinate system of the display. We can represent each change of coordinate systems by a matrix. We can represent successive changes in coordinate systems by multiplying, or **concatenating**, the individual matrices into a single matrix. In Chapter 3, we examine these operations in detail. Because multiplying one matrix by another matrix yields a third matrix, a sequence of transformations is an obvious candidate for a pipeline architecture. In addition, because the matrices that we use in computer graphics will always be small (4×4), we have the opportunity to use parallelism within the transformation blocks in the pipeline.

Eventually, after multiple stages of transformation, the geometry is transformed by a projection transformation. We shall see in Chapter 4 that we can implement this step using 4×4 matrices, and thus projection fits in the pipeline. In general, we want to keep three-dimensional information as long as possible, as objects pass through the pipeline. Consequently, the projection transformation is somewhat more general than the projections in Section 1.5. In addition to retaining three-dimensional information, there is a variety of projections that we can implement. We shall see these projections in Chapter 4.

The assignment of vertex colors can be as simple as the program specifying a color or as complex as the computation of a color from a physically realistic lighting model that incorporates the surface properties of the object and the characteristic light sources in the scene. We shall discuss lighting models in Chapter 5.

1.7.5 Clipping and Primitive Assembly

The second fundamental block in the implementation of the standard graphics pipeline is for clipping and primitive assembly. We must do clipping because of the limitation that no imaging system can see the whole world at once. The human retina has a limited size corresponding to an approximately 90-degree field of view. Cameras have film of limited size, and we can adjust their fields of view by selecting different lenses.

We obtain the equivalent property in the synthetic camera by considering a **clipping volume**, such as the pyramid in front of the lens in Figure 1.25. The projections of objects in this volume appear in the image. Those that are outside do not and are said to be clipped out. Objects that straddle the edges of the clipping volume are partly visible in the image. Efficient clipping algorithms are developed in Chapter 6.

Clipping must be done on a primitive-by-primitive basis rather than on a vertex-by-vertex basis. Thus, within this stage of the pipeline, we must assemble sets of vertices into primitives, such as line segments and polygons, before clipping can take place. Consequently, the output of this stage is a set of primitives whose projections can appear in the image.

1.7.6 Rasterization

The primitives that emerge from the clipper are still represented in terms of their vertices and must be converted to pixels in the frame buffer. For example, if three vertices specify a triangle with a solid color, the rasterizer must determine which pixels in the frame buffer are inside the polygon. We discuss this rasterization (or scan-conversion) process in Chapter 6 for line segments and polygons. The output of the rasterizer is a set of **fragments** for each primitive. A fragment can be thought of as a potential pixel that carries with it information, including its color and location, that is used to update the corresponding pixel in the frame buffer. Fragments can also carry along depth information that allows later stages to determine if a particular fragment lies behind other previously rasterized fragments for a given pixel.

1.7.7 Fragment Processing

The final block in our pipeline takes in the fragments generated by the rasterizer and updates the pixels in the frame buffer. If the application generated three-dimensional data, some fragments may not be visible because the surfaces that they define are behind other surfaces. The color of a fragment may be altered by texture mapping or bump mapping, as in Color Plates 6 and 7. The color of the pixel that corresponds to a fragment can also be read from the frame buffer and blended with the fragment's color to create translucent effects. These effects will be covered in Chapter 7.

1.8 PROGRAMMABLE PIPELINES

Graphics architectures have gone through multiple design cycles in which the importance of special-purpose hardware relative to standard CPUs has gone back and forth. However, the importance of the pipeline architecture has remained regardless of this cycle. None of the other approaches—ray tracing, radiosity, photon mapping—can achieve real-time behavior, that is, the ability to render complex dynamic scenes so that the viewer sees the display without defects. However, the term *real-time* is becoming increasingly difficult to define as graphics hardware improves. Although some approaches such as ray tracing can come close to real time, none can achieve the performance of pipeline architectures with simple application programs and simple GPU programs. Hence, the commodity graphics market is dominated by graphics cards that have pipelines built into the graphics processing unit. All of these commodity cards implement the pipeline that we have just described, albeit with more options, many of which we shall discuss in later chapters.

For many years, these pipeline architectures have had a fixed functionality. Although the application program could set many parameters, the basic operations available within the pipeline were fixed. Recently, there has been a major advance in pipeline architectures. Both the vertex processor and the fragment processor are now programmable by the application program. One of the most exciting aspects of this advance is that many of the techniques that formerly could not be done in real time because they were not part of the fixed-function pipeline can now be done in real time. Bump mapping, which we illustrated in Color Plate 6, is but one example of an algorithm that is now programmable but formerly could only be done off-line.

Vertex programs can alter the location or color of each vertex as it flows through the pipeline. Thus, we can implement a variety of light–material models or create new kinds of projections. Fragment programs allow us to use textures in new ways and to implement other parts of the pipeline, such as lighting, on a per-fragment basis rather than per vertex.

Programmability is now available at every level, including hand-held devices such as cell phones. WebGL is being built into Web browsers. At the high end, the speed and parallelism in programmable GPUs make them suitable for carrying out high-performance computing that does not involve graphics. The latest versions of OpenGL have responded to these advances first by adding programmability to the standard as an option that an application programmer could use as an alternative to the fixed-function pipeline and later through versions that require the application to provide both a vertex shader and a fragment shader. We will follow these new standards throughout. Although it will take a little more code for our first programs because we will not use a fixed-function pipeline, the rewards will be significant as our code will be efficient and easily extendable.

1.9   PERFORMANCE CHARACTERISTICS

There are two fundamentally different types of processing in our architecture. At the front end, there is geometric processing, based on processing vertices through the various transformations, vertex shading, clipping, and primitive assembly. This processing is ideally suited for pipelining, and it usually involves floating-point calculations. The geometry engine developed by Silicon Graphics, Inc. (SGI) was a VLSI implementation for many of these operations in a special-purpose chip that became the basis for a series of fast graphics workstations. Later, floating-point accelerator chips put 4×4 matrix-transformation units on the chip, reducing a matrix multiplication to a single instruction. Nowadays, graphics workstations and commodity graphics cards use graphics processing units (GPUs) that perform most of the graphics operations at the chip level. Pipeline architectures are the dominant type of high-performance system.

Beginning with rasterization and including many features that we discuss later, processing involves a direct manipulation of bits in the frame buffer. This back-end processing is fundamentally different from front-end processing, and we implement it most effectively using architectures that have the ability to move blocks of bits quickly. The overall performance of a system is characterized by how fast we can move geometric entities through the pipeline and by how many pixels per second we can alter in the frame buffer. Consequently, the fastest graphics workstations are characterized by geometric pipelines at the front ends and parallel bit processors at the back ends. Until about 10 years ago, there was a clear distinction between front- and back-end processing and there were different components and boards dedicated to each. Now commodity graphics cards use GPUs that contain the entire pipeline within a single chip. The latest cards implement the entire pipeline using floating-point arithmetic and have floating-point frame buffers. These GPUs are so powerful that even the highest level systems—systems that incorporate multiple pipelines—use these processors.

Pipeline architectures dominate the graphics field, especially where real-time performance is of importance. Our presentation has made a case for using such an architecture to implement the hardware in a system. Commodity graphics cards incorporate the pipeline within their GPUs. Cards that cost less than $100 can render millions of shaded texture-mapped polygons per second. However, we can also make as strong a case for pipelining being the basis of a complete software implementation of an API. The power of the synthetic-camera paradigm is that the latter works well in both cases.

However, where realism is important, other types of renderers can perform better at the expense of requiring more computation time. Pixar's RenderMan interface was created to interface to their off-line renderer. Physically based techniques, such as ray tracing and radiosity, can create photorealistic images with great fidelity, but usually not in real time.

SUMMARY AND NOTES

In this chapter, we have set the stage for our top-down development of computer graphics. We presented the overall picture so that you can proceed to writing graphics application programs in the next chapter without feeling that you are working in a vacuum.

We have stressed that computer graphics is a method of image formation that should be related to classical methods of image formation—in particular, to image formation in optical systems, such as in cameras. In addition to explaining the pinhole camera, we have introduced the human visual system; both are examples of imaging systems.

We described multiple image-formation paradigms, each of which has applicability in computer graphics. The synthetic-camera model has two important consequences for computer graphics. First, it stresses the independence of the objects and the viewer—a distinction that leads to a good way of organizing the functions that will be in a graphics library. Second, it leads to the notion of a pipeline architecture, in which each of the various stages in the pipeline performs distinct operations on geometric entities and then passes on the transformed objects to the next stage.

We also introduced the idea of tracing rays of light to obtain an image. This paradigm is especially useful in understanding the interaction between light and materials that is essential to physical image formation. Because ray tracing and other physically based strategies cannot render scenes in real time, we defer further discussion of them until Chapter 11.

The modeling–rendering paradigm is becoming increasingly important. A standard graphics workstation can generate millions of line segments or polygons per second at a resolution exceeding 2048 × 1546 pixels. Such a workstation can shade the polygons using a simple shading model and can display only visible surfaces at this rate. However, realistic images may require a resolution of up to 4000 × 6000 pixels to match the resolution of film and may use light and material effects that cannot be implemented in real time. Even as the power of available hardware and software continues to grow, modeling and rendering have such different goals that we can expect the distinction between a modeling and a rendering to survive.

Our next step will be to explore the application side of graphics programming. We use the OpenGL API, which is powerful, is supported on most platforms, and has a distinct architecture that will allow us to use it to understand how computer graphics works, from an application program to a final image on a display.

SUGGESTED READINGS

There are many excellent graphics textbooks. The book by Newman and Sproull [New73] was the first to take the modern point of view of using the synthetic-camera model. The various versions of Foley et al. [Fol90, Fol94] have been the standard references for over a decade. Other good texts include Hearn and Baker [Hea11], Hill [Hil07], and Shirley [Shi02].

Good general references include *Computer Graphics*, the quarterly journal of SIGGRAPH (the Association for Computing Machinery's Special Interest Group on Graphics), *IEEE Computer Graphics and Applications*, and *Visual Computer*. The proceedings of the annual SIGGRAPH conference include the latest techniques. These proceedings formerly were published as the summer issue of *Computer Graphics*. Now, they are published as an issue of the *ACM Transactions on Graphics* and are available on DVD. Of particular interest to newcomers to the field are the state-of-the-art animations available from SIGGRAPH and the notes from tutorial courses taught at that conference, both of which are now available on DVD or in ACM's digital library.

Sutherland's doctoral dissertation, published as *Sketchpad: A Man–Machine Graphical Communication System* [Sut63] was probably the seminal paper in the development of interactive computer graphics. Sutherland was the first person to realize the power of the new paradigm in which humans interacted with images on a CRT display. Videotape copies of film of his original work are still available.

Tufte's books [Tuf83, Tuf90, Tuf97] show the importance of good visual design and contain considerable historical information on the development of graphics. The article by Carlbom and Paciorek [Car78] gives a good discussion of some of the relationships between classical viewing, as used in fields such as architecture, and viewing by computer.

Many books describe the human visual system. Pratt [Pra78] gives a good short discussion for working with raster displays. Also see Glassner [Gla95], Wyszecki and Stiles [Wys82], and Hall [Hal89].

EXERCISES

1.1 What are the main advantages and disadvantages of the preferred method to form computer-generated images discussed in this chapter?

1.2 The human visual system has all the components of a physical imaging system, such as a camera or a microscope. What are the main cells or light sensors present in the human eye? List them, and explain their uses.

1.3 A different method of approximating a sphere starts with a regular tetrahedron, which is constructed from four triangles. Find its vertices, assuming that it is centered at the origin and has one vertex on the y-axis. Derive an algorithm for obtaining increasingly closer approximations to a unit sphere, based on subdividing the faces of the tetrahedron.

1.4 Consider the clipping of a point in three dimensions against a 3D rectangular clipping window or a cube. Mathematically demonstrate how the point should be clipped. Use the coordinates of the point and the equation of the plane of a 3D rectangular clipping window or a cube for your calculations.

1.5 Each image has a set of objects and each object comprises a set of graphical primitives. What does each primitive comprise? What are the major steps in the imaging process?

1.6 A display processor is a special type of processor. What are the significant advantages of display processors? Explain briefly.

1.7 Consider the perspective views of the cube shown in Figure 1.39. The one on the left is called a *one-point perspective* because parallel lines in one direction of the cube—along the sides of the top—converge to a *vanishing point* in the image. In contrast, the image on the right is a *two-point perspective*. Characterize the particular relationship between the viewer, or a simple camera, and the cube that determines why one is a two-point perspective and the other a one-point perspective.

1.8 The memory in a frame buffer must be fast enough to allow the display to be refreshed at a rate sufficiently high to avoid flicker. A typical workstation display can have a resolution of 1400×1200 pixels. If it is refreshed 60 times per second, how fast must the memory be? That is, how much time can we take

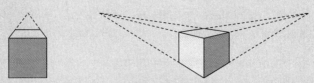

FIGURE 1.39   Perspective views of a cube.

to read one pixel from memory? What is this number for an 800 × 600 display that operates at 50 Hz but is interlaced?

1.9   A display device has a resolution of 800 × 600 pixels and uses 24 bit color for each pixel. If we generate a video with 25 frames per second which we want to upload onto the Internet, calculate the Internet speed required to transmit the video.

1.10   Consider the design of a two-dimensional graphical API for a specific application, such as for a power plant design. List all the primitives and attributes that you would include in your system.

1.11   It is possible to design a color CRT that uses a single electron gun and does not have a shadow mask. The single beam is turned on and off at the appropriate times to excite the desired phosphors. Why might such a CRT be more difficult to design, as compared to the shadow-mask CRT?

1.12   In a typical shadow-mask CRT, if we want to have a smooth display, the width of a pixel must be about three times the width of a triad. Assume that a monitor displays 800 × 600 pixels, has a CRT diameter of 55 cm, and has a CRT depth of 27 cm. Estimate the spacing between holes in the shadow mask.

1.13   This interesting exercise should help you understand how to organize the graphics utilities of your display device's properties. Go to the control panel and then display properties settings. Then, change screen resolution and color quality. What changes take place in the resolution and color quality of the display device? Does your operating system allow you to change the display properties settings?

CHAPTER 2

GRAPHICS PROGRAMMING

Our approach to computer graphics is programming oriented. Consequently, we want you to get started programming graphics as soon as possible. To this end, we will introduce a minimal application programming interface (API). This API will be sufficient to allow you to program many interesting two- and three-dimensional problems and to familiarize you with the basic graphics concepts.

We regard two-dimensional graphics as a special case of three-dimensional graphics. This perspective allows us to get started, even though we will touch on three-dimensional concepts lightly in this chapter. Our two-dimensional code will execute without modification on a three-dimensional system.

Our development will use a simple but informative problem: the Sierpinski gasket. It shows how we can generate an interesting and, to many people, unexpectedly sophisticated image using only a handful of graphics functions. We use OpenGL as our API, but our discussion of the underlying concepts is broad enough to encompass most modern systems. The functionality that we introduce in this chapter is sufficient to allow you to write basic two- and three-dimensional programs that do not require user interaction.

2.1 THE SIERPINSKI GASKET

We will use as a sample problem the drawing of the Sierpinski gasket—an interesting shape that has a long history and is of interest in areas such as fractal geometry. The Sierpinski gasket is an object that can be defined recursively and randomly; in the limit, however, it has properties that are not at all random. We start with a two-dimensional version, but as we will see in Section 2.10, the three-dimensional version is almost identical.

Suppose that we start with three points in space. As long as the points are not collinear, they are the vertices of a unique triangle and also define a unique plane. We assume that this plane is the plane $z = 0$ and that these points, as specified in some convenient coordinate system,[1] are $(x_1, y_1, 0)$, $(x_2, y_2, 0)$, and $(x_3, y_3, 0)$. The construction proceeds as follows:

1. Pick an initial point $\mathbf{p} = (x, y, 0)$ at random inside the triangle.

2. Select one of the three vertices at random.

3. Find the point $\mathbf{q}$ halfway between $\mathbf{p}$ and the randomly selected vertex.

4. Display $\mathbf{q}$ by putting some sort of marker, such as a small circle, at the corresponding location on the display.

5. Replace $\mathbf{p}$ with $\mathbf{q}$.

6. Return to step 2.

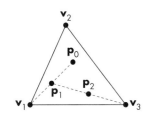

FIGURE 2.1 Generation of the Sierpinski gasket.

Thus, each time that we generate a new point, we display it on the output device. This process is illustrated in Figure 2.1, where $\mathbf{p}_0$ is the initial point, and $\mathbf{p}_1$ and $\mathbf{p}_2$ are the first two points generated by our algorithm.

Before we develop the program, you might try to determine what the resulting image will be. Try to construct it on paper; you might be surprised by your results.

A possible form for our graphics program might be this:

```
main( )
{
    initialize_the_system();
    p = find_initial_point();

    for(some_number_of_points)
    {
        q = generate_a_point(p);
        display_the_point(q);
        p = q;
    }
    cleanup();
}
```

This form can be converted into a real program fairly easily. However, even at this level of abstraction, we can see two other alternatives. Consider the pseudocode

```
main( )
{
    initialize_the_system();
    p = find_initial_point();
```

1. In Chapter 3, we expand the concept of a coordinate system to the more general formulation of a *frame*.

```
    for(some_number_of_points)
    {
        q = generate_a_point(p);
        store_the_point(q);
        p = q;
    }
    display_all_points();
    cleanup();
}
```

In this algorithm, we compute all the points first and put them into an array or some other data structure. We then display all the points through a single function call. This approach avoids the overhead of sending small amounts of data to the graphics processor for each point we generate at the cost of having to store all the data. The strategy used in the first algorithm is known as **immediate mode graphics** and, until recently, was the standard method for displaying graphics, especially where interactive performance was needed. One consequence of immediate mode is that there is no memory of the geometric data. With our first example, if we want to display the points again, we would have to go through the entire creation and display process a second time.

In our second algorithm, because the data are stored in a data structure, we can redisplay the data, perhaps with some changes such as altering the color or changing the size of a displayed point, by resending the array without regenerating the points. The method of operation is known as **retained mode graphics** and goes back to some of the earliest special purpose graphics display hardware. The architecture of modern graphics systems that employ a GPU leads to a third version of our program.

Our second approach has one major flaw. Suppose that, as we might in an animation, we wish to redisplay the same objects. The geometry of the objects is unchanged, but the objects may be moving. Displaying all the points involves sending the data from the CPU to the GPU each time we wish to display the objects in a new position. For large amounts of data, this data transfer is the major bottleneck in the display process. Consider the following alternative scheme:

```
main( )
{
    initialize_the_system();
    p = find_initial_point();

    for(some_number_of_points)
    {
        q = generate_a_point(p);
        store_the_point(q);
        p = q;
    }
}
```

```
        send_all_points_to_GPU();
        display_data_on_GPU();
        cleanup();
}
```

As before, we place data in an array, but now we have broken the display process into two parts: storing the data on the GPU and displaying the data that has been stored. If we only have to display our data once, there is no advantage over our previous method, but if we want to animate the display, our data are already on the GPU and redisplay does not require any additional data transfer, only a simple function call that alters the location of some spatial data describing the objects that have moved.

Although our final OpenGL program will have a slightly different organization, it will follow this third strategy. We develop the full program in stages. First, we concentrate on the core: generating and displaying points. We must answer two questions:

- How do we represent points in space?

- Should we use a two-dimensional, three-dimensional, or other representation?

Once we answer these questions, we will be able to place our geometry on the GPU in a form that can be rendered. Then, we will be able to address how we view our objects using the power of programmable shaders.

2.2   PROGRAMMING TWO-DIMENSIONAL APPLICATIONS

For two-dimensional applications, such as the Sierpinski gasket, although we could use a pen-plotter API, such an approach would limit us. Instead, we choose to start with a three-dimensional world; we regard two-dimensional systems, such as the one on which we will produce our image, as special cases. Mathematically, we view the two-dimensional plane, or a simple two-dimensional curved surface, as a subspace of a three-dimensional space. Hence, statements—both practical and abstract—about the larger three-dimensional world hold for the simpler two-dimensional world.

We can represent a point in the plane $z = 0$ as $\mathbf{p} = (x, y, 0)$ in the three-dimensional world, or as $\mathbf{p} = (x, y)$ in the two-dimensional plane. OpenGL, like most three-dimensional graphics systems, allows us to use either representation, with the underlying internal representation being the same, regardless of which form the user chooses. We can implement representations of points in a number of ways, but the simplest is to think of a three-dimensional point as being represented by a triplet $\mathbf{p} = (x, y, z)$ or a column matrix

$$\mathbf{p} = \begin{bmatrix} x \\ y \\ z \end{bmatrix},$$

whose components give the location of the point. For the moment, we can leave aside the question of the coordinate system in which **p** is represented.

We use the terms *vertex* and *point* in a somewhat different manner in OpenGL. A **vertex** is a position in space; we use two-, three-, and four-dimensional spaces in computer graphics. We use vertices to specify the atomic geometric primitives that are recognized by our graphics system. The simplest geometric primitive is a point in space, which is usually specified by a single vertex. Two vertices can specify a line segment, a second primitive object; three vertices can specify either a triangle or a circle; four vertices can specify a quadrilateral; and so on. Two vertices can also specify either a circle or a rectangle. Likewise, three vertices can also specify three points or two connected line segments, and four vertices can specify a variety of objects including two triangles.

The heart of our Sierpinski gasket program is generating the points. In order to go from our third algorithm to a working OpenGL program, we need to introduce a little more detail on OpenGL. We want to start with as simple a program as possible. One simplification is to delay a discussion of coordinate systems and transformations among them by putting all the data we want to display inside a cube centered at the origin whose diagonal goes from $(-1, -1, -1)$ and $(1, 1, 1)$. This system known as **clip coordinates** is the one that our vertex shader uses to send information to the rasterizer. Objects outside this cube will be eliminated, or **clipped**, and cannot appear on the display. Later, we will learn to specify geometry in our application program in coordinates better suited for our application—**object coordinates**—and use transformations to convert the data to a representation in clip coordinates.

We could write the program using a simple array of two elements to hold the x- and y-values of each point. We will have far clearer code if we first define a two-dimensional point type and operations for this type. We have created such classes and operators and put them in a file vec.h. The types in vec.h and the other types defined later in the three- and four-dimensional classes match the types in the OpenGL Shading Language and so should make all our coding examples clearer than if we had used ordinary arrays. In addition to defining these new types, vec.h and its companion file mat2.h also define overloaded operators and constructors for these types that match GLSL. Hence, code such as

```
vec2 a = vec2(1.0, 2.0);
vec2 b = vec2(3.0, 4.0);
vec2 c = a + b;
```

can appear either in a shader or in the application. We can input and output points using the usual stream operators cin and cout. We can access individual elements using either the usual membership operator, e.g., p.x or p.y, or by indexing as we would an array (p[0] and p[1]).

One small addition will make our applications even clearer. Rather than using the GLSL vec2, we typedef a point2

```
typedef vec2 point2;
```

Within vec.h, the type vec2 is specified as a struct with two elements of type GLfloat. In OpenGL, we often use basic OpenGL types, such as GLfloat and GLint, rather than the corresponding C types float and int. These types are defined in the OpenGL header files and usually in the obvious way—for example,

```
typedef float GLfloat;
```

However, use of the OpenGL types allows additional flexibility for implementations where, for example, we might want to change floats to doubles without altering existing application programs.

The following code generates 5000 points starting with the vertices of a triangle that lie in the plane $z = 0$:

```
#include "vec.h" // include point types and operations
#include <stdlib.h> //includes random number generator

typedef vec2 point2; //defines a point2 type identical to a vec2

void init()
{
    const int NumPoints = 5000;
    point2 points[NumPoints];

    // A triangle in the plane z= 0

    point2 vertices[3]={point2(-1.0,-1.0), point2(0.0,1.0),
                        point2(1.0,-1.0)};

    // An arbitrary initial point inside the triangle

    points[0] = point2(0.25, 0.50);

    // compute and store NumPoints-1 new points

    for(int k = 1; k < NumPoints; k++)
    {
        int j = rand() % 3; // pick a vertex at random

        // Compute the point halfway between selected
        // vertex and previous point
        points[k] = (points[k-1]+vertices[j])/2.0;
    }
}
```

Note that because every point we generate must lie inside the triangle determined by these vertices, we know that none of the generated points will be clipped out.

The function `rand()` is a standard random-number generator that produces a new random integer each time it is called. We use the modulus operator to reduce these random integers to the three integers 0, 1, and 2. For a small number of iterations, the particular characteristics of the random-number generator are not crucial, and any other random-number generator should work at least as well as `rand`.

We intend to generate the points only once and then place them on the GPU. Hence, we make their creation part of an initialization function `init`.

We specified our points in two dimensions. We could have also specified them in three dimensions by adding a z-coordinate, which is always zero through the three-dimensional types in `mat.h` and `vec.h`. The changes to the code would be minimal. We would have the code lines

```
#include "vec.h" // three-dimensional type

typedef vec3 point3;
```

and

```
point3 points [NumPoints];
point3 vertices[3] = {point3(-1.0,-1.0, 0.0), point3(0.0,1.0, 0.0),
                      point3(1.0,-1.0, 0.0)};
```

as part of initialization. Although we still do not have a complete program, Figure 2.2 shows the output that we expect to see.

Note that because any three noncollinear points specify a unique plane, had we started with three points (x_1, y_1, z_1), (x_2, y_2, z_2), and (x_3, y_3, z_3) along with an initial point in the same plane, then the gasket would be generated in the plane specified by the original three vertices.

We have now written the core of the program. Although we have some data, we have not placed these data on the GPU nor have we asked the GPU to display anything. We have not even introduced a single OpenGL function. Before we can display anything, we still have to address issues such as the following:

1. In what colors are we drawing?

2. Where on the display does our image appear?

3. How large will the image be?

4. How do we create an area of the display—a window—for our image?

5. How much of our infinite drawing surface will appear on the display?

6. How long will the image remain on the display?

The answers to all these questions are important, although initially they may appear to be peripheral to our major concerns. As we will see, the basic code that we develop to answer these questions and to control the placement and appearance of our

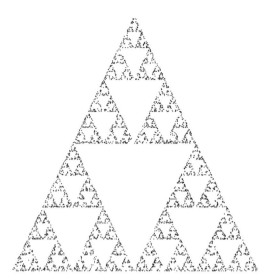

FIGURE 2.2   The Sierpinski gasket as generated with 5000 random points.

renderings will not change substantially across programs. Hence, the effort that we expend now will be repaid later.

2.3   THE OPENGL APPLICATION PROGRAMMING INTERFACE

We have the heart of a simple graphics program; now, we want to gain control over how our objects appear on the display. We also want to control the flow of the program, and we have to interact with the window system. Before completing our program, we describe the OpenGL Application Programming Interface (API) in more detail. Because vertices are represented in the same manner internally, whether they are specified as two- or three-dimensional entities, everything that we do here will be equally valid in three dimensions. Of course, we can do much more in three dimensions, but we are only getting started. In this chapter, we concentrate on how to specify primitives to be displayed.

OpenGL's structure is similar to that of most modern APIs, such as DirectX. Hence, any effort that you put into learning OpenGL will carry over to other software systems. Although OpenGL is easy to learn, compared with other APIs, it is nevertheless powerful. It supports the simple two- and three-dimensional programs that we will develop in Chapters 2 through 5; it also supports the advanced rendering techniques that we study in Chapters 7 through 11.

Our prime goal is to study computer graphics; we are using an API to help us attain that goal. Consequently, we do not present all OpenGL functions, and we omit many details. However, our sample programs will be complete. More detailed

FIGURE 2.3   Graphics system as a black box.

information on OpenGL and on other APIs is given in the Suggested Readings section at the end of the chapter.

2.3.1 Graphics Functions

Our basic model of a graphics package is a **black box**, a term that engineers use to denote a system whose properties are described only by its inputs and outputs; we may know nothing about its internal workings. We can think of the graphics system as a box whose inputs are function calls from an application program; measurements from input devices, such as the mouse and keyboard; and possibly other input, such as messages from the operating system. The outputs are primarily the graphics sent to our output devices. For now, we can take the simplified view of inputs as function calls and outputs as primitives displayed on our monitor, as shown in Figure 2.3.

A graphics system performs multiple tasks to produce output and handle user input. An API for interfacing with this system can contain hundreds of individual functions. It will be helpful to divide these functions into seven major groups:

1. Primitive functions
2. Attribute functions
3. Viewing functions
4. Transformation functions
5. Input functions
6. Control functions
7. Query functions

Although we will focus on OpenGL as the particular system that we use, all graphics APIs support similar functionality. What differs among APIs is where these functions are supported. OpenGL is designed around a pipeline architecture, and modern versions are based on using programmable shaders. Consequently, OpenGL and other APIs such as DirectX that support a similar architecture will have much in common, whereas OpenGL and an API for a ray tracer will have less overlap. Nevertheless, regardless of the underlying architecture and API, we still have to address all the seven tasks.

The **primitive functions** define the low-level objects or atomic entities that our system can display. Depending on the API, the primitives can include points, line segments, polygons, pixels, text, and various types of curves and surfaces. OpenGL supports a very limited set of primitives directly, only points, line segments, and triangles. Support for other primitives comes from the application approximating them with the supported primitives. For the most important objects such as regular polyhedra, quadrics, and Bezier curves and surfaces that are not directly supported by OpenGL, there are libraries that provide the necessary code. Support for expanded sets of primitives is usually done with great efficiency through programmable shaders.

If primitives are the *what* of an API—the primitive objects that can be displayed—then attributes are the *how*. That is, the attributes govern the way that a primitive appears on the display. **Attribute functions** allow us to perform operations ranging from choosing the color with which we display a line segment, to picking a pattern with which to fill the inside of a polygon, to selecting a typeface for the titles on a graph. In OpenGL, we can set colors by passing the information from the application to the shader or by having a shader compute a color, for example, through a lighting model that uses data specifying light sources and properties of the surfaces in our model.

Our synthetic camera must be described if we are to create an image. As we saw in Chapter 1, we must describe the camera's position and orientation in our world and must select the equivalent of a lens. This process will not only fix the view but also allow us to clip out objects that are too close or too far away. The **viewing functions** allow us to specify various views, although APIs differ in the degree of flexibility they provide in choosing a view. OpenGL does not provide any viewing functions but relies on the use of transformations in the shaders to provide the desired view.

One of the characteristics of a good API is that it provides the user with a set of **transformation functions** that allows her to carry out transformations of objects, such as rotation, translation, and scaling. Our developments of viewing in Chapter 4 and of modeling in Chapter 8 will make heavy use of matrix transformations. In OpenGL, we carry out transformations by forming transformations in our applications and then applying them either in the application or in the shaders.

For interactive applications, an API must provide a set of **input functions** to allow us to deal with the diverse forms of input that characterize modern graphics systems. We need functions to deal with devices such as keyboards, mice, and data tablets. Later in this chapter, we will introduce functions for working with different input modes and with a variety of input devices.

In any real application, we also have to worry about handling the complexities of working in a multiprocessing, multiwindow environment—usually an environment where we are connected to a network and there are other users. The **control functions** enable us to communicate with the window system, to initialize our programs, and to deal with any errors that take place during the execution of our programs.

If we are to write device-independent programs, we should expect the implementation of the API to take care of differences between devices, such as how many colors are supported or the size of the display. However, there are applications where we need to know some properties of the particular implementation. For example, we would probably choose to do things differently if we knew in advance that we were working with a display that could support only two colors rather than millions of colors. More generally, within our applications we can often use other information within the API, including camera parameters or values in the frame buffer. A good API provides this information through a set of **query functions**.

2.3.2 The Graphics Pipeline and State Machines

If we put together some of these perspectives on graphics APIs, we can obtain another view, one closer to the way OpenGL, in particular, is actually organized and implemented. We can think of the entire graphics system as a **state machine**, a black box that contains a finite-state machine. This state machine has inputs that come from the application program. These inputs may change the state of the machine or can cause the machine to produce a visible output. From the perspective of the API, graphics functions are of two types: those that specify primitives that flow through a pipeline inside the state machine and those that either change the state inside the machine or return state information. In OpenGL, there are very few functions that can cause any output. Most set the state, either by enabling various OpenGL features—hidden-surface removal, texture—or set parameters used for rendering.

Until recently, OpenGL defined many state variables and contained separate functions for setting the values of individual variables. The latest versions have eliminated most of these variables and functions. Instead, the application program can define its own state variables and use them or send their values to the shaders.

One important consequence of the state machine view is that most parameters are persistent; their values remain unchanged until we explicitly change them through functions that alter the state. For example, once we set a color, that color remains the *current color* until it is changed through a color-altering function. Another consequence of this view is that attributes that we may conceptualize as bound to objects—a red line or a blue circle—are in fact part of the state, and a line will be drawn in red only if the current color state calls for drawing in red. Although within our applications it is usually harmless, and often preferable, to think of attributes as bound to primitives, there can be annoying side effects if we neglect to make state changes when needed or lose track of the current state.

2.3.3 The OpenGL Interface

OpenGL functions are in a single library named GL (or OpenGL in Windows). Function names begin with the letters `gl`. Shaders are written in the OpenGL Shading Language (GLSL), which has a separate specification from OpenGL, although the functions to interface the shaders with the application are part of the OpenGL API.

To interface with the window system and to get input from external devices into our programs, we need at least one more library. For each major window system there is a system-specific library that provides the "glue" between the window system and OpenGL. For the X Window System, this library is called GLX, for Windows, it is wgl, and for the Macintosh, it is agl. Rather than using a different library for each system, we use two readily available libraries, the **OpenGL Extension Wrangler (GLEW)** and the **OpenGL Utility Toolkit (GLUT)**. GLEW removes operating system dependencies. GLUT provides the minimum functionality that should be expected in any modern

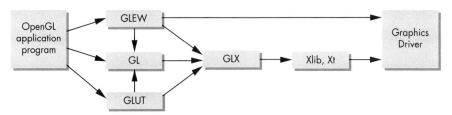

FIGURE 2.4 Library organization.

windowing system.[2] We introduce a few of its functions in this chapter and describe more of them in Chapter 3.

Figure 2.4 shows the organization of the libraries for an X Window System environment. For this window system, GLUT will use GLX and the X libraries. The application program, however, can use only GLUT functions and thus can be recompiled with the GLUT library for other window systems.

OpenGL makes heavy use of defined constants to increase code readability and avoid the use of magic numbers. Thus, strings such as GL_FILL and GL_POINTS are defined in header (.h) files. In most implementations, one of the include lines

```
#include <GL/glut.h>
```

or

```
#include <GLUT/glut.h>
```

is sufficient to read in glut.h and gl.h.

Although OpenGL is not object oriented, it supports a variety of data types through multiple forms for many functions. For example, we will use various forms of the function glUniform to transfer data to shaders. If we transfer a floating-point number such as a time value, we would use glUniform1f. We could use glUniform3iv to transfer an integer position in three dimensions through a pointer to a three-dimensional array of ints. Later, we will use the form glUniformMatrix4fv to transfer a 4 × 4 matrix of floats. We will refer to such functions using the notation

```
glSomeFunction*();
```

where the * can be interpreted as either two or three characters of the form nt or ntv, where n signifies the number of dimensions (2, 3, 4, or matrix); t denotes the data type, such as integer (i), float (f), or double (d); and v, if present, indicates that the variables are specified through a pointer to an array, rather than through an argument

---

2. A more up-to-date version of GLUT is provided by freeglut, which is available on the Web.

list. We will use whatever form is best suited for our discussion, leaving the details of the various other forms to the *OpenGL Programming Guide* [Shr10]. Regardless of which form an application programmer chooses, the underlying representation is the same, just as the plane on which we are constructing the gasket can be looked at as either a two-dimensional space or the subspace of a three-dimensional space corresponding to the plane $z = 0$. In Chapter 3, we will see that the underlying representation is four-dimensional; however, we do not need to worry about that fact yet. In general, the application programmer chooses the form to use that is best suited for her application.

2.3.4 Coordinate Systems

At this point, if we look back at our Sierpinski gasket code, you may be puzzled about how to interpret the values of x, y, and z in our specification of vertices. In what units are they? Are they in feet, meters, microns? Where is the origin? In each case, the simple answer is that it is up to you.

Originally, graphics systems required the user to specify all information, such as vertex locations, directly in units of the display device. If that were true for high-level application programs, we would have to talk about points in terms of screen locations in pixels or centimeters from a corner of the display. There are obvious problems with this method, not the least of which is the absurdity of using distances on the computer screen to describe phenomena where the natural unit might be light years (such as in displaying astronomical data) or microns (for integrated-circuit design). One of the major advances in graphics software systems occurred when the graphics systems allowed users to work in any coordinate system that they desired. The advent of **device-independent graphics** freed application programmers from worrying about the details of input and output devices. The user's coordinate system became known as the **world coordinate system**, or the **application** or **object coordinate system**. Within the slight limitations of floating-point arithmetic on our computers, we can use any numbers that fit our application.

We will refer to the units that the application program uses to specify vertex positions as **vertex coordinates**. In most applications, vertex coordinates will be the same as object or world coordinates, but depending on what we choose to do or not do in our shaders, vertex coordinates can be one of the other internal coordinate systems used in the pipeline. We will discuss these other coordinate systems in Chapters 3 and 4.

Units on the display were first called **physical-device coordinates** or just **device coordinates**. For raster devices, such as most CRT and flat panel displays, we use the term **window coordinates** or **screen coordinates**. Window coordinates are always expressed in some integer type, because the center of any pixel in the frame buffer must be located on a fixed grid or, equivalently, because pixels are inherently discrete and we specify their locations using integers.

At some point, the values in vertex coordinates must be mapped to window coordinates, as shown in Figure 2.5. The graphics system, rather than the user, is responsible for this task, and the mapping is performed automatically as part of the

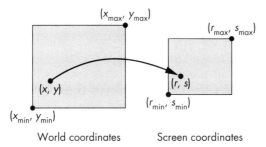

FIGURE 2.5   Mapping from vertex coordinates to screen coordinates.

rendering process. As we will see in the next few sections, to define this mapping the user needs to specify only a few parameters—such as the area of the world that she would like to see and the size of the display. However, between the application and the frame buffer are the two shaders and rasterizer, and, as we shall see when we discuss viewing, there are three other intermediate coordinate systems of importance.

2.4   PRIMITIVES AND ATTRIBUTES

Within the graphics community, there has been an ongoing debate about which primitives should be supported in an API. The debate is an old one and has never been fully resolved. On the minimalist side, the contention is that an API should contain a small set of primitives that all hardware can be expected to support. In addition, the primitives should be orthogonal, each giving a capability unobtainable from the others. Minimal systems typically support lines, polygons, and some form of text (strings of characters), all of which can be generated efficiently in hardware. On the other end are systems that can also support a variety of primitives, such as circles, curves, surfaces, and solids. The argument here is that users need more complex primitives to build sophisticated applications easily. However, because few hardware systems can be expected to support the large set of primitives that is the union of all the desires of the user community, a program developed with such a system probably would not be portable, because few implementations could be expected to support the entire set of primitives.

As graphics hardware has improved and real-time performance has become measured in the tens of millions of polygons per second, the balance has tilted toward supporting a minimum set of primitives. One reason is that GPUs achieve their speed largely because they are optimized for points, lines, and triangles. We will develop code later that will approximate various curves and surfaces with primitives that are supported on GPUs.

We can separate primitives into two classes: **geometric primitives** and **image**, or **raster, primitives**. Geometric primitives are specified in the problem domain and include points, line segments, polygons, curves, and surfaces. These primitives pass through a geometric pipeline, as shown in Figure 2.6, where they are subject to a series

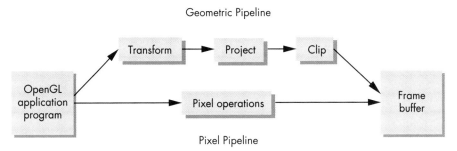

FIGURE 2.6   Simplified OpenGL pipeline.

of geometric operations that determine whether a primitive is visible, where on the display it appears if it is visible, and the rasterization of the primitive into pixels in the frame buffer. Because geometric primitives exist in a two- or three-dimensional space, they can be manipulated by operations such as rotation and translation. In addition, they can be used as building blocks for other geometric objects using these same operations. Raster primitives, such as arrays of pixels, lack geometric properties and cannot be manipulated in space in the same way as geometric primitives. They pass through a separate parallel pipeline on their way to the frame buffer. We will defer our discussion of raster primitives until Chapter 7.

The basic OpenGL geometric primitives are specified by sets of vertices. An application starts by computing vertex data—positions and other attributes—and putting the results into arrays that are sent to the GPU for display. When we want to display some geometry, we execute functions whose parameters specify how the vertices are to be interpreted. For example, we can display the vertices we computed for the Sierpinski gasket, starting with the first vertex, as points through the function call

```
glDrawArrays(GL_POINTS, 0, NumPoints);
```

after they have been placed on the GPU.

All OpenGL geometric primitives are variants of points, line segments, and triangular polygons. A point can be displayed as a single pixel or a small group of pixels. Finite sections of lines between two vertices, called **line segments**—in contrast to lines that are infinite in extent—are of great importance in geometry and computer graphics. You can use line segments to define approximations to curves, or you can use a sequence of line segments to connect data values for a graph. You can also use line segments to display the edges of closed objects, such as polygons, that have interiors. Consequently, it is often helpful to think in terms of both vertices and line segments.

If we wish to display points or line segments, we have a few choices in OpenGL (Figure 2.7). The primitives and their type specifications include the following:

Points (GL_POINTS)   Each vertex is displayed at a size of at least one pixel.

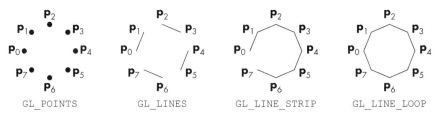

FIGURE 2.7   Point and line-segment types.

FIGURE 2.8   Filled objects.

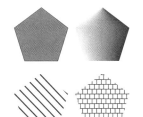

FIGURE 2.9   Methods of displaying a polygon.

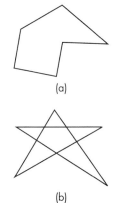

(a)

(b)

FIGURE 2.10   Polygons. (a) Simple. (b) Nonsimple.

Line segments (GL_LINES)   The line-segment type causes successive pairs of vertices to be interpreted as the endpoints of individual segments. Note that successive segments usually are disconnected because the vertices are processed on a pairwise basis.

Polylines (GL_LINE_STRIP, GL_LINE_LOOP)   If successive vertices (and line segments) are to be connected, we can use the line strip, or **polyline** form. Many curves can be approximated via a suitable polyline. If we wish the polyline to be closed, we can locate the final vertex in the same place as the first, or we can use the GL_LINE_LOOP type, which will draw a line segment from the final vertex to the first, thus creating a closed path.

2.4.1 Polygon Basics

Line segments and polylines can model the edges of objects, but closed objects have interiors (Figure 2.8). Usually we reserve the name **polygon** for an object that has a border that can be described by a line loop but also has a well-defined interior.[3] Polygons play a special role in computer graphics because we can display them rapidly and use them to approximate arbitrary surfaces. The performance of graphics systems is characterized by the number of polygons per second that can be rendered.[4] We can render a polygon in a variety of ways: We can render only its edges, we can render its interior with a solid color or a pattern, and we can render or not render the edges, as shown in Figure 2.9. Although the outer edges of a polygon are defined easily by an ordered list of vertices, if the interior is not well defined, then the list of vertices may not be rendered at all or rendered in an undesirable manner. Three properties will ensure that a polygon will be displayed correctly: It must be simple, convex, and flat.

In two dimensions, as long as no two edges of a polygon cross each other, we have a **simple** polygon. As we can see in Figure 2.10, simple two-dimensional polygons have well-defined interiors. Although the locations of the vertices determine whether or not a polygon is simple, the cost of testing is sufficiently high (see Exercise 2.12) that most graphics systems require that the application program does any necessary

---

3. The term *fill area* is sometimes used instead of *polygon*.

4. Measuring polygon rendering speeds involves both the number of vertices and the number of pixels inside.

testing. We can ask what a graphics system will do if it is given a nonsimple polygon to display and whether there is a way to define an interior for a nonsimple polygon. We will examine these questions further in Chapter 6.

From the perspective of implementing a practical algorithm to fill the interior of a polygon, simplicity alone is often not enough. Some APIs guarantee a consistent fill from implementation to implementation only if the polygon is convex. An object is **convex** if all points on the line segment between any two points inside the object, or on its boundary, are inside the object. Thus, in Figure 2.11, $\mathbf{p}_1$ and $\mathbf{p}_2$ are arbitrary points inside a polygon and the entire line segment connecting them is inside the polygon. Although so far we have been dealing with only two-dimensional objects, this definition makes reference neither to the type of object nor to the number of dimensions. Convex objects include triangles, tetrahedra, rectangles, circles, spheres, and parallelepipeds (Figure 2.12). There are various tests for convexity (see Exercise 2.19). However, like simplicity testing, convexity testing is expensive and usually left to the application program.

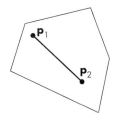

FIGURE 2.11   Convexity.

In three dimensions, polygons present a few more difficulties because, unlike all two-dimensional objects, all the vertices that specify the polygon need not lie in the same plane. One property that most graphics systems exploit, and that is the basis of OpenGL polygons, is that any three vertices that are not collinear determine both a triangle and the plane in which that triangle lies. Hence, if we always use triangles, we are safe—we can be sure that these objects will be rendered correctly. Often, we are almost forced to use triangles because typical rendering algorithms are guaranteed to be correct only if the vertices form a flat convex polygon. In addition, hardware and software often support a triangle type that is rendered faster than is a polygon with three vertices.

2.4.2 Polygons in OpenGL

Returning to the OpenGL types, the only OpenGL polygons (Figure 2.13) that OpenGL supports are triangles. Triangles can be displayed in three ways: as points corresponding to the vertices, as edges, or with the interiors filled. In OpenGL, we use the function `glPolygonMode` to tell the renderer to generate only the edges or just points for the vertices, instead of fill (the default). However, if we want to draw a

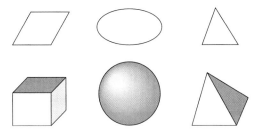

FIGURE 2.12   Convex objects.

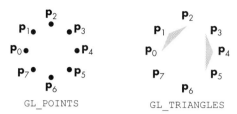

FIGURE 2.13   Triangle types.

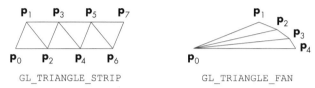

FIGURE 2.14   Triangle strip and triangle fan.

polygon that is filled and to display its edges, then we have to render it twice, once in each mode, or to draw a filled polygon and a line loop with the same vertices.

Here are the types:

Triangles (GL_TRIANGLES)   The edges are the same as they would be if we used line loops. Each successive group of three vertices specifies a new triangle.

Strips and Fans (GL_TRIANGLE_STRIP, GL_TRIANGLE_FAN)   These objects are based on groups of triangles that share vertices and edges. In the triangle strip, for example, each additional vertex is combined with the previous two vertices to define a new triangle (Figure 2.14). A triangle fan is based on one fixed point. The next two points determine the first triangle, and subsequent triangles are formed from one new point, the previous point, and the first (fixed) point.

2.4.3 Approximating a Sphere

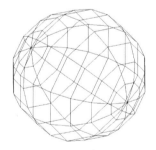

FIGURE 2.15   Sphere approximation with quadrilaterals.

Fans and strips allow us to approximate many curved surfaces simply. For example, one way to construct an approximation to a sphere is to use a set of polygons defined by lines of longitude and latitude, as shown in Figure 2.15. We can do so very efficiently using triangle strips. Consider a unit sphere. We can describe it by the following three equations:

$$x(\theta, \phi) = \sin \theta \cos \phi,$$

$$y(\theta, \phi) = \cos \theta \cos \phi,$$

$$z(\theta, \phi) = \sin \phi.$$

If we fix θ and draw curves as we change ϕ, we get circles of constant longitude. Likewise, if we fix ϕ and vary θ, we obtain circles of constant latitude. By generating points at fixed increments of θ and ϕ, we can specify quadrilaterals, as shown in Figure 2.15. However, because OpenGL supports triangles, not quadrilaterals, we generate the data for two triangles for each quadrilateral. Remembering that we must convert degrees to radians for the standard trigonometric functions, the code for the quadrilaterals corresponding to increments of 20 degrees in θ and to 20 degrees in ϕ is

```
const float DegreesToRadians = M_PI / 180.0; // M_PI = 3.14159...

point3 quad_data[342];    // 8 rows of 18 quads

int k = 0;
for(float phi = -80.0; phi <= 80.0; phi += 20.0)
{
    float phir   = phi*DegreesToRadians;
    float phir20 = (phi + 20.0)*DegreesToRadians;

    for(float theta = -180.0; theta <= 180.0; theta += 20.0)
    {
        float thetar = theta*DegreesToRadians;
        quad_data[k] = point3(sin(thetar)*cos(phir),
                          cos(thetar)*cos(phir), sin(phir));
        k++;
        quad_data[k] = point3(sin(thetar)*cos(phir20),
                          cos(thetar)*cos(phir20), sin(phir20));
        k++;
    }
}
```

Later we can render these data using `glDrawArrays(GL_LINE_LOOP,...)` or some other drawing function. However, we have a problem at the poles, where we can no longer use strips because all lines of longitude converge there. We can, however, use two triangle fans, one at each pole as follows:

```
const float DegreesToRadians = M_PI / 180.0; // M_PI = 3.14159...

int k = 0;
point3 strip_data[40];

strip_data[k] = point3(0.0, 0.0, 1.0);
k++;

float sin80 = sin(80.0*DegreesToRadians);
float cos80 = cos(80.0*DegreesToRadians);
```

```
for(float theta = -180.0; theta <= 180.0; theta += 20.0)
{
    float thetar = theta*DegreesToRadians;
    strip_data[k] = point3(sin(thetar)*cos80,
                           cos(thetar)*cos80, sin80);
    k++;
}

strip_data[k] = point3(0.0, 0.0, -1.0);
k++;

for(float theta = -180.0; theta <= 180.0; theta += 20.0)
{
    float thetar = theta;
    strip_data[k] = point3(sin(thetar)*cos80,
                           cos(thetar)*cos80, sin80);
    k++;
}
```

These data could be rendered with `glDrawArrays(GL_TRIANGLE_FAN, ....)` or another drawing function. Note that because triangle fans are polygons, if we want to get the line segment display in Figure 2.15, we would first have to set the polygon mode to lines instead of fill.

2.4.4 Triangulation

We have been using the terms polygon and triangle somewhat interchangeably. If we are interested in objects with interiors, general polygons are problematic. A set of vertices may not all lie in the same plane or specify a polygon that is neither simple nor convex. Such problems do not arise with triangles. As long as the three vertices of a triangle are not collinear, its interior is well defined and the triangle is simple, flat, and convex. Consequently, triangles are easy to render, and for these reasons triangles are the only fillable geometric entity that OpenGL recognizes. In practice, we need to deal with more general polygons. The usual strategy is to start with a list of vertices and generate a set of triangles consistent with the polygon defined by the list, a process known as **triangulation**.

Figure 2.16 shows a convex polygon and two different triangulations. Although every set of vertices can be triangulated, not all triangulations are equivalent. Consider the quadrilateral in Figure 2.17. If we triangulate it as in Figure 2.17(b), we create two long thin triangles rather than two triangles closer to being equilateral as in Figure 2.17(c). As we shall see when we discuss lighting in Chapter 5, long thin triangles can lead to visual artifacts when rendered. There are some simple algorithms that work for planar convex polygons. We can start with the first three vertices and form a triangle. We can then remove the second vertex from the list of vertices and repeat the process until we have only three vertices left, which form the final triangle. This process is illustrated in Figure 2.18, but it does not guarantee a good set of triangles nor can it handle concave polygons. In Chapter 6, we will discuss the triangulation of

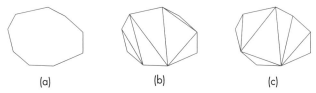

FIGURE 2.16   (a) Two-dimensional polygon. (b) A triangulation. (c) Another triangulation.

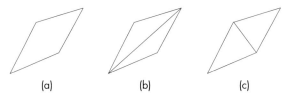

FIGURE 2.17   (a) Quadrilateral. (b) A triangulation. (c) Another triangulation.

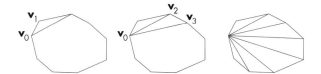

FIGURE 2.18   Recursive triangulation of a convex polygon.

simple but nonconvex polygons as part of rasterization. This technique will allows us to render more general polygons than triangles.

We will delay a discussion of more general triangulation algorithms until we discuss curves and surfaces in Chapter 10. One reason for this delay is that there are a number of related processes that arise when we consider modeling surfaces. For example, laser-scanning technology allows us to gather millions of unstructured three-dimensional vertices. We then have to form a surface from these vertices, usually in the form of a mesh of triangles. The **Delaunay triangulation** algorithm finds a best triangulation in the sense that if we consider the circle determined by any triangle, no other vertex lies in this circle. Triangulation is a special case of the more general problem of **tessellation**, which divides a polygon into a polygonal mesh, not all of which need be triangles. General tessellation algorithms are complex, especially when the initial polygon may contain holes.

Computer
Graphics

FIGURE 2.19 Stroke text
(PostScript font).

2.4.5 Text

Graphical output in applications such as data analysis and display requires annotation, such as labels on graphs. Although in nongraphical programs textual output is the norm, text in computer graphics is problematic. In nongraphical applications, we are usually content with a simple set of characters, always displayed in the same manner. In computer graphics, however, we often wish to display text in a multitude of fashions by controlling type styles, sizes, colors, and other parameters. We also want to have available a choice of fonts. **Fonts** are families of typefaces of a particular style, such as Times, Computer Modern, or Helvetica.

There are two forms of text: stroke and raster. **Stroke text** (Figure 2.19) is constructed as are other geometric objects. We use vertices to specify line segments or curves that outline each character. If the characters are defined by closed boundaries, we can fill them. The advantage of stroke text is that it can be defined to have all the detail of any other object, and because it is defined in the same way as other graphical objects are, it can be manipulated by our standard transformations and viewed like any other graphical primitive. Using transformations, we can make a stroke character bigger or rotate it, retaining its detail and appearance. Consequently, we need to define a character only once, and we can use transformations to generate it at the desired size and orientation.

Defining a full 128- or 256-character stroke font, however, can be complex, and the font can take up significant memory and processing time. The standard PostScript fonts are defined by polynomial curves, and they illustrate all the advantages and disadvantages of stroke text. The various PostScript fonts can be used for both high- and low-resolution applications. Often, developers mitigate the problem of slow rendering of such stroke characters by putting considerable processing power in the printer.

Raster text (Figure 2.20) is simple and fast. Characters are defined as rectangles of bits called **bit blocks**. Each block defines a single character by the pattern of 0 and 1 bits in the block. A raster character can be placed in the frame buffer rapidly by a **bit-block-transfer (bitblt)** operation, which moves the block of bits using a single function call. We will discuss bitblt in Chapter 7.

You can increase the size of raster characters by **replicating**, or duplicating, pixels, a process that gives larger characters a blocky appearance (Figure 2.21). Other transformations of raster characters, such as rotation, may not make sense, because

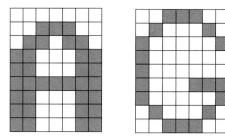

FIGURE 2.20   Raster text.

FIGURE 2.21   Raster-character replication.

the transformation may move the bits defining the character to locations that do not correspond to the location of pixels in the frame buffer.

Because stroke and bitmap characters can be created from other primitives, OpenGL does not have a text primitive. However, the GLUT library provides a few predefined bitmap and stroke character sets that are defined in software and are portable.

2.4.6 Curved Objects

The primitives in our basic set have all been defined through vertices. With the exception of the point type, all consist of line segments or use line segments to define the boundary of a region that can be filled with a solid color or a pattern. We can take two approaches to creating a richer set of objects.

First, we can use the primitives that we have to approximate curves and surfaces. For example, if we want a circle, we can use a regular polygon of n sides. Likewise, we have approximated a sphere with triangles and quadrilaterals. More generally, we approximate a curved surface by a mesh of convex polygons—a tessellation—which can occur either at the rendering stage or within the user program.

The other approach, which we will explore in Chapter 10, is to start with the mathematical definitions of curved objects and then build graphics functions to implement those objects. Objects such as quadric surfaces and parametric polynomial curves and surfaces are well understood mathematically, and we can specify them through sets of vertices. For example, we can specify a sphere by its center and a point on its surface, or we can specify a cubic polynomial curve using data at four points.

2.4.7 Attributes

Although we can describe a geometric object through a set of vertices, a given object can be displayed in many different ways. Properties that describe how an object should be rendered are called **attributes**. Available attributes depend on the type of object. For example, a line could be black or green. It could be solid or dashed. A polygon could be filled with a single color or with a pattern. We could display it as filled or only by its edges. Several of these attributes are shown in Figure 2.22 for lines and polygons.

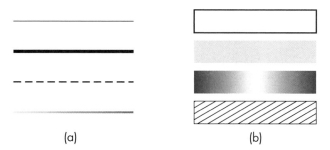

(a)   (b)

FIGURE 2.22   Attributes for (a) lines and (b) polygons.

Attributes may be associated with, or **bound** to, geometric objects, such as the color of a cube. Often we will find it better to model an object such as the cube by its individual faces and to specify attributes for the faces. Hence, a cube would be green because its six faces are green. Each face could then be described by two triangles so ultimately a green cube would be rendered as 12 green triangles.

If we go one step further, we see that each of the triangles is specified through three vertices. In a pipeline architecture, each vertex is processed independently through a vertex shader. Hence, we can associate properties with each vertex. For example, if we assign a different color to each vertex of a polygon, the rasterizer can interpolate these vertex colors to obtain different colors for each fragment. These **vertex attributes** may also be dependent on the application. For example, in a simulation of heat distribution of some object, the application might determine a temperature for each vertex defining the object. In Chapter 3, we will include vertex attribute data in the array with our vertex locations that is sent to the GPU.

In systems that use immediate-mode graphics and a pipeline architecture, some attributes are part of the state of the graphics systems. Hence, there would be a **current color** that would be used to render all primitives until changed by some state-changing function such as

```
set_current_color(color);
```

Likewise, there would be attribute-setting functions for a variety of attributes.[5]

Each geometric type has a set of attributes. For example, a point has a color attribute and a size attribute. Line segments can have color, thickness, and pattern (solid, dashed, or dotted). Filled primitives, such as polygons, have more attributes because we must use multiple parameters to specify how the fill should be done. We can fill with a solid color or a pattern. We can decide not to fill the polygon and to display only its edges. If we fill the polygon, we might also display the edges in a color different from that of the interior.

5. Earlier versions of OpenGL contained state-setting functions such as glColor, glLineWidth, and glStipple. These deprecated attributes can be implemented in your shaders.

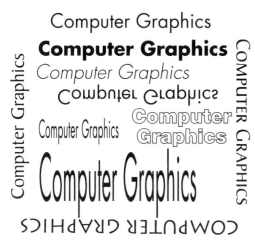

FIGURE 2.23   Stroke-text attributes.

In systems that support stroke text as a primitive, there is a variety of attributes. Some of these attributes are demonstrated in Figure 2.23; they include the direction of the text string, the path followed by successive characters in the string, the height and width of the characters, the font, and the style (bold, italic, underlined).

Although the notion of current state works well for interactive applications, it is inconsistent with our physical intuition. A box is green or red. It either contains a pattern on its surfaces or it doesn't. Object-oriented graphics takes a fundamentally different approach in which attributes are part of a geometric object. In Chapter 8, we will discuss scene graphs, which are fundamental to systems such as Open Scene Graph, and we will see that they provide another higher-level object-oriented approach to computer graphics.

2.5   COLOR

Color is one of the most interesting aspects of both human perception and computer graphics. We can use the model of the human visual system from Chapter 1 to obtain a simple but useful color model. Full exploitation of the capabilities of the human visual system using computer graphics requires a far deeper understanding of the human anatomy, physiology, and psychophysics. We will present a more sophisticated development in Chapter 6.

A visible color can be characterized by a function $C(\lambda)$ that occupies wavelengths from about 350 to 780 nm, as shown in Figure 2.24. The value for a given wavelength λ in the visible spectrum gives the intensity of that wavelength in the color.

Although this characterization is accurate in terms of a physical color whose properties we can measure, it does not take into account how we *perceive* color. As noted in Chapter 1, the human visual system has three types of cones responsible for

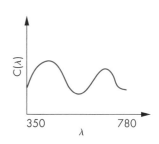

FIGURE 2.24   A color distribution.

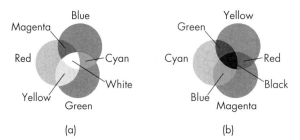

FIGURE 2.25   Color formation. (a) Additive color.
(b) Subtractive color.

color vision. Hence, our brains do not receive the entire distribution $C(\lambda)$ for a given color but rather three values—the **tristimulus values**—that are the responses of the three types of cones to the color. This reduction of a color to three values leads to the **basic tenet of three-color theory**: *If two colors produce the same tristimulus values, then they are visually indistinguishable.*

A consequence of this tenet is that, in principle, a display needs only three primary colors to produce the three tristimulus values needed for a human observer. We vary the intensity of each primary to produce a color, as we saw for the CRT in Chapter 1. The CRT is one example of the use of **additive color**, where the primary colors add together to give the perceived color. Other examples that use additive color include projectors and slide (positive) film. In such systems, the primaries are usually red, green, and blue. With additive color, primaries add light to an initially black display, yielding the desired color.

For processes such as commercial printing and painting, a **subtractive color model** is more appropriate. Here we start with a white surface, such as a sheet of paper. Colored pigments remove color components from light that is striking the surface. If we assume that white light hits the surface, a particular point will be red if all components of the incoming light are absorbed by the surface except for wavelengths in the red part of the spectrum, which are reflected. In subtractive systems, the primaries are usually the **complementary colors**: cyan, magenta, and yellow (CMY; Figure 2.25). We will not explore subtractive color here. You need to know only that an RGB additive system has a dual with a CMY subtractive system (see Exercise 2.8).

We can view a color as a point in a **color solid**, as shown in Figure 2.26 and in Color Plate 21. We draw the solid using a coordinate system corresponding to the three primaries. The distance along a coordinate axis represents the amount of the corresponding primary in the color. If we normalize the maximum value of each primary to be 1, then we can represent any color that we can produce with this set of primaries as a point in a unit cube. The vertices of the cube correspond to black (no primaries on); red, green, and blue (one primary fully on); the pairs of primaries, cyan (green and blue fully on), magenta (red and blue fully on), and yellow (red and green fully on); and white (all primaries fully on). The principal diagonal of

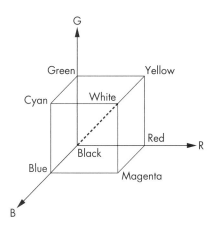

FIGURE 2.26 Color solid.

the cube connects the origin (black) with white. All colors along this line have equal tristimulus values and appear as shades of gray.

There are many matters that we are not exploring fully here and will return to in Chapter 6. Most concern the differences among various sets of primaries or the limitations conferred by the physical constraints of real devices. In particular, the set of colors produced by one device—its **color gamut**—is not the same as for other devices, nor will it match the human's color gamut. In addition, the tristimulus values used on one device will not produce the same visible color as the same tristimulus values used on another device.

2.5.1 RGB Color

Now we can look at how color is handled in a graphics system from the programmer's perspective—that is, through the API. There are two different approaches. We will stress the **RGB-color model** because an understanding of it will be crucial for our later discussion of shading. Historically, the **indexed-color model** (Section 2.5.2) was easier to support in hardware because of its lower memory requirements and the limited colors available on displays, but in modern systems RGB color has become the norm.

In a three-primary-color, additive-color RGB system, there are conceptually separate buffers for red, green, and blue images. Each pixel has separate red, green, and blue components that correspond to locations in memory (Figure 2.27). In a typical system, there might be a 1280×1024 array of pixels, and each pixel might consist of 24 bits (3 bytes): 1 byte for each of red, green, and blue. With present commodity graphics cards having up to 12GB of memory, there is no longer a problem of storing and displaying the contents of the frame buffer at video rates.

As programmers, we would like to be able to specify any color that can be stored in the frame buffer. For our 24-bit example, there are 2^{24} possible colors, sometimes referred to as 16M colors, where M denotes 1024^2. Other systems may

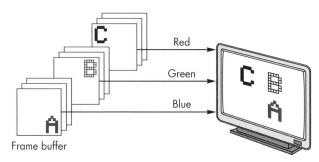

FIGURE 2.27   RGB color.

have as many as 12 (or more) bits per color or as few as 4 bits per color. Because our API should be independent of the particulars of the hardware, we would like to specify a color independently of the number of bits in the frame buffer and to let the drivers and hardware match our specification as closely as possible to the available display. A natural technique is to use the color cube and to specify color components as numbers between 0.0 and 1.0, where 1.0 denotes the maximum (or **saturated** value) of the corresponding primary and 0.0 denotes a zero value of that primary.

In applications in which we want to assign a color to each vertex, we can put colors into a separate data structure, such as

```
typedef vec3 color3;

color3 colors[3] = {color3(1.0, 0.0, 0.0), color3(0.0, 1.0, 0.0),
                    color3(0.0, 0.0. 1.0)};
```

which holds the colors red, green, and blue, or we could create a single array that contains both vertex locations and vertex colors. These data can be sent to the shaders, where colors will be applied to pixels in the frame buffer.

Later, we shall be interested in a four-color (RGBA) system. The fourth color (A, or **alpha**) also is stored in the frame buffer, as are the RGB values; it can be set with four-dimensional versions of the color functions. In Chapter 7, we will see various uses for alpha, such as combining images. Here we need to specify the alpha value as part of the initialization of an OpenGL program. If blending is enabled (Chapter 7), then the alpha value will be treated by OpenGL as either an **opacity** or **transparency** value. Transparency and opacity are complements of each other. An opaque object passes no light through it; a transparent object passes all light. Opacity values can range from fully transparent (A=0.0) to fully opaque (A=1.0).

One of the first tasks that we must do in a program is to clear an area of the screen—a drawing window—in which to display our output. We also must clear this window whenever we want to draw a new frame. By using the four-dimensional (RGBA) color system, the graphics and operating systems can interact to create effects where the drawing window interacts with other windows that may be beneath it by manipulating the opacity assigned to the window when it is cleared. The function call

```
glClearColor(1.0, 1.0, 1.0, 1.0);
```

specifies an RGB-color clearing color that is white, because the first three components are set to 1.0, and is opaque, because the alpha component is 1.0. We can then use the function `glClear` to make the window on the screen solid and white. Note that by default blending is not enabled. Consequently, the alpha value can be set in `glClearColor` to a value other than 1.0 and the default window will still be opaque.

2.5.2 Indexed Color

Early graphics systems had frame buffers that were limited in depth. For example, we might have had a frame buffer with a spatial resolution of 1280×1024, but each pixel was only 8 bits deep. We could divide each pixel's 8 bits into smaller groups of bits and assign red, green, and blue to each. Although this technique was adequate in a few applications, it usually did not give us enough flexibility with color assignment. Indexed color provided a solution that allowed applications to display a wide range of colors as long as the application did not need more colors than could be referenced by a pixel. Although indexed color is no longer part of recent versions of OpenGL, this technique can be created within an application.

We follow an analogy with an artist who paints in oils. The oil painter can produce an almost infinite number of colors by mixing together a limited number of pigments from tubes. We say that the painter has a potentially large color **palette**. At any one time, however, perhaps due to a limited number of brushes, the painter uses only a few colors. In this fashion, she can create an image that, although it contains a small number of colors, expresses her choices because she can select the few colors from a large palette.

Returning to the computer model, we can argue that if we can choose for each application a limited number of colors from a large selection (our palette), we should be able to create good-quality images most of the time.

We can select colors by interpreting our limited-depth pixels as indices into a table of colors rather than as color values. Suppose that our frame buffer has k bits per pixel. Each pixel value or index is an integer between 0 and $2^k - 1$. Suppose that we can display each color component with a precision of m bits; that is, we can choose from 2^m reds, 2^m greens, and 2^m blues. Hence, we can produce any of 2^{3m} colors on the display, but the frame buffer can specify only 2^k of them. We handle the specification through a user-defined **color-lookup table** that is of size $2^k \times 3m$ (Figure 2.28). The user program fills the 2^k entries (rows) of the table with the desired colors, using m bits for each of red, green, and blue. Once the user has constructed the table, she can specify a color by its index, which points to the appropriate entry in the color-lookup table (Figure 2.29). For $k = m = 8$, a common configuration, she can choose 256 out of 16 M colors. The 256 entries in the table constitute the user's color palette.

In systems that support color-index mode, the present color is selected by a function that selects a particular color out of the table. Setting and changing the entries in the color-lookup table involves interacting with the window system. One difficulty arises if the window system and underlying hardware support only a limited

Input		Red	Green	Blue
0		0	0	0
1		$2^m - 1$	0	0
.		0	$2^m - 1$	0
.		.	.	.
.		.	.	.
$2^k - 1$		.	.	.
		$\leftarrow$ m bits $\rightarrow$	$\leftarrow$ m bits $\rightarrow$	$\leftarrow$ m bits $\rightarrow$

FIGURE 2.28   Color-lookup table.

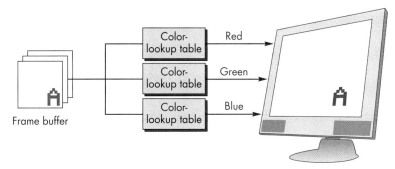

FIGURE 2.29   Indexed color.

number of colors because the window system may have only a single color table that must be used for all its windows, or it might have to juggle multiple tables, one for each window on the screen.

Historically, color-index mode was important because it required less memory for the frame buffer and fewer other hardware components. However, cost is no longer an issue, and color-index mode presents a few problems. When we work with dynamic images that must be shaded, usually we need more colors than are provided by color-index mode. In addition, the interaction with the window system is also more complex than with RGB color. Consequently, for the most part, we will assume that we are using RGB color.

The major exception is when we consider a technique called pseudocoloring, where we start with a monochromatic image. For example, we might have scalar values of a physical entity such as temperature that we wish to display in color. We can create a mapping of these values to red, green, and blue that are identical to the color-lookup tables used for indexed color.

2.5.3 Setting of Color Attributes

For our simple example program, we use RGB color. We have three attributes to set. The first is the clear color, which is set to white by the following function call:

```
glClearColor(1.0, 1.0, 1.0, 1.0);
```

Note this function uses RGBA color.

The color we use to render points is set in the shaders. We can set an RGB color in the application such as

```
typedef vec3 color3;
color3 point_color = color3(1.0, 0.0, 0.0);
```

or as an RGBA color as

```
typedef vec4 color4;
color4 point_color = color4(1.0, 0.0, 0.0, 1.0);
```

and send this color to the vertex shader. We could also set the color totally in the shader. We will see a few options later in this chapter. We can set the size of our rendered points to be 2 pixels wide by using the following OpenGL function:

```
glPointSize(2.0);
```

Note that attributes, such as the point size[6] and line width, are specified in terms of the pixel size. Hence, if two displays have different-sized pixels (due to their particular screen dimensions and resolutions), then the rendered images may appear slightly different. Certain graphics APIs, in an attempt to ensure that identical displays will be produced on all systems with the same user program, specify all attributes in a device-independent manner. Unfortunately, ensuring that two systems produce the same display has proved to be a difficult implementation problem. OpenGL has chosen a more practical balance between desired behavior and realistic constraints.

2.6 VIEWING

We can now put a variety of graphical information into our world, and we can describe how we would like these objects to appear, but we do not yet have a method for specifying exactly which of these objects should appear on the screen. Just as what we record in a photograph depends on where we point the camera and what lens we use, we have to make similar viewing decisions in our program.

A fundamental concept that emerges from the synthetic-camera model that we introduced in Chapter 1 is that the specification of the objects in our scene is completely independent of our specification of the camera. Once we have specified both the scene and the camera, we can compose an image. The camera forms an image by exposing the film, whereas the computer system forms an image by carrying out

---

6. Note that point size is one of the few state variables that can be set using an OpenGL function in the latest versions.

a sequence of operations in its pipeline. The application program needs to worry only about the specification of the parameters for the objects and the camera, just as the casual photographer is concerned about the resulting picture, not about how the shutter works or the details of the photochemical interaction of film with light.

There are default viewing conditions in computer image formation that are similar to the settings on a basic camera with a fixed lens. However, a camera that has a fixed lens and sits in a fixed location forces us to distort our world to take a picture. We can create pictures of elephants only if we place the animals sufficiently far from the camera, or we can photograph ants only if we put the insects relatively close to the lens. We prefer to have the flexibility to change the lens to make it easier to form an image of a collection of objects. The same is true when we use our graphics system.

2.6.1 The Orthographic View

The simplest and OpenGL's default view is the orthographic projection. We discuss this projection and others in detail in Chapter 4, but we introduce the orthographic projection here so that you can get started writing three-dimensional programs. Mathematically, the orthographic projection is what we would get if the camera in our synthetic-camera model had an infinitely long telephoto lens and we could then place the camera infinitely far from our objects. We can approximate this effect, as shown in Figure 2.30, by leaving the image plane fixed and moving the camera far from this plane. In the limit, all the projectors become parallel, and the center of projection is replaced by a **direction of projection**.

Rather than worrying about cameras an infinite distance away, suppose that we start with projectors that are parallel to the positive z-axis and the projection plane at $z = 0$, as shown in Figure 2.31. Note that not only are the projectors perpendicular or orthogonal to the projection plane, but also we can slide the projection plane along the z-axis without changing where the projectors intersect this plane.

For orthographic viewing, we can think of there being a special orthographic camera that resides in the projection plane, something that is not possible for other views. Perhaps more accurately stated, there is a reference point in the projection plane from which we can make measurements of a view volume and a direction of projection. In OpenGL, the reference point starts off at the origin and the camera points in the negative z-direction, as shown in Figure 2.32. The orthographic projection takes a point (x, y, z) and projects it into the point $(x, y, 0)$, as shown in Figure 2.33. Note that if we are working in two dimensions with all vertices in the plane $z = 0$, a point and its projection are the same; however, we can employ the machinery of a three-dimensional graphics system to produce our image.

In OpenGL, an orthographic projection with a right-parallelepiped viewing volume is the default. The volume is the cube defined by the planes

$x = \pm 1,$

$y = \pm 1,$

$z = \pm 1.$

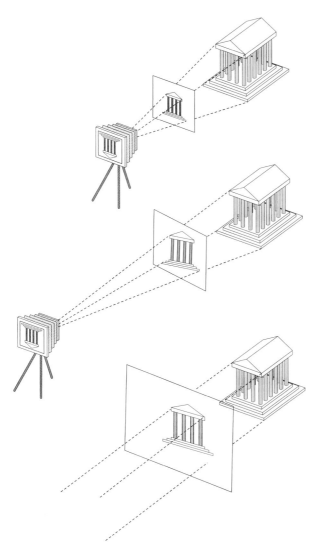

FIGURE 2.30 Creating an orthographic view by moving the camera away from the projection plane.

The orthographic projection "sees" only those objects in the volume specified by this viewing volume. Unlike a real camera, the orthographic projection can include objects behind the camera. Thus, because the plane $z = 0$ is located between -1 and 1, the two-dimensional plane intersects the viewing volume.

In Chapters 3 and 4, we will learn to use transformations to create other views. For now, we will scale and position our objects so those that we wish to view are inside the default volume.

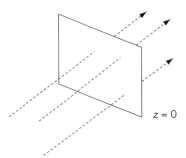

FIGURE 2.31 Orthographic projectors with projection plane $z = 0$.

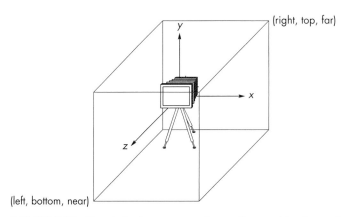

FIGURE 2.32 The default camera and an orthographic view volume.

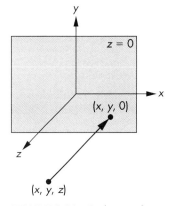

FIGURE 2.33 Orthographic projection.

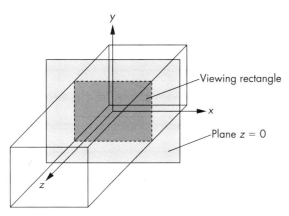

FIGURE 2.34   Viewing volume.

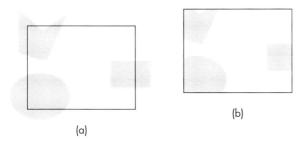

FIGURE 2.35   Two-dimensional viewing. (a) Objects before clipping.
(b) Image after clipping.

2.6.2 Two-Dimensional Viewing

Remember that, in our view, two-dimensional graphics is a special case of three-dimensional graphics. Our viewing area is in the plane $z = 0$ within a three-dimensional **viewing volume**, as shown in Figure 2.34.

We could also consider two-dimensional viewing directly by taking a rectangular area of our two-dimensional world and transferring its contents to the display, as shown in Figure 2.35. The area of the world that we image is known as the **viewing rectangle**, or **clipping rectangle**. Objects inside the rectangle are in the image; objects outside are **clipped out** and are not displayed. Objects that straddle the edges of the rectangle are partially visible in the image. The size of the window on the display and where this window is placed on the display are independent decisions that we examine in Section 2.7.

2.7   CONTROL FUNCTIONS

We are almost done with our first program, but we must discuss the minimal interactions with the window and operating systems. If we look at the details for a specific environment, such as the X Window System on a Linux platform or Microsoft Windows on a PC, we see that the programmer's interface between the graphics system and the operating and window systems can be complex. Exploitation of the possibilities open to the application programmer requires knowledge specific to these systems. In addition, the details can be different for two different environments, and discussing these differences will do little to enhance our understanding of computer graphics.

Rather than deal with these issues in detail, we look at a minimal set of operations that must take place from the perspective of the graphics application program. Earlier we discussed the OpenGL Utility Toolkit (GLUT); it is a library of functions that provides a simple interface between the systems. Details specific to the underlying windowing or operating system are inside the implementation, rather than being part of its API. Operationally, we add another library to our standard library search path. GLUT will help us to understand the interactions that characterize modern interactive graphics systems, including a wide range of APIs, operating systems, and window systems. The application programs that we produce using GLUT should run under multiple window systems.

2.7.1   Interaction with the Window System

The term *window* is used in a number of different ways in the graphics and workstation literature. We use **window**, or **screen window**, to denote a rectangular area of our display. We are concerned only with raster displays. A window has a height and width, and because the window displays the contents of the frame buffer, positions in the window are measured in **window** or **screen coordinates**,[7] where the units are pixels.

In a modern environment, we can display many windows on the monitor. Each can have a different purpose, ranging from editing a file to monitoring our system. We use the term *window system* to refer to the multiwindow environment provided by systems such as the X Window System and Microsoft Windows. The window in which the graphics output appears is one of the windows managed by the window system. Hence, to the window system, the graphics window is a particular type of window—one in which graphics can be displayed or rendered. References to positions in this window are relative to one corner of the window. We have to be careful about which corner is the origin. In science and engineering, the lower-left corner is the origin and has window coordinates (0, 0). However, virtually all raster systems display

---

7. In OpenGL, window coordinates are three-dimensional, whereas screen coordinates are two-dimensional. Both systems use units measured in pixels for x and y, but window coordinates retain depth information.

their screens in the same way as commercial television systems do—from top to bottom, left to right. From this perspective, the top-left corner should be the origin. Our OpenGL functions assume that the origin is bottom left, whereas information returned from the windowing system, such as the mouse position, often has the origin at the top left and thus requires us to convert the position from one coordinate system to the other.

Although our display may have a resolution of, say, 1280×1024 pixels, the window that we use can have any size. Thus, the frame buffer should have a resolution at least equal to the display size. Conceptually, if we use a window of 300×400 pixels, we can think of it as corresponding to a 300×400 frame buffer, even though it uses only a part of the real frame buffer.

Before we can open a window, there must be interaction between the windowing system and OpenGL. In GLUT, this interaction is initiated by the following function call:

```
glutInit(int *argc, char **argv);
```

The two arguments allow the user to pass command-line arguments, as in the standard C `main` function, and are usually the same as in `main`. We can now open an OpenGL window using the GLUT function

```
glutCreateWindow(char *title);
```

where the title at the top of the window is given by the string `title`.

The window that we create has a default size, a position on the screen, and characteristics such as the use of RGB color. We can also use GLUT functions before window creation to specify these parameters. For example, the code

```
glutInitDisplayMode(GLUT_RGB | GLUT_DEPTH | GLUT_DOUBLE);
glutInitWindowSize(640, 480);
glutInitWindowPosition(0, 0);
```

specifies a 640 width $\times$ 480 height window in the top-left corner of the display. We specify RGB rather than indexed (`GLUT_INDEX`) color, a depth buffer for hidden-surface removal, and double rather than single (`GLUT_SINGLE`) buffering. The defaults, which are all we need for now, are RGB color, no hidden-surface removal, and single buffering. Thus, we do not need to request these options explicitly, but specifying them makes the code clearer. Note that parameters are logically OR'ed together in the argument to `glutInitDisplayMode`.

2.7.2 Aspect Ratio and Viewports

The **aspect ratio** of a rectangle is the ratio of the rectangle's width to its height. The independence of the object, viewing, and workstation window specifications can cause undesirable side effects if the aspect ratio of the viewing rectangle, specified by camera parameters, is not the same as the aspect ratio of the window specified

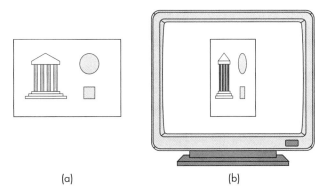

(a)   (b)

FIGURE 2.36   Aspect-ratio mismatch. (a) Viewing rectangle. (b) Display window.

by `glutInitWindowSize`. If they differ, as depicted in Figure 2.36, objects are distorted on the screen. This distortion is a consequence of our default mode of operation, in which the entire clipping rectangle is mapped to the display window. The only way that we can map the entire contents of the clipping rectangle to the entire display window is to distort the contents of the former to fit inside the latter. We can avoid this distortion if we ensure that the clipping rectangle and display window have the same aspect ratio.

Another, more flexible, method is to use the concept of a viewport. A **viewport** is a rectangular area of the display window. By default, it is the entire window, but it can be set to any smaller size in pixels via the function

```
void glViewport(GLint x, GLint y, GLsizei w, GLsizei h);
```

where (`x,y`) is the lower-left corner of the viewport (measured relative to the lower-left corner of the window) and `w` and `h` give the width and height, respectively. The types are all integers that allow us to specify positions and distances in pixels. Primitives are displayed in the viewport, as shown in Figure 2.37. For a given window, we can adjust the height and width of the viewport to match the aspect ratio of the clipping rectangle, thus preventing any object distortion in the image.

The viewport is part of the state. If we change the viewport between rendering objects or rerender the same objects with the viewport changed, we achieve the effect of multiple viewports with different images in different parts of the window. We will see further uses of the viewport in Chapter 3, where we consider interactive changes in the size and shape of the window.

2.7.3 The `main`, `display`, and `init` Functions

In principle, we should be able to combine the simple initialization code with our code from Section 2.1 to form a complete OpenGL program that generates the Sierpinski gasket. Unfortunately, life in a modern system is not that simple. There are

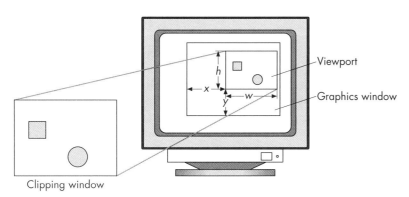

FIGURE 2.37   A mapping to the viewport.

two problems: One is generic to all graphics systems; the second has more to do with problems of interacting with the underlying windowing system.

Our basic mechanism for display will be to form a data structure that contains all the geometry and attributes we need to specify a primitive and how we would like it displayed. We then send this structure to the shaders that will process our data and display the results. Once the application has sent the data to the shaders, it is free to do other tasks. In an interactive application, we would continue to generate more primitives.

However, for an application such as our sample program, we draw a few primitives and are finished. As the application ends, the application window will disappear from the display before we have had a chance to see our output. A simple solution for this problem might be to insert a delay, for example, via a standard function such as `sleep(enough_time)` to give us enough time to view our output. For any but the most trivial applications, however, we need a more sophisticated mechanism.

The mechanism employed by most graphics and window systems is to use **event processing**, which gives us interactive control in our programs. **Events** are changes that are detected by the operating system and include such actions as a user pressing a key on the keyboard, the user clicking a mouse button or moving the mouse, or the user iconifying a window on the display. Events are varied, and usually only a subset of them is important to graphics applications. An event may generate data that are stored with the occurrence of the event. For example, if a key is pressed, the code for the key will be stored.

When events occur they are placed in queue, the **event queue**, that can be examined by an application program or by the operating system. A given event can be ignored or cause an action to take place. For example, an application that does not use the keyboard will ignore all pressing and releasing of keys, whereas an application that uses the keyboard might use keyboard events to control the flow of the application.

With GLUT, we can execute the function

```
glutMainLoop();
```

to begin an event-processing loop. If there are no events to process, the program will sit in a wait state, with our graphics on the screen, until we terminate the program through some external means—say, by hitting a special key or a combination of keys, such as Control-C—that terminates the execution of the program.

If there are events in the queue, our program responds to them through functions called **callbacks**. A callback function is associated with a specific type of event. Hence, a typical interactive application would use a mouse callback and perhaps a keyboard callback. For our simple example, we need only a single callback called the **display callback**. A display callback is generated when the application program or the operating system determines that the graphics in a window need to be redrawn. One of these times is when during initialization, the application creates a window on the display. Hence, virtually every program must have a display callback function that is executed when the callback occurs.

The display callback function is named through the GLUT function

```
void glutDisplayFunc(void (*func)(void));
```

and **registered** with the window system. Here the function named `func` will be called whenever the windowing system determines that the OpenGL window needs to be redisplayed. Because one of these times is when the window is first opened, if we put all our graphics into this function (for our noninteractive example), `func` will be executed once and our gasket will be drawn. Although it may appear that our use of the display function is merely a convenience for organizing our program, the display function is required by GLUT. A display callback is also invoked, for example, when the window is moved from one location on the screen to another and when a window in front of the OpenGL window is destroyed, making visible the whole OpenGL window.

Following is a `main` function that works for most noninteractive applications:

```
#include <glew.h>
#include <GL/glut.h>

int main(int argc, char **argv)
{
    glutInit(&argc, argv);
    glutInitDisplayMode (GLUT_SINGLE | GLUT_RGB);
    glutInitWindowSize(500, 500);
    glutInitWindowPosition(0, 0);
    glutCreateWindow("simple OpenGL example");
    glewInit();
    glutDisplayFunc(display);
    init();
    glutMainLoop();
}
```

We use an initialization function `init()` to set the OpenGL state variables dealing with viewing and attributes—parameters that we prefer to set once, independently of the display function. The standard `include` (`.h`) file for GLUT is loaded before the beginning of the function definitions. In most implementations, the compiler directive

```
#include <GL/glut.h>
```

will add in the header files for the GLUT library and the OpenGL library (`gl.h`). The macro definitions for our standard values, such as `GL_LINES` and `GL_RGB`, are in these files. If we are using the GLEW library, we usually need only add the include file and execute `glewInit`.

2.7.4 Program Structure

Every program we write will have a similar structure to our gasket program. We will always use the GLUT toolkit. The `main` function will then consist of calls to GLUT functions to set up our window(s) and to make sure that the local environment supports the required display properties. The `main` will also name the required callbacks and callback functions. Every program must have a `display` callback, and most will have other callbacks to set up interaction. The `init` function will set up user options, usually through OpenGL functions in the GL library. Although these options could be set in `main`, it is clearer to keep GLUT functions separate from OpenGL functions. In the majority of programs, the graphics output will be generated in the `display` callback.

Every application, no matter how simple, must provide both a vertex shader and a fragment shader. Setting up the shaders requires a number of steps, including reading the shader code from files, compiling the code, and linking the shaders with the application. These steps are almost identical for most applications. Hence, we will put this code into a function `initShaders`. These operations require a handful of OpenGL functions that have little to do with graphics. Consequently, we place the details of these functions in Appendix A.

2.8 THE GASKET PROGRAM

We can now complete our gasket program. We have already created the points and put them in an array. Now we have to get these data to our GPU and render them. We start by creating a **vertex-array object** that will allow us to bundle data associated with a vertex array. Use of multiple vertex-array objects will make it easy to switch among different vertex arrays. We use `glGenVertexArray` to find an unused name for the buffer. The first time the function `glBindVertexArray` is executed for a given name, the object is created. Subsequent calls to this function make the named object active. For this example, we need only a single vertex array buffer that we set up as follows:

```
GLuint abuffer;

glGenVertexArrays(1, &abuffer);
glBindVertexArray(abuffer);
```

Next, we create a **buffer object** on the GPU and place our data in that object. We need three functions that we can call after we have generated our points:

```
GLuint buffer;

glGenBuffers(1, &buffer);
glBindBuffer(GL_ARRAY_BUFFER, buffer);
glBufferData(GL_ARRAY_BUFFER, sizeof(points),
             points, GL_STATIC_DRAW);
```

First, we use `glGenBuffers` to give us an unused identifier for our buffer object that is put into the variable `buffer`. The function `glBindBuffer` creates the buffer with the identifier from `glGenBuffers`. The type `GL_ARRAY_BUFFER` indicates that the data in the buffer will be vertex attribute data rather than some one of the other storage types that we will encounter later. Finally, with `glBufferData`, we allocate sufficient memory on the GPU for our data and provide a pointer to the array holding the data. Once data is in GPU memory, we might, as in this example, simply display it once. But in more realistic applications we might alter the data, redisplay it many times, and even read data back from the GPU to the CPU. Modern GPUs can alter how they store data to increase efficiency depending on the type of application. The final parameter in `glBufferData` gives a hint of how the application plans to use the data. In our case, we are sending it once and displaying it so the choice of `GL_STATIC_DRAW` is appropriate. The code to compute the points and create the buffer object can be part of initialization.

2.8.1 Rendering the Points

When we want to display our points, we can use the function

```
glDrawArrays(GL_POINTS, 0, N);
```

which causes N data to be rendered starting with the first point. The value of the first parameter, `GL_POINTS`, tells the GPU we want the data to be used to display distinct points rather than other primitives such as lines or polygons that could be described by the same data. Thus, a simple display callback is

```
void mydisplay(void)
{
    glClear(GL_COLOR_BUFFER_BIT);
    glDrawArrays(GL_POINTS, 0, N);
    glFlush();
}
```

We clear the frame buffer and then render the point data that is on the GPU. The `glFlush` ensures that all the data are rendered as soon as possible. If you leave it out, the program should work correctly, but you notice a delay in a busy or networked environment.

But this is just the beginning of the story. The rendering process must be carried out by the pipeline of the vertex shader, the rasterizer, and the fragment shader in order to get the proper pixels displayed in the frame buffer. Because our example uses only points, we need only develop very simple shaders and put together the whole application. Even though our shaders will be almost trivial, we must provide both a vertex shader and fragment shader to have a complete application. There are no default shaders.

2.8.2 The Vertex Shader

The only information that we put in our buffer object is the location of each point. When we execute `glDrawArrays`, each of the `NumPoints` vertices generates an execution of a vertex shader that we must provide. If we leave the color determination to the fragment shader, all the vertex shader must do is pass the vertex's location to the rasterizer. Although we will see many more tasks that can be done in a vertex shader, the absolute minimum it must do is send a vertex location to the rasterizer.

We write our shader using the OpenGL Shading Language (GLSL), which is a C-like language with which we can write both vertex and fragment shaders. We will discuss GLSL in more detail later when we want to write more sophisticated shaders, but here is the code for a simple **pass-through** vertex shader:

```
in vec4 vPosition;

void main()
{
    gl_Position = vPosition;
}
```

Each shader is a complete program with `main` as its entry point. GLSL expands the C data types to include matrix and vector types. The type `vec4` is equivalent to a C++ class for a four-element array of `floats`. We have provided similar types for the application side in `vec.h` and will introduce more in Chapter 3. The input vertex's location is given by the four-dimensional vector `vPosition` whose specification includes the keyword `in` to signify that its value is input to the shader when the shader is initiated. There is one special state variable in our shader: `gl_Position`, which is the position that will be passed to the rasterizer and must be output by every vertex shader. Because `gl_Position` is known to OpenGL, we need not declare it in the shader.

In general, a vertex shader will transform the representation of a vertex location from whatever coordinate system in which it is specified to a representation in clip coordinates for the rasterizer. However, because we specified the values in our application in clip coordinates, our shader does not have to make any changes to the values input to the shader and merely passes them through via `gl_Position`.

We still have to establish a connection between the array `points` in the application and the input array `vPosition` in the shader. We will do this after we compile and link our shaders. First, we look at the fragment shader.

2.8.3 The Fragment Shader

Each invocation of the vertex shader outputs a vertex that then goes through primitive assembly and clipping before reaching the rasterizer. The rasterizer outputs fragments for each primitive inside the clipping volume. Each fragment invokes an execution of the fragment shader. At a minimum, each execution of the fragment shader must output a color for the fragment unless the fragment is to be discarded. Here is a minimum GLSL fragment shader:

```
void main()
{
    gl_FragColor = vec4(1.0, 0.0, 0.0, 1.0);
}
```

All this shader does is assign a four-dimensional RGBA color to each fragment through the built-in variable `gl_FragColor`. The A component of the color is its opacity. We want our points to be opaque and not translucent, so we use A = 1.0. Setting R to 1.0 and the other two components to 0.0 colors each fragment red.

2.8.4 Combining the Parts

We now have the pieces but need to put them together. In particular, we have to compile the shaders, connect variables in the application with their counterparts in the shaders, and link everything together. We start with the bare minimum. Shaders must be compiled and linked. Most of the time we will do these operations as part of initialization so we can put the necessary code in a function `initShader` that will remain almost unchanged from application to application.

2.8.5 The `initShader` Function

A typical application contains three distinct parts: the application program, which comprises a `main` function and other functions such as `init`, a vertex shader, and a fragment shader. The first part is a set of C (or C++) functions, whereas the shaders are written in GLSL. To obtain a module that we can execute, we have to connect these entities, a process that involves reading source code from files, compiling the individual parts, and linking everything together. We can control this process through our application using a set of OpenGL functions that we will discuss in detail in Chapter 3. Here it will be sufficient to describe the steps briefly.

Our first step is to create a container called a **program object** to hold our shaders and two shader objects, one for each type of shader. The program object has an integer identifier we can use to refer to it in the application. After we create these objects, we can attach the shaders to the program object. Generally, the shader source code will be in standard text files. We read them into strings that can be attached to the program and compiled. If the compilation is successful, the application and shaders can be linked together. Assuming we have the vertex shader source in a file `vshader.glsl` and the fragment shader in a file `fshader.glsl`, we can execute the above steps by a function call of the form

```
GLuint program;

program = InitShader("vsource.glsl", "fsource.glsl");
```

in the `main` function of the application.

When we link the program object and the shaders, the names of shader variables are bound to indices in tables that are created in the linking process. The function `glGetAttribLocation` returns the index of an attribute variable, such as the vertex location attribute `vPosition` in our vertex shader. From the perspective of the application program, the client, we have to do two things. We have to enable the vertex attributes that are in the shaders (`glEnableVertexAttribArray`), and we must describe the form of the data in the vertex array (`glVertexAttribPointer`), as in the code

```
GLuint loc;

loc = glGetAttribLocation(program, "vPosition");
glEnableVertexAttribArray(loc);
glVertexAttribPointer(loc, 2, GL_FLOAT, GL_FALSE, 0,
                      BUFFER_OFFSET(0));
```

In `glVertexAttribPointer`, the second and third parameters specify that the array `points` is a two-dimensional array of `floats`. The fourth parameter says that we do not want the data normalized to be the range (0.0, 1.0), whereas the fifth states that the values in the array are contiguous. We will deal with noncontiguous data in later examples. The last parameter is the address in the buffer where the data begin. In this example, we have only a single data array `points` so the zero value works. A more robust strategy is to specify a buffer offset and use it as follows:

```
#define BUFFER_OFFSET(bytes) ((GLvoid*) (bytes))

glVertexAttribPointer(loc, 2, GL_FLOAT, GL_FALSE, 0,
                      BUFFER_OFFSET(0));
```

Note that the data in `points` in the application consists of only x and y values, whereas the array `vPosition` in the vertex shader is four dimensional. This difference does not create a problem, because we have described the data correctly in our function parameters. The underlying reason for the differences is a fundamental aspect of how our graphics systems work. We want our application programs to be as close to the problem as possible. Some of our applications will be two dimensional; most will be three dimensional, and some may even be four dimensional.

A complete listing of this program, the `initShader` function and a function for reading shader source code, as well as other example programs that we generate in subsequent chapters, are given in Appendix A.

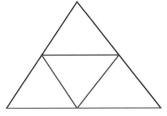

FIGURE 2.38 Bisecting the sides of a triangle.

2.9 POLYGONS AND RECURSION

The output from our gasket program (Figure 2.2) shows considerable structure. If we were to run the program with more iterations, then much of the randomness in the image would disappear. Examining this structure, we see that regardless of how many points we generate, there are no points in the middle. If we draw line segments connecting the midpoints of the sides of the original triangle, dividing the original triangle into four triangles, the middle one contains no points (Figure 2.38).

Looking at the other three triangles, we see that we can apply the same observation to each of them; that is, we can subdivide each of these triangles into four triangles by connecting the midpoints of the sides, and each middle triangle will contain no points.

This structure suggests a second method for generating the Sierpinski gasket—one that uses polygons instead of points and does not require the use of a random-number generator. One advantage of using polygons is that we can fill solid areas on our display. Our strategy is to start with a single triangle, subdivide it into four smaller triangles by bisecting the sides, and then to remove the middle triangle from further consideration. We repeat this procedure on the remaining triangles until the size of the triangles that we are removing is small enough—about the size of one pixel—that we can draw the remaining triangles.

We can implement the process that we just described through a recursive program. We start its development with a simple function that adds the locations of the three vertices that specify a triangle to an array `points`:

```
#include "vec.h"
typedef vec2 point2;

void triangle(point2 a, point2 b, point2 c)

/* specify one triangle */

{
    static int i = 0;

    points[i] = a;
    i++;
    points[i] = b;
    i++;
    points[i] = c;
    i++;
}
```

Hence, each time that `triangle` is called it adds three two-dimensional vertices to the data array.

Suppose that the vertices of our original triangle are given by the following array:

```
point2 v[3];
```

Then the midpoints of the sides are given by the array `mid[3]`, which can be computed using the following code:

```
point2 mid[3];

mid[0] = (v[0] + v[1])/2.0;
mid[1] = (v[0] + v[2])/2.0;
mid[2] = (v[1] + v[2])/2.0;
```

With these six locations, we can use `triangle` to place the data for the three triangles formed by (`v[0]`, `mid[0]`, `mid[1]`), (`v[2]`, `mid[1]`, `mid[2]`), and (`v[1]`, `mid[2]`, `mid[0]`) in `points`. However, we do not simply want to draw these triangles; we want to subdivide them. Hence, we make the process recursive. We specify a recursive function

```
divide_triangle(point2 a, point2 b, point2 c, int k);
```

that will draw the triangles only if *k* is zero. Otherwise, it will subdivide the triangle specified by a, b, and c and decrease k. Here is the code:

```
void divide_triangle(point2 a, point2 b, point2 c, int k)
{
    if(k > 0)
    {
        // compute midpoints of sides

        point2 ab = (a + b)/2.0;
        point2 ac = (a + c)/2.0;
        point2 bc = (b + c)/2.0;

        // subdivide all but inner triangle

        divide_triangle(a, ab, ac, k-1);
        divide_triangle(c, ac, bc, k-1);
        divide_triangle(b, bc, ab, k-1);
    }
    else triangle(a,b,c); /* draw triangle at end of recursion */
}
```

FIGURE 2.39 Triangles after five subdivisions.

The display function is now almost trivial. It uses a global[8] value of n determined by the main program to fix the number of subdivision steps we would like, and it calls `divide_triangle` once with the single function call

```
divide_triangle(v[0], v[1], v[2], Ndivisions);
```

where `Ndivisions` is the number of times we want to subdivide the original triangle. If we do not account for vertices shared by two vertices and treat each triangle independently, then each subdivision triples the number of vertices, giving us

$$Nvertices = 3^{Ndivisions+1}.$$

We set up the buffer object exactly as we did previously, and we can then render all the triangles by

```
void display( void )
{
    glClear(GL_COLOR_BUFFER_BIT);
    glDrawArrays(GL_TRIANGLES, 0, Nvertices);
    glFlush();
}
```

The rest of the program is almost identical to our previous gasket program. Output for five subdivision steps is shown in Figure 2.39. The complete program is given in Appendix A.

---

8. Note that often we have no convenient way to pass variables to GLUT callbacks other than through global parameters. Although we prefer not to pass values in such a manner, because the form of these functions is fixed, we have no good alternative.

2.10 THE THREE-DIMENSIONAL GASKET

We have argued that two-dimensional graphics is a special case of three-dimensional graphics, but we have not yet seen a complete three-dimensional program. Next, we convert our two-dimensional Sierpinski gasket program to a program that will generate a three-dimensional gasket; that is, one that is not restricted to a plane. We can follow either of the two approaches that we used for the two-dimensional gasket. Both extensions start in a similar manner, replacing the initial triangle with a tetrahedron (Figure 2.40).

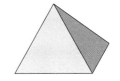

FIGURE 2.40 Tetrahedron.

2.10.1 Use of Three-Dimensional Points

Because every tetrahedron is convex, the midpoint of a line segment between a vertex and any point inside a tetrahedron is also inside the tetrahedron. Hence, we can follow the same procedure as before, but this time, instead of the three vertices required to specify a triangle, we need four initial vertices to specify the tetrahedron. Note that as long as no three vertices are collinear, we can choose the four vertices of the tetrahedron at random without affecting the character of the result.

The required changes are primarily in the function `display`. We declare and initialize an array to hold the vertices as follows:

```
// vertices of an arbitrary tetrahedron

point3 vertices[4] = { point3(-1.0, -1.0, -1.0),
                       point3( 1.0, -1.0, -1.0),
                       point3( 0.0,  1.0, -1.0),
                       point3( 0.0,  0.0,  1.0) };

// arbitrary initial location inside tetrahedron

point3 p = point3(0.0, 0.0, 0.0);
```

We now use the array

```
point3 points[NumPoints];
```

to store the vertex data. We compute a new location as before but add a midpoint computation for the z component:

```
// computes and plots a single new location

  point3 p;
  int rand();
  int j = rand() % 4; // pick a vertex at random

// compute point halfway between a vertex and the old location

  p = (p + vertices[j])/2.0;
```

We create vertex-array and buffer objects exactly as with the two-dimensional version and can use the same display function.

One problem with the three-dimensional gasket that we did not have with the two-dimensional gasket occurs because points are not restricted to a single plane; thus, it may be difficult to envision the three-dimensional structure from the two-dimensional image displayed, especially if we render each point in the same color.

To get around this problem, we can add a more sophisticated color-setting process to our shaders, one that makes the color of each point depend on that point's location. We can map the color cube to the default view volume by noting that both are cubes but that whereas x, y, and z range from -1 to 1, each color component must be between 0 and 1. If we use the mapping

$$r = \frac{1+x}{2},$$

$$g = \frac{1+y}{2},$$

$$b = \frac{1+z}{2},$$

every point in the viewing volume maps to a distinct color. In the vertex shader, we can set the color using the components of `vPosition`, so our shader becomes

```
in vec4 vPosition;
out vec4 color;

void main()
{
    color = vec4((1.0 + vPosition.xyz)/2.0, 1.0);
    gl_Position = vPosition;
}
```

This color is output to the rasterizer so the fragment shader can use it as input to set the color of a fragment, so the fragment shader becomes

```
in vec4 color;
void main()
{
  gl_FragColor = color;
}
```

Figure 2.41 shows that if we generate enough points, the resulting figure will look like the initial tetrahedron with increasingly smaller tetrahedrons removed.

2.10.2 Use of Polygons in Three Dimensions

There is a more interesting approach to the three-dimensional Sierpinski gasket that uses both polygons and subdivision of a tetrahedron into smaller tetrahedrons. Suppose that we start with a tetrahedron and find the midpoints of its six edges and

FIGURE 2.41   Three-dimensional Sierpinski gasket.

connect these midpoints as shown in Figure 2.42. There are now four smaller tetrahedrons, one for each of the original vertices, and another area in the middle that we will discard.

Following our second approach to a single triangle, we will use recursive subdivision to subdivide the four tetrahedrons that we keep. Because the faces of a tetrahedron are the four triangles determined by its four vertices, at the end of the subdivisions, we can render each of the final tetrahedrons by drawing four triangles.

Most of our code is almost the same as in two dimensions. Our triangle routine now uses points in three dimensions rather than in two dimensions:

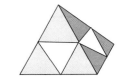

FIGURE 2.42   Subdivided tetrahedron.

```
#include "vec.h"
typedef vec3 point3;

void triangle(point3 a, point3 b, point3 c)

/* specify one triangle */

{
      static int i = 0;

      points[i] = a;
      i++;
      points[i] = b;
      i++;
      points[i]= c;
      i++;
}
```

We draw each tetrahedron, coloring each face with a different color by using the following function:

```
void tetra(point3 a, point3 b, point3 c, point3 d)
{
      triangle(a, b, c);
      triangle(a, c, d);
      triangle(a, d, b);
      triangle(b, d, c);
}
```

We subdivide a tetrahedron in a manner similar to subdividing a triangle. Our code for divide_triangle does the same:

```
void divide_tetra(point3 a, point3 b, point3 c, point3 d, int m)
{
    if(m > 0)
    {
        point3 mid[6];

        // compute six midpoints

        mid[0] = (a + b)/2.0;
        mid[1] = (a + c)/2.0;
        mid[2] = (a + d)/2.0;
        mid[3] = (b + c)/2.0;
        mid[4] = (c + d)/2.0;
        mid[5] = (b + d)/2.0;

        // create 4 tetrahedrons by subdivision

        divide_tetra(a, mid[0], mid[1], mid[2], m-1);
        divide_tetra(mid[0], b, mid[3], mid[5], m-1);
        divide_tetra(mid[1], mid[3], c, mid[4], m-1);
        divide_tetra(mid[2], mid[5], mid[5], d, m-1);

    }
    else tetra(a,b,c,d); /* draw tetrahedron at end of recursion */
}
```

We can now start with four vertices and do n subdivisions as follows:

```
divide_tetra(v[0], v[1], v[2], v[3], n);
```

There are two more problems that we must address before we have a useful three-dimensional program. The first is how to deal with color. If we use just a single color as in our first example, we won't be able to see any of the three-dimensional structure. Alternately, we could use the approach of our last example of letting the color of each fragment be determined by where the point is located in three dimensions. But we would prefer to use a small number of colors and color the face of each triangle with one of these colors. We can set this scheme by choosing some base colors in the application, such as

```
typedef vec3 color3;
color3 base_colors[4] = {color3(1.0, 0.0, 0.0), color3(0.0, 1.0, 0.0),
                         color3(0.0, 0.0, 1.0), color3(0.0, 0.0, 0.0)};
```

and then assigning colors to each point as it is generated. We set a color index as we generate the triangles

```
int colorindex;
void tetra(point3 a, point3 b, point3 c, point3 d)
{
    colorindex = 0;
    triangle(a,b,c);
    colorindex = 1;
    triangle(a,c,d);
    colorindex = 2;
    triangle(a,d,b);
    colorindex = 3;
    triangle(b,d,c);
}
```

and then form a color array with a color for each point:

```
color3 colors[NumVertices];
int i = 0;      // number of vertices

void triangle(point3 a, point3 b, point3 c)

/* specify one triangle */

{
        colors[i] = base_colors[colorindex];
        points[i] = a;
        i++;
        colors[i] = base_colors[colorindex];
        points[i] = b;
        i++;
        colors[i] = base_colors[colorindex];
        points[i] = c;
        i++;
}
```

We send these colors to the GPU along with their associated vertices in a buffer object. Inside of the buffer object, we'll place the vertex data at the start of the buffer's memory and then follow it with the color data. To do this, however, we'll need to first allocate a buffer large enough to contain all of the data, and then load data into the buffer in two operations using the OpenGL function `glBufferSubData`. The function `glBufferSubData` allows us to update parts of an existing buffer object with new data. The first parameter specifies which array in the buffer we want to update. The second parameter specifies which byte in the buffer to start writing data at, and the third parameter specifies how many bytes to read from the memory pointer, which is passed in using the fourth parameter. Consider the code:

```
GLuint buffer;

glGenBuffers(1, &buffer);
glBindBuffer(GL_ARRAY_BUFFER, buffer);

// Allocate a buffer of uninitialized data of the correct size
glBufferData(GL_ARRAY_BUFFER, sizeof(points) + sizeof(colors),
             NULL, GL_STATIC_DRAW);

// Load the separate arrays of data

glBufferSubData(GL_ARRAY_BUFFER, 0, sizeof(points), points );
glBufferSubData(GL_ARRAY_BUFFER, sizeof(points),
                sizeof(colors), colors );
```

In the above example, the first call updates the bytes in the range [0, `sizeof(points)-1`]. Since we need to write the data for the colors immediately after in the buffer, we start at the byte immediately following the vertex data, which is just the length (in bytes) of the `points` array, which is `sizeof(points)`. We use that size as the starting offset in the second `glBufferSubData` call.

If in the shader the color is named `vColor`, the second vertex array can be set up in the shader initialization:

```
loc2 = glGetAttribLocation(program, "vColor");
glEnableVertexAttribArray(loc2);
glVertexAttribPointer(loc2, 3, GL_FLOAT, GL_FALSE, 0,
                      BUFFER_OFFSET(sizeof(points)));
```

In the vertex shader, we use `vColor` to set a color to be sent to the fragment shader.

2.10.3 Hidden-Surface Removal

If you execute the code in the previous section, you might be confused by the results. The program draws triangles in the order that they are specified in the program. This order is determined by the recursion in our program and not by the geometric relationships among the triangles. Each triangle is drawn (filled) in a solid color and is drawn over those triangles that have already been rendered to the display.

Contrast this order to the way that we would see the triangles if we were to construct the three-dimensional Sierpinski gasket out of small solid tetrahedra. We would see only those faces of tetrahedra that were in front of all other faces as seen by a viewer. Figure 2.43 shows a simplified version of this **hidden-surface** problem. From the viewer's position, quadrilateral A is seen clearly, but triangle B is blocked from view, and triangle C is only partially visible. Without going into the details of any specific algorithm, you should be able to convince yourself that given the position of the viewer and the triangles, we should be able to draw the triangles such that the correct image is obtained. Algorithms for ordering objects so that they are drawn correctly are called **visible-surface algorithms** or **hidden-surface–removal algorithms**, depending on how we look at the problem. We discuss such algorithms in detail in Chapters 3 and 6.

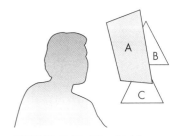

FIGURE 2.43 The hidden-surface problem.

For now, we can simply use a particular hidden-surface–removal algorithm, called the **z-buffer** algorithm, that is supported by OpenGL. This algorithm can be turned on (enabled) and off (disabled) easily. In our main program, we must request the auxiliary storage, a *z* (or depth) buffer, by modifying the initialization of the display mode to the following:

```
glutInitDisplayMode(GLUT_SINGLE | GLUT_RGB | GLUT_DEPTH);
```

Note that the *z*-buffer is one of the buffers that make up the frame buffer. We enable the algorithm by the function call

```
glEnable(GL_DEPTH_TEST);
```

either in `main` or in an initialization function such as `init`. Because the algorithm stores information in the depth buffer, we must clear this buffer whenever we wish to redraw the display; thus, we modify the clear procedure in the display function:

```
glClear(GL_COLOR_BUFFER_BIT | GL_DEPTH_BUFFER_BIT);
```

The display callback is as follows:

```
void display()
{
  glClear(GL_COLOR_BUFFER_BIT | GL_DEPTH_BUFFER_BIT);
  glDrawArrays(GL_TRIANGLES, 0, NumVertices);
  glFlush();
}
```

The results are shown in Figure 2.44 for a recursion of four steps. The complete program is given in Appendix A.

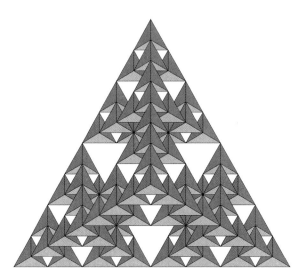

FIGURE 2.44   Three-dimensional gasket after four recursion steps.

2.11   ADDING INTERACTION

In this section, we develop event-driven input through a set of simple examples that use the callback mechanism that we introduced in Section 2.7. We examine various events that are recognized by the window system, and, for those of interest to our application, we write callback functions that govern how the application program responds to these events.

2.11.1 Using the Pointing Device

We start by altering the `main` function in the gasket program. In the original version, we used functions in the GLUT library to put a window on the screen and then entered the event loop by executing the function `glutMainLoop`. We entered the loop but could do nothing else because there were no callbacks other than the display callback. We could not even terminate the program, except through an external system-dependent mechanism, such as pressing control-c. Our first example will remedy this omission by using the pointing device to terminate a program. We accomplish this task by having the program execute a standard termination function called `exit` when a particular mouse button is depressed.

We discuss only those events recognized by GLUT. Standard window systems such as the X Window System or Microsoft Windows recognize many more events, which differ among systems. However, the GLUT library recognizes a small set of events that is common to most window systems and is sufficient for developing basic interactive graphics programs. Because GLUT has been implemented for the major window systems, we can use our simple applications on multiple systems by recompiling the application.

Two types of events are associated with the pointing device, which is conventionally assumed to be a mouse but could be a trackpad or a data tablet. A **move event** is generated when the mouse is moved with one of the buttons depressed. If the mouse is moved without a button being held down, this event is called a **passive move event**. After a move event, the position of the mouse is made available to the application program. A **mouse event** occurs when one of the mouse buttons is either depressed or released. When a button is depressed, the action generates a mouse down event. When it is released, a mouse up event is generated. The information returned includes the button that generated the event, the state of the button after the event (up or down), and the position of the cursor tracking the mouse in window coordinates (with the origin in the upper-left corner of the window). We register the mouse callback function, usually in the `main` function, by means of the GLUT function

```
glutMouseFunc(myMouse);
```

The mouse callback must have the form

```
void myMouse(int button, int state, int x, int y);
```

and is provided by the application programmer. Within the callback function, we define the actions that we want to take place if the specified event occurs. There may be multiple actions defined in the mouse callback function corresponding to the many possible button and state combinations. For our simple example, we want the depression of the left mouse button to terminate the program. The required callback is the single-line function

```
void myMouse(int button, int state, int x, int y)
{
    if(button == GLUT_LEFT_BUTTON && state == GLUT_DOWN)
            exit(0);
}
```

If any other mouse event—such as a depression of one of the other buttons—occurs, no response action will occur, because no action corresponding to these events has been defined in the callback function.

We will now develop an example that incorporates many of the aspects of CAD programs and adds some interactivity. Along the way, we will introduce some additional callbacks. We start by developing a simple program that will display a single triangle whose vertices are entered interactively using the pointing device. We will use the same shaders so most of the code will be similar to our previous examples.

We specify a global array to hold the three two-dimensional vertices

```
point2 points[3];
```

We can then use the mouse callback to capture the data each time the left mouse button is depressed. Consider the code

```
int w, h;
int count = 0;

void mouse(int button, int state, int x, int y)
{
    if(button == GLUT_RIGHT_BUTTON && state == GLUT_DOWN)
    {
        exit(0);
    }

    if(button == GLUT_LEFT_BUTTON  && state == GLUT_DOWN)
    {
        points[count].x = (float) x / (w/2) - 1.0;
        points[count].y = (float) (h-y) / (h/2) - 1.0;
        count++;
    }

    if(count == 3)
    {
        glutPostRedisplay();
        count =  0;
    }
}
```

The right mouse button is used to end the program. The left mouse button is used to provide the vertex data for our triangle. We use the globals h and w to hold the height and width of the OpenGL window. Hence, in our main we might see the code

```
w = 512;
h = 512;
glutInitWindowSize(w, h);
```

in our main function, which would give us the same 512×512 window we used previously. The basic idea is that each time the left mouse button is depressed, we put the scaled location of the mouse into points and then move on to the next vertex. Scaling is necessary because the mouse callback returns the position of the mouse in screen coordinates measured from the top-left corner of the window. Thus, for our w × h window, the top-left corner has coordinates $(0, 0)$ whereas the bottom right corner has coordinates $(w-1, h-1)$. This number of increasing y values from top to bottom is common in window systems and has its origins in television systems that display images top to bottom. The window we use in our application program has its origin in the center, the bottom-left corner is at $(-1.0, -1.0)$ and the top-right corner has coordinates $(1.0, 1.0)$. Because any primitives outside this region are clipped out, we want to scale the values returned by the mouse callback to this region and make sure to flip the y values so that our triangles appear upright. The two lines

```
points[count].x = (float) x / (w/2) - 1.0;
points[count].y = (float) (h-y) / (h/2) - 1.0;
```

carry out this transformation of coordinates.

Once we have the data for three vertices, we can draw the triangle. We cause the drawing of the triangle through the display callback. However, instead of invoking the display callback directly through an execution of `display`, we instead use

```
glutPostRedisplay();
```

What this function does is set an internal flag indicating that the display needs to be redrawn. Each time the system goes through the event loop, multiple events may occur whose callbacks require refreshing the display. Rather than each of these callbacks explicitly executing the display function, each uses `glutPostRedisplay` to set the display flag. Thus, at the end of the event loop, if the flag is set, the display callback is invoked and the flag unset. This method prevents the display from being redrawn multiple times in a single pass through the event loop.[9] Returning to our example, we see that each successive three depressions of the left mouse button specifies a new triangle that replaces the previous triangle on the display.

Although we have a program that has some interactivity, introducing a few more callbacks will lead to a much more interesting program that can be expanded to a painting or CAD program.

2.11.2 Window Events

Most window systems allow a user to resize the window interactively, usually by using the mouse to drag a corner of the window to a new location. This event is called a **reshape event** and is an example of a **window event**. Other window events include iconifying a window and exposing a window that was covered by another window. Each can have a callback that specified which actions to take if the event occurs. Unlike most other callbacks, there is a default reshape callback that simply changes the viewport to the new window size, an action that might not be what the user desires. If the window size changes, we have to consider the three questions:

1. Do we redraw all the objects that were in the window before it was resized?

2. What do we do if the aspect ratio of the new window is different from that of the old window?

3. Do we change the sizes or attributes of new primitives if the size of the new window is different from that of the old?

---

9. Some interactive applications may need to execute the display callback directly.

There is no single answer to any of these questions. If we are displaying the image of a real-world scene, our reshape function probably should make sure that no shape distortions occur. But this choice may mean that part of the resized window is unused or that part of the scene cannot be displayed in the window. If we want to redraw the objects that were in the window before it was resized, we need a mechanism for storing and recalling them. Often we do this recall by encapsulating all drawing in a single function, such as the display callback function used in our previous examples. In interactive applications that is probably not the best choice, because we decide what we draw interactively.

The reshape event returns in its measure the height and width of the new window. We can use these values to rescale the data that we use to specify the geometry. Thus, we have the callback

```
GLint windowHeight, windowWidth;

void reshape(GLsizei w, GLsizei h)
{
    windowWidth = w;
    windowHeight = h;
    glViewport(0, 0, windowWidth, windowHeight);
}
```

This function creates a new viewport that covers the entire resized window and copies the returned values of the new window width and height to the global variables `windowWidth` and `windowHeight` so they can be used by the mouse callback. Note that because the reshape callback generates a display callback, we do not need to call `glutPostRedisplay`.

2.11.3 Keyboard Events

We can also use the keyboard as an input device. Keyboard events can be generated when the mouse is in the window and one of the keys is depressed or released.[10] The GLUT function `glutKeyboardFunc` is the callback for events generated by depressing a key, whereas `glutKeyboardUpFunc` is the callback for events generated by release of a key.

When a keyboard event occurs, the ASCII code for the key that generated the event and the location of the mouse are returned. All the key-press callbacks are registered in a single callback function, such as

```
glutKeyboardFunc(myKey);
```

For example, if we wish to use the keyboard only to exit the program, we can use the callback function

---

10. Depending on the operating system, the mouse focus may have to set by first clicking inside the window before events are recognized.

```
void myKey(unsigned char key, int x, int y)
{
    if(key=='q' || key == 'Q') exit(0);
}
```

GLUT includes a function `glutGetModifiers` that allows the user to define actions using the meta keys, such as the Control and Alt keys. These special keys can be important when we are using one- or two-button mice because we can then define the same functionality as having left, right, and middle buttons as we have assumed in this chapter. More information about these functions is in the Suggested Readings section at the end of the chapter.

2.11.4 The Idle Callback

The **idle callback** is invoked when there are no other events. Its default is the null function pointer. A typical use of the idle callback is to continue to generate graphical primitives through a display function while nothing else is happening. Another is to produce an animated display.

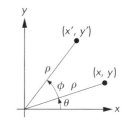

FIGURE 2.45 Two-dimensional rotation.

Let's do a simple extension to our triangle program that rotates the triangle about the center of the window. Consider the two-dimensional rotation in Figure 2.45. A point at (x, y) when rotated by ϕ degrees about the origin moves to a point (x', y'). We obtain the equations of rotation by expressing both points in polar coordinates. If the original point is at

$$x = r \cos(\theta),$$

$$y = r \sin(\theta),$$

then the rotated point is at

$$x' = r \cos(\theta + \phi) = r(\cos(\theta) \cos(\phi) - \sin(\theta) \sin(\phi)),$$

$$y' = r \sin(\theta + \phi) = r(\cos(\theta) \sin(\phi) + \sin(\theta) \cos(\phi)),$$

or

$$x' = x \cos(\phi) - y \sin(\phi),$$

$$y' = x \sin(\phi) + y \cos(\phi).$$

Instead of displaying a triangle using the entered vertex positions, first we will rotate the positions by a small angle each time. The idle callback need only post a redisplay. In `main`, we specify an idle callback,

```
glutIdleFunc(idle);
```

The display callback not only changes the vertex positions but must also send the new vertex data to the GPU as in the code for which the angle is 1/1000 of a degree:

```
const float  DegreesToRadians = M_PI / 180.0;

float angle = 0.001*DegreesToRadians;  // small angle in radians

void display()
{
    for( int i = 0; i < 3; i++)
    {
        float x = cos(angle)*points[i].x - sin(angle)*points[i].y;
        float y = sin(angle)*points[i].x + cos(angle)*points[i].y;
        points[i].x = x;
        points[i].y = y;
    }
    glBufferData(GL_ARRAY_BUFFER, sizeof(points), points,
                 GL_STATIC_DRAW);
    glClear(GL_COLOR_BUFFER_BIT);  // clear the window
    glDrawArrays(GL_TRIANGLES, 0, 3);
    glFlush();
}
```

The idle function is just

```
void idle()
{
    glutPostRedisplay();
}
```

Alternately, we could have incremented the angle by a small amount in the idle callback and always applied the rotation to the original points in the display callback.

We can change most callback functions during program execution by simply specifying a new callback function. We can also disable a callback by setting its callback function to NULL. In our example, we want to stop the rotation while we are collecting data and then restart it once a new triangle is completely specified. We can modify the display callback to accomplish this change:

```
void mouse(int button, int state, int x, int y)
{
    if(button == GLUT_RIGHT_BUTTON && state == GLUT_DOWN)
    {
        exit(0);
    }

    if(button == GLUT_LEFT_BUTTON && state == GLUT_DOWN)
    {
        glutIdleFunc(NULL);
        points[count].x = (float) x / (w/2) - 1.0;
        points[count].y = (float) (h-y) / (h/2) - 1.0;
        count++;
    }
```

```
   if(count == 3)
   {
      glutIdleFunc(idle);
      glutPostRedisplay();
      count = 0;
   }
}
```

2.11.5 Double Buffering

Although we have a complete program, depending on the speed of your computer and how much you increment the angle in the idle callback, you may see a display that does not show a rotating triangle but rather a somewhat broken-up display with pieces of the triangle showing. This problem can be far more severe if you try to generate a display with many objects in motion.

The reason for this behavior is the decoupling of the automatic display of the contents of the frame buffer from the application code that changes values in the frame buffer. Typically the frame buffer is redisplayed at a regular rate, known as the **refresh rate**, which is in the range of 60 to 100 Hz (or frames per second). However, an application program operates asynchronously and can cause changes to the frame buffer at any time. Hence, a redisplay of the frame buffer can occur when its contents are still being altered by the application and the viewer will see only a partially drawn display. There are a couple of solutions to this problem. Some operating systems give the user a parameter to set that will couple or sync the drawing into and display of the frame buffer.

The more common solution is **double buffering**. Instead of a single frame buffer, the hardware has two frame buffers. One, called the **front buffer**, is one that is displayed. The other, called the **back buffer**, is then available for constructing what we would like to display. Once the drawing is complete, we swap the front and back buffers. We then clear the new back buffer and can start drawing into it. Thus, rather than using glFlush at the end of the display callback, we use

```
glutSwapBuffers();
```

We have to make one other change to use double buffering. In our initialization, we have to request a double buffer. Hence, in main we use

```
glutInitDisplayMode(GLUT_RGBA | GLUT_DOUBLE | GLUT_DEPTH);
```

Note that the default in GLUT is equivalent to using GLUT_SINGLE rather than GLUT_DOUBLE. However, modern graphics hardware has sufficient memory that we can always use double rather than single buffering. Most graphics cards will also allow you to synchronize the display refresh with the application program.

2.11.6 Window Management

GLUT also supports both multiple windows and subwindows of a given window. We can open a second top-level window (with the label "second window") by

```
uint id = glutCreateWindow("second window");
```

The returned integer value allows us to select this window as the current window into which objects will be rendered by

```
glutSetWindow(id);
```

We can make this window have properties different from those of other windows by invoking the `glutInitDisplayMode` before `glutCreateWindow`. Furthermore, each window can have its own set of callback functions because callback specifications refer to the present window.

FIGURE 2.46   Slidebar.

2.12   MENUS

We could use our graphics primitives and our mouse callbacks to construct various graphical input devices. For example, we could construct a slidebar (Figure 2.46) using filled rectangles for the device, text for any labels, and the mouse to get the position. However, much of the code would be tedious to develop, especially if we tried to create visually appealing and effective graphical devices (widgets). Most window systems provide a toolkit that contains a set of widgets, but because our philosophy is not to restrict our discussion to any particular window system, we shall not discuss the specifics of such widget sets. Fortunately, GLUT provides one additional feature, **pop-up menus**, that we can use with the mouse to create sophisticated interactive applications.

Using menus involves taking a few simple steps. We must specify the actions corresponding to each entry in the menu. We must link the menu to a particular mouse button. Finally, we must register a callback function for each menu. We can demonstrate simple menus with the example of a pop-up menu that has three entries. The first selection allows us to exit our program. The second and third start and stop the rotation. The function calls to set up the menu and to link it to the right mouse button should be placed in our `main` function. They are

```
glutCreateMenu(demo_menu);
glutAddMenuEntry("quit", 1);
glutAddMenuEntry("start rotation", 2);
glutAddMenuEntry("stop rotation", 3);
glutAttachMenu(GLUT_RIGHT_BUTTON);
```

The function `glutCreateMenu` registers the callback function `demo_menu`.

The second argument in each entry's definition is the identifier passed to the callback when the entry is selected. Hence, our callback function is

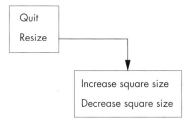

FIGURE 2.47   Structure of hierarchical menus.

```
void demo_menu(int id)
{
    switch(id)
    {
       case 1:
         exit(0);
         break;

       case 2:
         glutIdleFunc(idle);
         break;

       case 3:
         glutIdleFunc(NULL);
         break;
    }
    glutPostRedisplay();
}
```

The call to `glutPostRedisplay` requests a redraw through the `glutDisplayFunc` callback, so that the screen is drawn again without the menu.

GLUT also supports hierarchical menus, as shown in Figure 2.47. For example, suppose that we want the main menu that we create to have only two entries. The first entry still causes the program to terminate, but now the second causes a submenu to pop up. The submenu contains the two entries for turning the rotation on and off. The following code for the menu (which is in **main**) should be clear:

```
sub_menu = glutCreateMenu(rotation_menu);
glutAddMenuEntry("start rotation", 2);
glutAddMenuEntry("stop rotation", 3);
glutCreateMenu(top_menu);
glutAddMenuEntry("Quit", 1);
glutAddSubMenu("start/stop rotation", sub_menu);
glutAttachMenu(GLUT_RIGHT_BUTTON);
```

Writing the callback functions, `rotation_menu` and `top_menu`, should be a simple exercise.

SUMMARY AND NOTES

In this chapter, we introduced just enough of the OpenGL API to apply the basic concepts that we learned in Chapter 1. Although the first application we used to develop our first program was two dimensional, we took the path of looking at two-dimensional graphics as a special case of three-dimensional graphics. We then were able to extend the example to three dimensions with minimal work.

The Sierpinski gasket provides a nontrivial beginning application. A few extensions and mathematical issues are presented in the exercises at the end of this chapter. The texts in the Suggested Readings section provide many other examples of interesting curves and surfaces that can be generated with simple programs.

The historical development of graphics APIs and graphical models illustrates the importance of starting in three dimensions. The pen-plotter model from Chapter 1 was used for many years and is the basis of many important APIs, such as PostScript. Work to define an international standard for graphics APIs began in the 1970s and culminated with the adoption of GKS by the International Standards Organization (ISO) in 1984. However, GKS had its basis in the pen-plotter model and as a two-dimensional API was of limited utility in the CAD community. Although the standard was extended to three dimensions with GKS-3D, the limitations imposed by the original underlying model led to a standard that was lacking in many aspects. The PHIGS and PHIGS+ APIs, started in the CAD community, are inherently three dimensional and are based on the synthetic-camera model.

OpenGL is derived from the IrisGL API, which is based on implementing the synthetic-camera model with a pipeline architecture. IrisGL was developed for Silicon Graphics, Inc. (SGI) workstations, which incorporated a pipeline architecture originally implemented with special-purpose VLSI chips. Hence, although PHIGS and GL have much in common, GL was designed specifically for high-speed real-time rendering. OpenGL was a result of application users realizing the advantages of GL programming and wanting to carry these advantages to other platforms. Because it removed input and windowing functions from GL and concentrated on rendering, OpenGL emerged as a new API that was portable while retaining the features that make GL such a powerful API.

Although most application programmers who use OpenGL prefer to program in C, there is a fair amount of interest in higher-level interfaces. Using C++ rather than C requires minimal code changes but does not provide a true object-oriented interface to OpenGL. Among object-oriented programmers, there has been much interest in both OpenGL and higher-level APIs. Although there is no official Java binding to OpenGL, there have been multiple efforts to come up with one. The problem is not simple, because application users want to make use of the object orientation of Java and various Java toolkits, together with a non–object-oriented OpenGL specification. There are a few bindings available on the Internet, and Sun Microsystems recently released their Java bindings. Many Java programmers use the JOGL bindings.

In Chapter 8, we will introduce scene graphs, which provide a much higher-level, object-oriented interface to graphics hardware. Most scene graph APIs are built on top of OpenGL.

Within the game community, the dominance of Windows makes it possible for game developers to write code for a single platform. DirectX runs only on Windows platforms and is optimized for speed on these systems. Although much DirectX code looks like OpenGL code, the coder can use device-dependent features that are available in commodity graphics cards. Consequently, applications written in DirectX do not have the portability and stability of OpenGL applications. Thus, we see DirectX dominating the game world, whereas scientific and engineering applications generally are written in OpenGL. For OpenGL programmers who want to use features specific to certain hardware, OpenGL has an extension mechanism for accessing these features but at the cost of portability. Programming pipelines that are accessible through the OpenGL Shading Language and Cg are leading to small performance differences between OpenGL and DirectX for high-end applications.

Our examples and programs have shown how we describe and display geometric objects in a simple manner. In terms of the modeling–rendering paradigm that we presented in Chapter 1, we have focused on the modeling. However, our models are completely unstructured. Representations of objects are lists of vertices and attributes. In Chapter 8, we will learn to construct hierarchical models that can represent relationships among objects. Nevertheless, at this point, you should be able to write interesting programs. Complete the exercises at the end of the chapter and extend a few of the two-dimensional problems to three dimensions.

SUGGESTED READINGS

The Sierpinski gasket provides a good introduction to the mysteries of fractal geometry; there are good discussions in several texts [Bar93, Hil01, Man82, Pru90].

The pen-plotter API is used by PostScript [Ado85] and LOGO [Pap81]. LOGO provides turtle graphics, an API that is both simple to learn and capable of describing several of the two-dimensional mathematical curves that we use in Chapter 11 (see Exercise 2.4).

GKS [ANSI85], GKS-3D [ISO88], PHIGS [ANSI88], and PHIGS+[PHI89] are both U.S. and international standards. Their formal descriptions can be obtained from the American National Standards Institute (ANSI) and from ISO. Numerous textbooks use these APIs [Ang90, End84, Fol94, Hea04, Hop83, Hop91].

The X Window System [Sch88] has become the standard on UNIX workstations and has influenced the development of window systems on other platforms. The RenderMan interface is described in [Ups89].

The standard reference for OpenGL is the *OpenGL Programming Guide* [Shr10]. The *OpenGL Reference Manual* [Ope04] has the man pages for older versions. There is also a formal specification of OpenGL [Seg92]. The OpenGL Shading Language is described in [Ros09]. The standards documents as well as many other references and pointers to code examples are on the OpenGL Web site, www.opengl.org.

Starting with the second edition and continuing through the present edition, the *Programming Guide* uses the GLUT library that was developed by Mark Kilgard [Kil94b]. The *Programming Guide* provides many more code examples using OpenGL. GLUT was developed for use with the X Window System [Kil96], but there are also versions for Windows and the Macintosh. Much of this information and many of the example programs are available over the Internet. Representative sites are listed at the beginning of Appendix A.

OpenGL: A Primer [Ang08], the companion book to this text, contains details of the OpenGL functions used here and more example programs. Windows users can find more examples in [Wri11] and [Fos97]. Details for Mac OS X users are [Kue08]

The graphics part of the DirectX API was originally known as Direct3D. The present version is Version 11.0.

EXERCISES

2.1   A slight variation on generating the Sierpinski gasket with triangular polygons yields the *fractal mountains* used in computer-generated animations. After you find the midpoint of each side of the triangle, perturb this location before subdivision. Generate these triangles without fill. Later, you can do this exercise in three dimensions and add shading. After a few subdivisions, you should have generated sufficient detail that your triangles look like a mountain.

2.2   The Sierpinski gasket, as generated in Exercise 2.1, demonstrates many of the geometric complexities that are studied in fractal geometry [Man82]. Suppose that you construct the gasket with mathematical lines that have length but no width. In the limit, what percentage of the area of the original triangle remains after the central triangle has been removed after each subdivision? Consider the perimeters of the triangles remaining after each central triangle is removed. In the limit, what happens to the total perimeter length of all remaining triangles?

2.3   At the lowest level of processing, we manipulate bits in the frame buffer. OpenGL has pixel-oriented commands that allow users to access the frame buffer directly. You can experiment with simple raster algorithms, such as drawing lines or circles, through a function that generates a single point. Write a small library that will allow you to work in a virtual frame buffer that you create in memory. The core functions should be `WritePixel` and `ReadPixel`. Your library should allow you to set up and display your virtual frame buffer and to run a user program that reads and writes pixels.

2.4   *Turtle graphics* is an alternative positioning system that is based on the concept of a turtle moving around the screen with a pen attached to the bottom of its shell. The turtle's position can be described by a triplet (x, y, θ), giving the

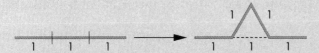

FIGURE 2.48   Generation of the Koch snowflake.

location of the center and the orientation of the turtle. A typical API for such a system includes functions such as the following:

```
init(x,y,theta); /* initialize position and orientation
                    of turtle */
forward(distance);
right(angle);
left(angle);
pen(up_down);
```

Implement a turtle-graphics library using OpenGL.

2.5   Triangulation is the process of generating a set of triangles consistent with the polygon defined by a list of vertices. What is the use of the Delaunay triangulation algorithm?

2.6   Space-filling curves have interested mathematicians for centuries. In the limit, these curves have infinite length, but they are confined to a finite rectangle and never cross themselves. Many of these curves can be generated iteratively. Consider the "rule" pictured in Figure 2.48 that replaces a single line segment with four shorter segments. Write a program that starts with a triangle and iteratively applies the replacement rule to all the line segments. The object that you generate is called the Koch snowflake. For other examples of space-filling curves, see [Hil07] and [Bar93].

2.7   You can generate a simple maze starting with a rectangular array of cells. Each cell has four sides. You remove sides (except from the perimeter of all the cells) until all the cells are connected. Then you create an entrance and an exit by removing two sides from the perimeter. A simple example is shown in Figure 2.49. Write a program using OpenGL that takes as input the two integers N and M and then draws an $N \times M$ maze.

2.8   Describe how you would adapt the RGB-color model in OpenGL to allow you to work with a subtractive color model.

2.9   We saw that a fundamental operation in graphics systems is to map a point (x, y) that lies within a clipping rectangle to a point (x_s, y_s) that lies in the viewport of a window on the screen. Assume that the two rectangles are defined by the viewport specified by

```
glViewport(u, v, w, h);
```

and a viewing rectangle specified by

FIGURE 2.49   Maze.

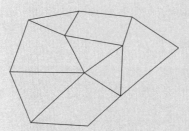

FIGURE 2.50   Polygonal mesh.

$$x_{min} \leq x \leq x_{max},$$

$$y_{min} \leq y \leq y_{max}.$$

Find the mathematical equations that map (x, y) into (x_s, y_s).

2.10   Many graphics APIs use relative positioning. In such a system, the API contains functions such as

```
move_rel(x,y);
line_rel(x,y);
```

for drawing lines and polygons. The `move_rel` function moves an internal position, or cursor, to a new position; the `line_rel` function moves the cursor and defines a line segment between the old cursor position and the new position. What are the advantages and disadvantages of relative positioning as compared to the absolute positioning used in OpenGL? Describe how you would add relative positioning to OpenGL.

2.11   In practice, testing each point in a line to determine whether it is inside or outside the polygon is extremely inefficient. Describe the general strategies that you might use to avoid point-by-point testing.

2.12   Describe the functions of strips and fans in OpenGL polygons.

2.13   Figure 2.50 shows a set of polygons called a *mesh*; these polygons share some edges and vertices. Find one or more simple data structures that represent the mesh. A good data structure should include information on shared vertices and edges. Using OpenGL, find an efficient method for displaying a mesh represented by your data structure. *Hint:* Start with an array or linked list that contains the locations of the vertices.

2.14   What is an aspect ratio? How is it related to a viewport? Explain how an aspect ratio is specified in OpenGL.

2.15   In OpenGL, we can associate a color with each vertex. If the endpoints of a line segment have different colors assigned to them, OpenGL will interpolate between the colors as it renders the line segment. It will do the same for polygons. Use this property to display the *Maxwell triangle*: an equilateral triangle whose vertices are red, green, and blue. What is the relationship between the Maxwell triangle and the color cube?

2.16 We can simulate many realistic effects using computer graphics by incorporating simple physics in the model. Simulate a bouncing ball in two dimensions incorporating both gravity and elastic collisions with a surface. You can model the ball with a closed polygon that has a sufficient number of sides to look smooth.

2.17 An interesting but difficult extension of Exercise 2.16 is to simulate a game of pool or billiards. You will need to have multiple balls that can interact with the sides of the table and with one another. *Hint:* Start with two balls and consider how to detect possible collisions.

2.18 A certain graphics system with a CRT display is advertised to display any four colors out of 256 colors. What does this statement tell you about the frame buffer and about the quality of the monitor?

2.19 Devise a test for the convexity of a two-dimensional polygon.

2.20 Another approach to the three-dimensional gasket is based on subdividing only the faces of an initial tetrahedron. Write a program that takes this approach. How do the results differ from the program that we developed in Section 2.10?

2.21 Each time that we subdivide the tetrahedron and keep only the four smaller tetrahedrons corresponding to the original vertices, we decrease the volume by a factor f. Find f. What is the ratio of the new surface area of the four tetrahedrons to the surface area of the original tetrahedron?

2.22 Creating simple games is a good way to become familiar with interactive graphics programming. Program the game of checkers. You can look at each square as an object that can be picked by the user. You can start with a program in which the user plays both sides.

2.23 Write an interactive program that will allow you to guide a graphical rat through the maze you generated in Exercise 2.7. You can use the left and right buttons to turn the rat and the middle button to move him forward.

2.24 A redisplay of the frame buffer can occur when its contents are still being altered by the application and the viewer will see only a partially drawn display. Devise a solution to this problem.

2.25 The required refresh rate for CRT displays of 55 to 85 Hz is based on the use of short-persistence phosphors that emit light for extremely short intervals when excited. Is it better to use an interlaced or noninterlaced system if the refresh rate is increased or decreased? Explain both perspectives.

2.26 Which hidden-surface-removal algorithm is supported by OpenGL? Derive the algorithm in OpenGL.

CHAPTER 3

GEOMETRIC OBJECTS AND TRANSFORMATIONS

We are now ready to concentrate on three-dimensional graphics. Much of this chapter is concerned with such matters as how to represent basic geometric types, how to convert between various representations, and what statements we can make about geometric objects independent of a particular representation.

We begin with an examination of the mathematical underpinnings of computer graphics. This approach should avoid much of the confusion that arises from a lack of care in distinguishing among a geometric entity, its representation in a particular reference system, and a mathematical abstraction of it.

We use the notions of affine and Euclidean vector spaces to create the necessary mathematical foundation for later work. One of our goals is to establish a method for dealing with geometric problems that is independent of coordinate systems. The advantages of such an approach will be clear when we worry about how to represent the geometric objects with which we would like to work. The coordinate-free approach will prove to be far more robust than one based on representing the objects in a particular coordinate system or frame. This coordinate-free approach also leads to the use of homogeneous coordinates, a system that not only enables us to explain this approach but also leads to efficient implementation techniques.

We use the terminology of abstract data types to reinforce the distinction between an object and its representation. Our development will show that the mathematics arise naturally from our desire to manipulate a few basic geometric objects. Much of what we present here is an application of vector spaces, geometry, and linear algebra. Appendices B and C summarize the formalities of vector spaces and matrix algebra, respectively.

In a vein similar to the approach we took in Chapter 2, we develop a simple application program to illustrate the basic principles and to see how the concepts are realized within an API. In this chapter, our example is focused on the representation and transformations of a cube. We also consider how to specify transformations interactively and apply them smoothly. Because transformations are key to both modeling and implementation, we will develop transformation capabilities that can be carried out in both the application code and in the shaders.

3.1 SCALARS, POINTS, AND VECTORS

In computer graphics, we work with sets of geometric objects, such as lines, polygons, and polyhedra. Such objects exist in a three-dimensional world and have properties that can be described using concepts such as length and angles. As we discovered working in two dimensions, we can define most geometric objects using a limited set of simple entities. These basic geometric objects and the relationships among them can be described using three fundamental types: scalars, points, and vectors.

Although we will consider each type from a geometric perspective, each of these types also can be defined formally, as in Appendix B, as obeying a set of axioms. Although ultimately we will use the geometric instantiation of each type, we want to take great care in distinguishing between the abstract definition of each entity and any particular example, or implementation, of it. By taking care here, we can avoid many subtle pitfalls later. Although we will work in three-dimensional spaces, virtually all our results will hold in *n*-dimensional spaces.

3.1.1 Geometric Objects

Our fundamental geometric object is a point. In a three-dimensional geometric system, a **point** is a location in space. The only property that a point possesses is that point's location; a mathematical point has neither a size nor a shape.

Points are useful in specifying geometric objects but are not sufficient by themselves. We need real numbers to specify quantities such as the distance between two points. Real numbers—and complex numbers, which we will use occasionally—are examples of **scalars**. Scalars are objects that obey a set of rules that are abstractions of the operations of ordinary arithmetic. Thus, addition and multiplication are defined and obey the usual rules such as commutivity and associativity. Every scalar has multiplicative and additive inverses, which implicitly define subtraction and division.

We need one additional type—the **vector**—to allow us to work with directions.[1] Physicists and mathematicians use the term *vector* for any quantity with direction and magnitude. Physical quantities, such as velocity and force, are vectors. A vector does not, however, have a fixed location in space.

FIGURE 3.1 Directed line segment that connects points.

In computer graphics, we often connect points with directed line segments, as shown in Figure 3.1. A directed line segment has both magnitude—its length—and direction—its orientation—and thus is a vector. Because vectors have no fixed position, the directed line segments shown in Figure 3.2 are identical because they have the same direction and magnitude. We will often use the terms *vector* and *directed line segment* synonymously.

Vectors can have their lengths altered by real numbers. Thus, in Figure 3.3(a), line segment *A* has the same direction as line segment *B*, but *B* has twice the length

FIGURE 3.2 Identical vectors.

---

1. The types such as vec3 used by GLSL and that we have used in our classes are not geometric types but rather storage types. Hence, we can use a vec3 to store information about a point, a vector, or a color. Unfortunately, the choice of names by GLSL can cause some confusion.

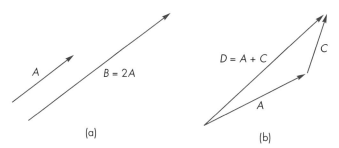

FIGURE 3.3 (a) Parallel line segments. (b) Addition of line segments.

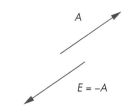

FIGURE 3.4 Inverse vectors.

that A has, so we can write $B = 2A$. We can also combine directed line segments by the **head-to-tail rule**, as shown in Figure 3.3(b). Here, we connect the head of vector A to the tail of vector C to form a new vector D, whose magnitude and direction are determined by the line segment from the tail of A to the head of C. We call this new vector, D, the **sum** of A and C and write $D = A + C$. Because vectors have no fixed positions, we can move any two vectors as necessary to form their sum graphically. Note that we have described two fundamental operations: the addition of two vectors and the multiplication of a vector by a scalar.

If we consider two directed line segments, A and E, as shown in Figure 3.4, with the same length but opposite directions, their sum as defined by the head-to-tail addition has no length. This sum forms a special vector called the **zero vector**, which we denote **0**, that has a magnitude of zero. Because it has no length, the orientation of this vector is undefined. We say that E is the **inverse** of A and we can write $E = -A$. Using inverses of vectors, scalar-vector expressions such as $A + 2B - 3C$ make sense.

Although we can multiply a vector by a scalar to change its length, there are no obvious sensible operations between two points that produce another point. Nor are there operations between a point and a scalar that produce a point. There is, however, an operation between points and directed line segments (vectors), as illustrated in Figure 3.5. We can use a directed line segment to move from one point to another. We call this operation **point-vector addition**, and it produces a new point. We write this operation as $P = Q + v$. We can see that the vector v displaces the point Q to the new location P.

FIGURE 3.5 Point-vector addition.

Looking at things slightly differently, any two points define a directed line segment or vector from one point to the second. We call this operation **point-point subtraction**, and we can write it as $v = P - Q$. Because vectors can be multiplied by scalars, some expressions involving scalars, vectors, and points make sense, such as $P + 3v$, or $2P - Q + 3v$ (because it can be written as $P + (P - Q) + 3v$, a sum of a point and a vector), whereas others, such as $P + 3Q - v$, do not.

3.1.2 Coordinate-Free Geometry

Points exist in space regardless of any reference or coordinate system. Thus, we do not need a coordinate system to specify a point or a vector. This fact may seem counter

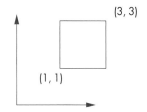

FIGURE 3.6 Object and coordinate system.

FIGURE 3.7 Object without coordinate system.

to your experiences, but it is crucial to understanding geometry and how to build graphics systems. Consider the two-dimensional example shown in Figure 3.6. Here we see a coordinate system defined by two axes, an origin, and a simple geometric object, a square. We can refer to the point at the lower-left corner of the square as having coordinates (1, 1) and note that the sides of the square are orthogonal to each other and that the point at (3, 1) is 2 units from the point at (1, 1). Now suppose that we remove the axes as shown in Figure 3.7. We can no longer specify where the points are. But those locations were relative to an arbitrary location of the origin and the orientation of the axes. What is more important is that the fundamental geometric relationships are preserved. The square is still a square, orthogonal lines are still orthogonal, and distances between points remain the same.

Of course, we may find it inconvenient, at best, to refer to a specific point as "that point over there" or "the blue point to the right of the red one." Coordinate systems and frames (see Section 3.3) solve this reference problem, but for now we want to see just how far we can get following a coordinate-free approach that does not require an arbitrary reference system.

3.1.3 The Mathematical View: Vector and Affine Spaces

If we view scalars, points, and vectors as members of mathematical sets, then we can look at a variety of abstract spaces for representing and manipulating these sets of objects. Mathematicians have explored a variety of such spaces for applied problems, ranging from the solution of differential equations to the approximation of mathematical functions. The formal definitions of the spaces of interest to us—vector spaces, affine spaces, and Euclidean spaces—are given in Appendix B. We are concerned with only those examples in which the elements are geometric types.

We start with a set of scalars, any pair of which can be combined to form another scalar through two operations, called *addition* and *multiplication*. If these operations obey the closure, associativity, commutivity, and inverse properties described in Appendix B, the elements form a **scalar field**. Familiar examples of scalars include the real numbers, complex numbers, and rational functions.

Perhaps the most important mathematical space is the **(linear) vector space**. A vector space contains two distinct types of entities: vectors and scalars. In addition to the rules for combining scalars, within a vector space, we can combine scalars and vectors to form new vectors through **scalar–vector multiplication** and vectors with vectors through **vector–vector addition**. Examples of mathematical vector spaces include n-tuples of real numbers and the geometric operations on our directed line segments.

In a linear vector space, we do not necessarily have a way of measuring a scalar quantity. A **Euclidean space** is an extension of a vector space that adds a measure of size or distance and allows us to define such things as the length of a line segment.

An **affine space** is an extension of the vector space that includes an additional type of object: the point. Although there are no operations between two points or between a point and a scalar that yield points, there is an operation of *vector–point addition* that produces a new point. Alternately, we can say there is an operation called *point–point subtraction* that produces a vector from two points. Examples of affine spaces include the geometric operations on points and directed line segments that we introduced in Section 3.1.1.

In these abstract spaces, objects can be defined independently of any particular representation; they are simply members of various sets. One of the major vector-space concepts is that of representing a vector in terms of one or more sets of basis vectors. Representation (Section 3.3) provides the tie between abstract objects and their implementation. Conversion between representations leads us to geometric transformations.

3.1.4 The Computer Science View

Although the mathematician may prefer to think of scalars, points, and vectors as members of sets that can be combined according to certain axioms, the computer scientist prefers to see them as **abstract data types** (**ADTs**). An ADT is a set of operations on data; the operations are defined independently of how the data are represented internally or of how the operations are implemented. The notion of *data abstraction* is fundamental to modern computer science. For example, the operation of adding an element to a list or of multiplying two polynomials can be defined independently of how the list is stored or of how real numbers are represented on a particular computer. People familiar with this concept should have no trouble distinguishing between objects (and operations on objects) and objects' representations (or implementations) in a particular system. From a computational point of view, we should be able to declare geometric objects through code such as

```
vector u,v;
point p,q;
scalar a,b;
```

regardless of the internal representation or implementation of the objects on a particular system. In object-oriented languages, such as C++, we can use language features, such as classes and overloading of operators, so we can write lines of code, such as

```
q = p+a*v;
```

using our geometric data types. Of course, first we must define functions that perform the necessary operations; so that we can write them, we must look at the mathematical functions that we wish to implement. First, we will define our objects. Then we will look to certain abstract mathematical spaces to help us with the operations among them.

3.1.5 Geometric ADTs

The three views of scalars, points, and vectors leave us with a mathematical and computational framework for working with our geometric entities. In summary, for computer graphics our scalars are the real numbers using ordinary addition and multiplication. Our geometric points are locations in space, and our vectors are directed line segments. These objects obey the rules of an affine space. We can also create the corresponding ADTs in a program.

Our next step is to show how we can use our types to form geometrical objects and to perform geometric operations among them. We will use the following notation:

- Greek letters α, β, γ, ... denote scalars;
- uppercase letters P, Q, R, ... denote points;
- lowercase letters u, v, w, ... denote vectors.

We have not as yet introduced any reference system, such as a coordinate system; thus, for vectors and points, this notation refers to the abstract objects, rather than to these objects' representations in a particular reference system. We use boldface letters for the latter in Section 3.3. The **magnitude** of a vector v is a real number denoted by $|v|$. The operation of vector–scalar multiplication (see Appendix B) has the property that

$$|\alpha v| = |\alpha||v|,$$

and the direction of αv is the same as the direction of v if α is positive and the opposite direction if α is negative.

We have two equivalent operations that relate points and vectors. First, there is the subtraction of two points, P and Q—an operation that yields a vector v denoted by

$$v = P - Q.$$

As a consequence of this operation, given any point Q and vector v, there is a unique point, P, that satisfies the preceding relationship. We can express this statement as follows: Given a point Q and a vector v, there is a point P such that

$$P = Q + v.$$

FIGURE 3.8   Point–point subtraction.

Thus, P is formed by a point–vector addition operation. Figure 3.8 shows a visual interpretation of this operation. The head-to-tail rule gives us a convenient way of visualizing vector–vector addition. We obtain the sum $u + v$ as shown in Figure 3.9(a) by drawing the sum vector as connecting the tail of u to the head of v. However, we can also use this visualization, as demonstrated in Figure 3.9(b), to show that for any three points P, Q, and R,

$$(P - Q) + (Q - R) = P - R.$$

3.1.6 Lines

The sum of a point and a vector (or the subtraction of two points) leads to the notion of a line in an affine space. Consider all points of the form

$$P(\alpha) = P_0 + \alpha d,$$

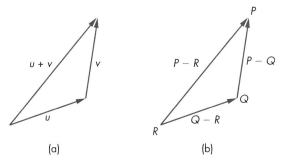

FIGURE 3.9 Use of the head-to-tail rule. (a) For vectors. (b) For points.

where P_0 is an arbitrary point, d is an arbitrary vector, and α is a scalar that can vary over some range of values. Given the rules for combining points, vectors, and scalars in an affine space, for any value of α, evaluation of the function $P(\alpha)$ yields a point. For geometric vectors (directed line segments), these points lie on a line, as shown in Figure 3.10. This form is known as the **parametric form** of the line because we generate points on the line by varying the parameter α. For $\alpha = 0$, the line passes through the point P_0, and as α is increased, all the points generated lie in the direction of the vector d. If we restrict α to nonnegative values, we get the **ray** emanating from P_0 and going in the direction of d. Thus, a line is infinitely long in both directions, a line segment is a finite piece of a line between two points, and a ray is infinitely long in one direction.

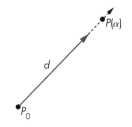

FIGURE 3.10 Line in an affine space.

3.1.7 Affine Sums

Whereas in an affine space the addition of two vectors, the multiplication of a vector by a scalar, and the addition of a vector and a point are defined, the addition of two arbitrary points and the multiplication of a point by a scalar are not. However, there is an operation called **affine addition** that has certain elements of these latter two operations. For any point Q, vector v, and positive scalar α,

$$P = Q + \alpha v$$

describes all points on the line from Q in the direction of v, as shown in Figure 3.11. However, we can always find a point R such that

$$v = R - Q;$$

thus,

$$P = Q + \alpha(R - Q) = \alpha R + (1 - \alpha)Q.$$

This operation looks like the addition of two points and leads to the equivalent form

$$P = \alpha_1 R + \alpha_2 Q,$$

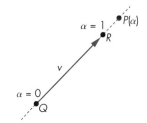

FIGURE 3.11 Affine addition.

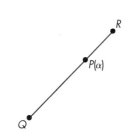

FIGURE 3.12   Line segment that connects two points.

where

$$\alpha_1 + \alpha_2 = 1.$$

3.1.8 Convexity

A **convex** object is one for which any point lying on the line segment connecting any two points in the object is also in the object. We saw the importance of convexity for polygons in Chapter 2. We can use affine sums to help us gain a deeper understanding of convexity. For $0 \le \alpha \le 1$, the affine sum defines the line segment connecting R and Q, as shown in Figure 3.12; thus, this line segment is a convex object. We can extend the affine sum to include objects defined by n points $P_1, P_2, \ldots, P_n$. Consider the form

$$P = \alpha_1 P_1 + \alpha_2 P_2 + \cdots + \alpha_n P_n.$$

We can show, by induction (see Exercise 3.29), that this sum is defined if and only if

$$\alpha_1 + \alpha_2 + \cdots + \alpha_n = 1.$$

The set of points formed by the affine sum of n points, under the additional restriction

$$\alpha_i \ge 0, \quad i = 1, 2, \ldots, n,$$

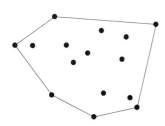

FIGURE 3.13   Convex hull.

is called the **convex hull** of the set of points (Figure 3.13). It is easy to verify that the convex hull includes all line segments connecting pairs of points in $\{P_1, P_2, \ldots, P_n\}$. Geometrically, the convex hull is the set of points that we form by stretching a tight-fitting surface over the given set of points—**shrink-wrapping** the points. It is the smallest convex object that includes the set of points. The notion of convexity is extremely important in the design of curves and surfaces; we will return to it in Chapter 10.

3.1.9 Dot and Cross Products

Many of the geometric concepts relating the orientation between two vectors are in terms of the **dot** (**inner**) and **cross** (**outer**) **products** of two vectors. The dot product of u and v is written $u \cdot v$ (see Appendix B). If $u \cdot v = 0$, u and v are said to be **orthogonal**. In a Euclidean space, the magnitude of a vector is defined. The square of the magnitude of a vector is given by the dot product

$$|u|^2 = u \cdot u.$$

The cosine of the angle between two vectors is given by

$$\cos \theta = \frac{u \cdot v}{|u||v|}.$$

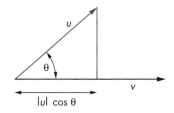

FIGURE 3.14   Dot product and projection.

In addition, $|u| \cos \theta = u \cdot v / |v|$ is the length of the orthogonal projection of u onto v, as shown in Figure 3.14. Thus, the dot product expresses the geometric result that the shortest distance from a point (the end of the vector u) to the line segment v is obtained by drawing the vector orthogonal to v from the end of u. We can also see that the vector u is composed of the vector sum of the orthogonal projection of u on v and a vector orthogonal to v.

In a vector space, a set of vectors is **linearly independent** if we cannot write one of the vectors in terms of the others using scalar-vector addition. A vector space has a **dimension**, which is the maximum number of linearly independent vectors that we can find. Given any three linearly independent vectors in a three-dimensional space, we can use the dot product to construct three vectors, each of which is orthogonal to the other two. This process is outlined in Appendix B. We can also use two non-parallel vectors, u and v, to determine a third vector n that is orthogonal to them (Figure 3.15). This vector is the **cross product**

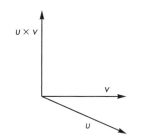

FIGURE 3.15　Cross product.

$$n = u \times v.$$

Note that we can use the cross product to derive three mutually orthogonal vectors in a three-dimensional space from any two nonparallel vectors. Starting again with u and v, we first compute n as before. Then, we can compute w by

$$w = u \times n,$$

and u, n, and w are mutually orthogonal.

The cross product is derived in Appendix C, using the representation of the vectors that gives a direct method for computing it. The magnitude of the cross product gives the magnitude of the sine of the angle θ between u and v,

$$|\sin \theta| = \frac{|u \times v|}{|u||v|}.$$

Note that the vectors u, v, and n form a **right-handed coordinate system**; that is, if u points in the direction of the thumb of the right hand and v points in the direction of the index finger, then n points in the direction of the middle finger.

3.1.10 Planes

A **plane** in an affine space can be defined as a direct extension of the parametric line. From simple geometry, we know that three points not on the same line determine a unique plane. Suppose that P, Q, and R are three such points in an affine space. The line segment that joins P and Q is the set of points of the form

$$S(\alpha) = \alpha P + (1 - \alpha)Q, \qquad 0 \le \alpha \le 1.$$

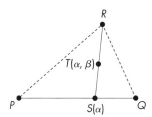

FIGURE 3.16　Formation of a plane.

Suppose that we take an arbitrary point on this line segment and form the line segment from this point to R, as shown in Figure 3.16. Using a second parameter β, we can describe points along this line segment as

$$T(\beta) = \beta S + (1 - \beta)R, \qquad 0 \le \beta \le 1.$$

Such points are determined by both α and β and form the plane determined by P, Q, and R. Combining the preceding two equations, we obtain one form of the equation of a plane:

$$T(\alpha, \beta) = \beta[\alpha P + (1 - \alpha)Q] + (1 - \beta)R.$$

We can rearrange this equation in the following form:

$$T(\alpha, \beta) = P + \beta(1 - \alpha)(Q - P) + (1 - \beta)(R - P).$$

Noting that $Q - P$ and $R - P$ are arbitrary vectors, we have shown that a plane can also be expressed in terms of a point, P_0, and two nonparallel vectors, u and v, as

$$T(\alpha, \beta) = P_0 + \alpha u + \beta v.$$

If we write T as

$$T(\alpha, \beta) = \beta\alpha P + \beta(1 - \alpha)Q + (1 - \beta)R,$$

this form is equivalent to expressing T as

$$T(\alpha, \beta', \gamma) = \alpha' P + \beta' Q + \gamma' R,$$

as long as

$$\alpha' + \beta' + \gamma' = 1.$$

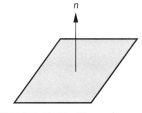

FIGURE 3.17 Normal to a plane.

The representation of a point by $(\alpha', \beta', \gamma')$ is called its **barycentric coordinate** representation.

We can also observe that for $0 \le \alpha, \beta \le 1$, all the points $T(\alpha, \beta)$ lie in the triangle formed by P, Q, and R. If a point P lies in the plane, then

$$P - P_0 = \alpha u + \beta v.$$

We can find a vector w that is orthogonal to both u and v, as shown in Figure 3.17. If we use the cross product

$$n = u \times v,$$

then the equation of the plane becomes

$$n \cdot (P - P_0) = 0.$$

The vector n is perpendicular, or orthogonal, to the plane; it is called the **normal** to the plane. The forms $P(\alpha)$, for the line, and $T(\alpha, \beta)$, for the plane, are known as **parametric forms** because they give the value of a point in space for each value of the parameters α and β.

3.2   THREE-DIMENSIONAL PRIMITIVES

In a three-dimensional world, we can have a far greater variety of geometric objects than we can in two dimensions. When we worked in a two-dimensional plane in Chapter 2, we considered objects that were simple curves, such as line segments, and flat objects with well-defined interiors, such as simple polygons. In three dimensions, we retain these objects, but they are no longer restricted to lie in the same plane. Hence, curves become curves in space (Figure 3.18), and objects with interiors can become surfaces in space (Figure 3.19). In addition, we can have objects with volumes, such as parallelepipeds and ellipsoids (Figure 3.20).

FIGURE 3.18   Curves in three dimensions.

We face two problems when we expand our graphics system to incorporate all these possibilities. First, the mathematical definitions of these objects can become complex. Second, we are interested in only those objects that lead to efficient implementations in graphics systems. The full range of three-dimensional objects cannot be supported on existing graphics systems, except by approximate methods.

Three features characterize three-dimensional objects that fit well with existing graphics hardware and software:

1. The objects are described by their surfaces and can be thought of as being hollow.

2. The objects can be specified through a set of vertices in three dimensions.

3. The objects either are composed of or can be approximated by flat, convex polygons.

FIGURE 3.19   Surfaces in three dimensions.

We can understand why we set these conditions if we consider what most modern graphics systems do best: They render triangles or meshes of triangles. Commodity graphics cards can render over 100 million small, flat triangles per second. Performance measurements for graphics systems usually are quoted for small three-dimensional triangles that can be generated by triangle strips. In addition, these triangles are shaded, lit, and texture mapped, features that are implemented in the hardware of modern graphics cards.

The first condition implies that we need only two-dimensional primitives to model three-dimensional objects because a surface is a two- rather than a three-dimensional entity. The second condition is an extension of our observations in Chapters 1 and 2. If an object is specified by vertices, we can use a pipeline architecture to process these vertices at high rates, and we can use the hardware to generate the images of the objects only during rasterization. The final condition is an extension from our discussion of two-dimensional polygons. Most graphics systems are optimized for the processing of points, line segments, and triangles. In three dimensions, a triangle is specified by an ordered list of three vertices.

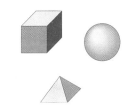

FIGURE 3.20   Volumetric objects.

However, for general polygons specified with more than three vertices, the vertices do not have to lie in the same plane. If they do not, there is no simple way to define the interior of the object. Consequently, most graphics systems require that the application either specify simple planar polygons or triangles. If a system allows polygons and the application does not specify a flat polygon, then the results of rasterizing the polygon are not guaranteed to be what the programmer might desire. Because triangular polygons are always flat, either the modeling system is designed to always produce triangles, or the graphics system provides a method to divide, or **tessellate**, an arbitrary polygon into triangular polygons. If we apply this same argument to a curved object, such as a sphere, we realize that we should use an approximation to the sphere composed of small, flat polygons. Hence, even if our modeling system provides curved objects, we assume that a triangle mesh approximation is used for implementation.

The major exception to this approach is **constructive solid geometry** (**CSG**). In such systems, we build objects from a small set of volumetric objects through a set of operations such as union and intersection. We consider CSG models in Chapter 8. Although this approach is an excellent one for modeling, rendering CSG models is more difficult than is rendering surface-based polygonal models. Although this situation may not hold in the future, we discuss in detail only surface rendering.

All the primitives with which we work can be specified through a set of vertices. As we move away from abstract objects to real objects, we must consider how we represent points in space in a manner that can be used within our graphics systems.

3.3   COORDINATE SYSTEMS AND FRAMES

So far, we have considered vectors and points as abstract objects, without representing them in an underlying reference system. In a three-dimensional vector space, we can represent any vector w uniquely in terms of any three linearly independent vectors, v_1, v_2, and v_3 (see Appendix B), as

$$w = \alpha_1 v_1 + \alpha_2 v_2 + \alpha_3 v_3.$$

The scalars α_1, α_2, and α_3 are the **components** of w with respect to the **basis** v_1, v_2, and v_3. These relationships are shown in Figure 3.21. We can write the **representation**

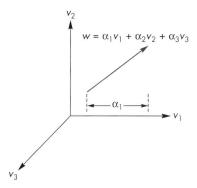

FIGURE 3.21   Vector derived from three basis vectors.

of w with respect to this basis as the column matrix

$$\mathbf{a} = \begin{bmatrix} \alpha_1 \\ \alpha_2 \\ \alpha_3 \end{bmatrix},$$

where boldface letters denote a representation in a particular basis, as opposed to the original abstract vector w. We can also write this relationship as

$$w = \mathbf{a}^T \begin{bmatrix} v_1 \\ v_2 \\ v_3 \end{bmatrix} = \mathbf{a}^T \mathbf{v},$$

where

$$\mathbf{v} = \begin{bmatrix} v_1 \\ v_2 \\ v_3 \end{bmatrix}.$$

We usually think of the basis vectors, v_1, v_2, v_3, as defining a **coordinate system**. However, for dealing with problems using points, vectors, and scalars, we need a more general method. Figure 3.22 shows one aspect of the problem. The three vectors form a coordinate system that is shown in Figure 3.22(a) as we would usually draw it, with the three vectors emerging from a single point. We could use these three basis vectors as a basis to represent any vector in three dimensions. Vectors, however, have direction and magnitude but lack a position attribute. Hence, Figure 3.22(b) is equivalent, because we have moved the basis vectors, leaving their magnitudes and directions unchanged. Most people find this second figure confusing, even though mathematically it expresses the same information as the first figure. We are still left with the problem of how to represent points—entities that have fixed positions.

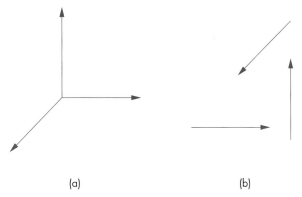

(a)   (b)

FIGURE 3.22   Coordinate systems. (a) Vectors emerging from a common point. (b) Vectors moved.

Because an affine space contains points, once we fix a particular reference point—the origin—in such a space, we can represent all points unambiguously. The usual convention for drawing coordinate axes as emerging from the origin, as shown in Figure 3.22(a), makes sense in the affine space where both points and vectors have representations. However, this representation requires us to know *both* the reference point and the basis vectors. The origin and the basis vectors determine a **frame**. Loosely, this extension fixes the origin of the vector coordinate system at some point P_0. Within a given frame, every vector can be written uniquely as

$$w = \alpha_1 v_1 + \alpha_2 v_2 + \alpha_3 v_3 = \mathbf{a}^T \mathbf{v},$$

just as in a vector space; in addition, every point can be written uniquely as

$$P = P_0 + \beta_1 v_1 + \beta_2 v_2 + \beta_3 v_3 = P_0 + \mathbf{b}^T \mathbf{v}.$$

Thus, the representation of a particular vector in a frame requires three scalars; the representation of a point requires three scalars and the knowledge of where the origin is located. As we will see in Section 3.3.4, by abandoning the more familiar notion of a coordinate system and a basis in that coordinate system in favor of the less familiar notion of a frame, we avoid the difficulties caused by vectors having magnitude and direction but no fixed position. In addition, we are able to represent points and vectors in a manner that will allow us to use matrix representations but that maintains a distinction between the two geometric types.

Because points and vectors are two distinct geometric types, graphical representations that equate a point with a directed line segment drawn from the origin to that point (Figure 3.23) should be regarded with suspicion. Thus, a correct interpretation of Figure 3.23 is that a given vector can be defined as going from a fixed reference point (the origin) to a particular point in space. Note that a vector, like a point, exists regardless of the reference system, but as we will see with both points and vectors, eventually we have to work with their representation in a particular reference system.

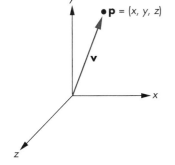

FIGURE 3.23   A dangerous representation of a vector.

3.3.1 Representations and N-Tuples

Suppose that vectors e_1, e_2, and e_3 form a basis. The representation of any vector, v, is given by the component $(\alpha_1, \alpha_2, \alpha_3)$ of a vector $\mathbf{a}$ where

$$v = \alpha_1 e_1 + \alpha_2 e_2 + \alpha_3 e_3.$$

The basis vectors[2] must themselves have representations that we can denote $\mathbf{e}_1$, $\mathbf{e}_2$, and $\mathbf{e}_3$, given by

---

2. Many textbooks on vectors refer to these vectors as the unit basis $\mathbf{i}$, $\mathbf{j}$, $\mathbf{k}$ and write other vectors in the form $v = \alpha_1 \mathbf{i} + \alpha_2 \mathbf{j} + \alpha_3 \mathbf{k}$.

$$\mathbf{e_1} = (1, 0, 0)^T,$$

$$\mathbf{e_2} = (0, 1, 0)^T,$$

$$\mathbf{e_3} = (0, 0, 1)^T.$$

In other words, the 3-tuple $(1, 0, 0)$ is the representation of the first basis vector. Consequently, rather than thinking in terms of abstract vectors, we can work with 3-tuples and we can write the representation of any vector v as a column matrix $\mathbf{a}$ or the 3-tuple $(\alpha_1, \alpha_2, \alpha_3)$, where

$$\mathbf{a} = \alpha_1\mathbf{e_1} + \alpha_2\mathbf{e_2} + \alpha_3\mathbf{e_3}.$$

The basis 3-tuples $\mathbf{e_1}$, $\mathbf{e_2}$, and $\mathbf{e_3}$ are vectors in the familiar Euclidean space $\mathbf{R}^3$. The vector space $\mathbf{R}^3$ is equivalent (or **homomorphic**) to the vector space of our original geometric vectors. From a practical perspective, it is almost always easier to work with 3-tuples (or more generally n-tuples) than with other representations.

3.3.2 Change of Coordinate Systems

Frequently, we are required to find how the representation of a vector changes when we change the basis vectors. For example, in OpenGL, we specify our geometry using the coordinate system or frame that is natural for the model, which is known as the **object** or **model frame**. Models are then brought into the **world frame**. At some point, we want to know how these objects appear to the camera. It is natural at that point to convert from the world frame to the **camera** or **eye frame**. The conversion from the object frame to the eye frame is done by the model-view matrix.

Let's consider changing representations for vectors first. Suppose that $\{v_1, v_2, v_3\}$ and $\{u_1, u_2, u_3\}$ are two bases. Each basis vector in the second set can be represented in terms of the first basis (and vice versa). Hence, there exist nine scalar components, $\{\gamma_{ij}\}$, such that

$$u_1 = \gamma_{11}v_1 + \gamma_{12}v_2 + \gamma_{13}v_3,$$

$$u_2 = \gamma_{21}v_1 + \gamma_{22}v_2 + \gamma_{23}v_3,$$

$$u_3 = \gamma_{31}v_1 + \gamma_{32}v_2 + \gamma_{33}v_3.$$

The 3×3 matrix

$$\mathbf{M} = \begin{bmatrix} \gamma_{11} & \gamma_{12} & \gamma_{13} \\ \gamma_{21} & \gamma_{22} & \gamma_{23} \\ \gamma_{31} & \gamma_{32} & \gamma_{33} \end{bmatrix}$$

is defined by these scalars, and

$$\begin{bmatrix} u_1 \\ u_2 \\ u_3 \end{bmatrix} = \mathbf{M} \begin{bmatrix} v_1 \\ v_2 \\ v_3 \end{bmatrix},$$

or

$\mathbf{u} = \mathbf{Mv}$.

The matrix $\mathbf{M}$ contains the information to go from a representation of a vector in one basis to its representation in the second basis. The inverse of $\mathbf{M}$ gives the matrix representation of the change from $\{u_1, u_2, u_3\}$ to $\{v_1, v_2, v_3\}$. Consider a vector w that has the representation $\{\alpha_1, \alpha_2, \alpha_3\}$ with respect to $\{v_1, v_2, v_3\}$; that is,

$w = \alpha_1 v_1 + \alpha_2 v_2 + \alpha_3 v_3$.

Equivalently,

$w = \mathbf{a}^T \mathbf{v}$,

where

$$\mathbf{a} = \begin{bmatrix} \alpha_1 \\ \alpha_2 \\ \alpha_3 \end{bmatrix},$$

$$\mathbf{v} = \begin{bmatrix} v_1 \\ v_2 \\ v_3 \end{bmatrix}.$$

Assume that $\mathbf{b}$ is the representation of w with respect to $\{u_1, u_2, u_3\}$; that is,

$w = \beta_1 u_1 + \beta_2 u_2 + \beta_3 u_3$,

or

$$w = \mathbf{b}^T \begin{bmatrix} u_1 \\ u_2 \\ u_3 \end{bmatrix} = \mathbf{b}^T \mathbf{u},$$

where

$$\mathbf{b} = \begin{bmatrix} \beta_1 \\ \beta_2 \\ \beta_3 \end{bmatrix}.$$

Then, using our representation of the second basis in terms of the first, we find that

$$w = \mathbf{b}^T \begin{bmatrix} u_1 \\ u_2 \\ u_3 \end{bmatrix} = \mathbf{b}^T \mathbf{M} \begin{bmatrix} v_1 \\ v_2 \\ v_3 \end{bmatrix} = \mathbf{a}^T \begin{bmatrix} v_1 \\ v_2 \\ v_3 \end{bmatrix}.$$

Thus,

$$\mathbf{a} = \mathbf{M}^T \mathbf{b}.$$

The matrix

$$\mathbf{T} = (\mathbf{M}^T)^{-1}$$

takes us from $\mathbf{a}$ to $\mathbf{b}$, through the simple matrix equation

$$\mathbf{b} = \mathbf{T}\mathbf{a}.$$

Thus, rather than working with our original vectors, typically directed line segments, we can work instead with their representations, which are 3-tuples or elements of $\mathbf{R}^3$. This result is important because it moves us from considering abstract vectors to working with column matrices of scalars—the vectors' representations. The important point to remember is that whenever we work with columns of real numbers as "vectors," there is an underlying basis of which we must not lose track, lest we end up working in the wrong coordinate system.

These changes in basis leave the origin unchanged. We can use them to represent rotation and scaling of a set of basis vectors to derive another basis set, as shown in Figure 3.24. However, a simple translation of the origin, or change of frame as shown in Figure 3.25, cannot be represented in this way. After we complete a simple example, we introduce homogeneous coordinates, which allow us to change frames yet still use matrices to represent the change.

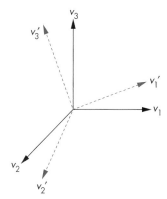

FIGURE 3.24 Rotation and scaling of a basis.

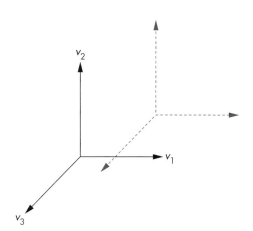

FIGURE 3.25 Translation of a basis.

3.3.3 Example Change of Representation

Suppose that we have a vector w whose representation in some basis is

$$\mathbf{a} = \begin{bmatrix} 1 \\ 2 \\ 3 \end{bmatrix}.$$

We can denote the three basis vectors as v_1, v_2, and v_3. Hence,

$$w = v_1 + 2v_2 + 3v_3.$$

Now suppose that we want to make a new basis from the three vectors v_1, v_2, and v_3 where

$$u_1 = v_1,$$
$$u_2 = v_1 + v_2,$$
$$u_3 = v_1 + v_2 + v_3.$$

The matrix $\mathbf{M}$ is

$$\mathbf{M} = \begin{bmatrix} 1 & 0 & 0 \\ 1 & 1 & 0 \\ 1 & 1 & 1 \end{bmatrix}.$$

The matrix that converts a representation in v_1, v_2, and v_3 to one in which the basis vectors are u_1, u_2, and u_3 is

$$\mathbf{T} = (\mathbf{M}^T)^{-1}$$

$$= \begin{bmatrix} 1 & 1 & 1 \\ 0 & 1 & 1 \\ 0 & 0 & 1 \end{bmatrix}^{-1}$$

$$= \begin{bmatrix} 1 & -1 & 0 \\ 0 & 1 & -1 \\ 0 & 0 & 1 \end{bmatrix}.$$

In the new system, the representation of w is

$$\mathbf{b} = \mathbf{Ta} = \begin{bmatrix} -1 \\ -1 \\ 3 \end{bmatrix}.$$

That is,

$$w = -u_1 - u_2 + 3u_3.$$

If we are working in the space of 3-tuples ($\mathbf{R}^3$), rather than in an abstract setting, then we can associate v_1, v_2, and v_3 with the unit basis in $\mathbf{R}^3$:

$$\mathbf{e}_1 = \begin{bmatrix} 1 \\ 0 \\ 0 \end{bmatrix}, \qquad \mathbf{e}_2 = \begin{bmatrix} 0 \\ 1 \\ 0 \end{bmatrix}, \qquad \mathbf{e}_3 = \begin{bmatrix} 0 \\ 0 \\ 1 \end{bmatrix}.$$

We can make this example a little more concrete by considering the following variant. Suppose that we are working with the default (x, y, z) coordinate system, which happens to be orthogonal. We are given the three direction vectors whose representations are $(1, 0, 0)$, $(1, 1, 0)$, and $(1, 1, 1)$. Thus, the first vector points along the x-axis, the second points in a direction parallel to the plane $z = 0$, and the third points in a direction symmetric to the three basis directions. These three new vectors, although they are not mutually orthogonal, are linearly independent and thus form a basis for a new coordinate system that we can call the x', y', z' system. The original directions have representations in the x', y', z' system given by the columns of the matrix $\mathbf{T}$.

3.3.4 Homogeneous Coordinates

The potential confusion between a vector and a point that we illustrated in Figure 3.23 still exists with a three-dimensional representation. Suppose that we start with the frame defined by the point P_0 and the vectors v_1, v_2, and v_3. Usually, our first inclination is to represent a point P located at (x, y, z) with the column matrix

$$\mathbf{p} = \begin{bmatrix} x \\ y \\ z \end{bmatrix},$$

where x, y, and z are the components of the basis vectors for this point, so that

$$P = P_0 + xv_1 + yv_2 + zv_3.$$

If we represent the point this way, then its representation is of the same form as the *vector*

$$w = xv_1 + yv_2 + zv_3.$$

Homogeneous coordinates avoid this difficulty by using a four-dimensional representation for both points and vectors in three dimensions. In the frame specified by (v_1, v_2, v_3, P_0), any point P can be written uniquely as

$$P = \alpha_1 v_1 + \alpha_2 v_2 + \alpha_3 v_3 + P_0.$$

If we agree to define the "multiplication" of a point by the scalars 0 and 1 as

$$0 \cdot P = \mathbf{0},$$

$$1 \cdot P = P,$$

then we can express this relation formally, using a matrix product, as

$$P = [\,\alpha_1 \quad \alpha_2 \quad \alpha_3 \quad 1\,] \begin{bmatrix} v_1 \\ v_2 \\ v_3 \\ P_0 \end{bmatrix}.$$

Strictly speaking, this expression is not a dot or inner product, because the elements of the matrices are dissimilar; nonetheless, the expression is computed as though it were an inner product by multiplying corresponding elements and summing the results. The four-dimensional row matrix on the right side of the equation is the **homogeneous-coordinate representation** of the point P in the frame determined by v_1, v_2, v_3, and P_0. Equivalently, we can say that P is represented by the column matrix

$$\mathbf{p} = \begin{bmatrix} \alpha_1 \\ \alpha_2 \\ \alpha_3 \\ 1 \end{bmatrix}.$$

In the same frame, any vector w can be written as

$$w = \delta_1 v_1 + \delta_2 v_2 + \delta_3 v_3$$

$$= [\,\delta_1 \quad \delta_2 \quad \delta_3 \quad 0\,]^T \begin{bmatrix} v_1 \\ v_2 \\ v_3 \\ P_0 \end{bmatrix}.$$

Thus, w can be represented by the column matrix

$$\mathbf{w} = \begin{bmatrix} \delta_1 \\ \delta_2 \\ \delta_3 \\ 0 \end{bmatrix}.$$

There are numerous ways to interpret this formulation geometrically. We simply note that we can carry out operations on points and vectors using their homogeneous-coordinate representations and ordinary matrix algebra. Consider, for example, a change of frames—a problem that caused difficulties when we used three-dimensional representations. If (v_1, v_2, v_3, P_0) and (u_1, u_2, u_3, Q_0) are two frames, then we can express the basis vectors and reference point of the second frame in terms of the first as

$$u_1 = \gamma_{11}v_1 + \gamma_{12}v_2 + \gamma_{13}v_3,$$
$$u_2 = \gamma_{21}v_1 + \gamma_{22}v_2 + \gamma_{23}v_3,$$
$$u_3 = \gamma_{31}v_1 + \gamma_{32}v_2 + \gamma_{33}v_3,$$
$$Q_0 = \gamma_{41}v_1 + \gamma_{42}v_2 + \gamma_{43}v_3 + P_0.$$

These equations can be written in the form

$$\begin{bmatrix} u_1 \\ u_2 \\ u_3 \\ Q_0 \end{bmatrix} = \mathbf{M} \begin{bmatrix} v_1 \\ v_2 \\ v_3 \\ P_0 \end{bmatrix},$$

where now $\mathbf{M}$ is the 4×4 matrix

$$\mathbf{M} = \begin{bmatrix} \gamma_{11} & \gamma_{12} & \gamma_{13} & 0 \\ \gamma_{21} & \gamma_{22} & \gamma_{23} & 0 \\ \gamma_{31} & \gamma_{32} & \gamma_{33} & 0 \\ \gamma_{41} & \gamma_{42} & \gamma_{43} & 1 \end{bmatrix}.$$

$\mathbf{M}$ is called the **matrix representation** of the change of frames.

We can also use $\mathbf{M}$ to compute the changes in the representations directly. Suppose that $\mathbf{a}$ and $\mathbf{b}$ are the homogeneous-coordinate representations either of two points or of two vectors in the two frames. Then

$$\mathbf{b}^T \begin{bmatrix} u_1 \\ u_2 \\ u_3 \\ Q_0 \end{bmatrix} = \mathbf{b}^T \mathbf{M} \begin{bmatrix} v_1 \\ v_2 \\ v_3 \\ P_0 \end{bmatrix} = \mathbf{a}^T \begin{bmatrix} v_1 \\ v_2 \\ v_3 \\ P_0 \end{bmatrix}.$$

Hence,

$$\mathbf{a} = \mathbf{M}^T \mathbf{b}.$$

When we work with representations, as is usually the case, we are interested in $\mathbf{M}^T$, which is of the form

$$\mathbf{M}^T = \begin{bmatrix} \alpha_{11} & \alpha_{12} & \alpha_{13} & \alpha_{14} \\ \alpha_{21} & \alpha_{22} & \alpha_{23} & \alpha_{24} \\ \alpha_{31} & \alpha_{32} & \alpha_{33} & \alpha_{34} \\ 0 & 0 & 0 & 1 \end{bmatrix}$$

and is determined by 12 coefficients.

There are other advantages to using homogeneous coordinates that we explore extensively in later chapters. Perhaps the most important is that all affine (line-preserving) transformations can be represented as matrix multiplications in homogeneous coordinates. Although we have to work in four dimensions to solve three-dimensional problems when we use homogeneous-coordinate representations, less arithmetic work is involved. The uniform representation of all affine transformations makes carrying out successive transformations (concatenation) far easier than in three-dimensional space. In addition, modern hardware implements homogeneous-coordinate operations directly, using parallelism to achieve high-speed calculations.

3.3.5 Example Change in Frames

Consider again the example of Section 3.3.3. If we again start with the basis vectors v_1, v_2, and v_3 and convert to a basis determined by the same u_1, u_2, and u_3, then the three equations are the same:

$$u_1 = v_1,$$

$$u_2 = v_1 + v_2,$$

$$u_3 = v_1 + v_2 + v_3.$$

The reference point does not change, so we add the equation

$$Q_0 = P_0.$$

Thus, the matrices in which we are interested are the matrix

$$\mathbf{M} = \begin{bmatrix} 1 & 0 & 0 & 0 \\ 1 & 1 & 0 & 0 \\ 1 & 1 & 1 & 0 \\ 0 & 0 & 0 & 1 \end{bmatrix},$$

its transpose, and their inverses.

Suppose that in addition to changing the basis vectors, we also want to move the reference point to the point that has the representation (1, 2, 3, 1) in the original system. The displacement vector $v = v_1 + 2v_2 + 3v_3$ moves P_0 to Q_0. The fourth component identifies this entity as a point. Thus, we add to the three equations from the previous example the equation

$$Q_0 = P_0 + v_1 + 2v_2 + 3v_3,$$

and the matrix $\mathbf{M}^T$ becomes

$$\mathbf{M}^T = \begin{bmatrix} 1 & 1 & 1 & 1 \\ 0 & 1 & 1 & 2 \\ 0 & 0 & 1 & 3 \\ 0 & 0 & 0 & 1 \end{bmatrix}.$$

Its inverse is

$$\mathbf{T} = (\mathbf{M}^T)^{-1} = \begin{bmatrix} 1 & -1 & 0 & 1 \\ 0 & 1 & -1 & 1 \\ 0 & 0 & 1 & -3 \\ 0 & 0 & 0 & 1 \end{bmatrix}.$$

This pair of matrices allows us to move back and forth between representations in the two frames. Note that $\mathbf{T}$ takes the *point* $(1, 2, 3)$ in the original frame, whose representation is

$$\mathbf{p} = \begin{bmatrix} 1 \\ 2 \\ 3 \\ 1 \end{bmatrix},$$

to

$$\mathbf{p}' = \begin{bmatrix} 0 \\ 0 \\ 0 \\ 1 \end{bmatrix},$$

the origin in the new system. However, the *vector* $(1, 2, 3)$, which is represented as

$$\mathbf{a} = \begin{bmatrix} 1 \\ 2 \\ 3 \\ 0 \end{bmatrix}$$

in the original system, is transformed to

$$\mathbf{b} = \begin{bmatrix} -1 \\ -1 \\ 3 \\ 0 \end{bmatrix},$$

a transformation that is consistent with the results from our example of change in coordinate systems and that also demonstrates the importance of distinguishing between points and vectors.

3.3.6 Working with Representations

Application programs almost always work with representations rather than abstract points. Thus, when we specify a point—for example, by putting its coordinates in an array—we are doing so with respect to some frame. In our earlier examples, we avoided dealing with changes in frames by specifying data in clip coordinates, a normalized system that OpenGL uses for its rendering. However, applications programs prefer to work in frames that have a relationship to the problem on which they are working and thus want to place the origin, orient the axes, and scale the units so they make sense in the problem space. Because OpenGL eventually needs its data in clip coordinates, at least one change of representation is required. As we shall see, in fact there are additional frames that we will find useful both for modeling and rendering. Hence, we will carry out a sequence of changes in representation.

Changes of representation are thus specified by a matrix of the form

$$\mathbf{a} = \mathbf{C}\mathbf{b},$$

where **a** and **b** are the two representations of a point or vector in homogeneous coordinates. As we have seen in Section 3.3.4, this matrix must be a homogeneous form so **C** is the transpose of a matrix **M** and is given by

$$\mathbf{C} = \mathbf{M}^T = \begin{bmatrix} \alpha_{11} & \alpha_{12} & \alpha_{13} & \alpha_{14} \\ \alpha_{21} & \alpha_{22} & \alpha_{23} & \alpha_{24} \\ \alpha_{31} & \alpha_{32} & \alpha_{33} & \alpha_{34} \\ 0 & 0 & 0 & 1 \end{bmatrix}.$$

The problem is how to find **C** when we are working with representations. It turns out to be quite easy. Suppose that we are working in some frame and we specify another frame by its representation in this frame. Thus, if in the original system we specify a frame by the representations of three vectors, u, v, and n, and give the origin of the new frame as the point p, in homogeneous coordinates all four of these entities are 4-tuples or elements of $\mathbf{R}^4$.

Let's consider the inverse problem. The matrix

$$\mathbf{T} = \mathbf{C}^{-1}$$

converts from representations in the (u, v, n, p) frame to representations in the original frame. Thus, we must have

$$\mathbf{T} \begin{bmatrix} 1 \\ 0 \\ 0 \\ 0 \end{bmatrix} = \mathbf{u} = \begin{bmatrix} u_1 \\ u_2 \\ u_3 \\ 0 \end{bmatrix}.$$

Likewise,

$$\mathbf{T} \begin{bmatrix} 0 \\ 1 \\ 0 \\ 0 \end{bmatrix} = \mathbf{v} = \begin{bmatrix} v_1 \\ v_2 \\ v_3 \\ 0 \end{bmatrix},$$

$$\mathbf{T} \begin{bmatrix} 0 \\ 0 \\ 1 \\ 0 \end{bmatrix} = \mathbf{n} = \begin{bmatrix} n_1 \\ n_2 \\ n_3 \\ 0 \end{bmatrix},$$

$$\mathbf{T} \begin{bmatrix} 0 \\ 0 \\ 0 \\ 1 \end{bmatrix} = \mathbf{p} = \begin{bmatrix} p_1 \\ p_2 \\ p_3 \\ 1 \end{bmatrix}.$$

Putting these results together, we find

$$\mathbf{TI} = \mathbf{T} = [\, u \quad v \quad n \quad p \,] = \begin{bmatrix} u_1 & v_1 & n_1 & p_1 \\ u_2 & v_2 & n_2 & p_2 \\ u_3 & v_3 & n_3 & p_3 \\ 0 & 0 & 0 & 1 \end{bmatrix},$$

or

$$\mathbf{C} = [\, u \quad v \quad n \quad p \,]^{-1} = \begin{bmatrix} u_1 & v_1 & n_1 & p_1 \\ u_2 & v_2 & n_2 & p_2 \\ u_3 & v_3 & n_3 & p_3 \\ 0 & 0 & 0 & 1 \end{bmatrix}^{-1}.$$

Thus, the representation of a frame in terms of another frame gives us the inverse of the matrix we need to convert from representations in the first frame to representations in the second. Of course, we must compute this inverse, but computing the inverse of a 4×4 matrix of this form should not present a problem.

3.4 FRAMES IN OPENGL

As we have seen, OpenGL is based on a pipeline model, the first part of which is a sequence of operations on vertices, many of which are geometric. We can characterize such operations by a sequence of transformations or, equivalently, as a sequence of changes of frames for the objects specified by an application program.

In versions of OpenGL with a fixed-function pipeline and immediate-mode rendering, six frames were specified in the pipeline. With programmable shaders, we have a great deal of flexibility to add additional frames or avoid some traditional frames. Although as we demonstrated in our first examples, we could use some knowledge of how the pipeline functions to avoid using all these frames, that would not be the best way to build our applications. Rather, each of the six frames we will discuss will prove to be useful, either for developing our applications or for implementation of the pipeline. Some will be applied in the application code, others in our shaders. Some may not be visible to the application. In each of these frames, a vertex has different coordinates. The following is the usual order in which the frames occur in the pipeline:

1. Object (or model) coordinates

2. World coordinates

3. Eye (or camera) coordinates

4. Clip coordinates

5. Normalized device coordinates

6. Window (or screen) coordinates

Let's consider what happens when an application program specifies a vertex. This vertex may be specified directly in the application program or indirectly through an instantiation of some object. In most applications, we tend to specify or use an object with a convenient size, orientation, and location in its own frame called the **model** or **object frame**. For example, a cube would typically have its faces aligned with axes of the frame, its center at the origin, and have a side length of 1 or 2 units. The coordinates in the corresponding function calls are in object or model coordinates.

An individual scene may comprise hundreds or even thousands of individual objects. The application program generally applies a sequence of transformations to each object to size, orient, and position it within a frame that is appropriate for the particular application. For example, if we were using an instance of a square for a window in an architectural application, we would scale it to have the correct proportions and units, which would probably be in feet or meters. The origin of application coordinates might be a location in the center of the bottom floor of the building. This application frame is called the **world frame**, and the values are in **world coordinates**. Note that if we do not model with predefined objects or apply any transformations before we specify our geometry, object and world coordinates are the same.

Object and world coordinates are the natural frames for the application program. However, the image that is produced depends on what the camera or viewer sees. Virtually all graphics systems use a frame whose origin is the center of the camera's lens[3] and whose axes are aligned with the sides of the camera. This frame

---

3. For a perspective view, the center of the lens is the center of projection (COP), whereas for an orthogonal view, the direction of projection is aligned with the sides of the camera.

is called the **camera frame** or **eye frame**. Because there is an affine transformation that corresponds to each change of frame, there are 4×4 matrices that represent the transformation from model coordinates to world coordinates and from world coordinates to eye coordinates. These transformations usually are concatenated together into the **model-view transformation**, which is specified by the model-view matrix. Usually, the use of the model-view matrix instead of the individual matrices should not pose any problems for the application programmer. In Chapter 5, where we discuss lighting and shading, we will see situations where we must separate the two transformations.

The last three representations are used primarily in the implementation of the pipeline, but, for completeness, we introduce them here. Once objects are in eye coordinates, OpenGL must check whether they lie within the view volume. If an object does not, it is clipped from the scene prior to rasterization. OpenGL can carry out this process most efficiently if it first carries out a projection transformation that brings all potentially visible objects into a cube centered at the origin in **clip coordinates**. We will study this transformation in Chapter 4. After this transformation, vertices are still represented in homogeneous coordinates. The division by the w component, called **perspective division**, yields three-dimensional representations in **normalized device coordinates**. The final transformation takes a position in normalized device coordinates and, taking into account the viewport, creates a three-dimensional representation in **window coordinates**. Window coordinates are measured in units of pixels on the display but retain depth information. If we remove the depth coordinate, we are working with two-dimensional **screen coordinates**.

The application programmer usually works with two frames: the eye frame and the object frame. By concatenating them together to form the model-view matrix, we have a transformation that positions the object frame relative to the eye frame. Thus, the model-view matrix converts the homogeneous-coordinate representations of points and vectors to their representations in the application space to their representations in the eye frame.

Although an application does not require us to use the model-view matrix, the model-view matrix is so important to most applications that we will almost always include it in our examples. One of the issues we will discuss in some detail is where we specify our transformations and where they are applied. For example, we could specify a transformation in the application and apply it to the data there. We could also define the parameters of a transformation in the application and send these parameters to the shaders and let the GPU carry out the transformations. We examine these approaches in the following sections.

Let's assume that we allocate a model-view matrix in our applications and initialize it to an identity matrix. Now the object frame and eye frame are identical. Thus, if we do not change the model-view matrix, we are working in eye coordinates. As we saw in Chapter 2, the camera is at the origin of its frame, as shown in Figure 3.26(a). The three basis vectors in eye space correspond to (1) the up direction of the camera, the y direction; (2) the direction the camera is pointing, the negative z direction; and (3) a third orthogonal direction, x, placed so that the x, y, z directions form a right-handed coordinate system. We obtain other frames in which to

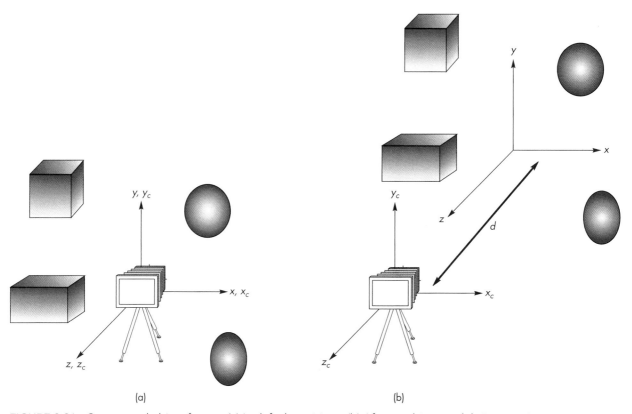

FIGURE 3.26   Camera and object frames. (a) In default positions. (b) After applying model-view matrix.

place objects by performing homogeneous coordinate transformations that specify new frames relative to the camera frame. In Section 3.5, we will learn how to specify these transformations; in Section 3.3, we used them to position the camera relative to our objects.

Because frame changes are represented by model-view matrices that can be stored, we can save frames and move between frames by changing the current model-view matrix. In Chapter 7, we will see that creating a data structure such as a stack to store transformations will be helpful in working with complex models.

When first working with multiple frames, there can be some confusion about which frames are fixed and which are varying. Because the model-view matrix positions the camera *relative* to the objects, it is usually a matter of convenience as to which frame we regard as fixed. Most of the time, we will regard the camera as fixed and the other frames as moving relative to the camera, but you may prefer to adopt a different view.

Before beginning a detailed discussion of transformations and how we use them in OpenGL, we present two simple examples. In the default settings shown in Figure 3.26(a), the camera and object frames coincide with the camera pointing in the negative z-direction. In many applications, it is natural to specify objects near the origin, such as a square centered at the origin or perhaps a group of objects whose center of mass is at the origin. It is also natural to set up our viewing conditions so that the camera sees only those objects that are in front of it. Consequently, to form images that contain all these objects, we must either move the camera away from the objects or move the objects away from the camera. Equivalently, we move the camera frame relative to the object frame. If we regard the camera frame as fixed and the model-view matrix as positioning the object frame relative to the camera frame, then the model-view matrix,

$$\mathbf{A} = \begin{bmatrix} 1 & 0 & 0 & 0 \\ 0 & 1 & 0 & 0 \\ 0 & 0 & 1 & -d \\ 0 & 0 & 0 & 1 \end{bmatrix},$$

moves a point (x, y, z) in the object frame to the point $(x, y, z - d)$ in the camera frame. Thus, by making d a suitably large positive number, we "move" the objects in front of the camera by moving the world frame relative to the camera frame, as shown in Figure 3.26(b). Note that, as far as the user—who is working in world coordinates—is concerned, she is positioning objects as before. The model-view matrix takes care of the relative positioning of the object and eye frames. This strategy is almost always better than attempting to alter the positions of the objects by changing their vertex positions to place them in front of the camera.

Let's look at another example. When we define our objects using vertices, we are working in the application frame (or world frame). The vertex positions specified there are the representation of points in that frame. Thus, we do not use the world frame directly but rather implicitly by representing points (and vectors) in it. Consider the situation illustrated in Figure 3.27.

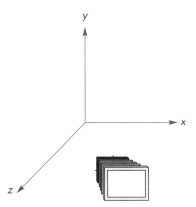

FIGURE 3.27   Camera at (1, 0, 1) pointing toward the origin.

Here we see the camera positioned in the object frame. Using homogeneous coordinates, it is centered at a point $p = (1, 0, 1, 1)^T$ in world coordinates and points at the origin in the world frame. Thus, the vector whose representation in the world frame is $\mathbf{n} = (-1, 0, -1, 0)^T$ is orthogonal to the back of the camera and points toward the origin. The camera is oriented so that its up direction is the same as the up direction in world coordinates and has the representation $\mathbf{v} = (0, 1, 0, 0)^T$. We can form an orthogonal coordinate system for the camera by using the cross product to determine a third orthogonal direction for the camera, which is $\mathbf{u} = (1, 0, -1, 0)^T$. We can now proceed as we did in Section 3.3.6 and derive the matrix $\mathbf{M}$ that converts the representation of points and vectors in the world frame to their representations in the camera frame. The transpose of this matrix in homogeneous coordinates is obtained by the inverse of a matrix containing the coordinates of the camera,

$$(\mathbf{M}^T)^{-1} = \begin{bmatrix} u^T \\ v^T \\ n^T \\ 0 \quad 0 \quad 0 \quad 1 \end{bmatrix} = \begin{bmatrix} 1 & 0 & -1 & 1 \\ 0 & 1 & 0 & 0 \\ -1 & 0 & -1 & 1 \\ 0 & 0 & 0 & 1 \end{bmatrix}^{-1} = \begin{bmatrix} \frac{1}{2} & 0 & -\frac{1}{2} & 0 \\ 0 & 1 & 0 & 0 \\ -\frac{1}{2} & 0 & -\frac{1}{2} & 1 \\ 0 & 0 & 0 & 1 \end{bmatrix}.$$

Note that the origin in the original frame is now one unit in the n direction from the origin in the camera frame or, equivalently, at the point whose representation is $(0, 0, 1, 1)$ in the camera frame.

In OpenGL, we can set a model-view matrix by sending an array of 16 elements to the vertex shader. For situations in which we have the representation of one frame in terms of another through the specification of the basis vectors and the origin, it is a direct exercise to find the required coefficients. However, such is not usually the case. For most geometric problems, we usually go from one frame to another by a sequence of geometric transformations such as rotations, translations, and scales. We will follow this approach in subsequent sections. But first, we will introduce some helpful C++ classes.

3.5 MATRIX AND VECTOR CLASSES

In Chapter 2, we saw how using some new data types could clarify our application code and were necessary for GLSL. Let's expand and formalize these notions by introducing the C++ classes that we will use in our applications. The code is in two files, `mat.h` and `vec.h`, that can both be included in your application through the include line

```
#include "mat.h"
```

The basic types are `mat2`, `mat3`, `mat4`, `vec2`, `vec3`, and `vec4`. The matrix classes are for 2×2, 3×3, and 4×4 matrices whereas the vector types are for 2-, 3-, and 4-element arrays. The arithmetic operators are overloaded, so we can write code such as

```
#include "mat.h"

vec4 x, y = vec4(1.0, 2.0, 3.0, 1.0);  // use of constructor
x = 2.0*y;
x[2] =  5.0;
mat4 a, b = mat4(vec4(y), vec4(x), vec4(y), vec4(x)); //matrix constructor
float s = 2.5;
a[2][1] = 3.5;
b = s*a;
vec4 z = b*x;
y =  x*b;
```

Thus, we can reference individual elements of either type and carry out the standard matrix operations, as described in Appendix B. Note that the products b*x and x*b will, in general, yield different results. The first is the product of a 1 × 4 row matrix times a 4 × 4 square matrix, whereas the second is the product of a 4 × 4 square matrix times a 4 × 1 column matrix. Both yield four elements and so can be stored as vec4s.

In light of our previous definition of points and vectors, the use of the names vec2, vec3, and vec4 may be a bit disconcerting. GLSL uses these types to store any quantity that has three or four elements, including vectors (directions) and points in homogeneous coordinates, colors (either RGB or RGBA), and, as we shall see later, texture coordinates. The advantage is that we can write code for all these types that uses the same operations. By using these same GLSL types in the classes in vec.h and mat.h, the code that manipulates points, vectors, and transformations in our applications will look similar to GLSL code. We will see that we will often have a choice as to where we carry out our algorithms, in the application or in one of the shaders. By having the same types available, we will be able to transfer an algorithm easily from an application to one of the shaders.

One trick that can make the application code a little clearer is to use a typedef to assign names to types that will make the code easier to understand. Some helpful examples we will use are

```
typedef vec3 color3;
typedef vec4 color4;
typedef vec3 point3;
typedef vec4 point4;
```

Of course we have not really created any new classes, but we prefer code such as

```
color3 red = color3(1.0, 0.0, 0.0);
```

to

```
vec3 red =  vec3(1.0, 0.0, 0.0);
```

FIGURE 3.28   One frame of cube animation.

3.6   MODELING A COLORED CUBE

We now have most of the basic conceptual and practical knowledge we need to build three-dimensional graphical applications. We will use them to produce a program that draws a rotating cube. One frame of an animation might be as shown in Figure 3.28. However, before we can rotate the cube, we will consider how we can model it efficiently. Although three-dimensional objects can be represented, like two-dimensional objects, through a set of vertices, we will see that data structures will help us to incorporate the relationships among the vertices, edges, and faces of geometric objects. Such data structures are supported in OpenGL through a facility called **vertex arrays,** which we introduce at the end of this section.

After we have modeled the cube, we can animate it by using affine transformations. We introduce these transformations in Section 3.7 and then use them to alter a model-view matrix. In Chapter 4, we use these transformations again as part of the viewing process. Our pipeline model will serve us well. Vertices will flow through a number of transformations in the pipeline, all of which will use our homogeneous-coordinate representation. At the end of the pipeline awaits the rasterizer. At this point, we can assume it will do its job automatically, provided we perform the preliminary steps correctly.

3.6.1 Modeling the Faces

The cube is as simple a three-dimensional object as we might expect to model and display. There are a number of ways, however, to model it. A CSG system would regard it as a single primitive. At the other extreme, the hardware processes the cube as an object defined by eight vertices. Our decision to use surface-based models implies that we regard a cube either as the intersection of six planes or as the six polygons, called **facets**, that define its faces. A carefully designed data structure should support both the high-level application view of the cube and the low-level view needed for the implementation.

We start by assuming that the vertices of the cube are available through an array of vertices. We will work with homogeneous coordinates, so

```
point4 vertices[8] = {
    point4(-1.0,-1.0,-1.0,1.0),point4(1.0,-1.0,-1.0,1.0),
    point4(1.0,1.0,-1.0,1.0), point4(-1.0,1.0,-1.0,1.0),
    point4(-1.0,-1.0,1.0,1.0), point4(1.0,-1.0,1.0,1.0)
    point4(1.0,1.0,1.0,1.0), point4(-1.0,1.0,1.0,1.0)};
```

We can then use the list of points to specify the faces of the cube. For example, one face is given by the sequence of vertices (0, 3, 2, 1). We can specify the other five faces similarly.

3.6.2 Inward- and Outward-Pointing Faces

We have to be careful about the order in which we specify our vertices when we are defining a three-dimensional polygon. We used the order 0, 3, 2, 1 for the first face. The order 1, 0, 3, 2 would be the same, because the final vertex in a polygon specification is always linked back to the first. However, the order 0, 1, 2, 3 is different. Although it describes the same boundary, the edges of the polygon are traversed in the reverse order—0, 3, 2, 1—as shown in Figure 3.29. The order is important because each polygon has two sides. Our graphics systems can display either or both of them. From the camera's perspective, we need a consistent way to distinguish between the two faces of a polygon. The order in which the vertices are specified provides this information.

We call a face **outward facing** if the vertices are traversed in a counterclockwise order when the face is viewed from the outside. This method is also known as the **right-hand rule** because if you orient the fingers of your right hand in the direction the vertices are traversed, the thumb points outward.

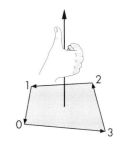

FIGURE 3.29 Traversal of the edges of a polygon.

In our example, the order 0, 3, 2, 1 specifies an outward face of the cube, whereas the order 0, 1, 2, 3 specifies the back face of the same polygon. Note that each face of an enclosed object, such as our cube, is an inside or outside face, regardless of from where we view it, as long as we view the face from outside the object. By specifying front and back carefully, we will be able to eliminate (or **cull**) faces that are not visible or to use different attributes to display front and back faces. We will consider culling further in Chapter 6.

3.6.3 Data Structures for Object Representation

We could now describe our cube through a set of vertex specifications. For example, we could use a two-dimensional array of positions

```
point3 faces[6][4];
```

or we could use a single array of 24 vertices

```
point3 cube_vertices[24];
```

where `cube_vertices[i]` contains the x, y, z coordinates of the ith vertex in the list. Both of these methods work, but they both fail to capture the essence of the cube's **topology**, as opposed to the cube's **geometry**. If we think of the cube as a polyhedron, we have an object—the cube—that is composed of six faces. The faces are each quadrilaterals that meet at vertices; each vertex is shared by three faces. In addition, pairs of vertices define edges of the quadrilaterals; each edge is shared by two faces. These statements describe the topology of a six-sided polyhedron. All are true, regardless of the location of the vertices—that is, regardless of the geometry of the object.[4]

Throughout the rest of this book, we will see that there are numerous advantages to building for our objects data structures that separate the topology from the

---

4. We are ignoring special cases (singularities) that arise, for example, when three or more vertices lie along the same line or when the vertices are moved so that we no longer have nonintersecting faces.

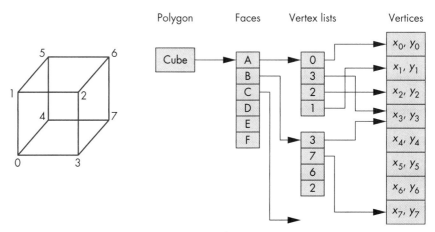

FIGURE 3.30   Vertex-list representation of a cube.

geometry. In this example, we use a structure, the vertex list, that is both simple and useful and can be expanded later.

The data specifying the location of the vertices contain the geometry and can be stored as a simple list or array, such as in vertices[8]—the **vertex list**. The top-level entity is a cube; we regard it as being composed of six faces. Each face consists of four ordered vertices. Each vertex can be specified indirectly through its index. This data structure is shown in Figure 3.30. One of the advantages of this structure is that each geometric location appears only once, instead of being repeated each time it is used for a facet. If, in an interactive application, the location of a vertex is changed, the application needs to change that location only once, rather than searching for multiple occurrences of the vertex.

3.6.4 The Color Cube

We can use the vertex list to define a color cube. We use a function quad that takes as input the indices of four vertices in outward pointing order and adds data to two arrays, as in Chapter 2, to store the vertex positions and the corresponding colors for each face in the arrays

```
vec4 quad_colors[36], vertices[36];

int i = 0; /* vertex and color index */
```

Note that because we can only display triangles, the quad function must generate two triangles for each face and thus six vertices. If we want each vertex to have its own color, then we need 24 vertices and 24 colors for our data. Using this quad function, we can specify our cube through the function

```
void colorcube()
{
   quad(0,3,2,1);
   quad(2,3,7,6);
   quad(3,0,4,7);
   quad(1,2,6,5);
   quad(4,5,6,7);
   quad(5,4,0,1);
}
```

We will assign the colors to the vertices using the colors of the corners of the color solid from Chapter 2 (black, white, red, green, blue, cyan, magenta, yellow). We assign a color for each vertex using the index of the vertex. Alternately, we could use the first index of the first vertex specified by quad to fix the color for the entire face. Here are the RGBA colors,

```
color4 colors[8] = {color4(0.0,0.0,0.0,1.0),
                     color4(1.0,0.0,0.0,1.0),
                     color4(1.0,1.0,0.0,1.0),
                     color4(0.0,1.0,0.0,1.0),
                     color4(0.0,0.0,1.0,1.0),
                     color4(1.0,0.0,1.0,1.0),
                     color4(0.0,1.0,1.0,1.0),
                     color4(1.0,1.0,1.0,1.0)};
```

and the vertices of a cube that corresponds to the clipping area in clip coordinates,

```
point4 vertices[8] = {point4(-1.0,-1.0,1.0,1.0), point4(-1.0,1.0,1.0,1.0),
                      point4(1.0,1.0,1.0,1.0), point4(1.0,-1.0,1.0,1.0),
                      point4(-1.0,-1.0,-1.0,1.0), point4(-1.0,1.0,-1.0,1.0),
                      point4(1.0,1.0,-1.0,1.0), point4(1.0,-1.0,-1.0,1.0)};
```

Here is the quad function that uses the first three vertices to specify one triangle and the first, third, and fourth to specify the second:

```
int i = 0;

void quad(int a, int b, int c, int d)
{
    quad_color[i] = colors[a];
    points[i] = vertices[a];
    i++;
    quad_color[i] = colors[b];
    points[i] = vertices[b];
    i++;
    quad_color[i] = colors[c];
    points[i] = vertices[c];
    i++;
```

```
        quad_color[i] = colors[a];
        points[i] = vertices[a];
        i++;
        quad_color[i] = colors[c];
        points[i] = vertices[c];
        i++;
        quad_color[i] = colors[d];
        points[i] = vertices[d];
        i++;
}
```

Note the initialization of `i` outside the `quad` function. If, as in later examples, we invoke `quad` multiple times, either because we change the colors or locations of the same vertices or we have multiple cubes, we must be careful as to where we start placing data in the `points` array. Our program is almost complete, but first we examine how the colors and other vertex attributes can be assigned to fragments by the rasterizer.

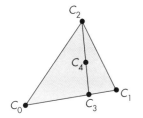

FIGURE 3.31 Interpolation using barycentric coordinates.

3.6.5 Interpolation

Although we have specified colors for the vertices of the cube, the graphics system must decide how to use this information to assign colors to points inside the polygon. There are many ways to use the colors of the vertices to fill in, or **interpolate**, colors across a polygon. Probably the most common method used in computer graphics is based on the barycentric coordinate representation of triangles that we introduced in Section 3.1. One of the major reasons for this approach is that triangles are the key object that we work with in rendering.

Consider the polygon shown in Figure 3.31. The colors C_0, C_1, and C_2 are the ones assigned to the vertices in the application program. Assume that we are using RGB color and that the interpolation is applied individually to each primary color. We first use linear interpolation to interpolate colors, along the edges between vertices 0 and 1, creating RGB colors along the edges through the parametric equations as follows:

$$C_{01}(\alpha) = (1 - \alpha)C_0 + \alpha C_1.$$

As α goes from 0 to 1, we generate colors, $C_{01}(\alpha)$ along this edge. For a given value of α, we obtain the color C_3. We can now interpolate colors along the line connecting C_3 with the color C_2 at the third vertex as follows:

$$C_{32}(\beta) = (1 - \beta)C_3 + \beta C_2,$$

which for a given value of β gives the color C_4 at an interior point. As the barycentric coordinates α and β range from 0 to 1, we get interpolated colors for all the interior points and thus a color for each fragment generated by the rasterizer. The same interpolation method can be used on any vertex attribute.[5]

We now have an object that we can display much as we did with the three-dimensional Sierpinski gasket in Section 2.9, using a basic orthographic projection. In Section 3.7, we introduce transformations, enabling us to animate the cube and also to construct more complex objects. First, however, we introduce an OpenGL feature that not only reduces the overhead of generating our cube but also gives us a higher-level method of working with the cube and with other polyhedral objects.

3.6.6 Displaying the Cube

The complete program is given in Appendix A. The parts of the application program to display the cube and the shaders are almost identical to the the code we used to display the three-dimensional gasket in Chapter 2. The differences are entirely in how we place data in the arrays for the vertex positions and vertex colors. The OpenGL parts, including the shaders, are the same.

However, the display of the cube is not very informative. Because the sides of the cube are aligned with the clipping volume, we see only the front face. The display also occupies the entire window. We could get a more interesting display by changing the data so that it corresponds to a rotated cube. We could scale the data to get a smaller cube. For example, we could scale the cube by half by changing the vertex data to

```
point4 vertices[8] = {point4(-0.5,-0.5,0.5,1.0),
                      point4(-0.5,0.5,0.5,1.0),
                      point4(0.5,0.5,0.5,1.0),
                      point4(0.5,-0.5,0.5,1.0),
                      point4(-0.5,-0.5,-0.5,1.0),
                      point4(-0.5,0.5,-0.5,1.0),
                      point4(0.5,0.5,-0.5,1.0),
                      point4(0.5,-0.5,-0.5,1.0)};
```

but that would not be a very flexible solution. We could put the scale factor in the quad function. A better solution might be to change the vertex shader to

```
in vec4 vPosition;
in vec4 vColor;
out vec4 color;

void main()
{
  gl_Position = 0.5*vPosition;
  color = vColor;
}
```

---

5. Modern graphics cards support interpolation methods that are correct under perspective viewing.

Note that we also changed the vertex shader to use input data in four-dimensional homogeneous coordinates. We also can simplify the fragment shader to

```
in vec4 color;
out vec4 fragColor;

void main()
{
   fragColor = color;
}
```

Rather than looking at these ad hoc approaches, we will develop a transformation capability that will enable us to rotate, scale, and translate data either in the application or in the shaders. We will also examine in greater detail how we convey data among the application and shaders that enable us to carry out transformations in the GPU and alter transformations dynamically.

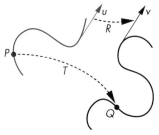

FIGURE 3.32   Transformation.

3.7   AFFINE TRANSFORMATIONS

A **transformation** is a function that takes a point (or vector) and maps it into another point (or vector). We can picture such a function by looking at Figure 3.32 or by writing down the functional form

$$Q = T(P)$$

for points, or

$$v = R(u)$$

for vectors. If we use homogeneous coordinate representations, then we can represent both vectors and points as four-dimensional column matrices and we can define the transformation with a single function,

$$\mathbf{q} = f(\mathbf{p}),$$

$$\mathbf{v} = f(\mathbf{u}),$$

that transforms the representations of both points and vectors in a given frame.

This formulation is too general to be useful, as it encompasses all single-valued mappings of points and vectors. In practice, even if we were to have a convenient description of the function f, we would have to carry out the transformation on every point on a curve. For example, if we transform a line segment, a general transformation might require us to carry out the transformation for every point between the two endpoints.

Consider instead a restricted class of transformations. Let's assume that we are working in four-dimensional, homogeneous coordinates. In this space, both points and vectors are represented as 4-tuples.[6] We can obtain a useful class of transformations if we place restrictions on f. The most important restriction is linearity. A function f is a **linear function** if and only if, for any scalars α and β and any two vertices (or vectors) p and q,

$$f(\alpha p + \beta q) = \alpha f(p) + \beta f(q).$$

The importance of such functions is that if we know the transformations of p and q, we can obtain the transformations of linear combinations of p and q by taking linear combinations of their transformations. Hence, we avoid having to calculate transformations for every linear combination.

Using homogeneous coordinates, we work with the representations of points and vectors. A linear transformation then transforms the representation of a given point (or vector) into another representation of that point (or vector) and can always be written in terms of the two representations, **u** and **v**, as a matrix multiplication:

$$\mathbf{v} = \mathbf{C}\mathbf{u},$$

where **C** is a square matrix. Comparing this expression with the expression we obtained in Section 3.3 for changes in frames, we can observe that as long as **C** is nonsingular, each linear transformation corresponds to a change in frame. Hence, we can view a linear transformation in two equivalent ways: (1) as a change in the underlying representation, or frame, that yields a new representation of our vertices, or (2) as a transformation of the vertices within the same frame.

When we work with homogeneous coordinates, **C** is a 4×4 matrix that leaves unchanged the fourth (w) component of a representation. The matrix **C** is of the form

$$\mathbf{C} = \begin{bmatrix} \alpha_{11} & \alpha_{12} & \alpha_{13} & \alpha_{14} \\ \alpha_{21} & \alpha_{22} & \alpha_{23} & \alpha_{24} \\ \alpha_{31} & \alpha_{32} & \alpha_{33} & \alpha_{34} \\ 0 & 0 & 0 & 1 \end{bmatrix}$$

and is the transpose of the matrix **M** that we derived in Section 3.3.4. The 12 values can be set arbitrarily, and we say that this transformation has 12 **degrees of freedom**. However, points and vectors have slightly different representations in our affine space. Any vector is represented as

$$\mathbf{u} = \begin{bmatrix} \alpha_1 \\ \alpha_2 \\ \alpha_3 \\ 0 \end{bmatrix}.$$

---

6. We consider only those functions that map vertices to other vertices and that obey the rules for manipulating points and vectors that we have developed in this chapter and in Appendix B.

Any point can be written as

$$\mathbf{p} = \begin{bmatrix} \beta_1 \\ \beta_2 \\ \beta_3 \\ 1 \end{bmatrix}.$$

If we apply an arbitrary $\mathbf{C}$ to a vector,

$$\mathbf{v} = \mathbf{Cu},$$

we see that only nine of the elements of $\mathbf{C}$ affect $\mathbf{u}$, and thus there are only nine degrees of freedom in the transformation of vectors. Affine transformations of points have the full 12 degrees of freedom.

We can also show that affine transformations preserve lines. Suppose that we write a line in the form

$$P(\alpha) = P_0 + \alpha d,$$

where P_0 is a point and d is a vector. In any frame, the line can be expressed as

$$\mathbf{p}(\alpha) = \mathbf{p}_0 + \alpha \mathbf{d},$$

where $\mathbf{p}_0$ and $\mathbf{d}$ are the representations of P_0 and d in that frame. For any affine transformation matrix $\mathbf{A}$,

$$\mathbf{Cp}(\alpha) = \mathbf{Cp}_0 + \alpha \mathbf{Cd}.$$

Thus, we can construct the transformed line by first transforming $\mathbf{p}_0$ and $\mathbf{d}$ and using whatever line-generation algorithm we choose when the line segment must be displayed. If we use the two-point form of the line,

$$\mathbf{p}(\alpha) = \alpha \mathbf{p}_0 + (1 - \alpha)\mathbf{p}_1,$$

a similar result holds. We transform the representations of $\mathbf{p}_0$ and $\mathbf{p}_1$ and then construct the transformed line. Because there are only 12 elements in $\mathbf{C}$ that we can select arbitrarily, there are 12 degrees of freedom in the affine transformation of a line or line segment.

We have expressed these results in terms of abstract mathematical spaces. However, their importance in computer graphics is practical. We need only to transform the homogeneous-coordinate representation of the endpoints of a line segment to determine completely a transformed line. Thus, we can implement our graphics systems as a pipeline that passes endpoints through affine-transformation units and generates the interior points at the rasterization stage.

Fortunately, most of the transformations that we need in computer graphics are affine. These transformations include rotation, translation, and scaling. With slight modifications, we can also use these results to describe the standard parallel and perspective projections discussed in Chapter 4.

3.8 TRANSLATION, ROTATION, AND SCALING

We have been going back and forth between looking at geometric objects as abstract entities and working with their representation in a given frame. When we work with application programs, we have to work with representations. In this section, first we show how we can describe the most important affine transformations independently of any representation. Then, we find matrices that describe these transformations by acting on the representations of our points and vectors. In Section 3.8, we will see how these transformations can be implemented in OpenGL.

We look at transformations as ways of moving the points that describe one or more geometric objects to new locations. Although there are many transformations that will move a particular point to a new location, there will almost always be only a single way to transform a collection of points to new locations while preserving the spatial relationships among them. Hence, although we can find many matrices that will move one corner of our color cube from P_0 to Q_0, only one of them, when applied to all the vertices of the cube, will result in a displaced cube of the same size and orientation.

3.8.1 Translation

Translation is an operation that displaces points by a fixed distance in a given direction, as shown in Figure 3.33. To specify a translation, we need only to specify a displacement vector d, because the transformed points are given by

$$P' = P + d$$

for all points P on the object. Note that this definition of translation makes no reference to a frame or representation. Translation has three degrees of freedom because we can specify the three components of the displacement vector arbitrarily.

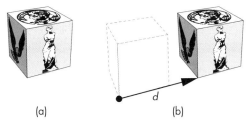

(a)　　　　　　　(b)

FIGURE 3.33 Translation. (a) Object in original position. (b) Object translated.

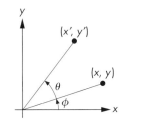

FIGURE 3.34   Two-dimensional rotation.

3.8.2 Rotation

Rotation is more difficult to specify than translation because we must specify more parameters. We start with the simple example of rotating a point about the origin in a two-dimensional plane, as shown in Figure 3.34. Having specified a particular point—the origin—we are in a particular frame. A two-dimensional point at (x, y) in this frame is rotated about the origin by an angle θ to the position (x', y'). We can obtain the standard equations describing this rotation by representing (x, y) and (x', y') in polar form:

$$x = \rho \cos \phi,$$

$$y = \rho \sin \phi,$$

$$x' = \rho \cos(\theta + \phi),$$

$$y' = \rho \sin(\theta + \phi).$$

Expanding these terms using the trigonometric identities for the sine and cosine of the sum of two angles, we find

$$x' = \rho \cos \phi \cos \theta - \rho \sin \phi \sin \theta = x \cos \theta - y \sin \theta,$$

$$y' = \rho \cos \phi \sin \theta + \rho \sin \phi \cos \theta = x \sin \theta + y \cos \theta.$$

These equations can be written in matrix form as

$$\begin{bmatrix} x' \\ y' \end{bmatrix} = \begin{bmatrix} \cos \theta & -\sin \theta \\ \sin \theta & \cos \theta \end{bmatrix} \begin{bmatrix} x \\ y \end{bmatrix}.$$

We expand this form to three dimensions in Section 3.9.

Note three features of this transformation that extend to other rotations:

1. There is one point—the origin, in this case—that is unchanged by the rotation. We call this point the **fixed point** of the transformation. Figure 3.35 shows a two-dimensional rotation about a fixed point in the center of the object rather than about the origin of the frame.

2. Knowing that the two-dimensional plane is part of three-dimensional space, we can reinterpret this rotation in three dimensions. In a right-handed system, when we draw the x- and y-axes in the standard way, the positive z-axis comes out of the page. Our definition of a positive direction of rotation is counterclockwise when we look down the positive z-axis toward the origin. We use this definition to define positive rotations about other axes.

3. Rotation in the two-dimensional plane $z = 0$ is equivalent to a three-dimensional rotation about the z-axis. Points in planes of constant z all rotate in a similar manner, leaving their z values unchanged.

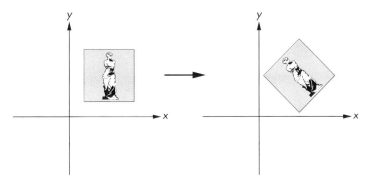

FIGURE 3.35   Rotation about a fixed point.

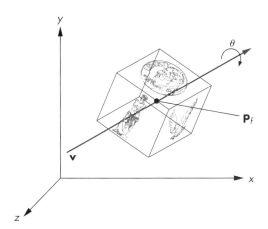

FIGURE 3.36   Three-dimensional rotation.

We can use these observations to define a general three-dimensional rotation that is independent of the frame. We must specify the three entities shown in Figure 3.36: a fixed point (P_f), a rotation angle (θ), and a line or vector about which to rotate. For a given fixed point, there are three degrees of freedom: the two angles necessary to specify the orientation of the vector and the angle that specifies the amount of rotation about the vector.

Rotation and translation are known as **rigid-body transformations**. No combination of rotations and translations can alter the shape or volume of an object; they can alter only the object's location and orientation. Consequently, rotation and translation alone cannot give us all possible affine transformations. The transformations shown in Figure 3.37 are affine, but they are not rigid-body transformations.

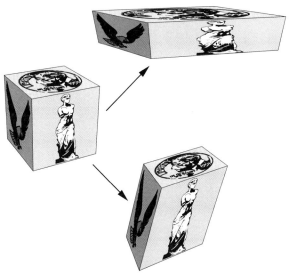

FIGURE 3.37   Non–rigid-body transformations.

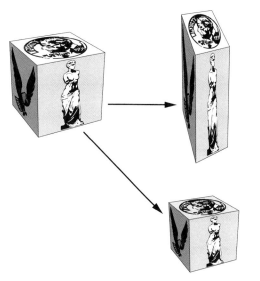

FIGURE 3.38   Uniform and nonuniform scaling.

3.8.3 Scaling

Scaling is an affine non–rigid-body transformation by which we can make an object bigger or smaller. Figure 3.38 illustrates both uniform scaling in all directions and scaling in a single direction. We need nonuniform scaling to build up the full set of

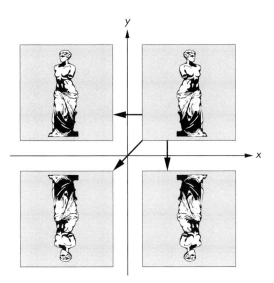

FIGURE 3.40 Reflection.

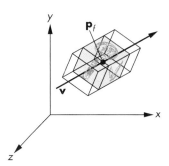

FIGURE 3.39 Effect of scale factor.

affine transformations that we use in modeling and viewing by combining a properly chosen sequence of scalings, translations, and rotations.

Scaling transformations have a fixed point, as we can see from Figure 3.39. Hence, to specify a scaling, we can specify the fixed point, a direction in which we wish to scale, and a scale factor (α). For $\alpha > 1$, the object gets longer in the specified direction; for $0 \leq \alpha < 1$, the object gets smaller in that direction. Negative values of α give us **reflection** (Figure 3.40) about the fixed point, in the scaling direction. Scaling has six degrees of freedom because we can specify an arbitrary fixed point and three independent scaling factors.

3.9 TRANSFORMATIONS IN HOMOGENEOUS COORDINATES

All graphics APIs force us to work within some reference system. Hence, we cannot work with high-level expressions such as

$$Q = P + \alpha v.$$

Instead, we work with representations in homogeneous coordinates and with expressions such as

$$\mathbf{q} = \mathbf{p} + \alpha \mathbf{v}.$$

Within a frame, each affine transformation is represented by a 4 × 4 matrix of the form

$$\mathbf{A} = \begin{bmatrix} \alpha_{11} & \alpha_{12} & \alpha_{13} & \alpha_{14} \\ \alpha_{21} & \alpha_{22} & \alpha_{23} & \alpha_{24} \\ \alpha_{31} & \alpha_{32} & \alpha_{33} & \alpha_{34} \\ 0 & 0 & 0 & 1 \end{bmatrix}.$$

3.9.1 Translation

Translation displaces points to new positions defined by a displacement vector. If we move the point $\mathbf{p}$ to $\mathbf{p}'$ by displacing by a distance $\mathbf{d}$, then

$$\mathbf{p}' = \mathbf{p} + \mathbf{d}.$$

Looking at their homogeneous-coordinate forms

$$\mathbf{p} = \begin{bmatrix} x \\ y \\ z \\ 1 \end{bmatrix}, \qquad \mathbf{p}' = \begin{bmatrix} x' \\ y' \\ z' \\ 1 \end{bmatrix}, \qquad \mathbf{d} = \begin{bmatrix} \alpha_x \\ \alpha_y \\ \alpha_z \\ 0 \end{bmatrix},$$

we see that these equations can be written component by component as

$$x' = x + \alpha_x,$$

$$y' = y + \alpha_y,$$

$$z' = z + \alpha_z.$$

This method of representing translation using the addition of column matrices does not combine well with our representations of other affine transformations. However, we can also get this result using the matrix multiplication:

$$\mathbf{p}' = \mathbf{T}\mathbf{p},$$

where

$$\mathbf{T} = \begin{bmatrix} 1 & 0 & 0 & \alpha_x \\ 0 & 1 & 0 & \alpha_y \\ 0 & 0 & 1 & \alpha_z \\ 0 & 0 & 0 & 1 \end{bmatrix}.$$

$\mathbf{T}$ is called the **translation matrix**. We sometimes write it as $\mathbf{T}(\alpha_x, \alpha_y, \alpha_z)$ to emphasize the three independent parameters.

It might appear that using a fourth fixed element in the homogeneous representation of a point is not necessary. However, if we use the three-dimensional forms

$$\mathbf{q} = \begin{bmatrix} x \\ y \\ z \end{bmatrix}, \qquad \mathbf{q}' = \begin{bmatrix} x' \\ y' \\ z' \end{bmatrix},$$

it is not possible to find a 3×3 matrix $\mathbf{D}$ such that $\mathbf{q}' = \mathbf{Dq}$ for the given displacement vector $\mathbf{d}$. For this reason, the use of homogeneous coordinates is often seen as a clever trick that allows us to convert the addition of column matrices in three dimensions to matrix–matrix multiplication in four dimensions.

We can obtain the inverse of a translation matrix either by applying an inversion algorithm or by noting that if we displace a point by the vector d, we can return to the original position by a displacement of $-d$. By either method, we find that

$$\mathbf{T}^{-1}(\alpha_x, \alpha_y, \alpha_z) = \mathbf{T}(-\alpha_x, -\alpha_y, -\alpha_z) = \begin{bmatrix} 1 & 0 & 0 & -\alpha_x \\ 0 & 1 & 0 & -\alpha_y \\ 0 & 0 & 1 & -\alpha_z \\ 0 & 0 & 0 & 1 \end{bmatrix}.$$

3.9.2 Scaling

For both scaling and rotation, there is a fixed point that is unchanged by the transformation. We let the fixed point be the origin, and we show how we can concatenate transformations to obtain the transformation for an arbitrary fixed point.

A scaling matrix with a fixed point of the origin allows for independent scaling along the coordinate axes. The three equations are

$$x' = \beta_x x,$$

$$y' = \beta_y y,$$

$$z' = \beta_z z.$$

These three equations can be combined in homogeneous form as

$$\mathbf{p}' = \mathbf{Sp},$$

where

$$\mathbf{S} = \mathbf{S}(\beta_x, \beta_y, \beta_z) = \begin{bmatrix} \beta_x & 0 & 0 & 0 \\ 0 & \beta_y & 0 & 0 \\ 0 & 0 & \beta_z & 0 \\ 0 & 0 & 0 & 1 \end{bmatrix}.$$

As is true of the translation matrix and, indeed, of all homogeneous coordinate transformations, the final row of the matrix does not depend on the particular transformation, but rather forces the fourth component of the transformed point to retain the value 1.

We obtain the inverse of a scaling matrix by applying the reciprocals of the scale factors:

$$\mathbf{S}^{-1}(\beta_x, \beta_y, \beta_z) = \mathbf{S}\left(\frac{1}{\beta_x}, \frac{1}{\beta_y}, \frac{1}{\beta_z}\right).$$

3.9.3 Rotation

We first look at rotation with a fixed point at the origin. There are three degrees of freedom corresponding to our ability to rotate independently about the three coordinate axes. We have to be careful, however, because matrix multiplication is not a commutative operation (Appendix C). Rotation about the x-axis by an angle θ followed by rotation about the y-axis by an angle ϕ does not give us the same result as the one that we obtain if we reverse the order of the rotations.

We can find the matrices for rotation about the individual axes directly from the results of the two-dimensional rotation that we developed in Section 3.7.2. We saw that the two-dimensional rotation was actually a rotation in three dimensions about the z-axis and that the points remained in planes of constant z. Thus, in three dimensions, the equations for rotation about the z-axis by an angle θ are

$$x' = x \cos \theta - y \sin \theta,$$

$$y' = x \sin \theta + y \cos \theta,$$

$$z' = z,$$

or, in matrix form,

$$\mathbf{p}' = \mathbf{R}_z \mathbf{p},$$

where

$$\mathbf{R}_z = \mathbf{R}_z(\theta) = \begin{bmatrix} \cos \theta & -\sin \theta & 0 & 0 \\ \sin \theta & \cos \theta & 0 & 0 \\ 0 & 0 & 1 & 0 \\ 0 & 0 & 0 & 1 \end{bmatrix}.$$

We can derive the matrices for rotation about the x- and y-axes through an identical argument. If we rotate about the x-axis, then the x values are unchanged, and we have a two-dimensional rotation in which points rotate in planes of constant x; for rotation about the y-axis, the y values are unchanged. The matrices are

$$\mathbf{R}_x = \mathbf{R}_x(\theta) = \begin{bmatrix} 1 & 0 & 0 & 0 \\ 0 & \cos \theta & -\sin \theta & 0 \\ 0 & \sin \theta & \cos \theta & 0 \\ 0 & 0 & 0 & 1 \end{bmatrix},$$

$$\mathbf{R}_y = \mathbf{R}_y(\theta) = \begin{bmatrix} \cos\theta & 0 & \sin\theta & 0 \\ 0 & 1 & 0 & 0 \\ -\sin\theta & 0 & \cos\theta & 0 \\ 0 & 0 & 0 & 1 \end{bmatrix}.$$

The signs of the sine terms are consistent with our definition of a positive rotation in a right-handed system.

Suppose that we let $\mathbf{R}$ denote any of our three rotation matrices. A rotation by θ can always be undone by a subsequent rotation by $-\theta$; hence,

$$\mathbf{R}^{-1}(\theta) = \mathbf{R}(-\theta).$$

In addition, noting that all the cosine terms are on the diagonal and the sine terms are off-diagonal, we can use the trigonometric identities

$$\cos(-\theta) = \cos\theta$$
$$\sin(-\theta) = -\sin\theta$$

to find

$$\mathbf{R}^{-1}(\theta) = \mathbf{R}^T(\theta).$$

In Section 3.10.1, we show how to construct any desired rotation matrix, with a fixed point at the origin, as a product of individual rotations about the three axes

$$\mathbf{R} = \mathbf{R}_z\mathbf{R}_y\mathbf{R}_x.$$

Using the fact that the transpose of a product is the product of the transposes in the reverse order, we see that for any rotation matrix,

$$\mathbf{R}^{-1} = \mathbf{R}^T.$$

A matrix whose inverse is equal to its transpose is called an **orthogonal matrix**. Normalized orthogonal matrices correspond to rotations about the origin.

3.9.4 Shear

Although we can construct any affine transformation from a sequence of rotations, translations, and scalings, there is one more affine transformation—the **shear** transformation—that is of such importance that we regard it as a basic type rather than deriving it from the others. Consider a cube centered at the origin, aligned with the axes, and viewed from the positive z-axis, as shown in Figure 3.41. If we pull the top to the right and the bottom to the left, we shear the object in the x-direction. Note that neither the y nor the z values are changed by the shear, so we can call this operation x shear to distinguish it from shears of the cube in other possible directions.

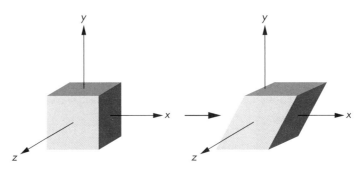

FIGURE 3.41   Shear.

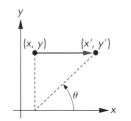

FIGURE 3.42   Computation of the shear matrix.

Using simple trigonometry on Figure 3.42, we see that each shear is characterized by a single angle θ; the equations for this shear are

$$x' = x + y \cot \theta,$$

$$y' = y,$$

$$z' = z,$$

leading to the shearing matrix

$$\mathbf{H}_x(\theta) = \begin{bmatrix} 1 & \cot \theta & 0 & 0 \\ 0 & 1 & 0 & 0 \\ 0 & 0 & 1 & 0 \\ 0 & 0 & 0 & 1 \end{bmatrix}.$$

We can obtain the inverse by noting that we need to shear in only the opposite direction; hence,

$$\mathbf{H}_x^{-1}(\theta) = \mathbf{H}_x(-\theta).$$

Shearing in the x-direction followed by a shear in z-direction, leaves the y values unchanged and can be regarded as a shear in the $x - z$ plane.

3.10   CONCATENATION OF TRANSFORMATIONS

In this section, we create examples of affine transformations by multiplying together, or **concatenating**, sequences of the basic transformations that we just introduced. Using this strategy is preferable to attempting to define an arbitrary transformation directly. The approach fits well with our pipeline architectures for implementing graphics systems.

Suppose that we carry out three successive transformations on a point $\mathbf{p}$, creating a new point $\mathbf{q}$. Because the matrix product is associative, we can write the sequence as

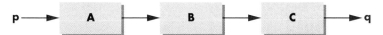

FIGURE 3.43   Application of transformations one at a time.

$$\mathbf{q} = \mathbf{CBAp},$$

without parentheses. Note that here the matrices **A**, **B**, and **C** (and thus **M**) can be arbitrary 4×4 matrices, although in practice they will most likely be affine. The order in which we carry out the transformations affects the efficiency of the calculation. In one view, shown in Figure 3.43, we can carry out **A**, followed by **B**, followed by **C**—an order that corresponds to the grouping

$$\mathbf{q} = (\mathbf{C}(\mathbf{B}(\mathbf{Ap}))).$$

If we are to transform a single point, this order is the most efficient because each matrix multiplication involves multiplying a column matrix by a square matrix. If we have many points to transform, then we can proceed in two steps. First, we calculate

$$\mathbf{M} = \mathbf{CBA}.$$

Then, we use this matrix on each point

$$\mathbf{q} = \mathbf{Mp}.$$

This order corresponds to the pipeline shown in Figure 3.44, where we compute **M** first, then load it into a pipeline transformation unit. If we simply count operations, we see that although we do a little more work in computing **M** initially, because **M** may be applied to tens of thousands of points, this extra work is insignificant compared with the savings we obtain by using a single matrix multiplication for each point. We now derive examples of computing **M**.

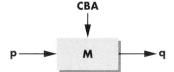

FIGURE 3.44   Pipeline transformation.

3.10.1 Rotation About a Fixed Point

Our first example shows how we can alter the transformations that we defined with a fixed point at the origin (rotation, scaling, shear) to have an arbitrary fixed point. We demonstrate for rotation about the z-axis; the technique is the same for the other cases.

Consider a cube with its center at $\mathbf{p}_f$ and its sides aligned with the axes. We want to rotate the cube about the z-axis, but this time about its center $\mathbf{p}_f$, which becomes the fixed point of the transformation, as shown in Figure 3.45. If $\mathbf{p}_f$ were the origin, we would know how to solve the problem: We would simply use $\mathbf{R}_z(\theta)$. This observation suggests the strategy of first moving the cube to the origin. We can then apply $\mathbf{R}_z(\theta)$ and finally move the object back such that its center is again at $\mathbf{p}_f$. This sequence is shown in Figure 3.46. In terms of our basic affine transformations,

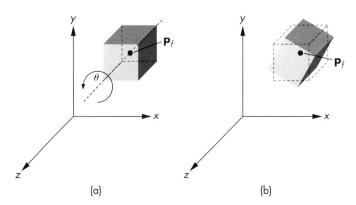

FIGURE 3.45   Rotation of a cube about its center.

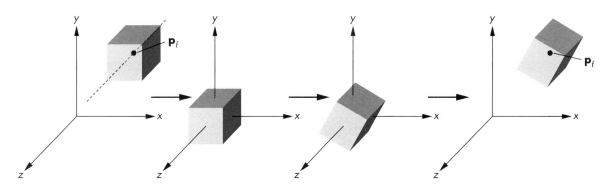

FIGURE 3.46   Sequence of transformations.

the first is $\mathbf{T}(-\mathbf{p}_f)$, the second is $\mathbf{R}_z(\theta)$, and the final is $\mathbf{T}(\mathbf{p}_f)$. Concatenating them together, we obtain the single matrix

$$\mathbf{M} = \mathbf{T}(\mathbf{p}_f)\mathbf{R}_z(\theta)\mathbf{T}(-\mathbf{p}_f).$$

If we multiply out the matrices, we find that

$$\mathbf{M} = \begin{bmatrix} \cos\theta & -\sin\theta & 0 & x_f - x_f\cos\theta + y_f\sin\theta \\ \sin\theta & \cos\theta & 0 & y_f - x_f\sin\theta - y_f\cos\theta \\ 0 & 0 & 1 & 0 \\ 0 & 0 & 0 & 1 \end{bmatrix}.$$

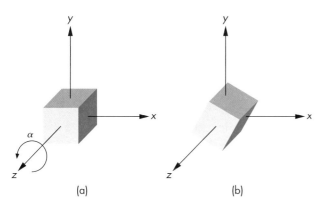

FIGURE 3.47   Rotation of a cube about the z-axis. (a) Cube before rotation. (b) Cube after rotation.

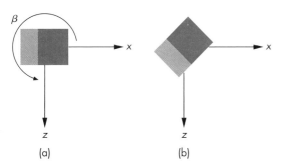

FIGURE 3.48   Rotation of a cube about the y-axis.

3.10.2 General Rotation

We now show that an arbitrary rotation about the origin can be composed of three successive rotations about the three axes. The order is not unique (see Exercise 3.10), although the resulting rotation matrix is. We form the desired matrix by first doing a rotation about the z-axis, then doing a rotation about the y-axis, and concluding with a rotation about the x-axis.

Consider the cube, again centered at the origin with its sides aligned with the axes, as shown in Figure 3.47(a). We can rotate it about the z-axis by an angle α to orient it, as shown in Figure 3.47(b). We then rotate the cube by an angle β about the y-axis, as shown in a top view in Figure 3.48. Finally, we rotate the cube by an angle γ about the x-axis, as shown in a side view in Figure 3.49. Our final rotation matrix is

$$\mathbf{R} = \mathbf{R}_x \mathbf{R}_y \mathbf{R}_z.$$

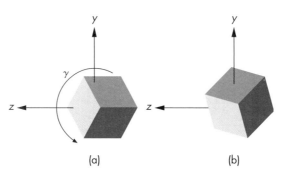

FIGURE 3.49   Rotation of a cube about the *x*-axis.

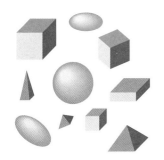

FIGURE 3.50   Scene of simple objects.

A little experimentation should convince you that we can achieve any desired orientation by proper choice of α, β, and γ, although, as we will see in the example of Section 3.10.4, finding these angles can be tricky.

3.10.3 The Instance Transformation

Our example of a cube that can be rotated to any desired orientation suggests a generalization appropriate for modeling. Consider a scene composed of many simple objects, such as those shown in Figure 3.50. One option is to specify each of these objects, through its vertices, in the desired location with the desired orientation and size. An alternative is to specify each of the object types once at a convenient size, in a convenient place, and with a convenient orientation. Each occurrence of an object in the scene is an **instance** of that object's prototype, and we can obtain the desired size, orientation, and location by applying an affine transformation—the **instance transformation**—to the prototype. We can build a simple database to describe a scene from a list of object identifiers (such as 1 for a cube and 2 for a sphere) and of the instance transformation to be applied to each object.

The instance transformation is applied in the order shown in Figure 3.51. Objects are usually defined in their own frames, with the origin at the center of mass and the sides aligned with the model frame axes. First, we scale the object to the desired size. Then we orient it with a rotation matrix. Finally, we translate it to the desired orientation. Hence, the instance transformation is of the form

$$\mathbf{M} = \mathbf{TRS}.$$

Modeling with the instance transformation works well not only with our pipeline architectures but also with other methods for retaining objects such as scene graphs that we will introduce in Chapter 8. A complex object that is used many times can be loaded into the server once as a display list. Displaying each instance of it requires only sending the appropriate instance transformation to the server before executing the display list.

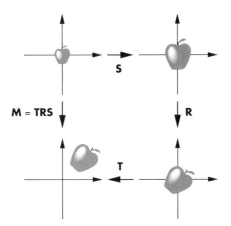

FIGURE 3.51   Instance transformation.

3.10.4 Rotation About an Arbitrary Axis

Our final rotation example illustrates not only how we can achieve a rotation about an arbitrary point and line in space but also how we can use direction angles to specify orientations. Consider rotating a cube, as shown in Figure 3.52. We need three entities to specify this rotation. There is a fixed point $\mathbf{p}_0$ that we assume is the center of the cube, a vector about which we rotate, and an angle of rotation. Note that none of these entities relies on a frame and that we have just specified a rotation in a coordinate-free manner. Nonetheless, to find an affine matrix to represent this transformation, we have to assume that we are in some frame.

The vector about which we wish to rotate the cube can be specified in various ways. One way is to use two points, $\mathbf{p}_1$ and $\mathbf{p}_2$, defining the vector

$$\mathbf{u} = \mathbf{p}_2 - \mathbf{p}_1.$$

Note that the order of the points determines the positive direction of rotation for θ and that even though we draw $\mathbf{u}$ as passing through $\mathbf{p}_0$, only the orientation of $\mathbf{u}$ matters. Replacing $\mathbf{u}$ with a unit-length vector

$$\mathbf{v} = \frac{\mathbf{u}}{|\mathbf{u}|} = \begin{bmatrix} \alpha_x \\ \alpha_y \\ \alpha_z \end{bmatrix}$$

in the same direction simplifies the subsequent steps. We say that $\mathbf{v}$ is the result of **normalizing u**. We have already seen that moving the fixed point to the origin is a helpful technique. Thus, our first transformation is the translation $\mathbf{T}(-\mathbf{p}_0)$, and the final one is $\mathbf{T}(\mathbf{p}_0)$. After the initial translation, the required rotation problem is as shown in Figure 3.53. Our previous example (see Section 3.10.2) showed that we could get an arbitrary rotation from three rotations about the individual axes. This problem is more difficult because we do not know what angles to use for the

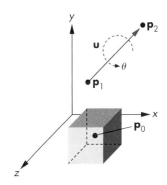

FIGURE 3.52   Rotation of a cube about an arbitrary axis.

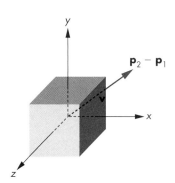

FIGURE 3.53   Movement of the fixed point to the origin.

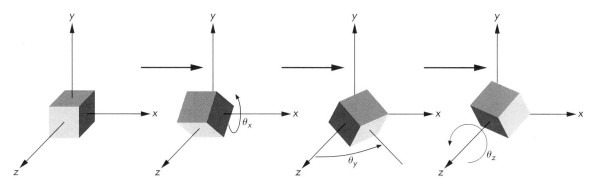

FIGURE 3.54   Sequence of rotations.

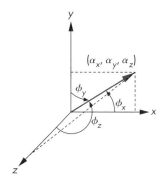

FIGURE 3.55   Direction angles.

individual rotations. Our strategy is to carry out two rotations to align the axis of rotation, **v**, with the z-axis. Then we can rotate by θ about the z-axis, after which we can undo the two rotations that did the aligning. Our final rotation matrix will be of the form

$$\mathbf{R} = \mathbf{R}_x(-\theta_x)\mathbf{R}_y(-\theta_y)\mathbf{R}_z(\theta)\mathbf{R}_y(\theta_y)\mathbf{R}_x(\theta_x).$$

This sequence of rotations is shown in Figure 3.54. The difficult part of the process is determining θ_x and θ_y.

We proceed by looking at the components of **v**. Because **v** is a unit-length vector,

$$\alpha_x^2 + \alpha_y^2 + \alpha_z^2 = 1.$$

We draw a line segment from the origin to the point $(\alpha_x, \alpha_y, \alpha_z)$. This line segment has unit length and the orientation of **v**. Next, we draw the perpendiculars from the point $(\alpha_x, \alpha_y, \alpha_z)$ to the coordinate axes, as shown in Figure 3.55. The three **direction angles**—ϕ_x, ϕ_y, ϕ_z—are the angles between the line segment (or **v**) and the axes. The **direction cosines** are given by

$$\cos \phi_x = \alpha_x,$$

$$\cos \phi_y = \alpha_y,$$

$$\cos \phi_z = \alpha_z.$$

Only two of the direction angles are independent, because

$$\cos^2 \phi_x + \cos^2 \phi_y + \cos^2 \phi_z = 1.$$

We can now compute θ_x and θ_y using these angles. Consider Figure 3.56. It shows that the effect of the desired rotation on the point $(\alpha_x, \alpha_y, \alpha_z)$ is to rotate the line segment into the plane $y = 0$. If we look at the projection of the line segment (before the rotation) on the plane $x = 0$, we see a line segment of length d on this plane. Another way to envision this figure is to think of the plane $x = 0$ as a wall and consider a distant light source located far down the positive x-axis. The line that we see on the wall is the shadow of the line segment from the origin to $(\alpha_x, \alpha_y, \alpha_z)$. Note that the length of the shadow is less than the length of the line segment. We can say the line segment has been **foreshortened** to $d = \sqrt{\alpha_y^2 + \alpha_z^2}$. The desired angle of rotation is determined by the angle that this shadow makes with the z-axis. However, the rotation matrix is determined by the sine and cosine of θ_x. Thus, we never need to compute θ_x; rather, we need to compute only

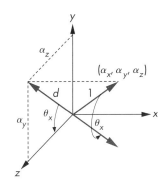

FIGURE 3.56 Computation of the x rotation.

$$\mathbf{R}_x(\theta_x) = \begin{bmatrix} 1 & 0 & 0 & 0 \\ 0 & \alpha_z/d & -\alpha_y/d & 0 \\ 0 & \alpha_y/d & \alpha_z/d & 0 \\ 0 & 0 & 0 & 1 \end{bmatrix}.$$

We compute $\mathbf{R}_y$ in a similar manner. Figure 3.57 shows the rotation. This angle is clockwise about the y-axis; therefore, we have to be careful of the sign of the sine terms in the matrix, which is

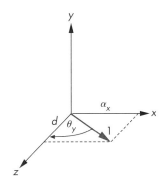

FIGURE 3.57 Computation of the y rotation.

$$\mathbf{R}_y(\theta_y) = \begin{bmatrix} d & 0 & -\alpha_x & 0 \\ 0 & 1 & 0 & 0 \\ \alpha_x & 0 & d & 0 \\ 0 & 0 & 0 & 1 \end{bmatrix}.$$

Finally, we concatenate all the matrices to find

$$\mathbf{M} = \mathbf{T}(\mathbf{p}_0)\mathbf{R}_x(-\theta_x)\mathbf{R}_y(-\theta_y)\mathbf{R}_z(\theta)\mathbf{R}_y(\theta_y)\mathbf{R}_x(\theta_x)\mathbf{T}(-\mathbf{p}_0).$$

Let's look at a specific example. Suppose that we wish to rotate an object by 45 degrees about the line passing through the origin and the point $(1, 2, 3)$. We leave the fixed point at the origin. The first step is to find the point along the line that is a unit distance from the origin. We obtain it by normalizing $(1, 2, 3)$ to $(1/\sqrt{14}, 2/\sqrt{14}, 3/\sqrt{14})$, or $(1/\sqrt{14}, 2/\sqrt{14}, 3/\sqrt{14}, 1)$ in homogeneous coordinates. The first part of the rotation takes this point to $(0, 0, 1, 1)$. We first rotate about the x-axis by the angle $\cos^{-1}\frac{3}{\sqrt{14}}$. This matrix carries $(1/\sqrt{14}, 2/\sqrt{14}, 3/\sqrt{14}, 1)$ to $(1/\sqrt{14}, 0, \sqrt{13/14}, 1)$, which is in the plane $y = 0$. The y rotation must be by the angle $-\cos^{-1}(\sqrt{13/14})$. This rotation aligns the object with the z-axis, and now we can rotate about the z-axis by the desired 45 degrees. Finally, we undo the first two rotations. If we concatenate these five transformations into a single rotation matrix $\mathbf{R}$, we find that

$$\mathbf{R} = \mathbf{R}_x\left(-\cos^{-1}\frac{3}{\sqrt{13}}\right)\mathbf{R}_y\left(\cos^{-1}\sqrt{\frac{13}{14}}\right)\mathbf{R}_z(45)\mathbf{R}_y\left(-\cos^{-1}\sqrt{\frac{13}{14}}\right)$$

$$\mathbf{R}_x\left(\cos^{-1}\frac{3}{\sqrt{13}}\right)$$

$$= \begin{bmatrix} \frac{2+13\sqrt{2}}{28} & \frac{2-\sqrt{2}-3\sqrt{7}}{14} & \frac{6-3\sqrt{2}+4\sqrt{7}}{28} & 0 \\ \frac{2-\sqrt{2}+3\sqrt{7}}{14} & \frac{4+5\sqrt{2}}{14} & \frac{6-3\sqrt{2}-\sqrt{7}}{14} & 0 \\ \frac{6-3\sqrt{2}-4\sqrt{7}}{28} & \frac{6-3\sqrt{2}+\sqrt{7}}{14} & \frac{18+5\sqrt{2}}{28} & 0 \\ 0 & 0 & 0 & 1 \end{bmatrix}.$$

This matrix does not change any point on the line passing through the origin and the point (1, 2, 3). If we want a fixed point other than the origin, we form the matrix

$$\mathbf{M} = \mathbf{T}(\mathbf{p_f})\mathbf{R}\mathbf{T}(-\mathbf{p_f}).$$

This example is not simple. It illustrates the powerful technique of applying many simple transformations to get a complex one. The problem of rotation about an arbitrary point or axis arises in many applications. The major variants lie in the manner in which the axis of rotation is specified. However, we can usually employ techniques similar to the ones that we have used here to determine direction angles or direction cosines.

3.11 TRANSFORMATION MATRICES IN OPENGL

We can now focus on the implementation of a homogeneous-coordinate transformation package and of that package's interface to the user. We have introduced a set of frames, including the world frame and the camera frame, that should be important for developing applications. In a shader-based implementation of OpenGL, the existence or nonexistence of these frames is entirely dependent on what the application programmer decides to do.[7] In a modern implementation of OpenGL, the application programmer not only can choose which frames to use but also where to carry out

---

7. In earlier versions of OpenGL that relied on the fixed-function pipeline, these frames were part of the specification and their state was part of the environment.

the transformations between frames. Some will best be carried out in the application, others in a shader.

As we develop a method for specifying and carrying out transformations, we should emphasize the importance of *state*. Although very few state variables are predefined in OpenGL, once we specify various attributes and matrices, they effectively define the state of the system. Thus, when a vertex is processed, how it is processed is determined by the values of these state variables.

The two transformations we will use most often are the model-view transformation and the projection transformation. The model-view transformation brings representations of geometric objects from application or model frame to the camera frame. The projection matrix will both carry out the desired projection and also change the representation to clip coordinates. We will use only the model-view matrix in this chapter. The model-view matrix normally is an affine-transformation matrix and has only 12 degrees of freedom, as discussed in Section 3.7. The projection matrix, as we will see in Chapter 4, is also a 4×4 matrix, but it is not affine.

3.11.1 Current Transformation Matrices

The generalization common to most graphics systems is of a **current transformation matrix (CTM)**. The CTM is part of the pipeline (Figure 3.58); thus, if **p** is a vertex specified in the application, then the pipeline produces **Cp**. Note that Figure 3.58 does not indicate where in the pipeline the current transformation matrix is applied. If we use a CTM, we can regard it as part of the state of the system.

First we will introduce a simple set of functions that we can use to form and manipulate 4×4 affine transformation matrices. Let **C** denote the CTM (or any other 4×4 affine matrix). Initially, we will set it to the 4×4 identity matrix; it can be reinitialized as needed. If we use the symbol $\leftarrow$ to denote replacement, we can write this initialization operation as

$$\mathbf{C} \leftarrow \mathbf{I}.$$

The functions that alter **C** are of two forms: those that load it with some matrix and those that modify it by premultiplication or postmultiplication by a matrix. The three transformations supported in most systems are translation, scaling with a fixed point of the origin, and rotation with a fixed point of the origin. Symbolically, we can write these operations in postmultiplication form as

$$\mathbf{C} \leftarrow \mathbf{CT},$$

$$\mathbf{C} \leftarrow \mathbf{CS},$$

FIGURE 3.58   Current transformation matrix (CTM).

$$\mathbf{C} \leftarrow \mathbf{CR},$$

and in load form as

$$\mathbf{C} \leftarrow \mathbf{T},$$

$$\mathbf{C} \leftarrow \mathbf{S},$$

$$\mathbf{C} \leftarrow \mathbf{R}.$$

Most systems allow us to load the CTM with an arbitrary matrix $\mathbf{M}$,

$$\mathbf{C} \leftarrow \mathbf{M},$$

or to postmultiply by an arbitrary matrix $\mathbf{M}$,

$$\mathbf{C} \leftarrow \mathbf{CM}.$$

Although we will occasionally use functions that set a matrix, most of the time we will alter an existing matrix; that is, the operation

$$\mathbf{C} \leftarrow \mathbf{CR},$$

is more common than the operation

$$\mathbf{C} \leftarrow \mathbf{R}.$$

3.11.2 Rotation, Translation, and Scaling

In our applications and shaders, the matrix that is most often applied to all vertices is the product of the model-view matrix and the projection matrix. We can think of the CTM as the product of these matrices (Figure 3.59), and we can manipulate each individually by working with the desired matrix.

Using the matrix and vector classes, we can form affine matrices for rotation, translation, and scaling by creating the following five functions:

```
RotateX(float xangle);
RotateY(float yangle);
RotateZ(float zangle);
Translate(float dx, float dy, float dz);
Scale(float sx, float sy, float sz);
```

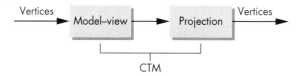

FIGURE 3.59 Model-view and projection matrices.

For example, the code for `Rotatez` is

```
mat4 Rotatez(const float theta)
{
   float s = M_PI/180.0*theta; //convert degrees to radians
   mat4 c;                     // an identity matrix
   c[2][2] = c[3][3] = 1.0;
   c[0][0] = c[1][1] = cos(s);
   c[1][0] = sin(s);
   c[0][1] = -c[1][0];
   return c;
}
```

For rotation, the angles are specified in degrees and the rotations are for a fixed point at the origin. In the translation function, the variables are the components of the displacement vector; for scaling, the variables determine the scale factors along the coordinate axes and the fixed point is the origin.

3.11.3 Rotation About a Fixed Point

In Section 3.10, we showed that we can perform a rotation about a fixed point, other than the origin, by first moving the fixed point to the origin, then rotating about the origin, and finally moving the fixed point back to its original location. Using the example from Section 3.11, the following sequence sets the matrix mode, then forms the required matrix for a 45-degree rotation about the line through the origin and the point $(1, 2, 3)$ with a fixed point of $(4, 5, 6)$:

```
mat4 R,  ctm;
float thetax, thetay;
const float Radians_To_Degrees = 180.0/M_PI;

thetax = Radians_To_Degrees*acos(3.0/sqrt(14.0));
thetay = Radians_To_Degrees*acos(sqrt(13.0/14.0));

R = RotateX(-thetax)*RotateY(-thetay)*RotateZ(-45.0)
     *RotateY(-thetax)*RotateX(thetax);
ctm = Translate(4.0, 5.0, 6.0)*R* Translate(-4.0, -5.0, -6.0);
```

Because we want to do arbitrary rotations so often, it is a good exercise (Exercise 3.31) to write functions `Rotate(float theta, vec3 d)` and `Rotate(float theta, float dx, float dy, float dz)` that will form an arbitrary rotation matrix for a rotation of `theta` degrees about a line in the direction of the vector $d = (dx, dy, dz)$.[8]

---

8. Although it is a good exercise to write the various matrix functions yourself, we also provide them in a separate include file `angel.h` that can be downloaded from the book's Web site.

3.11.4 Order of Transformations

You might be bothered by what appears to be a reversal of the required function calls. The rule in OpenGL is this: *The transformation specified last is the one applied first.* A little examination shows that this order is a consequence of multiplying the CTM on the right by the specified affine transformation and thus is both correct and reasonable. The sequence of operations that we specified was

$\mathbf{C} \leftarrow \mathbf{I}$,

$\mathbf{C} \leftarrow \mathbf{CT}(4.0, 5.0, 6.0)$,

$\mathbf{C} \leftarrow \mathbf{CR}(45.0, 1.0, 2.0, 3.0)$,

$\mathbf{C} \leftarrow \mathbf{CT}(-4.0, -5.0, -6.0)$.

In each step, we postmultiply at the end of the existing CTM, forming the matrix

$\mathbf{C} = \mathbf{T}(4.0, 5.0, 6.0)\mathbf{R}(45.0, 1.0, 2.0, 3.0)\mathbf{T}(-4.0, -5.0, -6.0)$,

which is the matrix that we expect from Section 3.11. Each vertex **p** that is specified *after* the model-view matrix has been set will be multiplied by **C**, thus forming the new vertex

$\mathbf{q} = \mathbf{Cp}$.

There are other ways to think about the order of operations. One way is in terms of a stack. Altering the CTM is similar to pushing matrices onto a stack; when we apply the final transformation, the matrices are popped off the stack in the reverse order in which they were placed there. The analogy is conceptual rather than exact because when we use a transformation function, the matrix is altered immediately.

3.12 SPINNING OF THE CUBE

We will now examine how we can manipulate the color cube interactively. We will take the cube that we defined in Section 3.6 and we rotate it using the three buttons of the mouse. Our program will be based on the following three callback functions:

```
glutDisplayFunc(display);
glutIdleFunc(spincube);
glutMouseFunc(mouse)
```

We will examine two fundamentally different ways of doing the updates to the display. In the first, we will form a new model-view matrix in the display callback and apply it to the vertex data to get new vertex positions. We must then send the new data to the GPU. In the second, we will send the model-view matrix to the vertex shader and apply it there. The mouse and idle callbacks will be the same in both cases, so let's examine them first.

The mouse callback selects the axis for rotation, using 0, 1, and 2 to denote rotation about the *x*, *y*, and *z* axes, respectively:

```
int axis = 0;

void mouse(int button, int state, int x, int y)
{
    if(button == GLUT_LEFT_BUTTON && state == GLUT_DOWN) axis = 0;
    if(button == GLUT_MIDDLE_BUTTON && state == GLUT_DOWN) axis = 1;
    if(button == GLUT_RIGHT_BUTTON && state == GLUT_DOWN) axis = 2;
}
```

The idle callback increments the angle associated with the chosen axis by 0.1 degrees each time:

```
void spinCube()
{
   theta[axis] += 0.1;
   if( theta[axis] > 360.0 ) theta[axis] -= 360.0;
   glutPostRedisplay();
}
```

3.12.1 Updating in the Display Callback

The function `display` starts by clearing the frame and depth buffers and then forms a model-view matrix using the values of three angles determined by the mouse callback

```
    glClear(GL_COLOR_BUFFER_BIT | GL_DEPTH_BUFFER_BIT);
    mat4 ctm = RotateX(theta[0])*RotateY(theta[1])*RotateZ(theta[2]);
```

The problem is how to apply this matrix. Suppose that we set up the data arrays as in our previous examples by executing the `colorcube` function as part of our initialization. Thus, we have color and position data in the arrays `quad_colors` and `points` for 36 vertices. We can use a second array

```
point4 new_points[36];
```

to hold the transformed points and then apply the rotations in the display callback

```
    for(i=0; i<36; i++)
    {
        new_points[i] = ctm*points[i];
    }
```

However, these transformed positions are on the CPU, not on the GPU. To get them into the pipeline, we can initialize the vertex array to be `new_points` rather than `points` initially,

```
loc = glGetAttribLocation(program, "vPosition");
glEnableVertexAttribArray(loc);
glVertexAttribPointer(loc, 4, GL_FLOAT, GL_FALSE, 0,
                      BUFFER_OFFSET(0));
```

and then in the display callback send these points to the GPU:

```
glBindVertexArray(abuffer);
glBindBuffer(GL_ARRAY_BUFFER, buffers[0]);
glBufferData(GL_ARRAY_BUFFER, sizeof(new_points), new_points,
             GL_STATIC_DRAW);
glDrawArrays(GL_TRIANGLES, 0, N);
glutSwapBuffers();
```

There is, however, a major weakness in this approach. We are applying the current transformation in the application program and sending the vertex positions to the GPU every time we want to update the display. Consequently, we are not using the power of the GPU and having the performance determined by how fast we can send data from the CPU to the GPU. In applications, where we have complex geometry, this approach will lead to poor performance.

Our second approach will be to send the vertex data to the GPU once. Every time we update the transformation matrix, we will send a new transformation matrix to the GPU and update the vertex positions on the GPU. First, we must examine how to get such data from the CPU to the GPU.

3.12.2 Uniform Variables

In a given application, a variable may change in a variety of ways. When we send vertex attributes to a shader, these attributes can be different for each vertex in a primitive. We may also want parameters that will remain the same for all vertices in a primitive or equivalently for all the vertices that are displayed when we execute a function such as glDrawArrays. Such variables are called **uniform qualified variables**. For example, in our present example, we want the same rotation matrix to apply to all the vertices in the points array.

We set up uniform variables in much the same way as we did for vertex attributes. Suppose that we want to send the elapsed time from the application to the vertex shader. In the application, we can use GLUT to get the elapsed time in milliseconds

```
float etime;

etime = 0.001*glutGet(GLUT_ELAPSED_TIME);
```

In the vertex shader, we might have a corresponding variable time. For example, the following shader varies the x component of each vertex sinusoidally:

```
uniform float time;
attribute vec4  vPosition;

void main()
{
    vPosition.x *= (1+sin(time));
    gl_Position = vPosition;
}
```

We still must establish a connection between the corresponding time variables in the application and the shader and get the values from the application to the shader.

After the shaders have been compiled and linked, we can get the correspondence in the application in a manner similar to vertex attributes. We get the location by

```
GLint timeParam;

timeParam = glGetUniformLocation(program, "time");
```

Now whenever we want to send the elapsed time to the shader, we execute

```
glUniform1f(timeParam, etime);
```

There are forms of `glUniform` corresponding to all the types supported by GLSL, including floats, ints, and two-, three-, and four-dimensional vectors and matrices. For the 4×4 rotation matrix, we use the form

```
glUniformMatrix4fv(matrix_loc, 1, GL_TRUE, ctm);
```

Here, `matrix_loc` is determined by

```
GLint matrix_loc;

matrix_loc = getUniformLocation(program, "rotation");
```

for the vertex shader

```
in vec4 vPosition;
in vec4 vColor;
out vec4 color;
uniform mat4 rotation;

void main()
{
  gl_Position = rotation*vPosition;
  color = vColor;
}
```

The second parameter, `glUniformMatrix`, is the number of elements of `ctm` that are sent. The third parameter declares that the data should be sent in row-major order. The display callback is now

```
mat4 ctm;

void display()
{
    glClear(GL_COLOR_BUFFER_BIT | GL_DEPTH_BUFFER_BIT);
    ctm = RotateX(theta[0])*RotateY(theta[1])*RotateZ(theta[2]);
    glUniformMatrix4fv(matrix_loc, 1, GL_TRUE, ctm);
    glDrawArrays(GL_TRIANGLES, 0, N);
    glutSwapBuffers();
}
```

Alternately, we could have computed the rotation matrix in the vertex shader by sending only the rotation angles to the vertex shader. A program that takes this approach is in Appendix A.

3.13 INTERFACES TO THREE-DIMENSIONAL APPLICATIONS

In Section 3.12, we used a three-button mouse to control the direction of rotation of our cube. This interface is limited. Rather than use all three mouse buttons to control rotation, we might want to use mouse buttons to control functions, such as pulling down a menu, that we would have had to assign to keys in our previous example.

In Section 3.10, we noted that there were many ways to obtain a given orientation. Rather than do rotations about the x-, y-, and z-axes in that order, we could do a rotation about the x-axis, followed by a rotation about the y-axis, and finish with another rotation about the x-axis. If we do our orientation this way, we can obtain our desired orientation using only two mouse buttons. However, there is still a problem: Our rotations are in a single direction. It would be easier to orient an object if we could rotate either forward or backward about an axis and could stop the rotation once we reached a desired orientation.

GLUT allows us to use the keyboard in combination with the mouse. We could, for example, use the left mouse button for a forward rotation about the x-axis and the Control key in combination with the left mouse button for a backward rotation about the x-axis.

However, neither of these options provides a good user interface, which should be more intuitive and less awkward. Let's consider a few options that provide a more interesting and smoother interaction.

3.13.1 Using Areas of the Screen

Suppose that we want to use one mouse button for orienting an object, one for getting closer to or farther from the object, and one for translating the object to the left or right. We can use the motion callback to achieve all these functions. The callback returns which button has been activated and where the mouse is located. We can use the location of the mouse to control how fast and in which direction we rotate or translate and to move in or out.

As just noted, we need the ability to rotate about only two axes to achieve any orientation. We could then use the left mouse button and the mouse position to control orientation. We can use the distance from the center of the screen to control the x and y rotations. Thus, if the left mouse button is held down but the mouse is located in the center of the screen, there will be no rotation; if the mouse is moved up, the object will be rotated about the y-axis in a clockwise manner; and if the mouse is moved down, the object will be rotated about the y-axis in a counterclockwise manner. Likewise, motion to the right or left will cause rotation about the x-axis. The distance from the center can control the speed of rotation. Motion toward the corners can cause simultaneous rotations about the x- and y-axes.

Using the right mouse button in a similar manner, we can translate the object right to left and up to down. We might use the middle mouse button to move the object toward or away from the viewer by having the mouse position control a translation in the z-direction. The code for such an interface is straightforward in GLUT; we leave it as an exercise (Exercise 3.20).

3.13.2 A Virtual Trackball

The use of the mouse position to control rotation about two axes provides us with most of the functionality of a trackball. We can go one step further and create a graphical or virtual trackball using our mouse and the display. One of the benefits of such a device is that we can create a frictionless trackball that, once we start it rotating, will continue to rotate until stopped by the user. Thus, the device will support continuous rotations of objects but will still allow changes in the speed and orientation of the rotation. We can also do the same for translation and other parameters that we can control from the mouse.

We start by mapping the position of a trackball to that of a mouse. Consider the trackball shown in Figure 3.60. We assume that the ball has a radius of 1 unit. We can

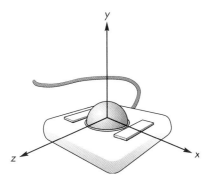

FIGURE 3.60   Trackball frame.

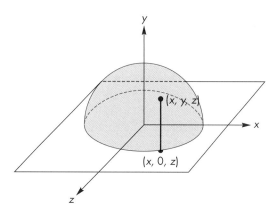

FIGURE 3.61   Projection of the trackball position to the plane.

map a position on its surface to the plane $y = 0$ by doing an orthogonal projection to the plane, as shown in Figure 3.61. The position (x, y, z) on the surface of the ball is mapped to $(x, 0, z)$ on the plane. This projection is reversible because we know that the three-dimensional point that is projected to the point on the plane must satisfy the equation of the sphere

$$x^2 + y^2 + z^2 = 1.$$

Thus, given the point on the plane $(x, 0, z)$, the corresponding point on the hemisphere must be (x, y, z), where

$$y = \sqrt{1 - x^2 - z^2}.$$

We can compute the three-dimensional information and track it as the mouse moves. Suppose that we have two positions on the hemisphere $\mathbf{p}_1$ and $\mathbf{p}_2$; then the vectors from the origin to these points determine the orientation of a plane, as shown in Figure 3.62, whose normal is defined by their cross product

$$\mathbf{n} = \mathbf{p}_1 \times \mathbf{p}_2.$$

The motion of the trackball that moves from $\mathbf{p}_1$ to $\mathbf{p}_2$ can be achieved by a rotation about $\mathbf{n}$. The angle of rotation is the angle between the vectors $\mathbf{p}_1$ and $\mathbf{p}_2$, which we can compute using the magnitude of the cross product. Because both $\mathbf{p}_1$ and $\mathbf{p}_2$ have unit length,

$$|\sin \theta| = |\mathbf{n}|.$$

If we are tracking the mouse at a high rate, then the changes in position that we detect will be small; rather than use an inverse trigonometric function to find θ, we can use

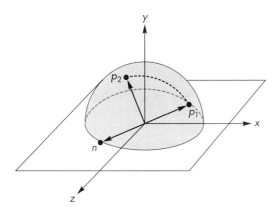

FIGURE 3.62   Computation of the plane of rotation.

the approximation

$$\sin\theta \approx \theta.$$

We can implement the virtual trackball through use of the idle, motion, and mouse callbacks in GLUT. We can think of the process in terms of three logical variables, or flags, that control the tracking of the mouse and of the display redrawing. These are set initially as follows:[9]

```
bool trackingMouse = false;
bool trackballMove = false;
bool redrawContinue = false;
```

If `redrawContinue` is true, the idle function posts a redisplay. If `tracking-Mouse` is true, we update the trackball position as part of the motion callback. If `trackballMove` is true, we update the rotation matrix that we use in our display routine.

The changes in these variables are controlled through the mouse callback. When we push a mouse button—either a particular button or any button, depending on exactly what we want—we start updating the trackball position by initializing it, and then letting the motion callback update it and post redisplays in response to changes in the position of the mouse. When the mouse button is released, we stop tracking the mouse. We can use the two most recent mouse positions to define a velocity vector so that we can continually update the rotation matrix. Thus, once the mouse button is released, the object will continue to rotate at a constant velocity—an effect that we

---

9. If the compiler does not support the Boolean type, we can use `typedef bool int;` and then define `true` and `false` as 1 and 0, respectively.

could achieve with an ideal frictionless trackball but not directly with either a real mouse or a real trackball.

3.13.3 Smooth Rotations

Our approach to orienting objects has been based on angles (the Euler angles) measured with respect to the three coordinate axes. This perspective led to our forming rotation matrices by concatenating simple rotations about the x-, y-, and z-axes to obtain a desired rotation about an arbitrary axis. Although OpenGL allows us to rotate about an arbitrary axis, we usually employ our concatenation strategy to determine this axis and the corresponding angle of rotation.[10]

Consider what happens if we wish to move between two orientations as part of an animation. In principle, we can determine an appropriate rotation matrix as the product of rotations about the three axes,

$$\mathbf{R}(\theta) = \mathbf{R}_x(\theta_x)\mathbf{R}_y(\theta_y)\mathbf{R}_z(\theta_z).$$

If we want to create a sequence of images that move between the two orientations, we can change the individual angles in small increments, either individually or simultaneously. Such a sequence would not appear smooth to a viewer; she would detect the individual rotations about each of the three axes.

With a device such as the trackball, we saw that we could rotate the cube smoothly about any axis. We did so by exploiting the equivalence between the two orientations of the cube and two points on a unit circle. A smooth rotation between the two orientations corresponds to a great circle on the surface of a sphere. This circle corresponds to a single rotation about a suitable axis that is the normal to the plane determined by the two points on the sphere and that sphere's center. If we increase this angle smoothly, our viewer will see a smooth rotation.

In one sense, what has failed us is our mathematical formulation, which relies on the use of coordinate axes. However, a deeper and less axis-dependent method is embedded within the matrix formulation. Suppose that we start with an arbitrary rotation matrix $\mathbf{R}$. All points on a line in the direction $\mathbf{d}$ are unaffected by the rotation. Thus, for any such point $\mathbf{p}$,

$$\mathbf{R}\mathbf{p} = \mathbf{p}.$$

In terms of the matrix $\mathbf{R}$, the column matrix $\mathbf{p}$ is an **eigenvector** of the matrix corresponding to the **eigenvalue** 1 (see Appendix C). In addition, for the direction $\mathbf{d}$,

$$\mathbf{R}\mathbf{d} = \mathbf{d},$$

---

10. This section and the next may be skipped on a first reading.

so that its direction is unaffected by the rotation. Consequently, **d** is also an eigen-vector of **R** corresponding to another eigenvalue of 1. The point **p** must be the fixed point of the rotation, and the vector **d** must be the normal to a plane perpendicular to the direction of rotation. In terms of the trackball, computing the axis of rota-tion was equivalent to finding a particular eigenvector of the desired rotation matrix. We could also go the other way. Given an arbitrary rotation matrix, by finding its eigenvalues and eigenvectors, we also determine the axis of rotation and the fixed point.

3.13.4 Incremental Rotation

Suppose that we are given two orientations of an object, such as a camera, and we want to go smoothly from one to the other. One approach is to find the great circle path as we did with the virtual trackball and make incremental changes in the angle that rotates us along this path. Thus, we start with the axis of rotation, a start angle, a final angle, and a desired increment in the angle determined by the number of steps we wish to take. The main loop in the code will be of the following form:

```
mat4 ctm;
for(i=0, i<imax; i++)
{
    thetax += dx;
    thetay += dy;
    thetaz += dz;
    ctm = RotateXm(thetax)*RotateYm(thetay)*RotateZm(thetaz);
    draw_object();
}
```

One problem with this approach is that the calculation of the rotation matrix requires the evaluation of the sines and cosines of three angles. We would do better if we compute the rotation matrix once and reuse it. We could also use the small angle approximations

$$\sin \theta \approx \theta,$$

$$\cos \theta \approx 1.$$

If we form an arbitrary rotation matrix through the Euler angles

$$\mathbf{R} = \mathbf{R}_z(\psi)\mathbf{R}_y(\phi)\mathbf{R}_x(\theta),$$

then we can use the approximations to write **R** as

$$\mathbf{R} = \begin{bmatrix} \cos\psi & -\sin\psi & 0 & 0 \\ \sin\psi & \cos\psi & 0 & 0 \\ 0 & 0 & 1 & 0 \\ 0 & 0 & 0 & 1 \end{bmatrix} \begin{bmatrix} \cos\phi & 0 & \sin\phi & 0 \\ 0 & 1 & 0 & 0 \\ -\sin\phi & 0 & \cos\phi & 0 \\ 0 & 0 & 0 & 1 \end{bmatrix}$$

$$\begin{bmatrix} 1 & 0 & 0 & 0 \\ 0 & \cos\theta & -\sin\theta & 0 \\ 0 & \sin\theta & \cos\theta & 0 \\ 0 & 0 & 0 & 1 \end{bmatrix}$$

$$\approx \begin{bmatrix} 1 & -\psi & \phi & 0 \\ \psi & 1 & -\theta & 0 \\ -\phi & \theta & 1 & 0 \\ 0 & 0 & 0 & 1 \end{bmatrix}.$$

3.14 QUATERNIONS

Quaternions are an extension of complex numbers that provide an alternative method for describing and manipulating rotations. Although less intuitive than our original approach, quaternions provide advantages for animation and hardware implementation of rotation.

3.14.1 Complex Numbers and Quaternions

In two dimensions, the use of complex numbers to represent operations such as rotation is well known to most students of engineering and science. For example, suppose that we let $\mathbf{i}$ denote the pure imaginary number such that $\mathbf{i}^2 = -1$. Recalling Euler's identity,

$$e^{\mathbf{i}\theta} = \cos\theta + \mathbf{i}\sin\theta,$$

we can write the polar representation of a complex number $\mathbf{c}$ as

$$\mathbf{c} = a + \mathbf{i}b = re^{\mathbf{i}\theta},$$

where $r = \sqrt{a^2 + b^2}$ and $\theta = \tan^{-1} b/a$.

If we rotate $\mathbf{c}$ about the origin by ϕ to $\mathbf{c}'$, then we can find $\mathbf{c}'$ using a rotation matrix, or we can use the polar representation to write

$$\mathbf{c}' = re^{\mathbf{i}(\theta+\phi)} = re^{\mathbf{i}\theta} e^{\mathbf{i}\phi}.$$

Thus, $e^{\mathbf{i}\phi}$ is a rotation operator in the complex plane and provides an alternative to using transformations that may prove more efficient in practice.

However, we are really interested in rotations in a three-dimensional space. In three dimensions, the problem is more difficult because to specify a rotation about the origin we need to specify both a direction (a vector) and the amount of rotation about it (a scalar). One solution is to use a representation that consists of both a vector and a scalar. Usually, this representation is written as the **quaternion**

$$a = (q_0, q_1, q_2, q_3) = (q_0, \mathbf{q}),$$

where $\mathbf{q} = (q_1, q_2, q_3)$. The operations among quaternions are based on the use of three "complex" numbers $\mathbf{i}, \mathbf{j}$, and $\mathbf{k}$ with the properties

$$\mathbf{i}^2 = \mathbf{j}^2 = \mathbf{k}^2 = \mathbf{ijk} = -1.$$

These numbers are analogous to the unit vectors in three dimensions, and we can write $\mathbf{q}$ as

$$\mathbf{q} = q_1\mathbf{i} + q_2\mathbf{j} + q_3\mathbf{k}.$$

Now we can use the relationships among $\mathbf{i}, \mathbf{j}$, and $\mathbf{k}$ to derive quaternion addition and multiplication. If the quaternion b is given by

$$b = (p_0, \mathbf{p}),$$

then using the dot and cross products for vectors,

$$a + b = (p_0 + q_0, \mathbf{p} + \mathbf{q}),$$

$$ab = (p_0q_0 - \mathbf{q} \cdot \mathbf{p}, q_0\mathbf{p} + p_0\mathbf{q} + \mathbf{q} \times \mathbf{p}).$$

We can also define a magnitude for quaternions in the normal manner as

$$|a|^2 = q_0^2 + q_1^2 + q_2^2 + q_3^2 = q_0^2 + \mathbf{q} \cdot \mathbf{q}.$$

Quaternions have a multiplicative identity, the quaternion $(1, \mathbf{0})$, and it is easy to verify that the inverse of a quaternion is given by

$$a^{-1} = \frac{1}{|a|^2}(q_0, -\mathbf{q}).$$

3.14.2 Quaternions and Rotation

So far, we have only defined a new mathematical object. For it to be of use to us, we must relate it to our geometric entities and show how it can be used to carry out operations such as rotation. Suppose that we use the vector part of a quaternion to represent a point in space

$$p = (0, \mathbf{p}).$$

Thus, the components of $\mathbf{p} = (x, y, z)$ give the location of the point. Consider the quaternion

$$r = \left(\cos \frac{\theta}{2}, \sin \frac{\theta}{2} \mathbf{v} \right),$$

where $\mathbf{v}$ has unit length. We can then show that the quaternion r is a unit quaternion ($|r| = 1$), and therefore

$$r^{-1} = \left(\cos \frac{\theta}{2}, -\sin \frac{\theta}{2} \mathbf{v} \right).$$

If we consider the quaternion product of the quaternion p that represents a point with r, we obtain the quaternion

$$p' = rpr^{-1}.$$

This quaternion has the form $(0, \mathbf{p}')$, where

$$\mathbf{p}' = \cos^2 \frac{\theta}{2} \mathbf{p} + \sin^2 \frac{\theta}{2} (\mathbf{p} \cdot \mathbf{v}) \mathbf{v} + 2 \sin \frac{\theta}{2} \cos \frac{\theta}{2} (\mathbf{v} \times \mathbf{p}) - \sin \frac{\theta}{2} (\mathbf{v} \times \mathbf{p}) \times \mathbf{v}$$

and thus p' is the representation of a point. What is less obvious is that p' is the result of rotating the point $\mathbf{p}$ by θ degrees about the vector $\mathbf{v}$. However, we can verify that this indeed is the case by comparing terms in p' with those of the general rotation. Before doing so, consider the implication of this result. Because we get the same result, the quaternion product formed from r and p is an alternate to transformation matrices as a representation of rotation with a fixed point of the origin about an arbitrary axis. If we count operations, quaternions are faster and have been built into both hardware and software implementations.

Let's consider a few examples. Suppose that we consider the rotation about the z-axis by θ with a fixed point at the origin. The desired unit vector v is $(0, 0, 1)$, yielding the quaternion

$$r = \cos \frac{\theta}{2} + \sin \frac{\theta}{2} (0, 0, 1).$$

The rotation of an arbitrary point $\mathbf{p} = (x, y, z)$ yields the quaternion

$$p' = rpr^{-1} = r(0, \mathbf{p})r^{-1} = (0, \mathbf{p}'),$$

where

$$\mathbf{p}' = (x \cos \theta - y \sin \theta, x \sin \theta + y \cos \theta, z).$$

Thus, we get the expected result but with fewer operations. If we consider a sequence of rotations about the coordinate axes that in matrix form yields the matrix $\mathbf{R} = \mathbf{R}_x(\theta_x)\mathbf{R}_y(\theta_y)\mathbf{R}_z(\theta_z)$, we instead can use the product of the corresponding quaternions to form $r_x r_y r_z$.

Returning to the rotation about an arbitrary axis, in Section 3.10.4, we derived a matrix of the form

$$\mathbf{M} = \mathbf{T}(\mathbf{p}_0)\mathbf{R}_x(-\theta_x)\mathbf{R}_y(-\theta_y)\mathbf{R}_z(\theta_z)\mathbf{R}_y(\theta_y)\mathbf{R}_x(\theta_x)\mathbf{T}(-\mathbf{p}_0).$$

Because of the translations at the beginning and end, we cannot use quaternions for the entire operation. We can, however, recognize that the elements of $p' = rpr^{-1}$ can be used to find the elements of the homogeneous coordinate rotation matrix embedded in $\mathbf{M}$. Thus, if again $r = (\cos\frac{\theta}{2}, \sin\frac{\theta}{2}\mathbf{v})$, then

$$\mathbf{R} = \begin{bmatrix} 1 - 2\sin^2\frac{\theta}{2}(v_y^2 + v_z^2) & 2\sin^2\frac{\theta}{2}v_xv_y - 2\cos\frac{\theta}{2}\sin\frac{\theta}{2}v_z \\ 2\sin^2\frac{\theta}{2}v_xv_y + 2\cos\frac{\theta}{2}\sin\frac{\theta}{2}v_z & 1 - 2\sin^2\frac{\theta}{2}(v_x^2 + v_z^2) \\ 2\sin^2\frac{\theta}{2}v_xv_z - 2\cos\frac{\theta}{2}\sin\frac{\theta}{2}v_y & 2\sin^2\frac{\theta}{2}v_yv_z + 2\cos\frac{\theta}{2}\sin\frac{\theta}{2}v_x \\ 0 & 0 \end{bmatrix}$$
$$\begin{bmatrix} 2\sin^2\frac{\theta}{2}v_xv_z + 2\cos\frac{\theta}{2}\sin\frac{\theta}{2}v_y & 0 \\ 2\sin^2\frac{\theta}{2}v_yv_z - 2\cos\frac{\theta}{2}\sin\frac{\theta}{2}v_x & 0 \\ 1 - 2\sin^2\frac{\theta}{2}(v_x^2 + v_y^2) & 0 \\ 0 & 1 \end{bmatrix}.$$

This matrix can be made to look more familiar if we use the trigonometric identities

$$\cos\theta = \cos^2\frac{\theta}{2} - \sin^2\frac{\theta}{2} = 1 - 2\sin^2\frac{\theta}{2},$$

$$\sin\theta = 2\cos\frac{\theta}{2}\sin\frac{\theta}{2},$$

and recall that $\mathbf{v}$ is a unit vector so that

$$v_x^2 + v_y^2 + v_z^2 = 1.$$

Thus, we can use quaternion products to form r and then form the rotation part of $\mathbf{M}$ by matching terms between $\mathbf{R}$ and r. We then use our normal transformation operations to add in the effect of the two translations.

Alternately, we can use the vec4 type to create quaternions either in the application (Exercise 3.26) or in the shaders (Exercise 3.30). In either case, we can carry out the rotation directly without converting back to a rotation matrix.

In addition to the efficiency of using quaternions instead of rotation matrices, quaternions can be interpolated to obtain smooth sequences of rotations for animation.

SUMMARY AND NOTES

In this chapter, we have presented two different—but ultimately complementary—points of view regarding the mathematics of computer graphics. One is that mathematical abstraction of the objects with which we work in computer graphics is necessary if we are to understand the operations that we carry out in our programs. The other is that transformations—and the techniques for carrying them out, such as the use of homogeneous coordinates—are the basis for implementations of graphics systems.

Our mathematical tools come from the study of vector analysis and linear algebra. For computer-graphics purposes, however, the order in which we have chosen to present these tools is the reverse of the order that most students learn them. In particular, linear algebra is studied first, and then vector-space concepts are linked to the study of n-tuples in $\mathbf{R}^n$. In contrast, our study of representation in mathematical spaces led to our use of linear algebra as a tool for implementing abstract types.

We pursued a coordinate-free approach for two reasons. First, we wanted to show that all the basic concepts of geometric objects and of transformations are independent of the ways the latter are represented. Second, as object-oriented languages become more prevalent, application programmers will work directly with the objects, instead of with those objects' representations. The references in Suggested Readings contain examples of geometric programming systems that illustrate the potential of this approach.

Homogeneous coordinates provided a wonderful example of the power of mathematical abstraction. By going to an abstract mathematical space—the affine space—we were able to find a tool that led directly to efficient software and hardware methods.

Finally, we provided the set of affine transformations supported in OpenGL and discussed ways that we could concatenate them to provide all affine transformations. The strategy of combining a few simple types of matrices to build a desired transformation is a powerful one; you should use it for a few of the exercises at the end of this chapter. In Chapter 4, we build on these techniques to develop viewing for three-dimensional graphics; in Chapter 8, we use our transformations to build hierarchical models.

SUGGESTED READINGS

There are many texts on vector analysis and linear algebra, although most treat the topics separately. Within the geometric-design community, the vector-space approach of coordinate-free descriptions of curves and surfaces has been popular; see the book by Faux and Pratt [Fau80]. See DeRose [DeR88, DeR89] for an introduction to geometric programming. Homogeneous coordinates arose in geometry [Max51] and were later discovered by the graphics community [Rob63, Rie81]. Their use in hardware started with Silicon Graphics' Geometry Engine [Cla82]. Modern hard-

ware architectures use application-specific integrated circuits (ASICs) that include homogeneous coordinate transformations.

Quaternions were introduced to computer graphics by Shoemake [Sho85] for use in animation. See the book by Kuipers [Kui99] for many examples of the use of rotation matrices and quaternions.

Software tools such as Mathematica [Wol91] and MATLAB [Mat95] are excellent aids for learning to manipulate transformation matrices.

EXERCISES

3.1 Show that the following sequences commute:
a. A rotation and a uniform scaling
b. Two rotations about the same axis
c. Two translations

3.2 *Twist* is similar to rotation about the origin except that the amount of rotation increases by a factor f the farther a point is from the origin. Write a program to twist the triangle-based Sierpinski gasket by a user-supplied value of f. Observe how the shape of the gasket changes with the number of subdivisions.

3.3 Write a library of functions that will allow you to do geometric programming. Your library should contain functions for manipulating the basic geometric types (points, lines, vectors) and operations on those types, including dot and cross products. It should allow you to change frames. You can also create functions to interface with OpenGL so that you can display the results of geometric calculations.

3.4 If we are interested in only two-dimensional graphics, we can use three-dimensional homogeneous coordinates by representing a point as $\mathbf{p} = [x\,y\,1]^T$ and a vector as $\mathbf{v} = [a\,b\,0]^T$. Find the 3×3 rotation, translation, scaling, and shear matrices. How many degrees of freedom are there in an affine transformation for transforming two-dimensional points?

3.5 We can specify an affine transformation by considering the location of a small number of points both before and after these points have been transformed. In three dimensions, how many points must we consider to specify the transformation uniquely? How does the required number of points change when we work in two dimensions?

3.6 Why is a directed line segment synonymous with a vector?

3.7 Which affine non-rigid-body transformation can make an object bigger or smaller? Besides rotation, translation and scaling, state one affine transformation.

3.8 Derive the shear transformation from the rotation, translation, and scaling transformations.

3.9 In two dimensions, we can specify a line by the equation $y = mx + h$. Find an affine transformation to reflect two-dimensional points about this line. Extend your result to reflection about a plane in three dimensions.

3.10 In Section 3.10, we showed that an arbitrary rotation matrix could be composed from successive rotations about the three axes. How many ways can we compose a given rotation if we can do only three simple rotations? Are all three of the simple rotation matrices necessary?

3.11 What is the advantage of the approach, independent of coordinate systems, that is used for dealing with geometric problems?

3.12 Define a point in a three-dimensional geometric system. What is the only property of this point?

3.13 What are the three fundamental types that represent the relationships among basic geometric objects?

3.14 Consider the solution of either constant-coefficient linear differential or difference equations (recurrences). Show that the solutions of the homogeneous equations form a vector space. Relate the solution for a particular inhomogeneous equation to an affine space.

3.15 Write a program to generate a Sierpinski gasket as follows. Start with a white triangle. At each step, use transformations to generate three similar triangles that are drawn over the original triangle, leaving the center of the triangle white and the three corners black.

FIGURE 3.63   Symmetric orientation of cube.

3.16 Start with a cube centered at the origin and aligned with the coordinate axes. Find a rotation matrix that will orient the cube symmetrically, as shown in Figure 3.63.

3.17 We have used vertices in three dimensions to define objects such as three-dimensional polygons. Given a set of vertices, find a test to determine whether the polygon that they determine is planar.

3.18 Mathematically explain rotating a point about the origin in a two-dimensional plane.

3.19 We defined an instance transformation as the product of a translation, a rotation, and a scaling. Can we accomplish the same effect by applying these three types of transformations in a different order?

3.20 Write a program that allows you to orient the cube with one mouse button, to translate it with a second, and to zoom in and out with a third.

3.21 A vector v displaces a point Q to a new location P. Write the expression to represent the point-vector addition and the point-point subtraction operation.

3.22 An incremental rotation about the z-axis can be approximated by the matrix

$$\begin{bmatrix} 1 & -\theta & 0 & 0 \\ \theta & 1 & 0 & 0 \\ 0 & 0 & 1 & 0 \\ 0 & 0 & 0 & 1 \end{bmatrix}.$$

What negative aspects are there if we use this matrix for a large number of steps? Can you suggest a remedy? *Hint:* Consider points a distance of 1 from the origin.

3.23 What is scalar-vector multiplication and vector-vector addition in a vector space? What are the extra features that a Euclidean space provides over a vector space?

3.24 For any point Q, vector v, and positive scalar α in an affine space, write an expression to describe all points on the line from Q in the direction of v.

3.25 Name the usual order in which frames occur in the pipeline.

3.26 Using the vec4 class, create a set of quaternion operations that can be carried out in an application. For example, you might start with the prototypes

```
typedef vec4 quaternion;
quaternion multq(const quaternion &, const quaternion &);
quaternion addq(const quaternion &, const quaternion &);
quaternion iverseq(const quaternion &);
point4 rotateq(float theta, const point4 &);
```

3.27 When are two vectors, u and v, said to be orthogonal? In a vector space, when is a set of vectors said to be linearly independent?

3.28 To specify a scaling, we can specify the fixed point, a direction in which we wish to scale, and a scale factor (α). For what value of α will:
a. the object grow longer in the specified direction?
b. the object grow smaller in the specified direction?

3.29 Show that the sum

$$P = \alpha_1 P_1 + \alpha_2 P_2 + \cdots + \alpha_n P_n$$

is defined if and only if

$$\alpha_1 + \alpha_2 + \cdots + \alpha_n = 1.$$

Hint: Start with the first two terms and write them as

$$P = \alpha_1 P_1 + \alpha_2 P_2 + \cdots = \alpha_1 P_1 + (\alpha_2 + \alpha_1 - \alpha_1)P_2 + \cdots$$
$$= \alpha_1 (P_1 - P_2) + (\alpha_1 + \alpha_2)P_2 + \cdots,$$

and then proceed inductively.

3.30 Write a vertex shader whose input is a quaternion and rotates the input vertex using quaternion rotation.

3.31 Write a function Rotate(float theta, vec3d) that will rotate by theta degrees about the axis d with a fixed point at the origin.

CHAPTER 4

VIEWING

We have completed our discussion of the first half of the synthetic camera model—specifying objects in three dimensions. We now investigate the multitude of ways in which we can describe our virtual camera. Along the way, we examine related topics, such as the relationship between classical viewing techniques and computer viewing and how projection is implemented using projective transformations.

There are three parts to our approach. First, we look at the types of views that we can create and why we need more than one type of view. Then we examine how an application program can specify a particular view within OpenGL. We will see that the viewing process has two parts. In the first, we use the model-view matrix to switch vertex representations from the object frame in which we defined our objects to their representation in the eye frame, in which the camera is at the origin. This representation of the geometry will allow us to use canonical viewing procedures. The second part of the process deals with the type of projection we prefer (parallel or perspective) and the part of the world we wish to image (the clipping or view volume). These specifications will allow us to form a projection matrix that is concatenated with the model-view matrix. Finally, we derive the projection matrices that describe the most important parallel and perspective views and investigate how to carry out these projections in OpenGL.

4.1 CLASSICAL AND COMPUTER VIEWING

Before looking at the interface between computer-graphics systems and application programs for three-dimensional viewing, we take a slight diversion to consider classical viewing. There are two reasons for examining classical viewing. First, many of the jobs that were formerly done by hand drawing—such as animation in movies, architectural rendering, drafting, and mechanical-parts design—are now routinely done with the aid of computer graphics. Practitioners of these fields need to be able to produce classical views—such as isometrics, elevations, and various perspectives—and thus must be able to use the computer system to produce such renderings. Second, the relationships between classical and computer viewing show many advantages of, and a few difficulties with, the approach used by most APIs.

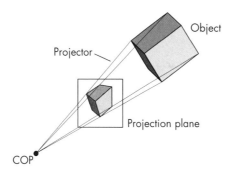

FIGURE 4.1   Viewing.

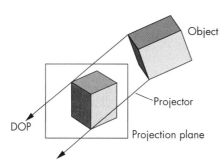

FIGURE 4.2   Movement of the center of projection (COP) to infinity.

When we introduced the synthetic-camera model in Chapter 1, we pointed out the similarities between classical and computer viewing. The basic elements in both cases are the same. We have objects, a viewer, projectors, and a projection plane (Figure 4.1). The projectors meet at the **center of projection** (**COP**). The COP corresponds to the center of the lens in the camera or in the eye, and in a computer-graphics system, it is the origin of the **camera frame** for perspective views. All standard graphics systems follow the model that we described in Chapter 1, which is based on geometric optics. The projection surface is a plane, and the projectors are straight lines. This situation is the one we usually encounter and is straightforward to implement, especially with our pipeline model.

Both classical and computer graphics allow the viewer to be an infinite distance from the objects. Note that as we move the COP to infinity, the projectors become parallel and the COP can be replaced by a **direction of projection** (**DOP**), as shown in Figure 4.2. Note also that as the COP moves to infinity, we can leave the projection plane fixed and the size of the image remains about the same, even though the COP is infinitely far from the objects. Views with a finite COP are called **perspective views**; views with a COP at infinity are called **parallel views**. For parallel views, the origin of the camera frame usually lies in the projection plane.

Color Plates 9 and 10 show a parallel and a perspective rendering, respectively. These plates illustrate the importance of having both types of view available in applications such as architecture; in an API that supports both types of viewing, the user can switch easily between various viewing modes. Most modern APIs support both parallel and perspective viewing. The class of projections produced by these systems is known as **planar geometric projections** because the projection surface is a plane and the projectors are lines. Both perspective and parallel projections preserve lines; they do not, in general, preserve angles. Although the parallel views are the limiting case of perspective viewing, both classical and computer viewing usually treat them as separate cases. For classical views, the techniques that people use to construct the two types by hand are different, as anyone who has taken a drafting class surely knows. From the computer perspective, there are differences in how we specify the two types of views. Rather than looking at a parallel view as the limit of the perspective view, we derive the limiting equations and use those equations directly to form the corresponding projection matrix. In modern pipeline architectures, the projection matrix corresponding to either type of view can be loaded into the pipeline.

Although computer-graphics systems have two fundamental types of viewing (parallel and perspective), classical graphics appears to permit a host of different views, ranging from multiview orthographic projections to one-, two-, and three-point perspectives. This seeming discrepancy arises in classical graphics as a result of the desire to show a specific relationship among an object, the viewer, and the projection plane, as opposed to the computer-graphics approach of complete independence of all specifications.

4.1.1 Classical Viewing

When an architect draws an image of a building, she knows which side she wishes to display and thus where she should place the viewer in relationship to the building. Each classical view is determined by a specific relationship between the objects and the viewer.

In classical viewing, there is the underlying notion of a **principal face**. The types of objects viewed in real-world applications, such as architecture, tend to be composed of a number of planar faces, each of which can be thought of as a principal face. For a rectangular object, such as a building, there are natural notions of the front, back, top, bottom, right, and left faces. In addition, many real-world objects have faces that meet at right angles; thus, such objects often have three orthogonal directions associated with them.

Figure 4.3 shows some of the main types of views. We start with the most restrictive view for each of the parallel and perspective types, and then move to the less restrictive conditions.

4.1.2 Orthographic Projections

Our first classical view is the **orthographic projection** shown in Figure 4.4. In all orthographic (or orthogonal) views, the projectors are perpendicular to the projection plane. In a **multiview orthographic projection**, we make multiple projections, in

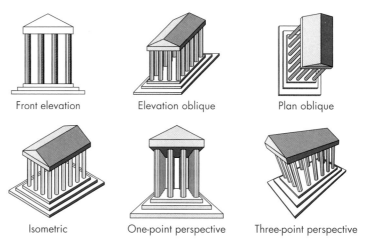

Front elevation   Elevation oblique   Plan oblique

Isometric   One-point perspective   Three-point perspective

FIGURE 4.3   Classical views.

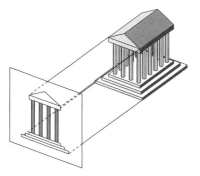

FIGURE 4.4   Orthographic projections.

each case with the projection plane parallel to one of the principal faces of the object. Usually, we use three views—such as the front, top, and right—to display the object. The reason that we produce multiple views should be clear from Figure 4.5. For a box-like object, only the faces parallel to the projection plane appear in the image. A viewer usually needs more than two views to visualize what an object looks like from its multiview orthographic projections. Visualization from these images can require skill on the part of the viewer. The importance of this type of view is that it preserves both distances and angles, and because there is no distortion of either distance or shape, multiview orthographic projections are well suited for working drawings.

4.1.3 Axonometric Projections

If we want to see more principal faces of our box-like object in a single view, we must remove one of our restrictions. In **axonometric** views, the projectors are still

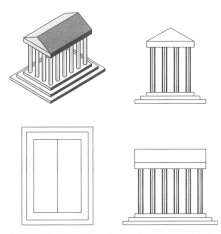

FIGURE 4.5   Temple and three multiview orthographic projections.

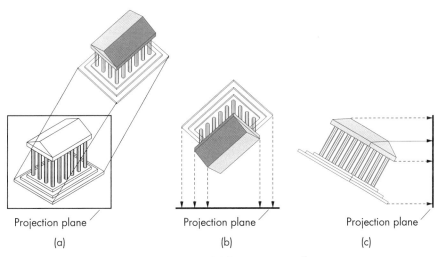

Projection plane

(a)

Projection plane

(b)

Projection plane

(c)

FIGURE 4.6   Axonometric projections. (a) Construction of trimetric-view projections. (b) Top view. (c) Side view.

orthogonal to the projection plane, as shown in Figure 4.6, but the projection plane can have any orientation with respect to the object. If the projection plane is placed symmetrically with respect to the three principal faces that meet at a corner of our rectangular object, then we have an **isometric** view. If the projection plane is placed symmetrically with respect to two of the principal faces, then the view is **dimetric**. The general case is a **trimetric** view. These views are shown in Figure 4.7. Note that in an isometric view, a line segment's length in the image space is shorter than its length measured in the object space. This **foreshortening** of distances is the same

Dimetric   Trimetric   Isometric

FIGURE 4.7   Axonometric views.

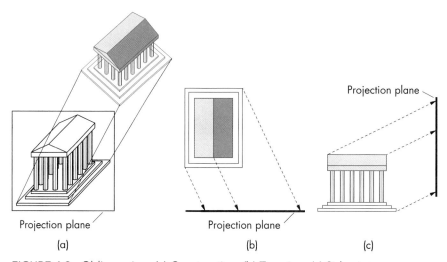

Projection plane

(a)   (b)   (c)

FIGURE 4.8   Oblique view. (a) Construction. (b) Top view. (c) Side view.

in the three principal directions, so we can still make distance measurements. In the dimetric view, however, there are two different foreshortening ratios; in the trimetric view, there are three. Also, although parallel lines are preserved in the image, angles are not. A circle is projected into an ellipse. This distortion is the price we pay for the ability to see more than one principal face in a view that can be produced easily either by hand or by computer. Axonometric views are used extensively in architectural and mechanical design.

4.1.4 Oblique Projections

The **oblique** views are the most general parallel views. We obtain an oblique projection by allowing the projectors to make an arbitrary angle with the projection plane, as shown in Figure 4.8. Consequently, angles in planes parallel to the projection plane are preserved. A circle in a plane parallel to the projection plane is projected into a circle, yet we can see more than one principal face of the object. Oblique views are the most difficult to construct by hand. They are also somewhat unnatural. Most physical viewing devices, including the human visual system, have a lens that is in a fixed relationship with the image plane—usually, the lens is parallel to the plane. Although these devices produce perspective views, if the viewer is far from the object, the views are approximately parallel, but orthogonal, because the projection plane is parallel to the lens. The bellows camera that we used to develop the synthetic-camera model in Section 1.6 has the flexibility to produce approximations to parallel oblique views. One use of such a camera is to create images of buildings in which the sides of the building are parallel rather than converging as they would be in an image created with an orthogonal view with the camera on the ground.

From the application programmer's point of view, there is no significant difference among the different parallel views. The application programmer specifies a type of view—parallel or perspective—and a set of parameters that describe the camera. The problem for the application programmer is how to specify these parameters in the viewing procedures so as best to view an object or to produce a specific classical view.

4.1.5 Perspective Viewing

All perspective views are characterized by **diminution** of size. When objects are moved farther from the viewer, their images become smaller. This size change gives perspective views their natural appearance; however, because the amount by which a line is foreshortened depends on how far the line is from the viewer, we cannot make measurements from a perspective view. Hence, the major use of perspective views is in applications such as architecture and animation, where it is important to achieve natural-looking images.

In the classical perspective views, the viewer is located symmetrically with respect to the projection plane, as shown in Figure 4.9. Thus, the pyramid determined by the window in the projection plane and the center of projection is a symmetric or right

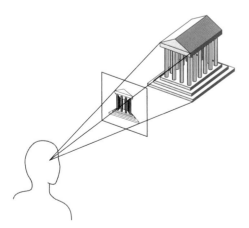

FIGURE 4.9   Perspective viewing.

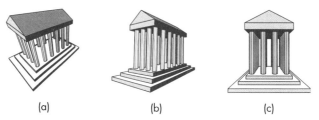

FIGURE 4.10   Classical perspective views. (a) Three-point. (b) Two-point. (c) One-point.

pyramid. This symmetry is caused by the fixed relationship between the back (retina) and lens of the eye for human viewing, or between the back and lens of a camera for standard cameras, and by similar fixed relationships in most physical situations. Some cameras, such as the bellows camera, have movable film backs and can produce general perspective views. The model used in computer graphics includes this general case.

The classical perspective views are usually known as **one-**, **two-**, and **three-point perspectives**. The differences among the three cases are based on how many of the three principal directions in the object are parallel to the projection plane. Consider the three perspective projections of the building shown in Figure 4.10. Any corner of the building includes the three principal directions. In the most general case—the three-point perspective—parallel lines in each of the three principal directions converges to a finite **vanishing point** (Figure 4.10(a)). If we allow one of the principal directions to become parallel to the projection plane, we have a two-point projection (Figure 4.10(b)), in which lines in only two of the principal directions converge. Finally, in the one-point perspective (Figure 4.10(c)), two of the principal directions are parallel to the projection plane, and we have only a single vanishing point. As with parallel viewing, it should be apparent from the programmer's point of view that the three situations are merely special cases of general perspective viewing, which we implement in Section 4.4.

4.2   VIEWING WITH A COMPUTER

We can now return to three-dimensional graphics from a computer perspective. Because viewing in computer graphics is based on the synthetic-camera model, we should be able to construct any of the classical views. However, there is a fundamental difference. All the classical views are based on a particular relationship among the objects, the viewer, and the projectors. In computer graphics, we stress the independence of the object specifications and camera parameters. Hence, to create one of the classical views, the application program must use information about the objects to create and place the proper camera.

Using OpenGL, we will have many options on how and where we carry out viewing. All our approaches will use the powerful transformation capabilities of the GPU. Because every transformation is equivalent to a change of frames, we can develop viewing in terms of the frames and coordinate systems we introduced in Chapter 3. In particular, we will work with object coordinates, camera coordinates, and clip coordinates.

A good starting point is the output of the vertex shader. In Chapters 2 and 3, we used the fact that as long as the vertices output by the vertex shader were within the clipping volume, they continued onto the rasterizer. Hence, in Chapter 2 we were able to specify vertex positions inside the default viewing cube. In Chapter 3, we learned how to scale positions using affine transformations so they would be mapped inside the cube. We also relied on the fact that objects that are sent to the rasterizer are projected with a simple orthographic projection.

Hidden-surface removal, however, occurs after the fragment shader. Consequently, although an object might be blocked from the camera by other objects, even with hidden-surface removal enabled, the rasterizer will still generate fragments for blocked objects within the clipping volume. However, we need more flexibility in both how we specify objects and how we view them. There are four major additions to address:

1. We need the ability to work in the units of the application.

2. We need to position the camera independently of the objects.

3. We want to be able to specify a clipping volume in units related to the application.

4. We want to be able to do either parallel or perspective projections.

We can accomplish all these additions by careful use of transformations: the first three using affine transformations, and the last using a process called perspective normalization. All of these transformations must be carried out either in the application code or in the vertex shader.

We approach all these tasks through the transformation capabilities we developed in Chapter 3. Of the frames that are used in OpenGL, three are important in the viewing process: the object frame, the camera frame, and the clip coordinate frame. In Chapters 2 and 3, we were able to avoid explicitly specifying the first two by using a default in which all three frames were identical. We either directly specified vertex positions in clip coordinates or used an affine transformation to scale objects we wanted to be visible to lie within the clipping cube in clip coordinates. The camera was fixed to be at the origin and pointing in the negative z-direction in clip coordinates.[1]

To get a more flexible way to do viewing, we will separate the process into two fundamental operations. First, we must position and orient the camera. This operation is the job of the model-view transformation. After vertices pass through this

---

1. The default camera can "see" objects behind it if they are in the clipping volume.

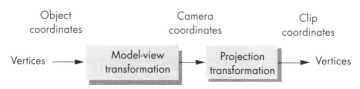

FIGURE 4.11   Viewing transformations.

transformation, they will be represented in eye or camera coordinates. The second step is the application of the projection transformation. This step applies the specified projection—orthographic or perspective—to the vertices and puts objects within the specified clipping volume into the same clipping cube in clip coordinates. One of the functions of either projection will be to allow us to specify a view volume in camera coordinates rather than having to scale our object to fit into the default view volume. These transformations are shown in Figure 4.11.

What we have called the current transformation matrix will be the product of two matrices: the model-view matrix and the projection matrix. The model-view matrix will take vertices in object coordinates and convert them to a representation in camera coordinates and thus must encapsulate the positioning and orientation of the camera. The projection matrix will both carry out the desired projection—either orthogonal or perspective—and convert a viewing volume specified in camera coordinates to fit inside the viewing cube in clip coordinates.

4.3 POSITIONING OF THE CAMERA

In this section, we deal with positioning and orientation of the camera; in Section 4.4, we discuss how we specify the desired projection. Although we will focus on an API that will work well with OpenGL, we also will examine briefly a few other APIs to specify a camera.

4.3.1 Positioning of the Camera Frame

As we saw in Chapter 3, we can specify vertices in any units we choose, and we can define a model-view matrix by a sequence of affine transformations that repositions these vertices. The model-view transformation is the concatenation of a modeling transformation that takes instances of objects in object coordinates and brings them into the world frame. The second part transforms world coordinates to eye coordinates. Because we usually do not need to access world coordinates, we can use the model-view matrix rather than separate modeling and viewing matrices.

Initially, we set the model-view matrix to an identity matrix, so the camera frame and the object frame are identical. Hence, the camera is initially pointing in the negative z-direction (Figure 4.12). In most applications, we model our objects as being located around the origin, so a camera located at the default position with the default orientation does not see all the objects in the scene. Thus, either we must

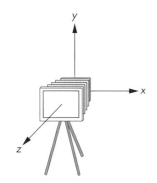

FIGURE 4.12   Initial camera position.

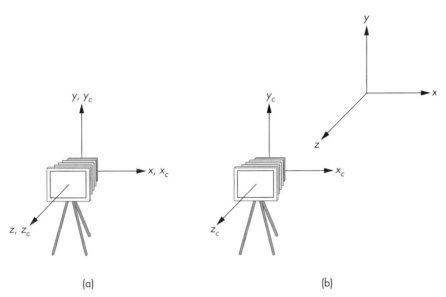

FIGURE 4.13   Movement of the camera and object frames. (a) Initial configuration. (b) Configuration after change in the model-view matrix.

move the camera away from the objects that we wish to have in our image, or the objects must be moved in front of the camera. These are equivalent operations, as either can be looked at as positioning the frame of the camera with respect to the frame of the objects.

It might help to think of a scene in which we have initially specified several objects by specifying all vertices and putting their positions into an array. We start with the model-view matrix set to an identity matrix. Changes to the model-view matrix move the object frame relative to the camera and affect the camera's view of all objects defined *afterward*, because their vertices are specified relative to the repositioned object frame. Equivalently, in terms of the flow of an application program, the projection and model-view matrices are part of its state. We will either apply them to the vertex positions in the application or, more likely, we will send them to the vertex shader where they will be applied automatically whenever vertex data is sent to the shader.

In either case, the sequence illustrated in Figure 4.13 shows the process. In part (a), we have the initial configuration. A vertex specified at $\mathbf{p}$ has the same representation in both frames. In part (b), we have changed the model-view matrix to $\mathbf{C}$ by a sequence of transformations. The two frames are no longer the same, although $\mathbf{C}$ contains the information to move from the camera frame to the object frame or, equivalently, contains the information that moves the camera away from its initial position at the origin of the object frame. A vertex specified at $\mathbf{q}$ *after* the change to the model-view matrix is at $\mathbf{q}$ in the object frame. However, its position in the camera frame is $\mathbf{Cq}$ and can be stored internally within the application or sent to the GPU, where it will be converted to camera coordinates. The viewing transformation will assume that vertex data it starts with is in camera coordinates.

An equivalent view is that the camera is still at the origin of its own frame, and the model-view matrix is applied to primitives specified in this system. In practice, you can use either view. But be sure to take great care regarding where in your program the primitives are specified relative to changes in the model-view matrix.

At any given time, the model-view matrix encapsulates the relationship between the camera frame and the object frame. Although combining the modeling and viewing transformations into a single matrix may initially cause confusion, on closer examination this approach is a good one. If we regard the camera as an object with geometric properties, then transformations that alter the position and orientation of objects should also affect the position and orientation of the camera relative to these objects.

The next problem is how we specify the desired position of the camera and then implement camera positioning in OpenGL. We outline three approaches, one in this section and two in Section 4.3.2. Two others are given as exercises (Exercises 4.2 and 4.3).

Our first approach is to specify the position indirectly by applying a sequence of rotations and translations to the model-view matrix. This approach is a direct application of the instance transformation that we presented in Chapter 3, but we must be careful for two reasons. First, we usually want to specify the camera's position and orientation *before* we position any objects in the scene.[2] Second, the order of transformations on the camera may appear to be backward from what you might expect.

Consider an object centered at the origin. The camera is in its initial position, also at the origin, pointing down the negative z-axis. Suppose that we want an image of the faces of the object that point in the positive z-direction. We must move the camera *away* from the origin. If we allow the camera to remain pointing in the negative z-direction, then we want to move the camera backward along the positive z-axis, and the proper transformation is

$$\mathbf{T} = \begin{bmatrix} 1 & 0 & 0 & 0 \\ 0 & 1 & 0 & 0 \\ 0 & 0 & 1 & -d \\ 0 & 0 & 0 & 1 \end{bmatrix},$$

where d is a positive number.

Many people find it helpful to interpret this operation as moving the camera frame relative to the object frame. This point of view has a basis in classical viewing. In computer graphics, we usually think of objects as being positioned in a fixed frame,

---

2. In an animation, where in the program we specify the position of the camera depends on whether we wish to attach the camera to a particular object or to place the camera in a fixed position in the scene (see Exercise 4.3).

and it is the viewer who must move to the right position to achieve the desired view. In classical viewing, the viewer dominates. Conceptually, we do viewing by picking up the object, orienting it as desired, and bringing it to the desired location. One consequence of the classical approach is that distances are measured from the viewer to the object, rather than—as in most physically based systems—from the object to the viewer. Classical viewing often resulted in a left-handed camera frame. Early graphics systems followed the classical approach by having modeling in right-handed coordinates and viewing in left-handed coordinates—a decision that, although technically correct, caused confusion among users. When we are working in camera coordinates, we will measure distances from the camera, which is consistent with classical viewing. In OpenGL, the internal frames are right handed. Fortunately, because the application program works primarily in object coordinates, the application programmer usually does not see any of the internal representations and thus does not have to worry about these alternate perspectives on viewing.

Suppose that we want to look at the same object from the positive *x*-axis. Now, not only do we have to move away from the object, but we also have to rotate the camera about the *y*-axis, as shown in Figure 4.14. We must do the translation after we rotate the camera by 90 degrees about the *y*-axis. In the program, the calls must be in the reverse order, as we discussed in Section 3.11, so we expect to see code like the following:

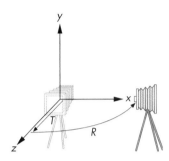

FIGURE 4.14   Positioning of the camera.

```
mat4 model_view;
model_view = Translate(0.0, 0.0, -d)*RotateX(-90.0);
```

In terms of the two frames, first we rotate the object frame relative to the camera frame, and then we move the two frames apart.

In Chapters 2 and 3, we were able to show simple three-dimensional examples by using an identity matrix as the default projection matrix. That default setting has the effect of creating an orthographic projection with the camera at the origin, pointed in the negative *z*-direction. In our cube example in Chapter 3, we rotated the cube to see the desired faces. As we just discussed, rotating the cube is equivalent to rotating the frame of the cube with respect to the frame of the camera; we could have achieved the same view by rotating the camera relative to the cube. We can extend this strategy of translating and rotating the camera to create other orthographic views. Perspective views require changes to the default projection.

Consider creating an isometric view of the cube. Suppose that again we start with a cube centered at the origin and aligned with the axes. Because the default camera is in the middle of the cube, we want to move the camera away from the cube by a translation. We obtain an isometric view when the camera is located symmetrically with respect to three adjacent faces of the cube; for example, anywhere along the line from the origin through the point (1, 1, 1). We can move the cube away from the camera and then rotate the cube to achieve the desired view or, equivalently, move the camera away from the cube and then rotate it to point at the cube.

Starting with the default camera, suppose that we are now looking at the cube from somewhere on the positive *z*-axis. We can obtain one of the eight isometric

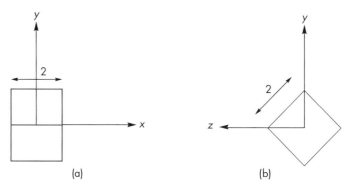

FIGURE 4.15   Cube after rotation about x-axis. (a) View from positive z-axis. (b) View from positive y-axis.

views—there is one for each vertex—by first rotating the cube about the x-axis until we see the two faces symmetrically, as shown in Figure 4.15(a). Clearly, we obtain this view by rotating the cube by 45 degrees. The second rotation is about the y-axis. We rotate the cube until we get the desired isometric. The required angle of rotation is -35.26 degrees about the y-axis. This second angle of rotation may not seem obvious. Consider what happens to the cube after the first rotation. From our position on the positive z-axis, the cube appears as shown in Figure 4.15(a). The original corner vertex at $(-1, 1, 1)$ has been transformed to $(-1, 0, \sqrt{2})$. If we look at the cube from the x-axis, as in Figure 4.15(b), we see that we want to rotate the right vertex to the y-axis. The right triangle that determines this angle has sides of 1 and $\sqrt{2}$, which correspond to an angle of 35.26 degrees. However, we need a clockwise rotation, so the angle must be negative. Finally, we move the camera away from the origin. Thus, our strategy is first to rotate the frame of the camera relative to the frame of the object and then to separate the two frames; the model-view matrix is of the form

$$\mathbf{M} = \mathbf{TR}_x\mathbf{R}_y.$$

We obtain this model-view matrix for an isometric by multiplying the matrices in homogeneous coordinates. The concatenation of the rotation matrices yields

$$\mathbf{R} = \mathbf{R}_x\mathbf{R}_y = \begin{bmatrix} 1 & 0 & 0 & 0 \\ 0 & \sqrt{6}/3 & -\sqrt{3}/3 & 0 \\ 0 & \sqrt{3}/3 & \sqrt{6}/3 & 0 \\ 0 & 0 & 0 & 1 \end{bmatrix} \begin{bmatrix} \sqrt{2}/2 & 0 & \sqrt{2}/2 & 0 \\ 0 & 1 & 0 & 0 \\ -\sqrt{2}/2 & 0 & \sqrt{2}/2 & 0 \\ 0 & 0 & 0 & 1 \end{bmatrix}$$

$$= \begin{bmatrix} \sqrt{2}/2 & 0 & \sqrt{2}/2 & 0 \\ \sqrt{6}/6 & \sqrt{6}/3 & -\sqrt{6}/6 & 0 \\ -\sqrt{3}/3 & \sqrt{3}/3 & \sqrt{3}/3 & 0 \\ 0 & 0 & 0 & 1 \end{bmatrix}.$$

It is simple to verify that the original vertex $(-1, 1, 1)$ is correctly transformed to $(0, 0, \sqrt{3})$ by this matrix. If we concatenate in the translation by $(0, 0, -d)$, the matrix becomes

$$\mathbf{TR} = \begin{bmatrix} \sqrt{2}/2 & 0 & \sqrt{2}/2 & 0 \\ \sqrt{6}/6 & \sqrt{6}/3 & -\sqrt{6}/6 & 0 \\ -\sqrt{3}/3 & \sqrt{3}/3 & \sqrt{3}/3 & -d \\ 0 & 0 & 0 & 1 \end{bmatrix}.$$

In OpenGL, the code for setting the model-view matrix is as follows:

```
mat4 model_view;
model_view = Translate(0.0, 0.0, -d)*RotateX(35.26)*RotateY(45.0);
```

We have gone from a representation of our objects in object coordinates to one in camera coordinates. Rotation and translation do not affect the size of an object nor, equivalently, the size of its orthographic projection. However, these transformations can affect whether or not objects are clipped. Because the clipping volume is measured relative to the camera, if, for example, we translate the object away from the camera, it may no longer lie within the clipping volume. Hence, even though the projection of the object is unchanged and the camera still points at it, the object would not be in the image.

4.3.2 Two Viewing APIs

The construction of the model-view matrix for an isometric view is a little unsatisfying. Although the approach was intuitive, an interface that requires us to compute the individual angles before specifying the transformations is a poor one for an application program. We can take a different approach to positioning the camera—an approach that is similar to that used by PHIGS, one of the original standard APIs for three-dimensional graphics. Our starting point is again the object frame. We describe the camera's position and orientation in this frame. The precise type of image that we wish to obtain—perspective or parallel—is determined separately by the specification of the projection matrix. This second part of the viewing process is often called the **normalization transformation**. We approach this problem as one of a change in frames. Again, we think of the camera as positioned initially at the origin, pointed in the negative z-direction. Its desired location is centered at a point called the **view-reference point** (**VRP**; Figure 4.16), whose position is given in the object frame. The user executes a function such as

```
set_view_reference_point(x, y, z);
```

to specify this position. Next, we want to specify the orientation of the camera. We can divide this specification into two parts: specification of the **view-plane normal** (**VPN**) and specification of the **view-up vector** (**VUP**). The VPN (**n** in Figure 4.16) gives the orientation of the projection plane or back of the camera. The orientation

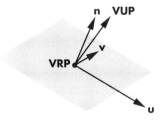

FIGURE 4.16   Camera frame.

of a plane is determined by that plane's normal, and thus part of the API is a function such as

```
set_view_plane_normal(nx, ny, nz);
```

The orientation of the plane does not specify what direction is up from the camera's perspective. Given only the VPN, we can rotate the camera with its back in this plane. The specification of the VUP fixes the camera and is performed by a function such as

```
set_view_up(vup_x, vup_y, vup_z);
```

FIGURE 4.17 Determination of the view-up vector.

We project the VUP vector on the view plane to obtain the up-direction vector $\mathbf{v}$ (Figure 4.17). Use of the projection allows the user to specify any vector not parallel to $\mathbf{v}$, rather than being forced to compute a vector lying in the projection plane. The vector $\mathbf{v}$ is orthogonal to $\mathbf{n}$. We can use the cross product to obtain a third orthogonal direction $\mathbf{u}$. This new orthogonal coordinate system usually is referred to as either the **viewing-coordinate system** or the **u-v-n system**. With the addition of the VRP, we have the desired camera frame. The matrix that does the change of frames is the **view-orientation matrix** and is equivalent to the viewing component of the model-view matrix.

We can derive this matrix using rotations and translations in homogeneous coordinates. We start with the specifications of the view-reference point,

$$\mathbf{p} = \begin{bmatrix} x \\ y \\ z \\ 1 \end{bmatrix},$$

the view-plane normal,

$$\mathbf{n} = \begin{bmatrix} n_x \\ n_y \\ n_z \\ 0 \end{bmatrix},$$

and the view-up vector,

$$\mathbf{v_{up}} = \begin{bmatrix} v_{up_x} \\ v_{up_y} \\ v_{up_z} \\ 0 \end{bmatrix}.$$

We construct a new frame with the view-reference point as its origin, the view-plane normal as one coordinate direction, and two other orthogonal directions that we call $\mathbf{u}$ and $\mathbf{v}$. Our default is that the original x, y, z axes become u, v, n, respectively. The view-reference point can be handled through a simple translation $\mathbf{T}(-x, -y, -z)$ from the viewing frame to the original origin. The rest of the model-view matrix is determined by a rotation so that the model-view matrix $\mathbf{V}$ is of the form

$$\mathbf{V} = \mathbf{TR}.$$

The direction $\mathbf{v}$ must be orthogonal to $\mathbf{n}$; hence,

$$\mathbf{n} \cdot \mathbf{v} = 0.$$

Figure 4.17 shows that $\mathbf{v}$ is the projection of $\mathbf{v_{up}}$ into the plane formed by $\mathbf{n}$ and $\mathbf{v_{up}}$ and thus must be a linear combination of these two vectors,

$$\mathbf{v} = \alpha\mathbf{n} + \beta\mathbf{v_{up}}.$$

If we temporarily ignore the length of the vectors, then we can set $\beta = 1$ and solve for

$$\alpha = -\frac{\mathbf{v_{up}} \cdot \mathbf{n}}{\mathbf{n} \cdot \mathbf{n}}$$

and

$$\mathbf{v} = \mathbf{v_{up}} - \frac{\mathbf{v_{up}} \cdot \mathbf{n}}{\mathbf{n} \cdot \mathbf{n}} \mathbf{n}.$$

We can find the third orthogonal direction by taking the cross product

$$\mathbf{u} = \mathbf{v} \times \mathbf{n}.$$

These vectors do not generally have unit length. We can normalize each independently, obtaining three unit-length vectors $\mathbf{u'}$, $\mathbf{v'}$, and $\mathbf{n'}$. The matrix

$$\mathbf{A} = \begin{bmatrix} u'_x & v'_x & n'_x & 0 \\ u'_y & v'_y & n'_y & 0 \\ u'_z & v'_z & n'_z & 0 \\ 0 & 0 & 0 & 1 \end{bmatrix}$$

is a rotation matrix that orients a vector in the $\mathbf{u'v'n'}$ system with respect to the original system. However, we really want to go in the opposite direction to obtain the representation of vectors in the original system in the $\mathbf{u'v'n'}$ system. We want $\mathbf{A}^{-1}$, but because $\mathbf{A}$ is a rotation matrix, the desired matrix $\mathbf{R}$ is

$$\mathbf{R} = \mathbf{A}^{-1} = \mathbf{A}^{T}.$$

Finally, multiplying by the translation matrix $\mathbf{T}$, we have

$$\mathbf{V} = \mathbf{RT} = \begin{bmatrix} u'_x & u'_y & u'_z & -xu'_x - yu'_y - zu'_z \\ v'_x & v'_y & v'_z & -xv'_x - yv'_y - zv'_z \\ n'_x & n'_y & n'_z & -xn'_x - yn'_y - zn'_z \\ 0 & 0 & 0 & 1 \end{bmatrix}.$$

Note that, in this case, the translation matrix is on the right, whereas in our first derivation it was on the left. One way to interpret this difference is that in our first derivation, we first rotated one of the frames and then pushed the frames apart in a direction represented in the camera frame. In the second derivation, the camera position was specified in the object frame. Another way to understand this difference is to note that the matrices $\mathbf{RT}$ and $\mathbf{TR}$ have similar forms. The rotation parts of the product—the upper-left 3×3 submatrices—are identical, as are the bottom rows. The top three elements in the right column differ because the frame of the rotation affects the translation coefficients in $\mathbf{RT}$ and does not affect them in $\mathbf{TR}$. For our isometric example,

$$\mathbf{n} = \begin{bmatrix} -1 \\ 1 \\ 1 \\ 0 \end{bmatrix},$$

$$\mathbf{v_{up}} = \begin{bmatrix} 0 \\ 1 \\ 0 \\ 0 \end{bmatrix}.$$

The camera position must be along a diagonal in the original frame. If we use

$$\mathbf{p} = \frac{\sqrt{3}}{3} \begin{bmatrix} -d \\ d \\ d \\ 1 \end{bmatrix},$$

we obtain the same model-view matrix that we derived in Section 4.3.1.

4.3.3 The Look-At Function

The use of the VRP, VPN, and VUP is but one way to provide an API for specifying the position of a camera. In many situations, a more direct method is appropriate. Consider the situation illustrated in Figure 4.18. Here a camera is located at a point $\mathbf{e}$ called the **eye point**, specified in the object frame, and it is pointed at a second point $\mathbf{a}$, called the **at point**. These points determine a VPN and a VRP. The VPN is given by

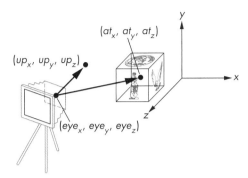

FIGURE 4.18   Look-at positioning.

the vector formed by point subtraction between the eyepoint and the at point,

$$\mathbf{vpn} = \mathbf{a} - \mathbf{e},$$

and normalizing it,

$$\mathbf{n} = \frac{\mathbf{vpn}}{|\mathbf{vpn}|}.$$

The view-reference point is the eye point. Hence, we need only to add the desired up direction for the camera, and a function to construct the desired matrix LookAt could be of the form[3]

```
mat4 LookAt(point4 eye, point4 at, vec4 up)
```

or the equivalent form

```
mat4 LookAt(GLfloat eyex, GLfloat eyey, GLfloat eyez,
            GLfloat atx, GLfloat aty, GLfloat atz,
            GLfloat upx, GLfloat upy, GLfloat upz);
```

Note that once we have computed the vector **vpn**, we can proceed as we did with forming the transformation in the previous section. A slightly simpler computation would be to form a vector perpendicular to $\mathbf{n}$ and $\mathbf{v_{up}}$ by taking their cross product and normalizing it,

$$\mathbf{u} = \frac{\mathbf{v_{up}} \times \mathbf{n}}{|\mathbf{v_{up}} \times \mathbf{n}|}.$$

3. Because we are working in homogeneous coordinates, vup can be a vec4 type if the fourth component is a zero.

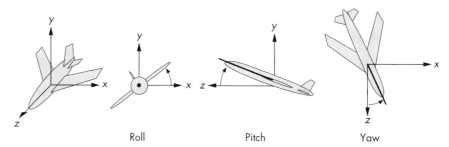

FIGURE 4.19   Roll, pitch, and yaw.

Finally, we get the normalized projection of the up vector onto the camera plane by taking a second cross product

$$\mathbf{v} = \frac{\mathbf{n} \times \mathbf{u}}{|\mathbf{n} \times \mathbf{u}|}.$$

Note that we can use the standard rotations, translations, and scalings as part of defining our objects. Although these transformations will also alter the model-view matrix, it is often helpful conceptually to consider the use of LookAt as positioning the objects and subsequent operations that affect the model-view matrix as positioning the camera.

Note that whereas functions, such as LookAt, that position the camera alter the model-view matrix and are specified in object coordinates, the functions that we introduce to form the projection matrix will be specified in eye coordinates.

4.3.4 Other Viewing APIs

In many applications, neither of the viewing interfaces that we have presented is appropriate. Consider a flight-simulation application. The pilot using the simulator usually uses three angles—**roll**, **pitch**, and **yaw**—to specify her orientation. These angles are specified relative to the center of mass of the vehicle and to a coordinate system aligned along the axes of the vehicle, as shown in Figure 4.19. Hence, the pilot sees an object in terms of the three angles and of the distance from the object to the center of mass of her vehicle. A viewing transformation can be constructed (Exercise 4.2) from these specifications from a translation and three simple rotations.

Viewing in many applications is most naturally specified in polar—rather than rectilinear—coordinates. Applications involving objects that rotate about other objects fit this category. For example, consider the specification of a star in the sky. Its direction from a viewer is given by its elevation and azimuth (Figure 4.20). The **elevation** is the angle above the plane of the viewer at which the star appears. By defining a normal at the point that the viewer is located and using this normal to define a plane, we define the elevation, regardless of whether or not the viewer is actually standing on a plane. We can form two other axes in this plane, creating a viewing-coordinate system. The **azimuth** is the angle measured from an axis in this plane to the projec-

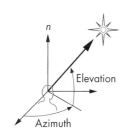

FIGURE 4.20   Elevation and azimuth.

tion onto the plane of the line between the viewer and the star. The camera can still be rotated about the direction it is pointed by a **twist angle**.

4.4 PARALLEL PROJECTIONS

A parallel projection is the limit of a perspective projection in which the center of projection is infinitely far from the objects being viewed, resulting in projectors that are parallel rather than converging at the center of projection. Equivalently, a parallel projection is what we would get if we had a telephoto lens with an infinite focal length. Rather than first deriving the equations for a perspective projection and computing their limiting behavior, we will derive the equations for parallel projections directly using the fact that we know in advance that the projectors are parallel and point in a direction of projection.

4.4.1 Orthogonal Projections

Orthogonal or **orthographic** projections are a special case of parallel projections, in which the projectors are perpendicular to the view plane. In terms of a camera, orthogonal projections correspond to a camera with a back plane parallel to the lens, which has an infinite focal length. Figure 4.21 shows an orthogonal projection with the projection plane $z = 0$. As points are projected into this plane, they retain their x and y values, and the equations of projection are

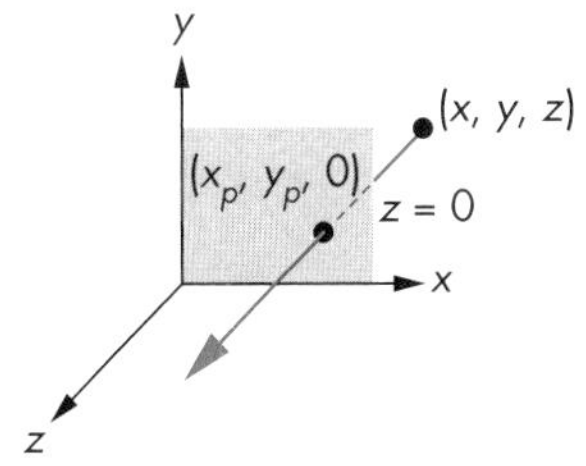

$$x_p = x,$$

$$y_p = y,$$

$$z_p = 0.$$

FIGURE 4.21   Orthogonal projection.

We can write this result using our original homogeneous coordinates:

$$
\begin{bmatrix} x_p \\ y_p \\ z_p \\ 1 \end{bmatrix}
=
\begin{bmatrix} 1 & 0 & 0 & 0 \\ 0 & 1 & 0 & 0 \\ 0 & 0 & 0 & 0 \\ 0 & 0 & 0 & 1 \end{bmatrix}
\begin{bmatrix} x \\ y \\ z \\ 1 \end{bmatrix}.
$$

To prepare ourselves for a more general orthogonal projection, we can write this expression as

$$\mathbf{q} = \mathbf{MIp},$$

where

$$
\mathbf{p} =
\begin{bmatrix} x \\ y \\ z \\ 1 \end{bmatrix},
$$

I is a 4 × 4 identity matrix, and

$$\mathbf{M} = \begin{bmatrix} 1 & 0 & 0 & 0 \\ 0 & 1 & 0 & 0 \\ 0 & 0 & 0 & 0 \\ 0 & 0 & 0 & 1 \end{bmatrix}.$$

The projection described by **M** is carried out by the hardware after the vertex shader. Hence, only those objects inside the cube of side length 2 centered at the origin will be projected and possibly visible. If we want to change which objects are visible, we can replace the identity matrix by a transformation **N** that we can carry out either in the application or in the vertex shader, which will give us control over the clipping volume. For example, if we replace **I** with a scaling matrix, we can see more or fewer objects.

4.4.2 Parallel Viewing with OpenGL

We will focus on a single orthogonal viewing function in which the view volume is a right parallelepiped, as shown in Figure 4.22. The sides of the clipping volume are the four planes

$x = right,$

$x = left,$

$y = top,$

$y = bottom.$

The near (front) clipping plane is located a distance `near` from the origin, and the far (back) clipping plane is at a distance `far` from the origin. All these values are in camera coordinates. We will derive a function

```
mat4 Ortho(GLfloat left, GLfloat right, GLfloat bottom, GLfloat top,
           GLfloat near, GLfloat far)
```

which will form the projection matrix **N**.[4]

Although mathematically we get a parallel view by moving the camera to infinity, because the projectors are parallel, we can slide this camera in the direction of projection without changing the projection. Consequently, it is helpful to think of an orthogonal camera located initially at the origin in camera coordinates with the view volume determined by

---

4. Users of Microsoft Windows may have to change the identifiers `near` and `far` because `far` is a reserved word in Visual C++.

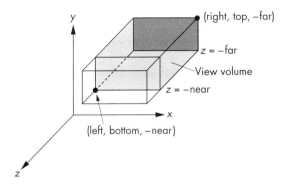

FIGURE 4.22   Orthographic viewing.

$$x = \pm 1,$$

$$y = \pm 1,$$

$$z = \pm 1$$

as the default behavior. Equivalently, we are applying an identity projection matrix for **N**. We will derive a nonidentity matrix **N** using translation and scaling that will transform vertices in camera coordinates to fit inside the default view volume, a process called **projection normalization.** This matrix is what will be produced by `Ortho`. Note that we are forced to take this approach because the final projection carried out by the GPU is fixed. Nevertheless, the normalization process is efficient and will allow us to carry out parallel and perspective projections with the same pipeline.

4.4.3 Projection Normalization

When we introduced projection in Chapter 1 and looked at classical projection earlier in this chapter, we viewed it as a technique that took the specification of points in three dimensions and mapped them to points on a two-dimensional projection surface. Such a transformation is not invertible, because all points along a projector map into the same point on the projection surface.

In computer graphics systems, we adopt a slightly different approach. First, we work in four dimensions using homogeneous coordinates. Second, we retain depth information—distance along a projector—as long as possible so that we can do hidden-surface removal later in the pipeline. Third, we use projection normalization, to convert all projections into orthogonal projections by first distorting the objects such that the orthogonal projection of the distorted objects is the same as the desired projection of the original objects. This technique is shown in Figure 4.23. The concatenation of the **normalization matrix**, which carries out the distortion and the

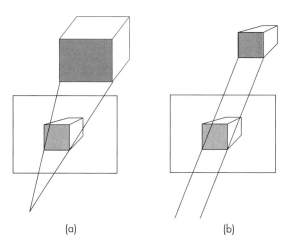

FIGURE 4.23   Predistortion of objects. (a) Perspective view. (b) Orthographic projection of distorted object.

FIGURE 4.24   Normalization transformation.

simple orthogonal projection matrix from Section 4.4.2, as shown in Figure 4.24, yields a homogeneous coordinate matrix that produces the desired projection.

One advantage of this approach is that we can design the normalization matrix so that view volume is distorted into the **canonical view volume**, which is the cube defined by the planes

$x \pm 1,$

$y \pm 1,$

$z \pm 1.$

Besides the advantage of having both perspective and parallel views supported by the same pipeline by loading in the proper normalization matrix, the canonical view volume simplifies the clipping process because the sides are aligned with the coordinate axes.

The normalization process defines what most systems call the **projection matrix**. The projection matrix brings objects into four-dimensional clip coordinates, and the subsequent perspective division converts vertices to a representation in three-dimensional normalized device coordinates. Values in normalized device coordinates are later mapped to window coordinates by the viewport transformation. Here we are concerned with the first step—deriving the projection matrix.

4.4.4 Orthogonal-Projection Matrices

Although parallel viewing is a special case of perspective viewing, we start with orthogonal parallel viewing and later extend the normalization technique to perspective viewing.

In OpenGL, the default projection matrix is an identity matrix, or equivalently, what we would get from the following code:

```
mat4 N = Ortho(-1.0, 1.0, -1.0, 1.0, -1.0, 1.0);
```

The view volume is in fact the canonical view volume. Points within the cube defined by the sides $x \pm 1$, $y \pm 1$, and $z \pm 1$ are mapped to the same cube. Points outside this cube remain outside the cube. As trivial as this observation may seem, it indicates that we can get the desired projection matrix for the general orthogonal view by finding a matrix that maps the right parallelepiped specified by Ortho to this same cube.

Before we do so, recall that the last two parameters in Ortho are distances to the near and far planes measured from a camera at the origin pointed in the negative z-direction. Thus, the near plane is at $z = 1.0$, which is behind the camera, and the far plane is at $z = -1.0$, which is in front of the camera. Although the projectors are parallel and an orthographic projection is conceptually akin to having a camera with a long telephoto lens located far from the objects, the importance of the near and far distances in Ortho is that they determine which objects are clipped out.

Now suppose that, instead, we set the Ortho parameters by the following function call:

```
mat4 N = Ortho(left, right, bottom, top, near, far);
```

We now have specified a right parallelepiped view volume whose right side (relative to the camera) is the plane $x = left$, whose left side is the plane $x = right$, whose top is the plane $y = top$, and whose bottom is the plane $y = bottom$. The front is the near clipping plane $z = -near$, and the back is the far clipping plane $z = -far$. The projection matrix that OpenGL sets up is the matrix that transforms this volume to the cube centered at the origin with sides of length 2, which is shown in Figure 4.25. This matrix converts the vertices that specify our objects to vertices within this canonical view volume, by scaling and translating them. Consequently, vertices are transformed such that vertices within the specified view volume are transformed to vertices within the canonical view volume, and vertices outside the specified view volume are transformed to vertices outside the canonical view volume. Putting everything together, we see that the projection matrix is determined by the type of view and the view volume specified in Ortho, and that these specifications are relative to the camera. The positioning and orientation of the camera are determined by the model-view matrix. These two matrices are concatenated together, and objects have their vertices transformed by this matrix product.

We can use our knowledge of affine transformations to find this projection matrix. There are two tasks that we need to do. First, we must move the center of the

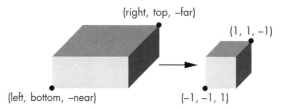

FIGURE 4.25 Mapping a view volume to the canonical view volume.

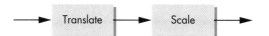

FIGURE 4.26 Affine transformations for normalization.

specified view volume to the center of the canonical view volume (the origin) by doing a translation. Second, we must scale the sides of the specified view volume to each
have a length of 2 (see Figure 4.25). Hence, the two transformations are

$$\mathbf{T} = \mathbf{T}(-(right + left)/2, -(top + bottom)/2, +(far + near)/2)$$

and

$$\mathbf{S} = \mathbf{S}(2/(right - left), 2/(top - bottom), 2/(near - far)),$$

and they can be concatenated together (Figure 4.26) to form the projection matrix

$$\mathbf{N} = \mathbf{ST} = \begin{bmatrix} \frac{2}{right-left} & 0 & 0 & -\frac{left+right}{right-left} \\ 0 & \frac{2}{top-bottom} & 0 & -\frac{top+bottom}{top-bottom} \\ 0 & 0 & -\frac{2}{far-near} & -\frac{far+near}{far-near} \\ 0 & 0 & 0 & 1 \end{bmatrix}.$$

This matrix maps the near clipping plane, $z = -near$, to the plane $z = -1$ and the
far clipping plane, $z = -far$, to the plane $z = 1$. Because the camera is pointing in the
negative z-direction, the projectors are directed from infinity on the negative z-axis
toward the origin.

4.4.5 Oblique Projections
Using Ortho, we have only a limited class of parallel projections—namely, only those
for which the projectors are orthogonal to the projection plane. As we saw earlier in

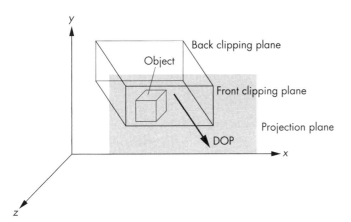

FIGURE 4.28 Oblique clipping volume.

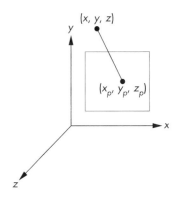

FIGURE 4.27 Oblique projection.

this chapter, oblique parallel projections are useful in many fields.[5] We could develop an oblique projection matrix directly; instead, however, we follow the process that we used for the general orthogonal projection. We convert the desired projection to a canonical orthogonal projection of distorted objects.

An oblique projection can be characterized by the angle that the projectors make with the projection plane, as shown in Figure 4.27. In APIs that support general parallel viewing, the view volume for an oblique projection has the near and far clipping planes parallel to the view plane, and the right, left, top, and bottom planes parallel to the direction of projection, as shown in Figure 4.28. We can derive the equations for oblique projections by considering the top and side views in Figure 4.29, which shows a projector and the projection plane $z = 0$. The angles θ and ϕ characterize the degree of obliqueness. In drafting, projections such as the cavalier and cabinet projections are determined by specific values of these angles. However, these angles are not the only possible interface (see Exercises 4.9 and 4.10).

If we consider the top view, we can find x_p by noting that

$$\tan \theta = \frac{z}{x_p - x},$$

and thus

$$x_p = x + z \cot \theta.$$

Likewise,

$$y_p = y + z \cot \phi.$$

---

5. Note that without oblique projections we cannot draw coordinate axes in the way that we have been doing in this book (see Exercise 4.15).

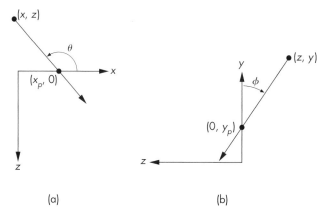

FIGURE 4.29   Oblique projection. (a) Top view. (b) Side view.

Using the equation for the projection plane

$$z_p = 0,$$

we can write these results in terms of a homogeneous-coordinate matrix

$$\mathbf{P} = \begin{bmatrix} 1 & 0 & \cot\theta & 0 \\ 0 & 1 & \cot\phi & 0 \\ 0 & 0 & 0 & 0 \\ 0 & 0 & 0 & 1 \end{bmatrix}.$$

Following our strategy of the previous example, we can break $\mathbf{P}$ into the product

$$\mathbf{P} = \mathbf{M}_{\text{orth}}\mathbf{H}(\theta, \phi) = \begin{bmatrix} 1 & 0 & 0 & 0 \\ 0 & 1 & 0 & 0 \\ 0 & 0 & 0 & 0 \\ 0 & 0 & 0 & 1 \end{bmatrix} \begin{bmatrix} 1 & 0 & \cot\theta & 0 \\ 0 & 1 & \cot\phi & 0 \\ 0 & 0 & 1 & 0 \\ 0 & 0 & 0 & 1 \end{bmatrix},$$

where $\mathbf{H}(\theta, \phi)$ is a shearing matrix. Thus, we can implement an oblique projection by first doing a shear of the objects by $\mathbf{H}(\theta, \phi)$ and then doing an orthographic projection. Figure 4.30 shows the effect of $\mathbf{H}(\theta, \phi)$ on an object—a cube—inside an oblique view volume. The sides of the clipping volume become orthogonal to the view plane, but the sides of the cube become oblique as they are affected by the same shear transformation. However, the orthographic projection of the distorted cube is identical to the oblique projection of the undistorted cube.

We are not finished, because the view volume created by the shear is not our canonical view volume. We have to apply the same scaling and translation matrices that we used in Section 4.4.4. Hence, the transformation

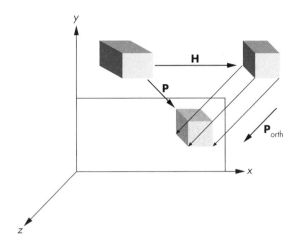

FIGURE 4.30   Effect of shear transformation.

$$
\mathbf{ST} = \begin{bmatrix}
\frac{2}{right-left} & 0 & 0 & -\frac{right+left}{right-left} \\
0 & \frac{2}{top-bottom} & 0 & -\frac{top+bottom}{top-bottom} \\
0 & 0 & -\frac{2}{far-near} & -\frac{far+near}{near-far} \\
0 & 0 & 0 & 1
\end{bmatrix}
$$

must be inserted after the shear and before the final orthographic projection, so the final matrix is

$$
\mathbf{N} = \mathbf{M}_{\text{orth}}\mathbf{STH}.
$$

The values of *left*, *right*, *bottom*, and *top* are the vertices of the right parallelepiped view volume created by the shear. These values depend on how the sides of the original view volume are communicated through the application program; they may have to be determined from the results of the shear to the corners of the original view volume. One way to do this calculation is shown in Figure 4.29.

The specification for an oblique projection can be through the angles θ and ψ that projectors make with the projection plane. The parameters *near* and *far* are not changed by the shear. However, the x and y values of where the sides of the view volume intersect the near plane are changed by the shear and become *left*, *right*, *top*, and *bottom*. If these points of intersection are $(x_{\min}, near)$, $(x_{\max}, near)$, $(y_{\min}, near)$, and $(y_{\max}, near)$, then our derivation of shear in Chapter 3 yields the relationships

$$left = x_{\min} - near * \cot \theta,$$

$$right = x_{\max} - near * \cot \theta,$$

$$top = y_{\max} - near * \cot \phi,$$

$$bottom = y_{\min} - near * \cot \phi.$$

4.4.6 An Interactive Viewer

In this section, we extend the rotating cube program to include both the model-view matrix and an orthogonal projection matrix whose parameters can be set interactively. As in our previous examples with the cube, we have choices as to where to apply our transformations. In this example, we will send the model-view and projection matrices to the vertex shader. Because the model-view matrix can be used to both transform an object and position the camera, in this example we will not use the mouse function and instead focus on camera position and the orthogonal projection. It will be straightforward to bring back the mouse and idle callbacks later to restart the rotation of the cube.

The colored cube is centered at the origin in object coordinates so wherever we place the camera, the `at` point is at the origin. Let's position the camera in polar coordinates so the `eye` point has coordinates

$$\mathbf{eye} = \begin{bmatrix} r\cos\theta \\ r\sin\theta\cos\phi \\ r\sin\theta\sin\phi \end{bmatrix},$$

where the radius r is the distance from the origin. We can let the up direction be the y-direction in object coordinates. These values specify a model-view matrix through the LookAt function. In this example, we will send both a model-view and a projection matrix to the vertex shader with the following display callback:

```
void display( )
{
    glClear(GL_COLOR_BUFFER_BIT | GL_DEPTH_BUFFER_BIT);
    eye[0] = radius*cos(theta);
    eye[1] = radius*sin(theta)*cos(phi);
    eye[2] = radius*sin(theta)*sin(phi);
    model_view = LookAt(eye, at, up);
    projection = Ortho(left, right, bottom, top, near, far);
    glUniformMatrix4fv(matrix_loc, 1, GL_TRUE, model_view);
    glUniformMatrix4fv(projection_loc, 1, GL_TRUE, projection);
    glDrawArrays(GL_TRIANGLES, 0, N);
    glutSwapBuffers();
}
```

The corresponding vertex shader is

```
in vec4 vPosition;
in vec4 vColor;
out vec4 color;
uniform mat4 model_view;
uniform mat4 projection;
void main()
{
  gl_Position = projection*model_view*vPosition;
  color = vColor;
}
```

We can use the keyboard callback to alter the projection matrix and the camera position. The position of the camera is controlled by the r, o, and p keys, and the sides of the viewing parallelpiped by the x, y, and z keys.

```
void mykey(unsigned char key, int mousex, int mousey)
{
    float dr = M_PI/180.0*5.0; // 5 degrees in radians
    if(key=='q'||key=='Q') exit(0);
    if(key == 'x') {left *= 1.1; right *= 1.1;}
    if(key == 'X') {left *= 0.9; right *= 0.9;}
    if(key == 'y') {bottom *= 1.1; top *= 1.1;}
    if(key == 'Y') {bottom *= 0.9; top *= 0.9;}
    if(key == 'z') {near  *= 1.1; far *= 1.1;}
    if(key == 'Z') {near *= 0.9; far *= 0.9;}
    if(key == 'r') radius *= 2.0;
    if(key == 'R') radius *= 0.5;
    if(key == 'o') theta += dr;
    if(key == 'O') theta -= dr;
    if(key == 'p') phi += dr;
    if(key == 'P') phi -= dr;
    glutPostRedisplay();
}
```

Note that as we move the camera around, the size of the image of the cube does not change, which is a consequence of using an orthogonal projection. However, depending on the radius, some or even all of the cube can be clipped out. This behavior is a consequence of the parameters in Ortho being measured relative to the camera. Hence, if we move the camera back by increasing the radius but leave the near and far distances unchanged, first the back of the cube will be clipped out. Eventually, as the radius becomes larger, the entire cube will be clipped out.

Now consider what happens as we change the parameters in Ortho. As we increase right and left, the cube elongates in the x-direction. A similar phenomenon occurs when we increase bottom and top in the y-direction. Although this distortion of the cube's image may be annoying, it is a consequence of using an $x - y$ rectangle in Ortho that is not square. This rectangle is mapped to the full viewport, which has been unchanged. We can alter the program so that we increase or decrease all of `left`, `right`, `bottom`, and `top` simultaneously or we can alter the viewport as part of any change to `Ortho` (see Exercise 4.28).

4.5 PERSPECTIVE PROJECTIONS

We now turn to perspective projections, which are what we get with a camera whose lens has a finite focal length or, in terms of our synthetic camera model, the center of projection is finite.

As with parallel projections, we will separate perspective viewing into two parts: the positioning of the camera and the projection. Positioning will be done the same way, and we can use the `LookAt` function. The projection part is equivalent to selecting a lens for the camera. As we saw in Chapter 1, it is the combination of the lens and the size of the film (or of the back of the camera) that determines how much of the world in front of a camera appears in the image. In computer graphics, we make an equivalent choice when we select the type of projection and the viewing parameters.

With a physical camera, a wide-angle lens gives the most dramatic perspectives, with objects near the camera appearing large compared to objects far from the lens. A telephoto lens gives an image that appears flat and is close to a parallel view.

First, we consider the mathematics for a simple projection. We can extend our use of homogeneous coordinates to the projection process, which allows us to characterize a particular projection with a 4×4 matrix.

4.5.1 Simple Perspective Projections

Suppose that we are in the camera frame with the camera located at the origin, pointed in the negative z-direction. Figure 4.31 shows two possibilities. In Figure 4.31(a), the back of the camera is orthogonal to the z-direction and is parallel to the lens. This configuration corresponds to most physical situations, including those of the human visual system and of simple cameras. The situation shown in Figure 4.31(b) is more general; the back of the camera can have any orientation with respect to the front. We consider the first case in detail because it is simpler. However, the derivation of the general result follows the same steps and should be a direct exercise (Exercise 4.6).

As we saw in Chapter 1, we can place the projection plane in front of the center of projection. If we do so for the configuration of Figure 4.32(a), we get the views shown in Figure 4.33. A point in space (x, y, z) is projected along a projector into the point (x_p, y_p, z_p). All projectors pass through the origin, and, because the projection plane is perpendicular to the z-axis,

$$z_p = d.$$

Because the camera is pointing in the negative z-direction, the projection plane is in the negative half-space $z < 0$, and the value of d is negative.

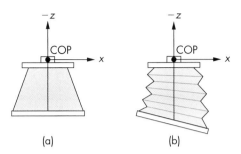

FIGURE 4.31 Two cameras. (a) Back parallel to front. (b) Back not parallel to front.

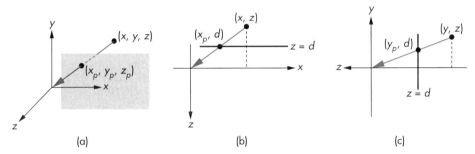

FIGURE 4.32 Three views of perspective projection. (a) Three-dimensional view. (b) Top view. (c) Side view.

From the top view shown in Figure 4.32(b), we see two similar triangles whose tangents must be the same. Hence,

$$\frac{x}{z} = \frac{x_p}{d},$$

and

$$x_p = \frac{x}{z/d}.$$

Using the side view shown in Figure 4.32(c), we obtain a similar result for y_p:

$$y_p = \frac{y}{z/d}.$$

These equations are nonlinear. The division by z describes **nonuniform foreshortening**: The images of objects farther from the center of projection are reduced in size (diminution) compared to the images of objects closer to the COP.

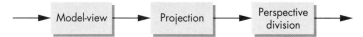

FIGURE 4.33   Projection pipeline.

We can look at the projection process as a transformation that takes points (x, y, z) to other points (x_p, y_p, z_p). Although this **perspective transformation** preserves lines, it is not affine. It is also irreversible. Because all points along a projector project into the same point, we cannot recover a point from its projection. In Sections 4.7 and 4.8, we will develop an invertible variant of the projection transformation that preserves distances that are needed for hidden-surface removal.

We can extend our use of homogeneous coordinates to handle projections. When we introduced homogeneous coordinates, we represented a point in three dimensions (x, y, z) by the point $(x, y, z, 1)$ in four dimensions. Suppose that, instead, we replace (x, y, z) by the four-dimensional point

$$\mathbf{p} = \begin{bmatrix} wx \\ wy \\ wz \\ w \end{bmatrix}.$$

As long as $w \neq 0$, we can recover the three-dimensional point from its four-dimensional representation by dividing the first three components by w. In this new homogeneous-coordinate form, points in three dimensions become lines through the origin in four dimensions. Transformations are again represented by 4×4 matrices, but now the final row of the matrix can be altered—and thus w can be changed by such a transformation.

Obviously, we would prefer to keep $w = 1$ to avoid the divisions otherwise necessary to recover the three-dimensional point. However, by allowing w to change, we can represent a larger class of transformations, including perspective projections. Consider the matrix

$$\mathbf{M} = \begin{bmatrix} 1 & 0 & 0 & 0 \\ 0 & 1 & 0 & 0 \\ 0 & 0 & 1 & 0 \\ 0 & 0 & 1/d & 0 \end{bmatrix}.$$

The matrix $\mathbf{M}$ transforms the point

$$\mathbf{p} = \begin{bmatrix} x \\ y \\ z \\ 1 \end{bmatrix}$$

to the point

$$\mathbf{q} = \begin{bmatrix} x \\ y \\ z \\ z/d \end{bmatrix}.$$

At first glance, $\mathbf{q}$ may not seem sensible; however, when we remember that we have to divide the first three components by the fourth to return to our original three-dimensional space, we obtain the results

$$x_p = \frac{x}{z/d},$$

$$y_p = \frac{y}{z/d},$$

$$z_p = \frac{z}{z/d} = d,$$

which are the equations for a simple perspective projection. In homogeneous coordinates, dividing $\mathbf{q}$ by its w component replaces $\mathbf{q}$ by the equivalent point

$$\mathbf{q}' = \begin{bmatrix} \frac{x}{z/d} \\ \frac{y}{z/d} \\ d \\ 1 \end{bmatrix} = \begin{bmatrix} x_p \\ y_p \\ z_p \\ 1 \end{bmatrix}.$$

We have shown that we can do at least a simple perspective projection, by defining a 4×4 projection matrix that we apply after the model-view matrix. However, we must perform a **perspective division** at the end. This division can be made a part of the pipeline, as shown in Figure 4.33.

4.6 PERSPECTIVE PROJECTIONS WITH OPENGL

The projections that we developed in Section 4.4 did not take into account the properties of the camera—the focal length of its lens or the size of the film plane. Figure 4.34 shows the **angle of view** for a simple pinhole camera, like the one that we discussed in Chapter 1. Only those objects that fit within the angle of view of the camera appear in the image. If the back of the camera is rectangular, only objects within a semi-infinite pyramid—the **view volume**—whose apex is at the COP can appear in the image. Objects not within the view volume are said to be **clipped** out of the scene. Hence, our description of simple projections has been incomplete; we did not include the effects of clipping.

With most graphics APIs, the application program specifies clipping parameters through the specification of a projection. The infinite pyramid in Figure 4.34 becomes

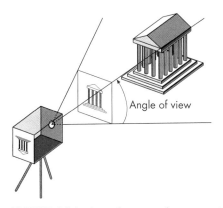

FIGURE 4.34   Specification of a view volume.

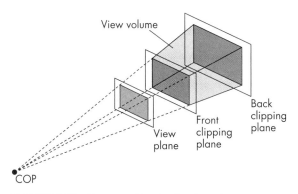

FIGURE 4.35   Front and back clipping planes.

a finite clipping volume by adding front and back clipping planes, in addition to the angle of view, as shown in Figure 4.35. The resulting view volume is a **frustum**—a truncated pyramid. We have fixed only one parameter by specifying that the COP is at the origin in the camera frame. In principle, we should be able to specify each of the six sides of the frustum to have almost any orientation. If we did so, however, we would make it difficult to specify a view in the application and complicate the implementation. In practice, we rarely need this flexibility, and usually we can get by with only two perspective viewing functions. Other APIs differ in their function calls but incorporate similar restrictions.

4.6.1 Perspective Functions

We will develop two functions for specifying perspective views and one for specifying parallel views. Alternatively, we can form the projection matrix directly, either by

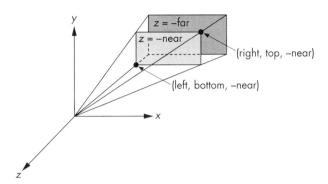

FIGURE 4.36   Specification of a frustum.

loading it or by applying rotations, translations, and scalings to an initial identity matrix. We can specify a perspective camera view by the function

```
mat4 Frustum(GLfloat left, GLfloat right, GLfloat bottom, GLfloat top,
             GLfloat near, GLfloat far);
```

whose parameters are similar to those in `Ortho`. These parameters are shown in Figure 4.36 in the camera frame. The near and far distances are measured from the COP (the origin in eye coordinates) to front and back clipping planes, both of which are parallel to the plane $z = 0$. Because the camera is pointing in the negative z-direction, the front (near) clipping plane is the plane $z = -near$ and the back (far) clipping plane is the plane $z = -far$. The left, right, top, and bottom values are measured in the near (front clipping) plane. The plane $x = left$ is to the left of the camera as viewed from the COP in the direction the camera is pointing. Similar statements hold for `right`, `bottom`, and `top`. Although in virtually all applications $far > near > 0$, as long as $near \neq far$, the resulting projection matrix is valid, although objects behind the center of projection—the origin—will be inverted in the image if they lie between the near and far planes.

Note that these specifications do not have to be symmetric with respect to the z-axis and that the resulting frustum also does not have to be symmetric (a right frustum). In Section 4.7, we show how the projection matrix for this projection can be derived from the simple perspective-projection matrix.

In many applications, it is natural to specify the angle of view, or field of view. However, if the projection plane is rectangular, rather than square, then we see a different angle of view in the top and side views (Figure 4.37). The angle *fovy* is the angle between the top and bottom planes of the clipping volume. The function

```
mat4 Perspective(GLfloat fovy, GLfloat aspect, GLfloat near, GLfloat far);
```

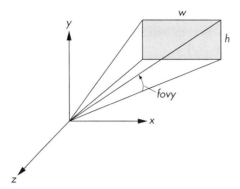

FIGURE 4.37   Specification using the field of view.

allows us to specify the angle of view in the up (y) direction, as well as the aspect ratio—width divided by height—of the projection plane. The near and far planes are specified as in `Frustum`.

4.7   PERSPECTIVE-PROJECTION MATRICES

For perspective projections, we follow a path similar to the one that we used for parallel projections: We find a transformation that allows us, by distorting the vertices of our objects, to do a simple canonical projection to obtain the desired image. Our first step is to decide what this canonical viewing volume should be. We then introduce a new transformation, the **perspective-normalization transformation**, that converts a perspective projection to an orthogonal projection. Finally, we derive the perspective-projection matrix we will use in OpenGL.

4.7.1   Perspective Normalization

In Section 4.5, we introduced a simple perspective-projection matrix. For the projection plane at $z = -1$ and the center of the projection at the origin, the projection matrix is

$$\mathbf{M} = \begin{bmatrix} 1 & 0 & 0 & 0 \\ 0 & 1 & 0 & 0 \\ 0 & 0 & 1 & 0 \\ 0 & 0 & -1 & 0 \end{bmatrix}.$$

To form an image, we also need to specify a clipping volume. Suppose that we fix the angle of view at 90 degrees by making the sides of the viewing volume intersect the projection plane at a 45-degree angle. Equivalently, the view volume is the semi-infinite view pyramid formed by the planes

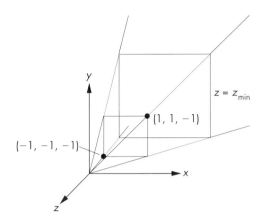

FIGURE 4.38   Simple perspective projection.

$x = \pm z,$

$y = \pm z,$

shown in Figure 4.38. We can make the volume finite by specifying the near plane to be $z = -near$ and the far plane to be $z = -far$, where both *near* and *far*, the distances from the center of projection to the near and far planes, satisfy

$0 < near < far.$

Consider the matrix

$$\mathbf{N} = \begin{bmatrix} 1 & 0 & 0 & 0 \\ 0 & 1 & 0 & 0 \\ 0 & 0 & \alpha & \beta \\ 0 & 0 & -1 & 0 \end{bmatrix},$$

which is similar to **M** but is nonsingular. For now, we leave α and β unspecified (but nonzero). If we apply **N** to the homogeneous-coordinate point $\mathbf{p} = [\, x \quad y \quad z \quad 1\,]^{T}$, we obtain the new point $\mathbf{q} = [\, x' \quad y' \quad z' \quad w' \,]^{T}$, where

$x' = x,$

$y' = y,$

$z' = \alpha z + \beta,$

$w' = -z.$

After dividing by w', we have the three-dimensional point

$$x'' = -\frac{x}{z},$$

$$y'' = -\frac{y}{z},$$

$$z'' = -\left(\alpha + \frac{\beta}{z}\right).$$

If we apply an orthographic projection along the z-axis to $\mathbf{N}$, we obtain the matrix

$$\mathbf{M}_{\text{orth}}\mathbf{N} = \begin{bmatrix} 1 & 0 & 0 & 0 \\ 0 & 1 & 0 & 0 \\ 0 & 0 & 0 & 0 \\ 0 & 0 & -1 & 0 \end{bmatrix},$$

which is a simple perspective-projection matrix, and the projection of the arbitrary point $\mathbf{p}$ is

$$\mathbf{p}' = \mathbf{M}_{\text{orth}}\mathbf{N}\mathbf{p} = \begin{bmatrix} x \\ y \\ 0 \\ -z \end{bmatrix}.$$

After we do the perspective division, we obtain the desired values for x_p and y_p:

$$x_p = -\frac{x}{z},$$

$$y_p = -\frac{y}{z}.$$

We have shown that we can apply a transformation $\mathbf{N}$ to points, and after an orthogonal projection, we obtain the same result as we would have for a perspective projection. This process is similar to how we converted oblique projections to orthogonal projections by first shearing the objects.

The matrix $\mathbf{N}$ is nonsingular and transforms the original viewing volume into a new volume. We choose α and β such that the new volume is the canonical clipping volume. Consider the sides

$$x = \pm z.$$

They are transformed by $x'' = -x/z$ to the planes

$$x'' = \pm 1.$$

Likewise, the sides $y = \pm z$ are transformed to

$$y'' = \pm 1.$$

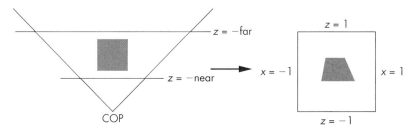

FIGURE 4.39 Perspective normalization of view volume.

The front clipping plane $z = -near$ is transformed to the plane

$$z'' = -\left(\alpha - \frac{\beta}{near}\right).$$

Finally, the far plane $z = -far$ is transformed to the plane

$$z'' = -\left(\alpha - \frac{\beta}{far}\right).$$

If we select

$$\alpha = -\frac{near + far}{near - far},$$

$$\beta = -\frac{2 * near * far}{near - far},$$

then the plane $z = -near$ is mapped to the plane $z'' = -1$, the plane $z = -far$ is mapped to the plane $z'' = 1$, and we have our canonical clipping volume. Figure 4.39 shows this transformation and the distortion to a cube within the volume. Thus, **N** has transformed the viewing frustum to a right parallelepiped, and an orthographic projection in the transformed volume yields the same image as does the perspective projection. The matrix **N** is called the **perspective-normalization matrix**. The mapping

$$z'' = -\left(\alpha + \frac{\beta}{z}\right)$$

is nonlinear but preserves the ordering of depths. Thus, if z_1 and z_2 are the depths of two points within the original viewing volume and

$$z_1 > z_2,$$

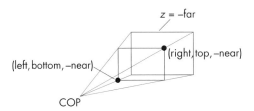

FIGURE 4.40   OpenGL perspective.

then their transformations satisfy

$$z_1'' > z_2''.$$

Consequently, hidden-surface removal works in the normalized volume, although the nonlinearity of the transformation can cause numerical problems because the depth buffer has a limited depth resolution. Note that although the original projection plane we placed at $z = -1$ has been transformed by $\mathbf{N}$ to the plane $z'' = \beta - \alpha$, there is little consequence to this result because we follow $\mathbf{N}$ by an orthographic projection.

Although we have shown that both perspective and parallel transformations can be converted to orthographic transformations, the effects of this conversion are greatest in implementation. As long as we can put a carefully chosen projection matrix in the pipeline before the vertices are defined, we need only one viewing pipeline for all possible views. In Chapter 6, where we discuss implementation in detail, we will see how converting all view volumes to right parallelepipeds by our normalization process simplifies both clipping and hidden-surface removal.

4.7.2 OpenGL Perspective Transformations

The function `Frustum` does not restrict the view volume to a symmetric (or right) frustum. The parameters are as shown in Figure 4.40. We can form the perspective matrix by first converting this frustum to the symmetric frustum with 45-degree sides (see Figure 4.39). The process is similar to the conversion of an oblique parallel view to an orthogonal view. First, we do a shear to convert the asymmetric frustum to a symmetric one. Figure 4.40 shows the desired transformation. The shear angle is determined by our desire to skew (shear) the point $((left + right)/2, (top + bottom)/2, -near)$ to $(0, 0, -near)$. The required shear matrix is

$$\mathbf{H}(\theta, \phi) = \mathbf{H}\left(\cot^{-1}\left(\frac{left + right}{-2near}\right), \cot^{-1}\left(\frac{top + bottom}{-2near}\right)\right).$$

The resulting frustum is described by the planes

$$x = \pm \frac{right - left}{-2 * near},$$

$$y = \pm \frac{top - bottom}{-2 * near},$$

$$z = -near,$$

$$z = -far.$$

The next step is to scale the sides of this frustum to

$$x = \pm z,$$

$$y = \pm z,$$

without changing either the near plane or the far plane. The required scaling matrix is $\mathbf{S}(-2 * near/(right - left), -2 * near/(top - bottom), 1)$. Note that this transformation is determined uniquely without reference to the location of the far plane $z = -far$ because in three dimensions, an affine transformation is determined by the results of the transformation on four points. In this case, these points are the four vertices where the sides of the frustum intersect the near plane.

To get the far plane to the plane $z = -1$ and the near plane to $z = 1$ after applying a projection normalization, we use the projection-normalization matrix $\mathbf{N}$:

$$\mathbf{N} = \begin{bmatrix} 1 & 0 & 0 & 0 \\ 0 & 1 & 0 & 0 \\ 0 & 0 & \alpha & \beta \\ 0 & 0 & -1 & 0 \end{bmatrix},$$

with α and β as in Section 4.7.1. The resulting projection matrix is in terms of the near and far distances,

$$\mathbf{P} = \mathbf{NSH} = \begin{bmatrix} \frac{2*near}{right-left} & 0 & \frac{right+left}{right-left} & 0 \\ 0 & \frac{2*near}{top-bottom} & \frac{top+bottom}{top-bottom} & 0 \\ 0 & 0 & -\frac{far+near}{far-near} & \frac{-2far*near}{far-near} \\ 0 & 0 & -1 & 0 \end{bmatrix}.$$

We obtain the projection matrix corresponding to Persective(fovy, aspect, near, far) by using symmetry in $\mathbf{P}$ so

$$left = -right,$$

$$bottom = -top,$$

and simple trigonometry to determine

$$top = near * \tan(fovy),$$

$$right = top * aspect,$$

simplifying **P** to

$$\mathbf{P} = \mathbf{NSH} = \begin{bmatrix} \frac{near}{right} & 0 & 0 & 0 \\ 0 & \frac{near}{top} & 0 & 0 \\ 0 & 0 & \frac{-far+near}{far-near} & \frac{-2far*near}{far-near} \\ 0 & 0 & -1 & 0 \end{bmatrix}.$$

4.7.3 Perspective Example

We have to make almost no changes to our previous example to go from an orthogonal projection to a perspective projection. We can substitute `Frustum` for `Ortho` and the parameters are the same. However, for a perspective view we should have

$$far > near > 0.$$

Note that if we want to see the foreshortening we associate with perspective views, we can either move the cube off the z-axis or add additional cubes to the right or left.

We can add the perspective division to our vertex shader, so it becomes

```
in vec4 vPosition;
in vec4 vColor;
out vec4 color;
uniform mat4 model_view;
uniform mat4 projection;
void main()
{
   gl_Position = projection*model_view*vPosition/vPosition.w;
   color = vColor;
}
```

The full program is in Appendix A.

4.8   HIDDEN-SURFACE REMOVAL

Before introducing a few additional examples and extensions of viewing, we need to deepen our understanding of the hidden-surface–removal process. Let's start with the cube we have been using in our examples. When we look at a cube that has opaque sides, depending on its orientation, we see only one, two, or three front-facing sides. From the perspective of our basic viewing model, we can say that we see only these faces because they block the projectors from reaching any other surfaces.

From the perspective of computer graphics, however, all six faces of the cube have been specified and travel down the graphics pipeline; thus, the graphics system must be careful about which surfaces it displays. Conceptually, we seek algorithms that either remove those surfaces that should not be visible to the viewer, called **hidden-surface–removal algorithms**, or find which surfaces are visible, called **visible-surface algorithms**. There are many approaches to the problem, several of which we investigate in Chapter 6. OpenGL has a particular algorithm associated with it, the **z-buffer algorithm**, to which we can interface through three function calls. Hence, we introduce that algorithm here, and we return to the topic in Chapter 6.

Hidden-surface–removal algorithms can be divided into two broad classes. **Object-space algorithms** attempt to order the surfaces of the objects in the scene such that rendering surfaces in a particular order provides the correct image. For example, for our cube, if we were to render the back-facing surfaces first, we could "paint" over them with the front surfaces and would produce the correct image. This class of algorithms does not work well with pipeline architectures in which objects are passed down the pipeline in an arbitrary order. In order to decide on a proper order in which to render the objects, the graphics system must have all the objects available so it can sort them into the desired back-to-front order.

Image-space algorithms work as part of the projection process and seek to determine the relationship among object points on each projector. The z-buffer algorithm is of the latter type and fits in well with the rendering pipeline in most graphics systems because we can save partial information as each object is rendered.

The basic idea of the z-buffer algorithm is shown in Figure 4.41. A projector from the COP passes through two surfaces. Because the circle is closer to the viewer than to the triangle, it is the circle's color that determines the color placed in the color buffer at the location corresponding to where the projector pierces the projection plane. The difficulty is determining how we can make this idea work regardless of the order in which the triangle and the circle pass through the pipeline.

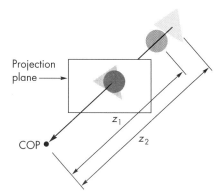

FIGURE 4.41   The z-buffer algorithm.

Let's assume that all the objects are polygons. If, as the polygons are rasterized, we can keep track of the distance from the COP or the projection plane to the closest point on each projector that already has been rendered, then we can update this information as successive polygons are projected and filled. Ultimately, we display only the closest point on each projector. The algorithm requires a **depth buffer**, or *z-buffer*, to store the necessary depth information as polygons are rasterized. Because we must keep depth information for each pixel in the color buffer, the *z*-buffer has the same spatial resolution as the color buffers. Its depth resolution is usually 32 bits with recent graphics cards that store this information as floating-point numbers. The *z*-buffer is one of the buffers that constitute the frame buffer and is usually part of the memory on the graphics card.

The depth buffer is initialized to a value that corresponds to the farthest distance from the viewer. When each polygon inside the clipping volume is rasterized, the depth of each fragment—how far the corresponding point on the polygon is from the viewer—is calculated. If this depth is greater than the value at that fragment's location in the depth buffer, then a polygon that has already been rasterized is closer to the viewer along the projector corresponding to the fragment. Hence, for this fragment we ignore the color of the polygon and go on to the next fragment for this polygon, where we make the same test. If, however, the depth is less than what is already in the *z*-buffer, then along this projector the polygon being rendered is closer than any one we have seen so far. Thus, we use the color of the polygon to replace the color of the pixel in the color buffer and update the depth in the *z* buffer.[6]

For the example shown in Figure 4.41, we see that if the triangle passes through the pipeline first, its colors and depths will be placed in the color and *z*-buffers. When the circle passes through the pipeline, its colors and depths will replace the colors and depths of the triangle where they overlap. If the circle is rendered first, its colors and depths will be placed in the buffers. When the triangle is rendered, in the areas where there is overlap the depths of the triangle are greater than the depth of the circle, and at the corresponding pixels no changes will be made to the color or depth buffers.

Major advantages of this algorithm are that its complexity is proportional to the number of fragments generated by the rasterizer and that it can be implemented with a small number of additional calculations over what we have to do to project and display polygons without hidden-surface removal. We will return to this issue in Chapter 6.

From the application programmer's perspective, she must initialize the depth buffer and enable hidden-surface removal by using

```
glutInitDisplayMode(GLUT_DOUBLE | GLUT_RGB | GLUT_DEPTH);
glEnable(GL_DEPTH_TEST);
```

---

6. The color of the polygon is determined by shading (Chapter 5) and texture mapping (Chapter 7) if these features are enabled.

Here we use the GLUT library for the initialization and specify a depth buffer in addition to our usual RGB color and double buffering. The programmer can clear the color and depth buffers as necessary for a new rendering by using

```
glClear(GL_COLOR_BUFFER_BIT | GL_DEPTH_BUFFER_BIT);
```

4.8.1 Culling

For a convex object, such as the cube, faces whose normals point away from the viewer are never visible and can be eliminated or culled before the rasterizer. We can turn on culling in OpenGL by enabling it as follows:

```
glEnable(GL_CULL_FACE);
```

However, culling is guaranteed to produce a correct image only if we have a single convex object. Often we can use culling in addition to the z-buffer algorithm (which works with any collection of polygons). For example, suppose that we have a scene composed of a collection of n cubes. If we use only the z-buffer algorithm, we pass $6n$ polygons through the pipeline. If we enable culling, half the polygons can be eliminated early in the pipeline, and thus only $3n$ polygons pass through all stages of the pipeline. We consider culling further in Chapter 6.

4.9 DISPLAYING MESHES

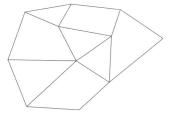

FIGURE 4.42 Mesh.

We now have the tools to walk through a scene interactively by having the camera parameters change in response to user input. Before introducing a simple interface, let's consider another example of data display: mesh plots. A **mesh** is a set of polygons that share vertices and edges. A general mesh, as shown in Figure 4.42, may contain polygons with any number of vertices and require a moderately sophisticated data structure to store and display efficiently. Rectangular and triangular meshes, such as we introduced in Chapter 2 for modeling a sphere, are much simpler to work with and are useful for a wide variety of applications. Here we introduce rectangular meshes for the display of height data. Height data determine a surface, such as terrain, through either a function that gives the heights above a reference value, such as elevations above sea level, or through samples taken at various points on the surface.

Suppose that the heights are given by y through a function

$$y = f(x, z),$$

where x and z are the points on a two-dimensional surface such as a rectangle. Thus, for each x, z we get exactly one y, as shown in Figure 4.43. Such surfaces are sometimes called **2-1/2–dimensional surfaces** or **height fields**. Although all surfaces cannot be represented this way, they have many applications. For example, if we use an x, z coordinate system to give positions on the surface of the earth, then we can use such a function to represent the height or altitude at each location. In many situations

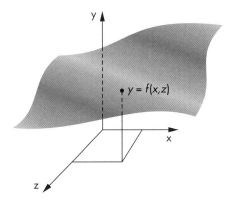

FIGURE 4.43   Height field.

the function f is known only discretely, and we have a set of samples or measurements of experimental data of the form

$$y_{ij} = f(x_i, z_j).$$

We assume that these data points are equally spaced such that

$$x_i = x_0 + i\Delta x, \quad i = 0, \ldots, N,$$

$$z_j = z_0 + j\Delta z, \quad j = 0, \ldots, M,$$

where Δx and Δz are the spacing between the samples in the x- and z-directions, respectively. If f is known analytically, then we can sample it to obtain a set of discrete data with which to work.

Probably the simplest way to display the data is to draw a line strip for each value of x and another for each value of z, thus generating $N + M$ line strips. Suppose that the height data are in an array `data`. We can form a single array with the data converted to vertices arranged by rows with the code

```
float data[N][M];
point4 vertices[2*N*M]

int k =0;
for(int i = 0; i<N; i++) for(int j=0; j<M; j++)
{
    vertices[k] = vec4(i, data[i][j], j, 1.0);
    k++;
}
```

We can form an array for the vertices by column by switching roles of `i` and `j` as follows:

```
point4 vertices[N*M];

int k =0;
for(int i = 0; i<M; i++) for(int j=0; j<N; j++)
{
    vertices[k] = point4(j, data[j][i],i,1.0);
    k++;
}
```

We usually will want to scale the data to be over a convenient range, such as (0, 1), and scale the x and z values to make them easier to display as part of the model-view matrix or, equivalently, by adjusting the size of the view volume.

We can display these vertices by sending both arrays to the vertex shader. So in the initialization we set up the vertex buffer object with the correct size but without sending any data:

```
GLuint buffer;

glBindVertexArray(buffer);

loc = glGetAttribLocation(program, "vPosition");
glEnableVertexAttribArray(loc);
glVertexAttribPointer(loc, 4, GL_FLOAT, GL_FALSE, 0,
                    BUFFER_OFFSET(0));

glGenBuffers(1, &buffer);
glBindBuffer(GL_ARRAY_BUFFER, buffer);
glBufferData(GL_ARRAY_BUFFER, sizeof(vertices), NULL,
            GL_DYNAMIC_DRAW)
```

In the display callback, we load the two vertex arrays successively and display them:

```
/* form array of vertices by row here */

glBufferData(GL_ARRAY_BUFFER, sizeof(vertices), vertices,
            GL_DYNAMIC_DRAW);
glDrawArrays(GL_LINE_STRIP, 0, N*M);

/* form array of vertices by column here */

glBufferData(GL_ARRAY_BUFFER, sizeof(vertices), vertices,
            GL_DYNAMIC_DRAW);
glDrawArrays(GL_LINE_STRIP, 0, N*M);
```

You should now be able to complete a program to display the data. Figure 4.44 shows a rectangular mesh from height data for a part of Honolulu, Hawaii. These data are available on the Web site for the book. There are a few problems with this simple

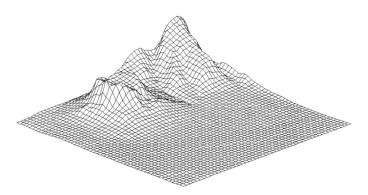

FIGURE 4.44   Mesh plot of Honolulu data using line strips.

approach. One is that we have to load data onto the GPU twice every time we want to display the mesh and thus are wasting a lot of time moving data from the CPU to the GPU. A second problem is that we are not doing any hidden-surface removal, so we see the lines from parts of the original surface that should be hidden from the viewer. Third, there are some annoying "extra" lines that appear from the end of one row (or column) to the next row (or column). These lines are a consequence of putting all rows (and columns) into a single line strip.

We can get around the last problem by assigning vertex colors carefully. The first two problems can be avoided by displaying the data as a surface using polygons. An added advantage in using polygons is that we will be able to extend our code to displaying the mesh with lights and material properties in Chapter 5.

4.9.1 Displaying Meshes as a Surface

One simple way to generate a surface is through a triangular mesh. We can use the four points y_{ij}, $y_{i+1, j}$, $y_{i+1, j+1}$, and $y_{i, j+1}$ to generate two triangles. Thus, the height data specify a mesh of $2NM$ triangles.

The basic OpenGL program is straightforward. We can form the array of triangle data in the `main` function or as part of initialization as in the following code, which normalizes the data to be in the range $(0, 1)$, the x values to be over $(-1, 1)$, and the z values to be over $(-1, 0)$:

```
float data[N][M]; // all values assumed non negative
float fmax;       // maximum of data
point4 triangles[6*N*M] // vertex positions
float fn = float(N);
float fm = float(M);

int k =0;
for(i=0; i<N-1; i++) for(j=0; j<M-1;j++)
   //NM quads, 2 triangles/quad
```

```
{
    triangles[k] = vec4(2.0*(i/fn-0.5), data[i][j]/fmax,  -j/fm,
                        1.0); k++;
    triangles[k] = vec4(2.0*((i+1)/fn-0.5), data[i+1][j]/fmax,
                        -j/fm, 1.0); k++;
    triangles[k] = vec4(2.0*((i+1)/fn-0.5), data[i+1][j+1]/fmax,
                        -(j+1)/fm,1.0); k++;
    triangles[k] = vec4(2.0*((i+1)/fn-0.5),data[i+1][j]/fmax,
                        -j/fm, 1.0); k++;
    triangles[k] = vec4(2.0*((i+1)/fn-0.5), data[i+1][j+1]/fmax,
                        -(j+1)/fm,1.0); k++;
    triangles[k] = vec4(2.0*(i/fn-0.5), data[i][j+1]/fmax,
                        -(j+1)/fm, 1.0); k++;
}
```

We initialize the vertex array as before,

```
glBindVertexArray(abuffer);

loc = glGetAttribLocation(program, "vPosition");
glEnableVertexAttribArray(loc);
glVertexAttribPointer(loc, 4, GL_FLOAT, GL_FALSE, 0,
                      BUFFER_OFFSET(0));

glGenBuffers(1, buffers);
glBindBuffer(GL_ARRAY_BUFFER, buffers[0]);
glBufferData(GL_ARRAY_BUFFER, sizeof(triangles), triangles,
             GL_STATIC_DRAW);
```

and display it as

```
    glPolygonMode(GL_FRONT_AND_BACK, GL_LINE);
    glDrawArrays(GL_TRIANGLES, 0, 6*N*M);
```

If we integrate this code with our previous example using line strips, the output will look almost identical. Although we have designed a surface, by choosing to display only the edges by using a polygon mode of GL_LINE, we do not generate any fragments corresponding to the inside of the polygon, and thus we see the edges of polygons that would be hidden if the mode were GL_FILL. We can fix this problem by rendering the data twice, first as a filled white surface and second as black lines. Because the data are already on the GPU, we do not have to send any vertex data to the GPU for the second rendering. We can specify two colors in the initialization that we will send to the fragment shader

```
    color4 white = vec4(1.0, 1.0, 1.0, 1.0);
    color4 black = vec4(0.0, 0.0, 0.0, 1.0);

    color_loc = glGetUniformLocation(program, "fcolor");
```

and then modify to the display callback to have the code

```
glPolygonMode(GL_FRONT_AND_BACK, GL_FILL);
glUniform4fv(color_loc, 1, white);
glDrawArrays(GL_TRIANGLES, 0, 6*N*M);
glPolygonMode(GL_FRONT_AND_BACK, GL_LINE);
glUniform4fv(color_loc, 1, black);
glDrawArrays(GL_TRIANGLES, 0, 6*N*M);
```

The modified fragment shader is

```
uniform vec4 fcolor;
void main()
{
  gl_FragColor = fcolor;
}
```

4.9.2 Polygon Offset

There are interesting aspects to this OpenGL program, and we can make various modifications. First, if we use all the data, the resulting plot may contain many small polygons. The resulting density of lines in the display may be annoying and can contain moiré patterns. Hence, we might prefer to subsample the data either by using every kth point for some k or by averaging groups of data points to obtain a new set of samples with smaller N and M.

There is one additional trick that we used in the display of Figure 4.44. If we draw both a polygon and a line loop with the code in the previous section, then each triangle is rendered twice in the same plane, once filled and once by its edges. Even though the second rendering of just the edges is done with filled rendering, numerical inaccuracies in the renderer often cause parts of second rendering to lie behind the corresponding fragments in the first rendering. We can avoid this problem by enabling the **polygon offset mode** and setting the offset parameters using `glPolygonOffset`. Polygon fill offset moves fragments slightly away from the viewer, so all the desired lines should be visible. In initialization, we can set up polygon offset by

```
glEnable(GL_POLYGON_OFFSET_FILL);
glPolygonOffset(1.0, 1.0);
```

The two parameters in `PolygonOffset` are combined with the slope of the polygon and an implementation-dependent constant. Consequently, you may have to do a little experimentation to find the best values.

Perhaps the greatest weakness of our code is that we are sending too much data to the GPU and not using the most efficient rendering method. Consider a mesh consisting of a single row of N quadrilaterals. If we render it as 2N triangles using

```
point4 vertices[6*N];
```

```
glDrawArrays(GL_TRIANGLES, 0, 6*N);
```

we send 6*N* vertices to the GPU. If we instead set our vertices as a triangle strip, then these two lines of code become

```
point4 vertices[2*N-2];
```

```
glDrawArrays(GL_TRIANGLE_STRIP, 0, 2*N-2);
```

Not only are we sending less data and requiring less of the GPU's memory, but the GPU will render the triangles much faster as a triangle strip as opposed to individual triangles. For a $1 \times M$ mesh, we can easily construct the array for a triangle strip. For an $N \times M$ mesh, the process is more complex. Although it would be simple to repeat the process for the $1 \times M$ mesh N times, setting up N triangle strips, this approach would have us repeatedly sending data to the GPU. What we need is a single triangle strip for the entire mesh. Exercises 4.22 and 4.23 outline two approaches.

4.9.3 Walking Through a Scene

The next step is to specify the camera and add interactivity. In this version, we use perspective viewing, and we allow the viewer to move the camera by pressing the x, X, y, Y, z, and Z keys on the keyboard, but we have the camera always pointing at the center of the cube. The LookAt function provides a simple way to reposition and reorient the camera.

The changes that we have to make to our previous program in Section 4.4 are minor. We define an array viewer[3] to hold the camera position. Its contents are altered by the simple keyboard callback function keys as follows:

```
void keys(unsigned char key, int x, int y)
{
   if(key == 'x') viewer[0]-= 1.0;
   if(key == 'X') viewer[0]+= 1.0;
   if(key == 'y') viewer[1]-= 1.0;
   if(key == 'Y') viewer[1]+= 1.0;
   if(key == 'z') viewer[2]-= 1.0;
   if(key == 'Z') viewer[2]+= 1.0;
   glutPostRedisplay();
}
```

The display function calls LookAt using viewer for the camera position and uses the origin for the at position. The cube is rotated, as before, based on the mouse input. Note the order of the function calls in display that alter the model-view matrix:

```
mat4 model_view;
void display()
{
   glClear(GL_COLOR_BUFFER_BIT | GL_DEPTH_BUFFER_BIT);

   model_view = LookAt(viewer[0],viewer[1],viewer[2],
              0.0, 0.0, 0.0, 0.0, 1.0, 0.0)
              *RotateX(theta[0])*RotateY(theta[1])*RotateZ(theta[2]);

/* draw mesh or other objects here */

   glutSwapBuffers();
}
```

We can invoke `Frustum` from the reshape callback to specify the camera lens through the following code:

```
mat4 projection;

void myReshape(int w, int h)
{
   glViewport(0, 0, w, h);

GLfloat left = -2.0, right = 2.0, bottom = -2.0, top = 2.0;
GLfloat aspect = (GLfloat) w / h;

if ( aspect <= 1.0 ) {
   bottom /= aspect;
   top /= aspect;
} else {
   left *= aspect;
   right *= aspect;
}

projection = Frustum(left, right, bottom, top, 2.0, 20.0);
   glUniformMatrix4fv(projection_loc, 1, GL_TRUE, projection);
}
```

Note that we chose the values of the parameters in `Frustum` based on the aspect ratio of the window. Other than the added specification of a keyboard callback function in `main`, the rest of the program is the same as the program in Section 4.4. If you run this program, you should note the effects of moving the camera, the lens, and the sides of the viewing frustum. Note what happens as you move toward the mesh. You should also consider the effect of always having the viewer look at the center of the mesh as she is moving.

Note that we could have used the mouse buttons to move the viewer. We could use the mouse buttons to move the user forward or to turn her right or left (see

Exercise 4.14). However, by using the keyboard for moving the viewer, we can use the mouse to move the object as with the rotating cube in Chapter 3.

In this example, we are using direct positioning of the camera through `LookAt`. There are other possibilities. One is to use rotation and translation matrices to alter the model-view matrix incrementally. If we want to move the viewer through the scene without having her looking at a fixed point, this option may be more appealing. We could also keep a position variable in the program and change it as the viewer moves. In this case, the model-view matrix would be computed from scratch rather than changed incrementally. Which option we choose depends on the particular application, and often on other factors as well, such as the possibility that numerical errors might accumulate if we were to change the model-view matrix incrementally many times.

The basic mesh rendering can be extended in many ways. In Chapter 5, we will learn to add lights and surface properties to create a more realistic image; in Chapter 7, we will learn to add a texture to the surface. The texture map might be an image of the terrain from a photograph or other data that might be obtained by digitization of a map. If we combine these techniques, we can generate a display in which we can make the image depend on the time of day by changing the position of the light source. It is also possible to obtain smoother surfaces by using the data to define a smoother surface with the aid of one of the surface types that we will introduce in Chapter 10.

4.10 PROJECTIONS AND SHADOWS

The creation of simple shadows is an interesting application of projection matrices. Although shadows are not geometric objects, they are important components of realistic images and give many visual clues to the spatial relationships among the objects in a scene. Starting from a physical point of view, shadows require a light source to be present. A point is in shadow if it is not illuminated by any light source or, equivalently, if a viewer at that point cannot see any light sources. However, if the only light source is at the center of projection, there are no visible shadows, because any shadows are behind visible objects. This lighting strategy has been called the "flashlight in the eye" model and corresponds to the simple lighting we have used thus far.

To add physically correct shadows, we must understand the interaction between light and materials, a topic that we investigate in Chapter 5. There we show that global calculations are difficult; normally, they cannot be done in real time.

Nevertheless, the importance of shadows in applications such as flight simulators led to a number of special approaches that can be used in many circumstances. Consider the shadow generated by the point source in Figure 4.45. We assume for simplicity that the shadow falls on the ground or the surface,

$y = 0$.

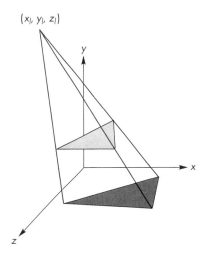

(x_l, y_l, z_l)

FIGURE 4.45   Shadow from a single polygon.

Not only is the shadow a flat polygon, called a **shadow polygon**, but it also is the projection of the original polygon onto the surface. Specifically, the shadow polygon is the projection of the polygon onto the surface with the center of projection at the light source. Thus, if we do a projection onto the plane of a surface in a frame in which the light source is at the origin, we obtain the vertices of the shadow polygon. These vertices must then be converted back to a representation in the object frame. Rather than do the work as part of an application program, we can find a suitable projection matrix and use it to compute the vertices of the shadow polygon.

Suppose that we start with a light source at (x_l, y_l, z_l), as shown in Figure 4.46(a). If we reorient the figure such that the light source is at the origin, as shown in Figure 4.46(b), by a translation matrix $\mathbf{T}(-x_l, -y_l, -z_l)$, then we have a simple perspective projection through the origin. The projection matrix is

$$\mathbf{M} = \begin{bmatrix} 1 & 0 & 0 & 0 \\ 0 & 1 & 0 & 0 \\ 0 & 0 & 1 & 0 \\ 0 & \frac{1}{-y_l} & 0 & 0 \end{bmatrix}.$$

Finally, we translate everything back with $\mathbf{T}(x_l, y_l, z_l)$. The concatenation of this matrix and the two translation matrices projects the vertex (x, y, z) to

$$x_p = x_l - \frac{x - x_l}{(y - y_l)/y_l},$$

$$y_p = 0,$$

$$z_p = z_l - \frac{z - z_l}{(y - y_l)/y_l}.$$

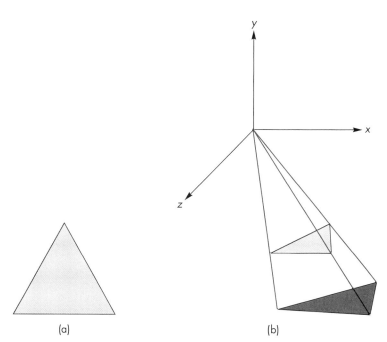

FIGURE 4.46   Shadow polygon projection. (a) From a light source.
(b) With source moved to the origin.

However, with an OpenGL program, we can alter the model-view matrix to form the
desired polygon as follows. If the light source is fixed, we can compute the shadow
projection matrix once as part of initialization. Otherwise, we need to recompute
it, perhaps in the idle callback function, if the light source is moving. The code for
setting up the matrix is as follows:

```
float light[3];   // location of light
mat4 m;    // shadow projection matrix initially an identity matrix

m[3][1] = -1.0/light[1];
```

Let's project a single square polygon parallel onto the plane $y = 0$. We can specify the
square through the vertices

```
point4 square[4] = {vec4(-0.5, 0.5, -0.5, 1.0), vec4(-0.5, 0.5, 0.5, 1.0),
    vec4(0.5, 0.5, -0.5, 1.0), vec4(0.5, 0.5, 0.5, 1.0)};
```

Note that the vertices are ordered so that we can render them using a triangle strip.
We initialize a red color for the square and a black color for its shadow, which we will
send to the fragment shader. We initialize a vertex array and a buffer object, as we did
in our previous examples:

```
GLuint abuffer, buffer;
glGenVertexArrays(1, &abuffer);
glBindVertexArray(abuffer);

int loc = glGetAttribLocation(program, "vPosition");
glEnableVertexAttribArray(loc);
glVertexAttribPointer(loc, 4, GL_FLOAT, GL_FALSE, 0,
                      BUFFER_OFFSET(0));
color_loc = glGetUniformLocation(program, "fcolor");

glGenBuffers(1, &buffer);
glBindBuffer(GL_ARRAY_BUFFER, buffer);
glBufferData(GL_ARRAY_BUFFER, sizeof(square), square,
             GL_STATIC_DRAW);
```

If the data do not change, we can also set the projection matrix and model-view matrix as part of initialization and send them to the vertex shader:

```
model_view = LookAt(eye, at, up);
projection = Ortho(left, right, bottom, top, near, far);
glUniformMatrix4fv(matrix_loc, 1, GL_TRUE, model_view);
glUniformMatrix4fv(projection_loc, 1, GL_TRUE, projection);
```

The core of the display callback is

```
void display()
{
    mat4 mm;
    // clear the window
    glClear(GL_COLOR_BUFFER_BIT | GL_DEPTH_BUFFER_BIT);

    // render red square

    glUniform4fv(color_loc, 1, red);
    glDrawArrays(GL_TRIANGLE_STRIP, 0, 4);

    //  matrix to compute vertices of shadow polygon

    mm = model_view*Translate(light[0], light[1],
    light[2])*m*Translate(-light[0], -light[1], -light[2]);
    glUniformMatrix4fv(matrix_loc, 1, GL_TRUE, mm);

    // render shadow polygon

    glUniform4fv(color_loc, 1, black);
    glDrawArrays(GL_TRIANGLE_STRIP, 0, 4);
    glutSwapBuffers();
}
```

Note that although we are performing a projection with respect to the light source, the matrix that we use is the model-view matrix. We render the same polygon twice: the first time as usual and the second time with an altered model-view matrix that transforms the vertices. The same viewing conditions are applied to both the polygon and its shadow polygon. The results of computing shadows for the colored cube are shown in Color Plate 29.

For a simple environment, such as an airplane flying over flat terrain casting a single shadow, this technique works well. It is also easy to convert from point sources to distant (parallel) light sources (see Exercise 4.17). However, when objects can cast shadows on other objects, this method becomes impractical. In Chapter 11, we address more general, but slower, rendering methods that will create shadows automatically as part of the rendering process.

SUMMARY AND NOTES

We have come a long way. We can now write complete, nontrivial, three-dimensional applications. Probably the most instructive activity that you can do now is to write such an application. Developing skill with manipulating the model-view and projection functions takes practice.

We have presented the mathematics of the standard projections. Although most APIs obviate the application programmer from writing projection functions, understanding the mathematics leads to understanding a pipeline implementation based on concatenation of 4×4 matrices. Until recently, application programs had to do the projections within the applications, and most hardware systems did not support perspective projections.

There are three major themes in the remainder of this book. First, we explore modeling further by expanding our basic set of primitives. In Chapter 8, we incorporate more complex relationships between simple objects through hierarchical models. In Chapter 9, we explore approaches to modeling that allow us to describe objects through procedures rather than as geometric objects. This approach allows us to model objects with only as much detail as is needed, to incorporate physical laws into our models, and to model natural phenomena that cannot be described by polygons. In Chapter 10, we leave the world of flat objects, adding curves and curved surfaces. These objects are defined by vertices, and we can implement them by breaking them into small flat primitives, so we can use the same viewing pipeline.

The second major theme is realism. Although more complex objects allow us to build more realistic models, we also explore more complex rendering options. In Chapter 5, we consider the interaction of light with the materials that characterize our objects. We look more deeply at hidden-surface–removal methods, at shading models, and in Chapter 7 at techniques such as texture mapping that allow us to create complex images from simple objects using advanced rendering techniques.

Third, we look more deeply at implementation in Chapter 6. At this point, we have introduced the major functional units of the graphics pipeline. We discuss the details of the algorithms used in each unit. We will also see additional possibilities for creating images by working directly in the frame buffer.

SUGGESTED READINGS

Carlbom and Paciorek [Car78] discuss the relationships between classical and computer viewing. Rogers and Adams [Rog90] give many examples of the projection matrices corresponding to the standard views used in drafting. Foley et al. [Fol90], Watt [Wat00], and Hearn and Baker [Hea04] derive canonical projection transformations. All follow a PHIGS orientation, so the API is slightly different from the one used here, although Foley derives the most general case. The references differ in whether they use column or row matrices, in where the COP is located, and in whether the projection is in the positive or negative z-direction. See the *OpenGL Programming Guide* [Shr10] for a further discussion of the use of the model-view and projection matrices in OpenGL.

EXERCISES

4.1 Not all projections are planar geometric projections. Give an example of a projection in which the projection surface is not a plane and another in which the projectors are not lines.

4.2 Consider an airplane whose position is specified by the roll, pitch, and yaw and by the distance from an object. Find a model-view matrix in terms of these parameters.

4.3 Consider a satellite orbiting the earth. Its position above the earth is specified in polar coordinates. Find a model-view matrix that keeps the viewer looking at the earth. Such a matrix could be used to show the earth as it rotates.

4.4 Show how to compute u and v directions from the VPN, VRP, and VUP using only cross products.

4.5 Can we obtain an isometric of the cube by a single rotation about a suitably chosen axis? Explain your answer.

4.6 Derive the perspective-projection matrix when the COP can be at any point and the projection plane can be at any orientation.

4.7 What is a parallel projection? What specialty do orthogonal projections provide? What is the advantage of the normalization transformation process?

4.8 Any attempt to take the projection of a point in the same plane as the COP will lead to a division by zero. What is the projection of a line segment that has endpoints on either side of the projection plane?

4.9 Define one or more APIs to specify oblique projections. You do not need to write the functions; just decide which parameters the user must specify.

4.10   Derive an oblique-projection matrix from specification of front and back clipping planes and top-right and bottom-left intersections of the sides of the clipping volume with the front clipping plane.

4.11   Our approach of normalizing all projections seems to imply that we could predistort all objects and support only orthographic projections. Explain any problems we would face if we took this approach to building a graphics system.

4.12   Hidden-surface-removal algorithms can be divided into two broad classes. What are these classes? Explain each.

4.13   We can create an interesting class of three-dimensional objects by extending two-dimensional objects into the third dimension by extrusion. For example, a circle becomes a cylinder, a line becomes a quadrilateral, and a quadrilateral in the plane becomes a parallelepiped. Use this technique to convert the two-dimensional maze from Exercise 2.7 to a three-dimensional maze.

4.14   Extend the maze program of Exercise 4.13 to allow the user to walk through the maze. A click on the middle mouse button should move the user forward; a click on the right or left button should turn the user 90 degrees to the right or left, respectively.

4.15   If we were to use orthogonal projections to draw the coordinate axes, the x- and y-axes would lie in the plane of the paper, but the z-axis would point out of the page. Instead, we can draw the x- and y-axes meeting at a 90-degree angle, with the z-axis going off at -135 degrees from the x-axis. Find the matrix that projects the original orthogonal-coordinate axes to this view.

4.16   Write a program to display a rotating cube in a box with three light sources. Each light source should project the cube onto one of the three visible sides of the box.

4.17   Find the projection of a point onto the plane $ax + by + cz + d = 0$ from a light source located at infinity in the direction (d_x, d_y, d_z).

4.18   Using one of the three-dimensional interfaces discussed in Chapter 3, write a program to move the camera through a scene composed of simple objects.

4.19   The specification of the orientation of a camera can be divided into the specification of the view-plane normal (VPN) and the specification of the view-up vector (VUP). Explain each of these.

4.20   In animation, often we can save effort by working with two-dimensional patterns that are mapped onto flat polygons that are always parallel to the camera, a technique known as **billboarding**. Write a program that will keep a simple polygon facing the camera as the camera moves.

4.21   Stereo images are produced by creating two images with the viewer in two slightly different positions. Consider a viewer who is at the origin but whose eyes are separated by Δx units. What are the appropriate viewing specifications to create the two images?

4.22 In Section 4.9, we displayed a mesh by drawing two line strips. How would you alter this approach to not draw the extra line from the end of one row (or column) to the begining of the next row (or column)?

4.23 Derive a method for displaying a mesh using a single triangle strip.

4.24 Why are projections produced by parallel and perspective viewing known as planar geometric projections?

4.25 What is the default projection matrix in OpenGL? Explain nonuniform fore-shortening.

4.26 The classical perspective views are usually known as one-, two-, and three-point perspectives. What are the differences between these perspectives?

4.27 What should the position of the center of projection (COP) be for
a. perspective views?
b. parallel views?

4.28 Write a reshape callback that does not distort the shape of objects as the window is altered.

CHAPTER 5

LIGHTING AND SHADING

We have learned to build three-dimensional graphical models and to display them. However, if you render one of our models, you might be disappointed to see images that look flat and thus fail to show the three-dimensional nature of the model. This appearance is a consequence of our unnatural assumption that each surface is lit such that it appears to a viewer in a single color. Under this assumption, the orthographic projection of a sphere is a uniformly colored circle, and a cube appears as a flat hexagon. If we look at a photograph of a lit sphere, we see not a uniformly colored circle but rather a circular shape with many gradations, or **shades**, of color. It is these gradations that give two-dimensional images the appearance of being three-dimensional.

What we have left out is the interaction between light and the surfaces in our models. This chapter begins to fill that gap. We develop separate models of light sources and of the most common light–material interactions. Our aim is to add shading to a fast pipeline graphics architecture. Consequently, we develop only local lighting models. Such models, as opposed to global lighting models, allow us to compute the shade to assign to a point on a surface, independent of any other surfaces in the scene. The calculations depend only on the material properties assigned to the surface, the local geometry of the surface, and the locations and properties of the light sources. In this chapter, we introduce the lighting models used most often in OpenGL applications. We shall see that we have choices as to where to apply a given lighting model: in the application, in the vertex shader, or in the fragment shader.

Following our previous development, we investigate how we can apply shading to polygonal models. We develop a recursive approximation to a sphere that will allow us to test our shading algorithms. We then discuss how light and material properties are specified in OpenGL applications and can be added to our sphere-approximating program.

We conclude the chapter with a short discussion of the two most important methods for handling global lighting effects: ray tracing and radiosity.

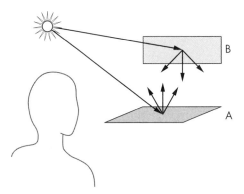

FIGURE 5.1   Reflecting surfaces.

5.1   LIGHT AND MATTER

In Chapters 1 and 2, we presented the rudiments of human color vision, delaying until now any discussion of the interaction between light and surfaces. Perhaps the most general approach to rendering is based on physics, where we use principles such as conservation of energy to derive equations that describe how light is reflected from surfaces.

From a physical perspective, a surface can either emit light by self-emission, as a light bulb does, or reflect light from other surfaces that illuminate it. Some surfaces may both reflect light and emit light from internal physical processes. When we look at a point on an object, the color that we see is determined by multiple interactions among light sources and reflective surfaces. These interactions can be viewed as a recursive process. Consider the simple scene in Figure 5.1. Some light from the source that reaches surface A is scattered. Some of this reflected light reaches surface B, and some of it is then scattered back to A, where some of it is again reflected back to B, and so on. This recursive scattering of light between surfaces accounts for subtle shading effects, such as the bleeding of colors between adjacent surfaces. Mathematically, the limit of this recursive process can be described using an integral equation, the **rendering equation**, which in principle we could use to find the shading of all surfaces in a scene. Unfortunately, this equation generally cannot be solved analytically. Numerical methods for computing a solution are not fast enough for real-time rendering. There are various approximate approaches, such as radiosity and ray tracing, each of which is an excellent approximation to the rendering equation for particular types of surfaces. Although ray tracing can render moderately complex scenes in real time, these methods cannot render scenes at the rate at which we can pass polygons through the modeling-projection pipeline. Consequently, we focus on a simpler rendering model, based on the Phong reflection model, that provides a compromise between physical correctness and efficient calculation. We will introduce global methods in Section 5.10 and then consider the rendering equation, radiosity, and ray tracing in greater detail in Chapter 11.

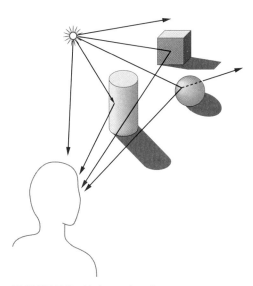

FIGURE 5.2   Light and surfaces.

Rather than looking at a global energy balance, we follow rays of light from light-emitting (or self-luminous) surfaces that we call **light sources**. We then model what happens to these rays as they interact with reflecting surfaces in the scene. This approach is similar to ray tracing, but we consider only single interactions between light sources and surfaces. There are two independent parts of the problem. First, we must model the light sources in the scene. Then we must build a reflection model that deals with the interactions between materials and light.

To get an overview of the process, we can start following rays of light from a point source, as shown in Figure 5.2. As we noted in Chapter 1, our viewer sees only the light that leaves the source and reaches her eyes—perhaps through a complex path and multiple interactions with objects in the scene. If a ray of light enters her eye directly from the source, she sees the color of the source. If the ray of light hits a surface visible to our viewer, the color she sees is based on the interaction between the source and the surface material: She sees the color of the light reflected from the surface toward her eyes.

In terms of computer graphics, we replace the viewer by the projection plane, as shown in Figure 5.3. Conceptually, the clipping window in this plane is mapped to the screen; thus, we can think of the projection plane as ruled into rectangles, each corresponding to a pixel. The color of the light source and of the surfaces determines the color of one or more pixels in the frame buffer.

We need to consider only those rays that leave the source and reach the viewer's eye, either directly or through interactions with objects. In the case of computer viewing, these are the rays that reach the center of projection (COP) after passing through the clipping rectangle. Note that in scenes for which the image shows a lot

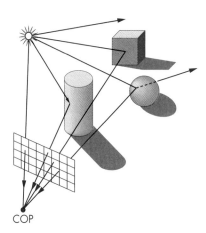

COP

FIGURE 5.3   Light, surfaces, and computer imaging.

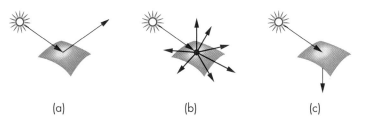

(a)   (b)   (c)

FIGURE 5.4   Light–material interactions. (a) Specular surface. (b) Diffuse surface. (c) Translucent surface.

of the background, most rays leaving a source do not contribute to the image and are thus of no interest to us. We make use of this observation in Section 5.10.

Figure 5.2 shows both single and multiple interactions between rays and objects. It is the nature of these interactions that determines whether an object appears red or brown, light or dark, dull or shiny. When light strikes a surface, some of it is absorbed and some of it is reflected. If the surface is opaque, reflection and absorption account for all the light striking the surface. If the surface is translucent, some of the light is transmitted through the material and emerges to interact with other objects. These interactions depend on wavelength. An object illuminated by white light appears red because it absorbs most of the incident light but reflects light in the red range of frequencies. A shiny object appears so because its surface is smooth. Conversely, a dull object has a rough surface. The shading of objects also depends on the orientation of their surfaces, a factor that we shall see is characterized by the normal vector at each point. These interactions between light and materials can be classified into the three groups depicted in Figure 5.4.

1. **Specular surfaces** appear shiny because most of the light that is reflected or **scattered** is in a narrow range of angles close to the angle of reflection. Mirrors are **perfectly specular surfaces**; the light from an incoming light ray may be partially absorbed, but all reflected light from a given angle emerges at a single angle, obeying the rule that the angle of incidence is equal to the angle of reflection.

2. **Diffuse surfaces** are characterized by reflected light being scattered in all directions. Walls painted with matte or flat paint are diffuse reflectors, as are many natural materials, such as terrain viewed from an airplane or a satellite. **Perfectly diffuse surfaces** scatter light equally in all directions, and thus a flat perfectly diffuse surface appears the same to all viewers.

3. **Translucent surfaces** allow some light to penetrate the surface and to emerge from another location on the object. This process of **refraction** characterizes glass and water. Some incident light may also be reflected at the surface.

We shall model all these surfaces in Section 5.3. First, we consider light sources.

5.2 LIGHT SOURCES

Light can leave a surface through two fundamental processes: self-emission and reflection. We usually think of a light source as an object that emits light only through internal energy sources. However, a light source, such as a light bulb, can also reflect some light that is incident on it from the surrounding environment. We will usually omit the emissive term in our simple models. When we discuss lighting in Section 5.7, we will see that we can easily add a self-emission term.

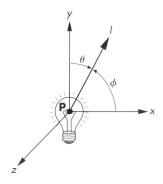

FIGURE 5.5 Light source.

If we consider a source such as the one in Figure 5.5, we can look at it as an object with a surface. Each point (x, y, z) on the surface can emit light that is characterized by the direction of emission (θ, ϕ) and the intensity of energy emitted at each wavelength λ. Thus, a general light source can be characterized by a six-variable **illumination function** $I(x, y, z, \theta, \phi, \lambda)$. Note that we need two angles to specify a direction, and we are assuming that each frequency can be considered independently. From the perspective of a surface illuminated by this source, we can obtain the total contribution of the source (Figure 5.6) by integrating over its surface, a process that accounts for the emission angles that reach this surface and must also account for the distance between the source and the surface. For a distributed light source, such as a light bulb, the evaluation of this integral is difficult, whether we use analytic or numerical methods. Often, it is easier to model the distributed source with polygons, each of which is a simple source, or with an approximating set of point sources.

We consider four basic types of sources: ambient lighting, point sources, spotlights, and distant light. These four lighting types are sufficient for rendering most simple scenes.

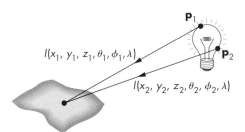

FIGURE 5.6   Adding the contribution from a source.

5.2.1 Color Sources

Not only do light sources emit different amounts of light at different frequencies, but their directional properties can vary with frequency as well. Consequently, a physically-correct model can be complex. However, our model of the human visual system is based on three-color theory, which tells us we perceive three tristimulus values rather than a full-color distribution. For most applications, we can thus model light sources as having three components—red, green, and blue—and can use each of the three color sources to obtain the corresponding color components that a human observer sees.

We describe a source through a three-component intensity, or **luminance**, function

$$\mathbf{I} = \begin{bmatrix} I_r \\ I_g \\ I_b \end{bmatrix},$$

each of whose components is the intensity of the independent red, green, and blue components. Thus, we use the red component of a light source for the calculation of the red component of the image. Because light–material computations involve three similar but independent calculations, we will tend to present a single scalar equation, with the understanding that it can represent any of the three color components.

5.2.2 Ambient Light

In many rooms, such as classrooms or kitchens, the lights have been designed and positioned to provide uniform illumination throughout the room. Such illumination is often achieved through large sources that have diffusers whose purpose is to scatter light in all directions. We could create an accurate simulation of such illumination, at least in principle, by modeling all the distributed sources and then integrating the illumination from these sources at each point on a reflecting surface. Making such a model and rendering a scene with it would be a daunting task for a graphics system, especially one for which real-time performance is desirable. Alternatively, we can look at the desired effect of the sources: to achieve a uniform light level in the room. This uniform lighting is called **ambient light**. If we follow this second approach, we can postulate an ambient intensity at each point in the environment. Thus, ambient

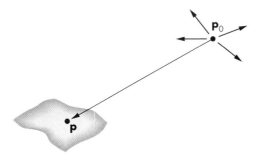

FIGURE 5.7   Point source illuminating a surface.

illumination is characterized by an intensity, $\mathbf{I}_a$, that is identical at every point in the scene.

Our ambient source has three color components:

$$\mathbf{I}_a = \begin{bmatrix} I_{ar} \\ I_{ag} \\ I_{ab} \end{bmatrix}.$$

We will use the *scalar* I_a to denote any one of the red, green, or blue components of $\mathbf{I}_a$. Although every point in our scene receives the same illumination from $\mathbf{I}_a$, each surface can reflect this light differently.

5.2.3 Point Sources

An ideal **point source** emits light equally in all directions. We can characterize a point source located at a point $\mathbf{p}_0$ by a three-component color matrix:

$$\mathbf{I}(\mathbf{p_0}) = \begin{bmatrix} I_r(\mathbf{p_0}) \\ I_g(\mathbf{p_0}) \\ I_b(\mathbf{p_0}) \end{bmatrix}.$$

The intensity of illumination received from a point source is proportional to the inverse square of the distance between the source and surface. Hence, at a point $\mathbf{p}$ (Figure 5.7), the intensity of light received from the point source is given by the matrix

$$\mathbf{i}(\mathbf{p}, \mathbf{p_0}) = \frac{1}{|\mathbf{p} - \mathbf{p_0}|^2} \mathbf{I}(\mathbf{p_0}).$$

As with ambient light, we will use $I(\mathbf{p_0})$ to denote any of the components of $\mathbf{I}(\mathbf{p_0})$.

The use of point sources in most applications is determined more by their ease of use than by their resemblance to physical reality. Scenes rendered with only point sources tend to have high contrast; objects appear either bright or dark. In the real world, it is the large size of most light sources that contributes to softer scenes, as we can see from Figure 5.8, which shows the shadows created by a source of finite size. Some areas are fully in shadow, or in the **umbra**, whereas others are in partial

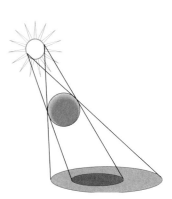

FIGURE 5.8   Shadows created by finite-size light source.

shadow, or in the **penumbra**. We can mitigate the high-contrast effect from point-source illumination by adding ambient light to a scene.

The distance term also contributes to the harsh renderings with point sources. Although the inverse-square distance term is correct for point sources, in practice it is usually replaced by a term of the form $(a + bd + cd^2)^{-1}$, where d is the distance between $\mathbf{p}$ and $\mathbf{p}_0$. The constants a, b, and c can be chosen to soften the lighting. Note that if the light source is far from the surfaces in the scene, the intensity of the light from the source is sufficiently uniform that the distance term is constant over each surface.

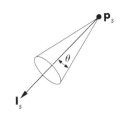

FIGURE 5.9   Spotlight.

5.2.4 Spotlights

Spotlights are characterized by a narrow range of angles through which light is emitted. We can construct a simple spotlight from a point source by limiting the angles at which light from the source can be seen. We can use a cone whose apex is at $\mathbf{p}_s$, which points in the direction $\mathbf{l}_s$, and whose width is determined by an angle θ, as shown in Figure 5.9. If $\theta = 180$, the spotlight becomes a point source.

More realistic spotlights are characterized by the distribution of light within the cone—usually with most of the light concentrated in the center of the cone. Thus, the intensity is a function of the angle ϕ between the direction of the source and a vector $\mathbf{s}$ to a point on the surface (as long as this angle is less than θ; Figure 5.10). Although this function could be defined in many ways, it is usually defined by $\cos^e \phi$, where the exponent e (Figure 5.11) determines how rapidly the light intensity drops off.

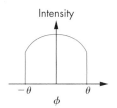

FIGURE 5.10   Attenuation of a spotlight.

As we shall see throughout this chapter, cosines are convenient functions for lighting calculations. If $\mathbf{u}$ and $\mathbf{v}$ are any unit-length vectors, we can compute the cosine of the angle θ between them with the dot product

$$\cos \theta = \mathbf{u} \cdot \mathbf{v},$$

a calculation that requires only three multiplications and two additions.

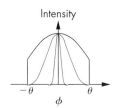

FIGURE 5.11   Spotlight exponent.

5.2.5 Distant Light Sources

Most shading calculations require the direction from the point on the surface to the light source position. As we move across a surface, calculating the intensity at each point, we should recompute this vector repeatedly—a computation that is a significant part of the shading calculation. However, if the light source is far from the surface, the vector does not change much as we move from point to point, just as the light from the sun strikes all objects that are in close proximity to one another at the same angle. Figure 5.12 illustrates that we are effectively replacing a point source of light with a source that illuminates objects with parallel rays of light—a parallel source. In practice, the calculations for distant light sources are similar to the calculations for parallel projections; they replace the *location* of the light source with the *direction* of the light source. Hence, in homogeneous coordinates, a point light source at $\mathbf{p}_0$ is represented internally as a four-dimensional column matrix:

FIGURE 5.12   Parallel light source.

$$\mathbf{p}_0 = \begin{bmatrix} x \\ y \\ z \\ 1 \end{bmatrix}.$$

In contrast, the distant light source is described by a direction vector whose representation in homogeneous coordinates is the matrix

$$\mathbf{p}_0 = \begin{bmatrix} x \\ y \\ z \\ 0 \end{bmatrix}.$$

The graphics system can carry out rendering calculations more efficiently for distant light sources than for near ones. Of course, a scene rendered with distant light sources looks different from a scene rendered with near sources. Fortunately, our models will allow both types of sources.

5.3 THE PHONG REFLECTION MODEL

Although we could approach light–material interactions through physical models, we have chosen to use a model that leads to efficient computations, especially when we use it with our pipeline-rendering model. The reflection model that we present was introduced by Phong and later modified by Blinn. It has proved to be efficient and to be a close-enough approximation to physical reality to produce good renderings under a variety of lighting conditions and material properties.

The Phong model uses the four vectors shown in Figure 5.13 to calculate a color for an arbitrary point $\mathbf{p}$ on a surface. If the surface is curved, all four vectors can change as we move from point to point. The vector $\mathbf{n}$ is the normal at $\mathbf{p}$; we discuss its calculation in Section 5.4. The vector $\mathbf{v}$ is in the direction from $\mathbf{p}$ to the viewer or COP. The vector $\mathbf{l}$ is in the direction of a line from $\mathbf{p}$ to an arbitrary point on the source for a distributed light source or, as we are assuming for now, to the point-light source. Finally, the vector $\mathbf{r}$ is in the direction that a perfectly reflected ray from $\mathbf{l}$ would take. Note that $\mathbf{r}$ is determined by $\mathbf{n}$ and $\mathbf{l}$. We calculate it in Section 5.4.

The Phong model supports the three types of material–light interactions—ambient, diffuse, and specular—that we introduced in Section 5.1. Suppose that we have a set of point sources. We assume that each source can have separate ambient, diffuse, and specular components for each of the three primary colors. Although this assumption may appear unnatural, remember that our goal is to create realistic shading effects in as close to real time as possible. We use a local model to simulate effects that can be global in nature. Thus, our light-source model has ambient, diffuse, and specular terms. We need nine coefficients to characterize these terms at any point $\mathbf{p}$ on the surface. We can place these nine coefficients in a 3×3 illumination matrix for the ith light source:

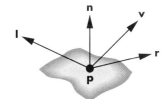

FIGURE 5.13 Vectors used by the Phong model.

$$\mathbf{L}_i = \begin{bmatrix} L_{ira} & L_{iga} & L_{iba} \\ L_{ird} & L_{igd} & L_{ibd} \\ L_{irs} & L_{igs} & L_{ibs} \end{bmatrix}.$$

The first row of the matrix contains the ambient intensities for the red, green, and blue terms from source i. The second row contains the diffuse terms; the third contains the specular terms. We assume that any distance-attenuation terms have not yet been applied. This matrix is only a simple way of storing the nine lighting terms we need. In practice, we will use constructs such as

```
vec3 light_i_ambient, light_i_diffuse, light_i_specular;
```

or

```
vec4 light_i_ambient, light_i_diffuse, light_i_specular;
```

for each source in our code. The four-dimensional form will be useful when we consider lighting with materials that are not opaque.

We construct the model by assuming that we can compute how much of each of the incident lights is reflected at the point of interest. For example, for the red diffuse term from source i, L_{ird}, we can compute a reflection term R_{ird}, and the latter's contribution to the intensity at $\mathbf{p}$ is $R_{ird}L_{ird}$. The value of R_{ird} depends on the material properties, the orientation of the surface, the direction of the light source, and the distance between the light source and the viewer. Thus, for each point, we have nine coefficients that we can place in a matrix of reflection terms of the form

$$\mathbf{R}_i = \begin{bmatrix} R_{ira} & R_{iga} & R_{iba} \\ R_{ird} & R_{igd} & R_{ibd} \\ R_{irs} & R_{igs} & R_{ibs} \end{bmatrix}.$$

We can then compute the contribution for each color source by adding the ambient, diffuse, and specular components. For example, the red intensity that we see at $\mathbf{p}$ from source i is

$$I_{ir} = R_{ira}L_{ira} + R_{ird}L_{ird} + R_{irs}L_{irs}$$
$$= I_{ira} + I_{ird} + I_{irs}.$$

We obtain the total intensity by adding the contributions of all sources and, possibly, a global ambient term. Thus, the red term is

$$I_r = \sum_i (I_{ira} + I_{ird} + I_{irs}) + I_{ar},$$

where I_{ar} is the red component of the global ambient light.

We can simplify our notation by noting that the necessary computations are the same for each source and for each primary color. They differ depending on whether we are considering the ambient, diffuse, or specular terms. Hence, we can omit the subscripts i, r, g, and b. We write

$$I = I_a + I_d + I_s = L_a R_a + L_d R_d + L_s R_s,$$

with the understanding that the computation will be done for each of the primaries and each source; the global ambient term can be added at the end. As with the lighting terms, when we get to code we will use forms such as

```
vec4 reflect_i_ambient, reflect_i_diffuse, reflect_i_specular;
```

Note that these terms are all for a single surface and in general we will have different reflectivity properties for each material.

5.3.1 Ambient Reflection

The intensity of ambient light I_a is the same at every point on the surface. Some of this light is absorbed and some is reflected. The amount reflected is given by the ambient reflection coefficient, $R_a = k_a$. Because only a positive fraction of the light is reflected, we must have

$$0 \le k_a \le 1,$$

and thus

$$I_a = k_a L_a.$$

Here L_a can be any of the individual light sources, or it can be a global ambient term.

A surface has, of course, three ambient coefficients—k_{ar}, k_{ag}, and k_{ab}—and they can differ. Hence, for example, a sphere appears yellow under white ambient light if its blue ambient coefficient is small and its red and green coefficients are large.

5.3.2 Diffuse Reflection

A perfectly diffuse reflector scatters the light that it reflects equally in all directions. Hence, such a surface appears the same to all viewers. However, the amount of light reflected depends both on the material—because some of the incoming light is absorbed—and on the position of the light source relative to the surface. Diffuse reflections are characterized by rough surfaces. If we were to magnify a cross section of a diffuse surface, we might see an image like that shown in Figure 5.14. Rays of light that hit the surface at only slightly different angles are reflected back at markedly different angles. Perfectly diffuse surfaces are so rough that there is no preferred angle of reflection. Such surfaces, sometimes called **Lambertian surfaces**, can be modeled mathematically with Lambert's law.

Consider a diffuse planar surface, as shown in Figure 5.15, illuminated by the sun. The surface is brightest at noon and dimmest at dawn and dusk because, according to Lambert's law, we see only the vertical component of the incoming light.

FIGURE 5.14   Rough surface.

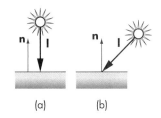

FIGURE 5.15   Illumination of a diffuse surface. (a) At noon. (b) In the afternoon.

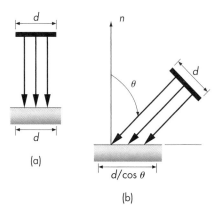

FIGURE 5.16   Vertical contributions by Lambert's law. (a) At noon. (b) In the afternoon.

One way to understand this law is to consider a small parallel light source striking a plane, as shown in Figure 5.16. As the source is lowered in the (artificial) sky, the same amount of light is spread over a larger area, and the surface appears dimmer. Returning to the point source of Figure 5.15, we can characterize diffuse reflections mathematically. Lambert's law states that

$$R_d \propto \cos \theta,$$

where θ is the angle between the normal at the point of interest $\mathbf{n}$ and the direction of the light source $\mathbf{l}$. If both $\mathbf{l}$ and $\mathbf{n}$ are unit-length vectors,[1] then

$$\cos \theta = \mathbf{l} \cdot \mathbf{n}.$$

If we add in a reflection coefficient k_d representing the fraction of incoming diffuse light that is reflected, we have the diffuse reflection term:

$$I_d = k_d(\mathbf{l} \cdot \mathbf{n})L_d.$$

If we wish to incorporate a distance term, to account for attenuation as the light travels a distance d from the source to the surface, we can again use the quadratic attenuation term:

$$I_d = \frac{k_d}{a + bd + cd^2}(\mathbf{l} \cdot \mathbf{n})L_d.$$

---

1. Direction vectors, such as $\mathbf{l}$ and $\mathbf{n}$, are used repeatedly in shading calculations through the dot product. In practice, both the programmer and the graphics software should seek to normalize all such vectors as soon as possible.

There is a potential problem with this expression because $(\mathbf{l} \cdot \mathbf{n})L_d$ will be negative if the light source is below the horizon. In this case, we want to use zero rather than a negative value. Hence, in practice we use $\max((\mathbf{l} \cdot \mathbf{n})L_d, 0)$.

5.3.3 Specular Reflection

If we employ only ambient and diffuse reflections, our images will be shaded and will appear three-dimensional, but all the surfaces will look dull, somewhat like chalk. What we are missing are the highlights that we see reflected from shiny objects. These highlights usually show a color different from the color of the reflected ambient and diffuse light. For example, a red plastic ball viewed under white light has a white highlight that is the reflection of some of the light from the source in the direction of the viewer (Figure 5.17).

FIGURE 5.17   Specular highlights.

Whereas a diffuse surface is rough, a specular surface is smooth. The smoother the surface is, the more it resembles a mirror. Figure 5.18 shows that as the surface gets smoother, the reflected light is concentrated in a smaller range of angles centered about the angle of a perfect reflector—a mirror or a perfectly specular surface. Modeling specular surfaces realistically can be complex because the pattern by which the light is scattered is not symmetric. It depends on the wavelength of the incident light, and it changes with the reflection angle.

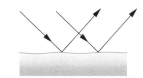

FIGURE 5.18   Specular surface.

Phong proposed an approximate model that can be computed with only a slight increase over the work done for diffuse surfaces. The model adds a term for specular reflection. Hence, we consider the surface as being rough for the diffuse term and smooth for the specular term. The amount of light that the viewer sees depends on the angle ϕ between $\mathbf{r}$, the direction of a perfect reflector, and $\mathbf{v}$, the direction of the viewer. The Phong model uses the equation

$$I_s = k_s L_s \cos^\alpha \phi.$$

The coefficient k_s ($0 \leq k_s \leq 1$) is the fraction of the incoming specular light that is reflected. The exponent α is a **shininess** coefficient. Figure 5.19 shows how, as α is increased, the reflected light is concentrated in a narrower region centered on the angle of a perfect reflector. In the limit, as α goes to infinity, we get a mirror; values in the range 100 to 500 correspond to most metallic surfaces, and smaller values (< 100) correspond to materials that show broad highlights.

The computational advantage of the Phong model is that if we have normalized $\mathbf{r}$ and $\mathbf{n}$ to unit length, we can again use the dot product, and the specular term becomes

$$I_s = k_s L_s \max((\mathbf{r} \cdot \mathbf{v})^\alpha, 0).$$

We can add a distance term, as we did with diffuse reflections. What is referred to as the **Phong model**, including the distance term, is written

$$I = \frac{1}{a + bd + cd^2}(k_d L_d \max(\mathbf{l} \cdot \mathbf{n}, 0) + k_s L_s \max((\mathbf{r} \cdot \mathbf{v})^\alpha, 0)) + k_a L_a.$$

This formula is computed for each light source and for each primary.

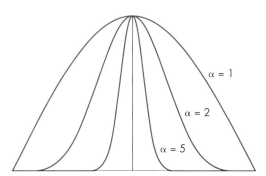

FIGURE 5.19   Effect of shininess coefficient.

It might seem to make little sense either to associate a different amount of ambient light with each source or to allow the components for specular and diffuse lighting to be different. Because we cannot solve the full rendering equation, we must use various tricks in an attempt to obtain realistic renderings.

Consider, for example, an environment with many objects. When we turn on a light, some of that light hits a surface directly. These contributions to the image can be modeled with specular and diffuse components of the source. However, much of the rest of the light from the source is scattered from multiple reflections from other objects and makes a contribution to the light received at the surface under consideration. We can approximate this term by having an ambient component associated with the source. The shade that we should assign to this term depends on *both* the color of the source and the color of the objects in the room—an unfortunate consequence of our use of approximate models. To some extent, the same analysis holds for diffuse light. Diffuse light reflects among the surfaces, and the color that we see on a particular surface depends on other surfaces in the environment. Again, by using carefully chosen diffuse and specular components with our light sources, we can approximate a global effect with local calculations.

We have developed the Phong model in object space. The actual shading, however, is not done until the objects have passed through the model-view and projection transformations. These transformations can affect the cosine terms in the model (see Exercise 5.19). Consequently, to make a correct shading calculation, we must either preserve spatial relationships as vertices and vectors pass through the pipeline, perhaps by sending additional information through the pipeline from object space, or go backward through the pipeline to obtain the required shading information.

5.3.4 The Modified Phong Model

If we use the Phong model with specular reflections in our rendering, the dot product $\mathbf{r} \cdot \mathbf{v}$ should be recalculated at every point on the surface. We can obtain an interesting approximation by using the unit vector halfway between the viewer vector and the light-source vector:

$$\mathbf{h} = \frac{\mathbf{l} + \mathbf{v}}{|\mathbf{l} + \mathbf{v}|}.$$

Figure 5.20 shows all five vectors. Here we have defined ψ as the angle between $\mathbf{n}$ and $\mathbf{h}$, the **halfway angle**. When $\mathbf{v}$ lies in the same plane as do $\mathbf{l}$, $\mathbf{n}$, and $\mathbf{r}$, we can show (see Exercise 5.7) that

$$2\psi = \phi.$$

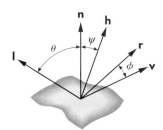

FIGURE 5.20 Determination of the halfway vector.

If we replace $\mathbf{r} \cdot \mathbf{v}$ with $\mathbf{n} \cdot \mathbf{h}$, we avoid calculation of $\mathbf{r}$. However, the halfway angle ψ is smaller than ϕ, and if we use the same exponent e in $(\mathbf{n} \cdot \mathbf{h})^e$ that we used in $(\mathbf{r} \cdot \mathbf{v})^e$, then the size of the specular highlights will be smaller. We can mitigate this problem by replacing the value of the exponent e with a value e' so that $(\mathbf{n} \cdot \mathbf{h})^{e'}$ is closer to $(\mathbf{r} \cdot \mathbf{v})^e$. It is clear that avoiding recalculation of $\mathbf{r}$ is desirable. However, to appreciate fully where savings can be made, you should consider all the cases of flat and curved surfaces, near and far light sources, and near and far viewers (see Exercise 5.8).

When we use the halfway vector in the calculation of the specular term, we are using the **Blinn-Phong**, or **modified Phong, lighting model**. This model is the default in systems with a fixed-function pipeline and is the one we will use in our first shaders that carry out lighting.

Color Plate 17 shows a group of Utah teapots (Section 10.10) that have been rendered in OpenGL using the modified Phong model. Note that it is only our ability to control material properties that makes the teapots appear different from one another. The various teapots demonstrate how the modified Phong model can create a variety of surface effects, ranging from dull surfaces to highly reflective surfaces that look like metal.

5.4 COMPUTATION OF VECTORS

The illumination and reflection models that we have derived are sufficiently general that they can be applied to either curved or flat surfaces, to parallel or perspective views, and to distant or near surfaces. Most of the calculations for rendering a scene involve the determination of the required vectors and dot products. For each special case, simplifications are possible. For example, if the surface is a flat polygon, the normal is the same at all points on the surface. If the light source is far from the surface, the light direction is the same at all points.

In this section, we examine how the vectors are computed for the general case. In Section 5.5, we see what additional techniques can be applied when our objects are composed of flat polygons. This case is especially important because most renderers, including OpenGL, render curved surfaces by approximating those surfaces with many small, flat polygons.

5.4.1 Normal Vectors

For smooth surfaces, the vector normal to the surface exists at every point and gives the local orientation of the surface. Its calculation depends on how the surface is represented mathematically. Two simple cases—the plane and the sphere—illustrate both how we compute normals and where the difficulties lie.

A plane can be described by the equation

$$ax + by + cz + d = 0.$$

As we saw in Chapter 3, this equation could also be written in terms of the normal to the plane, $\mathbf{n}$, and a point, $\mathbf{p}_0$, known to be on the plane as

$$\mathbf{n} \cdot (\mathbf{p} - \mathbf{p}_0) = 0,$$

where $\mathbf{p}$ is any point (x, y, z) on the plane. Comparing the two forms, we see that the vector $\mathbf{n}$ is given by

$$\mathbf{n} = \begin{bmatrix} a \\ b \\ c \end{bmatrix},$$

or, in homogeneous coordinates,

$$\mathbf{n} = \begin{bmatrix} a \\ b \\ c \\ 0 \end{bmatrix}.$$

However, suppose that instead we are given three noncollinear points—$\mathbf{p}_0$, $\mathbf{p}_1$, $\mathbf{p}_2$—that are in this plane and thus are sufficient to determine it uniquely. The vectors $\mathbf{p}_2 - \mathbf{p}_0$ and $\mathbf{p}_1 - \mathbf{p}_0$ are parallel to the plane, and we can use their cross product to find the normal

$$\mathbf{n} = (\mathbf{p}_2 - \mathbf{p}_0) \times (\mathbf{p}_1 - \mathbf{p}_0).$$

We must be careful about the order of the vectors in the cross product: Reversing the order changes the surface from outward pointing to inward pointing, and that reversal can affect the lighting calculations. Some graphics systems use the first three vertices in the specification of a polygon to determine the normal automatically. OpenGL does not do so, but as we shall see in Section 5.5, forcing users to compute normals creates more flexibility in how we apply our lighting model.

For curved surfaces, how we compute normals depends on how we represent the surface. In Chapter 10, we discuss three different methods for representing curves and surfaces. We can see a few of the possibilities by considering how we represent a unit sphere centered at the origin. The usual equation for this sphere is the **implicit equation**

$$f(x, y, z) = x^2 + y^2 + z^2 - 1 = 0,$$

or in vector form,

$$f(\mathbf{p}) = \mathbf{p} \cdot \mathbf{p} - 1 = 0.$$

The normal is given by the **gradient vector**, which is defined by the column matrix

$$\mathbf{n} = \begin{bmatrix} \frac{\partial f}{\partial x} \\ \frac{\partial f}{\partial y} \\ \frac{\partial f}{\partial z} \end{bmatrix} = \begin{bmatrix} 2x \\ 2y \\ 2z \end{bmatrix} = 2\mathbf{p}.$$

The sphere could also be represented in **parametric form**. In this form, the x, y, and z values of a point on the sphere are represented independently in terms of two parameters u and v:

$$x = x(u, v),$$

$$y = y(u, v),$$

$$z = z(u, v).$$

As we shall see in Chapter 10, this form is preferable in computer graphics, especially for representing curves and surfaces; although, for a particular surface, there may be multiple parametric representations. One parametric representation for the sphere is

$$x(u, v) = \cos u \sin v,$$

$$y(u, v) = \cos u \cos v,$$

$$z(u, v) = \sin u.$$

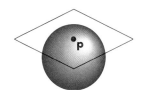

FIGURE 5.21   Tangent plane to sphere.

As u and v vary in the range $-\pi/2 < u < \pi/2$, $-\pi < v < \pi$, we get all the points on the sphere. When we are using the parametric form, we can obtain the normal from the **tangent plane**, shown in Figure 5.21, at a point $\mathbf{p}(u, v) = [x(u, v)\, y(u, v)\, z(u, v)]^T$ on the surface. The tangent plane gives the local orientation of the surface at a point; we can derive it by taking the linear terms of the Taylor series expansion of the surface at $\mathbf{p}$. The result is that at $\mathbf{p}$, lines in the directions of the vectors represented by

$$\frac{\partial \mathbf{p}}{\partial u} = \begin{bmatrix} \frac{\partial x}{\partial u} \\ \frac{\partial y}{\partial u} \\ \frac{\partial z}{\partial u} \end{bmatrix}, \qquad \frac{\partial \mathbf{p}}{\partial v} = \begin{bmatrix} \frac{\partial x}{\partial v} \\ \frac{\partial y}{\partial v} \\ \frac{\partial z}{\partial v} \end{bmatrix}$$

lie in the tangent plane. We can use their cross product to obtain the normal

$$\mathbf{n} = \frac{\partial \mathbf{p}}{\partial u} \times \frac{\partial \mathbf{p}}{\partial v}.$$

For our sphere, we find that

$$\mathbf{n} = \cos u \begin{bmatrix} \cos u \sin v \\ \cos u \cos v \\ \sin u \end{bmatrix} = (\cos u)\mathbf{p}.$$

We are interested in only the direction of $\mathbf{n}$; thus, we can divide by $\cos u$ to obtain the unit normal to the sphere

$$\mathbf{n} = \mathbf{p}.$$

In Section 5.9, we use this result to shade a polygonal approximation to a sphere.

Within a graphics system, we usually work with a collection of vertices, and the normal vector must be approximated from some set of points close to the point where the normal is needed. The pipeline architecture of real-time graphics systems makes this calculation difficult because we process one vertex at a time, and thus the graphics system may not have the information available to compute the approximate normal at a given point. Consequently, graphics systems often leave the computation of normals to the user program.

In OpenGL, we will usually set up a normal as a vertex attribute by a mechanism such as

```
typedef normal vec4;

normal n = vec4(nx, ny, nz, 0.0);
```

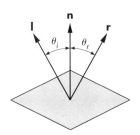

FIGURE 5.22   A mirror.

and then send the normal as needed to a vertex shader as an attribute qualified variable.

5.4.2 Angle of Reflection

Once we have calculated the normal at a point, we can use this normal and the direction of the light source to compute the direction of a perfect reflection. An ideal mirror is characterized by the following statement: *The angle of incidence is equal to the angle of reflection.* These angles are as pictured in Figure 5.22. The **angle of incidence** is the angle between the normal and the light source (assumed to be a point source); the **angle of reflection** is the angle between the normal and the direction in which the light is reflected. In two dimensions, there is but a single angle satisfying the angle condition. In three dimensions, however, our statement is insufficient to compute the required angle: There is an infinite number of angles satisfying our condition. We must add the following statement: *At a point* $\mathbf{p}$ *on the surface, the incoming light ray, the reflected light ray, and the normal at the point must all lie in the same plane.* These two conditions are sufficient for us to determine $\mathbf{r}$ from $\mathbf{n}$ and $\mathbf{l}$. Our primary interest is the direction, rather than the magnitude, of $\mathbf{r}$. However, many of our rendering calculations will be easier if we deal with unit-length vectors. Hence, we assume that both $\mathbf{l}$ and $\mathbf{n}$ have been normalized such that

$$|\mathbf{l}| = |\mathbf{n}| = 1.$$

We also want

$|\mathbf{r}| = 1.$

If $\theta_i = \theta_r$, then

$\cos \theta_i = \cos \theta_r.$

Using the dot product, the angle condition is

$\cos \theta_i = \mathbf{l} \cdot \mathbf{n} = \cos \theta_r = \mathbf{n} \cdot \mathbf{r}.$

The coplanar condition implies that we can write $\mathbf{r}$ as a linear combination of $\mathbf{l}$ and $\mathbf{n}$:

$\mathbf{r} = \alpha \mathbf{l} + \beta \mathbf{n}.$

Taking the dot product with $\mathbf{n}$, we find that

$\mathbf{n} \cdot \mathbf{r} = \alpha \mathbf{l} \cdot \mathbf{n} + \beta = \mathbf{l} \cdot \mathbf{n}.$

We can get a second condition between α and β from our requirement that $\mathbf{r}$ also be of unit length; thus,

$1 = \mathbf{r} \cdot \mathbf{r} = \alpha^2 + 2\alpha\beta \mathbf{l} \cdot \mathbf{n} + \beta^2.$

Solving these two equations, we find that

$\mathbf{r} = 2(\mathbf{l} \cdot \mathbf{n})\mathbf{n} - \mathbf{l}.$

Some of the shaders we develop will use this calculation to compute a reflection vector for use in the application; others that need the reflection vector only in a shader can use the GLSL `reflect` function to compute it. Methods such as environment maps will use the reflected-view vector (see Exercise 5.26) that is used to determine what a viewer would see if she looked at a reflecting surface such as a highly polished sphere.

5.5 POLYGONAL SHADING

Assuming that we can compute normal vectors, given a set of light sources and a viewer, the lighting models that we have developed can be applied at every point on a surface. Unfortunately, even if we have simple equations to determine normal vectors, as we did in our example of a sphere (Section 5.4), the amount of computation required can be large. We have already seen many of the advantages of using polygonal models for our objects. A further advantage is that for flat polygons, we can significantly reduce the work required for shading. Most graphics systems, including

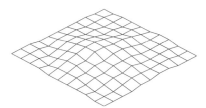

FIGURE 5.23   Polygonal mesh.

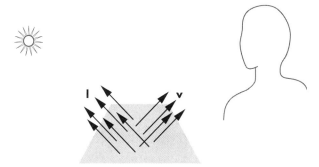

FIGURE 5.24   Distant source and viewer.

OpenGL, exploit the efficiencies possible for rendering flat polygons by decomposing curved surfaces into many small, flat polygons.

Consider a polygonal mesh, such as that shown in Figure 5.23, where each polygon is flat and thus has a well-defined normal vector. We consider three ways to shade the polygons: flat shading, smooth or Gouraud shading, and Phong shading.

5.5.1 Flat Shading

The three vectors—$\mathbf{l}$, $\mathbf{n}$, and $\mathbf{v}$—can vary as we move from point to point on a surface. For a flat polygon, however, $\mathbf{n}$ is constant. If we assume a distant viewer, $\mathbf{v}$ is constant over the polygon. Finally, if the light source is distant, $\mathbf{l}$ is constant. Here *distant* could be interpreted in the strict sense of meaning that the source is at infinity. The necessary adjustments, such as changing the *location* of the source to the *direction* of the source, could then be made to the shading equations and to their implementation. *Distant* could also be interpreted in terms of the size of the polygon relative to how far the polygon is from the source or viewer, as shown in Figure 5.24. Graphics systems or user programs often exploit this definition.

If the three vectors are constant, then the shading calculation needs to be carried out only once for each polygon, and each point on the polygon is assigned the same shade. This technique is known as **flat**, or **constant**, **shading**.

Flat shading will show differences in shading among the polygons in our mesh. If the light sources and viewer are near the polygon, the vectors $\mathbf{l}$ and $\mathbf{v}$ will be dif-

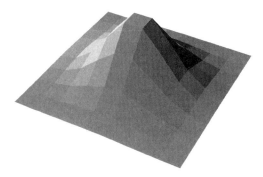

FIGURE 5.25　Flat shading of polygonal mesh.

ferent for each polygon. However, if our polygonal mesh has been designed to model a smooth surface, flat shading will almost always be disappointing because we can see even small differences in shading between adjacent polygons, as shown in Figure 5.25. The human visual system has a remarkable sensitivity to small differences in light intensity, due to a property known as **lateral inhibition**. If we see an increasing sequence of intensities, as is shown in Figure 5.26, we perceive the increases in brightness as overshooting on one side of an intensity step and undershooting on the other, as shown in Figure 5.27. We see stripes, known as **Mach bands**, along the edges. This phenomenon is a consequence of how the cones in the eye are connected to the optic nerve, and there is little that we can do to avoid it, other than to look for smoother shading techniques that do not produce large differences in shades at the edges of polygons.

FIGURE 5.26　Step chart.

5.5.2 Smooth and Gouraud Shading

In our rotating-cube example of Section 3.12, we saw that the rasterizer interpolates colors assigned to vertices across a polygon. Suppose that the lighting calculation is made at each vertex using the material properties and the vectors $\mathbf{n}$, $\mathbf{v}$, and $\mathbf{l}$ computed for each vertex. Thus, each vertex will have its own color that the rasterizer can use to interpolate a shade for each fragment. Note that if the light source is distant, and either the viewer is distant or there are no specular reflections, then smooth (or interpolative) shading shades a polygon in a constant color.

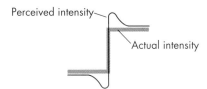

FIGURE 5.27　Perceived and actual intensities at an edge.

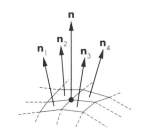

FIGURE 5.28 Normals near interior vertex.

If we consider our mesh, the idea of a normal existing at a vertex should cause concern to anyone worried about mathematical correctness. Because multiple polygons meet at interior vertices of the mesh, each of which has its own normal, the normal at the vertex is discontinuous. Although this situation might complicate the mathematics, Gouraud realized that the normal at the vertex could be *defined* in such a way as to achieve smoother shading through interpolation. Consider an interior vertex, as shown in Figure 5.28, where four polygons meet. Each has its own normal. In **Gouraud shading**, we define the normal at a vertex to be the normalized average of the normals of the polygons that share the vertex. For our example, the **vertex normal** is given by

$$\mathbf{n} = \frac{\mathbf{n}_1 + \mathbf{n}_2 + \mathbf{n}_3 + \mathbf{n}_4}{|\mathbf{n}_1 + \mathbf{n}_2 + \mathbf{n}_3 + \mathbf{n}_4|}.$$

From an OpenGL perspective, Gouraud shading is deceptively simple. We need only to set the vertex normals correctly. Often, the literature makes no distinction between smooth and Gouraud shading. However, the lack of a distinction causes a problem: How do we find the normals that we should average together? If our program is linear, specifying a list of vertices (and other properties), we do not have the necessary information about which polygons share a vertex. What we need, of course, is a data structure for representing the mesh. Traversing this data structure can generate the vertices with the averaged normals. Such a data structure should contain, at a minimum, polygons, vertices, normals, and material properties. One possible structure is the one shown in Figure 5.29. The key information that must be represented in the data structure is which polygons meet at each vertex.

Color Plates 4 and 5 show the shading effects available in OpenGL. In Color Plate 4, there is a single light source, but each polygon has been rendered with a single shade (constant shading), computed using the Phong model. In Color Plate 5,

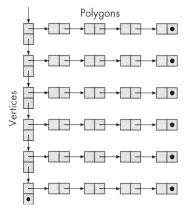

FIGURE 5.29 Mesh data structure.

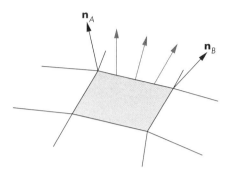

FIGURE 5.30   Edge normals.

normals have been assigned to all the vertices. OpenGL has then computed shades for the vertices and has interpolated these shades over the faces of the polygons.

Color Plate 21 contains another illustration of the smooth shading provided by OpenGL. We used this color cube as an example in both Chapters 2 and 3, and the programs are in Appendix A. The eight vertices are colored black, white, red, green, blue, cyan, magenta, and yellow. Once smooth shading is enabled, OpenGL interpolates the colors across the faces of the polygons automatically.

5.5.3 Phong Shading

Even the smoothness introduced by Gouraud shading may not prevent the appearance of Mach bands. Phong proposed that instead of interpolating vertex intensities, as we do in Gouraud shading, we interpolate normals across each polygon. Consider a polygon that shares edges and vertices with other polygons in the mesh, as shown in Figure 5.30. We can compute vertex normals by interpolating over the normals of the polygons that share the vertex. Next, we can use interpolation, as we did in Chapter 3, to interpolate the normals over the polygon. Consider Figure 5.31. We can use the interpolated normals at vertices A and B to interpolate normals along the edge between them:

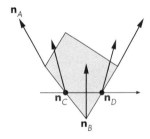

FIGURE 5.31   Interpolation of normals in Phong shading.

$$\mathbf{n}_C(\alpha) = (1 - \alpha)\mathbf{n}_A + \alpha\mathbf{n}_B.$$

We can do a similar interpolation on all the edges. The normal at any interior point can be obtained from points on the edges by

$$\mathbf{n}(\alpha, \beta) = (1 - \beta)\mathbf{n}_C + \beta\mathbf{n}_D.$$

Once we have the normal at each point, we can make an independent shading calculation. Usually, this process can be combined with rasterization of the polygon. Until recently, Phong shading could only be carried out off-line because it requires the interpolation of normals across each polygon. In terms of the pipeline, Phong shading requires that the lighting model be applied to each fragment, hence, the name **per-fragment shading**. We will implement Phong shading through a fragment shader.

5.6 APPROXIMATION OF A SPHERE BY RECURSIVE SUBDIVISION

We have used the sphere as an example curved surface to illustrate shading calculations. However, the sphere is not an object supported within OpenGL, so we will generate approximations to a sphere using triangles through a process known as **recursive subdivision**, a technique we introduced in Chapter 2 for constructing the Sierpinski gasket. Recursive subdivision is a powerful technique for generating approximations to curves and surfaces to any desired level of accuracy. The sphere approximation provides a basis for us to write simple programs that illustrate the interactions between shading parameters and polygonal approximations to curved surfaces.

Our starting point is a tetrahedron, although we could start with any regular polyhedron whose facets could be divided initially into triangles.[2] The regular tetrahedron is composed of four equilateral triangles, determined by four vertices. We start with the four vertices $(0, 0, 1)$, $(0, 2\sqrt{2}/3, -1/3)$, $(-\sqrt{6}/3, -\sqrt{2}/3, -1/3)$, and $(\sqrt{6}/3, -\sqrt{2}/3, -1/3)$. All four lie on the unit sphere, centered at the origin. (Exercise 5.6 suggests one method for finding these points.)

We get a first approximation by drawing a wireframe for the tetrahedron. We specify the four vertices as follows:

```
point4 v[4]= {vec4(0.0, 0.0, 1.0, 1.0),
              vec4(0.0, 0.942809, -0.333333, 1.0),
              vec4(-0.816497, -0.471405, -0.333333, 1.0),
              vec4(0.816497, -0.471405, -0.333333, 1.0)};
```

We then put the vertices into an array

```
point4 data[12];
```

so we can display the triangles using line loops. Each triangle adds three points to this array using the function

```
static int k = 0;

void triangle(point4 a, point4 b, point4 c)
{
    data[k]= a;
```

---

2. The regular icosahedron is composed of 20 equilateral triangles; it makes a nice starting point for generating spheres. See [Shr10].

```
      k++;
      data[k] = b;
      k++;
      data[k] = c;
      k++
}
```

All the data for the tetrahedron is put into `data` as follows:

```
void tetrahedron()
{
   triangle(v[0], v[1], v[2]);
   triangle(v[3], v[2], v[1]);
   triangle(v[0], v[3], v[1]);
   triangle(v[0], v[2], v[3]);
}
```

The order of vertices obeys the right-hand rule, so we can convert the code to draw shaded polygons with little difficulty. If we add the usual code for initialization, setting up a vertex buffer object and drawing the array, our program will generate an image such as that in Figure 5.32: a simple regular polyhedron, but a poor approximation to a sphere.

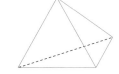

FIGURE 5.32　Tetrahedron.

We can get a closer approximation to the sphere by subdividing each facet of the tetrahedron into smaller triangles. Subdividing into triangles will ensure that all the new facets will be flat. There are at least three ways to do the subdivision, as shown in Figure 5.33. We can bisect each of the angles of the triangle and draw the three bisectors, which meet at a common point, thus generating three new triangles. We can also compute the center of mass (centroid) of the vertices by simply averaging them and then draw lines from this point to the three vertices, again generating three triangles. However, these techniques do not preserve the equilateral triangles that make up the regular tetrahedron. Instead—recalling a construction for the Sierpinski gasket of Chapter 2—we can connect the bisectors of the sides of the triangle, forming four equilateral triangles, as shown in Figure 5.33(c). We use this technique for our example.

After we have subdivided a facet as just described, the four new triangles will still be in the same plane as the original triangle. We can move the new vertices that

(a)　　　　　　(b)　　　　　　(c)

FIGURE 5.33　Subdivision of a triangle by (a) bisecting angles, (b) computing the centroid, and (c) bisecting sides.

we created by bisection to the unit sphere by normalizing each bisected vertex, using the normalization function `normalize` in `vec.h`. We can now subdivide a single triangle, defined by the vertices a, b, and c:

```
point4 v1, v2, v3;
v1 = normalize(a + b);
v2 = normalize(a + c);
v3 = normalize(b + c);

triangle(a, v2, v1);
triangle(c, v3, v2);
triangle(b, v1, v3);
triangle(v1, v2, v3);
```

We can use this code in our tetrahedron routine to generate 16 triangles rather than 4, but we would rather be able to repeat the subdivision process *n* times to generate successively closer approximations to the sphere. By calling the subdivision routine recursively, we can control the number of subdivisions.

First, we make the tetrahedron routine depend on the depth of recursion by adding an argument n:

```
void tetrahedron(int n)
{
   divide_triangle(v[0], v[1], v[2], n);
   divide_triangle(v[3], v[2], v[1], n);
   divide_triangle(v[0], v[3], v[1], n);
   divide_triangle(v[0], v[2], v[3], n);
}
```

The `divide_triangle` function calls itself to subdivide further if n is greater than zero but generates triangles if n has been reduced to zero. Here is the code:

```
void divide_triangle(point4 a, point4 b, point4 c, int n)
{
   point4 v1, v2, v3;
   if (n>0)
   {
      v1 = normalize(v[a] + v[b]);
      v2 = normalize(v[a] + v[c]);
      v3 = normalize(v[b] + v[c]);
      divide_triangle(a ,v2, v1, n-1);
      divide_triangle(c ,v3, v2, n-1);
      divide_triangle(b ,v1, v3, n-1);
      divide_triangle(v1 ,v2, v3, n-1);
   }
   else triangle(a, b, c);
}
```

Figure 5.34 shows an approximation to the sphere drawn with this code. We now turn to adding lighting and shading to our sphere approximation.

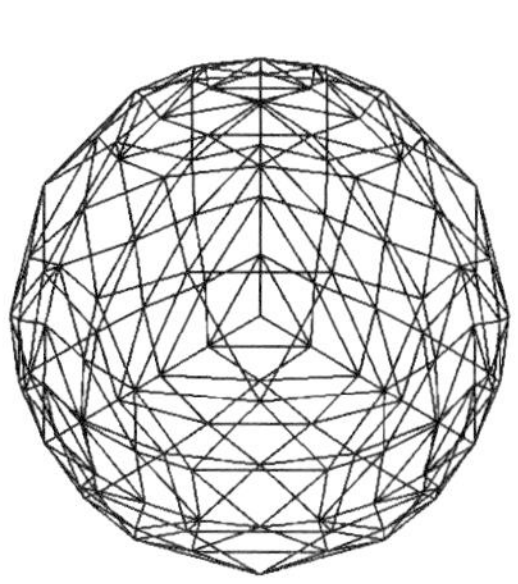

5.7 SPECIFYING LIGHTING PARAMETERS

For many years, the Blinn-Phong lighting model was the standard in computer graphics. It was implemented in hardware and was specified as part of the OpenGL fixed-functionality pipeline. With the present emphasis on shaders, we are free to implement other lighting models with no loss of efficiency. We can also choose where to apply a light model. Consequently, we must specify a group of lighting and material parameters and then either use them in the application code or send them to the shaders.

FIGURE 5.34 Sphere approximations using subdivision.

5.7.1 Light Sources

In Section 5.2. we introduced four types of light sources: ambient, point, spotlight, and distant. However, because spotlights and distant light sources can be derived from a point source, we will focus on point sources and ambient light. An ideal point source emits light uniformly in all directions. To get a spotlight from a point source, we need only limit the directions of the point source and make the light emissions follow a desired profile. To get a distant source from a point source, we need to allow the location of the source to go to infinity so the position of the source becomes the direction of the source. Note that this argument is similar to the argument that parallel viewing is the limit of perspective viewing as the center of projection moves to infinity. As we argued in deriving the equations for parallel projections, we will find it easier to derive the equations for lighting with distant sources directly rather than by taking limits.

Although the contribution of ambient light is the same everywhere in a scene, ambient light is dependent on the sources in the environment. For example, consider a closed room with a single white point source. When the light is turned off, there is no light in the room of any kind. When the light is turned on, at any point in the room that can see the light source there is a contribution from the light hitting surfaces directly contributing to the diffuse or specular reflection we see at that point. There is also a contribution from the white light bouncing off of multiple surfaces in the room and giving a contribution that is almost the same at every point in the room. It is this latter contribution that we call ambient light. Its color depends not only on the color of the source but also on the reflective properties of the surfaces in the room. Thus if the room has red walls, we would expect the ambient component to have a dominant red component. However, the existence of an ambient component to the shade we see on a surface is ultimately tied to the light sources in the environment and hence becomes part of the specification of the sources.

For every light source, we must specify its color and either its location or its direction. As in Section 5.2, the color of a source will have three components—diffuse, specular, and ambient—that we can specify for a single light as

```
color4 light_diffuse, light_specular, light_ambient;
```

We can specify the position of the light as follows:

```
point4 light_position;
```

For a point source, its position will be in homogeneous coordinates, so a light might be specified as

```
point4 light_position = vec4(1.0, 2.0, 3.0, 1.0);
```

If the fourth component is changed to zero as in

```
point4 light_position = vec4(1.0, 2.0, 3.0, 0.0);
```

the source becomes a directional source in the direction (1.0, 2.0, 3.0).

For positional light sources, we may also want to account for the attenuation of light received due to its distance from the source. Although for an ideal source the attenuation is inversely proportional to the square of the distance d, we can gain more flexibility by using the distance-attenuation model,

$$f(d) = \frac{1}{a + bd + cd^2},$$

which contains constant, linear, and quadratic terms. We can use three floats for these values,

```
float attenuation_constant, attenuation_linear, attenuation_quadratic;
```

and use them in the application or send them to the shaders as uniform variables.

We can also convert a positional source to a spotlight by setting its direction, the angle of the cone or the spotlight cutoff, and the drop off rate or spotlight exponent. These three parameters can be specified by three floats.

5.7.2 Materials

Material properties should match up directly with the supported light sources and with the chosen reflection model. We may also want the flexibility to specify different material properties for the front and back faces of a surface.

For example, we might specify ambient, diffuse, and specular reflectivity coefficients (k_a, k_d, k_s) for each primary color through three colors using either RGB or RGBA colors as

```
color3 ambient = color3(0.2, 0.2, 0.2);
color3 diffuse = color3(1.0, 0.8, 0.0);
color3 specular = color3(1.0, 1.0, 1.0);
```

or, assuming the surface is opaque,

```
color4 ambient = color4(0.2, 0.2, 0.2, 1.0);
color4 diffuse = color4(1.0, 0.8, 0.0, 1.0);
color4 specular = color4(1.0, 1.0, 1.0, 1.0);
```

Here we have defined a small amount of white ambient reflectivity, yellow diffuse properties, and white specular reflections. Note that often the diffuse and specular reflectivity are the same. For the specular component, we also need to specify its shininess:

```
float shininess;
```

If we have different reflectivity properties for the front and back faces, we can also specify three additional parameters,

```
color4 back_ambient, back_diffuse, back_specular;
```

that can be used to render the back faces.

We also want to allow for scenes in which a light source is within the view volume and thus might be visible. For example, for an outdoor night scene, we might see the moon in an image. We could model the moon with a simple polygonal approximation to a circle. However, when we render the moon, its color should be constant and not be affected by other light sources. We can create such effects by including an emissive component that models self-luminous sources. This term is unaffected by any of the light sources, and it does not affect any other surfaces. It adds a fixed color to the surfaces and is specified in a manner similar to other material properties. For example,

```
color4 emission = color4(0.0, 0.3, 0.3, 1.0);
```

specfies a small amount of blue-green (cyan) emission.

From an application programmer's perspective, we would like to have material properties that we can specify with a single function call. We can achieve this goal by defining material objects in the application using `structs` or `classes`. For example, consider the `typedef`

```
typedef struct materialStruct {
    color4 ambient;
    color4 diffuse;
    color4 specular;
    color4 emission;
    float shininess;
} materialStruct;
```

We can now define materials by code such as

```
materialStruct brassMaterials =
{
    {0.33, 0.22, 0.03, 1.0},
    {0.78, 0.57, 0.11, 1.0},
    {0.99, 0.91, 0.81, 1.0},
    {0.0, 0.0, 0.0, 1.0},
    27.8
};
```

and access this code through a pointer,

```
currentMaterial = &brassMaterials;
```

5.8   IMPLEMENTING A LIGHTING MODEL

Thus far, we have only looked at parameters that we might use in a light model. We have yet to build a particular model. Nor have we worried about where to apply a lighting model. We focus on a simple version of the Blinn-Phong model using a single point source. Because light from multiple sources is additive, we can repeat the calculation for each source and add up the individual contributions. We have three choices as to where we do the calculation: in the application, in the vertex shader, or in the fragment shader. Although the basic model can be the same for each, there will major differences both in efficiency and appearance, depending on where the calculation is done.

5.8.1 Applying the Lighting Model in the Application

We have used two methods to assign colors to filled triangles. In the first, we sent a single color for each polygon to the shaders as a uniform variable and used this color for each fragment. In the second, we assigned a color to each vertex as a vertex attribute. The rasterizer then interpolated these vertex colors across the polygon. Both these approaches can be applied to lighting. In constant or flat shading, we apply a lighting model once for each polygon and use the computed color for the entire polygon. In the interpolative shading, we apply the model at each vertex to compute a vertex color attribute. The vertex shader can then output these colors and the rasterizer will interpolate them to determine a color for each fragment.

Let's do a simple example with ambient, diffuse, and specular lighting. Assume that the following parameters have been specified for a single point light source:

```
color4 light_ambient, light_diffuse, light_specular;
point4 light_position;
```

Also assume that there is a single material whose parameters are

```
color4 reflect_ambient, reflect_diffuse, reflect_specular;
```

The color we need to compute is the sum of the ambient, diffuse, and specular contributions:

```
color4 color_out, ambient, diffuse, specular;

color_out = ambient + diffuse + specular;
```

Each component of the ambient term is the product of the corresponding terms from the ambient light source and the material reflectivity. We can use the function

```
vec4 product(vec4 a, vec4 b)
{
    return vec4(a[0]*b[0], a[1]*b[1], a[2]*b[2], a[3]*b[3]);
}
```

Hence,

```
ambient  = product(light_ambient, reflect_ambient);
```

We need the normal to compute the diffuse term. Because we are working with triangles, we have the three vertices and these vertices determine a unique plane and its normal. Suppose that we have three vertices v0, v1, and v2. The cross product of v1-v0 and v2-v1 is perpendicular to the plane determined by the three vertices. Thus, we get the desired unit normal as follows:

```
vec4 v0, v1, v2;

vec4 n = normalize(cross(v1-v0, v2-v1));
```

Note that the direction of the normal depends on the order of the vertices and assumes we are using the right-hand rule to determine an outward face.

Next, we need to take the dot product of the unit normal with the vector in the direction of the light source. There are four cases we must consider:

1. Constant shading with a distant source

2. Interpolative shading with a distant source

3. Constant shading with a finite source

4. Interpolative shading with a finite source

For constant shading, we only need to compute a single diffuse color for each triangle. For a distant source, we have the direction of the source that is the same for all points on the triangle. Hence, we can simply take the dot product of the unit normal with a normalized source direction. The diffuse contribution is then

```
color4 diffuse = product(light_diffuse, reflect_ambient)*dot(n, normalize(light_position));
```

There is one additional step we should take. The diffuse term only makes sense if the dot product is nonnegative, so we must modify the calculation to

```
color4 diffuse;

float d = dot(n, normalize(light_position));
if (d>0) diffuse = product(light_diffuse, reflect_ambient)*d;
else diffuse = vec4(0.0, 0.0, 0.0, 1.0);
```

For a distant light source, the diffuse contribution at each vertex is identical, so we need do only one diffuse calculation per polygon, and thus interpolative and constant diffuse shading are the same.

For a finite or near source, we have two choices: We either compute a single diffuse contribution for the entire polygon and use constant shading, or we compute the diffuse term at each vertex and use interpolative shading. Because we are working with triangles, the normal is the same at each vertex, but with a near source the vector from any point on the polygon to the light source will be different. If we use a single color, we can use the point at the center of the triangle to compute the direction:

```
point4 v  = (1.0/3.0)* (v0 + v1 + v2);
vector4 light_vector = light_position - v;
float d = dot(n, normalize(light_vector));
if (d>0) diffuse = product(light_diffuse, reflect_ambient)*d;
    else diffuse = vec4(0.0, 0.0, 0.0, 1.0);
```

The calculation for the specular term appears to be similar to the calculation for the diffuse, but there is one tricky issue. We need to compute the halfway vector. For a distance source, the light position becomes a direction, so

```
vec4 half = normalize(light_position + view_direction);
```

The view direction is a vector from a point on the surface to the eye. The default is that the camera is at the origin in object space, so for a vertex v, the vector is

```
vec4 origin = vec4(0.0, 0.0, 0.0, 1.0);
vec4 view_direction = v - origin;
```

Thus, even though each triangle has a single normal, there is a different halfway vector for each vertex, and consequently the specular term will vary across the surface as the rasterizer interpolates the vertex shades. The specular term for vertex v can be computed as

```
color4 specular;

float s = dot(half, n);
```

```
if (s>0.0) specular =
    pow(s, material_shininess)*product(light_specular, material_specular);
else specular = vec4(0.0, 0.0, 0.0, 1.0);
```

where the expression `exp(material_shininess*log(s))` evaluates `s` to the power `material_shininess`.

5.8.2 Efficiency

For a static scene, the lighting computation is done once so we can send the vertex positions and vertex colors to the GPU once. Consider what happens if we add lighting to our rotating-cube program. Each time the cube rotates about a coordinate axis, the normal to four of the faces changes as does the position of each of the six vertices. Hence, we must recompute the diffuse and specular components at each of the vertices. If we do all the calculations in the CPU, both the vertex positions and colors must then be sent to the GPU. For large data sets, this process is extremely inefficient. Not only are we doing a lot of computation on the CPU, but we are also causing a potential bottleneck by sending so much vertex data to the GPU. Consequently, we will almost always want to do lighting calculation in the shaders.

Before examining shaders for lighting, there are a few other efficiency measures we can employ, either in the application or in a shader. We can obtain many efficiencies if we assume that either or both of the viewer and the light source are far from the polygon we are rendering. Hence, even if the source is a point source with a finite location, it might be far enough away that the distances from the vertices to the source are all about the same. In this case, the diffuse term at each vertex would be identical and we would need do only one calculation per polygon. Note that a definition of far and near in this context depends both on the distance to the light source and the size of the polygon. A small polygon will not show much variation in the diffuse component even if the source is fairly close to the polygon. The same argument holds for the specular term when we consider the distance between vertices and the viewer. We can add parameters that allow the application to specify if it wants to use these simplified calculations.

In Chapter 3, we saw that a surface has both a front face and a back face. For polygons, we determine front and back by the order in which the vertices are specified, using the right-hand rule. For most objects, we see only the front faces, so we are not concerned with how OpenGL shades the back-facing surfaces. For example, for convex objects, such as a sphere or a parallelepiped (Figure 5.35), the viewer can never see a back face, regardless of where she is positioned. However, if we remove a side from a cube or slice the sphere, as shown in Figure 5.36, a properly placed viewer may see a back face; thus, we must shade both the front and back faces correctly. In many situations, we can ignore all back faces by either culling them out in the application or by not rendering any face whose normal does not point toward the viewer. If we render back faces, they may have different material properties than the front faces, so we must specify a set of back face properties.

FIGURE 5.35   Shading of convex objects.

FIGURE 5.36   Visible back surfaces.

Light sources are special types of geometric objects and have geometric attributes, such as position, just like polygons and points. Hence, light sources can be affected by transformations. We can specify them at the desired position or specify them in a convenient position and move them to the desired position by the model-view transformation. The basic rule governing object placement is that vertices are converted to eye coordinates by the model-view transformation in effect at the time the vertices are defined. Thus, by careful placement of the light-source specifications relative to the definition of other geometric objects, we can create light sources that remain stationary while the objects move, light sources that move while objects remain stationary, and light sources that move with the objects.

We also have choices as to which coordinate system to use for lighting computations. For now, we will do our lighting calculations in object coordinates. Depending on whether or not the light source or objects are moving, it may be more efficient to use eye coordinates. Later when we add texture mapping to our skills, we will introduce lighting methods that will use local coordinate systems.

5.8.3 Lighting in the Vertex Shader

When we presented transformations, we saw that a transformation such as the model-view transformation could be carried out either in the application or the vertex shader, but for most applications it was far more efficient to implement the transformation in the shader. The same is true for lighting. To implement lighting in the vertex shader, we must carry out three steps.

First, we must choose a lighting model. Do we use the Blinn-Phong or some other model? Do we include distance attenuation? Do we want two-sided lighting? Once we make these decisions, we can write a vertex shader to implement the model. Finally, we have to transfer the necessary data to the shader. Some data can be transferred using uniform variables, and other data can be transferred as vertex attributes.

Let's go through the process for the model we just developed, the Blinn-Phong model without distance attenuation with a single point light source. We can transfer the ambient, diffuse, and specular components of the source plus its position as uniform variables. We can do likewise for the material properties. Rather than writing the application code first, because we know how to transfer information to a shader, first we will write the vertex shader.

The vertex shader must output a vertex position in clip coordinates and a vertex color to the rasterizer. If we send a model-view matrix and a projection matrix to the shader, then the computation of the vertex position is identical to our examples from Chapters 3 and 4. Hence, this part of the code will look something like

```
in vec4 vPosition;
uniform mat4 ModelView;
uniform mat4 Projection;
void main()
{
    gl_Position = Projection*ModelView*vPosition;
}
```

The output color is the sum of the ambient, diffuse, and specular contributions,

```
out vec4 color
vec4 ambient, diffuse, specular;

color = ambient + diffuse + specular;
```

so the part we must address is computation of these three terms.

Rather than sending all the reflectivity and light colors separately to the shader, we send only the product term for each contribution. Thus, in the ambient computation, we use the products of the red, green, and blue ambient light with the red, green, and blue ambient reflectivities. We can compute these products and send them to the shader as the uniform vector

```
in vec4 AmbientProduct;
```

We can do the same for the diffuse and specular products:

```
uniform vec4 DiffuseProduct, SpecularProduct;
```

The ambient term is then simply

```
ambient = AmbientProduct;
```

The diffuse term requires a normal for each vertex. Because triangles are flat, the normal is the same for each vertex in a triangle so we can send the normal to the shader as a uniform variable.[3] We can use the `normalize` function to get a unit-length normal from the `vec4` type we used in the application:

```
uniform vec4 Normal;

vec3 N = normalize(Normal.xyz);
```

The unit vector in the direction of the light source is given by

```
vec3 L = normalize(LightPosition - vPosition).xyz;
```

The diffuse term is then

```
 diffuse =  max(dot(L, N), 0.0)*DiffuseProduct;
```

The specular term is computed in a similar manner. Because the viewer is at the origin in object coordinates, the normalized vector in the direction of the viewer is

---

3. In Section 5.9, we will consider methods that assign a different normal to each vertex of a polygon.

```
vec3 E = -normalize(vPosition.xyz);
```

and the halfway vector is

```
vec3 H = normalize(L+E);
```

The specular term is then

```
specular = pow(max(dot(N, H), 0.0), Shininess)*SpecularProduct;
```

However, if the light source is behind the surface, there cannot be a specular term, so we add a simple test:

```
specular = max(pow(max(dot(N, H), 0.0), Shininess)
            *SpecularProduct, 0.0);
```

Here is the full shader:

```
in vec4 vPosition;
in vec4 Normal;
out vec4 color;
uniform vec4 AmbientProduct, DiffuseProduct, SpecularProduct;
uniform mat4 ModelView;
uniform mat4 Projection;
uniform vec4 LightPosition;
uniform float Shininess;

void main()
{
    vec4 ambient, diffuse, specular;
    gl_Position = Projection*ModelView*vPosition;
    vec3 N = normalize(Normal.xyz);
    vec3 L = normalize(LightPosition.xyz - (ModelView*vPosition).xyz);
    vec3 E = -normalize((ModelView*vPosition).xyz);
    vec3 H = normalize(L+E);
    float Kd = max(dot(L, N), 0.0);
    float Ks = pow(max(dot(N, H), 0.0), Shininess);
    ambient = AmbientProduct;
    diffuse = Kd*DiffuseProduct;
    specular = max(pow(max(dot(N, H), 0.0), Shininess)
                *SpecularProduct, 0.0);
    color = vec4((ambient + diffuse + specular).xyz, 1.0);
}
```

Because the colors are set in the vertex shader, the simple fragment shader that we have used previously,

```
in vec4 color;
void main()
{
  gl_FragColor = color;
}
```

will take the interpolated colors from the rasterizer and assign them to fragments.

Let's return to the cube-shading example. The main change we have to make is to set up uniform variables for the light and material parameters. Thus, for the ambient component we might have an ambient light term and an ambient reflectivity given as

```
color4 light_ambient = color4(0.2, 0.2, 0.2, 1.0);
color4 material_ambient = color4(1.0, 0.0, 1.0, 1.0);
```

We compute the ambient product

```
color4 ambient_product = product(light_ambient, material_ambient);
```

We get these values to the shader as follows:

```
GLuint ambient_product_loc;
ambient_product_loc = glGetUniformLocation(program, "AmbientProduct");
glUniform4fv(ambient_product_loc, 4, ambient_product);
```

We can do the same for the rest of the uniform variables in the vertex shader. Note that the normal vector depends on more than one vertex and so cannot be computed in the shader, because the shader has the position information only for the vertex that initiated its execution.

There is an additional issue that has to do with the fact that the cube is rotating. As the cube rotates, the positions of all the vertices and all the normals to the surface change. When we first developed the program, we applied the rotation transformation in the application, and each time that the rotation matrix was updated we resent the vertices to the GPU. Later, we argued that it was far more efficient to send the rotation matrix to the shader and let the transformation be carried out in the GPU. The same is true with this example. We can send a projection matrix and a model-view matrix as uniform variables. This example has only one object, the cube, and thus the rotation matrix and the model-view matrix are identical. If we want to apply the rotation to the normal vector in the GPU, then we need to make the following change to the shader:

```
    vec4 NN = ModelView*Normal;
    vec3 N = normalize(NN.xyz);
```

The complete program is in Appendix A.

However, if there are multiple objects in the scene or the viewing parameters change, we have to be a little careful with this construct. Suppose that there is a second, nonrotating cube in the scene and we also use nondefault viewing parameters. Now we have two different model-view matrices, one for each cube. One is constant and the other is changing as one of the cubes rotates. What is really changing is the modeling part of the model-view matrix and not the viewing part that positions the camera. We can handle this complication in a number of ways. We could compute the two model-view matrices in the application and send them to the vertex shader each time there is a rotation. We could also use separate modeling and viewing transformations and send only the modeling matrix—the rotation matrix—to the shader after initialization. We would then form the model-view matrix in the shader. We could also just send the rotation angles to the shader and do all the work there. If the light source is also changing its position, we have even more options.

5.9   SHADING OF THE SPHERE MODEL

The rotating cube is a simple example to demonstrate lighting, but because there are only six faces and they meet at right angles, it is not a good example for testing the smoothness of a lighting model. Consider instead the sphere model that we developed in Section 5.6. Although the model comprises many small triangles, unlike the cube, we do not want to see the edges. Rather, we want to shade the polygons so that we cannot see the edges where triangles meet and the smoother the shading, the fewer polygons we need to model the sphere.

To shade the sphere model, we can start with the same shaders we used for the rotating cube. The differences are in the application program. We replace the generation of the cube with the tetrahedron subdivision from Section 5.6, adding the computation of the normals, which are sent to the vertex shader as attribute qualified variables. The result is shown in Figure 5.37. Note that even as we increase the number of subdivisions so that the interiors of the spheres appear smooth, we can still see edges of polygons around the outside of the sphere image. This type of outline is called a **silhouette edge**.

The differences in this example between constant shading and smooth shading are minor. Because each triangle is flat, the normal is the same at each vertex. If the source is far from the object, the diffuse component will be constant for each triangle. Likewise, if the camera is far from the viewer, the specular term will be constant for each triangle. However, because two adjacent triangles will have different normals and thus are shaded with different colors, we still can see the lack of smoothness even if we create many triangles.

One way to get an idea of how smooth a display we can get with relatively few triangles is to use the actual normals of the sphere for each vertex in the approximation. In Section 5.4, we found that for the sphere centered at the origin, the normal at a point **p** is simply **p**. Hence, in the `triangle` function, the position of a vertex gives the normal:

FIGURE 5.37   Shaded sphere model.

```
void triangle(point4 a, point4 b, point4 c)
{
    normals[k] = a;
    data[k]= a;
    k++;
    normals[k] = b;
    data[k] = b;
    k++;
    normals[k] = c;
    data[k] = c;
    k++;
}
```

FIGURE 5.38 Shading of the sphere with the true normals.

The results of this definition of the normals are shown in Figure 5.38 and Color Plate 29.

Although using the true normals produces a rendering more realistic than flat shading, the example is not a general one, because we have used normals that are known analytically. We also have not provided a true Gouraud-shaded image. Suppose we want a Gouraud-shaded image of our approximate sphere. At each vertex, we need to know the normals of all polygons incident at the vertex. Our code does not have a data structure that contains the required information. Try Exercises 5.9 and 5.10, in which you construct such a structure. Note that six polygons meet at a vertex created by subdivision, whereas only three polygons meet at the original vertices of the tetrahedron.

5.10 PER-FRAGMENT LIGHTING

There is another option we can use to obtain a smoother shading. We can do the lighting calculation on a per-fragment basis rather than on a per-vertex basis. When we did all our lighting calculations in the vertex shader, visually there was no advantage over doing the same computation in the application and then sending the computed vertex colors to the vertex shader, which would then pass them on to the rasterizer. Thus, whether we did lighting in the vertex shader or in the application, the rasterizer interpolated the same vertex colors to obtain fragment colors.

With a fragment shader, we can do an independent lighting calculation for each fragment. The fragment shader needs to get the interpolated values of the normal vector, light source position, and eye position from the rasterizer. The vertex shader can compute these values and output them to the rasterizer. In addition, the vertex shader must output the vertex position in clip coordinates. Here is the vertex shader:

```
in vec4 vPosition;
in vec4 Normal;

uniform mat4 ModelView;
uniform vec4 LightPosition;
uniform mat4 Projection;
```

```
out vec3 N;
out vec3 L;
out vec3 E;

void main()
{
    gl_Position = Projection*ModelView*vPosition;
    N = Normal.xyz;
    L = LightPosition.xyz - vPosition.xyz;
    if (LightPosition.w == 0.0)  L = LightPosition.xyz;
    E = vPosition.xyz;
}
```

The fragment shader can now apply the Blinn-Phong lighting model to each fragment using the light and material parameters passed in from the application as uniform variables and the interpolated vectors from the rasterizer. The following shader corresponds to the vertex shader we used in the previous example:

```
uniform vec4 AmbientProduct, DiffuseProduct, SpecularProduct;
uniform mat4 ModelView;
uniform vec4 LightPosition;
uniform float Shininess;

in vec3 N;
in vec3 L;
in vec3 E;

void main()
{
    vec3 NN = normalize(N);
    vec3 EE = normalize(E);
    vec3 LL = normalize(L);
    vec4 ambient, diffuse, specular;
    vec3 H = normalize(LL+EE);
    float Kd = max(dot(LL, NN), 0.0);
    Kd = dot(LL, NN);
    float Ks = pow(max(dot(NN, H), 0.0), Shininess);
    ambient = AmbientProduct;
    diffuse = Kd*DiffuseProduct;
    if (dot(LL, NN) < 0.0) specular = vec4(0.0, 0.0, 0.0, 1.0);
    else specular = Ks*SpecularProduct;
    gl_FragColor = vec4((ambient + diffuse + specular).xyz, 1.0);
}
```

Note that we normalize vectors in the fragment shader rather than in the vertex shaders. If we were to normalize a variable such as the normals in the vertex shader, it would not guarantee that the interpolated normals produced by the rasterizer would have the unit magnitude needed for the lighting computation.

5.10.1 Nonphotorealistic Shading

Programmable shaders make it possible to not only incorporate more realistic lighting models in real time but also to create interesting nonphotorealistic effects. Two such examples are the use of only a few colors and emphasizing the edges in objects. Both these effects are techniques that we might want to use to obtain a cartoonlike effect in an image.

Suppose that we use only two colors in a vertex shader:

```
vec4 color1 = vec4(1.0, 1.0, 0.0, 1.0); // yellow
vec4 color2 = vec4(1.0, 0.0, 0.0, 1.0); // red
```

We could then switch between the colors based, for example, on the magnitude of the diffuse color. Using the light and normal vectors, we could assign colors as

```
if (dot(lightv, norm) > 0.5) gl_FrontColor = color1;
   else gl_FrontColor = color2;
```

Although we could have used two colors in simpler ways, by using the diffuse color to determine a threshold, the color of the object changes with its shape and the position of the light source.

We can also try to draw the silhouette edge of an object. One way to identify such edges is to look at sign changes in dot(lightv, norm). This value should be positive for any vertex facing the viewer and negative for a vertex pointed away from the viewer. Thus, we can test for small values of this value and assign a color such as black to the vertex:

```
vec4 color3 = vec4(0.0, 0.0, 0.0, 1.0); // black
```

```
if (abs(dot(viewv, norm) < 0.01)) glFrontColor = color3;
```

5.11 GLOBAL ILLUMINATION

There are limitations imposed by the local lighting model that we have used. Consider, for example, an array of spheres illuminated by a distant source, as shown in Figure 5.39(a). The spheres close to the source block some of the light from the source from reaching the other spheres. However, if we use our local model, each sphere is shaded independently; all appear the same to the viewer (Figure 5.39(b)). In addition, if these spheres are specular, some light is scattered among spheres. Thus, if the spheres were very shiny, we should see the reflection of multiple spheres in some of the spheres and possibly even the multiple reflections of some spheres in themselves. Our lighting model cannot handle this situation. Nor can it produce shadows, except by using the tricks for some special cases, as we saw in Chapter 4.

All of these phenomena—shadows, reflections, blockage of light—are global effects and require a global lighting model. Although such models exist and can be quite elegant, in practice they are incompatible with the pipeline model. With the

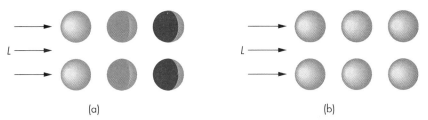

FIGURE 5.39   Array of shaded spheres. (a) Global lighting model.
(b) Local lighting model.

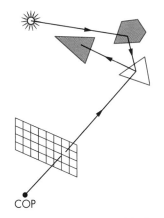

FIGURE 5.40   Polygon blocked
from light source.

pipeline model, we must render each polygon independently of the other polygons, and we want our image to be the same regardless of the order in which the application produces the polygons. Although this restriction limits the lighting effects that we can simulate, we can render scenes very rapidly.

There are alternative rendering strategies, including ray tracing and radiosity, that can handle global effects. Each is best at different lighting conditions. Ray tracing starts with the synthetic-camera model but determines for each projector that strikes a polygon if that point is indeed illuminated by one or more sources before computing the local shading at each point. Thus, in Figure 5.40, we see three polygons and a light source. The projector shown intersects one of the polygons. A local renderer might use the modified Phong model to compute the shade at the point of intersection. The ray tracer would find that the light source cannot strike the point of intersection directly but that light from the source is reflected from the third polygon and this reflected light illuminates the point of intersection. In Chapter 11, we shall show how to find this information and make the required calculations.

A radiosity renderer is based upon energy considerations. From a physical point of view, all the light energy in a scene is conserved. Consequently, there is an energy balance that accounts for all the light that radiates from sources and is reflected by various surfaces in the scene. A radiosity calculation thus requires the solution of a large set of equations involving all the surfaces. As we shall see in Chapter 11, a ray tracer is best suited to a scene consisting of highly reflective surfaces, whereas a radiosity renderer is best suited for a scene in which all the surfaces are perfectly diffuse.

Although a pipeline renderer cannot take into account many global phenomena exactly, this observation does not mean we cannot produce realistic imagery with OpenGL or another API that is based upon a pipeline architecture. What we can do is use our knowledge of OpenGL and of the effects that global lighting produces to approximate what a global renderer would do. For example, our use of projective shadows in Chapter 4 shows that we can produce simple shadows. Many of the most exciting advances in computer graphics over the past few years have been in the use of pipeline renderers for global effects. We will study many such techniques in the next few chapters, including mapping methods, multipass rendering, and transparency.

SUMMARY AND NOTES

We have developed a lighting model that fits well with our pipeline approach to graphics. With it, we can create a variety of lighting effects, and we can employ different types of light sources. Although we cannot create the global effects of a ray tracer, a typical graphics workstation can render a polygonal scene using the modified Phong reflection model and smooth shading in the same amount of time as it can render a scene without shading. From the perspective of an application program, adding shading requires setting parameters that describe the light sources and materials and can be implemented with programmable shaders. In spite of the limitations of the local lighting model that we have introduced, our simple renderer performs remarkably well; it is the basis of the reflection model supported by most APIs.

Programmable shaders have changed the picture considerably. Not only can we create new methods of shading each vertex, we can use fragment shaders to do the lighting calculation for each fragment, thus avoiding the need to interpolate colors across each polygon. Methods such as Phong shading that were not possible within the standard pipeline can now be programmed by the user and will execute in about the same amount of time as the modified Phong shader. It is also possible to create a myriad of new shading effects.

The recursive-subdivision technique that we used to generate an approximation to a sphere is a powerful one that will reappear in various guises in Chapter 10, where we use variants of this technique to render curves and surfaces. It will also arise when we introduce modeling techniques that rely on the self-similarity of many natural objects.

This chapter concludes our development of polygonal-based graphics. You should now be able to generate scenes with lighting and shading. Techniques for creating even more sophisticated images, such as texture mapping and compositing, involve using the pixel-level capabilities of graphics systems—topics that we consider in Chapter 7.

Now is a good time for you to write an application program. Experiment with various lighting and shading parameters. Try to create light sources that move, either independently or with the objects in the scene. You will probably face difficulties in producing shaded images that do not have small defects, such as cracks between polygons through which light can enter. Many of these problems are artifacts of small numerical errors in rendering calculations. There are many tricks of the trade for mitigating the effects of these errors. Some you will discover on your own; others are given in the Suggested Readings for this chapter.

We turn to rasterization issues in Chapter 6. Although we have seen some of the ways in which the different modules in the rendering pipeline function, we have not yet seen the details. As we develop these details, you will see how the pieces fit together such that each successive step in the pipeline requires only a small increment of work.

SUGGESTED READINGS

The use of lighting and reflection in computer graphics has followed two parallel paths: the physical and the computational. From the physical perspective, Kajiya's rendering equation [Kaj86] describes the overall energy balance in an environment and requires knowledge of the reflectivity function for each surface. Reflection models, such as the Torrance-Sparrow model [Tor67] and Cook-Torrance model [Coo82], are based on modeling a surface with small planar facets. See Hall [Hal89] and Foley [Fol90] for discussions of such models.

Phong [Pho75] is credited with putting together a computational model that included ambient, diffuse, and specular terms. The use of the halfway vector was first suggested by Blinn [Bli77]. The basic model of transmitted light was used by Whitted [Whi80]. It was later modified by Heckbert and Hanrahan [Hec84]. Gouraud [Gou71] introduced interpolative shading.

The *OpenGL Programming Guide* [Shr10] contains many good hints on effective use of OpenGL's rendering capabilities and discusses the fixed-function lighting pipeline that uses functions that have been deprecated in shader-based OpenGL.

EXERCISES

5.1   Most graphics systems and APIs use the simple lighting and reflection models that we introduced for polygon rendering. Describe the ways in which each of these models is incorrect. For each defect, give an example of a scene in which you would notice the problem.

5.2   Often, when a large polygon that we expect to have relatively uniform shading is shaded by OpenGL, it is rendered brightly in one area and more dimly in others. Explain why the image is uneven. Describe how you can avoid this problem.

5.3   Explain the following rendering strategies:
a. Ray tracing
b. Radiosity

5.4   How should the distance between the viewer and the surface enter the rendering calculations?

5.5   How are interactions between light and materials categorized? Give the different categories into which they might fall.

5.6   Find four points equidistant from one another on a unit sphere. These points determine a tetrahedron. *Hint:* You can arbitrarily let one of the points be at $(0, 1, 0)$ and let the other three be in the plane $y = -d$ for some positive value of d.

5.7   Show that if $\mathbf{v}$ lies in the same plane as $\mathbf{l}$, $\mathbf{n}$, and $\mathbf{r}$, then the halfway angle satisfies

$$2\psi = \phi.$$

What relationship is there between the angles if **v** is not coplanar with the other vectors?

5.8 Consider all the combinations of near or far viewers, near or far light sources, flat or curved surfaces, and diffuse and specular reflections. For which cases can you simplify the shading calculations? In which cases does the use of the halfway vector help? Explain your answers.

5.9 Construct a data structure for representing the subdivided tetrahedron. Traverse the data structure such that you can Gouraud-shade the approximation to the sphere based on subdividing the tetrahedron.

5.10 Repeat Exercise 5.9 but start with an icosahedron instead of a tetrahedron.

5.11 Construct a data structure for representing meshes of quadrilaterals. Write a program to shade the meshes represented by your data structure.

5.12 A general light source can be characterized by a six-variable illumination function. State the six variables.

5.13 Consider two materials that meet along a planar boundary. Suppose that the speed of light in the two materials are v_1 and v_2. Show that Snell's law is a statement that light travels from a point in one material to a point in the second material in the minimum time.

5.14 What are the four basic types of general light sources? Which of these sources emits light equally in all directions?

5.15 Although we have yet to discuss frame-buffer operations, you can start constructing a ray tracer using a single routine of the form `write_pixel(x, y, color)` that places the value of `color` (either an RGB color or an intensity) at the pixel located at `(x, y)` in the frame buffer. Write a pseudocode routine `ray` that recursively traces a cast ray. You can assume that you have a function available that will intersect a ray with an object. Consider how to limit how far the original ray will be traced.

5.16 If you have a pixel-writing routine available on your system, write a ray tracer that will ray-trace a scene composed of only spheres. Use the mathematical equations for the spheres rather than a polygonal approximation.

5.17 What is a silhouette edge?

5.18 Using the sphere-generation program in Appendix A as a starting point, construct an interactive program that will allow you to position one or more light sources and to alter material properties. Use your program to try to generate images of surfaces that match familiar materials, such as various metals, plastic, and carbon.

5.19 As geometric data pass through the viewing pipeline, a sequence of rotations, translations, scalings, and a projection transformation is applied to the vectors that determine the cosine terms in the Phong reflection model. Which, if any, of these operations preserve(s) the angles between the vectors? What are the implications of your answer for implementation of shading?

5.20 What is the specialty of diffuse surfaces? Why are they called Lambertian surfaces?

5.21 Describe the flat, or constant, shading technique. Due to which property does the human visual system exhibit remarkable sensitivity to small differences in light intensity?

5.22 What is ambient light? Explain how ambient light is dependent on environmental sources.

5.23 How is a point source located at a point p_0 represented using a three-component color matrix?

5.24 Convert the shadow-generation algorithm (Section 4.10) to an algorithm for distant sources. *Hint:* The perspective projection should become a parallel projection.

5.25 Compare the shadow-generation algorithm of Section 4.10 to the generation of shadows by a global-rendering method. What types of shadows can be generated by one method but not the other?

5.26 Consider a highly reflective sphere centered at the origin with a unit radius. If a viewer is located at **p**, describe the points she would see reflected in the sphere at a point on its surface.

CHAPTER 6

FROM VERTICES TO FRAGMENTS

We now turn to the next steps in the pipeline: clipping, rasterization, and hidden-surface removal. Although we have yet to consider some major parts of OpenGL that are available to the application programmer, including discrete primitives, texture mapping, and curves and surfaces, there are several reasons for considering these topics at this point. First, you may be wondering how your programs are processed by the system that you are using: how lines are drawn on the screen, how polygons are filled, and what happens to primitives that lie outside the viewing volumes defined in your program. Second, our contention is that if we are to use a graphics system efficiently, we need to have a deeper understanding of the implementation process: which steps are easy, and which tax our hardware and software. Third, our discussion of implementation will open the door to new capabilities that are supported by the latest hardware.

Learning implementation involves studying algorithms. As when we study any algorithm, we must be careful to consider such issues as theoretical versus practical performance, hardware versus software implementations, and the specific characteristics of an application. Although we can test whether an OpenGL implementation works correctly in the sense that it produces the correct pixels on the screen, there are many choices for the algorithms employed. We focus on the basic operations that are both necessary to implement a standard API and required whether the rendering is done by a pipeline architecture or by another method, such as ray tracing. Consequently, we present a variety of the basic algorithms for each of the principal tasks in an implementation.

In this chapter, we are concerned with the basic algorithms that are used to implement the rendering pipeline employed by OpenGL. We shall focus on three issues: clipping, rasterization, and hidden-surface removal. Clipping involves eliminating objects that lie outside the viewing volume and thus cannot be visible in the image. Rasterization produces fragments from the remaining objects. These fragments can contribute to the final image. Hidden-surface removal determines which fragments correspond to objects that are visible, namely, those that are in the view volume and are not blocked from view by other objects closer to the camera.

FIGURE 6.1   High-level view of the graphics process.

6.1   BASIC IMPLEMENTATION STRATEGIES

Let us begin with a high-level view of the implementation process. In computer graphics, we start with an application program, and we end with an image. We can again consider this process as a black box (Figure 6.1) whose inputs are the vertices and states defined in the program—geometric objects, attributes, camera specifications—and whose output is an array of colored pixels in the frame buffer.

Within the black box, we must do many tasks, including transformations, clipping, shading, hidden-surface removal, and rasterization of the primitives that can appear on the display. These tasks can be organized in a variety of ways, but regardless of the strategy that we adopt, we must always do two things: We must pass every geometric object through the system, and we must assign a color to every pixel in the color buffer that is displayed.

Suppose that we think of what goes into the black box in terms of a single program that carries out the entire process. This program takes as input a set of vertices specifying geometric objects and produces as output pixels in the frame buffer. Because this program must assign a value to every pixel and must process every geometric primitive (and every light source), we expect this program to contain at least two loops that iterate over these basic variables.

If we wish to write such a program, then we must immediately address the following question: Which variable controls the outer loop? The answer we choose determines the flow of the entire implementation process. There are two fundamental strategies, often called the **image-oriented** and the **object-oriented** approaches.

In the object-oriented approach, the outer loop is over the objects. We can think of the program as controlled by a loop of this form:

```
for (each_object) render(object);
```

A pipeline renderer fits this description. Vertices are defined by the program and flow through a sequence of modules that transforms them, colors them, and determines whether they are visible. A polygon might flow through the steps illustrated in Figure 6.2. Note that after a polygon passes through geometric processing, the rasterization of this polygon can potentially affect any pixels in the frame buffer. Most implementations that follow this approach are based on construction of a rendering pipeline containing hardware or software modules for each of the tasks. Data (vertices) flow forward through the system.

In the past, the major limitations of the object-oriented approach were the large amount of memory required and the high cost of processing each object indepen-

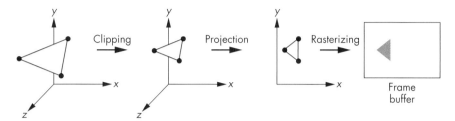

FIGURE 6.2   Object-oriented approach.

dently. Any geometric primitive that emerges from the geometric processing can po-tentially affect any set of pixels in the frame buffer; thus, the entire color buffer—and various other buffers, such as the depth buffer used for hidden-surface removal—must be of the size of the display and must be available at all times. Before memory became both inexpensive and dense, this requirement was considered to be a serious problem. Now various pipelined geometric processors are available that can process tens of millions of polygons per second. In fact, precisely because we are doing the same operations on every primitive, the hardware to build an object-based system is fast and relatively inexpensive, with many of the functions implemented with special-purpose chips.

Today, the main limitation of object-oriented implementations is that they can-not handle most global calculations. Because each geometric primitive is processed independently—and in an arbitrary order—complex shading effects that involve multiple geometric objects, such as reflections, cannot be handled except by approx-imate methods. The major exception is hidden-surface removal, where the z buffer is used to store global information.

Image-oriented approaches loop over pixels, or rows of pixels called **scanlines**, that constitute the frame buffer. In pseudocode, the outer loop of such a program is of the following form:

```
for (each_pixel) assign_a_color(pixel);
```

For each pixel, we work backward, trying to determine which geometric prim-itives can contribute to its color. The advantages of this approach are that we need only limited display memory at any time and that we can hope to generate pixels at the rate and in the order required to refresh the display. Because the results of most calculations do not differ greatly from pixel to pixel (or scanline to scanline), we can use this coherence in our algorithms by developing incremental forms for many of the steps in the implementation. The main disadvantage of this approach is that, unless we first build a data structure from the geometric data, we do not know which primitives affect which pixels. Such a data structure can be complex and may imply that all the geometric data must be available at all times during the rendering process. For problems with very large databases, even having a good data representation may

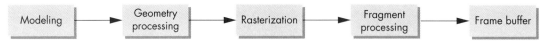

FIGURE 6.3   Implementation tasks.

not avoid memory problems. However, because image-space approaches have access to all objects for each pixel, they are well suited to handle global effects such as shadows and reflections. Ray tracing (Chapter 11) is an example of the image-based approach.

We lean toward the object-based approach, although we look at examples of algorithms suited for both approaches.

6.2 FOUR MAJOR TASKS

We start by reviewing the blocks in the pipeline, focusing on those blocks that we have yet to discuss in detail. There are four major tasks that any graphics system must perform to render a geometric entity, such as a three-dimensional polygon, as that entity passes from definition in a user program to possible display on an output device:

1. Modeling
2. Geometry processing
3. Rasterization
4. Fragment processing

Figure 6.3 shows how these tasks might be organized in a pipeline implementation. Regardless of the approach, all four tasks must be carried out.

6.2.1 Modeling

The usual results of the modeling process are sets of vertices that specify a group of geometric objects supported by the rest of the system. We have seen a few examples that required some modeling by the user, such as the approximation of spheres in Chapter 5. In Chapters 8 and 9, we explore other modeling techniques.

We can look at the modeler as a black box that produces geometric objects and is usually a user program. Yet, there are other tasks that the modeler might perform. Consider, for example, clipping: the process of eliminating parts of objects that cannot appear on the display because they lie outside the viewing volume. A user can generate geometric objects in her program, and she can hope that the rest of the system can process these objects at the rate at which they are produced, or the modeler can attempt to ease the burden on the rest of the system by minimizing the number of objects that it passes on. The latter approach often means that the modeler may do some of the same jobs as the rest of the system, albeit with different algorithms. In the case of clipping, the modeler, knowing more about the specifics of the application, can often use a good heuristic to eliminate many, if not most, primitives before they are sent on through the standard viewing process.

6.2.2 Geometry Processing

Geometry processing works with vertices. The goals of the geometry processor are to determine which geometric objects can appear on the display and to assign shades or colors to the vertices of these objects. Four processes are required: projection, primitive assembly, clipping, and shading.

Usually, the first step in geometry processing is to change representations from object coordinates to camera or eye coordinates using the model-view transformation. As we saw in Chapter 3, the conversion to camera coordinates is only the first part of the viewing process. The second step is to transform vertices using the projection transformation to a normalized view volume in which objects that might be visible are contained in a cube centered at the origin. Vertices are now represented in clip coordinates. Not only does this normalization convert both parallel and orthographic projections to a simple orthographic projection in a simple volume but, in addition, we simplify the clipping process, as we shall see in Section 6.7.

Geometric objects are transformed by a sequence of transformations that may reshape and move them (modeling) or may change their representations (viewing). Eventually, only those primitives that fit within a specified volume, the **view volume**, can appear on the display after rasterization. We cannot, however, simply allow all objects to be rasterized, hoping that the hardware will take care of primitives that lie wholly or partially outside the view volume. The implementation must carry out this task before rasterization. One reason is that rasterizing objects that lie outside the view volume is inefficient because such objects cannot be visible. Another reason is that when vertices reach the rasterizer, they can no longer be processed individually and first must be assembled into primitives. Primitives that lie partially in the viewing volume can generate new primitives with new vertices for which we must carry out shading calculations. Before clipping can take place, vertices must be grouped into objects, a process known as **primitive assembly**.

Note that even though an object lies inside the view volume, it will not be visible if it is obscured by other objects. Algorithms for **hidden-surface removal** (or **visible-surface determination**) are based on the three-dimensional spatial relationships among objects. This step is normally carried out as part of fragment processing.

As we saw in Chapter 5, colors can be determined on either a per-vertex or per-fragment basis. If they are assigned on a per-vertex basis, they can be sent from the application as vertex attributes or computed in the vertex shader. If lighting is enabled, vertex colors are computed using a lighting model that can be implemented in the application or in the vertex shader.

After clipping takes place, the remaining vertices are still in four-dimensional homogeneous coordinates. Perspective division converts them to three-dimensional representation in normalized device coordinates.

Collectively, these operations constitute what has been called **front-end processing**. All involve three-dimensional calculations, and all require floating-point arithmetic. All generate similar hardware and software requirements. All are carried out on a vertex-by-vertex basis. We will discuss clipping, the only geometric step that we have yet to discuss, in Section 6.3.

6.2.3 Rasterization

Even after geometric processing has taken place, we still need to retain depth information for hidden-surface removal. However, only the x, y values of the vertices are needed to determine which pixels in the frame buffer can be affected by the primitive. For example, after perspective division, a line segment that was specified originally in three dimensions by two vertices becomes a line segment specified by a pair of three-dimensional vertices in normalized device coordinates. To generate a set of fragments that give the locations of the pixels in the frame buffer corresponding to these vertices, we only need their x, y components or, equivalently, the results of the orthogonal projection of these vertices. We determine these fragments through a process called **rasterization** or **scan conversion**. For line segments, rasterization determines which fragments should be used to approximate a line segment between the projected vertices. For polygons, rasterization determines which pixels lie inside the two-dimensional polygon determined by the projected vertices.

The colors that we assign to these fragments can be determined by the vertex attributes or obtained by interpolating the shades at the vertices that are computed, as in Chapter 5. Objects more complex than line segments and polygons are usually approximated by multiple line segments and polygons, and thus most graphics systems do not have special rasterization algorithms for them. We shall see exceptions to this rule for some special curves and surfaces in Chapter 10.

The rasterizer starts with vertices in normalized device coordinates but outputs fragments whose locations are in units of the display—**window coordinates**. As we saw in Chapters 2 and 4, the projection of the clipping volume must appear in the assigned viewport. In OpenGL, this final transformation is done after projection and is two-dimensional. The preceding transformations have normalized the view volume such that its sides are of length 2 and line up with the sides of the viewport (Figure 6.4), so this transformation is simply

$$x_v = x_{v\min} + \frac{x + 1.0}{2.0}(x_{v\max} - x_{v\min}),$$

$$y_v = y_{v\min} + \frac{y + 1.0}{2.0}(y_{v\max} - y_{v\min}),$$

$$z_v = z_{v\min} + \frac{z + 1.0}{2.0}(z_{v\max} - z_{v\min}).$$

Recall that for perspective viewing, these z-values have been scaled nonlinearly by perspective normalization. However, they retain their original depth order, so they

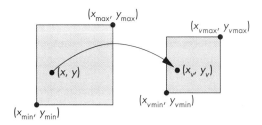

FIGURE 6.4   Viewport transformation.

can be used for hidden-surface removal. We shall use the term **screen coordinates** to refer to the two-dimensional system that is the same as window coordinates but lacks the depth coordinate.

6.2.4 Fragment Processing

In the simplest situations, each fragment is assigned a color by the rasterizer and this color is placed in the frame buffer at the locations corresponding to the fragment's location. However, there are many other possibilities.

The separate pixel pipeline (Chapter 7), supported by architectures such as OpenGL, merges with the results of the geometric pipeline at the rasterization stage. Consider what happens when a shaded and texture-mapped polygon is processed. Vertex lighting is computed as part of the geometric processing. The texture values are not needed until after rasterization when the renderer has generated fragments that correspond to locations inside a polygon. At this point, interpolation of per-vertex colors and texture coordinates takes place, and the texture parameters determine how to combine texture colors and fragment colors to determine final colors in the color buffer.

As we have noted, objects that are in the view volume will not be visible if they are blocked by any opaque objects closer to the viewer. The required hidden-surface removal process is typically carried out on a fragment-by-fragment basis.

Until now, we have assumed that all objects are opaque and thus an object located behind another object is not visible. We can also assume that objects are **translucent** and allow some light to pass through. In this case, fragment colors may have to be blended with the colors of pixels already in the color buffer. We consider this possibility in Chapter 7.

In most displays, the process of taking the image from the frame buffer and displaying it on a monitor happens automatically and is not of concern to the application program. However, there are numerous problems with the quality of display, such as the jaggedness associated with images on raster displays. In Chapter 7, we introduce algorithms for reducing this jaggedness, or **aliasing**, and we discuss problems with color reproduction on displays.

6.3 CLIPPING

We can now turn to clipping, the process of determining which primitives, or parts of primitives, fit within the clipping or view volume defined by the application program. Clipping is done before the perspective division that is necessary if the w component of a clipped vertex is not equal to 1. The portions of all primitives that can possibly be displayed—we have yet to apply hidden-surface removal—lie within the cube

$$w \geq x \geq -w,$$

$$w \geq y \geq -w,$$

$$w \geq z \geq -w.$$

This coordinate system is called **normalized device coordinates** because it depends on neither the original application units nor the particulars of the display device, although the information to produce the correct image is retained in this coordinate system. Note also that projection has been carried out only partially. We still must do the perspective division and the final orthographic projection.

We shall concentrate on clipping of line segments and polygons because they are the most common primitives to pass down the pipeline. Although the OpenGL pipeline does clipping on three-dimensional objects, there are other systems in which the objects are first projected into the x, y plane. Fortunately, many of the most efficient algorithms are almost identical in two and three dimensions, and we will focus on these algorithms.

6.4 LINE-SEGMENT CLIPPING

A **clipper** decides which primitives, or parts of primitives, can possibly appear on the display and be passed on to the rasterizer. Primitives that fit within the specified view volume pass through the clipper, or are **accepted**. Primitives that cannot appear on the display are eliminated, or **rejected** or **culled**. Primitives that are only partially within the view volume must be clipped such that any part lying outside the volume is removed.

Clipping can occur at one or more places in the viewing pipeline. The modeler may clip to limit the primitives that the hardware must handle. The primitives may be clipped after they have been projected from three- to two-dimensional objects. In OpenGL, primitives are clipped against a three-dimensional view volume before rasterization. We shall develop a sequence of clippers. For both pedagogic and historic reasons, we start with two two-dimensional line-segment clippers. Both extend directly to three dimensions and to clipping of polygons.

6.4.1 Cohen-Sutherland Clipping

The two-dimensional clipping problem for line segments is shown in Figure 6.5. We can assume for now that this problem arises after three-dimensional line segments have been projected onto the projection plane and that the window is part of the

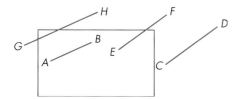

FIGURE 6.5   Two-dimensional clipping.

projection plane mapped to the viewport on the display. All values are specified as real numbers. We can see that the entire line segment AB appears on the display, whereas none of CD appears. EF and GH have to be shortened before being displayed. Although a line segment is completely determined by its endpoints, GH shows that even if both endpoints lie outside the clipping window, part of the line segment may still appear on the display.

We could compute the intersections of the lines (of which the segments are parts) with the sides of the window and could thus determine the necessary information for clipping. However, we want to avoid intersection calculations, if possible, because each intersection requires a floating-point division. The Cohen-Sutherland algorithm was the first to seek to replace most of the expensive floating-point multiplications and divisions with a combination of floating-point subtractions and bit operations.

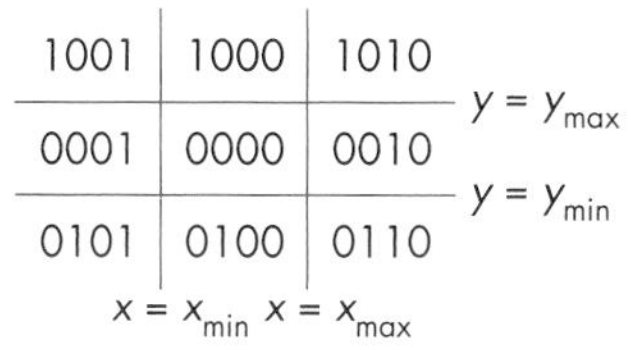

The algorithm starts by extending the sides of the window to infinity, thus breaking up space into the nine regions shown in Figure 6.6. Each region can be assigned a unique 4-bit binary number, or **outcode**, $b_0 b_1 b_2 b_3$, as follows. Suppose that (x, y) is a point in the region; then

1001	1000	1010
0001	0000	0010
0101	0100	0110

$y = y_{max}$
$y = y_{min}$

$x = x_{min}$ $x = x_{max}$

FIGURE 6.6   Breaking up of space and outcodes.

$$b_0 = \begin{cases} 1 & \text{if } y > y_{max}, \\ 0 & \text{otherwise.} \end{cases}$$

Likewise, b_1 is 1 if $y < y_{min}$, and b_2 and b_3 are determined by the relationship between x and the left and right sides of the window. The resulting codes are indicated in Figure 6.7. For each endpoint of a line segment, we first compute the endpoint's outcode, a step that can require eight floating-point subtractions per line segment.

Consider a line segment whose outcodes are given by $o_1 = outcode(x_1, y_1)$ and $o_2 = outcode(x_2, y_2)$. We can now reason on the basis of these outcodes. There are four cases:

1. ($o_1 = o_2 = 0$). Both endpoints are inside the clipping window, as is true for segment *AB* in Figure 6.7. The entire line segment is inside, and the segment can be sent on to be rasterized.

2. ($o_1 \neq 0$, $o_2 = 0$; or vice versa). One endpoint is inside the clipping window; one is outside (see segment *CD* in Figure 6.7). The line segment must be shortened. The nonzero outcode indicates which edge or edges of the window are crossed by the segment. One or two intersections must be computed. Note that after one intersection is computed, we can compute the outcode of the

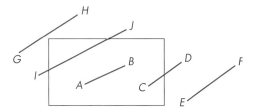

FIGURE 6.7   Cases of outcodes in Cohen-Sutherland algorithm.

point of intersection to determine whether another intersection calculation is required.

3. (o_1 & $o_2 \neq 0$). By taking the bitwise AND of the outcodes, we determine whether or not the two endpoints lie on the same outside side of the window. If so, the line segment can be discarded (see segment *EF* in Figure 6.7).

4. (o_1 & $o_2 = 0$). Both endpoints are outside, but they are on the outside of different edges of the window. As we can see from segments *GH* and *IJ* in Figure 6.7, we cannot tell from just the outcodes whether the segment can be discarded or must be shortened. The best we can do is to intersect with one of the sides of the window and to check the outcode of the resulting point.

All our checking of outcodes requires only Boolean operations. We do intersection calculations only when they are needed, as in the second case, or where the outcodes did not contain enough information, as in the fourth case.

The Cohen-Sutherland algorithm works best when there are many line segments but few are actually displayed. In this case, most of the line segments lie fully outside one or two of the extended sides of the clipping rectangle and can thus be eliminated on the basis of their outcodes. The other advantage is that this algorithm can be extended to three dimensions. The main disadvantage of the algorithm is that it must be used recursively. Consider line segment *GH* in Figure 6.7. It must be clipped against both the left and top sides of the clipping window. Generally, the simplest way to do so is to use the initial outcodes to determine the first side of the clipping window to clip against. After this first shortening of the original line segment, a new outcode is computed for the new endpoint created by shortening, and the algorithm is reexecuted.

We have not discussed how to compute any required intersections. The form this calculation takes depends on how we choose to represent the line segment, although only a single division should be required in any case. If we use the standard explicit form of a line,

$$y = mx + h,$$

where m is the slope of the line and h is the line's y intercept, then we can compute m and h from the endpoints. However, vertical lines cannot be represented in this form—a critical weakness of the explicit form. If we were interested in only the

Cohen-Sutherland algorithm, it would be fairly simple to program all cases directly because the sides of the clipping rectangle are parallel to the axes. However, we are interested in more than just clipping; consequently, other representations of the line and line segment are of importance. In particular, parametric representations are almost always used in computer graphics. We have already seen the parametric form of the line in Chapter 4; the parametric representation of other types of curves is considered in Chapter 10.

6.4.2 Liang-Barsky Clipping

If we use the parametric form for lines, we can approach the clipping of line segments in a different—and ultimately more efficient—manner. Suppose that we have a line segment defined by the two endpoints $\mathbf{p}_1 = [x_1, y_1]^T$ and $\mathbf{p}_2 = [x_2, y_2]^T$. We can use these endpoints to define a unique line that we can express parametrically, either in matrix form,

$$\mathbf{p}(\alpha) = (1 - \alpha)\mathbf{p}_1 + \alpha\mathbf{p}_2,$$

or as two scalar equations,

$$x(\alpha) = (1 - \alpha)x_1 + \alpha x_2,$$

$$y(\alpha) = (1 - \alpha)y_1 + \alpha y_2.$$

Note that this form is robust and needs no changes for horizontal or vertical lines. As the parameter α varies from 0 to 1, we move along the segment from $\mathbf{p}_1$ to $\mathbf{p}_2$. Negative values of α yield points on the line on the other side of $\mathbf{p}_1$ from $\mathbf{p}_2$. Similarly, values of $\alpha > 1$ give points on the line past $\mathbf{p}_2$ going off to infinity.

Consider a line segment and the line of which it is part, as shown in Figure 6.8(a). As long as the line is not parallel to a side of the window (if it is, we can handle that situation with ease), there are four points where the line intersects the extended sides of the window. These points correspond to the four values of the parameter: α_1, α_2, α_3, and α_4. One of these values corresponds to the line entering the window; another corresponds to the line leaving the window. Leaving aside, for the moment, how we

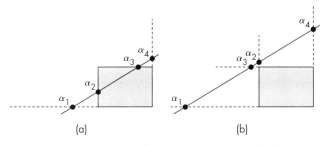

FIGURE 6.8 Two cases of a parametric line and a clipping window.

compute these intersections, we can order them and determine which correspond to intersections that we need for clipping. For the given example,

$$1 > \alpha_4 > \alpha_3 > \alpha_2 > \alpha_1 > 0.$$

Hence, all four intersections are inside the original line segment, with the two innermost (α_2 and α_3) determining the clipped line segment. We can distinguish this case from the case in Figure 6.8(b), which also has the four intersections between the endpoints of the line segment, by noting that the order for this case is

$$1 > \alpha_4 > \alpha_2 > \alpha_3 > \alpha_1 > 0.$$

The line intersects both the top and the bottom of the window before it intersects either the left or the right; thus, the entire line segment must be rejected. Other cases of the ordering of the points of intersection can be argued in a similar way.

Efficient implementation of this strategy requires that we avoid computing intersections until they are needed. Many lines can be rejected before all four intersections are known. We also want to avoid floating-point divisions where possible. If we use the parametric form to determine the intersection with the top of the window, we find the intersection at the value

$$\alpha = \frac{y_{max} - y_1}{y_2 - y_1}.$$

Similar equations hold for the other three sides of the window. Rather than computing these intersections, at the cost of a division for each, we instead write the equation as

$$\alpha(y_2 - y_1) = \alpha \Delta y = y_{max} - y_1 = \Delta y_{max}.$$

All the tests required by the algorithm can be restated in terms of Δy_{max}, Δy, and similar terms can be computed for the other sides of the windows. Thus, all decisions about clipping can be made without floating-point division. Only if an intersection is needed (because a segment has to be shortened) is the division done. The efficiency of this approach, compared to that of the Cohen-Sutherland algorithm, is that we avoid multiple shortening of line segments and the related reexecutions of the clipping algorithm. We forgo discussion of other efficient two-dimensional, line-clipping algorithms because, unlike the Cohen-Sutherland and Liang-Barsky algorithms, these algorithms do not extend to three dimensions.

6.5 POLYGON CLIPPING

Polygon clipping arises in a number of ways. Certainly, we want to be able to clip polygons against rectangular windows for display. However, we may at times want windows that are not rectangular. Other parts of an implementation, such as shadow generation and hidden-surface removal, can require clipping of polygons against

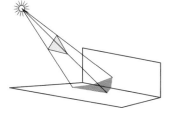

FIGURE 6.9 Polygon clipping in shadow generation.

other polygons. For example, Figure 6.9 shows the shadow of a polygon that we create by clipping a polygon that is closer to the light source against polygons that are farther away. Many antialiasing methods rely on our ability to clip polygons against other polygons.

We can generate polygon-clipping algorithms directly from line-clipping algorithms by clipping the edges of the polygon successively. However, we must be careful to remember that a polygon is a two-dimensional object with an interior, and depending on the form of the polygon, we can generate more than one polygonal object by clipping. Consider the nonconvex (or **concave**) polygon in Figure 6.10(a). If we clip it against a rectangular window, we get the result shown in Figure 6.10(b). Most viewers looking at this figure would conclude that we have generated three polygons by clipping. Unfortunately, implementing a clipper that can increase the number of objects can be a problem. We could treat the result of the clipper as a single polygon, as shown in Figure 6.11, with edges that overlap along the sides of the window, but this choice might cause difficulties in other parts of the implementation.

Convex polygons do not present such problems. Clipping a convex polygon against a rectangular window can leave at most a single convex polygon (see Exercise 6.3). A graphics system might then either forbid the use of concave polygons or divide (tessellate) a given polygon into a set of convex polygons, as shown in Figure 6.12. (OpenGL 4.1 includes tessellation functions.)

For rectangular clipping regions, both the Cohen-Sutherland and the Liang-Barsky algorithms can be applied to polygons on an edge-by-edge basis. There is another approach, developed by Sutherland and Hodgeman, that fits well with the pipeline architectures that we have discussed.

A line-segment clipper can be envisioned as a black box whose input is the pair of vertices from the segment to be tested and clipped and whose output either is a pair of vertices corresponding to the clipped line segment or is nothing if the input line segment lies outside the window (Figure 6.13).

Rather than considering the clipping window as four line segments, we can consider it as the object created by the intersection of four infinite lines that determine the top, bottom, right, and left sides of the window. We can then subdivide our clipper into a pipeline of simpler clippers, each of which clips against a single line that is the extension of an edge of the window. We can use the black-box view on each of the individual clippers.

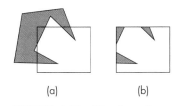

FIGURE 6.10 Clipping of a concave polygon. (a) Before clipping. (b) After clipping.

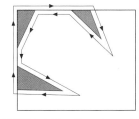

FIGURE 6.11 Creation of a single polygon.

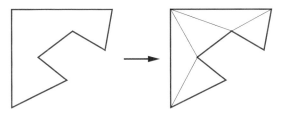

FIGURE 6.12 Tessellation of a concave polygon.

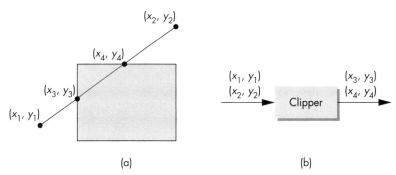

FIGURE 6.13   Two views of clipping. (a) Clipping against a rectangle. (b) Clipper as a black box.

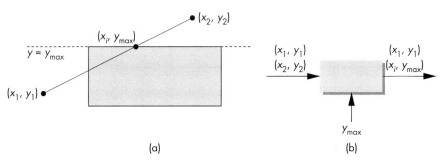

FIGURE 6.14   Clipping against top. (a) Graphically. (b) Black-box view.

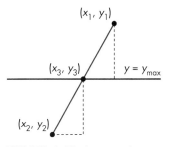

FIGURE 6.15   Intersection with the top of the window.

Suppose that we consider clipping against only the top of the window. We can think of this operation as a black box whose input and output are pairs of vertices, with the value of y_{max} as a parameter known to the clipper (Figure 6.14). Using the similar triangles in Figure 6.15, we see that if there is an intersection, it lies at

$$x_3 = x_1 + (y_{max} - y_1)\frac{x_2 - x_1}{y_2 - y_1},$$

$$y_3 = y_{max}.$$

Thus, the clipper returns one of three pairs: $\{(x_1, y_1), (x_2, y_2)\}$; $\{(x_1, y_1), (x_i, y_{max})\}$; or $\{(x_i, y_{max}), (x_2, y_2)\}$. We can clip against the bottom, right, and left lines independently, using the same equations, with the roles of x and y exchanged as necessary and the values for the sides of the window inserted. The four clippers can now be arranged in the pipeline of Figure 6.16. If we build this configuration in hardware, we have a clipper that is working on four vertices concurrently. Figure 6.17 shows a simple example of the effect of successive clippers on a polygon.

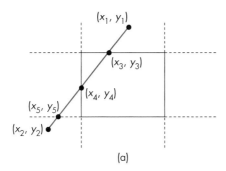

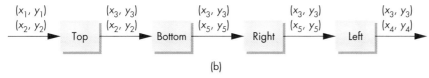

FIGURE 6.16 Pipeline clipping. (a) Clipping problem. (b) Pipeline clippers.

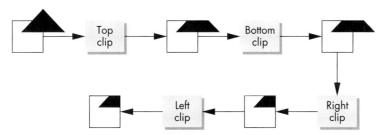

FIGURE 6.17 Example of pipeline clipping.

6.6 CLIPPING OF OTHER PRIMITIVES

Our emphasis in Chapters 1 through 5 was on writing programs in which the objects are built from line segments and triangles. We often render the curved objects that we discuss in Chapter 10 by subdividing them into small, approximately flat polygons. In pipeline architectures, we usually find some variant of the clippers that we have presented. Nevertheless, there are situations in which we want either to clip objects before they reach the hardware or to employ algorithms optimized for other primitives.

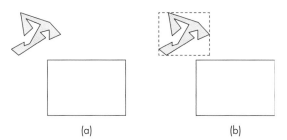

FIGURE 6.18   Using bounding boxes. (a) Polygon and clipping window.
(b) Polygon, bounding box, and clipping window.

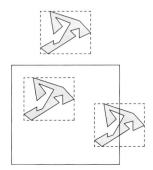

FIGURE 6.19   Clipping with
bounding boxes.

6.6.1 Bounding Boxes and Volumes

Suppose that we have a many-sided polygon, as shown in Figure 6.18(a). We could apply one of our clipping algorithms, which would clip the polygon by individually clipping all that polygon's edges. However, we can see that the entire polygon lies outside the clipping window. We can exploit this observation through the use of the axis-aligned bounding box or the extent of the polygon (Figure 6.18(b)): the smallest rectangle, aligned with the window, that contains the polygon. Calculating the bounding box requires merely going through the vertices of the polygon to find the minimum and maximum of both the x and y values.

Once we have the bounding box, we can often avoid detailed clipping. Consider the three cases in Figure 6.19. For the polygon above the window, no clipping is necessary, because the minimum y for the bounding box is above the top of the window. For the polygon inside the window, we can determine that it is inside by comparing the bounding box with the window. Only when we discover that the bounding box straddles the window do we have to carry out detailed clipping, using all the edges of the polygon. The use of extents is such a powerful technique—in both two and three dimensions—that modeling systems often compute a bounding box for each object automatically and store the bounding box with the object.

Axis-aligned bounding boxes work in both two and three dimensions. In three dimensions, they can be used in the application to perform clipping to reduce the burden on the pipeline. Other volumes, such as spheres, can also work well. One of the other applications of bounding volumes is in collision detection (Chapter 9). One of the fundamental operations in animating computer games is to determine if two moving entities have collided. For example, consider two animated characters moving in a sequence of images. We need to know when they collide so that we can alter their paths. This problem has many similarities to the clipping problem because we want to determine when the volume of one intersects the volume of the other. The complexity of the objects and the need to do these calculations very quickly make this problem difficult. A common approach is to place each object in a bounding volume, either an axis-aligned bounding box or a sphere, and to determine if the volumes intersect. If they do, then detailed calculations can be done.

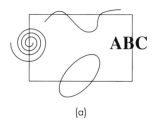 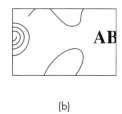

(a)   (b)

FIGURE 6.20   Curve clipping.

6.6.2 Curves, Surfaces, and Text

The variety of curves and surfaces that we can define mathematically makes it difficult to find general algorithms for processing these objects. The potential difficulties can be seen from the two-dimensional curves in Figure 6.20. For a simple curve, such as a quadric, we can compute intersections, although at a cost higher than that for lines. For more complex curves, such as the spiral, not only must intersection calculations be computed with numerical techniques, but even determining how many intersections we must compute may be difficult. We can avoid such problems by approximating curves with line segments and surfaces with planar polygons. The use of bounding boxes can also prove helpful, especially in cases such as quadratics, where we can compute intersections exactly but would prefer to make sure that the calculation is necessary before carrying it out.

The handling of text differs from API to API, with many APIs allowing the user to specify how detailed a rendering of text is required. There are two extremes. On one end, text is stored as bit patterns and is rendered directly by the hardware without any geometric processing. Any required clipping is done in the frame buffer. At the other extreme, text is defined like any other geometric object and is then processed through the standard viewing pipeline. OpenGL allows both these cases by not having a separate text primitive. The user can choose which mode she prefers by defining either bitmapped characters, using pixel operations, or stroke characters, using the standard primitives.

6.6.3 Clipping in the Frame Buffer

We might also consider delaying clipping until after objects have been projected and converted into screen coordinates. Clipping can be done in the frame buffer through a technique called **scissoring**. However, it is usually better to clip geometric entities before the vertices reach the frame buffer; thus, clipping within the frame buffer generally is required only for raster objects, such as blocks of pixels.

6.7   CLIPPING IN THREE DIMENSIONS

In three dimensions, we clip against a bounded volume rather than against a bounded region in the plane. The simplest extension of two-dimensional clipping to three

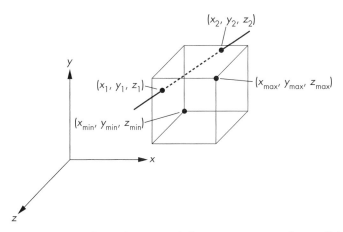

FIGURE 6.21   Three-dimensional clipping against a right parallelepiped.

dimensions is for the right parallelepiped clipping region (Figure 6.21):

$$x_{\min} \leq x \leq x_{\max},$$

$$y_{\min} \leq y \leq y_{\max},$$

$$z_{\min} \leq z \leq z_{\max}$$

or in clip space

$$-w \leq x \leq w,$$

$$-w \leq y \leq w,$$

$$-w \leq z \leq w.$$

Our three clipping algorithms (Cohen-Sutherland, Liang-Barsky, and Sutherland-Hodgeman) and the use of extents can be extended to three dimensions. For the Cohen–Sutherland algorithm, we replace the 4-bit outcode with a 6-bit outcode. The additional 2 bits are set if the point lies either in front of or behind the clipping volume (Figure 6.22). The testing strategy is virtually identical for the two- and three-dimensional cases.

For the Liang-Barsky algorithm, we add the equation

$$z(\alpha) = (1 - \alpha)z_1 + \alpha z_2$$

to obtain a three-dimensional parametric representation of the line segment. We have to consider six intersections with the surfaces that form the clipping volume, but we can use the same logic as we did in the two-dimensional case. Pipeline clippers add two modules to clip against the front and back of the clipping volume.

The major difference between two- and three-dimensional clippers is that in three dimensions we are clipping either lines against planes or polygons against

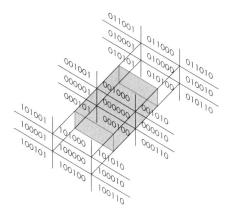

FIGURE 6.22   Cohen-Sutherland regions in three dimensions.

planes instead of clipping lines against lines as we do in two dimensions. Consequently, our intersection calculations must be changed. A typical intersection calculation can be posed in terms of a parametric line in three dimensions intersecting a plane (Figure 6.23). If we write the line and plane equations in matrix form (where $\mathbf{n}$ is the normal to the plane and $\mathbf{p}_0$ is a point on the plane), we must solve the equations

$$\mathbf{p}(\alpha) = (1 - \alpha)\mathbf{p}_1 + \alpha\mathbf{p}_2,$$

$$\mathbf{n} \cdot (\mathbf{p}(\alpha) - \mathbf{p}_0) = 0$$

for the α corresponding to the point of intersection. This value is

$$\alpha = \frac{\mathbf{n} \cdot (\mathbf{p}_0 - \mathbf{p}_1)}{\mathbf{n} \cdot (\mathbf{p}_2 - \mathbf{p}_1)},$$

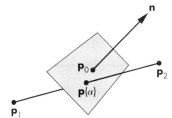

FIGURE 6.23   Plane–line intersection.

and computation of an intersection requires six multiplications and a division. However, if we look at the standard viewing volumes, we see that simplifications are possible. For orthographic viewing (Figure 6.24), the view volume is a right parallelepiped, and each intersection calculation reduces to a single division, as it did for two-dimensional clipping.

When we consider an oblique view (Figure 6.25), we see that the clipping volume no longer is a right parallelepiped. Although you might think that we have to compute dot products to clip against the sides of the volume, here is where the normalization process that we introduced in Chapter 4 pays dividends. We showed that an oblique projection is equivalent to a shearing of the data followed by an orthographic projection. Although the shear transformation distorts objects, they are distorted such that they project correctly by an orthographic projection. The shear also distorts the clipping volume from a general parallelepiped to a right parallelepiped. Figure 6.26(a) shows a top view of an oblique volume with a cube inside the volume. Figure 6.26(b)

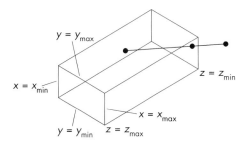

FIGURE 6.24   Clipping for orthographic viewing.

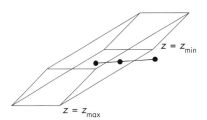

FIGURE 6.25   Clipping for oblique viewing.

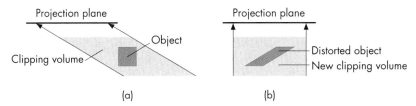

FIGURE 6.26   Distortion of view volume by shear. (a) Top view before shear. (b) Top view after shear.

shows the volume and object after they have been distorted by the shear. As far as projection is concerned, carrying out the oblique transformation directly or replacing it by a shear transformation and an orthographic projection requires the same amount of computation. When we add in clipping, it is clear that the second approach has a definite advantage because we can clip against a right parallelepiped. This example illustrates the importance of considering the incremental nature of the steps in an implementation. Analysis of either projection or clipping in isolation fails to show the importance of the normalization process.

For perspective projections, the argument for normalization is just as strong. By carrying out the perspective-normalization transformation from Chapter 4, but not the orthographic projection, we again create a rectangular clipping volume and simplify all subsequent intersection calculations.

6.8   RASTERIZATION

We are now ready to take the final step in the journey from the specification of geometric entities in an application program to the formation of fragments: rasterization of primitives. In this chapter, we are concerned with only line segments and polygons, both of which are defined by vertices. We can assume that we have clipped the primitives such that each remaining primitive is inside the view volume.

Fragments are potential pixels. Each fragment has a color attribute and a location in screen coordinates that corresponds to a location in the color buffer. Fragments also carry depth information that can be used for hidden-surface removal. To clarify the discussion, we will ignore hidden-surface removal until Section 6.11 and thus we can work directly in screen coordinates. Because we are not considering hidden-surface removal, translucent fragments, or antialiasing, we can develop rasterization algorithms in terms of the pixels that they color.

We further assume that the color buffer is an $n \times m$ array of pixels, with $(0, 0)$ corresponding to the lower-left corner. Pixels can be set to a given color by a single function inside the graphics implementation of the form

```
write_pixel(int ix, int iy, int value);
```

The argument `value` can be either an index, in color-index mode, or a pointer to an RGBA color. On the one hand, a color buffer is inherently discrete; it does not make sense to talk about pixels located at places other than integer values of ix and iy. On the other hand, screen coordinates, which range over the same values as do ix and iy, are real numbers. For example, we can compute a fragment location such as $(63.4, 157.9)$ in screen coordinates but must realize that the nearest pixel is centered either at $(63, 158)$ or at $(63.5, 157.5)$, depending on whether pixels are considered to be centered at whole or half integer values.

Pixels have attributes that are colors in the color buffer. Pixels can be displayed in multiple shapes and sizes that depend on the characteristics of the display. We address this matter in Section 6.13. For now, we can assume that a pixel is displayed as a square, whose center is at the location associated with the pixel and whose side is equal to the distance between pixels. In OpenGL, the centers of pixels are located at values halfway between integers. There are some advantages to this choice (see Exercise 6.19). We also assume that a concurrent process reads the contents of the color buffer and creates the display at the required rate. This assumption, which holds in many systems that have dual-ported memory, allows us to treat the rasterization process independently of the display of the contents of the frame buffer.

The simplest scan-conversion algorithm for line segments has become known as the **DDA algorithm**, after the digital differential analyzer, an early electromechanical device for digital simulation of differential equations. Because a line satisfies the differential equation $dy/dx = m$, where m is the slope, generating a line segment is equivalent to solving a simple differential equation numerically.

Suppose that we have a line segment defined by the endpoints (x_1, y_1) and (x_2, y_2). Because we are working in a color buffer, we assume that these values have

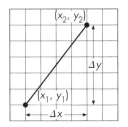

FIGURE 6.27 Line segment in window coordinates.

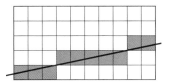

FIGURE 6.28 Pixels generated by DDA algorithm.

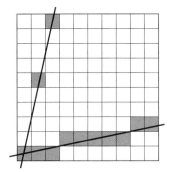

FIGURE 6.29 Pixels generated by high- and low-slope lines.

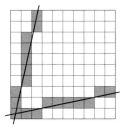

FIGURE 6.30 Pixels generated by revised DDA algorithm.

been rounded to have integer values, so the line segment starts and ends at a known pixel.[1] The slope is given by

$$m = \frac{y_2 - y_1}{x_2 - x_1} = \frac{\Delta y}{\Delta x}.$$

We assume that

$$0 \le m \le 1.$$

We can handle other values of m using symmetry. Our algorithm is based on writing a pixel for each value of ix in `write_pixel` as x goes from x_1 to x_2. If we are on the line segment, as shown in Figure 6.27, for any change in x equal to Δx, the corresponding changes in y must be

$$\Delta y = m \Delta x.$$

As we move from x_1 to x_2, we increase x by 1 in each iteration; thus, we must increase y by

$$\Delta y = m.$$

Although each x is an integer, each y is not, because m is a floating-point number and we must round it to find the appropriate pixel, as shown in Figure 6.28. Our algorithm, in pseudocode, is

```
for (ix=x1; ix <= x2; ix++)
{
    y+=m;
    write_pixel(x, round(y), line_color);
}
```

where `round` is a function that rounds a real number to an integer. The reason that we limited the maximum slope to 1 can be seen from Figure 6.29. Our algorithm is of this form: For each x, find the best y. For large slopes, the separation between pixels that are colored can be large, generating an unacceptable approximation to the line segment. If, however, for slopes greater than 1, we swap the roles of x and y, the algorithm becomes this: For each y, find the best x. For the same line segments, we get the approximations in Figure 6.30. Note that the use of symmetry removes any potential problems from either vertical or horizontal line segments. You may want to derive the parts of the algorithm for negative slopes.

Because line segments are determined by vertices, we can use interpolation to assign a different color to each pixel that we generate. We can also generate various

---

1. This assumption is not necessary to derive an algorithm. If we use a fixed-point representation for the endpoints and do our calculations using fixed-point arithmetic, then we retain the computational advantages of the algorithm and produce a more accurate rasterization.

dash and dot patterns by changing the color that we use as we generate pixels. Neither of these effects has much to do with the basic rasterization algorithm, as the latter's job is to determine only which pixels to color rather than to determine the color that is used.

6.9 BRESENHAM'S ALGORITHM

The DDA algorithm appears efficient. Certainly it can be coded easily, but it requires a floating-point addition for each pixel generated. Bresenham derived a line-rasterization algorithm that, remarkably, avoids all floating-point calculations and has become the standard algorithm used in hardware and software rasterizers.

We assume, as we did with the DDA algorithm, that the line segment goes between the integer points (x_1, y_1) and (x_2, y_2) and that the slope satisfies

$$0 \leq m \leq 1.$$

This slope condition is crucial for the algorithm, as we can see with the aid of Figure 6.31. Suppose that we are somewhere in the middle of the scan conversion of our line segment and have just placed a pixel at $(i + \frac{1}{2}, j + \frac{1}{2})$. We know that the line of which the segment is part can be represented as

$$y = mx + h.$$

At $x = i + \frac{1}{2}$, this line must pass within one-half the length of the pixel at $(i + \frac{1}{2}, j + \frac{1}{2})$;[2] otherwise, the rounding operation would not have generated this pixel. If we move ahead to $x = i + \frac{3}{2}$, the slope condition indicates that we must set the color of one of only two possible pixels: either the pixel at $(i + \frac{3}{2}, j + \frac{1}{2})$ or the pixel at $(i + \frac{3}{2}, j + \frac{3}{2})$. Having reduced our choices to two pixels, we can pose the problem anew in terms of the **decision variable** $d = a - b$, where a and b are the distances between the line and the upper and lower candidate pixels at $x = i + \frac{3}{2}$, as shown in Figure 6.32. If d is positive, the line passes closer to the lower pixel, so we choose the pixel at $(i + \frac{3}{2}, j + \frac{1}{2})$; otherwise, we choose the pixel at $(i + \frac{3}{2}, j + \frac{3}{2})$. Although we could compute d by computing $y = mx + b$, we hesitate to do so because m is a floating-point number.

We obtain the computational advantages of Bresenham's algorithm through two further steps. First, we replace floating-point operations with fixed-point operations. Second, we apply the algorithm incrementally. We start by replacing d with the new decision variable

$$d = (x_2 - x_1)(a - b) = \Delta x(a - b),$$

---

2. We are assuming that the pixels' centers are located halfway between integers.

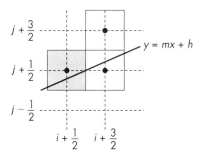

FIGURE 6.31   Conditions for Bresenham's algorithm.

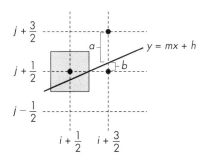

FIGURE 6.32   Decision variable for Bresenham's algorithm.

a change that cannot affect which pixels are drawn, because it is only the sign of the decision variable that matters. If we substitute for a and b, using the equation of the line and noting that

$$m = \frac{y_2 - y_1}{x_2 - x_1} = \frac{\Delta y}{\Delta x},$$

$$h = y_2 - mx_2,$$

then we can see that d is an integer. We have eliminated floating-point calculations, but the direct computation of d requires a fair amount of fixed-point arithmetic.

Let us take a slightly different approach. Suppose that d_k is the value of d at $x = k + \frac{1}{2}$. We would like to compute d_{k+1} incrementally from d_k. There are two situations, depending on whether or not we incremented the y location of the pixel at the previous step; these situations are shown in Figure 6.33. By observing that a is the distance between the location of the upper candidate location and the line, we see that a increases by m only if x was increased by the previous decision; otherwise, it decreases by $m - 1$. Likewise, b either decreases by $-m$ or increases by $1 - m$ when we increment x. Multiplying by Δx, we find that the possible changes in d are either $-2\Delta y$ or $2(\Delta x - \Delta y)$. We can state this result in the form

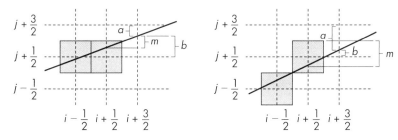

FIGURE 6.33   Incrementing of the values of a and b.

$$d_{k+1} = d_k - \begin{cases} 2\Delta y & \text{if } d_k > 0; \\ 2(\Delta y - \Delta x) & \text{otherwise.} \end{cases}$$

The calculation of each successive pixel in the color buffer requires only an addition and a sign test. This algorithm is so efficient that it has been incorporated as a single instruction on graphics chips. See Exercise 6.14 for calculation of the initial value d_0.

6.10 POLYGON RASTERIZATION

One of the major advantages that the first raster systems brought to users was the ability to display filled polygons. At that time, coloring each point in the interior of a polygon with a different shade was not possible in real time, and the phrases *rasterizing polygons* and *polygon scan conversion* came to mean filling a polygon with a single color. Unlike rasterization of lines, where a single algorithm dominates, there are many viable methods for rasterizing polygons. The choice depends heavily on the implementation architecture. We concentrate on methods that fit with our pipeline approach and can also support shading. In Sections 6.10.4 through 6.10.6, we survey a number of other approaches.

6.10.1 Inside–Outside Testing

Flat simple polygons have well-defined interiors. If they are also convex, they are guaranteed to rendered correctly by OpenGL and by other graphics systems. More general polygons arise in practice, however, and we can render them in multiple ways. For nonflat polygons,[3] we can work with their projections (Section 6.10.2), or we can use the first three vertices to determine a plane to use for the interior. For flat nonsimple polygons, we must decide how to determine whether a given point is

---

3. Strictly speaking, there is no such thing as a nonflat polygon because the interior is not defined unless it is flat. However, from a programming perspective, we can *define* a polygon by simply giving a list of vertices, regardless of whether or not they lie in the same plane.

FIGURE 6.34 Filling with the odd–even test.

inside or outside of the polygon. Conceptually, the process of filling the inside of a polygon with a color or pattern is equivalent to deciding which points in the plane of the polygon are interior (inside) points.

The **crossing** or **odd–even test** is the most widely used test for making inside–outside decisions. Suppose that **p** is a point inside a polygon. Any ray emanating from **p** and going off to infinity must cross an odd number of edges. Any ray emanating from a point outside the polygon and entering the polygon crosses an even number of edges before reaching infinity. Hence, a point can be defined as being inside if after drawing a line through it and following this line, starting on the outside, we cross an odd number of edges before reaching it. For the star-shaped polygon in Figure 6.34, we obtain the inside coloring shown. Odd–even testing is easy to implement and integrates well with the standard rendering algorithms. Usually, we replace rays through points with scanlines, and we count the crossing of polygon edges to determine inside and outside.

However, we might want our fill algorithm to color the star polygon as shown in Figure 6.35 rather than as shown in Figure 6.34. The **winding** test allows us to make that happen. This test considers the polygon as a knot being wrapped around a point or a line. To implement the test, we consider traversing the edges of the polygon from any starting vertex and going around the edge in a particular direction (which direction does not matter) until we reach the starting point. We illustrate the path by labeling the edges, as shown in Figure 6.35(b). Next we consider an arbitrary point. The **winding number** for this point is the number of times it is encircled by the edges of the polygon. We count clockwise encirclements as positive and counterclockwise encirclements as negative (or vice versa). Thus, points outside the star in Figure 6.35 are not encircled and have a winding number of 0, points that were filled in Figure 6.34 all have a winding number of 1, and points in the center that were not filled by the odd–even test have a winding number of 2. If we change our fill rule to be that a point is inside the polygon if its winding number is not zero, then we fill the inside of the polygon as shown in Figure 6.35(a).

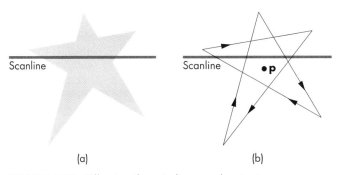

(a)   (b)

FIGURE 6.35 Fill using the winding number test.

6.10.2 OpenGL and Concave Polygons

Because OpenGL only renders triangles, which are always flat and convex, we still have the problem of what to do with more general polygons. One approach is to work with the application to ensure that they only generate triangles. Another is to provide software that can tessellate a given polygon into flat convex polygons, usually triangles. There are many ways to divide a given polygon into triangles. A good tessellation should not produce triangles that are long and thin; it should, if possible, produce sets of triangles that can use supported features, such as triangle strips and triangle fans.

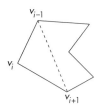

FIGURE 6.36   Removal of a triangle from a polygon.

Let's consider one approach to tessellating or triangularizing an arbitrary simple polygon with n vertices. From the construction, it will be clear that we always obtain a triangularization using exactly $n-2$ triangles. We assume our polygon is specified by an ordered list of vertices $v_0, v_1, \ldots, v_{n-1}$. Thus, there is an edge from v_0 to v_1, from v_1 to v_2, and finally from v_{n-1} to v_0. The first step is to find the left-most vertex, v_i, a calculation that requires a simple scan of the x components of the vertices. Let v_{i-1} and v_{i+1} be the two neighbors of v_i (where the indices are computed modulo n). These three vertices form the triangle v_{i-1}, v_i, v_{i+1}. If the situation is as in Figure 6.36, then we can proceed recursively by removing v_i from the original list and we will have a triangle and a polygon with $n-1$ vertices.

However, because the polygon may not be convex, the line segment from v_{i-1} to v_{i+1} can cross other edges, as shown in Figure 6.37. We can test for this case by checking if any of the other vertices lie to the left of the line segment and inside the triangle determined by v_{i-1}, v_i, v_{i+1}. If we connect v_i to the left-most of these vertices, we split the original triangle into two polygons (as in Figure 6.38), each of which has at least two vertices fewer than the original triangle. Using the leftmost vertex ensures that the two polygons are simple. Hence, we can proceed recursively with these two triangles, knowing that in the end we will have all triangles.

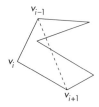

FIGURE 6.37   Vertex inside triangle.

Note that the worst-case performance of this method occurs when there are no vertices in the triangle formed by v_{i-1}, v_i, v_{i+1}. We require $O(n)$ tests to make sure that this is the case and if it is we then remove only one vertex from the original polygon. Consequently, the worst-case performance is $O(n^2)$. However, if we know in advance that the polygon is convex, these tests are not needed and the method is $O(n)$. The best performance in general occurs when the splitting results in two polygons with an equal number of vertices. If such a split occurs on each step, the method would be $O(n \log n)$. The Suggested Readings at the end of the chapter include methods that are guaranteed to be $O(n \log n)$, but they are more complex than the method outlined here. In practice, we rarely work with polygons with so many vertices that we need the more complex methods.

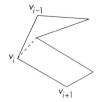

FIGURE 6.38   Splitting into two polygons.

6.10.3 Fill and Sort

A different approach to rasterization of polygons starts with the idea of a polygon processor: a black box whose inputs are the vertices for a set of two-dimensional polygons and whose output is a frame buffer with the correct pixels set. Suppose that we consider filling each polygon with a constant color—a choice we make only to clarify the discussion. First, consider a single polygon. The basic rule for filling a polygon is as follows: *If a point is inside the polygon, color it with the inside (fill) color.* This conceptual algorithm indicates that polygon fill is a sorting problem, where we sort all the pixels in the frame buffer into those that are inside the polygon and those that are not. From this perspective, we obtain different polygon-fill algorithms using different ways of sorting the points. We introduce three possibilities:

- Flood fill
- Scanline fill
- Odd–even fill

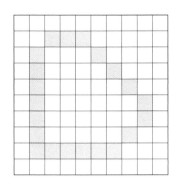

FIGURE 6.39 Polygon displayed by edges.

6.10.4 Flood Fill

We can display an unfilled polygon by rasterizing its edges into the frame buffer using Bresenham's algorithm. Suppose that we have only two colors: a background color (white) and a foreground, or drawing, color (black). We can use the foreground color to rasterize the edges, resulting in a frame buffer colored as shown in Figure 6.39 for a simple polygon. If we can find an initial point (x, y) inside the polygon— a **seed point**—then we can look at its neighbors recursively, coloring them with the foreground color if they are not edge points. The **flood-fill algorithm** can be expressed in pseudocode, assuming that there is a function `read_pixel` that returns the color of a pixel:

```
flood_fill(int x, int y)
{
    if (read_pixel(x,y) == WHITE)
    {
        write_pixel(x,y,BLACK);
        flood_fill(x-1,y);
        flood_fill(x+1,y);
        flood_fill(x,y-1);
        flood_fill(x,y+1);
    }
}
```

We can obtain a number of variants of flood fill by removing the recursion. One way to do so is to work one scanline at a time.

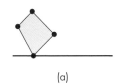

(a)

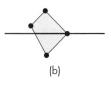

(b)

FIGURE 6.40 Singularities. (a) Zero or two edge crossings. (b) One edge crossing.

6.10.5 Singularities

We can extend most polygon-fill algorithms to other shapes if we use care (see Exercise 6.17). Polygons have the distinct advantage that the locations of their edges are known exactly. Even polygons can present problems, however, when vertices lie on scanlines. Consider the two cases in Figure 6.40. If we are using an odd–even fill definition, we have to treat these two cases differently. For case (a), we can count the intersection of the scanline with the vertex as either zero or two edge crossings; for case (b), the vertex–scanline intersection must be counted as one edge crossing.

We can fix our algorithm in one of two ways. We can check to see which of the two situations we have and then count the edge crossings appropriately. Or we can prevent the special case of a vertex lying on an edge—a **singularity**—from ever arising. We rule it out by ensuring that no vertex has an integer y value. If we find one that does, we perturb its location slightly. Another method—one that is especially valuable if we are working in the frame buffer—is to consider a virtual frame buffer of twice the resolution of the real frame buffer. In the virtual frame buffer, pixels are located only at even values of y, and all vertices are located only at odd values of y. Placing pixel centers halfway between integers, as OpenGL does, is equivalent to using this approach.

6.11 HIDDEN-SURFACE REMOVAL

Although every fragment generated by rasterization corresponds to a location in a color buffer, we do not want to display the fragment by coloring the corresponding pixel if the fragment is from an object behind another opaque object. Hidden-surface removal (or visible-surface determination) is done to discover what part, if any, of each object in the view volume is visible to the viewer or is obscured from the viewer by other objects. We describe a number of techniques for a scene composed purely of planar polygons. Because most renderers will have subdivided surfaces into polygons at this point, this choice is appropriate. Line segments can be handled by slight modifications (see Exercise 6.7).

6.11.1 Object-Space and Image-Space Approaches

The study of hidden-surface–removal algorithms clearly illustrates the variety of available algorithms, the differences between working with objects and working with images, and the importance of evaluating the incremental effects of successive algorithms in the implementation process.

Consider a scene composed of k three-dimensional opaque flat polygons, each of which we can consider to be an individual object. We can derive a generic **object-space approach** by considering the objects pairwise, as seen from the center of projection. Consider two such polygons, A and B. There are four possibilities (Figure 6.41):

1. A completely obscures B from the camera; we display only A.

2. B obscures A; we display only B.

3. A and B both are completely visible; we display both A and B.

4. A and B partially obscure each other; we must calculate the visible parts of each polygon.

For complexity considerations, we can regard the determination of which case we have and any required calculation of the visible part of a polygon as a single operation. We proceed iteratively. We pick one of the k polygons and compare it pairwise

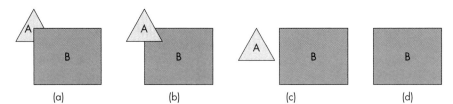

FIGURE 6.41   Two polygons. (a) *B* partially obscures *A*. (b) *A* partially obscures *B*. (c) Both *A* and *B* are visible. (d) *B* totally obscures *A*.

with the remaining $k - 1$ polygons. After this procedure, we know which part (if any) of this polygon is visible, and we render the visible part. We are now done with this polygon, so we repeat the process with any of the other $k - 1$ polygons. Each step involves comparing one polygon, pairwise, with the other remaining polygons until we have only two polygons remaining, and we compare these to each other. We can easily determine that the complexity of this calculation is $O(k^2)$. Thus, without deriving any of the details of any particular object-space algorithm, we should suspect that the object-space approach works best for scenes that contain relatively few polygons.

The **image-space approach** follows our viewing and ray-casting model, as shown in Figure 6.42. Consider a ray that leaves the center of projection and passes through a pixel. We can intersect this ray with each of the planes determined by our k polygons, determine for which planes the ray passes through a polygon, and finally, for those rays, find the intersection closest to the center of projection. We color this pixel with the shade of the polygon at the point of intersection. Our fundamental operation is the intersection of rays with polygons. For an $n \times m$ display, we have to carry out this operation nmk times, giving $O(k)$ complexity.[4] Again, without looking at the details of the operations, we were able to get an upper bound. In general, the $O(k)$ bound accounts for the dominance of image-space methods. The $O(k)$ bound is a worst-case bound. In practice, image-space algorithms perform much better (see Exercise 6.9). However, because image-space approaches work at the fragment or pixel level, their accuracy is limited by the resolution of the frame buffer.

6.11.2 Sorting and Hidden-Surface Removal

The $O(k^2)$ upper bound for object-oriented hidden-surface removal might remind you of the poorer sorting algorithms, such as bubble sort. Any method that involves brute-force comparison of objects by pairs has $O(k^2)$ complexity. But there is a more direct connection, which we exploited in the object-oriented sorting algorithms in Section 6.8.5. If we could organize objects by their distances from the camera, we should be able to come up with a direct method of rendering them.

But if we follow the analogy, we know that the complexity of good sorting algorithms is $O(k \log k)$. We should expect the same to be true for object-oriented

---

4. We can use more than one ray for each pixel to increase the accuracy of the rendering.

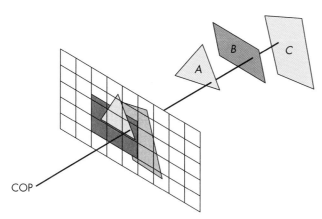

FIGURE 6.42   Image-space hidden-surface removal.

hidden-surface removal, and, in fact, such is the case. As with sorting, there are multiple algorithms that meet these bounds. In addition, there are related problems involving comparison of objects, such as collision detection, that start off looking as if they are $O(k^2)$ when, in fact, they can be reduced to $O(k \log k)$.

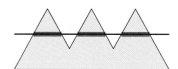

FIGURE 6.43   Polygon with spans.

6.11.3 Scanline Algorithms

The attraction of a **scanline algorithm** is that such a method has the potential to generate pixels as they are displayed. Consider the polygon in Figure 6.43, with one scanline shown. If we use our odd–even rule for defining the inside of the polygon, we can see three groups of pixels, or **spans**, on this scanline that are inside the polygon. Note that each span can be processed independently for lighting or depth calculations, a strategy that has been employed in some hardware that has parallel span processors. For our simple example of constant fill, after we have identified the spans, we can color the interior pixels of each span with the fill color.

The spans are determined by the set of intersections of polygons with scanlines. The vertices contain all the information that we need to determine these intersections, but the method that we use to represent the polygon determines the order in which these intersections are generated. For example, consider the polygon in Figure 6.43, which has been represented by an ordered list of vertices. The most obvious way to generate scanline–edge intersections is to process edges defined by successive vertices. Figure 6.44 shows these intersections, indexed in the order in which this method would generate them. Note that this calculation can be done incrementally (see Exercise 6.18). However, as far as fill is concerned, this order is far from the one we want. If we are to fill one scanline at a time, we would like the intersections sorted, first by scanlines and then by order of x on each scanline, as shown in Figure 6.45. A brute-force approach might be to sort all the intersections into the desired order. However, a large or jagged polygon might intersect so many edges that the n intersections can be large enough that the $O(n \log n)$ complexity of the sort makes the

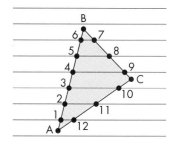

FIGURE 6.44   Polygon generated by vertex list.

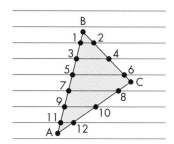

FIGURE 6.45   Desired order of vertices.

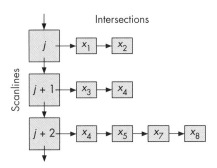

FIGURE 6.46   Data structure for y–x algorithm.

calculation too slow for real-time implementations; consider, for example, a polygon that spans one-half of the scan lines.

A number of methods avoid the general search. One, originally known as the **y–x algorithm**, creates a bucket for each scanline. As edges are processed, the intersections with scanlines are placed in the proper buckets. Within each bucket, an insertion sort orders the x values along each scanline. The data structure is shown in Figure 6.46. Once again, we see that a properly chosen data structure can speed up the algorithm. We can go even further by reconsidering how to represent polygons. If we do so, we arrive at the scanline method that was introduced in Section 6.8.

6.11.4 Back-Face Removal

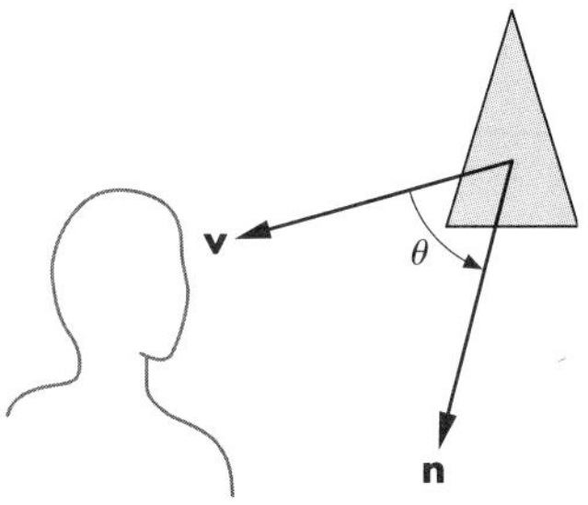

In Chapter 5, we noted that in OpenGL we can choose to render only front-facing polygons. For situations where we cannot see back faces, such as scenes composed of convex polyhedra, we can reduce the work required for hidden-surface removal by eliminating all back-facing polygons before we apply any other hidden-surface–removal algorithm. The test for **culling** a back-facing polygon can be derived from Figure 6.47. We see the front of a polygon if the normal, which comes out of the front face, is pointed toward the viewer. If θ is the angle between the normal and the viewer, then the polygon is facing forward if and only if

$$-90 \leq \theta \leq 90$$

or, equivalently,

$$\cos \theta \geq 0.$$

The second condition is much easier to test because, instead of computing the cosine, we can use the dot product:

$$\mathbf{n} \cdot \mathbf{v} \geq 0.$$

FIGURE 6.47   Back-face test.

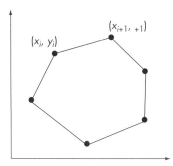

FIGURE 6.48   Computing the area of a polygon.

We can simplify this test even further if we note that usually it is applied after transformation to normalized device coordinates. In this system, all views are orthographic, with the direction of projection along the z-axis. Hence, in homogeneous coordinates,

$$
\mathbf{v} = \begin{bmatrix} 0 \\ 0 \\ 1 \\ 0 \end{bmatrix}.
$$

Thus, if the polygon is on the surface

$$
ax + by + cz + d = 0
$$

in normalized device coordinates, we need only to check the sign of c to determine whether we have a front- or back-facing polygon. This test can be implemented easily in either hardware or software; we must simply be careful to ensure that removing back-facing polygons is correct for our application.

There is another interesting approach to determining back faces. The algorithm is based on computing the area of the polygon in screen coordinates. Consider the polygon in Figure 6.48 with n vertices. Its area a is given by

$$
a = \frac{1}{2} \sum_i (y_{i+1} + y_i)(x_{i+1} - x_i),
$$

where the indices are taken modulo n (see Exercise 6.28). A negative area indicates a back-facing polygon.

6.11.5 The z-Buffer Algorithm

The **z-buffer algorithm** is the most widely used hidden-surface–removal algorithm. It has the advantages of being easy to implement, in either hardware or software, and of being compatible with pipeline architectures, where it can execute at the speed at

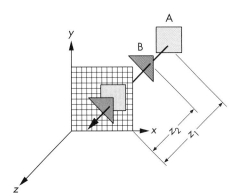

FIGURE 6.49   The z-buffer algorithm.

which fragments are passing through the pipeline. Although the algorithm works in image space, it loops over the polygons rather than over pixels and can be regarded as part of the scan-conversion process that we discussed in Section 6.10.

Suppose that we are in the process of rasterizing one of the two polygons shown in Figure 6.49. We can compute a color for each point of intersection between a ray from the center of projection and a pixel, using interpolated values of the vertex shades computed as in Chapter 5. In addition, we must check whether this point is visible. It will be visible if it is the closest point of intersection along the ray. Hence, if we are rasterizing B, its shade will appear on the screen if the distance z_2 is less than the distance z_1 to polygon A. Conversely, if we are rasterizing A, the pixel that corresponds to the point of intersection will not appear on the display. Because we are proceeding polygon by polygon, however, we do not have the information on all other polygons as we rasterize any given polygon. However, if we keep depth information with each fragment, then we can store and update depth information for each location in the frame buffer as fragments are processed.

Suppose that we have a buffer, the z-buffer, with the same resolution as the frame buffer and with depth consistent with the resolution that we wish to use for distance. For example, if we have a 1024×1280 display and we use standard integers for the depth calculation, we can use a 1024×1280 z-buffer with 32-bit elements. Initially, each element in the depth buffer is initialized to a depth corresponding to the maximum distance away from the center of projection.[5] The color buffer is initialized to the background color. At any time during rasterization and fragment processing,

5. If we have already done perspective normalization, we should replace the center of projection with the direction of projection because all rays are parallel. However, this change does not affect the z-buffer algorithm, because we can measure distances from any arbitrary plane, such as the plane $z = 0$, rather than from the COP.

each location in the z-buffer contains the distance along the ray corresponding to the location of the closest intersection point on any polygon found so far.

The calculation proceeds as follows. We rasterize, polygon by polygon, using one of the methods from Section 6.10. For each fragment on the polygon corresponding to the intersection of the polygon with a ray through a pixel, we compute the depth from the center of projection. We compare this depth to the value in the z-buffer corresponding to this fragment. If this depth is greater than the depth in the z-buffer, then we have already processed a polygon with a corresponding fragment closer to the viewer, and this fragment is not visible. If the depth is less than the depth in the z-buffer,[6] then we have found a fragment closer to the viewer. We update the depth in the z-buffer and place the shade computed for this fragment at the corresponding location in the color buffer. Note that for perspective views, the depth we are using in the z-buffer algorithm is the distance that has been altered by the normalization transformation that we discussed in Chapter 4. Although this transformation is nonlinear, it preserves relative distances. However, this nonlinearity can introduce numerical inaccuracies, especially when the distance to the near clipping plane is small.

Unlike other aspects of rendering where the particular implementation algorithms may be unknown to the user, for hidden-surface removal, OpenGL uses the z-buffer algorithm. This exception arises because the application program must initialize the z-buffer explicitly every time a new image is to be generated.

The z-buffer algorithm works well with image-oriented approaches to implementation because the amount of incremental work is small. Suppose that we are rasterizing a polygon, scanline by scanline—an option we examined in Section 6.9. The polygon is part of a plane (Figure 6.50) that can be represented as

$$ax + by + cz + d = 0.$$

Suppose that (x_1, y_1, z_1) and (x_2, y_2, z_2) are two points on the polygon (and the plane). If

$$\Delta x = x_2 - x_1,$$

$$\Delta y = y_2 - y_1,$$

$$\Delta z = z_2 - z_1,$$

then the equation for the plane can be written in differential form as

$$a\Delta x + b\Delta y + c\Delta z = 0.$$

---

6. In OpenGL, we can use the function `glDepthFunc` to decide what to do when the distances are equal.

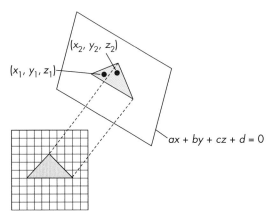

FIGURE 6.50   Incremental z-buffer algorithm.

This equation is in window coordinates, so each scanline corresponds to a line of constant y and $\Delta y = 0$ as we move across a scanline. On a scanline, we increase x in unit steps, corresponding to moving one pixel in the frame buffer, and Δx is constant. Thus, as we move from point to point across a scanline,

$$\Delta z = -\frac{a}{c} \Delta x.$$

This value is a constant that needs to be computed only once for each polygon.

Although the worst-case performance of an image-space algorithm is proportional to the number of primitives, the performance of the z-buffer algorithm is proportional to the number of fragments generated by rasterization, which depends on the area of the rasterized polygons.

6.11.6 Scan Conversion with the z-Buffer

We have already presented most of the essentials of polygon rasterization. In Section 6.10.1, we discussed the odd–even and winding tests for determining whether a point is inside a polygon. In Chapter 5, we learned to shade polygons by interpolation. Here we have only to put together the pieces and to consider efficiency.

Suppose that we follow the pipeline once more, concentrating on what happens to a single polygon. The vertices and normals pass through the geometric transformations one at a time. The vertices must be assembled into a polygon before the clipping stage. If our polygon is not clipped out, its vertices and normals can be passed on for shading and hidden-surface removal. At this point, although projection normalization has taken place, we still have depth information. If we wish to use an interpolative shading method, we can compute the lighting at each vertex.

Three tasks remain: computation of the final orthographic projection, hidden-surface removal, and shading. Careful use of the z-buffer algorithm can accomplish

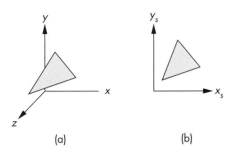

FIGURE 6.51   Dual representations of a polygon. (a) Normalized device coordinates. (b) Screen coordinates.

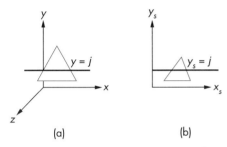

FIGURE 6.52   Dual representations of a scanline. (a) In normalized device coordinates. (b) In screen coordinates.

all three tasks simultaneously. Consider the dual representations of a polygon illustrated in Figure 6.51. In (a) the polygon is represented in three-dimensional normalized device coordinates; in (b) it is shown after projection in screen coordinates.

The strategy is to process each polygon, one scanline at a time. If we work again in terms of these dual representations, we can see that a scanline, projected backward from screen coordinates, corresponds to a line of constant y in normalized device coordinates (Figure 6.52). Suppose that we simultaneously march across this scanline and its back projection. For the scanline in screen coordinates, we move one pixel width with each step. We use the normalized-device-coordinate line to determine depths incrementally and to see whether or not the pixel in screen coordinates corresponds to a visible point on the polygon. Having computed shading for the vertices of the original polygon, we can use interpolation to obtain the correct color for visible pixels. This process requires little extra effort over the individual steps that we have already discussed. It is controlled, and thus limited, by the rate at which we can send polygons through the pipeline. Modifications such as applying bit patterns, called stipple patterns, or texture to polygons require only slight changes.

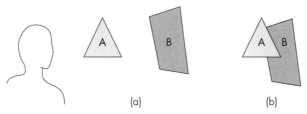

FIGURE 6.53   Painter's algorithm. (a) Two polygons and a viewer are shown. (b) Polygon *A* partially obscures *B* when viewed.

6.11.7 Depth Sort and the Painter's Algorithm

Although image-space methods are dominant in hardware due to the efficiency and ease of implementation of the z-buffer algorithm, often object-space methods are used within the application to lower the polygon count. **Depth sort** is a direct implementation of the object-space approach to hidden-surface removal. We present the algorithm for a scene composed of planar polygons; extensions to other classes of objects are possible. Depth sort is a variant of an even simpler algorithm known as the **painter's algorithm**.

Suppose that we have a collection of polygons that is sorted based on how far from the viewer the polygons are. For the example in Figure 6.53(a), we have two polygons. To a viewer, they appear as shown in Figure 6.53(b), with the polygon in front partially obscuring the other. To render the scene correctly, we could find the part of the rear polygon that is visible and render that part into the frame buffer—a calculation that requires clipping one polygon against the other. Or we could use an approach analogous to the way a painter might render the scene. She probably would paint the rear polygon in its entirety and then the front polygon, painting over that part of the rear polygon not visible to the viewer in the process. Both polygons would be rendered completely, with the hidden-surface removal being done as a consequence of the **back-to-front rendering** of the polygons.[7] The two questions related to this algorithm are how to do the sort and what to do if polygons overlap. Depth sort addresses both, although in many applications more efficiencies can be found (see, for example, Exercise 6.10).

Suppose we have already computed the extent of each polygon. The next step of depth sort is to order all the polygons by how far away from the viewer their maximum z-value is. This step gives the algorithm the name *depth sort*. Suppose that the order is as shown in Figure 6.54, which depicts the z-extents of the polygons after the sort. If the minimum depth—the z-value—of a given polygon is greater than the maximum depth of the polygon behind the one of interest, we can paint the polygons back to front and we are done. For example, polygon *A* in Figure 6.54 is behind all

---

7. In ray tracing and scientific visualization, we often use *front-to-back rendering* of polygons.

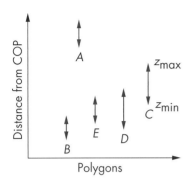

FIGURE 6.54   The z-extents of sorted polygons.

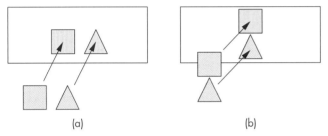

FIGURE 6.55   Test for overlap in x- and y-extents. (a) Nonoverlapping x-extents. (b) Nonoverlapping y-extents.

the other polygons and can be painted first. However, the others cannot be painted based solely on the z-extents.

If the z-extents of two polygons overlap, we still may be able to find an order to paint (render) the polygons individually and yield the correct image. The depth-sort algorithm runs a number of increasingly more difficult tests, attempting to find such an ordering. Consider a pair of polygons whose z-extents overlap. The simplest test is to check their x- and y-extents (Figure 6.55). If either of the x- or y-extents do not overlap,[8] neither polygon can obscure the other and they can be painted in either order. Even if these tests fail, it may still be possible to find an order in which we can paint the polygons individually. Figure 6.56 shows such a case. All the vertices of one polygon lie on the same side of the plane determined by the other. We can process the vertices (see Exercise 6.12) of the two polygons to determine whether this case exists.

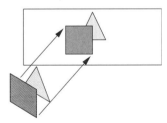

FIGURE 6.56   Polygons with overlapping extents.

---

8. The x- and y-extent tests apply to only a parallel view. Here is another example of the advantage of working in normalized device coordinates *after* perspective normalization.

FIGURE 6.57 Cyclic overlap.

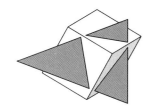

FIGURE 6.58 Piercing polygons.

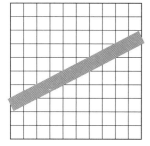

FIGURE 6.59 Ideal raster line.

Two troublesome situations remain. If three or more polygons overlap cyclically, as shown in Figure 6.57, there is no correct order for painting. The best we can do is to divide at least one of the polygons into two parts and attempt to find an order to paint the new set of polygons. The second problematic case arises if a polygon can pierce another polygon, as shown in Figure 6.58. If we want to continue with depth sort, we must derive the details of the intersection—a calculation equivalent to clipping one polygon against the other. If the intersecting polygons have many vertices, we may want to try another algorithm that requires less computation. A performance analysis of depth sort is difficult because the particulars of the application determine how often the more difficult cases arise. For example, if we are working with polygons that describe the surfaces of solid objects, then no two polygons can intersect. Nevertheless, it should be clear that, because of the initial sort, the complexity must be at least $O(k \log k)$, where k is the number of objects.

6.12 ANTIALIASING

Rasterized line segments and edges of polygons look jagged. Even on a display device that has a resolution as high as 1024×1280, we can notice these defects in the display. This type of error arises whenever we attempt to go from the continuous representation of an object, which has infinite resolution, to a sampled approximation, which has limited resolution. The name **aliasing** has been given to this effect because of the tie with aliasing in digital signal processing.

Aliasing errors are caused by three related problems with the discrete nature of the frame buffer. First, if we have an $n \times m$ frame buffer, the number of pixels is fixed, and we can generate only certain patterns to approximate a line segment. Many different continuous line segments may be approximated by the same pattern of pixels. We can say that all these segments are **aliased** as the same sequence of pixels. Given the sequence of pixels, we cannot tell which line segment generated the sequence. Second, pixel locations are fixed on a uniform grid; regardless of where we would like to place pixels, we cannot place them at other than evenly spaced locations. Third, pixels have a fixed size and shape.

At first glance, it might appear that there is little we can do about such problems. Algorithms such as Bresenham's algorithm are optimal in that they choose the closest set of pixels to approximate lines and polygons. However, if we have a display that supports more than two colors, there are other possibilities. Although mathematical lines are one-dimensional entities that have length but not width, rasterized lines must have a width in order to be visible. Suppose that each pixel is displayed as a square of width 1 unit and can occupy a box of 1-unit height and width on the display. Our basic frame buffer can work only in multiples of one pixel;[9] we can think of an idealized line segment in the frame buffer as being one pixel wide, as shown in Figure 6.59. Of course, we cannot draw this line, because it does not consist of our square

---

9. Some frame buffers permit operations in units of less than one pixel through multisampling methods.

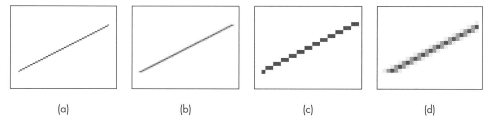

     (a)   (b)   (c)   (d)

FIGURE 6.60   Aliased versus antialiased line segments. (a) Aliased line segment. (b) Antialiased line segment. (c) Magnified aliased line segment. (d) Magnified antialiased line segment.

pixels. We can view Bresenham's algorithm as a method for approximating the ideal one-pixel-wide line with our real pixels. If we look at the ideal one-pixel-wide line, we can see that it partially covers many pixel-sized boxes. It is our scan-conversion algorithm that forces us, for lines of slope less than 1, to choose exactly one pixel value for each value of x. If, instead, we shade each box by the percentage of the ideal line that crosses it, we get the smoother appearing image shown in Figure 6.60(b). This technique is known as **antialiasing by area averaging**. The calculation is similar to polygon clipping. There are other approaches to antialiasing, as well as antialiasing algorithms that can be applied to other primitives, such as polygons. Color Plate 8 shows aliased and antialiased versions of a small area of the object in Color Plate 1.

A related problem arises because of the simple way that we are using the z-buffer algorithm. As we have specified that algorithm, the color of a given pixel is determined by the shade of a single primitive. Consider the pixel shared by the three polygons shown in Figure 6.61. If each polygon has a different color, the color assigned to the pixel is the one associated with the polygon closest to the viewer. We could obtain a much more accurate image if we could assign a color based on an area-weighted average of the colors of the three triangles. Such algorithms can be implemented with fragment shaders on hardware with floating point frame buffers.

FIGURE 6.61   Polygons that share a pixel.

We have discussed only one type of aliasing: **spatial-domain aliasing**. When we generate sequences of images, such as for animations, we also must be concerned with **time-domain aliasing**. Consider a small object moving in front of the projection plane that has been ruled into pixel-sized units, as shown in Figure 6.62. If our rendering process sends a ray through the center of each pixel and determines what it hits, then sometimes we intersect the object and sometimes, if the projection of the object is small, we miss the object. The viewer will have the unpleasant experience of seeing the object flash on and off the display as the animation progresses. There are several ways to deal with this problem. For example, we can use more than one ray per pixel—a technique common in ray tracing. What is common to all antialiasing techniques is that they require considerably more computation than does rendering without antialiasing. In practice, for high-resolution images, antialiasing is done off-line and only when a final image is needed.

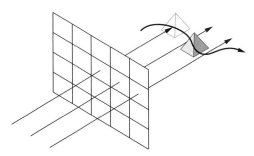

FIGURE 6.62 Time-domain aliasing.

6.13 DISPLAY CONSIDERATIONS

In most interactive applications, the application programmer need not worry about how the contents of the frame buffer are displayed. From the application programmer's perspective, as long as she uses double buffering, the process of writing into the frame buffer is decoupled from the process of reading the frame buffer's contents for display. The hardware redisplays the present contents of the frame buffer at a rate sufficient to avoid flicker—usually 60 to 85 Hz—and the application programmer worries only about whether or not her program can execute and fill the frame buffer fast enough. As we saw in Chapter 2, the use of double buffering allows the display to change smoothly, even if we cannot push our primitives through the system as fast as we would like.

Numerous other problems affect the quality of the display and often cause users to be unhappy with the output of their programs. For example, the displays of two monitors may have the same nominal resolution but may display pixels of different sizes (see Exercises 6.22 and 6.23).

Perhaps the greatest source of problems with displays concerns the basic physical properties of displays: the range of colors they can display and how they map software-defined colors to the values of the primaries for the display. The color gamuts of different displays can differ greatly. In addition, because the primaries on different systems are different, even when two different monitors can produce the same visible color, they may require different values of the primaries to be sent to the displays from the graphics system. In addition, the mapping between brightness values defined by the program and what is displayed is nonlinear.

OpenGL does not address these issues directly, because colors are specified as RGB values that are independent of any display properties. In addition, because RGB primaries are limited to the range from 0.0 to 1.0, it is often difficult to account for the full range of color and brightness detectable by the human visual system. However, if we expand on our discussion of color and the human visual system from Chapter 2, we can gain some additional control over color in OpenGL.

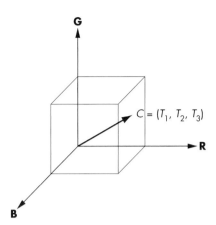

FIGURE 6.63   Color cube.

6.13.1 Color Systems

Our basic assumption about color, supported by the three-color theory of human vision, is that the three color values that we determine for each pixel correspond to the tristimulus values that we introduced in Chapter 2. Thus, a given color is a point in a color cube, as in Figure 6.63, and can be written symbolically as

$$C = T_1\mathbf{R} + T_2\mathbf{G} + T_3\mathbf{B}.$$

However, there are significant differences across RGB systems. For example, suppose that we have a yellow color that OpenGL has represented with the RGB triplet (0.8, 0.6, 0.0). If we use these values to drive both a CRT and a film-image recorder, we will see different colors, even though in both cases the red is 80 percent of maximum, the green is 60 percent of maximum, and there is no blue. The reason is that the film dyes and the CRT phosphors have different color distributions. Consequently, the range of displayable colors (or the color **gamut**) is different for each.

The emphasis in the graphics community has been on device-independent graphics; consequently, the real differences among display properties are not addressed by most APIs. Fortunately, the colorimetry literature contains the information we need. The standards for many of the common color systems exist. For example, CRTs are based on the National Television Systems Committee (NTSC) RGB system. We can look at differences in color systems as being equivalent to different coordinate systems for representing our tristimulus values. If $\mathbf{C}_1 = [R_1, G_1, B_1]^T$ and $\mathbf{C}_2 = [R_2, G_2, B_2]^T$ are the representations of the same color in two different systems, then there is a 3×3 color-conversion matrix $\mathbf{M}$ such that

$$\mathbf{C}_2 = \mathbf{M}\mathbf{C}_1.$$

Whether we determine this matrix from the literature or by experimentation, it allows us to produce similar displays on different output devices.

There are numerous potential problems even with this approach. The color gamuts of the two systems may not be the same. Hence, even after the conversion of tristimulus values, a color may not be producible on one of the systems. Second, the printing and graphic arts industries use a four-color subtractive system (CMYK) that adds black (K) as a fourth primary. Conversion between RGB and CMYK often requires a great deal of human expertise. Third, there are limitations to our linear color theory. The distance between colors in the color cube is not a measure of how far apart the colors are perceptually. For example, humans are particularly sensitive to color shifts in blue. Color systems such as YUV and CIE Lab have been created to address such issues.

Most RGB color systems are based on the primaries in real systems, such as CRT phosphors and film dyes. None can produce all the colors that we can see. Most color standards are based on a theoretical three-primary system called the **XYZ color system**. Here, the Y primary is the luminance of the color. In the XYZ system, all colors can be specified with positive tristimulus values. We use 3×3 matrices to convert from an XYZ color representation to representations in the standard systems. Color specialists often prefer to work with **chromaticity coordinates** rather than tristimulus values. The chromaticity of a color consists of the three fractions of the color in the three primaries. Thus, if we have the tristimulus values, T_1, T_2, and T_3, for a particular RGB color, its chromaticity coordinates are

$$t_1 = \frac{T_1}{T_1 + T_2 + T_3},$$

$$t_2 = \frac{T_2}{T_1 + T_2 + T_3},$$

$$t_3 = \frac{T_3}{T_1 + T_2 + T_3}.$$

Adding the three equations, we have

$$t_1 + t_2 + t_3 = 1,$$

and thus we can work in the two-dimensional t_1, t_2 space, finding t_3 only when its value is needed. The information that is missing from chromaticity coordinates, which was contained in the original tristimulus values, is the sum $T_1 + T_2 + T_3$, a value related to the intensity of the color. When working with color systems, this intensity is often not important to issues related to producing colors or matching colors across different systems.

Because each color fraction must be nonnegative, the chromaticity values are limited by

$$1 \geq t_i \geq 0.$$

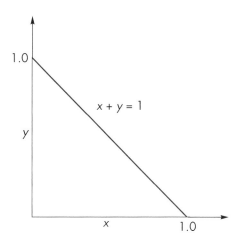

FIGURE 6.64   Triangle of producible colors in chromaticity coordinates.

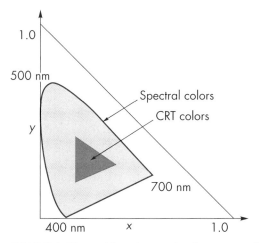

FIGURE 6.65   Visible colors and color gamut of a display.

All producible colors must lie inside the triangle in Figure 6.64. Figure 6.65 shows this triangle for the XYZ system and a curve of the representation for each visible spectral line. For the XYZ system, this curve must lie inside the triangle. Figure 6.65 also shows the range of colors (in x, y chromaticity coordinates) that are producible on a typical color printer or CRT. If we compare the two figures, we see that the colors inside the curve of pure spectral lines but outside the gamut of the physical display cannot be displayed on the physical device.

One defect of our development of color is that RGB color is based on how color is produced and measured rather than on how we perceive a color. When we see a given

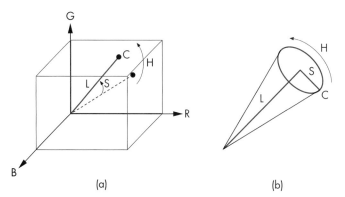

FIGURE 6.66   Hue–lightness–saturation color. (a) Using the RGB color cube. (b) Using a single cone.

color, we describe it not by three primaries but based on other properties, such as the name we give the color and how bright a shade we see. The hue–saturation–lightness (HLS) system is used by artists and some display manufacturers. The **hue** is the name we give to a color: red, yellow, gold. The **lightness** is how bright the color appears. **Saturation** is the color attribute that distinguishes a pure shade of a color from a shade of the same hue that has been mixed with white, forming a pastel shade. We can relate these attributes to a typical RGB color, as shown in Figure 6.66(a). Given a color in the color cube, the lightness is a measure of how far the point is from the origin (black). If we note that all the colors on the principal diagonal of the cube, going from black to white, are shades of gray and are totally unsaturated, then the saturation is a measure of how far the given color is from this diagonal. Finally, the hue is a measure of where the color vector is pointing. HLS colors are usually described in terms of a color cone, as shown in Figure 6.66(b), or a double cone that also converges at the top. From our perspective, we can look at the HLS system as providing a representation of an RGB color in polar coordinates.

6.13.2 The Color Matrix

RGB colors and RGBA colors can be manipulated as any other vector type. In particular, we can alter their components by multiplying by a matrix we call the **color matrix**. For example, if we use an RGBA color representation, the matrix multiplication converts a color, $rgba$, to a new color, $r'g'b'a'$, by the matrix multiplication

$$\begin{bmatrix} r' \\ g' \\ b' \\ a' \end{bmatrix} = \mathbf{C} \begin{bmatrix} r \\ g \\ b \\ a \end{bmatrix}.$$

Thus, if we are dealing with opaque surfaces for which $A = 1$, the matrix

$$\mathbf{C} = \begin{bmatrix} -1 & 0 & 0 & 1 \\ 0 & -1 & 0 & 1 \\ 0 & 0 & -1 & 1 \\ 0 & 0 & 0 & 1 \end{bmatrix}$$

converts the additive representation of a color to its subtractive representation.

6.13.3 Gamma Correction

In Chapter 2, we defined brightness as perceived intensity and observed that the human visual system perceives intensity in a logarithmic manner, as depicted in Figure 6.67. One consequence of this property is that if we want the brightness steps to appear to be uniformly spaced, the intensities that we assign to pixels should increase exponentially. These steps can be calculated from the measured minimum and maximum intensities that a display can generate.

In addition, the intensity I of a CRT is related to the voltage V applied by

$$I \propto V^{\gamma}$$

or

$$\log I = c_0 + \gamma \log V,$$

where the constants γ and c_0 are properties of the particular CRT. One implication of these two results is that two monitors may generate different brightnesses for the same values in the frame buffer. One way to correct for this problem is to have a lookup table in the display whose values can be adjusted for the particular characteristics of the monitor—the **gamma correction**.

There is an additional problem with CRTs. It is not possible to have a CRT whose display is totally black when no signal is applied. The minimum displayed intensity is called the **dark field** value and can be problematic, especially when CRT technology is used to project images. The contrast ratio of a display is the ratio of the maximum to minimum brightness. Newer display technologies have contrast ratios in the thousands.

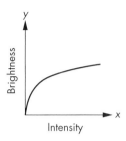

FIGURE 6.67 Logarithmic brightness.

6.13.4 Dithering and Halftoning

We have specified a color buffer by its spatial resolution (the number of pixels) and by its precision (the number of colors it can display). If we view these separate numbers as fixed, we say that a high-resolution black-and-white laser printer can display only 1-bit pixels. This argument also seems to imply that any black-and-white medium, such as a book, cannot display images with multiple shades. We know from experience that that is not the case; the trick is to trade spatial resolution for grayscale or color precision. **Halftoning** techniques in the printing industry use photographic means to simulate gray levels by creating patterns of black dots of varying size. The

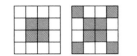

FIGURE 6.68 Digital halftone patterns.

human visual system tends to merge small dots together and sees not the dots, but rather an intensity proportional to the ratio of white to black in a small area.

Digital halftones differ because the size and location of displayed pixels are fixed. Consider a 4×4 group of 1-bit pixels, as shown in Figure 6.68. If we look at this pattern from far away, we see not the individual pixels but rather a gray level based on the number of black pixels. For our 4×4 example, although there are 2^{16} different patterns of black and white pixels, there are only 17 possible shades, corresponding to 0 to 16 black pixels in the array. There are many algorithms for generating halftone, or **dither**, patterns. The simplest picks 17 patterns (for our example) and uses them to create a display with 17 rather than two gray levels, although at the cost of decreasing the spatial resolution by a factor of 4.

The simple algorithm—always using the same array to simulate a shade—can generate beat, or moiré, patterns when displaying anything regular. Such patterns arise whenever we image two regular phenomena, because we see the sum and differences of their frequencies. Such effects are closely related to the aliasing problems we shall discuss in Chapter 7.

Many dithering techniques are based on simply randomizing the least significant bit of the luminance or of each color component. More sophisticated dither algorithms use randomization to create patterns with the correct average properties but avoid the repetition that can lead to moiré effects (see Exercise 6.26).

Halftoning (or dithering) is often used with color, especially with hard-copy displays, such as ink-jet printers, that can produce only fully on or off colors. Each primary can be dithered to produce more visual colors. OpenGL supports such displays and allows the user to enable dithering (`glEnable(GL_DITHER)`). Color dithering allows color monitors to produce smooth color displays, and normally dithering is enabled. Because dithering is so effective, displays can work well with a limited number of bits per color, allowing frame buffers to have a limited amount of memory. In many applications, we need to use the OpenGL query function `glGetIntegerv` to find out how many bits are being used for each color since this information is important when we use some of the techniques from Chapter 7 that read pixels from the frame buffer. If dithering is enabled and we read pixels out of the frame buffer, pixels that were written with the same RGB values may return different values when read. If these small differences are important, dithering should be disabled before reading from the frame buffer.

SUMMARY AND NOTES

We have presented an overview of the implementation process, including a sampling of the most important algorithms. Regardless of what the particulars of an implementation are—whether the tasks are done primarily in hardware or in software, whether we are working with a special-purpose graphics workstation or with a simple graphics terminal, and what the API is—the same tasks must be done. These tasks include implementation of geometric transformations, clipping, and rasterization. The relationship among hardware, software, and APIs is an interesting one.

The Geometry Engine that was the basis of many Silicon Graphics workstations is a VLSI chip that performed geometric transformations and clipping through a hardware pipeline. GL, the predecessor of OpenGL, was developed as an API for users of these workstations. Much of the OpenGL literature also follows the pipeline approach. We should keep in mind, however, that OpenGL is an API: It does not say anything about the underlying implementation. In principle, an image defined by an OpenGL program could be obtained from a ray tracer. We should carry away two lessons from our emphasis on pipeline architectures. First, this architecture provides an aid to the applications programmer in understanding the process of creating images. Second, at present, the pipeline view can lead to efficient hardware and software implementations.

The example of the z-buffer algorithm is illustrative of the relationship between hardware and software. Fifteen years ago, many hidden-surface–removal algorithms were used, of which the z-buffer algorithm was only one. The availability of fast, dense, inexpensive memory has made the z-buffer algorithm the dominant method for hidden-surface removal.

A related example is that of workstation architectures, where special-purpose graphics chips have made remarkable advances in just the past few years. Not only has graphics performance increased at a rate that exceeds Moore's law, but many new features have become available in the graphics processors. The whole approach we have taken in this book is based on these architectures.

So what does the future hold? Certainly, graphics systems will get faster and less expensive. More than any other factor, advances in hardware probably will dictate what future graphics systems will look like. At the present, hardware development is being driven by the video game industry. For less than $100, we can purchase a graphics card that exceeds the performance of graphics workstations that a few years ago would have cost more than $100,000. The features and performance of these cards are optimized for the needs of the computer game industry. Thus, we do not see uniform speedups in the various graphics functions that we have presented. In addition, new hardware features are appearing far faster than they can be incorporated into standard APIs. However, the speed at which these processors operate has challenged both the graphics and scientific communities to discover new algorithms to solve problems that until now had always been solved using conventional architectures.

On the software side, the low cost and speed of recent hardware has enabled software developers to produce rendering software that allows users to balance rendering time and quality of rendering. Hence, a user can add some ray-traced objects to a scene, the number depending on how long she is willing to wait for the rendering. The future of standard APIs is much less clear. On one hand, users in the scientific community prefer stable APIs so that application codes will have a long lifetime. On the other hand, users want to exploit new hardware features that are not supported on all systems. OpenGL has tried to take a middle road. Until OpenGL 3.1, all releases were backward compatible, so applications developed on earlier versions were guaranteed to run on new releases. OpenGL 3.1 and later versions deprecated many core features of earlier versions, including immediate mode rendering and most of the default behavior of the fixed-function pipeline. This major change in philosophy has allowed OpenGL to rapidly incorporate new hardware features. For those who need to run older code, almost all implementations support a compatibility extension with all the deprecated functions.

Numerous advanced architectures under exploration use massive parallelism. How parallelism can be exploited most effectively for computer graphics is still an open issue. Our two approaches to rendering—object-oriented and image-oriented—lead to two entirely different ways to develop a parallel renderer, which we shall explore further in Chapter 11.

We have barely scratched the surface of implementation. The literature is rich with algorithms for every aspect of the implementation process. The references should help you to explore this topic further.

SUGGESTED READINGS

The books by Rogers [Rog85] and by Foley and colleagues [Fol90] contain many more algorithms than we can present here. Also see the series *Graphic Gems* [Gra90, Gra91, Gra92, Gra94, Gra95] and *GPU Gems* [Ngu07, Pha05]. Books such as Möller and Haines [Mol02] and Eberly [Ebe01] cover the influence of recent advances in hardware.

The Cohen-Sutherland [Sut63] clipping algorithm goes back to the early years of computer graphics, as does Bresenham's algorithm [Bre63, Bre87], which was originally proposed for pen plotters. See [Lia84] and [Sut74a] for the Liang-Barsky and Sutherland-Hogman clippers.

Algorithms for triangulation can be found in references on Computational Geometry. See, for example, de Berg[deB08], which also discusses Delaunay triangulation, which we discuss in Chapter 10.

The z-buffer algorithm was developed by Catmull [Cat75]. See Sutherland [Sut74b] for a discussion of various approaches to hidden-surface removal.

Our decision to avoid details of the hardware does not imply that the hardware is either simple or uninteresting. The rate at which a modern graphics processor can display graphical entities requires sophisticated and clever hardware designs [Cla82, Ake88, Ake93]. The discussion by Molnar and Fuchs in [Fol90] shows a variety of approaches.

Pratt [Pra78] provides matrices to convert among various color systems. Halftone and dithering are discussed by Jarvis [Jar76] and by Knuth [Knu87].

EXERCISES

6.1   Explain the following occurrences, with respect to bounding boxes and detailed clipping:
   a. The polygon above the window
   b. The polygon inside the window
   c. The bounding box straddling the window.

6.2   State the different processes that are required in geometry processing. What are the steps involved?

6.3   Prove that clipping a convex object against another convex object results in at most one convex object.

6.4   Why is the coordinate system used in the clipping process called normalized device coordinates? What is the role of a clipper in line segment clipping?

6.5   What is the major difference between two- and three-dimensional clippers? Give a scan-conversion algorithm for line segments.

6.6   Derive the viewport transformation. Express it in terms of the three-dimensional scaling and translation matrices used to represent affine transformations in two dimensions.

6.7   Pre–raster-graphics systems were able to display only lines. Programmers produced three-dimensional images using hidden-line–removal techniques. Many current APIs allow us to produce wireframe images, composed of only lines, in which the hidden lines that define nonvisible surfaces have been removed. How does this problem differ from that of the polygon hidden-surface removal that we have considered? Derive a hidden-line–removal algorithm for objects that consist of the edges of planar polygons.

6.8   Often we display functions of the form $y = f(x, z)$ by displaying a rectangular mesh generated by the set of values $\{f(x_i, z_j)\}$ evaluated at regular intervals in x and z. Hidden-surface removal should be applied because parts of the surface can be obscured from view by other parts. Derive two algorithms, one using hidden-surface removal and the other using hidden-line removal, to display such a mesh.

6.9   Although we argued that the complexity of the image-space approach to hidden-surface removal is proportional to the number of polygons, performance studies have shown almost constant performance. Explain this result.

6.10 Consider a scene composed of only solid, three-dimensional polyhedra. Can you devise an object-space, hidden-surface–removal algorithm for this case? How much does it help if you know that all the polyhedra are convex?

6.11 We can look at object-space approaches to hidden-surface removal as analogous to sorting algorithms. However, we argued that the former's complexity is $O(k^2)$. We know that only the worst-performing sorting algorithms have such poor performance, and most are $O(k \log k)$. Does it follow that object-space, hidden-surface–removal algorithms have similar complexity? Explain your answer.

6.12 Devise a method for testing whether one planar polygon is fully on one side of another planar polygon.

6.13 What are the differences between our image-space approaches to hidden-surface removal and to ray tracing? Can we use ray tracing as an alternate technique to hidden-surface removal? What are the advantages and disadvantages of such an approach?

6.14 Write a program to generate the locations of pixels along a rasterized line segment using Bresenham's algorithm. Check that your program works for all slopes and all possible locations of the endpoints. What is the initial value of the decision variable?

6.15 Bresenham's algorithm can be extended to circles. Convince yourself of this statement by considering a circle centered at the origin. Which parts of the circle must be generated by an algorithm and which parts can be found by symmetry? Can you find a part of the circle such that if we know a point generated by a scan-conversion algorithm, we can reduce the number of candidates for the next pixel?

6.16 What is the crossing or odd-even test? Explain it with respect to a point p inside a polygon.

6.17 Suppose that you try to extend flood fill to arbitrary closed curves by scan-converting the curve and then applying the same fill algorithm that we used for polygons. What problems can arise if you use this approach?

6.18 Consider the edge of a polygon between vertices at (x_1, y_1) and (x_2, y_2). Derive an efficient algorithm for computing the intersection of all scan lines with this edge. Assume that you are working in window coordinates.

6.19 Vertical and horizontal edges are potentially problematic for polygon-fill algorithms. How would you handle these cases for the algorithms that we have presented?

6.20 In two-dimensional graphics, if two polygons overlap, we can ensure that they are rendered in the same order by all implementations by associating a priority attribute with each polygon. Polygons are rendered in reverse-priority order; that is, the highest-priority polygon is rendered last. How should we modify our polygon-fill algorithms to take priority into account?

6.21 Write the pseudocode for the flood-fill algorithm. Assume that there is a function `read_pixel` that returns the color of the pixel.

6.22 Although an ideal pixel is a square of 1 unit per side, most CRT systems generate round pixels that can be approximated as circles of uniform intensity. If a completely full unit square has intensity 1.0 and an empty square has intensity 0.0, how does the intensity of a displayed pixel vary with the radius of the circle?

6.23 Consider a bilevel display with round pixels. Do you think it is wiser to use small circles or large circles for foreground-colored pixels? Explain your answer.

6.24 What are the goals of the geometry processor?

6.25 There are various issues with how lines are drawn on the screen, how polygons are filled, and what happens to primitives that lie outside the viewing volumes defined in a program. How are these problems to be approached in OpenGL?

6.26 Generate a halftone algorithm based on the following idea. Suppose that gray levels vary from 0.0 to 1.0 and that we have a random-number generator that produces random numbers that are uniformly distributed over this interval. If we pick a gray level g, $g/100$ percent of the random numbers generated will be less than g.

6.27 Express the chromaticity coordinates in terms of tristimulus values.

6.28 Show that the area of a two-dimensional polygon, specified by the vertices $\{x_1, y_i\}$, is given by $\frac{1}{2} \sum_i (y_{i+1} + y_i)(x_{i+1} - x_i)$. What is the significance of a negative area? *Hint:* Consider the areas of the trapezoids formed by two successive vertices and corresponding values on the x-axis.

6.29 What are the advantages and disadvantages of the Cohen-Sutherland algorithm?

6.30 Axis-aligned bounding boxes work both in two and three dimensions. In three dimensions, why are axis-aligned bounding boxes used in the application to perform clipping?

CHAPTER 7

DISCRETE TECHNIQUES

Thus far, we have worked directly with geometric objects, such as lines, polygons, and polyhedra. Although we understood that, if visible, these entities would eventually be rasterized into pixels in the frame buffer, we did not have to concern ourselves with working with pixels directly. Over the last 25 years, the major advances in hardware and software have evolved to allow the application program to access the frame buffer both directly and indirectly. Many of the most exciting methods that have evolved over the past two decades rely on interactions between the application program and various buffers. Texture mapping, antialiasing, compositing, and alpha blending are only a few of the techniques that become possible when the API allows us to work with discrete buffers. At the same time, GPUs have evolved to include a large amount of memory to support discrete techniques. This chapter introduces these techniques, focusing on those that are supported by OpenGL and by similar APIs.

We start by looking at the frame buffer in more detail and the basis for working with arrays of pixels. We then consider mapping methods. These techniques are applied during the rendering process, and they enable us to give the illusion of a surface of great complexity, although the surface might be a single polygon. All these techniques use arrays of pixels to define how the shading process that we studied in Chapter 5 is augmented to create these illusions. We shall then look at some of the other buffers that are supported by the OpenGL API and how these buffers can be used for new applications. In particular, we examine techniques for combining or compositing images. Here we use the fourth "color" in RGBA mode, and we shall see that we can use this channel to blend images and to create effects such as transparency. We conclude with a discussion of the aliasing problems that arise whenever we work with discrete elements.

7.1 BUFFERS

We have already used two types of standard buffers: color buffers and depth buffers. There may be others supported by the hardware and software for special purposes. What all buffers have in common is that they are inherently discrete: They have

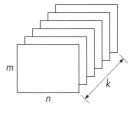

FIGURE 7.1   Buffer.

limited resolution, both spatially and in depth. We can define a (two-dimensional)[1] **buffer** as a block of memory with $n \times m$ k-bit elements (Figure 7.1).

We have used the term *frame buffer* to mean the set of buffers that the graphics system uses for rendering, including the front and back color buffers, the depth buffer, and other buffers the hardware may provide. These buffers generally reside on the graphics card. Later in this chapter, we will extend the notion of a frame buffer to include other buffers that a system might provide for off-screen rendering operations. For now, we will work with just the standard frame buffer.

At a given spatial location in the frame buffer, the k bits can include 32-bit RGBA colors, integers representing depths, or bits that can be used for masks. Groups of bits can store 1-byte representations of color components, integers for depths, or floating-point numbers for colors or depths. Figure 7.2 shows the OpenGL frame buffer and some of its constituent parts. If we consider the entire frame buffer, the values of n and m match the spatial resolution of the display. The depth of the frame buffer—the value of k—can exceed a few hundred bits. Even for the simple cases that we have seen so far, we have 64 bits for the front and back color buffers and 32 bits for the depth buffer. The numerical accuracy or **precision** of a given buffer is determined by its depth. Thus, if a frame buffer has 32 bits each for its front and back color buffers, each RGBA color component is stored with a precision of 8 bits.

When we work with the frame buffer, we usually work with one constituent buffer at a time. Thus, we shall use the term *buffer* in what follows to mean a particular buffer within the frame buffer. Each of these buffers is $n \times m$ and is k bits deep. However, k can be different for each buffer. For a color buffer, its k is determined by how many colors the system can display, usually 24 for RGB displays and 32 for RGBA displays. For the depth buffer, its k is determined by the depth precision that the system can support, often 32 bits to match the size of a floating-point number or an integer. We use the term **bitplane** to refer to any of the k $n \times m$ planes in a buffer, and **pixel** to refer to all k of the bits at a particular spatial location. With this definition, a pixel can be a byte, an integer, or even a floating-point number, depending on which buffer is used and how data are stored in the buffer.

The applications programmer generally will not know how information is stored in the frame buffer, because the frame buffer is inside the implementation which the programmer sees as a black box. Thus, the application program sends (writes or draws) information into the frame buffer or obtains (reads) information from the frame buffer through OpenGL functions. When the application program reads or writes pixels, not only are data transferred between ordinary processor memory and graphics memory on the graphics card, but usually these data must be reformatted to be compatible with the frame buffer. Consequently, what are ordinarily thought of as digital images, for example JPEG, PNG, or TIFF images, exist only on the application side of the process. Not only must the application programmer worry how to decode particular images so they can be sent to the frame buffer through OpenGL functions, but the programmer also must be aware of the time that is spent in the movement

---

1. We can also have one-, three-, and four-dimensional buffers.

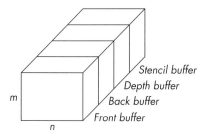

FIGURE 7.2   OpenGL frame buffer.

of digital data between processor memory and the frame buffer. If the application programmer also knows the internal format of how data are stored in any of the buffers, she can often write application programs that execute more efficiently.

7.2   DIGITAL IMAGES

Before we look at how the graphics system can work with digital images through pixel and bit operations, let's first examine what we mean by a digital image.[2] Within our programs, we generally work with images that are arrays of pixels. These images can be of a variety of sizes and data types, depending on the type of image with which we are working. For example, if we are working with RGB images, we usually represent each of the color components with 1 byte whose values range from 0 to 255. Thus, we might declare a 512×512 image in our application program as

```
GLubyte myimage[512][512][3];
```

or, if we are using a floating-point representation,

```
typedef vec3 color3;

color3 myimage[512][512];
```

If we are working with monochromatic or **luminance** images, each pixel represents a gray level from black (0) to white (255), so we would use

```
GLubyte myimage[512][512];
```

---

2. Most references often use the term *image* instead of *digital image*. This terminology can be confused with using the term *image* to refer to the result of combining geometric objects and a camera, through the projection process, to obtain what we have called an image. In this chapter, the context should be clear so that there should not be any confusion.

One way to form digital images is through code in the application program. For example, suppose that we want to create a 512×512 image that consists of an 8×8 checkerboard of alternating red and black squares, such as we might use for a game. The following code will work:

```
color3 check[512][512];
color3 red = color3(1.0, 0.0, 0.0);
color3 black = color3(0.0, 0.0, 0.0);

for ( int i = 0; i < 512; i++)
    for( int j = 0; j < 512; j++)
    {
        check[i][j] = ((8*i+j)/64) % 64 ? red : black;
    }
```

Usually, writing code to form images is limited to those that contain regular patterns. More often, we obtain images directly from data. For example, if we have an array of real numbers that we have obtained from an experiment or a simulation, we can scale them to go over the range 0 to 255 and then convert these data to form an unsigned-byte luminance image or over 0.0 to 1.0 for a floating-point image.

There is a third method of obtaining images that has become much more prevalent because of the influence of the Internet. Images are produced by scanning continuous images, such as photographs, or produced directly using digital cameras. Each image is in one of many possible "standard" formats. Some of the most popular formats are GIF, TIFF, PNG, PDF, and JPEG. These formats include direct coding of the values in some order, compressed but lossless coding, and compressed lossy coding. Each format arose from the particular needs of a group of applications. For example, PostScript (PS) images are defined by the PostScript language used to control printers. These images are an exact encoding of the image data—either RGB or luminance—into the 7-bit ASCII character set. Consequently, PostScript images can be understood by a large class of printers and other devices but tend to be very large. Encapsulated PostScript (EPS) are similar but include additional information that is useful for previewing images. GIF images are color index images and thus store a color table and an array of indices for the image.

TIFF images can have two forms. In one form, all the image data are coded directly. A header describes how the data are arranged. In the second form, the data are compressed. Compression is possible because most images contain much redundant data. For example, large areas of most images show very little variation in color or intensity. This redundancy can be removed by algorithms that result in a compressed version of the original image that requires less storage. Compressed TIFF images are formed by the Lempel-Ziv algorithm that provides optimal lossless compression allowing the original image to be compressed and recovered exactly. JPEG images are compressed by an algorithm that allows small errors in the compression and reconstruction of the image. Consequently, JPEG images have very high **compression ratios**, that is, the ratio of the number of bits in the original file to the number of bits in the compressed data file, with little or no visible distortion. Figure 7.3 shows

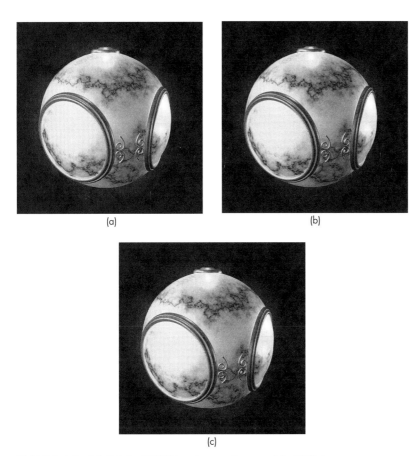

(a)   (b)

(c)

FIGURE 7.3   (a) Original TIFF luminance image. (b) JPEG image compressed by a factor of 18. (c) JPEG image compressed by a factor of 37.

three versions of a single 1200×1200 luminance image: uncompressed, as a TIFF image (Figure 7.3(a)); and as two JPEG images, compressed with different ratios (Figure 7.3(b) and Figure 7.3(c)). The corresponding file sizes are 1,440,198; 80,109; and 38,962 bytes, respectively. Thus, the TIFF image has 1 byte for each pixel plus 198 bytes of header and trailer information. For the JPEG images, the compression ratios are approximately 18 and 37. Even with the higher compression ratio, there is little visible distortion in the image. If we store the original image as a PostScript image, the file will be approximately twice as large as the TIFF image because each byte will be converted into two 7-bit ASCII characters, each pair requiring 2 bytes of storage. If we store the image as a compressed TIFF file, we need only about one-half of the storage. Using a zip file—a popular format used for compressing arbitrary files—would give about the same result. This amount of compression is image-dependent. Although this compression method is lossless, the compression ratio is far worse than is obtainable with lossy JPEG images, which are visibly almost indistinguishable from the original. This closeness accounts for the popularity of the JPEG format for sending images over the Internet. Most digital cameras produce images in JPEG and RAW formats. The RAW format gives the unprocessed RGB data plus a large amount of header information, including the date, the resolution, and the distribution of the colors.

The large number of image formats poses problems for a graphics API. Although some image formats are simple, others are quite complex. The OpenGL API avoids the problem by supporting only blocks of pixels, as compared to images formatted for files. Most of these OpenGL formats correspond to internal formats that differ in the number of bits for each color component and the order of the components in memory. There is limited support for compressed texture images but not for the standard formats such as JPEG. Hence, although OpenGL can work with images that are arrays of standard data types in memory, it is the application programmer's responsibility to read any formatted images into processor memory and write them out as formatted files. We will not deal with these issues here, as any discussion would require us to discuss the details of particular image formats. The necessary information can be found in the Suggested Readings at the end of the chapter.

We can also obtain digital images directly from our graphics system by forming images of three-dimensional scenes using the geometric pipeline and then reading these images back. We will see how to do the required operations later in the chapter.

7.3 WRITING INTO BUFFERS

In a modern graphics system, a user program can both write into and read from the buffers. There are two factors that make these operations different from the usual reading and writing into computer memory. First, we only occasionally want to read or write a single pixel or bit. Rather, we tend to read and write rectangular blocks of pixels (or bits), known as **bit blocks**. For example, we rasterize an entire scan line at a time when we fill a polygon; we write a small block of pixels when we display a raster character; we change the values of all pixels in a buffer when we do a clear operation. Hence, it is important to have both the hardware and software support a set of operations that work on rectangular blocks of pixels, known as **bit-block transfer** (**bitblt**) operations, as efficiently as possible. These operations are also known as **raster operations** (**raster-ops**).

Suppose that we want to take an $n \times m$ block of pixels from one of our buffers, the **source buffer**, and to copy it into either the same buffer or another buffer, the **destination buffer**. This transfer is shown in Figure 7.4. A typical form for a bitblt write operation is

```
write_block(source, n, m, x, y, destination, u, v);
```

where `source` and `destination` are the buffers. The operation writes an n × m source block whose lower-left corner is at (x,y) to the destination buffer starting at

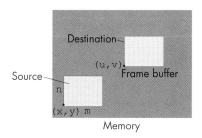

FIGURE 7.4   Writing of a block.

a location (u,v). Although there are numerous details that we must consider, such as what happens if the source block goes over the boundary of the destination block, the essence of bitblt is that a single function call alters the entire destination block. Note that, from the hardware perspective, the type of processing involved has none of the characteristics of the processing of geometric objects. Consequently, the hardware that optimizes bitblt operations has a completely different architecture from the geometric pipeline. Thus, the OpenGL architecture contains both a geometry pipeline and a pixel pipeline, each of which usually is implemented separately.

7.3.1 Writing Modes

A second difference between normal writing into memory and bitblt operations is the variety of ways we can write into the buffers. OpenGL supports 16 different modes (**writing modes**) for putting pixel data into a buffer. To understand the full range of possibilities, let's consider how we might write into a buffer.

The usual concept of a write-to memory is replacement. The execution of a statement in a C program such as

```
y=x;
```

results in the value at the location where y is stored being replaced with the value at the location of x.

There are other possibilities. Suppose that we can work one bit at a time in our buffers. Consider the writing model in Figure 7.5. The bit that we wish to place in memory, perhaps in an altered form, is called the **source bit**, s; the place in memory where we want to put it is called the **destination bit**, d. If, as in Chapter 3, we are allowed to read before writing, as depicted in Figure 7.5, then writing can be described by a replacement function f such that

$$d \leftarrow f(d, s).$$

For a 1-bit source and destination, there are only 16 possible ways to define the function f—namely, the 16 logical operations between two bits. These operations are shown in Figure 7.6, where each of the 16 columns on the right corresponds to one possible f. We can use the binary number represented by each column to

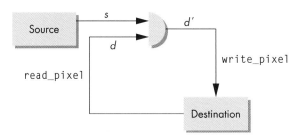

FIGURE 7.5 Writing model.

s	d	0	1	2	3	4	5	6	7	8	9	10	11	12	13	14	15
0	0	0	0	0	0	0	0	0	0	1	1	1	1	1	1	1	1
0	1	0	0	0	0	1	1	1	1	0	0	0	0	1	1	1	1
1	0	0	0	1	1	0	0	1	1	0	0	1	1	0	0	1	1
1	1	0	1	0	1	0	1	0	1	0	1	0	1	0	1	0	1

FIGURE 7.6 Writing modes.

denote a writing mode; equivalently, we can denote writing modes by the logical operation defined by the column. Suppose that we think of the logical value "1" as corresponding to a background color (say, white) and "0" as corresponding to a foreground color (say, black). We can examine the effects of various choices of f. Writing modes 0 and 15 are clear operations that change the value of the destination to either the foreground or the background color. The new value of the destination bit is independent of both the source and the destination values. Modes 3 and 7 are the normal writing modes. Mode 3 is the function

$$d \leftarrow s.$$

It simply replaces the value of the destination bit with the source. Mode 7 is the logical OR operation:

$$d \leftarrow s + d.$$

Figure 7.7 shows that these two writing modes can have different effects on the contents of the frame buffer. In this example, we write a dashed line into a frame buffer that already had a black (foreground colored) rectangle rendered into it. Both modes write the foreground color over the background color, but they differ if we try to write the background color over the foreground color. Which mode should be used depends on what effect the application programmer wishes to create.

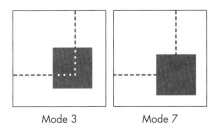

Mode 3   Mode 7

FIGURE 7.7   Writing in modes 3 and 7.

7.3.2 Writing with XOR

Mode 6 is the exclusive-or operation XOR, denoted by $\oplus$; it is the most interesting of the writing modes. Unlike modes 3 and 7, mode 6 cannot be implemented without a read of the destination bit. The power of the XOR write mode comes from the property that, if s and d are binary variables, then

$$d = (d \oplus s) \oplus s.$$

Thus, if we apply XOR twice to a bit, we return that bit to its original state.

The most important applications of this mode involve interaction. Consider what happens when we use menus in an interactive application, such as in a painting program. In response to a mouse click, a menu appears, covering a portion of the screen. After the user indicates an action from the menu, the menu disappears, and the area of the screen that it covered is returned to that area's original state. What has transpired involves the use of off-screen memory, known as **backing store**. Suppose that the menu has been stored off-screen as an array of bits, M, and that the area of the screen where the menu appears is an array of bits, S. Consider the sequence of operations

$$S \leftarrow S \oplus M,$$

$$M \leftarrow S \oplus M,$$

$$S \leftarrow S \oplus M,$$

where we assume that the XOR operation is applied to corresponding bits in S and M. If we substitute the result of the first equation in the second, and the result of the second in the third, we find that, at the end of the three operations, the menu appears on the screen. The original contents of the screen, where the menu is now located, are now off-screen, where the menu was originally. We have swapped the menu with an area of the screen using three bitblt operations. This method of swapping is considerably different from the normal mode of swapping, which uses replacement-mode writing, but requires temporary storage to effect the swap.

There are numerous variants of this technique. One is to move a cursor around the screen without affecting the area under it. Another is filling polygons with a solid color as part of scan conversion. Note that, because many APIs trace their backgrounds to the days before raster displays became the norm, the XOR-write mode was not always available. In OpenGL, the standard mode of writing into the frame buffer is mode 3. Fragments are copied into the frame buffer. We can change the mode by enabling logic operations

```
glLogicOp(mode);
glEnable(GL_COLOR_LOGIC_OP);
```

where `mode` can be any of the 16 modes. The usual ones are the `GL_COPY` (the default) and `GL_XOR`.

7.4 MAPPING METHODS

One of the most powerful uses of discrete data is for surface rendering. The process of modeling an object by a set of geometric primitives and then rendering these primitives has its limitations. Consider, for example, the task of creating a virtual orange by computer. Our first attempt might be to start with a sphere. From our discussion in Chapter 5, we know that we can build an approximation to a sphere out of triangles, and can render these triangles using material properties that match those of a real orange. Unfortunately, such a rendering would be far too regular to look much like an orange. We could instead follow the path that we shall explore in Chapter 10: We could try to model the orange with some sort of curved surface, and then render the surface. This procedure would give us more control over the shape of our virtual orange, but the image that we would produce still would not look right. Although it might have the correct overall properties, such as shape and color, it would lack the fine surface detail of the real orange. If we attempt to add this detail by adding more polygons to our model, even with hardware capable of rendering tens of millions of polygons per second, we can still overwhelm the pipeline.

An alternative is not to attempt to build increasingly more complex models, but rather to build a simple model and to add detail as part of the rendering process. As we saw in Chapter 6, as the implementation renders a surface—be it a polygon or a curved surface—it generates sets of fragments, each of which corresponds to a pixel in the frame buffer. Fragments carry color, depth, and other information that can be used to determine how they contribute to the pixels to which they correspond. As part of the rasterization process, we must assign a shade or color to each fragment. We started in Chapter 5 by using the modified-Phong model to determine vertex colors that could be interpolated across surfaces. However, these colors can be modified during fragment processing after rasterization. The mapping algorithms can be thought of as either modifying the shading algorithm based on a two-dimensional array, the map, or as modifying the shading by using the map to alter surface parameters, such as material properties and normals. There are three major techniques:

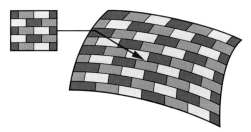

FIGURE 7.8   Texture mapping a pattern to a surface.

- Texture mapping
- Bump mapping
- Environment mapping

Texture mapping uses an image (or texture) to influence the color of a fragment. Textures can be specified using a fixed pattern, such as the regular patterns often used to fill polygons; by a procedural texture-generation method; or through a digitized image. In all cases, we can characterize the resulting image as the mapping of a texture to a surface, as shown in Figure 7.8, as part of the rendering of the surface.

Whereas texture maps give detail by painting patterns onto smooth surfaces, **bump maps** distort the normal vectors during the shading process to make the surface appear to have small variations in shape, such as the bumps on a real orange. **Reflection maps**, or **environment maps**, allow us to create images that have the appearance of reflected materials without our having to trace reflected rays. In this technique, an image of the environment is painted onto the surface as that surface is being rendered.

The three methods have much in common. All three alter the shading of individual fragments as part of fragment processing. All rely on the map being stored as a one-, two-, or three-dimensional digital image. All keep the geometric complexity low while creating the illusion of complex geometry. However, all are also subject to aliasing errors.

There are various examples of two-dimensional mappings in the color plates. Color Plate 7 was created using an OpenGL environment map and shows how a single texture map can create the illusion of a highly reflective surface while avoiding global calculations. Color Plate 15 uses a texture map for the surface of the table; Color Plate 10 uses texture mapping to create a brick pattern. In virtual reality, visualization simulations, and interactive games, real-time performance is required. Hardware support for texture mapping in modern systems allows the detail to be added, without significantly degrading the rendering time.

However, in terms of the standard pipeline, there are significant differences among the three techniques. Standard texture mapping is supported by the basic OpenGL pipeline and makes use of both the geometric and pixel pipelines. Environment maps are a special case of standard texture mapping but can be altered to create a variety of new effects if we can alter fragment processing. Bump mapping requires us to process each fragment independently, something we can do with a fragment shader.

7.5   TEXTURE MAPPING

Textures are patterns. They can range from regular patterns, such as stripes and checkerboards, to the complex patterns that characterize natural materials. In the real world, we can distinguish among objects of similar size and shape by their textures. Thus, if we want to create detailed virtual objects, we can extend our present capabilities by mapping a texture to the objects that we create.

Textures can be one, two, three, or four dimensional. For example, a one-dimensional texture might be used to create a pattern for coloring a curve. A three-dimensional texture might describe a solid block of material from which we could sculpt an object. Because the use of surfaces is so important in computer graphics, mapping two-dimensional textures to surfaces is by far the most common use of texture mapping and will be the only form of texture mapping that we shall consider in detail. However, the processes by which we map these entities is much the same regardless of the dimensionality of the texture, and we lose little by concentrating on two-dimensional texture mapping.

7.5.1 Two-Dimensional Texture Mapping

Although there are multiple approaches to texture mapping, all require a sequence of steps that involve mappings among three or four different coordinate systems. At various stages in the process, we shall be working with screen coordinates, where the final image is produced; object coordinates, where we describe the objects upon which the textures will be mapped; texture coordinates, which we use to locate positions in the texture; and parametric coordinates, which we use to help us define curved surfaces. Methods differ according to the types of surfaces we are using and the type of rendering architecture we have. Our approach will be to start with a fairly general discussion of texture, introducing the various mappings, and then to show how texture mapping is handled by a real-time pipeline architecture, such as that employed by OpenGL.

In most applications, textures start out as two-dimensional images of the sorts we introduced in Section 7.2. Thus, they might be formed by application programs or scanned in from a photograph, but, regardless of their origin, they are eventually brought into processor memory as arrays. We call the elements of these arrays **texels**, or texture elements, rather than pixels to emphasize how they will be used. However, at this point, we prefer to think of this array as a continuous rectangular two-dimensional texture pattern $T(s, t)$. The independent variables s and t are known as **texture coordinates**.[3] With no loss of generality, we can scale our texture coordinates to vary over the interval $[0,1]$.

---

3. In four dimensions, the coordinates are in (s, t, r, q) space.

A **texture map** associates a texel with each point on a geometric object that is itself mapped to screen coordinates for display. If the object is represented in homogeneous or (x, y, z, w) coordinates, then there are functions such that

$$x = x(s, t),$$

$$y = y(s, t),$$

$$z = z(s, t),$$

$$w = w(s, t).$$

One of the difficulties we must confront is that although these functions exist conceptually, finding them may not be possible in practice. In addition, we are worried about the inverse problem: Having been given a point (x, y, z) or (x, y, z, w) on an object, how do we find the corresponding texture coordinates, or equivalently, how do we find the "inverse" functions

$$s = s(x, y, z, w),$$

$$t = t(x, y, z, w)$$

to use to find the texel $T(s, t)$?

If we define the geometric object using parametric (u, v) surfaces, such as we did for the sphere in Section 5.6, there is an additional mapping function that gives object coordinate values, (x, y, z) or (x, y, z, w) in terms of u and v. Although this mapping is known for simple surfaces, such as spheres and triangles, and for the surfaces that we shall discuss in Chapter 10, we also need the mapping from parametric coordinates (u, v) to texture coordinates and sometimes the inverse mapping from texture coordinates to parametric coordinates.

We also have to consider the projection process that take us from object coordinates to screen coordinates, going through eye coordinates, clip coordinates, and window coordinates along the way. We can abstract this process through a function that takes a texture coordinate pair (s, t) and tells us where in the color buffer the corresponding value of $T(s, t)$ will make its contribution to the final image. Thus, there is a mapping of the form

$$x_s = x_s(s, t),$$

$$y_s = y_s(s, t)$$

into coordinates, where (x_s, y_s) is a location in the color buffer.

Depending on the algorithm and the rendering architecture, we might also want the function that takes us from a pixel in the color buffer to the texel that makes a contribution to the color of that pixel.

One way to think about texture mapping is in terms of two concurrent mappings: the first from texture coordinates to object coordinates, and the second from parametric coordinates to object coordinates, as shown in Figure 7.9. A third mapping takes us from object coordinates to screen coordinates.

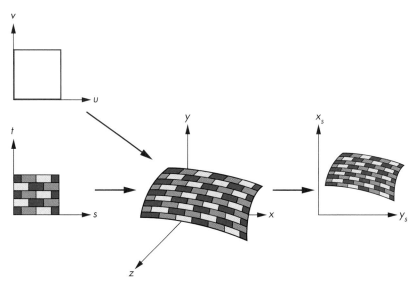

FIGURE 7.9   Texture maps for a parametric surface.

Conceptually, the texture-mapping process is simple. A small area of the texture pattern maps to the area of the geometric surface, corresponding to a pixel in the final image. If we assume that the values of T are RGB color values, we can use these values either to modify the color of the surface that might have been determined by a lighting model or to assign a color to the surface based on only the texture value. This color assignment is carried out as part of the assignment of fragment colors.

On closer examination, we face a number of difficulties. First, we must determine the map from texture coordinates to object coordinates. A two-dimensional texture usually is defined over a rectangular region in texture space. The mapping from this rectangle to an arbitrary region in three-dimensional space may be a complex function or may have undesirable properties. For example, if we wish to map a rectangle to a sphere, we cannot do so without distortion of shapes and distances. Second, owing to the nature of the rendering process, which works on a pixel-by-pixel basis, we are more interested in the inverse map from screen coordinates to texture coordinates. It is when we are determining the shade of a pixel that we must determine what point in the texture image to use—a calculation that requires us to go from screen coordinates to texture coordinates. Third, because each pixel corresponds to a small rectangle on the display, we are interested in mapping not points to points, but rather areas to areas. Here again is a potential aliasing problem that we must treat carefully if we are to avoid artifacts, such as wavy sinusoidal or moiré patterns.

Figure 7.10 shows several of the difficulties. Suppose that we are computing a color for the square pixel centered at screen coordinates (x_s, y_s). The center (x_s, y_s) corresponds to a point (x, y, z) in object space, but, if the object is curved, the projection of the corners of the pixel backward into object space yields a curved

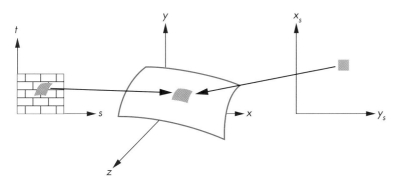

FIGURE 7.10 Preimages of a pixel.

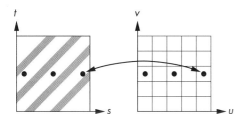

FIGURE 7.11 Aliasing in texture generation.

preimage of the pixel. In terms of the texture image $T(s, t)$, projecting the pixel back yields a preimage in texture space that is the area of the texture that ideally should contribute to the shading of the pixel.

Let's put aside for a moment the problem of how we find the inverse map, and let us look at the determination of colors. One possibility is to use the location that we get by back projection of the pixel center to find a texture value. Although this technique is simple, it is subject to serious aliasing problems, which are especially visible if the texture is periodic. Figure 7.11 illustrates the aliasing problem. Here, we have a repeated texture and a flat surface. The back projection of the center of each pixel happens to fall in between the dark lines, and the texture value is always the lighter color. More generally, not taking into account the finite size of a pixel can lead to moiré patterns in the image. A better strategy—but one more difficult to implement—is to assign a texture value based on averaging of the texture map over the preimage. Note that this method is imperfect, too. For the example in Figure 7.11, we would assign an average shade, but we would still not get the striped pattern of the texture. Ultimately, we still have aliasing defects due to the limited resolution of both the frame buffer and the texture map. These problems are most visible when there are regular high-frequency components in the texture.

Now we can turn to the mapping problem. In computer graphics, most curved surfaces are represented parametrically. A point **p** on the surface is a function of two

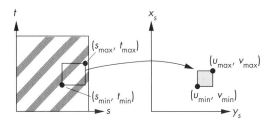

FIGURE 7.12   Linear texture mapping.

parameters u and v. For each pair of values, we generate the point

$$\mathbf{p}(u, v) = \begin{bmatrix} x(u, v) \\ y(u, v) \\ z(u, v) \end{bmatrix}.$$

In Chapter 10, we study in detail the derivation of such surfaces. Given a parametric surface, we can often map a point in the texture map $T(s, t)$ to a point on the surface $\mathbf{p}(u, v)$ by a linear map of the form

$$u = as + bt + c,$$
$$v = ds + et + f.$$

As long as $ae \neq bd$, this mapping is invertible. Linear mapping makes it easy to map a texture to a group of parametric surface patches. For example, if, as shown in Figure 7.12, the patch determined by the corners (s_{min}, t_{min}) and (s_{max}, t_{max}) corresponds to the surface patch with corners (u_{min}, v_{min}) and (u_{max}, v_{max}), then the mapping is

$$u = u_{min} + \frac{s - s_{min}}{s_{max} - s_{min}}(u_{max} - u_{min}),$$

$$v = v_{min} + \frac{t - t_{min}}{t_{max} - t_{min}}(v_{max} - v_{min}).$$

This mapping is easy to apply, but it does not take into account the curvature of the surface. Equal-sized texture patches must be stretched to fit over the surface patch.

Another approach to the mapping problem is to use a two-part mapping. The first step maps the texture to a simple three-dimensional intermediate surface, such as a sphere, cylinder, or cube. In the second step, the intermediate surface containing the mapped texture is mapped to the surface being rendered. This two-step mapping process can be applied to surfaces defined in either geometric or parametric coordinates. The following example is essentially the same in either system.

Suppose that our texture coordinates vary over the unit square, and that we use the surface of a cylinder of height h and radius r as our intermediate object, as shown

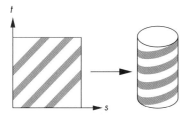

FIGURE 7.13 Texture mapping with a cylinder.

in Figure 7.13. Points on the cylinder are given by the parametric equations

$$x = r \cos(2\pi u),$$

$$y = r \sin(2\pi u),$$

$$z = v/h,$$

as u and v vary over $(0,1)$. Hence, we can use the mapping

$$s = u,$$

$$t = v.$$

By using only the curved part of the cylinder, and not the top and bottom, we were able to map the texture without distorting its shape. However, if we map to a closed object, such as a sphere, we must introduce shape distortion. This problem is similar to the problem of creating a two-dimensional image of the earth for a map. If you look at the various maps of the earth in an atlas, all distort shapes and distances. Both texture-mapping and map-design techniques must choose among a variety of representations, based on where we wish to place the distortion. For example, the familiar Mercator projection puts the most distortion at the poles. If we use a sphere of radius r as the intermediate surface, a possible mapping is

$$x = r \cos(2\pi u),$$

$$y = r \sin(2\pi u) \cos(2\pi v),$$

$$z = r \sin(2\pi u) \sin(2\pi v).$$

We can also use a rectangular box, as shown in Figure 7.14. Here, we map the texture to a box that can be unraveled, like a cardboard packing box. This mapping often is used with environment maps (Section 7.8).

The second step is to map the texture values on the intermediate object to the desired surface. Figure 7.15 shows three possible strategies. In Figure 7.15(a), we take the texture value at a point on the intermediate object, go from this point in the direction of the normal until we intersect the object, and then place the texture value at the point of intersection. We could also reverse this method, starting at a point on the surface of the object and going in the direction of the normal at this point until

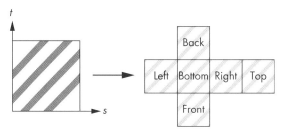

FIGURE 7.14   Texture mapping with a box.

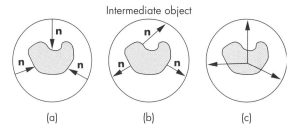

FIGURE 7.15   Second mapping. (a) Using the normal from the intermediate surface. (b) Using the normal from the object surface. (c) Using the center of the object.

we intersect the intermediate object, where we obtain the texture value, as shown in Figure 7.15(b). A third option, if we know the center of the object, is to draw a line from the center through a point on the object, and to calculate the intersection of this line with the intermediate surface, as shown in Figure 7.15(c). The texture at the point of intersection with the intermediate object is assigned to the corresponding point on the desired object.

7.6   TEXTURE MAPPING IN OPENGL

OpenGL supports a variety of texture-mapping options. The first version of OpenGL contained the functionality to map one- and two-dimensional textures to one- through four-dimensional graphical objects. Mapping of three-dimensional textures now is part of OpenGL and is supported by most hardware. We will focus on mapping two-dimensional textures to surfaces.

OpenGL's texture maps rely on its pipeline architecture. We have seen that there are actually two parallel pipelines: the geometric pipeline and the pixel pipeline. For texture mapping, the pixel pipeline merges with fragment processing after rasterization, as shown in Figure 7.16. This architecture determines the type of texture mapping that is supported. In particular, texture mapping is done as part of fragment processing. Each fragment that is generated is then tested for visibility with the z-buffer. We can think of texture mapping as a part of the shading process, but a part

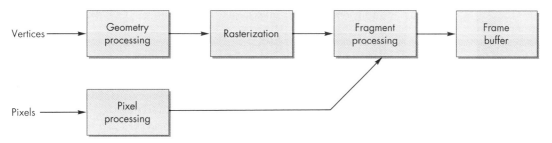

FIGURE 7.16 Pixel and geometry pipelines.

that is done on a fragment-by-fragment basis. Texture coordinates are handled much like normals and colors. They are associated with vertices through the OpenGL state, and the required texture values can then be obtained by interpolating the texture coordinates at the vertices across polygons.

7.6.1 Two-Dimensional Texture Mapping

Texture mapping requires interaction among the application program, the vertex shader, and the fragment shader. There are three basic steps. First, we must form a texture image and place it in texture memory on the GPU. Second, we must assign texture coordinates to each fragment. Finally, we must apply the texture to each fragment. Each of these steps can be accomplished in multiple ways, and there are many parameters that we can use to control the process. As texture mapping has become more important and GPUs have evolved to support more texture-mapping options, APIs have added more and more texture-mapping functions.

7.6.2 Texture Objects

In early versions of OpenGL, there was only a single texture, the *current texture*, that existed at any time. Each time that a different texture was needed—for example, if we wanted to apply different textures to different surfaces in the same scene—we had to set up a new texture map. This process was very inefficient. Each time another texture image was needed, it had to be loaded into texture memory, replacing the texels that were already there.

In a manner analogous to having multiple program objects, **texture objects** allow the application program to define objects that consist of the texture array and the various texture parameters that control its application to surfaces. As long as there is sufficient memory to retain them, these objects reside in texture memory.

We create a two-dimensional texture object by first getting some unused identifiers by calling `glGenTextures`. For a single texture, we could use the following code:

```
GLuint mytex[1];

glGenTextures(1, mytex);
```

We start forming a new texture object with the function `glBindTexture`, as in the following code:

```
glBindTexture(GL_TEXTURE_2D, mytex[0]);
```

Subsequent texture functions specify the texture image and its parameters, which become part of the texture object. Another call to `glBindTexture` with a new name starts a new texture object. A later execution of `glBindTexture` with an existing name makes that texture object the current texture object. We can delete unused texture objects by `glDeleteTextures`.

7.6.3 The Texture Array

Two-dimensional texture mapping starts with an array of texels, which is a two-dimensional pixel rectangle. Suppose that we have a 512×512 image `my_texels` that was generated by our program, or perhaps was read in from a file into an array:

```
GLubyte my_texels[512][512][3];
```

We specify that this array is to be used as a two-dimensional texture after a call to `glBindTexture` by

```
glTexImage2D(GL_TEXTURE_2D, 0, GL_RGB, 512, 512, 0,
             GL_RGB, GL_UNSIGNED_BYTE, my_texels);
```

More generally, two-dimensional textures are specified through the functions

```
glTexImage2D(GLenum target, GLint level, GLint iformat,
    GLsizei width, GLsizei height, GLint border, GLenum format,
    GLenum type, GLvoid *tarray)
```

The `target` parameter lets us choose a single image, as in our example, set up a cube map (Section 7.9), or test if there is sufficient texture memory for a texture image. The `level` parameter is used for mipmapping (Section 7.6.5), where 0 denotes the highest level (or resolution) or that we are not using mipmapping. The third parameter specifies how we would like the texture stored in texture memory. The fourth and fifth parameters (width and height) specify the size of the image in memory. The `border` parameter is no longer used and should be set to 0. The format and type parameters describe how the pixels in the image in processor memory are stored, so that OpenGL can read those pixels and store them in texture memory.

7.6.4 Texture Coordinates and Samplers

The key element in applying a texture in the fragment shader is the mapping between the location of a fragment and the corresponding location within the texture image where we will get the texture color for that fragment. Because each fragment has a

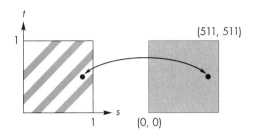

FIGURE 7.17   Mapping to texture coordinates.

location in the frame buffer that is one of its attributes, we need not refer to this position explicitly in the fragment shader. The potential difficulty is identifying the desired location in the texture image. In many applications, we could compute this location from a mathematical model of the objects. In others, we might use some sort of approximation. OpenGL does not have any preferred method and simply requires that we provide the location to the fragment shader or compute it within the shader.

Rather than having to use integer texel locations that depend on the dimensions of the texture image, we use two floating-point texture coordinates, s and t, both of which range over the interval (0.0, 1.0) as we traverse the texture image. For our example of a 512×512 two-dimensional texture image, the value (0.0, 0.0) corresponds to the texel `my_texels[0][0]`, and (1.0, 1.0) corresponds to the texel `my_texels[511][511]`, as shown in Figure 7.17. Any values of s and t in the unit interval correspond to a unique texel.

It is up to the application and the shaders to determine the appropriate texture coordinates for a fragment. The most common method is to treat texture coordinates as a vertex attribute. Thus, we could provide texture coordinates just as we provide vertex colors in the application. We then would pass these coordinates to the vertex shader and let the rasterizer interpolate the vertex texture coordinates to fragment texture coordinates.

Let's consider a simple example of using our checkerboard texture image for each side of the cube example. The example is particularly simple because we have an obvious mapping between each face of the cube and the texture coordinates for each vertex; namely, we assign texture coordinates (0.0, 0.0), (0.0, 1.0), (1.0, 1.0), and (1.0, 0.0) to the four corners of each face.

Recall that we form 36 triangles for the six faces. We add an array to hold the texture coordinates:

```
#define N 36

GLfloat tex_coord[N][2];
```

Here is the code of the quad function:

```
typedef vec2 point2;

void quad(int a, int b, int c, int d)
{
    static int i =0; /* vertex and color index */
    quad_color[i] = colors[a];
    points[i] = vertices[a];
    tex_coord[i] =  point2(0.0, 0.0);
    i++;
    quad_color[i] = colors[a];
    points[i] = vertices[b];
    tex_coord[i] =  point2(0.0, 1.0);
    i++;
    quad_color[i] = colors[a];
    points[i] = vertices[c];
    tex_coord[i] =  point2(1.0, 1.0);
     i++;
    quad_color[i] = colors[a];
    points[i] = vertices[a];
    tex_coord[i] =  point2(0.0, 0.0);
    i++;
    quad_color[i] = colors[a];
    points[i] = vertices[c];
    tex_coord[i] =  point2(1.0, 1.0);
    i++;
    quad_color[i] = colors[a];
    points[i] = vertices[d];
    tex_coord[i] =  point2(1.0, 0.0);
    i++;
}
```

We also need to do our initialization so we can pass the texture coordinates as a vertex attribute with the identifier texcoord in the vertex shader:

```
GLuint loc3;

loc3 = glGetAttribLocation(program, "texcoord");
glEnableVertexAttribArray(loc3);
glVertexAttribPointer(loc3, 2, GL_FLOAT, GL_FALSE, 0, tex_coord);
```

Next, we need to initialize the buffer object to store all of the data. Since we have three separate arrays of data, we will need to load them into an appropriately sized buffer in three operations using glBufferSubData:

```
GLintptr  offset;
GLsizeiptr size =
           sizeof(points) + sizeof(quad_color) + sizeof(tex_coord);
```

```
glGenBuffers(1, buffer);
glBindBuffer(GL_ARRAY_BUFFER, buffers[0]);
glBufferData(GL_ARRAY_BUFFER, size, NULL, GL_STATIC_DRAW);
offset = 0;
glBufferData(GL_ARRAY_BUFFER, offset, sizeof(points), points);
offset += sizeof(points);
glBufferData(GL_ARRAY_BUFFER, offset, sizeof(quad_color), quad_color);
offset += sizeof(quad_color);
glBufferData(GL_ARRAY_BUFFER, offset, sizeof(tex_coord), tex_coord);
```

Turning to the vertex shader, we add the texture coordinate attribute and output the texture coordinates. Here is the vertex shader for the rotating cube with texture coordinates:

```
in vec2 texcoord;
in vec4 vPosition;
in vec4 vColor;

out vec4 color;
out vec2 st;

uniform vec3 theta;

void main()
{
   mat4 rx, ry, rz;
   vec3 c =  cos(theta);
   vec3 s =  sin(theta);
   rz = mat4(c.z, -s.z, 0.0, 0.0,
             s.z, c.z, 0.0, 0.0,
             0.0, 0.0, 1.0, 0.0,
             0.0, 0.0, 0.0, 1.0);
   ry = mat4(c.y, 0.0, s.y, 0.0,
             0.0, 1.0, 0.0, 0.0,
             -s.y, 0.0, c.y, 0.0,
             0.0, 0.0, 0.0, 1.0);
   rx = mat4(1.0, 0.0, 0.0, 0.0,
             0.0, c.x, -s.x, 0.0,
             0.0, s.x, c.x, 0.0,
             0.0, 0.0, 0.0, 1.0);
   gl_Position = rz*ry*rx*vPosition;
   color = vColor;
   st = texcoord;
}
```

The output texture coordinates st are interpolated by the rasterizer and can be inputs to the fragment shader.

Note that the vertex shader is only concerned with the texture coordinates and has nothing to do with the texture object we created earlier. We should not be surprised because the texture itself is not needed until we are ready to assign a color to a fragment, that is in the fragment shader. Note also that many of the complexities of how we can apply the texture, many of which we have yet to discuss, are inside the texture object and thus will allow us to use very simple fragment shaders.

The key to putting everything together is a new type of variable called a **sampler** which most often appears only in a fragment shader. A sampler variable provides access to a texture object, including all its parameters. There are sampler variables for the types of textures supported by OpenGL, including one-dimensional (`sampler1D`), two-dimensional (`sampler2D`), and three-dimensional (`sampler3D`) textures and special types such as cube maps (`samplerCube`).

We link the texture object `mytex` we created in the application with the shader using a uniform variable

```
GLuint tex_loc;

tex_loc = glGetUniformLocation(program, "texMap");

glUniform1i(tex_loc, 0);
```

where `texMap` is the name of the sampler in the fragment shader and the second parameter in `glUniform1i` refers to the default texture unit. We will discuss mutliple texture units in Section 7.6.7.

The fragment shader is almost trivial. The interpolated vertex colors and the texture coordinates are input variables. If we want the texture values to multiply the colors as if we were using the checkerboard texture to simulate glass that alternates between clear and opaque, we could multiply the colors from the application by the values in the texture image as in the following fragment shader:

```
in vec2 st;
in vec4 color;
uniform sampler2D texMap;

void main()
{
  gl_FragColor = color * texture2D(texMap, st);
}
```

In the example shown in Figure 7.18(a), we use the whole texture on a rectangle. If we used only part of the range of s and t—for example, (0.0, 0.5)—we would use only part of `my_texels` for the texture map, and would get an image like that in Figure 7.18(b). OpenGL interpolates s and t across the quadrilateral, then maps these values back to the appropriate texel in `my_texels`. The quadrilateral example is simple because there is an obvious mapping of texture coordinates to vertices. For general polygons, the application programmer must decide how to assign the texture

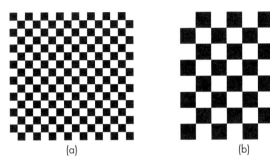

FIGURE 7.18   Mapping of a checkerboard texture to a quadrilateral. (a) Using the entire texel array. (b) Using part of the texel array.

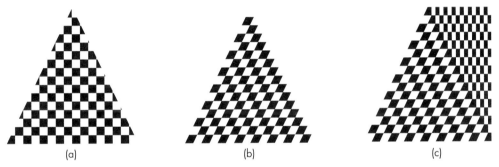

FIGURE 7.19   Mapping of texture to polygons. (a and b) Mapping of a checkerboard texture to a triangle. (c) Mapping of a checkerboard texture to a trapezoid.

coordinates. Figure 7.19 shows a few of the possibilities with the same texture map. Figures 7.19(a) and (b) use the same triangle but different texture coordinates. Note the artifacts of the interpolation and how quadrilaterals are treated as two triangles as they are rendered in Figure 7.19(c).

The basics of OpenGL texture mapping are simple: Specify an array of colors for the texture values, then assign texture coordinates. Unfortunately, there are a few nasty details that we must discuss before we can use texture effectively. Solving the resulting problems involves making trade-offs between quality of the images and efficiency.

One problem is how to interpret a value of s or t outside of the range (0.0, 1.0). Generally, we want the texture either to repeat if we specify values outside this range or to clamp the values to 0.0 or 1.0—that is, we want to use the values at 0.0 and 1.0 for values below and above the interval (0.0, 1.0), respectively. For repeated textures, we set these parameters via

```
glTexParameteri(GL_TEXTURE_2D, GL_TEXTURE_WRAP_S, GL_REPEAT);
```

For t, we use GL_TEXTURE_WRAP_T; for clamping, we use GL_CLAMP_TO_EDGE. By executing these functions after the glBindTexture, the parameters become part of the texture object.

7.6.5 Texture Sampling

Aliasing of textures is a major problem. When we map texture coordinates to the array of texels, we rarely get a point that corresponds to the center of a texel. One option is to use the value of the texel that is closest to the texture coordinate output by the rasterizer. This option is known as **point sampling**, but it is the one most subject to visible aliasing errors. A better strategy, although one that requires more work, is to use a weighted average of a group of texels in the neighborhood of the texel determined by point sampling. This option is known as **linear filtering**. Thus, in Figure 7.20 we see the location within a texel that is given by bilinear interpolation from the texture coordinates at the vertices and the four texels that would be used to obtain a smoother value. If we are using linear filtering, there is a problem at the edges of the texel array as we need additional texel values outside the array.

There is a further complication, however, in deciding how to use the texel values to obtain a texture value. The size of the pixel that we are trying to color on the screen may be smaller or larger than one texel, as shown in Figure 7.21.

In the first case, the texel is larger than one pixel (**magnification**); in the second, it is smaller (**minification**). In both cases, the fastest strategy is to use the value of the nearest point sampling. We can specify this option for both magnification and minification of textures as follows:

```
glTexParameteri(GL_TEXTURE_2D, GL_TEXTURE_MAG_FILTER, GL_NEAREST);
glTexParameteri(GL_TEXTURE_2D, GL_TEXTURE_MIN_FILTER, GL_NEAREST);
```

Alternatively, we can use filtering to obtain a smoother, less aliased image if we specify GL_LINEAR instead of GL_NEAREST.

OpenGL has another way to deal with the minification problem; it is called **mipmapping**. For objects that project to an area of screen space that is small compared with the size of the texel array, we do not need the resolution of the original

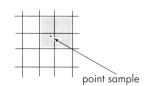

FIGURE 7.20   Texels used with linear filtering.

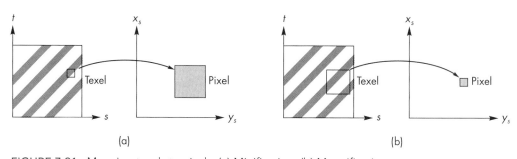

FIGURE 7.21   Mapping texels to pixels. (a) Minification. (b) Magnification.

texel array. OpenGL allows us to create a series of texture arrays at reduced sizes; it will then automatically use the appropriate size. For a 64×64 original array, we can set up 32×32, 16×16, 8×8, 4×4, 2×2, and 1×1 arrays for the current texture object by executing the function call

```
glGenerateMipmap(GL_TEXTURE_2D);
```

We can also set up the maps directly using the `level` parameter in `glTexImage2D`. This parameter is the level in the mipmap hierarchy for the specified texture array. Thus, level 0 refers to the original image, level 1 to the image at half resolution, and so on. However, we can give a pointer to any image in different calls to `glTexImage2D` and thus can have entirely different images used at different levels of the mipmap hierarchy. These mipmaps are invoked automatically if we specify

```
glTexParameteri(GL_TEXTURE_2D,
    GL_TEXTURE_MIN_FILTER,GL_NEAREST_MIPMAP_NEAREST);
```

This option asks OpenGL to use point sampling with the best mipmap. We can also do filtering within the best mipmap (`GL_NEAREST_MIPMAP_LINEAR`), point sampling using linear filtering between mipmaps (`GL_LINEAR_MIPMAP_NEAREST`), or both filters (`GL_LINEAR_MIPMAP_LINEAR`). Figure 7.22 shows the differences in mapping a texture using the nearest texel, linear filtering, and mipmapping, both with using the nearest texel and with linear filtering. The object is a quadrilateral that appears almost as a triangle when shown in perspective. The texture is a series of black and white lines that is applied so that the lines converge at the far side of the quadrilateral. Note that this texture map, because of its regularity, shows dramatic aliasing effects. The use of the nearest texel shows moiré patterns and jaggedness in the lines. Using linear filtering makes the lines smoother, but there are still clear moiré patterns. The texels between the black and white stripes are gray because of the filtering. Mipmapping also replaces many of the blacks and whites of the two-color patterns with grays that are the average of the two color values. For the parts of the object that are farthest from the viewer, the texels are gray and blend with the background. The mipmapped texture using the nearest texel in the proper mipmap still shows the jaggedness that is smoothed out when we use linear filtering with the mipmap. Advances in the speed of graphics processors (GPUs) and the inclusion of large amounts of texture memory in these GPUs often allows applications to use filtering and mipmapping without a performance penalty.

A final issue in using textures in OpenGL is the interaction between texture and shading. For RGB colors, there are multiple options. The texture can modulate the shade that we would have assigned without texture mapping by multiplying the color components of the texture by the color components from the shader. We could let the color of the texture totally determine the color of a fragment—a technique called **decaling**. These and other options are easily implemented in the fragment shader.

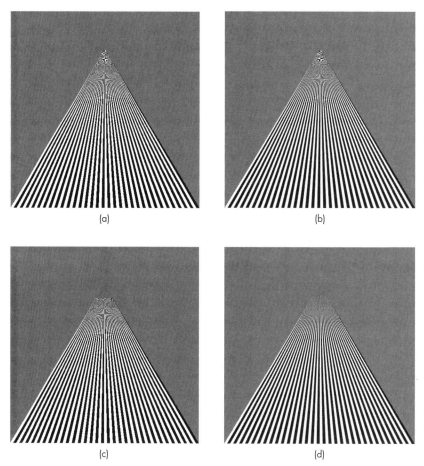

FIGURE 7.22 Texture mapping to a quadrilateral. (a) Point sampling. (b) Linear filtering. (c) Mipmapping point sampling. (d) Mipmapping linear filtering.

7.6.6 Working with Texture Coordinates

Our examples so far have assumed implicitly that we know how to assign texture coordinates. If we work with rectangular polygons of the same size, then it is fairly easy to assign coordinates. We can also use the fact that texture coordinates can be stored as one-, two-, three-, or four-dimensional arrays, just as are vertices. Thus, texture coordinates can be transformed by matrices and manipulated in the same manner as we transformed positions with the model-view and projection matrices. We can use a texture matrix to scale and orient textures and to create effects in which the texture moves with the object, the camera, or the lights.

However, if the set of polygons is an approximation to a curved object, then assigning texture coordinates is far more difficult. Consider the polygonal approxima-

FIGURE 7.23   Polygonal model of Utah teapot.

FIGURE 7.24   Texture-mapped Utah teapot.

tion of the Utah teapot[4] in Figure 7.23. Although the model uses only quadrilaterals, these quadrilaterals differ in size, with smaller quadrilaterals in areas where the object has higher curvature and larger quadrilaterals in flatter areas. Figure 7.24 shows our checkerboard texture mapped to the teapot without making any adjustment for the different sizes of the polygons. As we can see, by assigning the same set of texture coordinates to each polygon, the texture mapping process adjusts to the individual sizes of the polygons by scaling the texture map as needed. Hence, in areas such as the handle, where many small polygons are needed to give a good approximation to the curved surface, the black and white boxes are small compared to those on the body of the teapot. In some applications, these patterns are acceptable. However, if all surfaces of the teapot were made from the same material, we would expect to see the same pattern on all its parts. In principle, we could use the texture matrix to scale texture coordinates to achieve the desired display. However, in practice, it is almost impossible to determine the necessary information from the model to form the matrix.

One solution to this problem is to generate texture coordinates for each vertex in terms of the distance from a plane in either eye coordinates or object coordinates. Mathematically, each texture coordinate is given as a linear combination of the homogeneous coordinate values. Thus, for s and t,

---

4. We shall discuss the Utah teapot in detail in Chapter 10.

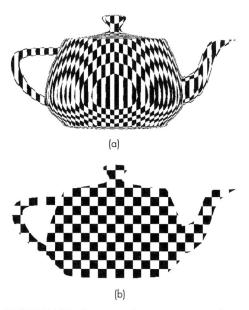

FIGURE 7.25   Teapot using texture coordinate generation. (a) In object coordinates. (b) In eye coordinates.

$$s = a_s x + b_s y + c_s z + d_s w,$$

$$t = a_t x + b_t y + c_t z + d_t w.$$

Figure 7.25(a) shows the teapot with texture coordinate generation in object space. Figure 7.25(b) uses the same equations but with the calculations in eye space. By doing the calculation in object space, the texture is fixed to the object and thus will rotate with the object. Using eye space, the texture pattern changes as we apply transformations to the object and give the illusion of the object moving through a texture field. One of the important applications of this technique is in terrain generation and mapping. We can map surface features as textures directly onto a three-dimensional mesh.

7.6.7 Multitexturing

Thus far, we have looked at applying a single texture to an object. However, there are many surface rendering effects that can best be implemented by more than a single application of a texture. For example, suppose that we want to apply a shadow to an object whose surface shades are themselves determined by a texture map. We could use a texture map for the shadow, but if there were only a single texture application, this method would not work.

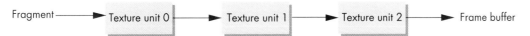

FIGURE 7.26   Sequence of texture units.

If, instead, we have multiple texture units as in Figure 7.26, then we can accomplish this task. Each unit acts as an independent texturing stage starting with the results of the previous stage. This facility is supported in recent versions of OpenGL.

Suppose that we want to use two texture units. We can define two texture objects as part of our initialization. We then activate each in turn and decide how its texture should be applied. The usual code is of the form

```
glActiveTexture(GL_TEXTURE0); /* unit 0 */
glBindTexture(GL_TEXTURE_2D, object0);
          /* how to apply texture 0 */
glActiveTexture(GL_TEXTURE1); /* unit 1 */
glBindTexture(GL_TEXTURE_2D, object1);
          /* how to apply texture 1 */
```

Each texture unit can use different texture coordinates, and the application needs to provide those texture coordinates for each unit.

7.7   TEXTURE GENERATION

One of the most powerful uses of texture mapping is to provide detail without generating numerous geometric objects. High-end graphics systems can do two-dimensional texture mapping in real time; for every frame, the texture is mapped to objects as part of the rendering process at almost the same rate as non-texture-mapped objects are processed. Graphics boards for personal computers now contain a significant amount of texture memory and allow game developers to use texture mapping to create complex animated environments.

If, for example, we want to simulate grass in a scene, we can texture map an image of grass that we might have obtained by, say, scanning a photograph, faster than we can generate two- or three-dimensional objects that look like grass. In mapping applications, rather than generating realistic surface detail for terrain, we can digitize a real map and paint it on a three-dimensional surface model by texture mapping.

We can also look for procedural methods for determining texture patterns. Of particular interest are patterns that we see in nature, such as the textures of sand, grass, or minerals. These textures show both structure (regular patterns) and considerable randomness. Most approaches to generating such textures algorithmically start with a random-number generator and process its output, as shown in Figure 7.27. We shall study procedural noise in detail in Chapter 9.

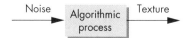

FIGURE 7.27 Texture generation.

The generation of a three-dimensional texture field $T(s, t, r)$ is a direct extension of two-dimensional texture-generation techniques. There are some practical advantages to using three-dimensional textures. Most important is that by associating each (s, t, r) value directly with an (x, y, z) point, we can avoid the mapping problem entirely. The user needs only to define a function $T(s, t, r)$ with the desired properties. Conceptually, this process is similar to sculpting the three-dimensional object from a solid block whose volume is colored by the specified texture. This technique has been used to generate objects that look as if they have been carved from solid rock. The texture-generation process defines a function $T(s, t, r)$ that displays the graininess we associate with materials such as marble and granite.

There are other advantages to using three-dimensional textures. Suppose that we have a two-dimensional texture that we obtained by photographing or modeling some natural material, such as stone. Now suppose that we want to create a cube that looks like it was formed from this stone. If we use two-dimensional texture mapping, we have to map the same pattern to the six sides of the cube. To make the cube look real, we must try to make the texture map appear continuous at the edges of the cube, where two texture maps meet. When we work with natural patterns, it is virtually impossible to ensure that we can do this matching. Note that the problem is even more serious at the vertices of the cube, where three texture maps meet (see Exercise 7.26). Often we can use filtering and texture borders to give visually acceptable results. However, if we use three-dimensional textures, this problem does not arise.

7.8 ENVIRONMENT MAPS

Highly reflective surfaces are characterized by specular reflections that mirror the environment. Consider, for example, a shiny metal ball in the middle of a room. We can see the contents of the room, in a distorted form, on the surface of the ball. Obviously, this effect requires global information, as we cannot shade the ball correctly without knowing about the rest of the scene. A physically based rendering method, such as a ray tracer, can produce this kind of image, although in practice ray-tracing calculations usually are too time-consuming to be practical for real-time applications. We can, however, use variants of texture mapping that can give approximate results that are visually acceptable through **environment maps** or **reflection maps**.

The basic idea is simple. Consider the mirror in Figure 7.28, which we can look at as a polygon whose surface is a highly specular material. From the point of view of a renderer, the position of the viewer and the normal to the polygon are known, so that the angle of reflection is determined as in Chapter 5. If we follow along this

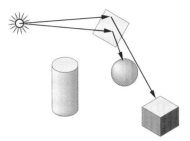

FIGURE 7.28   Scene with a mirror.

angle until we intersect the environment, we obtain the shade that is reflected in the mirror. Of course, this shade is the result of a shading process that involves the light sources and materials in the scene. We can obtain an approximately correct value of this shade as part of a two-step rendering pass, similar in some respects to the two-step texture-mapping process that we outlined in Section 7.5. In the first pass, we render the scene without the mirror polygon, with the camera placed at the center of the mirror pointed in the direction of the normal of the mirror. Thus, we obtain an image of the objects in the environment as "seen" by the mirror. This image is not quite correct (Exercise 7.3), but is usually good enough. We can then use this image to obtain the shades (texture values) to place on the mirror polygon for the second normal rendering with the mirror placed back in the scene.

There are two difficulties with this approach. First, the images that we obtain in the first pass are not quite correct, because they have been formed without one of the objects—the mirror—in the environment. Second, we must confront the mapping issue. Onto what surface should we project the scene in the first pass, and where should we place the camera? Potentially, we want all the information in the scene as we may want to do something like have our mirror move so that we should see different parts of the environment on successive frames, and thus a simple projection will not suffice.

There have been a variety of approaches to this projection problem. The classic approach is to project the environment onto a sphere centered at the center of projection. In Figure 7.29, we see some polygons that are outside the sphere and their projections on the sphere. Note that a viewer located at the center of the sphere cannot tell whether she is seeing the polygons in their original positions or their projections on the sphere. This illusion is similar to what we see in a planetarium. The "stars" that appear to be an infinite distance away are actually the projection of lights onto the hemisphere which encloses the audience.

In the original version of environment mapping, the surface of the sphere was then converted to a rectangle using lines of longitude and latitude for the mapping. Although conceptually simple, there are problems at the poles where the shape distortion becomes infinite. Computationally, this mapping does not preserve areas very well and requires evaluating a large number of trigonometric functions.

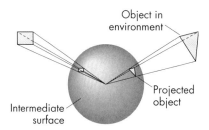

FIGURE 7.29   Mapping of the environment.

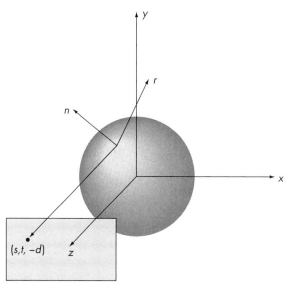

FIGURE 7.30   Reflection map.

OpenGL supports a variation of this method called **sphere mapping**. The application program supplies a circular image that is the orthographic projection of the sphere onto which the environment has been mapped. The advantage of this method is that the mapping from the reflection vector to two-dimensional texture coordinates on this circle is simple and can be implemented in either hardware or software. The difficult part is obtaining the required circular image. It can be approximated by taking a perspective projection with a very wide-angle lens or by remapping some other type of projection, such as the cube projection that we discuss next. We load the texture image in texture memory through `glTexImage2D`.

The equations for generating the texture coordinates can be understood with the help of Figure 7.30. It is probably easiest if we work backward from the viewer to the image. Suppose that the texture map is in the plane $z = -d$, where d is positive and we project backward orthogonally toward a unit sphere centered at the origin. Thus, if the texture coordinates in the plane are (s, t), then the projector intersects the sphere at $(s, t, \sqrt{(1.0 - s^2 - t^2)})$. For the unit sphere centered at the origin, the coordinates of any point on the sphere are also the components of the unit normal at that point. We can then compute the direction of reflection, as in Chapter 5, by

$$\mathbf{r} = 2(\mathbf{n} \cdot \mathbf{v})\mathbf{n} - \mathbf{v},$$

where

$$\mathbf{v} = \begin{bmatrix} s \\ t \\ 0 \end{bmatrix},$$

$$\mathbf{n} = \begin{bmatrix} s \\ t \\ \sqrt{1.0 - s^2 - t^2} \end{bmatrix}.$$

The vector $\mathbf{r}$ points into the environment. Thus, any object that $\mathbf{r}$ intersects has texture coordinates (s, t). However, this argument is backward because we start with an object defined by vertices. Given $\mathbf{r}$, we can solve for s and t and find that if

$$\mathbf{r} = \begin{bmatrix} r_x \\ r_y \\ r_z \end{bmatrix},$$

then

$$s = \frac{r_x}{f} + \frac{1}{2},$$

$$t = \frac{r_y}{f} + \frac{1}{2},$$

where

$$f = 2\sqrt{r_x^2 + r_y^2 + (r_z + 1)^2}.$$

If we put everything into eye coordinates, we compute $\mathbf{r}$ using the unit vector from the origin to the vertex for $\mathbf{v}$ and the vertex normal for $\mathbf{n}$.

This process reveals some issues that show that this method is only approximate. The reflection map is only correct for the vertex at the origin. In principle, each vertex should have its own reflection map. Actually each point on the object should have its own map and not an approximate value computed by interpolation. The errors are most significant the farther the object is from the origin. Nevertheless, reflection

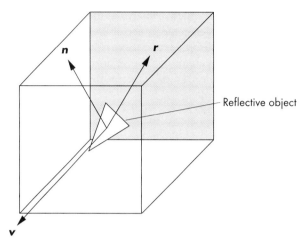

FIGURE 7.31 Reflective cube map.

mapping gives visually acceptable results in most situations, especially when there is animation as in films and games.

If we want to compute an environment map using the graphics system, we prefer to use the standard projections that are supported by the graphics systems. For an environment such as a room, the natural intermediate object is a box. We compute six projections, corresponding to the walls, floor, and ceiling, using six virtual cameras located at the center of the box, each pointing in a different direction. At this point, we can treat the six images as a single environment map and derive the textures from it, as in Figure 7.31. Color Plate 23 shows one frame from Pixar Animation Studio's *Geri's Game*. A reflection map was computed on a box (Color Plate 24) and then mapped to Geri's glasses.

We could also compute the six images in our program and use them to compute the circular image required by OpenGL's spherical maps. Note that all these methods can suffer from geometric distortions and aliasing problems. In addition, unless the application recomputes the environment maps, they are not correct if the viewer moves.

Regardless of how the images are computing, once we have them, we can specify a cube map in OpenGL with six function calls, one for each face of a cube centered at the origin. Thus, if we have a 512×512 RGBA image `imagexp` for the positive-x face, we have the following:

```
glTexImage2D(GL_TEXTURE_CUBE_MAP_POSITIVE_X, 0, GL_RGBA, 512, 512,
             0, GL_RGBA, GL_UNSIGNED_BYTE, imagexp);
```

For reflection maps, the calculation of texture coordinates can be done automatically. However, cube maps are fundamentally different from sphere maps, which are much like standard two-dimensional texture maps with special coordinate calculations. Here, we must use three-dimensional texture coordinates, which are often computed in the shader.

These techniques are examples of **multipass rendering** (or **multirendering**), where, in order to compute a single image, we compute multiple images, each using the rendering pipeline. Multipass methods are becoming increasingly more important as the power of graphics cards has increased to the point that we can render a scene multiple times from different perspectives in less time than is needed for reasonable refresh rates. Equivalently, most of these techniques can be done within the fragment shader.

7.9 REFLECTION MAP EXAMPLE

Let's look at a simple example of a reflection map based on our rotating cube example. In this example, we will use a cube map in which each of the six texture maps is a single texel. Our rotating cube will be totally reflective and placed inside a box, each of whose sides is one of the six colors: red, green, blue, cyan, magenta, and yellow. Here's how we can set up the cube map as part of initialization using texture unit 1:

```
GLuint tex[1];

GLubyte red[3] = {255, 0, 0};
GLubyte green[3] = {0, 255, 0};
GLubyte blue[3] = {0, 0, 255};
GLubyte cyan[3] = {0, 255, 255};
GLubyte magenta[3] = {255, 0, 255};
GLubyte yellow[3] = {255, 255, 0};

glActiveTexture(GL_TEXTURE1);
glGenTextures(1, tex);
glBindTexture(GL_TEXTURE_CUBE_MAP, tex);

glTexImage2D(GL_TEXTURE_CUBE_MAP_POSITIVE_X ,0,GL_RGB,1,1,0,GL_RGB,
             GL_UNSIGNED_BYTE, red);
glTexImage2D(GL_TEXTURE_CUBE_MAP_NEGATIVE_X ,0,GL_RGB,1,1,0,GL_RGB,
             GL_UNSIGNED_BYTE, green);
glTexImage2D(GL_TEXTURE_CUBE_MAP_POSITIVE_Y ,0,GL_RGB,1,1,0,GL_RGB,
             GL_UNSIGNED_BYTE, blue);
glTexImage2D(GL_TEXTURE_CUBE_MAP_NEGATIVE_Y ,0,GL_RGB,1,1,0,GL_RGB,
             GL_UNSIGNED_BYTE, cyan);
glTexImage2D(GL_TEXTURE_CUBE_MAP_POSITIVE_Z ,0,GL_RGB,1,1,0,GL_RGB,
             GL_UNSIGNED_BYTE, magenta);
glTexImage2D(GL_TEXTURE_CUBE_MAP_NEGATIVE_Z ,0,GL_RGB,1,1,0,GL_RGB,
             GL_UNSIGNED_BYTE, yellow);
glTexParameteri(GL_TEXTURE_CUBE_MAP,GL_TEXTURE_MIN_FILTER,GL_NEAREST);
```

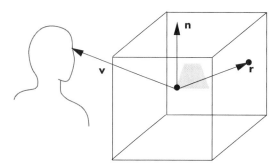

FIGURE 7.32   Reflection cube map.

The texture map will be applied using a sampler in the fragment shader. We set up the required uniform variables as in our other examples:

```
GLuint texMapLocation;

texMapLocation = glGetUniformLocation(program, "texMap");
glUniform1i(texMapLocation, 1);  // corresponding to unit 1
```

Now that we have set up the cube map, we can turn to the determination of the texture coordinates. The required computations for a reflection or environment map are shown in Figure 7.32. We assume that the environment has already been mapped to the cube. The difference between a reflection map and a simple cube texture map is that we use the reflection vector to access the texture for a reflection map rather than the view vector. We can compute the reflection vector at each vertex in our vertex program and then let the fragment program interpolate these values over the primitive.

However, to compute the reflection vector, we need the normal to each side of the rotating cube. We can compute normals in the application and send them to the vertex shader as a vertex attribute through the quad function

```
point4 normals[N];
vec4 normal;

void quad(int a, int b, int c, int d)
{
    static int i =0;

    normal = normalize(cross(vertices[b]-vertices[a],
                       vertices[c]-vertices[b]));

    normals[i] = normal;
    points[i] = vertices[a];
    i++;
```

```
        normals[i] = normal;
        points[i] = vertices[b];
        i++;
        normals[i] = normal;
        points[i] = vertices[c];
        i++;
        normals[i] = normal;
        points[i] = vertices[a];
        i++;
        normals[i] = normal;
        points[i] = vertices[c];
        i++;
        normals[i] = normal;
        points[i] = vertices[d];
        i++;
}
```

and combining the normal data in a vertex array

```
    glBindBuffer(GL_ARRAY_BUFFER, buffer);
    glBufferData(GL_ARRAY_BUFFER, sizeof(points) + sizeof(normals),
                NULL, GL_STATIC_DRAW);
    glBufferSubData(GL_ARRAY_BUFFER, 0, sizeof(points), points);
    glBufferSubData(GL_ARRAY_BUFFER, sizeof(points),
                    sizeof(normals), normals)
```

that is aligned with the shader

```
    loc2 = glGetAttribLocation(program, "Normal");
    glEnableVertexAttribArray(loc2);
```

We will assume that the rotation to the cube is applied in the application and its effect is incorporated in the model-view matrix. We also assume that the camera location is fixed. The normals must then be rotated in the vertex shader before we can use the **reflect** function to compute the direction of reflection. Our vertex shader is

```
in vec4 vPosition;
in vec4 Normal;
out vec3 R;

uniform mat4 ModelView;
uniform mat4 Projection;

void main()
{
    gl_Position = Projection*ModelView*vPosition;
    vec3 eyePos = vPosition.xyz;
```

```
    vec4 NN = ModelView*Normal;
    vec3 N = normalize(NN.xyz);
    R = reflect(eyePos, N);
}
```

It computes the reflection vector in eye coordinates as a varying variable. If we want the color to be totally determined by the texture, the fragment shader is simply as follows:

```
in vec3 R;
uniform samplerCube texMap;

void main()
{
    vec4 texColor = textureCube(texMap, R);
    gl_FragColor = texColor;
}
```

We can create more complex lighting by having the color determined in part by the specular, diffuse, and ambient lighting as we did for the modified-Phong lighting model.

However, we must be careful as to which frame we want to use in our shaders. The difference between this example and previous ones is that the environment map usually is computed in world coordinates. Object positions and normals are specified in object coordinates and are brought into the world frame by modeling transformations in the application. We usually never see the object-coordinate representation of objects because the model-view transformation converts object coordinates directly to eye coordinates. In many applications, we define our objects directly without modeling transformations so that model and object coordinates are the same. However, we want to write our program in a manner that allows for modeling transformations when we do reflection mapping. One way to accomplish this task is to compute the modeling matrix in the application and pass it to the fragment program as a uniform variable. Also note that we need the inverse transpose of the modeling matrix to transform the normal. However, if we pass in the inverse matrix as another uniform variable, we can postmultiply the normal to obtain the desired result. Color Plate 12 shows the use of a reflection map to determine the colors on the teapot. The teapot is set inside a cube, each of whose sides is one of the colors red, green, blue, cyan, magenta, or yellow.

7.10   BUMP MAPPING

Bump mapping is a texture-mapping technique that can give the appearance of great complexity in an image without increasing the geometric complexity. Unlike simple texture mapping, bump mapping will show changes in shading as the light source or object moves, making the object appear to have variations in surface smoothness.

Let's start by returning to our example of creating an image of an orange. If we take a photograph of a real orange, we can apply this image as a texture map to a surface. However, if we move the lights or rotate the object, we immediately notice that we have the image of a model of an orange rather than the image of a real orange. The problem is that a real orange is characterized primarily by small variations in its surface rather than by variations in its color, and the former are not captured by texture mapping. The technique of **bump mapping** varies the apparent shape of the surface by perturbing the normal vectors as the surface is rendered; the colors that are generated by shading then show a variation in the surface properties. Unlike techniques such as environment mapping that can be implemented without programmable shaders, bump mapping cannot be done in real time without them.

7.10.1 Finding Bump Maps

We start with the observation that the normal at any point on a surface characterizes the orientation of the surface at that point. If we perturb the normal at each point on the surface by a small amount, then we create a surface with small variations in its shape. If this perturbation to the normal can be applied only during the shading process, we can use a smooth model of the surface, which must have a smooth normal, but we can shade it in a way that gives the appearance of a complex surface. Because the perturbations are to the normal vectors, the rendering calculations are correct for the altered surface, even though the more complex surface defined by the perturbed normals need never be created.

We can perturb the normals in many ways. The following procedure for parametric surfaces is an efficient one. Let $\mathbf{p}(u, v)$ be a point on a parametric surface. The partial derivatives at the point

$$\mathbf{p}_u = \begin{bmatrix} \frac{\partial x}{\partial u} \\ \frac{\partial y}{\partial u} \\ \frac{\partial z}{\partial u} \end{bmatrix}, \qquad \mathbf{p}_v = \begin{bmatrix} \frac{\partial x}{\partial v} \\ \frac{\partial y}{\partial v} \\ \frac{\partial z}{\partial v} \end{bmatrix}$$

lie in the plane tangent to the surface at the point. Their cross product can be normalized to give the unit normal at that point:

$$\mathbf{n} = \frac{\mathbf{p}_u \times \mathbf{p}_v}{|\mathbf{p}_u \times \mathbf{p}_v|}.$$

Suppose that we displace the surface in the normal direction by a function called the **bump**, or **displacement**, **function**, $d(u, v)$, which we can assume is known and small ($|d(u, v)| \ll 1$). The displaced surface is given by

$$\mathbf{p}' = \mathbf{p} + d(u, v)\mathbf{n}.$$

We would prefer not to create the displaced surface because such a surface would have a higher geometric complexity than the undisplaced surface and would thus slow down the rendering process. We just want to make it look as though we have displaced the original surface. We can achieve the desired look by altering the normal **n**, instead of **p**, and using the perturbed normal in our shading calculations.

The normal at the perturbed point $\mathbf{p}'$ is given by the cross product

$$\mathbf{n}' = \mathbf{p}'_u \times \mathbf{p}'_v.$$

We can compute the two partial derivatives by differentiating the equation for $\mathbf{p}'$, obtaining

$$\mathbf{p}'_u = \mathbf{p}_u + \frac{\partial d}{\partial u}\mathbf{n} + d(u, v)\mathbf{n}_u,$$

$$\mathbf{p}'_v = \mathbf{p}_v + \frac{\partial d}{\partial v}\mathbf{n} + d(u, v)\mathbf{n}_v.$$

If d is small, we can neglect the term on the right of these two equations and take their cross product, noting that $\mathbf{n} \times \mathbf{n} = 0$, to obtain the approximate perturbed normal:

$$\mathbf{n}' \approx \mathbf{n} + \frac{\partial d}{\partial u}\mathbf{n} \times \mathbf{p}_v + \frac{\partial d}{\partial v}\mathbf{n} \times \mathbf{p}_u.$$

The two terms on the right are the displacement, the difference between the original and perturbed normals. The cross product of two vectors is orthogonal to both of them. Consequently, both cross products yield vectors that lie in the tangent plane at **p**, and their sum must also be in the tangent plane.

Although $\mathbf{p}'_u$ and $\mathbf{p}'_v$ lie in the tangent plane perpendicular to $\mathbf{n}'$, they are not necessarily orthogonal to each other. We can obtain an orthogonal basis and a corresponding rotation matrix using the cross product. First, we normalize $\mathbf{n}'$ and $\mathbf{p}'_u$, obtaining the vectors

$$\mathbf{m} = \frac{\mathbf{n}'}{|\mathbf{n}'|},$$

$$\mathbf{t} = \frac{\mathbf{p}'_u}{|\mathbf{p}'_u|}.$$

We obtain the third orthogonal vector, **b**, by

$$\mathbf{b} = \mathbf{m} \times \mathbf{t}.$$

The vector **t** is called the **tangent vector** at **p**, and **b** is called the **binormal vector** at **p**. The matrix

$$\mathbf{M} = [\,\mathbf{t} \quad \mathbf{b} \quad \mathbf{m}\,]^T$$

is the rotation matrix that will convert representations in the original space to representations in terms of the three vectors. The new space is sometimes called **tangent**

space. Because the tangent and binormal vectors can change for each point on the surface, tangent space is a local coordinate system.

To better understand the implication of having introduced another frame, one that is local to the point on the surface, let's consider a bump from the plane $z = 0$. The surface can be written in implicit form as

$$f(x, y) = ax + by + c = 0.$$

If we let $u = x$ and $v = y$, then, if $a \neq 0$, we have

$$\mathbf{p}(u, v) = \begin{bmatrix} u \\ -\dfrac{b}{a}v - \dfrac{c}{a} \\ 0 \end{bmatrix}.$$

The vectors $\partial \mathbf{p}/\partial u$ and $\partial \mathbf{p}/\partial v$ can be normalized to give the orthogonal vectors

$$\frac{\mathbf{p}'_u}{|\mathbf{p}'_u|} = [\,1 \quad 0 \quad 0\,]^T,$$

$$\frac{\mathbf{p}'_v}{|\mathbf{p}'_v|} = [\,0 \quad 1 \quad 0\,]^T.$$

Because these vectors turned out to be orthogonal, they serve as the tangent binormal vectors. The unit normal is

$$\mathbf{n} = [\,0 \quad 0 \quad 1\,]^T.$$

For this case, the displacement function is a function $d(x, y)$. To specify the bump map, we need two functions that give the values of $\partial d/\partial x$ and $\partial d/\partial y$. If these functions are known analytically, we can evaluate them either in the application or in the shader. More often, however, we have a sampled version of $d(x, y)$ as an array of pixels $\mathbf{D} = [d_{ij}]$. The required partial derivatives can be approximated by the difference between adjacent elements in the following array:

$$\frac{\partial d}{\partial x} \propto d_{ij} - d_{i-1,j},$$

$$\frac{\partial d}{\partial y} \propto d_{ij} - d_{i,j-1}.$$

These arrays can be precomputed in the application and stored as a texture called a **normal map**. The fragment shader can obtain the values using a sampler.

Before we develop the necessary shaders, consider what is different for the general case when the surface is not described by the plane $z = 0$. In our simple case, the tangent space axes aligned with the object or world axes. In general, the normal from a surface will not point in the z-direction nor along any particular axis. In addition, the tangent and binormal vectors, although orthogonal to each other and the normal, will have no particular orientation with respect to the world or object axes. The displacement function is measured along the normal so its partial derivatives are in an arbitrary plane. However, in tangent space this displacement is along the z-coordinate axis. Hence, the importance of the matrix **M** composed of the normal, tangent, and binormal vectors is that it allows us to go to the local coordinate system in which the bump map calculations match what we just did. The usual implementation of bump mapping is to find this matrix and transform object-space vectors into vectors in a tangent space local coordinate system. Because tangent space is local, the change in representation can be different for every fragment. With polygonal meshes, the calculation can be simpler if we use the same normal across each polygon and the application can send the tangent and binormal to the vertex shader once for each polygon.

We are almost ready to write vertex and fragment shaders for bump mapping. The entities that we need for lighting—the surface normal, the light vector(s), the half-angle vector, the vertex location—are usually in eye or object coordinates at the point in the process when we do lighting. Whether we use a normal map or compute the perturbation of the normal procedurally in a fragment shader, the displacements are in texture-space coordinates. For correct shading, we have to convert either the normal map to object-space coordinates or the object-space coordinates to texture-space coordinates. In general, the latter requires less work because it can be carried out on a per-vertex basis in the vertex shader rather than on a per-fragment basis. As we have seen, the matrix needed to convert from object space to texture space is precisely the matrix composed of the normal, tangent, and binormal.

We can send the normal to the vertex shader as a vertex attribute if it changes at each vertex, or, if we are working with a single flat polygon at a time, we can use a uniform variable. The application can also provide tangent vectors in a similar manner. The binormal can then be computed in the shader using the cross-product function. These computations are done in the vertex shader, which produces a light vector and view vector in tangent coordinates for use in the fragment shader. Because the normal vector in tangent coordinates always points in the positive z-direction, the view and light vectors are sufficient for doing lighting in tangent space.

7.10.2 Bump Map Example

Our example is a single square in the plane $y = 0$ with a light source above the plane that rotates in the plane $y = 10.0$. We will include only diffuse lighting to minimize the amount of code we need. Our displacement is a small square in the center of the original square. Before developing the code, the output is shown in Figure 7.33. The image on the left is with the light source in its original position; the image on the left is with the light source rotated 45 degrees in the $x - z$ plane at the same height above the surface.

First, let's look at the application program. We will use two triangles for the square polygon, and each of the six vertices will have a texture. So that part of the code will be much as in previous examples:

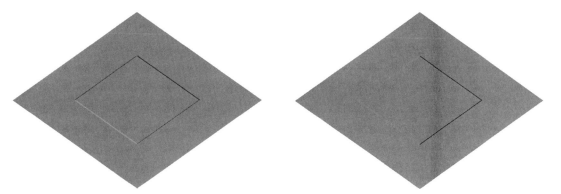

FIGURE 7.33 Bump mapping of a square displacement.

```
point4 points[6];
point2 tex_coord[6];

void mesh()
{
    point4 vertices[4] = {
        point4(0.0, 0.0, 0.0, 1.0),
        point4(1.0, 0.0, 0.0, 1.0),
        point4(1.0, 0.0, 1.0, 1.0),
        point4(0.0, 0.0, 1.0, 1.0)
    };

    points[0] = vertices[0];
    tex_coord[0] = point2(0.0, 0.0);
    points[1] = vertices[1];
    tex_coord[1] = point2(1.0, 0.0);
    points[2] = vertices[2];
    tex_coord[2] = point2(1.0, 1.0);
    points[3] = vertices[2];
    tex_coord[3] = point2(1.0, 1.0);
    points[4] = vertices[3];
    tex_coord[4] = point2(0.0, 1.0);
    points[5] = vertices[0];
    tex_coord[5] = point2(0.0, 0.0);
}
```

We send these data to the GPU as vertex attributes.

The displacement map is generated as an array in the application. The displacement data are in the array `data`. The normal map is computing by taking the differences to approximate the partial derivatives for two of the components and using 1.0 for the third to form the array `normals`. Because these values are stored as colors in a texture image, the components are scaled to the interval (0.0, 1.0).

```
const int N = 256;

float data[N+1][N+1];
vec3 normals[N][N];

for(int i = 0; i < N+1; i++)
    for(int j = 0; j < N+1; j++)
        data[i][j]=0.0;

for(int i = N/4; i < 3*N/4; i++)
    for(int j = N/4; j < 3*N/4; j++)
        data[i][j] = 1.0;

for(int i = 0;i < N; i++)
    for(int j = 0;j < N; j++)
    {
        vec4 n = vec3(data[i][j] - data[i+1][j], 0.0, data[i][j] -
                    data[i][j+1]);
        normals[i][j] = 0.5*normalize(n) + 0.5;
    }
```

The array `normals` is then sent to the GPU by building a texture object. We send a projection matrix, a model-view matrix, the light position, and the diffuse lighting parameters to the shaders as uniform variables. Because the surface is flat, the normal is constant and can be sent to the shader as a uniform variable. Likewise, the tangent vector is constant and can be any vector in the same plane as the polygon and can also be sent to the vertex shader as a uniform variable.

We now turn to the vertex shader. In this simple example, we want to do the calculations in texture space. Hence, we must transform both the light vector and eye vector to this space. The required transformation matrix is composed of the normal, tangent, and binormal vectors.

The normal and tangent are specified in object coordinates and must first be converted to eye coordinates. The required transformation matrix is the **normal matrix**, which is the inverse transpose of the upper-left 3×3 submatrix of the model-view matrix (see Exercise 7.30). We assume this matrix is computed in the application and sent to the shader as another uniform variable. We can then use the transformed normal and tangent to give the binormal in eye coordinates. Finally, we use these three vectors to transform the view vector and light vector to texture space. Here is the vertex shader:

```
/* bump map vertex shader */

out vec3 L; /* light vector in texture-space coordinates */
out vec3 V; /* view vector in texture-space coordinates */
out vec2 st; /* texture coordinates */

in vec2 texcoord;
in vec4 vPosition;
```

```
uniform vec3 Normal;
uniform vec4 LightPosition;
uniform mat4 ModelView;
uniform mat4 Projection;
uniform mat4 NormalMatrix;
uniform vec3 objTangent;

void main()
{
    gl_Position = Projection*ModelView*vPosition;

    st = texcoord;

    vec3 eyePosition = vec3(ModelView*vPosition);
    vec3 eyeLightPos = LightPosition.xyz;

    /* normal, tangent, and binormal in eye coordinates */

    vec3 N = normalize(NormalMatrix*Normal);
    vec3 T = normalize(NormalMatrix*objTangent);
    vec3 B = cross(N, T);

    /* light vector in texture space */

    L.x = dot(T, eyeLightPos-eyePosition);
    L.y = dot(B, eyeLightPos-eyePosition);
    L.z = dot(N, eyeLightPos-eyePosition);

    L = normalize(L);

    /* view vector in texture space */

    V.x = dot(T, -eyePosition);
    V.y = dot(B, -eyePosition);
    V.z = dot(N, -eyePosition);

    V = normalize(V);
}
```

Our strategy for the fragment shader is to provide the normalized perturbed normals as a texture map from the application as a normal map. The fragment shader is given by the following code:

```
in vec3 L;
in vec3 V;
in vec2 st;
uniform vec4 DiffuseProduct;
uniform sampler2D texMap;
```

```
void main()
{

   vec4 N = texture2D(texMap, st);
   vec3 NN = normalize(2.0*N.xyz-1.0);
   vec3 LL = normalize(L);
   float Kd = max(dot(NN.xyz, LL), 0.0);
   gl_FragColor = Kd*DiffuseProduct;
}
```

The values in the texture map are scaled back to the interval $(-1.0, 1.0)$. The diffuse product is a vector computed in the application, each of whose components is the product of a diffuse light component and a diffuse material component.

Note that this example does not use the texture-space view vectors computed in the vertex shader. These vectors would be necessary if we wanted to add a specular term. We have only touched the surface (so to speak) of bump mapping. Many of its most powerful applications are when it is combined with procedural texture generation, which we explore further in Chapter 8.

7.11   COMPOSITING TECHNIQUES

Thus far, we have assumed that we want to form a single image and that the objects that form this image have surfaces that are opaque. OpenGL provides a mechanism, through **alpha (α) blending**, that can, among other effects, create images with translucent objects. The **alpha channel** is the fourth color in RGBA (or RGBα) color mode. Like the other colors, the application program can control the value of A (or α) for each pixel. However, in RGBA mode, if blending is enabled, the value of α controls how the RGB values are written into the frame buffer. Because fragments from multiple objects can contribute to the color of the same pixel, we say that these objects are **blended** or **composited** together. We can use a similar mechanism to blend together images.

7.11.1 Opacity and Blending

The **opacity** of a surface is a measure of how much light penetrates through that surface. An opacity of 1 ($\alpha = 1$) corresponds to a completely opaque surface that blocks all light incident on it. A surface with an opacity of 0 is transparent; all light passes through it. The **transparency** or **translucency** of a surface with opacity α is given by $1 - \alpha$.

Consider the three uniformly lit polygons shown in Figure 7.34. Assume that the middle polygon is opaque, and the front polygon, nearest to the viewer, is transparent. If the front polygon were perfectly transparent, the viewer would see only the middle polygon. However, if the front polygon is only partially opaque (partially transparent), similar to colored glass, the color that viewer sees is a blending of the colors of the front and middle polygon. Because the middle polygon is opaque, the

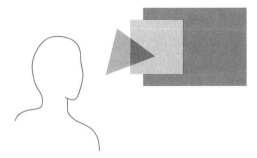

FIGURE 7.34   Translucent and opaque polygons.

viewer does not see the back polygon. If the front polygon is red and the middle is blue, she sees magenta, due to the blending of the colors. If we let the middle polygon be only partially opaque, she sees the blending of the colors of all three polygons.

In computer graphics, we usually render polygons one at a time into the frame buffer. Consequently, if we want to use blending or compositing, we need a way to apply opacity as part of fragment processing. We can use the notion of source and destination pixels, just as we used source and destination bits in Section 7.3. As a polygon is processed, pixel-sized fragments are computed and, if they are visible, are assigned colors based on the shading model in use. Until now, we have used the color of a fragment—as computed by the shading model and by any mapping techniques— to determine the color of the pixel in the frame buffer at the location in screen coordinates of the fragment. If we regard the fragment as the source pixel and the frame-buffer pixel as the destination, we can combine these values in various ways. Using α values is one way of controlling the blending on a fragment-by-fragment basis. Combining the colors of polygons is similar to joining two pieces of colored glass into a single piece of glass that has a higher opacity and a color different from either of the original pieces.

If we represent the source and destination pixels with the four-element (RGBα) arrays

$$\mathbf{s} = [\, s_r \quad s_g \quad s_b \quad s_a \,],$$

$$\mathbf{d} = [\, d_r \quad d_g \quad d_b \quad d_a \,],$$

then a compositing operation replaces $\mathbf{d}$ with

$$\mathbf{d}' = [\, b_r s_r + c_r d_r \quad b_g s_g + c_g d_g \quad b_b s_b + c_b d_b \quad b_a s_a + c_a d_a \,].$$

The arrays of constants $\mathbf{b} = [\, b_r \quad b_g \quad b_b \quad b_a \,]$ and $\mathbf{c} = [\, c_r \quad c_g \quad c_b \quad c_a \,]$ are the **source** and **destination blending factors**, respectively. As occurs with RGB colors, a value of α over 1.0 is limited (or clamped) to the maximum of 1.0, and negative values are clamped to 0.0. We can choose both the values of α and the method of combining source and destination values to achieve a variety of effects.

7.11.2 Image Compositing

The most straightforward use of α blending is to combine and display several images that exist as pixel maps or equivalently, as sets of data that have been rendered independently. In this case, we can regard each image as a radiant object that contributes equally to the final image. Usually, we wish to keep our RGB colors between 0 and 1 in the final image, without having to clamp those values greater than 1. Hence, we can either scale the values of each image or use the source and destination blending factors.

Suppose that we have n images that should contribute equally to the final display. At a given pixel, image i has components $\mathbf{C}_i \alpha_i$. Here, we are using $\mathbf{C}_i$ to denote the color triplet (R_i, G_i, B_i). If we replace $\mathbf{C}_i$ by $\frac{1}{n}\mathbf{C}_i$ and α_i by $\frac{1}{n}$, then we can simply add each image into the frame buffer (assuming the frame buffer is initialized to black with an $\alpha = 0$). Alternately, we can use a source blending factor of $\frac{1}{n}$ by setting the α value for each pixel in each image to be $\frac{1}{n}$, and using 1 for the destination blending factor and α for the source blending factor. Although these two methods produce the same image, if the hardware supports compositing, the second may be more efficient. Note that if n is large, blending factors of the form $\frac{1}{n}$ can lead to significant loss of color resolution. Recent frame buffers support floating point arithmetic and thus can avoid this problem.

7.11.3 Blending and Compositing in OpenGL

The mechanics of blending in OpenGL are straightforward. We enable blending by

```
glEnable(GL_BLEND);
```

Then we set up the desired source and destination factors by

```
glBlendFunc(source_factor, destination_factor);
```

OpenGL has a number of blending factors defined, including the values 1 (`GL_ONE`) and 0 (`GL_ZERO`), the source α and $1 - \alpha$ (`GL_SRC_ALPHA` and `GL_ONE_MINUS_SRC_ALPHA`), and the destination α and $1 - \alpha$ (`GL_DST_ALPHA` and `GL_ONE_MINUS_DST_ALPHA`). The application program specifies the desired options and then uses RGBA color.

The major difficulty with compositing is that for most choices of the blending factors the order in which we render the polygons affects the final image. For example, many applications use the source α as the source blending factor and $1 - \alpha$ for the destination factor. The resulting color and opacity are

$$(R_{d'}, G_{d'}, B_{d'}, \alpha_{d'}) = (\alpha_s R_s + (1 - \alpha_s)R_d, \alpha_s G + (1 - \alpha_s)G_d, \alpha_s B_s$$

$$+ (1 - \alpha_s)B_d, \alpha_s \alpha_d + (1 - \alpha_s)\alpha_d).$$

This formula ensures that neither colors nor opacities can saturate. However, the resulting color and α values depend on the order in which the polygons are rendered.

Consequently, unlike in most OpenGL programs, where the user does not have to worry about the order in which polygons are rasterized, to get a desired effect we must now control this order within the application.

A more subtle but visibly apparent problem occurs when we combine opaque and translucent objects in a scene. Normally, when we use blending, we do not enable hidden-surface removal, because polygons behind any polygon already rendered would not be rasterized and thus would not contribute to the final image. In a scene with both opaque and transparent polygons, any polygon behind an opaque polygon should not be rendered, but translucent polygons in front of opaque polygons should be composited. There is a simple solution to this problem that does not require the application program to order the polygons. We can enable hidden-surface removal as usual and can make the z-buffer read-only for any polygon that is translucent. We do so by calling

```
glDepthMask(GL_FALSE);
```

When the depth buffer is read-only, a translucent polygon that lies behind any opaque polygon already rendered is discarded. A translucent polygon that lies in front of any polygon that has already been rendered is blended with the color of the polygons it is in front of. However, because the z-buffer is read-only for this polygon, the depth values in the buffer are unchanged. Opaque polygons set the depth mask to true and are rendered normally. Note that because the result of compositing depends on the order in which we composite individual elements, we may notice defects in images in which we render translucent polygons in an arbitrary order. If we are willing to sort the translucent polygons, then we can render all the opaque polygons first and then render the translucent polygons in a back-to-front order with the z-buffer in a read-only mode.

7.11.4 Antialiasing Revisited

One of the major uses of the α channel is for antialiasing. Because a line must have a finite width to be visible, the default width of a line that is rendered should be one pixel wide. We cannot produce a thinner line. Unless the line is horizontal or vertical, such a line partially covers a number of pixels in the frame buffer, as shown in Figure 7.35. Suppose that, as part of the geometric-processing stage of the rendering process, as we process a fragment, we set the α value for the corresponding pixel to be a number between 0 and 1 that is the amount of that pixel covered by the fragment. We can then use this α value to modulate the color as we render the fragment to the frame buffer. We can use a destination blending factor of $1 - \alpha$ and a source destination factor of α. However, if there is overlap of fragments within a pixel, then there are numerous possibilities, as we can see from Figure 7.35. In Figure 7.36(a), the fragments do not overlap; in Figure 7.36(b), they do overlap. Consider the problem from the perspective of a renderer that works one polygon a time. For our simple example, suppose that we start with an opaque background and that the frame buffer starts with the background color $\mathbf{C}_0$. We can set $\alpha_0 = 0$, because no part of the pixel

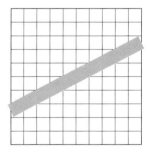

FIGURE 7.35   Raster line.

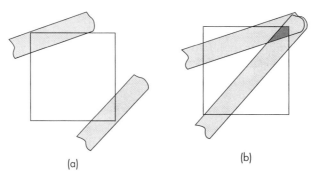

(a)   (b)

FIGURE 7.36   Fragments. (a) Nonoverlapping. (b) Overlapping.

has yet been covered with fragments from polygons. The first polygon is rendered. The color of the destination pixel is set to

$$\mathbf{C}_d = (1 - \alpha_1)\mathbf{C}_0 + \alpha_1 \mathbf{C}_1,$$

and its α value is set to

$$\alpha_d = \alpha_1.$$

Thus, a fragment that covers the entire pixel ($\alpha_1 = 1$) will have its color assigned to the destination pixel, and the destination pixel will be opaque. If the background is black, the destination color will be $\alpha_1 \mathbf{C}_1$. Now consider the fragment from the second polygon that subtends the same pixel. How we add in its color and α value depends on how we wish to interpret the overlap. If there is no overlap, we can assign the new color by blending the color of the destination with the color of the fragment, resulting in the color and α:

$$\mathbf{C}_d = (1 - \alpha_2)((1 - \alpha_1)\mathbf{C}_0 + \alpha_1 \mathbf{C}_1) + \alpha_2 \mathbf{C}_2,$$
$$\alpha_d = \alpha_1 + \alpha_2.$$

This color is a blending of the two colors and does not need to be clamped. The resulting value of α represents the new fraction of the pixel that is covered. However, the resulting color is affected by the order in which the polygons are rendered. The more difficult questions are what to do if the fragments overlap and how to tell whether there is an overlap. One tactic is to take a probabilistic view. If fragment 1 occupies a fraction α_1 of the pixel, fragment 2 occupies a fraction α_2 of the same pixel, and we have no other information about the location of the fragments within the pixel, then the average area of overlap is $\alpha_1 \alpha_2$. We can represent the average case as shown in Figure 7.37. Hence, the new destination α should be

$$\alpha_d = \alpha_1 + \alpha_2 - \alpha_1 \alpha_2.$$

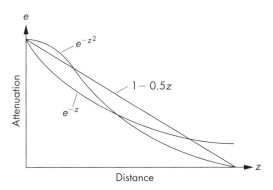

FIGURE 7.37   Average overlap.

How we should assign the color is a more complex problem, because we have to decide whether the second fragment is in front of the first or the first is in front of the second, or even whether the two should be blended. We can define an appropriate blending for whichever assumption we wish to make. Note that, in a pipeline renderer, polygons can be generated in an order that has nothing to do with their distances from the viewer. However, if we couple α blending with hidden-surface removal, we can use the depth information to make front-versus-back decisions.

In OpenGL, we can invoke antialiasing without having the user program combine α values explicitly if we enable blending and smoothing for lines or polygons; for example, we can use

```
glEnable(GL_LINE_SMOOTH);
glEnable(GL_POLYGON_SMOOTH);
glEnable(GL_BLEND);
glBlendFunc(GL_SRC_ALPHA, GL_ONE_MINUS_SRC_ALPHA);
```

to enable antialiasing. There may be a considerable performance penalty associated with antialiasing. Color Plate 8 shows OpenGL's antialiasing of polygons.

7.11.5 Back-to-Front and Front-to-Back Rendering

Although using the α channel gives us a way of creating the appearance of translucency, it is difficult to handle transparency in a physically correct manner without taking into account how an object is lit and what happens to rays and projectors that pass through translucent objects. In Figure 7.38, we can see several of the difficulties. We ignore refraction of light through translucent surfaces—an effect than cannot be handled easily with a pipeline polygon renderer. Suppose that the rear polygon is opaque, but reflective, and that the two polygons closer to the viewer are translucent. By following various rays from the light source, we can see a number of possibilities. Some rays strike the rear polygon, and the corresponding pixels can be colored with the shade at the intersection of the projector and the polygon. For these rays, we

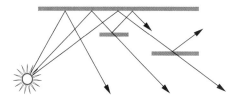

FIGURE 7.38   Scene with translucent objects.

should also distinguish between points illuminated directly by the light source and points for which the incident light passes through one or both translucent polygons. For rays that pass through only one translucent surface, we have to adjust the color based on the color and opacity of the polygon. We should also add a term that accounts for the light striking the front polygon that is reflected toward the viewer. For rays passing through both translucent polygons, we have to consider their combined effect.

For a pipeline renderer, the task is even more difficult—if not impossible—because we have to determine the contribution that each polygon makes as it is passed through the pipeline, rather than considering the contributions of all polygons to a given pixel at the same time. In applications where handling of translucency must be done in a consistent and realistic manner, we often must sort the polygons from front to back within the application. Then depending on the application, we can do a front-to-back or back-to-front rendering using OpenGL's blending functionality (see Exercise 7.27).

7.11.6 Scene Antialiasing and Multisampling

Rather than antialiasing individual lines and polygons, as we discussed in Section 7.11.4, we can antialias the entire scene using a technique called **multisampling**. In this mode, every pixel in the frame buffer contains a number of **samples**. Each sample is capable of storing a color, depth, and other values. When a scene is rendered, it is as if the scene is rendered at an enhanced resolution. However, when the image must be displayed in the frame buffer, all of the samples for each pixel are combined to produce the final pixel color.

In OpenGL, the number of samples per pixel is a function of how the frame buffer is created when the application initializes. In our programs, since we use GLUT, you would add the additional option `GLUT_MULTISAMPLE` to the `glutInitDisplayMode`. This will request that the pixels in the frame buffer have multiple samples.

Just as line and polygon antialiasing can be enabled and disabled during the rendering of a frame, so too with multisampling. To turn on multisampling and begin antialiasing all of the primitives rendered in the frame, simply call `glEnable(GL_MULTISAMPLE)`. Likewise, calling `glDisable(GL_MULTISAMPLE)` will stop the multisampled rendering. Generally speaking, an application will almost always either multisample all the time, or never.

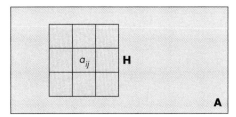

FIGURE 7.39   Filtering and convolution.

7.11.7 Image Processing

We can use pixel mapping to perform various image-processing operations. Suppose that we start with a discrete image. Perhaps this image was generated by a rendering, or perhaps we obtained it by digitizing a continuous image using a scanner. We can represent the image with an $N \times M$ matrix,

$$\mathbf{A} = [\, a_{ij} \,],$$

of scalar levels. If we process each color component of a color image independently, we can regard the entries in $\mathbf{A}$ as either individual color components or gray (luminance) levels. A **linear filter** produces a filtered matrix $\mathbf{B}$ whose elements are

$$b_{ij} = \sum_{k=-m}^{m} \sum_{l=-n}^{n} h_{kl}\, a_{i+k,\,j+l}.$$

We say that $\mathbf{B}$ is the result of **convolving** $\mathbf{A}$ with a filter matrix $\mathbf{H}$. In general, the values of m and n are small, and we can represent $\mathbf{H}$ by a small $(2m + 1 \times 2n + 1)$ **convolution matrix**.

We can view the filtering operation as shown in Figure 7.39 for $m = n = 1$. For each pixel in $\mathbf{A}$, we place the convolution matrix over a_{ij} and take a weighted average of the surrounding points. The values in the matrix are the weights. For example, for $n = m = 1$, we can average each pixel with its four surrounding neighbors using the 3×3 matrix

$$\mathbf{H} = \frac{1}{5}\begin{bmatrix} 0 & 1 & 0 \\ 1 & 1 & 1 \\ 0 & 1 & 0 \end{bmatrix}.$$

This filter can be used for antialiasing. We can use more points and can weight the center more heavily with

$$\mathbf{H} = \frac{1}{16}\begin{bmatrix} 1 & 2 & 1 \\ 2 & 4 & 2 \\ 1 & 2 & 1 \end{bmatrix}.$$

Note that we must define a border around **A** if we want **B** to have the same dimensions. Other operations are possible with small matrices. For example, we can use the matrix

$$\mathbf{H} = \begin{bmatrix} 0 & -1 & 0 \\ -1 & 4 & -1 \\ 0 & -1 & 0 \end{bmatrix}$$

to detect changes in value or edges in the image. If the matrix **H** is $k \times k$, we can implement a filter by accumulating k^2 images in the frame buffer, each time adding in a shifted version of **A**.

7.11.8 Other Multipass Methods

We can also use blending for filtering in time and depth. For example, if we jitter an object and render it multiple times, leaving the positions of the other objects unchanged, we get dimmer copies of the jittered object in the final image. If the object is moved along a path, rather than randomly jittered, we see the trail of the object. This **motion-blur** effect is similar to the result of taking a photograph of a moving object using a long exposure time. We can adjust the object's α value so as to render the final position of the object with greater opacity or to create the impression of speed differences.

We can use filtering in depth to create focusing effects. A real camera cannot produce an image with all objects in focus. Objects within a certain distance from the camera, the camera's **depth of field**, are in focus; objects outside it are out of focus and appear blurred. Computer graphics produces images with an infinite depth of field because we do not have to worry about the limitations of real lenses. Occasionally, however, we want to create an image that looks as though it were produced by a real camera, or to defocus part of a scene so as to emphasize the objects within a desired depth of field. This time, the trick is to move the viewer in a manner that leaves a particular plane fixed, as shown in Figure 7.40. Suppose that we wish to keep the plane at $z = z_f$ in focus and to leave the near ($z = z_{\min}$) and far ($z = z_{\max}$) clipping distances unchanged. If we use `Frustum`, we specify the near clipping rectangle $(x_{\min}, x_{\max}, y_{\min}, y_{\max})$. If we move the viewer from the origin in the x-direction by

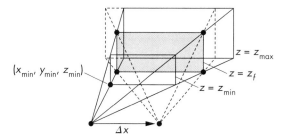

$z = z_{\max}$

$(x_{\min}, y_{\min}, z_{\min})$

$z = z_f$

$z = z_{\min}$

Δx

FIGURE 7.40 Depth-of-field jitter.

Δx, we must change x_{min} to

$$x'_{min} = x_{min} + \frac{\Delta x}{z_f}(z_f - z_{near}).$$

Similar equations hold for x_{max}, y_{min}, and y_{max}. As we increase Δx and Δy, we create a narrower depth of field.

7.12 SAMPLING AND ALIASING

We have seen a variety of applications in which the conversion from a continuous representation of an entity to a discrete approximation of that entity leads to visible errors in the display. We have used the term *aliasing* to characterize these errors. When we work with buffers, we are always working with digital images, and, if we are not careful, these errors can be extreme. In this section, we examine the nature of digital images and gather facts that will help us to understand where aliasing errors arise and how the effects of these errors can be mitigated.

We start with a continuous two-dimensional image $f(x, y)$. We can regard the value of f as either a gray level in a monochromatic image or the value of one of the primaries in a color image. In the computer, we work with a digital image that is an array of nm pixels arranged as n rows of m pixels. Each pixel has k bits. There are two processes involved in going from a continuous image to a discrete image. First, we must **sample** the continuous image at nm points on some grid to obtain a set of values $\{f_{ij}\}$. Each of these samples of the continuous image is the value of f measured over a small area in the continuous image. Then, we must convert each of these samples into a k-bit pixel by a process known as **quantization.**

7.12.1 Sampling Theory

Suppose that we have a rectangular grid of locations where we wish to obtain our samples of f, as in Figure 7.41. If we assume that the grid is equally spaced, then an ideal sampler would produce a value

$$f_{ij} = f(x_0 + ih_x, y_0 + jh_y),$$

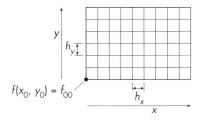

FIGURE 7.41   Sampling grid.

where h_x and h_y are the distances between the grid points in the x- and y-directions, respectively. Leaving aside for now the fact that no real sampler can make such a precise measurement, there are two important questions. First, what errors have we made in this idealized sampling process? That is, how much of the information in the original image is included in the sampled image? Second, can we go back from the digital image to a continuous image without incurring additional errors? This latter step is called **reconstruction** and describes display processes such as are required in displaying the contents of a frame buffer on a monitor.

The mathematical analysis of these issues uses Fourier analysis, a branch of applied mathematics particularly well suited for explaining problems of digital signal processing. The essence of Fourier theory is that a function, of either space or time, can be decomposed into a set of sinusoids, at possibly an infinite number of frequencies. This concept is most familiar with sound, where we routinely think of a particular sound in terms of its frequency components, or **spectrum**. For a two-dimensional image, we can think of it as being composed of sinusoidal patterns in two spatial frequencies that when added together produce the image. Figure 7.42(a) shows a one-dimensional function; Figure 7.42(b) shows the two sinusoids that form it. Figure 7.43 shows two-dimensional periodic functions. Thus, every two-dimensional spatial function $f(x, y)$ has two equivalent representations. One is its spatial form $f(x, y)$; the other is a representation in terms of its spectrum—the frequency-domain representation $g(\xi, \eta)$. The value of g is the contribution to f at the two-dimensional spatial frequency (ξ, η). By using these alternate representations of functions, we find that many phenomena, including sampling, can be explained much more easily in the frequency domain.

We can explain the consequences of sampling, without being overwhelmed by the mathematics, if we accept, without proof, the fundamental theorem known as the Nyquist sampling theorem. There are two parts to the theorem: The first allows us to discuss sampling errors, whereas the second governs reconstruction. We examine the second in Section 7.12.2.

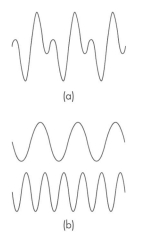

FIGURE 7.42   One-dimensional decomposition. (a) Function. (b) Components.

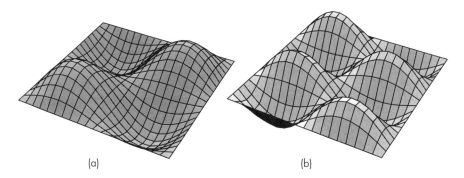

FIGURE 7.43   Two-dimensional periodic functions.

Nyquist sampling theorem (part 1): The ideal samples of a continuous function contain all the information in the original function if and only if the continuous function is sampled at a frequency greater than twice the highest frequency in the function.

Thus, if we are to have any chance of not losing information, we must restrict ourselves to functions that are zero in the frequency domain except in a window of width less than the sampling frequency, centered at the origin. The lowest frequency that cannot be in the data so as to avoid aliasing—one-half of the sampling frequency—is called the **Nyquist frequency**. Functions whose spectra are zero outside of some window are known as **band-limited** functions. For a two-dimensional image, the sampling frequencies are determined by the spacing of a two-dimensional grid with x and y spacing of $1/h_x$ and $1/h_y$, respectively. The theorem assumes an ideal sampling process that gathers an infinite number of samples, each of which is the exact value at the grid point. In practice, we can take only a finite number of samples—the number matching the resolution of our buffer. Consequently, we cannot produce a truly band-limited function. Although this result is a mathematical consequence of Fourier theory, we can observe that there will always be some ambiguity inherent in a finite collection of sampled points, simply because we do not know the function outside the region from which we obtained the samples.[5]

The consequences of violating the Nyquist criteria are aliasing errors. We can see from where the name *aliasing* comes by considering an ideal sampling process. Both the original function and its set of samples have frequency-domain representations. The spectral components of the sampled function are replicas of the spectrum of the original function, with their centers separated by the sampling frequency. Consider the one-dimensional function in Figure 7.44(a), with the samples indicated. Figure 7.44(b) shows its spectrum; in Figure 7.44(c), we have the spectrum of the sampled function, showing the replications of the spectrum in Figure 7.44(b).[6] Because we have sampled at a rate higher than the Nyquist frequency, there is a separation between the replicas.

Now consider the case in Figure 7.45. Here, we have violated the Nyquist criterion, and the replicas overlap. Consider the central part of the plot, which is magnified in Figure 7.46 and shows only the central replica, centered at the origin, and the replica to its right, centered at ξ_s. The frequency ξ_0 is above the Nyquist frequency $\xi_s/2$. There is, however, a replica of ξ_0, generated by the sampling process from the replica on the right, at $\xi_s - \xi_0$, a frequency less than the Nyquist frequency. The energy at this frequency can be heard, if we are dealing with digital sound, or seen, if we are considering two-dimensional images. We say that the frequency ξ_0 has an **alias** at

5. This statement assumes no knowledge of the underlying function f, other than a set of its samples. If we have additional information, such as knowledge that the function is periodic, knowledge of the function over a finite interval can be sufficient to determine the entire function.

6. We show the magnitude of the spectrum because the Fourier transform produces complex numbers for the frequency-domain components.

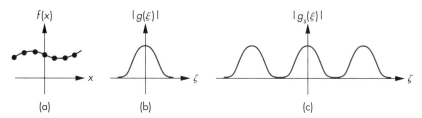

FIGURE 7.44 Band-limited function. (a) Function and its samples in the spatial domain. (b) Spectrum of the function. (c) Spectrum of the samples.

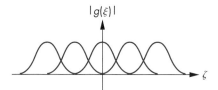

FIGURE 7.45 Overlapping replicas.

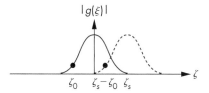

FIGURE 7.46 Aliasing.

$\xi_s - \xi_0$. Note that once aliasing has occurred, we cannot distinguish between information that was at a frequency in the original data and information that was placed at this frequency by the sampling process.

We can demonstrate aliasing and ambiguity without using Fourier analysis by looking at a single sinusoid, as shown in Figure 7.47. If we sample this sinusoid at twice its frequency, we can recover it from two samples. However, these same two samples are samples of a sinusoid of twice this frequency, and they can also be samples of sinusoids of other multiples of the basic frequency. All these frequencies are aliases of the same original frequency. If we know that the data were band limited, however, then the samples can describe only the original sinusoid.

If we were to do an analysis of the frequency content of real-world images, we would find that the spectral components of most images are concentrated in the lower frequencies. Consequently, although it is impossible to construct a finite-sized image that is band limited, the aliasing errors often are minimal because there is little content in frequencies above the Nyquist frequency, and little content is aliased into

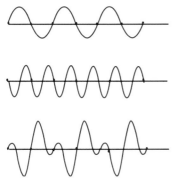

FIGURE 7.47   Aliasing of sinusoid.

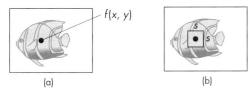

(a)   (b)

FIGURE 7.48   Scanning of an image.
(a) Point sampling. (b) Area averaging.

frequencies below the Nyquist frequency. The exceptions to this statement arise when there is regular (periodic) information in the continuous image. In the frequency representation, regularity places most of the information at a few frequencies. If any of these frequencies is above the Nyquist limit, the aliasing effect is noticeable as beat or moiré patterns. Examples that you might have noticed include the patterns that appear on video displays when people in the images wear striped shirts or plaid ties, and wavy patterns that arise both in printed (halftoned) figures derived from computer displays and in digital images of farmland with plowed fields.

Often, we can minimize aliasing by prefiltering before we scan an image or by controlling the area of the data that the scanner uses to measure a sample. Figure 7.48 shows two possible ways to scan an image. In Figure 7.48(a), we see an ideal scanner. It measures the value of a continuous image at a point, so the samples are given by

$$f_{ij} = f(x_i, y_i).$$

In Figure 7.48(b), we have a more realistic scanner that obtains samples by taking a weighted average over a small interval to produce samples of the form

$$f_{ij} = \int_{x_i - s/2}^{x_i + s/2} \int_{y_i - s/2}^{y_i + s/2} f(x, y) w(x, y) \, dy \, dx.$$

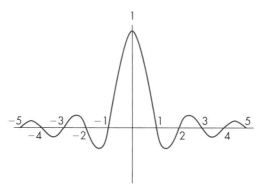

FIGURE 7.49   Sinc function.

By selecting the size of the window s and the weighting function w, we can attenuate high-frequency components in the image, and thus we can reduce aliasing. Fortunately, real scanners must take measurements over a finite region, called the **sampling aperture**; thus, some antialiasing takes place even if the user has no understanding of the aliasing problem.

7.12.2 Reconstruction

Suppose that we have an (infinite) set of samples, the members of which have been sampled at a rate greater than the Nyquist frequency. The reconstruction of a continuous function from the samples is based on part 2 of the Nyquist sampling theorem.

Nyquist sampling theorem (part 2): We can reconstruct a continuous function $f(x)$ from its samples $\{f_i\}$ by the formula

$$f(x) = \sum_{i=-\infty}^{\infty} f_i \operatorname{sinc}(x - x_i).$$

The function $\operatorname{sinc}(x)$ (see Figure 7.49) is defined as

$$\operatorname{sinc}(x) = \frac{\sin \pi x}{\pi x}.$$

The two-dimensional version of the reconstruction formula for a function $f(x, y)$ with ideal samples $\{f_{ij}\}$ is

$$f(x, y) = \sum_{i=-\infty}^{\infty} \sum_{j=-\infty}^{\infty} f_{ij} \operatorname{sinc}(x - x_i) \operatorname{sinc}(y - y_j).$$

These formulas follow from the fact that we can recover an unaliased function in the frequency domain by using a filter that is zero except in the interval $(-\xi_s/2, \xi_s/2)$—a low-pass filter—to obtain a single replica from the infinite number

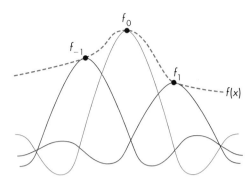

FIGURE 7.50   One-dimensional reconstruction.

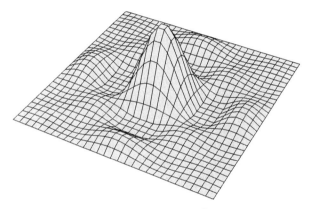

FIGURE 7.51   Two-dimensional sinc function.

of replicas generated by the sampling process shown in Figure 7.44. The reconstruction of a one-dimensional function is shown in Figure 7.50. In two dimensions, the reconstruction involves use of a two-dimensional sinc, as shown in Figure 7.51. Unfortunately, the sinc function cannot be produced in a physical display, because of its negative side lobes. Consider the display problem for a CRT display. We start with a digital image that is a set of samples. For each sample, we can place a spot of light centered at a grid point on the display surface, as shown in Figure 7.52. The value of the sample controls the intensity of the spot, or modulates the beam. We can control the shape of the spot by using techniques such as focusing the beam. The reconstruction formula tells us that the beam should have the shape of a two-dimensional sinc, but because the beam puts out energy, the spot must be nonnegative at all points. Consequently, the display process must make errors. We can evaluate a real display by considering how well its spot approximates the desired sinc. Figure 7.53 shows the sinc and several one-dimensional approximations. The Gaussian-shaped spot corresponds to the shape of many CRT spots, whereas the rectangular spot might corre-

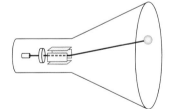

FIGURE 7.52   Display of a point on CRT.

FIGURE 7.53   Display spots. (a) Ideal spot. (b) Rectangular approximation. (c) Piecewise-linear approximation. (d) Gaussian approximation.

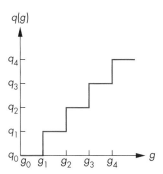

FIGURE 7.54   Quantizer.

spond to an LCD display with square pixels. Note that we can make either approximation wider or narrower. If we analyze the spot profiles in the frequency domain, we find that the wider spots are more accurate at low frequencies but are less accurate at higher frequencies. In practice, the spot size that we choose is a compromise. Visible differences across monitors often can be traced to different spot profiles.

7.12.3 Quantization

The mathematical analysis of sampling explains a number of important effects. However, we have not included the effect of each sample being quantized into k discrete levels. Given a scalar function g with values in the range

$$g_{\min} \le g \le g_{\max},$$

a **quantizer** is a function q such that, if $g_i \le g \le g_{i+1}$,

$$q(g) = q_i.$$

Thus, for each value of g, we assign it one of k values, as shown in Figure 7.54. In general, designing a quantizer involves choosing the $\{q_i\}$, the quantization levels, and the $\{g_i\}$, the threshold values. If we know the probability distribution for g, $p(g)$, we can solve for the values that minimize the mean square error:

$$e = \int (g - q(g))^2 p(g) dg.$$

However, we often design quantizers based on the perceptual issues that we discussed in Chapter 1. A simple rule of thumb is that we should not be able to detect one-level changes, but should be able to detect all two-level changes. Given the threshold for the visual system to detect a change in luminance, we usually need at least 7 or 8 bits (or 128 to 256 levels). We should also consider the logarithmic intensity-brightness response of humans. To do so, we usually distribute the levels exponentially, to give approximately equal perceptual errors as we go from one level to the next.

SUMMARY AND NOTES

In the early days of computer graphics, practitioners worked with only two- and three-dimensional geometric objects, whereas those practitioners who were involved with only two-dimensional images were considered to be working in image processing. Advances in hardware have made graphics and image-processing systems practically indistinguishable. For those practitioners involved with synthesizing images— certainly a major part of computer graphics—this merging of fields has brought forth a multitude of new techniques. The idea that a two-dimensional image or texture can be mapped to a three-dimensional surface in no more time than it takes to render the surface with constant shading would have been unthinkable 15 years ago. Now, these techniques are routine.

Techniques such as texture mapping have had an enormous effect on real-time graphics. In fields such as animation, virtual reality, and scientific visualization, we use hardware texture mapping to add detail to images without burdening the geometric pipeline. The use of compositing techniques through the alpha channel allows the application programmer to perform tasks, such as antialiasing, and to create effects, such as fog and depth of field, that until recently were done on different types of architectures, after the graphics had been created.

Mapping methods provide some of the best examples of the interactions among graphics hardware, software, and applications. Consider texture mapping. Although it was first described and implemented purely as a software algorithm, once people saw its ability to create scenes with great visual complexity, hardware developers started putting large amounts of texture memory in graphics systems. Once texture mapping was implemented in hardware, it could be done in real time, a development that led to the redesign of many applications, notably computer games.

Recent advances in GPUs provide many new possibilities. One is that the pipeline is now programmable. The programmability of the fragment processor makes possible many new texture-manipulation techniques while preserving interactive speeds. Second, the inclusion of large amounts of memory on the GPU removes one of the major bottlenecks in discrete methods, namely, many of the transfers of image data between processor memory and the GPU. Third, GPU architectures are designed for rapid processing of discrete data by incorporating a high degree of parallelism for fragment processing. Finally, the availability of floating-point frame buffers eliminates many of the precision issues that plagued techniques that manipulated image data.

In this chapter, we have concentrated on techniques that are supported by recently available hardware and APIs. Many of the techniques introduced here are recent. Many more have appeared in the recent literature and are available only for programmable processors.

SUGGESTED READINGS

Environment mapping was developed by Blinn and Newell [Bli76]. Texture mapping was first used by Catmull; see the review by Heckbert [Hec86]. Hardware support for texture mapping came with the SGI Reality Engine; see Akeley [Ake93]. Perlin and Hoffert [Per89] designed a noise function to generate two- and three-dimensional texture maps. Many texture synthesis techniques are discussed in Ebert et al. [Ebe02].

The aliasing problem in computer graphics has been of importance since the advent of raster graphics; see Crow [Cro81]. The first concerns were with rasterization of lines, but later other forms of aliasing arose with animations [Mag85] and ray tracing [Gla89]. The image-processing books [Pra78, Gon08, Cas96] provide an introduction to signal processing and aliasing in two dimensions. The books by Glassner [Gla95] and Watt and Policarpo [Wat98] are aimed at practitioners of computer graphics.

Many of the compositing techniques, including use of the α channel, were suggested by Porter and Duff [Por84]. The *OpenGL Programming Guide* [Shr10] contains many examples of how buffers can be used. The recent literature includes many new examples of the use of buffers. See the recent issues of the journals *Computer Graphics* and *IEEE Computer Graphics and Applications*.

Technical details on most of the standard image formats can be found in [Mia99, Mur94].

EXERCISES

7.1   Show how you can use the XOR writing mode to implement an odd–even fill algorithm.

7.2   What are the visual effects of using XOR to move a cursor around on the screen?

7.3   How is an image produced with an environment map different from a ray-traced image of the same scene?

7.4   In the movies and television, the wheels of cars and wagons often appear to be spinning in the wrong direction. What causes the effect? Can anything be done to fix this problem? Explain your answer.

7.5   We can attempt to display sampled data by simply plotting the points and letting the human visual system merge the points into shapes. Why is this technique dangerous if the data are close to the Nyquist limit?

7.6   Why do the patterns of striped shirts and ties change as an actor moves across the screen of your television?

7.7   What is meant by the opacity of a surface? What would the opacity of a transparent surface be? What about the opacity of an opaque surface?

7.8   Suppose that we have two translucent surfaces characterized by opacities α_1 and α_2. What is the opacity of the translucent material that we create by using the two in series? Give an expression for the transparency of the combined material.

7.9   Assume that we view translucent surfaces as filters of the light passing through them. Develop a blending model based on the complementary colors CMY.

7.10 In Section 7.11 we used $1 - \alpha$ and α for the destination and source blending factors, respectively. What would be the visual difference if we used 1 for the destination factor and kept α for the source factor?

7.11 Create interactive paintbrushes that add color gradually to image. Also use blending to add erasers that gradually remove images from the screen.

7.12 What is point sampling? Why is linear filtering a better choice than point sampling in the context of aliasing of textures?

7.13 Show how to use the luminance histogram of an image to derive a lookup table that will make the altered image have a flat histogram.

7.14 Texture mapping requires interaction between the application program, the vertex shader and the fragment shader. What are the three basic steps for texture mapping?

7.15 The generation of a three-dimensional texture field is a direct extension of two-dimensional texture-generation techniques. What are the advantages of using three-dimensional textures over two-dimensional textures?

7.16 Consider a scene composed of simple objects, such as parallelepipeds, that are instanced at different sizes. Suppose that you have a single texture map and you are asked to map this texture to all the objects. How would you map the texture so that the pattern would be the same size on each face of each object?

7.17 Explain the following mapping techniques:
a. Texture map
b. Bump map
c. Environment map

7.18 Using either your own image-processing code for convolution or the imaging extensions of OpenGL, implement a general 3×3 filtering program for luminance images.

7.19 Take an image from a digital camera or from some other source and apply 3×3 smoothing and sharpening filters, repetitively. Pay special attention to what happens at the edges of the filtered images.

7.20 Repeat Exercise 7.19 but first add a small amount of random noise to the image. Describe the differences between the results of the two exercises.

7.21 If your system supports the imaging extensions, compare the performance of filtering using the extensions with filtering done by your own code using processor memory.

7.22 One of the most effective methods of altering the contrast of an image is to allow the user to design a lookup interactively. Consider a graph in which a curve is approximated with three connected line segments. Write a program that displays an image, allows the user to specify the line segments interactively, and shows the image after it has been altered by the curve.

7.23 What does the term "frame buffer" mean?

7.24 Devise a method to convert the values obtained from a cube map to values for a spherical map.

7.25 How many bits are required to store each RGBA color component if a frame buffer has 32 bits each for its front and back color buffers?

7.26 Suppose we want to create a cube that has a black and white checkerboard pattern texture mapped to its faces. Can we texture map the cube so that the colors alternate as we traverse the cube from face to face?

7.27 In what types of applications might you prefer a front-to-back rendering instead of a back-to-front rendering?

7.28 For monochromatic images, what is the gray level for black and white? Also, what are some of the popular standard formats used for storing images?

7.29 TIFF images can have two forms. In one form, all the image data are coded directly. What is the second form? What algorithm is this based on?

7.30 Show that the normal matrix is the inverse transpose of the upper-left 3×3 submatrix of the model-view matrix.

CHAPTER 8

MODELING AND HIERARCHY

Models are abstractions of the world—both of the real world in which we live and of virtual worlds that we create with computers. We are all familiar with mathematical models that are used in all areas of science and engineering. These models use equations to model the physical phenomena that we wish to study. In computer science, we use abstract data types to model organizations of objects; in computer graphics, we model our worlds with geometric objects. When we build a mathematical model, we must choose carefully which type of mathematics fits the phenomena that we wish to model. Although ordinary differential equations may be appropriate for modeling the dynamic behavior of a system of springs and masses, we would probably use partial differential equations to model turbulent fluid flow. We go through analogous processes in computer graphics, choosing which primitives to use in our models and how to show relationships among them. Often, as is true of choosing a mathematical model, there are multiple approaches, so we seek models that can take advantage of the capabilities of our graphics systems.

In this chapter, we explore multiple approaches to developing and working with models of geometric objects. We consider models that use as building blocks a set of simple geometric objects: either the primitives supported by our graphics systems or a set of user-defined objects built from these primitives. We extend the use of transformations from Chapter 3 to include hierarchical relationships among the objects. The techniques that we develop are appropriate for applications, such as robotics and figure animation, where the dynamic behavior of the objects is characterized by relationships among the parts of the model.

The notion of hierarchy is a powerful one and is an integral part of object-oriented methodologies. We extend our hierarchical models of objects to hierarchical models of whole scenes, including cameras, lights, and material properties. Such models allow us to extend our graphics APIs to more object-oriented systems and also give us insight into using graphics over networks and distributed environments, such as the World Wide Web.

8.1   SYMBOLS AND INSTANCES

Our first concern is how we can store a model that may include many sophisticated objects. There are two immediate issues: how we define an object more complex than the ones we have dealt with until now and how we represent a collection of these objects. Most APIs take a minimalist attitude toward primitives: They contain only a few primitives, leaving it to the user to construct more complex objects from these primitives. Sometimes additional libraries provide objects built on top of the basic primitives. We assume that we have available a collection of basic three-dimensional objects provided by these options.

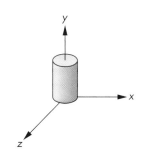

FIGURE 8.1   Cylinder symbol.

We can take a nonhierarchical approach to modeling by regarding these objects as **symbols** and by modeling our world as a collection of symbols. Symbols can include geometric objects, fonts, and application-specific sets of graphical objects. Symbols are usually represented at a convenient size and orientation. For example, a cylinder is usually oriented parallel to one of the axes, as shown in Figure 8.1, often with a unit height, a unit radius, and its bottom centered at the origin.

Most APIs, including OpenGL, make a distinction between the frame in which the symbol is defined, sometimes called the **model frame**, and the **object** or **world frame**. This distinction can be helpful when the symbols are purely shapes, such as the symbols that we might use for circuit elements in a CAD application, and have no physical units associated with them. In OpenGL, we have to set up the transformation from the frame of the symbol to the object coordinate frame within the application. Thus, the model-view matrix for a given symbol is the concatenation of an instance transformation that brings the symbol into object coordinates and a matrix that brings the symbol into the eye frame.

The instance transformation that we introduced in Chapter 3 allows us to place instances of each symbol in the model, at the desired size, orientation, and location. Thus, the instance transformation

M = TRS

is a concatenation of a translation, a rotation, and a scale (and possibly a shear), as shown in Figure 8.2. Consequently, OpenGL programs often contain repetitions of code in the following form:

```
mat4 instance;
mat4 model_view;

instance = Translate(dx, dy, dz)*RotateZ(rz)*
           RotateY(ry)*RotateX(rx)*Scale(sx, sy, sz);

model_view = model_view*instance;
cylinder(); /* or some other symbol */
```

In this example, the instance matrix is computed and alters the model-view matrix. The resulting model-view matrix is sent to the vertex shader using `glUniform`. The

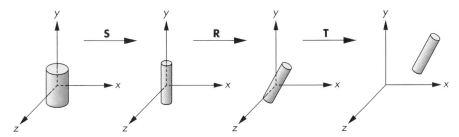

FIGURE 8.2   Instance transformation.

Symbol	Scale	Rotate	Translate
1	s_x, s_y, s_z	$\theta_x, \theta_y, \theta_z$	d_x, d_y, d_z
2			
3			
1			
1			
.			
.			

FIGURE 8.3   Symbol–instance transformation table.

code for `cylinder` generates vertices and can send them to the vertex shader using `glDrawArrays`. Alternately, we can apply the model-view matrix in the application as we generate the vertices.

We can also think of such a model in the form of a table, as shown in Figure 8.3. Here, each symbol is assumed to have a unique numerical identifier. The table stores this identifier and the parameters necessary to build the instance transformation matrix. The table shows that this modeling technique contains no information about relationships among objects. However, the table contains all the information that we require to draw the objects and is thus a simple data structure or model for a group of geometric objects. We could search the table for an object, change the instance transformation for an object, and add or delete objects. However, the flatness of the representation limits us.

8.2   HIERARCHICAL MODELS

Suppose that we wish to build a model of an automobile that we can animate. We can compose the model from five parts—the chassis and the four wheels (Figure 8.4)—each of which we can describe by using our standard graphics primitives. Two frames of a simple animation of the model are shown in Figure 8.5. We could write a program

FIGURE 8.4   Automobile model.

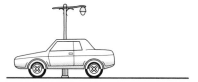

FIGURE 8.5   Two frames of animation.

to generate this animation by noting that if each wheel has a radius r, then a 360-degree rotation of a wheel must correspond to the car moving forward (or backward) a distance of $2\pi r$. The program could then contain one function to generate each wheel and another to generate the chassis. All these functions could use the same input, such as the desired speed and direction of the automobile. In pseudocode, our program might look like this:

```
{
    float s; /* speed */
    float d[3]; /* direction */
    float t; /* time */

    /* determine speed and direction at time t*/

    draw_right_front_wheel(s,d);
    draw_left_front_wheel(s,d);
    draw_right_rear_wheel(s,d);
    draw_left_rear_wheel(s,d);
    draw_chassis(s,d);
}
```

This program is just the kind that we do *not* want to write. It is linear and shows none of the relationships among the components of the automobile. There are two types of relationships that we would like to exploit. First, we cannot separate the movement of the car from the movement of the wheels. If the car moves forward, the wheels must turn.[1] Second, we would like to use the fact that all the wheels of the automobile are identical; they are merely located in different places, with different orientations.

We can represent the relationships among parts of the models, both abstractly and visually, with graphs. Mathematically, a **graph** consists of a set of **nodes** (or vertices) and a set of **edges**. Edges connect pairs of nodes or possibly connect a node to itself. Edges can have a direction associated with them; the graphs we use here are all **directed graphs**, which are graphs that have their edges leaving one node and entering another.

---

1. It is not clear whether we should say the wheels move the chassis or the chassis moves the wheels. From a graphics perspective, the latter view is probably more useful.

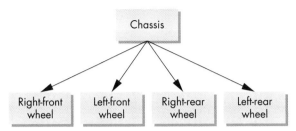

FIGURE 8.6 Tree structure for an automobile.

The most important type of graph we use is a tree. A (connected) **tree** is a directed graph without closed paths or loops. In addition, each node but one—the **root node**—has one edge entering it. Thus, every node except the root has a **parent node**, the node from which an edge enters, and can have one or more **child nodes**, nodes to which edges are connected. A node without children is called a **terminal node**, or **leaf**. Figure 8.6 shows a tree that represents the relationships in our car model. The chassis is the root node, and all four wheels are its children. Although the mathematical graph is a collection of set elements, in practice, both the edges and nodes can contain additional information. For our car example, each node can contain information defining the geometric objects associated with it. The information about the location and orientation of the wheels can be stored either in their nodes or in the edges connecting them with their parent.

In most cars the four wheels are identical, so storing the same information on how to draw each one at four nodes is inefficient. We can use the ideas behind the instance transformation to allow us to use a single prototype wheel in our model. If we do so, we can replace the tree structure by the **directed acyclic graph** (**DAG**) in Figure 8.7. In a DAG, although there are loops, we cannot follow directed edges around any loop. Thus, if we follow any path of directed edges from a node, the path terminates at another node, and in practice, working with DAGs is no more difficult than working with trees. For our car, we can store the information that positions each instance of the single prototype wheel in the chassis node, in the wheel node, or with the edges.

Both forms—trees and DAGs—are **hierarchical** methods of expressing the relationships in the physical model. In each form, various elements of a model can be related to other parts—their parents and their children. We will explore how to express these hierarchies in a graphics program.

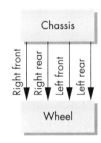

FIGURE 8.7 Directed-acyclic-graph (DAG) model of an automobile.

8.3 A ROBOT ARM

Robotics provides many opportunities for developing hierarchical models. Consider the simple robot arm illustrated in Figure 8.8(a). We can model it with three simple objects, or symbols, perhaps using only two parallelepipeds and a cylinder. Each of the symbols can be built up from our basic primitives.

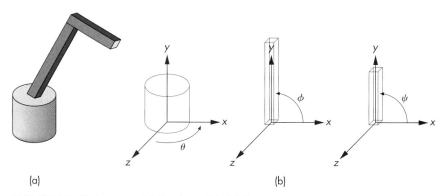

(a)   (b)

FIGURE 8.8 Robot arm. (a) Total model. (b) Components.

The robot arm consists of the three parts shown in Figure 8.8(b). The mechanism has three degrees of freedom, two of which can be described by **joint angles** between components and the third by the angle the base makes with respect to a fixed point on the ground. In our model, each joint angle determines how to position a component with respect to the component to which it is attached, or in the case of the base, the joint angle positions it relative to the surrounding environment. Each joint angle is measured in each component's own frame. We can rotate the base about its vertical axis by an angle θ. This angle is measured from the x-axis to some fixed point on the bottom of the base. The lower arm of the robot is attached to the base by a joint that allows the arm to rotate in the plane $z = 0$ in the arm's frame. This rotation is specified by an angle ϕ that is measured from the x-axis to the arm. The upper arm is attached to the lower arm by a similar joint, and it can rotate by an angle ψ, measured like that for the lower arm, in its own frame. As the angles vary, we can think of the frames of the upper and lower arms as moving relative to the base. By controlling the three angles, we can position the tip of the upper arm in three dimensions.

Suppose that we wish to write a program to render our simple robot model. Rather than specifying each part of the robot and its motion independently, we take an incremental approach. The base of the robot can rotate about the y-axis in its frame by the angle θ. Thus, we can describe the motion of any point **p** on the base by applying a rotation matrix $\mathbf{R}_y(\theta)$ to it.

The lower arm is rotated about the z-axis in its own frame, but this frame must be shifted to the top of the base by a translation matrix $\mathbf{T}(0, h_1, 0)$, where h_1 is the height above the base to the point where the joint between the base and the lower arm is located. However, if the base has rotated, then we must also rotate the lower arm, using $\mathbf{R}_y(\theta)$. We can accomplish the positioning of the lower arm by applying $\mathbf{R}_y(\theta)\mathbf{T}(0, h_1, 0)\mathbf{R}_z(\phi)$ to the arm's vertices. We can interpret the matrix $\mathbf{R}_y(\theta)\mathbf{T}(0, h_1, 0)$ as the matrix that positions the lower arm *relative* to the object or world frame and $\mathbf{R}_z(\phi)$ as the matrix that positions the lower arm *relative* to the base. Equivalently, we can interpret these matrices as positioning the frames of the lower arm and base relative to some world frame, as shown in Figure 8.9.

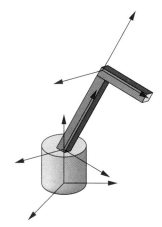

FIGURE 8.9 Movement of robot components and frames.

When we apply similar reasoning to the upper arm, we find that this arm has to be translated by a matrix $\mathbf{T}(0, h_2, 0)$ relative to the lower arm and then rotated by $\mathbf{R}_z(\psi)$. The matrix that controls the upper arm is thus $\mathbf{R}_y(\theta)\mathbf{T}(0, h_1, 0)\mathbf{R}_z(\phi)\mathbf{T}(0, h_2, 0)\mathbf{R}_z(\psi)$. The form of the display function for an OpenGL program to display the robot as a function of the joint angles (using the array `theta[3]` for θ, ϕ, and ψ) shows how we can alter the model-view matrix incrementally to display the various parts of the model efficiently:

```
void display()
{
    glClear(GL_COLOR_BUFFER_BIT);
    model_view = RotateY(theta[0]);
    base();
    model_view = model_view*Translate(0.0, BASE_HEIGHT, 0.0)
                          *RotateZ(theta[1]);
    lower_arm();
    model_view = model_view*Translate(0.0, LOWER_ARM_HEIGHT, 0.0)
                          *RotateZ(theta[2]);
    upper_arm();
    glutSwapBuffers();
}
```

Note that we have described the positioning of the arm independently of the details of the individual parts. As long as the positions of the joints do not change, we can alter the form of the robot by changing only the functions that draw the three parts. This separation makes it possible to write separate functions to describe the components and to animate the robot. Figure 8.10 shows the relationships among the parts of the robot arm as a tree. The complete program implements the structure and uses the mouse to animate the robot through a menu. It uses three parallelepipeds for the base and arms. If we use our cube code from Chapter 3 with an instance transformation for the parts, then the robot is rendered by the code:

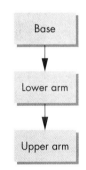

FIGURE 8.10 Tree structure for the robot arm in Figure 8.8.

```
mat4 instance;
mat4 model_view;

void base()
{
    instance = Translate(0.0, 0.5*BASE_HEIGHT, 0.0)
             *Scale(BASE_WIDTH, BASE_HEIGHT, BASE_WIDTH);
    glUniformMatrix4fv(model_view_loc, 16, GL_TRUE, model_view*instance);
    glDrawArrays(GL_TRIANGLES, 0, N);
}

void upper_arm()
{
    instance = Translate(0.0, 0.5*UPPER_ARM_HEIGHT, 0.0)
             *Scale(UPPER_ARM_WIDTH, UPPER_ARM_HEIGHT, UPPER_ARM_WIDTH);
```

```
        glUniformMatrix4fv(model_view_loc, 16, GL_TRUE, model_view*instance);
        glDrawArrays(GL_TRIANGLES, 0, N);
}

void lower_arm()
{
        instance = Translate(0.0, 0.5*LOWER_ARM_HEIGHT, 0.0)
                        *Scale(LOWER_ARM_WIDTH, LOWER_ARM_HEIGHT, LOWER_ARM_WIDTH);
        glUniformMatrix4fv(model_view_loc, 16, GL_TRUE, model_view*instance);
        glDrawArrays(GL_TRIANGLES, 0, N);
}
```

In each case, the instance transformation must scale the cube to the desired size, and because the cube vertices are centered at the origin, each cube must be raised to have its bottom in the place $y = 0$. The product of the model-view and instance transformations is sent to the vertex shader followed by the vertices (and colors if desired) for each part of the robot. Because the model-view matrix is different for each part of the robot, we render each part once its data have been sent to the GPU. Note that in this example, because we are using cubes for all the parts, we need to send the points to the GPU only once. However, if the parts were using different symbols, then we would need to use `glDrawArrays` in each drawing function.

Returning to the tree in Figure 8.10, we can look at it as a tree data structure of nodes and edges—as a graph. If we store all the necessary information in the nodes, rather than in the edges, then each node (Figure 8.11) must store at least three items:

1. A pointer to a function that draws the object represented by the node

2. A homogeneous-coordinate matrix that positions, scales, and orients this node (and its children) relative to the node's parent

3. Pointers to children of the node

Certainly, we can include other information in a node, such as a set of attributes (color, texture, material properties) that applies to the node. Drawing an object described by such a tree requires performing a tree **traversal**. That is, we must visit every node; at each node, we must compute the matrix that applies to the primitives pointed to by the node and must display these primitives. Our OpenGL program shows an incremental approach to this traversal.

This example is a simple one: There is only a single child for each of the parent nodes in the tree. The next example shows how we handle more complex models.

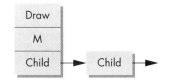

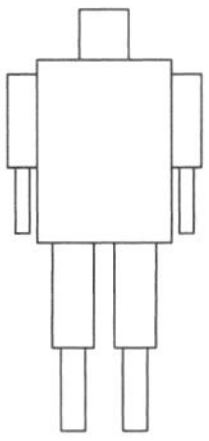

FIGURE 8.11 Node representation.

8.4 TREES AND TRAVERSAL

Figure 8.12 shows a boxlike representation of a humanoid that might be used for a robot model or in a virtual reality application. If we take the torso as the root element, we can represent this figure with the tree shown in Figure 8.13. Once we have positioned the torso, the position and orientation of the other parts of the model are determined by the set of joint angles. We can animate the figure by defining the motion of its joints. In a basic model, the knee and elbow joints might each have only

FIGURE 8.12 A humanoid figure.

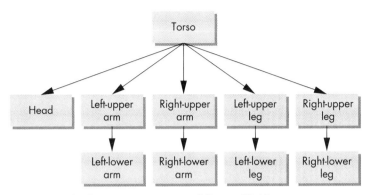

FIGURE 8.13 Tree representation of Figure 10.12.

a single degree of freedom, like the robot arm, whereas the joint at the neck might have two or three degrees of freedom.

Let's assume that we have functions, such as `head` and `left_upper_arm`, that draw the individual parts (symbols) in their own frames. We can now build a set of nodes for our tree by defining matrices that position each part relative to its parent, exactly as we did for the robot arm. If we assume that each body part has been defined at the desired size, each of these matrices is the concatenation of a translation matrix with a rotation matrix. We can show these matrices, as we do in Figure 8.14, by using the matrices to label the edges of the tree. Remember that each matrix represents the incremental change when we go from the parent to the child.

The interesting part of this example is how we do the traversal of the tree to draw the figure. In principle, we could use any tree-traversal algorithm, such as a depth-first or breadth-first search. Although in many applications it is insignificant which traversal algorithm is used, we will see that there are good reasons for always using the same algorithm for traversing our graphs. We will always traverse our trees left to right, depth first. That is, we start with the left branch, follow it to the left as deep

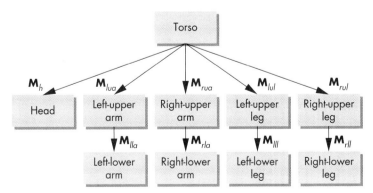

FIGURE 8.14 Tree with matrices.

as we can go, then go back up to the first right branch, and proceed recursively. This order of traversal is called a **pre-order traversal**.

We can write a tree-traversal function in one of two ways. We can do the traversal explicitly in the application code, using stacks to store the required matrices and attributes as we move through the tree. We can also do the traversal recursively. In this second approach, the code is simpler because the storage of matrices and attributes is done implicitly. We develop both approaches because both are useful and because their development yields further insights into how we can build graphics systems.

8.4.1 A Stack-Based Traversal

Consider the drawing of the figure by a function `figure`. This function might be called from the display callback or from a mouse callback in an animation that uses the mouse to control the joint angles. The model-view matrix, $\mathbf{M}$, in effect when this function is invoked, determines the position of the figure relative to the rest of the scene (and to the camera). The first node that we encounter results in the torso being drawn with $\mathbf{M}$ applied to all the torso's primitives. We then trace the leftmost branch of the tree to the node for the head. There we invoke the function `head` with the model-view matrix updated to $\mathbf{MM}_h$. Next, we back up to the torso node, then go down the subtree defining the left arm. This part looks just like the code for the robot arm; we draw the left-upper arm with the matrix $\mathbf{MM}_{lua}$ and the left-lower arm with matrix $\mathbf{MM}_{lua}\mathbf{M}_{lla}$. Then we move on to the right arm, left leg, and right leg. Each time we switch limbs, we must back up to the root and recover $\mathbf{M}$.

It is probably easiest to think in terms of the current transformation matrix of Chapter 3—the model-view matrix $\mathbf{C}$ that is applied to the primitives defined at a node.[2] The matrix $\mathbf{C}$ starts out as $\mathbf{M}$, is updated to $\mathbf{MM}_h$ for the head, and later to $\mathbf{MM}_{lul}\mathbf{M}_{lll}$, and so on. The application program must manipulate $\mathbf{C}$ before each call to a function defining a part of the figure. Note that as we back up the tree to start the right upper arm, we need $\mathbf{M}$ again. Rather than reforming it (or any other matrix we might need to reuse in a more complex model), we can store (push) it on a stack and recover it with pop. Here is a simple stack class with a capacity of 50 matrices:

```
class matrix_stack
{
   public:
      static const int MAX = 50;
      matrix_stack() {index = 0;}
      void push(const mat4& matrix);
      mat4 pop();
   private:
      mat4 matrices[MAX];
      int index;
};
```

---

2. We can ignore the projection matrix for now.

```
void matrix_stack::push(const mat4& matrix)
{
    matrices[index] = matrix;
    index++;
}

mat4 matrix_stack::pop()
{
    index--;
    return matrices[index];
}
```

Our traversal code will have translations and rotations intermixed with pushes and pops of the model-view matrix. Consider the code (without parameter values) for the beginning of the function figure:

```
mat4 model_view;
matrix_stack mvstack;
figure()
{
        mvstack.push(model_view);
        torso();
        model_view = model_view*Translate()*Rotate();
        head();

        model_view = mvstack.pop();
        mvstack.push(model_view);
        model_view = model_view*Translate()*Rotate();
        left_upper_arm();

        model_view = mvstack.pop();
        mvstack.push(model_view);
        model_view = Translate()*Rotate();
        left_lower_arm();

        model_view = mvstack.pop();
        mvstack.push(model_view);
        model_view = Translate()*Rotate();
        right_upper_arm();

        model_view = mvstack.pop();
        mvstack.push(model_view);
        .
        .
        .
}
```

The first push duplicates the current model-view matrix putting the copy on the top of the model-view–matrix stack. This method of pushing allows us to work immediately with the other transformations that alter the model-view matrix, knowing that we have preserved a copy on the stack. The following calls to `Translate` and `Rotate` determine $\mathbf{M}_h$ and concatenate it with the initial model-view matrix. We can then generate the primitives for the head. The subsequent pop recovers the original model-view matrix. Note that we must do another push to leave a copy of the original model-view matrix that we can recover when we come back to draw the right leg.

The functions for the individual parts are similar to the previous example. Here is the `torso` function:

```
void torso()
{
   mvstack.push(model_view);
   instance = Translate(0.0, 0.5*TORSO_HEIGHT,0.0)
                      *Scale(TORSO_WIDTH, TORSO_HEIGHT, TORSO_WIDTH);
   glUniformMatrix4fv(model_view_loc, 16, GL_TRUE, model_view*instance);
   colorcube();
   glDrawArrays(GL_TRIANGLES, 0, N);
   model_view = mvstack.pop();
}
```

Note the use of a push at the beginning and a pop at the end of the function. These serve to isolate the code and protect other parts of the program from being affected by state changes in this function. You should be able to complete this function by continuing in a similar manner.

Appendix A contains a complete program that implements this figure with a menu that will allow you to change the various joint angles. The individual parts are implemented using parallelepipeds, and the entire model can be shaded as we discussed in Chapter 5.

We have not considered how attributes such as color and material properties are handled by our traversal of a hierarchical model. Attributes are state variables: Once set, they remain in place until changed again. Hence, we must be careful as we traverse our tree. For example, suppose that within the code for `torso` we set the color to red and then within the code for `head` set the color to blue. If there are no other color changes, the color will still be blue as we traverse the rest of the tree and may remain blue after we leave the code for `figure`. Here is an example in which the particular traversal algorithm can make a difference, because the current state can be affected differently depending on the order in which the nodes are visited.

This situation may be disconcerting, but there is a solution. We can create other stacks that allow us to deal with attributes in a manner similar to our use of the model-view matrix. If we push the attributes on the attribute stack on entrance to the function `figure`, and pop on exit, we have restored the attributes to their original state. Moreover, we can use additional pushes and pops within `figure` to control how attributes are handled in greater detail.

In a more complex model, we can apply these ideas recursively. If, for example, we want to use a more detailed model of the head—one incorporating eyes, ears, a nose, and a mouth—then we could model these parts separately. The head would then itself be modeled hierarchically, and its code would include the pushing and popping of matrices and attributes.

Although we have discussed only trees, if two or more nodes call the same function, we really have a DAG, but DAGs present no additional difficulties.

Color Plates 22 and 27 show hierarchical models of robots and figures used in simulations. These objects were created with high-level interactive software that relies on our ability to traverse hierarchical structures to render the models.

The approach that we used to describe hierarchical objects is workable but has limitations. The code is explicit and relies on the application programmer to push and pop the required matrices and attributes. In reality, we implemented a stack-based representation of a tree. The code was hardwired for the particular example and thus would be difficult to extend or use dynamically. The code also does not make a clear distinction between building a model and rendering it. Although many application programmers write code in this form, we prefer to use it primarily to illustrate the flow of an OpenGL program that implements tree hierarchies. We now turn to a more general and powerful approach to working with tree-structured hierarchies.

8.5 USE OF TREE DATA STRUCTURES

Our second approach is to use a standard tree data structure to represent our hierarchy and then to render it with a traversal algorithm that is independent of the model. We use a **left-child, right-sibling** structure.

Consider the alternate representation of a tree in Figure 8.15. It is arranged such that all the elements at the same level are linked left to right. The children of a given node are represented as a second list arranged from the leftmost child to the rightmost. This second list points downward in Figure 8.15. This representation describes the structure of our hierarchical figure, but the structure still lacks the graphical information.

At each node, we must store the information necessary to draw the object: a function that defines the object and the homogeneous coordinate matrix that positions the object relative to its parent. Consider the following node structure:

```
typedef struct treenode
{
    mat m;
    void (*f)();
    struct treenode *sibling;
    struct treenode *child;
} treenode;
```

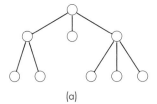

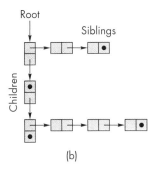

FIGURE 8.15 (a) Tree. (b) Left-child, right-sibling representation.

The array m stores a 4×4 homogeneous coordinate matrix. When we render the node, this matrix must first multiply the current model-view matrix; then the function f, which includes the graphics primitives, is executed. We also store a pointer to the sibling node on the right and a pointer to the leftmost child. If one or the other does not exist, then we store the null pointer (NULL). For our figure, we specify 10 nodes corresponding to the 10 parts of our model:

```
treenode torso_node, head_node, lua_node, rua_node, lll_node,
        rll_node, lla_node, rla_node, rul_node, lul_node;
```

We can specify the nodes either in the main function or in myinit. For example, consider the root of the figure tree—the torso node. It can be oriented by a rotation about the y-axis. We can form the required rotation matrix using our matrix functions, and the function to be executed after forming the matrix is torso. The torso node has no siblings, and its leftmost child is the head node, so the torso node is given as follows:

```
torso_node.m = RotateY(theta[0]);
torso_node.f = torso;
torso_node.sibling = NULL;
torso_node.child = &head_node;
```

If we use a cube as the basis for the torso, the drawing function might look as follows:

```
void torso()
{
   mvstack.push(model_view);
   instance = Translate(0.0, 0.5*TORSO_HEIGHT, 0.0)
                     *Scale(TORSO_WIDTH, TORSO_HEIGHT, TORSO_WIDTH);
   glUniformMatrix4fv(model_view_loc, 16, GL_TRUE, model_view*instance);
   colorcube();
   glDrawArrays(GL_TRIANGLES, 0, N);
   model_view = mvstack.pop();
}
```

The instance transformation first scales the cube to the desired size and then translates it so its bottom lies in the plane $y = 0$.

The torso is the root node of the figure, so its code is a little different from the other nodes. Consider the specification for the left-upper arm node:

```
lua_node.m = Translate(-(TORSO_WIDTH+UPPER_ARM_WIDTH),
                        0.9*TORSO_HEIGHT, 0.0)*RotateX(theta[3]);
lua_node.f = left_upper_arm;
lua_node.sibling =  &rua_node;
lua_node.child = &lla_node;
```

and the left_upper_arm function

```
void left_upper_arm()
{
   mvstack.push(model_view);
   instance = Translate(0.0, 0.5*UPPER_ARM_HEIGHT, 0.0)
                      *Scale(UPPER_ARM_WIDTH, UPPER_ARM_HEIGHT, UPPER_ARM_WIDTH);
   glUniformMatrix4fv(model_view_loc, 16, GL_TRUE, model_view*instance);
   colorcube();
   glDrawArrays(GL_TRIANGLES, 0, N);
   model_view = mvstack.pop();
}
```

The upper arm must be translated relative to the torso and its own width to get the center of rotation in the correct place. The node for the upper arm has both a sibling (the upper right arm) and a child (the lower left arm). To render the left upper arm, we first compute an instance transformation that gives it the desired size and positions so its bottom is also on the plane $y = 0$. This instance matrix is concatenated with the current model-view matrix to position the upper left arm correctly in object coordinates. The other nodes are specified in a similar manner.

Traversing the tree in the same order (preorder traversal) as in Section 8.4 can be accomplished by the recursive code as follows:

```
void traverse(treenode* root)
{
   if (root == NULL) return;
   mvstack.push(model_view);
   model_view = model_view*root->m;
   root->f();
   if (root->child != NULL) traverse(root->child);
   model_view = mvstack.pop();
   if (root->sibling != NULL) traverse(root->sibling);
}
```

To render a nonnull node, we first save the graphics state with `mvpush(model_view)`. We then use the matrix at the node to modify the model-view matrix. We then draw the objects at the node with the function pointed to by `f`. Finally, we traverse all the children recursively. Note that because we have multiplied the model-view matrix by the local matrix, we are passing this altered matrix to the children. For the siblings, however, we do not want to use this matrix, because each has its own local matrix. Hence, we must return to the original state (`mvstack.pop()`) before traversing the children. If we are changing attributes within nodes, either we can push and pop attributes within the rendering functions, or we can push the attributes when we push the model-view matrix.

One of the nice aspects of this traversal method is that it is completely independent of the particular tree; thus, we can use a generic display callback such as the following:

```
void display(void)
{
  glClear(GL_COLOR_BUFFER_BIT|GL_DEPTH_BUFFER_BIT);
  traverse(&torso_node);
  glutSwapBuffers();
}
```

We again animate the figure by controlling individual joint angles, which are selected from a menu and are incremented and decremented through the mouse buttons. Thus, the dynamics of the program are in the mouse callback, which changes an angle, recomputes the appropriate node matrix, and then posts a redisplay:

```
mymouse(int button, int state, int x, int y)
{
    if (button == GLUT_LEFT_BUTTON && state == GLUT_DOWN)
    {
        theta[angle] += 5.0;
        if (theta[angle] > 360.0 ) theta[angle] -= 360.0;
    }
    if (button == GLUT_RIGHT_BUTTON && state == GLUT_DOWN)
    {
        theta[angle] -= 5.0;
        if (theta[angle] < 360.0 ) theta[angle] += 360.0;
    }

    mvstack.push(model_view);
    switch (angle)
    {
    case 0 :
        torso_node.m = RotateY(theta[0]);
        break;
    case 1 : case 2 :
        head_node.m = Translate(0.0, TORSO_HEIGHT+0.5*HEAD_HEIGHT, 0.0)
            *RotateX(theta[1])*RotateY(theta[2])
            *Translate(0.0, -0.5*HEAD_HEIGHT, 0.0);
        break;
    // rest of cases
    }
}
```

There is one more feature that we can add to show the flexibility of this approach. As the program executes, we can add or remove dynamic nodes rather than static nodes. We can create dynamic nodes with the following code:

```
typedef treenode* tree_ptr;
tree_ptr torso_ptr = new treenode;
```

Nodes are defined as before. For example,

```
lua_node->m = Translate(-(TORSO_WIDTH+UPPER_ARM_WIDTH),
                        0.9*TORSO_HEIGHT, 0.0)*RotateX(theta[3]);
lua_node->f = left_upper_arm;
lua_node->sibling = &rua_node;
lua_node->child = &lla_node;
```

with the traversal by

```
traverse(torso_ptr);
```

For our figure example, there is no particular advantage to the dynamic approach. In a more general setting, however, we can use the dynamic approach to create structures that change interactively. For example, we can use this form to write an application that will let us edit figures, adding and removing parts as desired. This type of implementation is the basis for the scene trees that we discuss in Section 8.8. Color Plate 27 shows one frame of an animation with the figure using cylinders for most of the parts and adding lighting.

Note that as we have coded our examples, there is a fixed traversal order for the graph. If we had applied some other traversal algorithm, we could have produced a different image if we made any state changes within the graph, such as changing transformations or attributes. We can avoid some of these potential problems if we are careful to isolate parts of our code by pushing and popping attributes and matrices in each node (although there is a performance penalty for doing so too often).

8.6 ANIMATION

The models that we developed for our two examples—the robot arm and the figure—are **articulated**: The models consist of rigid parts connected by joints. We can make such models change their positions in time—animate them—by altering the values of a small set of parameters. Hierarchical models allow us to model the compound motions incorporating the physical relationships among the parts of the model. What we have not discussed is how to alter the parameters over time so as to achieve the desired motion.

Of the many approaches to animation, a few basic techniques are of particular importance when we work with articulated figures. These techniques arise both from traditional hand animation and from robotics.

In the case of our robot model, consider the problem of moving the tip of the upper arm from one position to another. The model has three degrees of freedom—the three angles that we can specify. Although each set of angles has a unique position for the tip, the converse is not true. Given a desired position of the tip of the arm, there may be no set of angles that place the tip as desired, a single set of angles that yields the specified position, or multiple sets of angles that place the tip at the desired position.

Studying **kinematics** involves describing the position of the parts of the model based on only the joint angles. We can use our hierarchical-modeling methods either to determine positions numerically or to find explicit equations that give the position of any desired set of points in the model in terms of the joint angles. Thus, if θ is an array of the joint angles and $\mathbf{p}$ is an array whose elements are the vertices in our model, a kinematic model is of the form

$$\mathbf{p} = f(\theta).$$

Likewise, if we specify the rates of change of the joint angles—the joint velocities—then we can obtain velocities of points on the model.

The kinematic model neglects matters such as the effects of inertia and friction. We could derive more complex differential equations that describe the dynamic behavior of the model in terms of applied forces—a topic that is studied in robotics.

Whereas both kinematics and dynamics are ways of describing the forward behavior of the model, in animation we are more concerned with **inverse kinematics** and **inverse dynamics**: Given a desired state of the model, how can we adjust the joint angles so as to achieve this position? There are two major concerns. First, given an environment including the robot and other objects, we must determine whether there exists a sequence of angles that achieves the desired state. There may be no single-valued function of the form

$$\theta = f^{-1}(\mathbf{p}).$$

For a given $\mathbf{p}$, in general we cannot tell if there is any θ that corresponds to this position or if there are multiple values of θ that satisfy the equation. Even if we can find a sequence of joint angles, we must ensure that as we go through this sequence our model does not hit any obstacles or violate any physical constraints. Although, for a model as simple as our robot, we might be able to find equations that give the joint angles in terms of the position, we cannot do so in general, because the forward equations do not have unique inverses. The figure model, which has 11 degrees of freedom, should give you an idea of how difficult it is to solve this problem.

A basic approach to overcoming these difficulties comes from traditional hand-animation techniques. In **key-frame animation**, the animator positions the objects at a set of times—the key frames. In hand animation, animators then can fill in the remaining frames, a process called **in-betweening**. In computer graphics, we can automate in-betweening by interpolating the joint angles between the key frames or, equivalently, using simple approximations to obtain the required dynamic equations between key frames. Using GPUs, much of the work required for in-betweening can now be automated as part of the pipeline, often using the programmability of recent GPUs. We can also use the spline curves that we develop in Chapter 10 to give smooth methods of going between key frames. Although we can develop code for the interpolation, both a skillful (human) animator and good interactive methods are crucial if we are to choose the key frames and the positions of objects in these frames.

8.7 GRAPHICAL OBJECTS

Although we have introduced multiple graphics paradigms, our development has been heavily based on a pipeline implementation of the synthetic-camera model. We made this choice because we want to support interactive three-dimensional applications with currently available hardware and software. Consequently, we have emphasized a mode of graphics in which geometric data are placed on the GPU and rendered to the screen almost immediately afterward. We have not made full use of the fact that once data are on the GPU, they can be reused without regenerating them in the application.

In addition, our desire to present the basics of implementation has led us to develop graphics in a manner that was never far from the details of the implementation. For all its benefits, this approach has not let us exploit many high-level alternatives to developing graphical applications.

Now we move to a higher level of abstraction and introduce two major concepts. First, we expand our notion of objects from geometric objects, such as polygons and vectors, to include most of the elements within a graphics program, such as viewers, lights, and material properties. Second, we focus on objects that exist even after their images have been drawn and even if we never display them. We investigate other approaches, such as the use of classes in C++ or structures in C. Although the OpenGL API does not support this approach directly, we do not have to abandon OpenGL. We still use OpenGL for rendering, and we regard what we develop as a software layer on top of OpenGL.

8.7.1 Methods, Attributes, and Messages

Our programs manipulate data. The data may be in many forms, ranging from numbers to strings to the geometric entities that we build in our applications. In traditional imperative programming, the programmer writes code to manipulate the data, usually through functions. The data are passed to a function through the function's parameters. Data are returned in a similar manner. To manipulate the data sent to it, the function must be aware of how those data are organized. Consider, for example, the cube that we have used in many of our previous examples. We have seen that we can model it in various ways, including with vertex pointers, edge lists, and lists of polygon vertices. The application programmer may care little about which model is used and may prefer to regard the cube as an atomic entity or an *object*. In addition, she may care little about the details of how the cube is rendered to the screen: which shading model or which polygon-fill algorithm is used. She can assume that the cube "knows how to render itself" and that conceptually the rendering algorithm is tied to the object itself. In some ways, OpenGL supports this view by using the state of the graphics system to control rendering. For example, the color of the cube, its orientation, and the lights that are applied to its surfaces can all be part of the state of the graphics system and may not depend on how the cube is modeled.

FIGURE 8.16   Imperative programming paradigm.

FIGURE 8.17   Object-oriented paradigm.

However, if we are working with a physical cube, we might find this view a bit strange. The location of a physical cube is tied to the physical object, as are its color, size, and orientation. Although we could use OpenGL to tie some properties to a virtual cube—through pushing and popping various attributes and matrices— the underlying programming model does not support these ideas well. For example, a function that transforms the cube would have to know exactly how the cube is represented and would work as shown in Figure 8.16.

The application programmer would write a function that would take as its inputs a pointer to the cube's data and the parameters of the transformation. It would then manipulate the data for the cube and return control to the application program (perhaps also returning some values).

Object-oriented design and object-oriented programming look at manipulation of objects in a fundamentally different manner. Even in the early days of object-oriented programming, languages such as Smalltalk recognized that computer graphics provides excellent examples of the power of the object-oriented approach. Recent trends within the software community indicate that we can combine our pipeline orientation with an object orientation to build even more expressive and high-performance graphics systems.

Object-oriented programming languages define **objects** as modules with which we build programs. These modules include the data that define the module, such as the vertices for our cube, properties of the module (**attributes**), and the functions (**methods**) that manipulate the module and its attributes. We send **messages** to objects to invoke a method. This model is shown in Figure 8.17.

The advantage to the writer of the application program is that she now does not need to know how the cube is represented; she needs to know only what functionality the cube object supports—what messages she can send to it.

Although the C `struct` has some of the properties of objects, the C language does not support the full power of an object-oriented approach. In C++, the `struct` is replaced with the `class`. C++ classes have two important properties that we can exploit to get the flavor of the object-oriented approach. C programmers should have no trouble understanding these concepts.

8.7.2 A Cube Object

Suppose that we wish to create a cube object in C that has a color attribute and a homogeneous coordinate transformation associated with it. In C, we could use a `struct` of the following form:

```
struct  cube
{
   float color[3];
   float matrix[4][4];

/* implementation goes here */

}
```

The implementation part of the structure contains the information on how a cube is actually represented. Typically, an application programmer does not need this information and needs to change only the color or matrix associated with the cube.

Once the `struct` has been defined, **instances** of the cube object can be created as are other basic data types:

```
cube a, b;
```

Attributes that are part of the class definition can be changed for each instance of the cube. Thus, we can set the color of cube `a` to red as follows:

```
a.color[0] = 1.0;
a.color[1] = a.color[2] = 0.0;
```

It should be clear how such a `struct` can be implemented within an OpenGL system.

Although we have created a retained cube object, we are limited in how we can manipulate it or render it. We could write a function that would render the cube through code such as

```
render_cube(a);
```

Or we could rotate the cube by invoking the method

```
rotate_cube(a, theta, d);
```

where d is the vector about which we wish to rotate.

This approach is workable but has limitations. One is that we need separate rendering and rotation functions for each type of object. A second is that the implementation part of the code is accessible to application programs. C++ classes solve both of these problems. A C++ class can have public, private, and protected members. The **public members** are similar to the members of C struct and can be altered by any function. The **private members** neither are visible to nor can be altered by a function that uses the class. The **protected members** are visible to classes within the same hierarchy. A programmer can also declare classes to be **friends** to give access to specific classes. Thus, in C++, we define the cube as

```
class  cube
{
 public:
   vec4 color;
   mat4 model;
 private:

/* implementation goes here */

}
```

thereby protecting and hiding the details of the implementation. Furthermore, C++ classes allow us to have members that are functions or methods. Once we add such functions, the object-orientation becomes clearer. Suppose that we add member functions to the public part of the cube class as follows:

```
void render();
void translate(float x, float y, float z);
void rotate(float theta, float axis_x, float axis_y,
            float axis_z);
```

Now an application program could create, translate, rotate, and render a cube through the following code:

```
cube a;
a.rotate(45.0, 1.0, 0.0, 0.0);
a.translate(1.0, 2.0, 3.0);
a.render();
```

Conceptually, this code assumes that an instance of the cube "knows" how to rotate itself and that by executing the code a.rotate, we are sending a message to a cube object that we would like it to carry out such a rotation. We could easily write an implementation of the rotation and translation methods that would use our rotation and translation functions to change the matrix member of the cube object.

It is less clear what a function call such as a.render really does. Each instance of an object persists and can be altered by further code in the application program. What is most important is that we have created an object that continues to exist somewhere in our system in a form that is not visible to the application program. The attributes of the object are also in the system and can be altered by functions such as `rotate`. The `render` function causes the object to be redrawn using the object's state rather than the system's current state. Hence, the render step involves sending data to the GPU with the necessary vertex attribute data coming from the implementation part of the object and using a function such as `glDrawArrays` to display the object.

8.7.3 Implementing the Cube Object

As an example of the choices that go into developing the private part of an object, let's consider the cube. One basic implementation would be similar to what we did for our rotating cube examples; we look at the cube as comprised of six faces, each of which consists of two triangles. Thus, the private part of the cube might be of the form

```
private:
    vec4 points[36];
    vec4 colors[36];
```

Note that we are allowing for different colors at each vertex. The constructor for a cube would set values for the points with a default of a unit cube.

We can do far better if we include more information in the implementation. Of particular interest is information that might help in the rendering. Thus, whereas OpenGL will do hidden-surface removal correctly through the z-buffer algorithm, we can often do much better by eliminating objects earlier through a separate visibility test, as we will discuss in Section 8.11. To support this functionality, we might want to include information that determines a bounding volume for the object. For example, we can include the axis-aligned bounding box for objects within the private part of the code. For polygonal objects, we need simply save the minimum and maximum of the x, y, and z of the vertices (after they have been transformed by any transformation matrix stored with the object).

8.7.4 Objects and Hierarchy

One of the major advantages of object-oriented design is the ability to reuse code and to build more sophisticated objects from a small set of simple objects. As in Section 8.4, we can build a figure object from cubes and have multiple instances of this new object, each with its own color, size, location, and orientation. A class for the humanoid figure could refer to the classes for arms and legs; the class for a car could refer to classes for wheels and a chassis. Thus, we would once more have tree-like representations similar to those that we developed in Section 8.5.

Often in object-oriented design, we want the representations to show relationships more complex than the parent–child relationship that characterizes trees. As we have used trees, the structure is such that the highest level of complexity is at the root and the relationship between a parent and child is a "has-a" relationship. Thus, the stick figure has two arms and two legs, whereas the car has four wheels and a chassis.

We can look at hierarchy in a different manner, with the simplest objects being the top of the hierarchy and the relationship between parents and children being an "is-a" relationship. This type of hierarchy is typical of taxonomies. A mammal is an animal. A human is a mammal. We used this relationship in describing projections. A parallel projection is a planar geometric projection; an oblique projection is a parallel projection. "Has-a" relationships allow us to define multiple complex objects from simpler objects and also allow the more complex object to inherit properties from the simpler object. Thus, if we write the code for a parallel projection, the oblique-projection code can use this code and refine only the parts that are necessary to convert the general parallel projection to an oblique one. For geometric objects, we can define base objects with a default set of properties such as their color and material properties. An application programmer could then use these properties or change them in subobjects. These concepts are supported by languages such as C++ that allow for subclasses and inheritance.

8.7.5 Geometric Objects

Suppose that we now want to build an object-oriented graphics system. What objects should we include? Although it is clear that we want to have objects such as points, vectors, polygons, rectangles, and triangles (possibly using subclasses), it is less clear how we should deal with attributes, light sources, and viewers. For example, should a material property be associated with an object such as a cube, or is it a separate object? The answer can be either or both. We could create a cube class in which there is a member for each of the ambient, diffuse, and specular material properties that we introduced with the Phong model in Chapter 5. We could also define a material class using code such as the following:

```
class material
{
 public:
   vec4 specular;
   float shininess;
   vec4 diffuse;
   vec4 ambient;
}
```

We could then assign the material to a geometric object through a member function of the cube class as follows:

```
cube a;
material b;
a.setMaterial(b);
```

Light sources are geometric objects—they have position and orientation among their features—and we can easily add a light source object:

```
class light
{
  public:
     boolean type;
     boolean near;
     vec4 position;
     vec4 orientation;
     vec4 specular;
     vec4 diffuse;
     vec4 ambient;
}
```

Once we have built up a collection of geometric objects, we can use it to describe a scene. To take advantage of the hierarchical relationships that we have introduced, we develop a new tree structure called a **scene graph**.

8.8 SCENE GRAPHS

If we think about what goes into describing a scene, we can see that in addition to our graphical primitives and geometric objects derived from these primitives, we have other objects, such as lights and a camera. These objects may also be defined by vertices and vectors and may have attributes, such as color, that are similar to the attributes associated with geometric primitives. It is the totality of these objects that describes a scene, and there may be hierarchical relationships among these objects. For example, when a primitive is defined in a program, the camera parameters that exist at that time are used to form the image. If we alter the camera lens between the definition of two geometric objects, we may produce an image in which each object is viewed differently. Although we cannot create such an image with a real camera, the example points out the power of our graphics systems. We can extend our use of tree data structures to describe these relationships among geometric objects, cameras, lights, and attributes.

Knowing that we can write a graphical application program to traverse a graph, we can expand our notion of the contents of a graph to describe an entire scene. One possibility is to use a tree data structure and to include various attributes at each node—in addition to the instance matrix and a pointer to the drawing function. Another possibility is to allow new types of nodes, such as attribute-definition nodes and matrix-transformation nodes. Consider the tree in Figure 8.18. Here we have set up individual nodes for the colors and for the model-view matrices. The place where there are branches at the top can be considered a special type of node, a **group node** whose function is to isolate the two children. The group node allows us to preserve the state that exists at the time that we enter a node and thus isolates the state of the subtree beginning at a group node from the rest of the tree. Using our preorder traversal algorithm, the corresponding application code is of the following form:

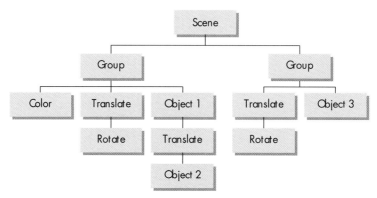

FIGURE 8.18   Scene tree.

```
pushAttrib
pushMatrix
   color
   translate
   rotate
   object1
  translate
   object2
popMatrix
pushMatrix
   translate
   rotate
   object3
popMatrix
popAttrib
```

The group nodes correspond to the OpenGL push and pop functions. This code preserves and restores both the attributes and the model-view matrix before exiting. It sets a drawing color that applies to the rest of the tree and traverses the tree in a manner similar to the figure example.

We can go further and note that we can use the attribute and matrix stacks to store the viewing conditions; thus, we can create a camera node in the tree. Although we probably do not want a scene in which individual objects are viewed with different cameras, we may want to view the same set of objects with multiple cameras, producing, for example, the multiview orthographic projections and isometric view that are used by architects and engineers. Such images can be created with a scene graph that has multiple cameras.

The scene graph we have just described is equivalent to an OpenGL program in the sense that we can use the tree to generate the program in a totally mechanical fashion. This approach was taken by Open Inventor and later by Open Scene Graph (OSG), both object-oriented APIs that were built on top of OpenGL. Open Inventor and OSG programs build, manipulate, and render a scene graph. Execution of a program causes traversal of the scene graph, which in turn executes graphics functions that are implemented in OpenGL.

The notion of scene graphs couples nicely with the object-oriented paradigm introduced in Section 8.7. We can regard all primitives, attributes, and transformations as software objects, and we can define classes to manipulate these entities. From this perspective, we can make use of concepts such as data encapsulation to build up scenes of great complexity with simple programs that use predefined software objects. We can even support animations through software objects that appear as nodes in the scene graph but cause parameters to change and the scene to be redisplayed. Although, in Open Inventor, the software objects are rendered using OpenGL, the scene graph itself is a database that includes all the elements of the scene. OpenGL is the rendering engine that allows the database to be converted to an image, but it is not used in the specification of the scene. Game engines employ a similar strategy in which the game play modifies a scene graph that can be traversed and rendered at an interactive rate.

Graphics software systems are evolving to the configuration shown in Figure 8.19. OpenGL is the rendering engine. It usually sits on top of another layer known as the **hardware abstraction layer** (**HAL**), which is a virtual machine that communicates with the physical hardware. Above OpenGL is an object-oriented layer that supports scene graphs and a storage mechanism. User programs can be written for any of the layers, depending on what facilities are required by the application.

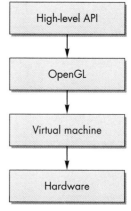

FIGURE 8.19 Modern graphics architecture.

8.9 OPEN SCENE GRAPH

Open Scene Graph is probably the most popular of the full scene graph APIs and provides much of the functionality lacking in our example. In addition to supporting a wider variety of nodes, there are two additional concepts that are key to OSG.

First, one of the benefits of a higher level of software than OpenGL is that such software can balance the workload between the CPU and the graphics processor. Consider how we process geometry in OpenGL. An application produces primitives that are specified through sets of vertices. As we have seen, OpenGL's main concern is rendering. All geometric primitives pass down at least part of the pipeline. It is only at the end of vertex processing that primitives that lie outside the view volume are clipped out. If a primitive is blocked from the viewer by another opaque geometric object and cannot appear in the final image, it nevertheless passes through most of the pipeline and only during hidden-surface removal will it be eliminated. Although present GPUs can process millions of vertices per second, many applications have such complex geometry that even these GPUs cannot render the geometry at a sufficiently high frame rate. OSG uses two strategies, occlusion culling and level of detail rendering, to lower the rendering load.

Occlusion culling seeks to eliminate objects that cannot be visible because they are blocked by other objects before they enter the rendering pipeline. In Figure 8.20,

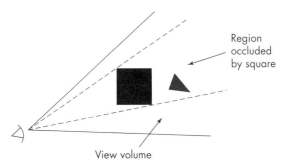

FIGURE 8.20   Occlusion.

we see that the square lies in the view volume and blocks the triangle from view. Although the z-buffer algorithm would yield a correct rendering, because OpenGL processes each object independently it cannot discover the occlusion. However, all the geometry is stored in the OSG scene graph, as is the information on the viewer. Hence, OSG can use one of many algorithms to go through the scene graph and cull objects. We will examine an approach to occlusion culling that uses binary spatial partitioning in Section 8.11.

The second strategy is based on an argument similar to the one that we used to justify mipmaps for texture mapping. If we can tell that a geometric object will render to a small area of the display, we do not need to render all the detail that might be its geometry. Once more, the necessary information can be placed in the scene graph. OSG has a level-of-detail node whose children are the models of an object with different levels of geometric complexity. The application program sets up these nodes. During the traversal of the scene graph, OSG determines which level of detail to use.

Level-of-detail rendering is important not only to OSG but also to real-time applications such as interactive games that are built using proprietary game engines. Game engines are very large complex software objects that may comprise millions of lines of code. Although a game engine may use OpenGL or DirectX to render the graphics and make extensive use of programmable shaders, a game engine also has to handle the game play and manage complex interactions that might involve multiple players. Game engines use scene graphs to maintain all the needed information, including the geometry and texture maps, and use level of detail extensively in processing their scene graphs. In the next section, we will examine some related issues involving graphics over the Internet.

The second major concept is how the scene graph is processed for each frame. OSG uses three traversals rather than the single traversal in our simple scene graph. The goal of the traversal process is to create a list of the geometry that can be rendered. This list contains the geometry at the best level of detail and only the geometry that has survived occlusion culling. In addition, the geometry has been sorted so that translucent surfaces will be rendered correctly.

The first traversal deals with updates to the scene graph that might be generated by callbacks that handle interaction or changes to the geometry from the application program. The second traversal builds a list of the geometry that has to be rendered. This traversal uses occlusion culling, translucency, level of detail, and bounding volumes. The final traversal goes through the geometry list and issues the necessary OpenGL calls to render the geometry.

8.10 GRAPHICS AND THE INTERNET

Before leaving the subject of scene graphs, we consider some of the issues that govern how graphics can be conveyed over the Internet. Of particular interest are multiplayer games that can involve thousands of concurrent participants, each of whom potentially can affect the scene graph of any other participant, and applications with large models that may be distributed over multiple sites.

The Internet has had an enormous effect on virtually all communications and computer applications. It allows us to communicate information in a multitude of forms and makes possible new methods of interaction. In order to use the Internet to its full potential, we need to move graphical information efficiently, to build applications that are viewable from many locations, and to access resources distributed over many sites. OpenGL and its extensions have had a major influence on the development of net-based three-dimensional applications and standards. We will take a graphics-oriented approach and see what extensions we need to develop Internet applications. Some of the concepts will be familiar. We use the client–server model to allow efficient rendering. We also look at how we can implement graphical applications that are independent of the API.

8.10.1 Hypermedia and HTML

As the Internet evolved, a series of standard high-level protocols became widely accepted for transferring mail, files, and other types of information. Systems such as the X Window system allowed users to open windows on remote systems and to transfer basic graphical information. As the Internet grew, however, more and more information became publicly available, and users needed more sophisticated methods to share information that was stored in a distributed way in diverse formats.

There are three key elements necessary for sharing such information: (1) an addressing scheme that allows users to identify resources over the network, (2) a method of encoding information in addition to simple text, such as pictures and references (or **links**) to other resources, and (3) a method of searching for resources interactively.

The first two needs were addressed by researchers at the European Particle Physics Center (CERN), who created the World Wide Web, which is essentially a networked hypertext system. Resources—files—are identified by a unique **Uniform Resource Locator** (**URL**) that consists of three parts: the protocol for transferring the document, the server where the document is located, and the location on the server where the document is to be found. For example, the URL for support for this text can be found at http://www.cs.unm.edu/~angel/BOOK. The first part (http) indicates that the information will be transferred using the hypertext transfer protocol http. The second part (www.cs.unm.edu) identifies the server as the World Wide Web site of the Computer Science Department at the University of New Mexico. The final part indicates that the information is stored in user account angel under the directory public_html/BOOK. Because no document is indicated, a default document—the home page—will be displayed.

The second contribution of CERN was the **Hypertext Markup Language** (**HTML**), which provided a simple way to describe a document consisting of text, references to other documents (links), and images. HTML documents are text documents, typically in ASCII code or one of the standard extended character sets.

The combination of URL addressing and HTML documents provided a way of making resources available. But until the National Center for SuperComputer Applications (NCSA) came up with its browser, Mosaic, it was not easy for a user to find resources and to search the Web. **Browsers** are interactive programs that allow the user to search for and download documents on the Web. Mosaic, and later Netscape Navigator, opened the door to "surfing" the Web.

8.10.2 Java and Applets

One issue with interactive computer graphics on the Internet is the heterogenous collection of computer hardware and operating systems. An application programmer cannot create an application that will execute on any machine connected to the Web, even if they use an industry standard API like OpenGL.

Java solves a portion of this problem by creating a machine in software that can be implemented on any computer. Java programs are compiled into **byte code** that can be run on any Java machine, regardless of what the underlying hardware is. Thus, the client and server exchange byte code over the Web. Small programs in byte code, called **applets**, are understood by the standard Web browsers and have added a tremendous amount of dynamic behavior to the Web.

8.10.3 Interactive Graphics and the Web

While HTML is useful for structuring information for layout on a rendered Web page, until HTML version 5 it lacked any rendering capabilities. Most often, any interactive rendering that was done in a browser was originally done using a Java applet; however, the requirement of downloading an applet combined with support of Java virtual machines dimished Java's promise of application portability, particularly when related to three-dimensional computer graphics.

As Web browsers became more capable of supporting various formats, other technologies evolved. Adobe's Flash technology uses a plugin to a Web browser to provide interactivity, but it lacks (at the time of this writing) a comprehensive solution for doing three-dimensional graphics, with most of its focus on rendering video or simple user interfaces.

Another technology that evolved was JavaScript. JavaScript is a derivative language of Java that is interpreted and executed by the Web browser, as compared to a virtual machine plugin. This allows tighter integration of normal Web page rendering, as interactive, user-controlled rendering. Once again, however, JavaScript's rendering capabilities were mostly focused on two-dimensional operations, and most three-dimensional renderings were done through software renderers implemented in JavaScript. Until recently, there wasn't a widely adopted standard for interactive three-dimensional graphics.

8.10.4 WebGL

WebGL is a derivative of OpenGL (or more specifically, OpenGL ES version 2.0, the embedded system version of OpenGL). It provides JavaScript bindings for OpenGL functions and allows an HTML page using WebGL to render using any GPU resources available in the system where the Web browser is running.

WebGL is currently under development by the Khronos Group (the same industry consortium that develops OpenGL) at the time of this writing. It integrates the rendering capabilities of HTML5's Canvas element. As with modern OpenGL applications, all rendering is controlled by vertex and fragment shaders.

8.11 OTHER TREE STRUCTURES

Tree and DAG structures provide powerful tools to describe scenes; trees are also used in a variety of other ways in computer graphics, of which we consider three. The first is the use of expression trees to describe an object hierarchy for solid objects; the other two describe spatial hierarchies that we can use to increase the efficiency of many rendering algorithms.

8.11.1 CSG Trees

The polygonal representation of objects that we have used has many strengths and a few weaknesses. The most serious weakness is that polygons describe only the surfaces that enclose the interior of a three-dimensional object, such as a polyhedron. In CAD applications, this limitation causes difficulties whenever we must employ any volumetric properties of the graphical object, such as its weight or its moment of inertia. In addition, because we display an object by drawing its edges or surfaces, there can be ambiguities in the display. For example, the wireframe shown in Figure 8.21 can be interpreted either as a cube with a hole through it created by removal of a cylinder or as a solid cube composed of two different materials.

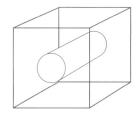

FIGURE 8.21 Wireframe that has two possible interpretations.

Constructive solid geometry (CSG) addresses these difficulties. Assume that we start with a set of atomic solid geometric entities, such as parallelepipeds, cylinders, and spheres. The attributes of these objects can include surface properties, such as color or reflectivity, but also volumetric properties, such as size and density. In describing scenes of such objects, we consider those points in space that constitute each object. Equivalently, each object is a set of points, and we can use set algebra to form new objects from these solid primitives.

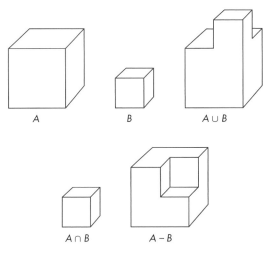

FIGURE 8.22   Set operations.

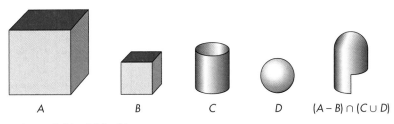

FIGURE 8.23   CSG object.

CSG modeling uses three set operations: union, intersection, and set difference. The **union** of two sets A and B, written $A \cup B$, consists of all points that are either in A or in B. The **intersection** of A and B, $A \cap B$, is the set of all points that are in both A and B. The **set difference**, $A - B$, is the set of points that are in A and are not in B. Figure 8.22 shows two objects and possible objects created by the three set operations.

Objects are described by algebraic expressions. The expression $(A - B) \cap (C \cup D)$ might describe an object such as the one illustrated in Figure 8.23.

Typically, we store and parse algebraic expressions using expression trees, where internal nodes store operations and terminal nodes store operands. For example, the tree in Figure 8.24 is a CSG tree that represents the object $(A - B) \cap (C \cup D)$ in Figure 8.23. We can evaluate or render the CSG tree by a **postorder** traversal; that is, we recursively evaluate the tree to the left of a node and the tree on the right of the node, and finally use these values to evaluate the node itself. Rendering of objects in CSG often is done with a variant of ray tracing; see Exercise 8.10 and Chapter 11.

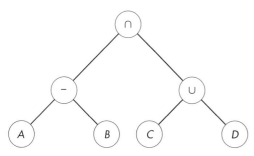

FIGURE 8.24   CSG tree.

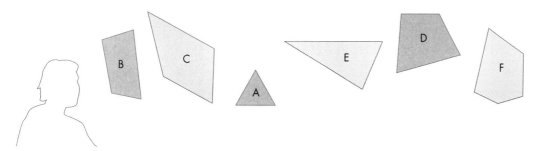

FIGURE 8.25   Collection of polygons and a viewer.

8.11.2 BSP Trees

Scene graphs and CSG trees describe hierarchical relationships among the parts of an object. We can also use trees to describe the world object space and encapsulate the spatial relationships among groups of objects. These relationships can lead to fast methods of **visibility testing** to determine which objects might be seen by a camera, thus avoiding processing all objects with tests such as the z-buffer algorithm. These techniques have become very important in real-time animations for computer games.

One approach to spatial hierarchy starts with the observation that a plane divides or partitions three-dimensional space into two parts (half spaces). Successive planes subdivide space into increasingly smaller partitions. In two dimensions, we can use lines to partition space.

Consider the polygons shown in Figure 8.25, with the viewer located as indicated. Arguing as we did in Chapter 7, there is an order in which to paint these polygons so that the image will be correct. Rather than using a method such as depth sort each time we want to render these polygons, we can store the relative-positioning information in a tree. We start the construction of the tree using the plane of one polygon to separate groups of polygons that are in front of it from those that are behind it. For example, consider a simple world in which all the polygons are parallel and are oriented with their normals parallel to the z-axis. This assumption makes it easier to illustrate the algorithm but does not affect the algorithm as long as the plane

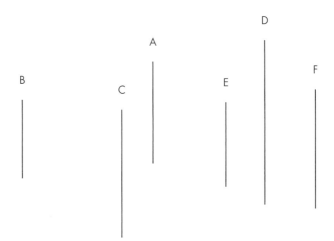

FIGURE 8.26   Top view of polygons.

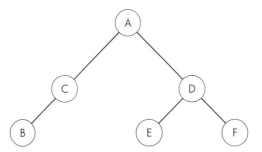

FIGURE 8.27   Binary space partitioning (BSP) tree.

of any polygon separates the other polygons into two groups. In this world, the view from the z-direction is as shown in Figure 8.26.

Plane A separates the polygons into two groups, one containing B and C, which are in front of A, and the second containing D, E, and F, which are behind A. We use this plane to start a **binary space partitioning tree** (**BSP tree**) that stores the separating planes and the order in which they are applied. Thus, in the BSP tree in Figure 8.27, A is at the root, B and C are in the left subtree, and D, E, and F are in the right subtree. Proceeding recursively, C is behind the plane of B, so we can complete the left subtree. The plane of D separates E and F, thus completing the right subtree. Note that for a given set of polygons, there are multiple possible BSP trees corresponding to the order in which we choose to make our partitions. In the general case, if a separating plane intersects a polygon, then we can break up the polygon into two polygons, one in front of the plane and one behind it, similar to what we did with overlapping polygons in the depth-sort algorithm in Chapter 6.

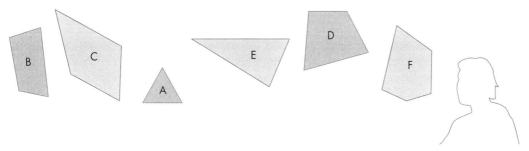

FIGURE 8.28 Movement of the viewer to back.

We can use this tree to paint the polygons by doing a **backward in-order traversal**. That is, we traverse the tree recursively, drawing the right subtree first, followed by the root, and finally by the left subtree. One of the advantages of BSP trees is that we can use the same tree even if the viewer moves by changing the traversal algorithm. If the viewer moves to the back, as shown in Figure 8.28, then we can paint the polygons using a standard in-order traversal—left subtree, root, right subtree. Also note that we can use the algorithm recursively wherever planes separate sets of polygons or other objects into groups, called **clusters**. Thus, we might group polygons into polyhedral objects, then group these polyhedra into clusters. We can then apply the algorithm within each cluster. In applications such as flight simulators, where the world model does not change but the viewer's position does, the use of BSP trees can be efficient for doing visible surface determination during rendering. The tree contains all the required information to paint the polygons; the viewer's position determines the traversal algorithm.

BSP trees are but one form of hierarchy to divide space. Another is the use of bounding volumes, such as spheres. The root of a tree of bounding spheres would be the sphere that contains all the objects in a scene. Subtrees would then correspond to groups of objects within the larger sphere, and the root nodes would be the bounding spheres for each object. We could use the same idea with other types of bounding volumes, such as the bounding boxes that we discussed in Chapter 6. Spheres are particularly good for interactive games because we can quickly determine if an object is potentially visible or whether two objects might collide.

8.11.3 Quadtrees and Octrees

One limitation of BSP trees is that the planes that separate polygons can have an arbitrary orientation so that construction of the tree can be costly, involving ordering and often splitting of polygons. Octrees and quadtrees avoid this problem by using separating planes and lines parallel to the coordinate axes.

Consider the two-dimensional picture in Figure 8.29. We assume that this picture is composed of black and white pixels, perhaps formed by the rendering of a three-dimensional scene. If we wish to store the scene, we can save it as a binary array. But notice the great deal of coherence in the picture. Pixels of each color are clustered

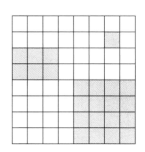

FIGURE 8.29 Two-dimensional space of pixels.

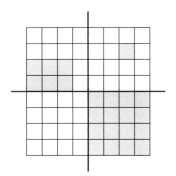

FIGURE 8.30   First subdivision of space.

together. We can draw two lines, as in Figure 8.30, dividing the region into quadrants. Noting that one quadrant is all white, we can assign a single color to it. For the other three, we can subdivide again and continue subdividing any quadrant that contains pixels of more than a single color. This information can be stored in a tree called a **quadtree**, in which each level corresponds to a subdivision and each node has four children. Thus, the quadtree for our original simple picture is as shown in Figure 8.31.

Because we construct the quadtree by subdividing space with lines parallel to the coordinate axes, formation and traversal of the tree are simpler than are the corresponding operations for a BSP tree. One of the most important advantages of quadtrees is that they can reduce the amount of memory needed to store images.

Quadtrees partition two-dimensional space. They can also be used to partition object space in a manner similar to BSP trees and thus can be traversed in an order depending on the position of the viewer so as to render correctly the objects in each region. In three dimensions, quadtrees extend to **octrees**. The partitioning is done by planes parallel to the coordinate axes, and each step of the partitioning subdivides space into eight octants, as shown in Figure 8.32.

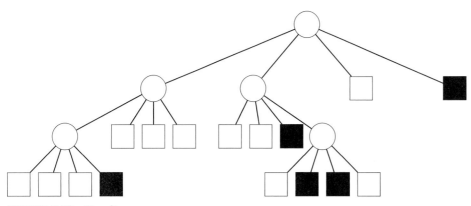

FIGURE 8.31   Quadtree.

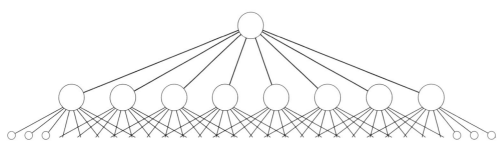

FIGURE 8.32   Octree.

Octrees are used for representing volume data sets that consist of volume elements called **voxels**, as shown in Figure 8.33. The arguments that have been made for quadtrees and octrees can also be applied to the spatial partitioning of objects, rather than pixels or voxels. For example, we can use recursive subdivision of two- or three-dimensional space for clipping. After each subdivison, we compare the bounding box of each object with each subdivided rectangle or cube to determine if the object lies in that region of the subdivided space.

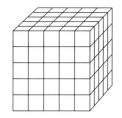

FIGURE 8.33   Volume data set.

SUMMARY AND NOTES

The speed at which modern hardware can render geometric objects has opened up the possibilities of a variety of modeling systems. As users of computer graphics, we need a large arsenal of techniques if we are to make full use of our graphics systems. We have introduced hierarchical modeling. Not only are there the many other forms that we investigate in this chapter and the next, but we can combine these techniques to generate new ones. The Suggested Readings will help you to explore modeling methods.

We have presented basic themes that apply to most approaches to modeling. One is the use of hierarchy to incorporate relationships among objects in a scene. We have seen that we can use fundamental data structures, such as trees and DAGs, to represent such relationships; traversing these data structures becomes part of the rendering process. The use of scene graphs in Open Scene Graph, VRML, and Java3D allows the application programmer to build complex animated scenes from a combination of predefined and user-defined software modules. Tree-structured models are also used to describe complex shaders that involve the interaction of light sources, material properties, atmospheric effects, and a variety of local reflection models. These could be implemented with RenderMan, Cg, or GLSL.

Object-oriented approaches are standard for complex applications and for applications that are distributed over networks. Unfortunately, there has not been agreement on a single object-oriented API. However, the actual rendering in most high-end systems is done at the OpenGL level because the closeness of this API to the hardware makes for efficient use of the hardware. Consequently, both application programmers and system developers need to be familiar with multiple levels of APIs.

Chapter 9 presents an entirely different, but complementary, approach to modeling based on procedural methods.

SUGGESTED READINGS

Hierarchical transformations through the use of a matrix stack were described in the graphics literature more than 30 years ago [New73]. The PHIGS API [ANSI88] was the first to incorporate them as part of a standard package. See Watt [Wat92] for an introduction to the use of articulated figures in animation. The paper by Lassiter

[Las87] shows the relationship between traditional animation techniques as practiced in the movie industry and animation in computer graphics.

BSP trees were first proposed by Fuchs, Kedem, and Naylor [Fuc80] for use in visibility testing and were later used in many other applications, such as CSG. See [Mol02] for additional applications.

Scene graphs are the heart of Open Inventor [Wer94]. The Open Inventor database format was the basis of VRML [Har96]. Most recent APIs, such as Java3D [Swo00] and DirectX [Kov97], are object oriented. For a discussion of Java and applets, see [Cha98] and [Arn96]. Trees are integral to the RenderMan Shading Language [Ups89], where they are used to construct shaders. Modeling systems, such as Maya, allow the user to specify different shaders and rendering algorithms for different objects. See [Ma07] for an introduction to Open Scene Graph.

Many applications of visibility testing can be found in [Mol02].

The use of scene graphs in game engine design is discussed in [Ebe01]. How the engine looks for a game programmer is described for the Torque engine in [Mau06].

EXERCISES

8.1 For our simple robot model, describe the set of points that can be reached by the tip of the upper arm.

8.2 Find equations for the position of any point on the simple robot in terms of the joint angles. Can you determine the joint angles from the position of the tip of the upper arm? Explain your answer.

8.3 Given two points in space that are reachable by the robot, describe a path between them in terms of the joint angles.

8.4 Write a simple circuit-layout program in terms of a symbol–instance transformation table. Your symbols should include the shapes for circuit elements—such as resistors, capacitors, and inductors for electrical circuits— or the shapes for various gates (AND, OR, NOT) for logical circuits.

8.5 We can write a description of a binary tree, such as we might use for a search, as a list of nodes with pointers to its children. Write an OpenGL program that will take such a description and display the tree graphically.

8.6 Robotics is only one example in which the parts of the scene show compound motion, where the movement of some objects depends on the movement of other objects. Other examples include bicycles (with wheels), airplanes (with propellers), and merry-go-rounds (with horses). Pick an example of compound motion. Write a graphics program to simulate your selection.

8.7 Use a directed graph to model an automobile. Which parts could the root and leaf nodes be used to represent?

8.8 Starting with the tree node in Section 8.5, add an attribute to the node and make any required changes to the traversal algorithm.

8.9 What is the relationship between a tree and a graph? In a tree, how are the root node and the terminal node different?

8.10 Why is ray tracing or ray casting a good strategy for rendering a scene described by a CSG tree?

8.11 If a tree structure is used to represent the robot arm, what information needs to be stored in each of the nodes of the tree?

8.12 Write a program that will allow the user to construct simple articulated figures from a small collection of basic shapes. Your program should allow the user to place the joints, and it should animate the resulting figures.

8.13 A graphical application program can be written to traverse a graph. How are the contents of a graph used to describe an entire scene?

8.14 "The scene graph is equivalent to an OpenGL program." Do you think this statement is justified? Explain why.

8.15 How are applets used in computer graphics?

8.16 What are the weaknesses of the polygonal representation of objects? Describe a technique that can be used to overcome these weaknesses.

8.17 What is the limitation of a BSP tree? Describe a technique that can be used to overcome this limitation.

8.18 BSP trees can be made more efficient if they are used hierarchically with objects grouped in clusters. Visibility checking is then done using the bounding volumes of the clusters. Implement such an algorithm and use it with a scene graph renderer.

PROCEDURAL METHODS

Thus far, we have assumed that the geometric objects that we wish to create can be described by their surfaces, and that these surfaces can be modeled (or approximated) by convex planar polygons. Our use of polygonal objects was dictated by the ease with which we could describe these objects and our ability to render them on existing systems. The success of computer graphics attests to the importance of such models.

Nevertheless, even as these models were being used in large CAD applications for flight simulators, in computer animations, in interactive video games, and to create special effects in films, both users and developers recognized the limitations of these techniques. Physical objects such as clouds, smoke, and water did not fit this style of modeling. Adding physical constraints and modeling complex behaviors of objects were not part of polygonal modeling. In response to such problems, researchers have developed procedural models, which use algorithmic methods to build representations of the underlying phenomena, generating polygons only as needed during the rendering process.

9.1 ALGORITHMIC MODELS

When we review the history of computer graphics, we see that the desire to create increasingly more realistic graphics has always outstripped advances in hardware. Although we can render more than 50 million polygons per second on existing commodity hardware, applications such as flight simulation, virtual reality, and computer games can demand rendering speeds greater than 500 million polygons per second. Furthermore, as rendering speeds have increased, database sizes also have increased dramatically. A single data set may contain more than 1 billion polygons.

Often, however, applications have such needs because they use existing software and modeling paradigms. Astute researchers and application programmers have suggested that we would not require as many polygons if we could render a model generating only those polygons that both are visible and project to an area at least the size of one pixel. We have seen examples of this idea in previous chapters, for example, when we considered culling polygons before they reached the rendering pipeline.

Nevertheless, a more productive approach has been to reexamine the way in which we do our modeling and seek techniques, known as **procedural methods**, that generate geometrical objects in a different manner from what we have seen thus far. Procedural methods span a wide range of techniques. What they have in common is that they describe objects in an algorithmic manner and produce polygons only when needed as part of the rendering process.

In many ways, procedural models can be understood by an analogy with methods that we use to represent irrational numbers—such as square roots, sines, and cosines—in a computer. Consider, for example, three ways of representing $\sqrt{2}$. We can say that numerically

$$\sqrt{2} = 1.414 \ldots ,$$

filling in as many digits as we like; or, more abstractly, we can define the $\sqrt{2}$ as the positive number x such that

$$x^2 = 2.$$

However, within the computer, $\sqrt{2}$ might be the result of executing an algorithm. For example, consider Newton's method. Starting with an initial approximation $x_0 = 1$, we compute the recurrence

$$x_{k+1} = \frac{x_k}{2} + \frac{1}{x_k}.$$

Each successive value of x_k is a better approximation to the $\sqrt{2}$. From this perspective, $\sqrt{2}$ is defined by an algorithm; equivalently, it is defined through a program. For objects we deal with in computer graphics, we can take a similar approach. For example, a sphere centered at the origin can be defined as the mathematical object that satisfies the equation

$$x^2 + y^2 + z^2 = r^2.$$

It also is the result of the tetrahedron subdivision process that we developed in Chapter 5 and of our program for doing that subdivision. A potential benefit of the second view is that when we render spheres, we can render small spheres (in screen space) with fewer triangles than we would need for large spheres.

A second type of problem with polygonal modeling has been the difficulty of combining computer graphics with physical laws. Although we can build and animate polygonal models of real-world objects, it is far more difficult to make these graphical objects act as solids and not penetrate one another.

We introduce four of many possible approaches to procedural modeling. In the first, we work with particles that obey Newton's laws. We then design systems of particles that are capable of complex behaviors that arise from solving sets of differential equations—a routine numerical task for up to thousands of particles. The positions of the particles yield the locations at which to place our standard geometric objects in a world model.

The second approach—language-based models—enables us to control complexity by replacing polygonal models with models similar to those used for both natural and computer languages. With these models we can approximate many natural objects with a few rules that generate the required graphical entities. Combined with fractal geometry, these models allow us to generate images using only the number of polygons required for display.

The third approach—fractal geometry—is based on the self-similarity that we see in many natural phenomena. Fractal geometry gives us a way of generating models at any desired level of detail. Finally, we introduce procedural noise as a method of introducing a controlled amount of randomness into our models. Procedural noise has been used to create texture maps, turbulent behavior in fluid models, realistic motion in animations, and fuzzy objects such as clouds.

9.2 PHYSICALLY BASED MODELS AND PARTICLE SYSTEMS

One of the great strengths—and weaknesses—of modeling in computer graphics is that we can build models based on any principles we choose. The graphical objects that we create may have little connection with physical reality. Historically, the attitude was that if something looked right, that was sufficient for most purposes. Not being constrained by physical models, which were often either not known or too complex to simulate in real time, allows the creation of the special effects that we see in computer games and movies. In fields such as scientific visualization, this flexibility allows mathematicians to "see" shapes that do not exist in the usual three-dimensional space and to display information in new ways. Researchers and engineers can construct prototypes of objects that are not limited by our ability to construct them with present materials and equipment.

However, when we wish to simulate objects in the real world and to see the results of this simulation on our display, we can get into trouble. Often, it is easy to make a model for a group of objects moving through space, but it is far more difficult to keep track of when two objects collide and to have the graphics system react in a physically correct manner. Indeed, it is far easier in computer graphics to let a ball go directly through a wall than to model the ball bouncing off the surface, incorporating the correct elastic rebound.

Recently, researchers have become interested in **physically based modeling**, a style of modeling in which the graphical objects obey physical laws. Such modeling can follow either of two related paths. In one, we model the physics of the underlying process and use the physics to drive the graphics. For example, if we want a solid object to appear to tumble in space and to bounce from various surfaces, we can, at least in principle, use our knowledge of dynamics and continuum mechanics to derive the required equations. This approach is beyond the scope of a first course in computer graphics, and we shall not pursue it. The other approach is to use a combination of basic physics and mathematical constraints to control the dynamic behavior of our objects. We follow this approach for a group of particles.

Particle systems are collections of particles, typically point masses, in which the dynamic behavior of the particles can be determined by the solution of sets of coupled differential equations. Particle systems have been used to generate a wide variety of behaviors in a number of fields. In fluid dynamics, people use particle systems to model turbulent behavior. Rather than solving partial differential equations, we can simulate the behavior of the system by following a group of particles that is subject to a variety of forces and constraints. We can also use particles to model solid objects. For example, a deformable solid can be modeled as a three-dimensional array of particles that are held together by springs. When the object is subjected to external forces, the particles move and their positions approximate the shape of the solid object.

Computer graphics practitioners have used particles to model such diverse phenomena as fireworks, the flocking behavior of birds, and wave action. In these applications, the dynamics of the particle system gives the positions of the particles, but at each location we can place a graphical object, rather than a point.

In all these cases, we work with a group of particles, each member of which we can regard as a point mass. We use physical laws to write equations that we can solve numerically to obtain the state of these particles at each time step. As a final step, we can render each particle as a graphical object—perhaps as a colored point for a fireworks application or a cartoon character in an animation.

9.3   NEWTONIAN PARTICLES

We consider a set of particles that is subject to Newton's laws. Although there is no reason that we could not use other physical laws or construct a set of our own (virtual) physical laws, the advantage of starting with Newtonian particles is that we can obtain a wide range of behaviors using simple, well-understood physics. A Newtonian particle must obey Newton's second law, which states that the mass of the particle (m) times that particle's acceleration ($\mathbf{a}$) is equal to the sum of the forces ($\mathbf{f}$) acting on the particle, or symbolically,

$$m\mathbf{a} = \mathbf{f}.$$

Note that both the acceleration and force are vectors, usually in three dimensions. One consequence of Newton's laws is that for an ideal point-mass particle—one whose total mass is concentrated at a single point—its state is completely determined by its position and velocity. Thus, in three-dimensional space, an ideal particle has 6 degrees of freedom, and a system of n particles has $6n$ state variables—the positions and velocities of all the particles. Within some reference frame, the state of the ith particle is given by two three-element column matrices,[1] a position matrix

$$\mathbf{p}_i = \begin{bmatrix} x_i \\ y_i \\ z_i \end{bmatrix}$$

and a velocity matrix

$$\mathbf{v}_i = \begin{bmatrix} \dot{x}_i \\ \dot{y}_i \\ \dot{z}_i \end{bmatrix} = \begin{bmatrix} \frac{dx}{dt} \\ \frac{dy}{dt} \\ \frac{dz}{dt} \end{bmatrix}.$$

Knowing that acceleration is the derivative of velocity and that velocity is the derivative of position, we can write Newton's second law for a particle as the six coupled, first-order differential equations

$$\dot{\mathbf{p}}_i = \mathbf{v}_i,$$

$$\dot{\mathbf{v}}_i = \frac{1}{m_i} \mathbf{f}_i(t).$$

Hence, the dynamics of a system of n particles is governed by a set of $6n$ coupled, ordinary differential equations.

In addition to its state, each particle may have a number of attributes, including its mass (m_i), and a set of properties that can alter what its behavior is and how it is displayed. For example, some attributes govern how we render the particle and determine its color, shape, and surface properties. Note that although the dynamics of a simple particle system is based on each particle being treated as a point mass, the user can specify how each particle should be rendered. For example, each particle may represent a person in a crowd scene, or a molecule in a chemical-synthesis application, or a piece of cloth in the simulation of a flag blowing in the wind. In each case, the underlying particle system governs the location and the velocity of the center of mass of the particle. Once we have the location of a particle, we can place the desired graphical object at this location.

The set of forces on the particles, $\{\mathbf{f}_i\}$, determines the behavior of the system. These forces are based on the state of the particle system and can change with time. We can base these forces on simple physical principles, such as spring forces, or on physical constraints that we wish to impose on the system, or we can base them on external forces, such as gravity, that we wish to apply to the system. By designing the forces carefully, we can obtain the desired system behavior.

---

1. We have chosen to use three-dimensional arrays here, rather than homogeneous coordinate representations, both to be consistent with the way these equations are usually written in the physics literature and to simplify the resulting differential equations.

The dynamic state of the system is obtained by numerical methods that in-volve stepping through approximations to the set of differential equations. A typical time step is based on computing the forces that apply to the n particles through a user-defined function, using these forces to update the state through a numerical differential-equation solver, and finally using the new positions of the particles and their attributes to render whatever graphical objects we wish to place at the particles' locations. Thus, in pseudocode, we have a loop of the form

```
float time, delta; float state[6n], force[3n];
state=get_initial_state();
for(time=t0; time<time_final; time+=delta)
 {
 /* compute forces */
    force=force_function(state, time);

 /* apply standard differential equation solver */
    state=ode(force, state, time, delta);

 /* display result */
    render(state, time);
}
```

The main component that we must design in a given application is the function that computes the forces on each particle.

9.3.1 Independent Particles

There are numerous simple ways that particles can interact and determine the forces that act on each particle. If the forces that act on a given particle are independent of other particles, the force on the ith particle can be described by the equation

$$\mathbf{f}_i = \mathbf{f}_i(\mathbf{p}_i, \mathbf{v}_i).$$

A simple case occurs where each particle is subject only to a constant gravitational force

$$\mathbf{f}_i/m_i = \mathbf{g}.$$

If this force points down, then

$$\mathbf{g} = \begin{bmatrix} 0 \\ -g \\ 0 \end{bmatrix},$$

where g is positive, and each particle will trace out a parabolic arc. If we add a term proportional to the velocity, we can have the particle subject to frictional forces, such as drag. If some of the attributes, such as color, change with time and if we give each particle a (random) lifetime, then we can simulate phenomena such as fireworks.

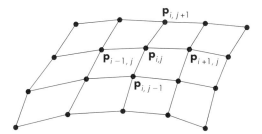

FIGURE 9.1   Mesh of particles.

More generally, external forces are applied independently to each point. If we allow the particles to drift randomly and render each as a large object, rather than as a point, we can model clouds or flows with independent particles.

9.3.2 Spring Forces

If in a system of n particles all particles are independent, then the force calculation is $O(n)$. In the most general case, the computation of the forces on a given particle may involve contributions due to pairwise interactions with all the other particles, an $O(n^2)$ computation. For large particle systems, an $O(n^2)$ computation can be too slow to be useful. Often, we can reduce this complexity by having a particle interact with only those particles that are close to it.

Consider the example of using particles to create a surface whose shape varies over time, such as a curtain or a flag blowing in the wind. We can use the location of each particle as a vertex for a rectangular mesh, as shown in Figure 9.1. The shape of the mesh changes over time, as a result both of external forces that act on each particle, such as gravity or wind, and of forces between particles that hold the mesh together, giving it the appearance of a continuous surface. We can approximate this second type of force by considering the forces between a particle and its closest neighbors. Thus, if $\mathbf{p}_{ij}$ is the location of the particle at row i, column j of the mesh, the force calculation for $\mathbf{p}_{ij}$ needs to consider only the forces between $\mathbf{p}_{ij}$ and $\mathbf{p}_{i+1,\,j}$, $\mathbf{p}_{i-1,\,j}$, $\mathbf{p}_{i,\,j+1}$, and $\mathbf{p}_{i,\,j-1}$—an $O(n)$ calculation.

One method to model the forces among particles is to consider adjacent particles as connected by a spring. Consider two adjacent particles, located at $\mathbf{p}$ and $\mathbf{q}$, connected by a spring, as shown in Figure 9.2. Let $\mathbf{f}$ denote the force acting on $\mathbf{p}$ from $\mathbf{q}$. A force $-\mathbf{f}$ acts on $\mathbf{q}$ from $\mathbf{p}$. The spring has a resting length s, which is the distance between particles if the system is not subject to external forces and is allowed to come to rest. When the spring is stretched, the force acts in the direction $\mathbf{d} = \mathbf{p} - \mathbf{q}$; that is, it acts along the line between the points. This force obeys **Hooke's law**:

$$\mathbf{f} = -k_s(|\mathbf{d}| - s)\frac{\mathbf{d}}{|\mathbf{d}|},$$

FIGURE 9.2   Particles connected by a spring.

where k_s is the spring constant and s is the length of the spring when it is at rest. This law shows that the farther apart the two particles are stretched, the stronger is the force attracting them back to the resting position. Conversely, when the ends of the spring are pushed together, the force pulls them back such that their positions move to a separation by the resting length. As we have stated Hooke's law, however, there is no damping (or friction) in the system. A system of masses and springs defined in such a manner will oscillate forever when perturbed. We can include a **drag**, or **damping term**, in Hooke's law. The damping force operates in the same direction as the spring force, but depends on the velocity between the particles. The fraction of the velocity that contributes to damping is proportional to the projection of the velocity vector onto the vector defined by the two points as shown in Figure 9.3. Mathematically, Hooke's law with the damping term is given by

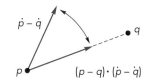

FIGURE 9.3 Computation of the spring damping force.

$$\mathbf{f} = -\left(k_s(|\mathbf{d}| - s) + k_d \frac{\dot{\mathbf{d}} \cdot \mathbf{d}}{|\mathbf{d}|} \right) \frac{\mathbf{d}}{|\mathbf{d}|}.$$

Here, k_d is the damping constant, and

$$\dot{\mathbf{d}} = \dot{\mathbf{p}} - \dot{\mathbf{q}}.$$

A system of masses and springs with damping that is not subjected to external forces will eventually come to rest.

The four images in Color Plate 31 show a mesh that is generated from the locations of a set of particles. Each interior particle is connected to its four neighbors by springs. The particles are also subject to external forces—the wind. At each time step, once the positions of the particles are determined, we can render the mesh using techniques such as texture mapping (Section 7.5) to create the detailed appearance of the surface.

9.3.3 Attractive and Repulsive Forces

Whereas spring forces are used to keep a group of particles together, repulsive forces push particles away from one another and attractive forces pull particles toward one another. We could use repulsive forces to distribute particles over a surface, or if the particles represent locations of objects, to keep objects from hitting one another. We could use attractive forces to build a model of the solar system or to create applications that model satellites revolving about the earth. The equations for attraction and repulsion are essentially the same except for a sign. Physical models of particle behavior may include both attractive and repulsive forces. See Exercise 9.14.

For a pair of particles, located at $\mathbf{p}$ and $\mathbf{q}$, the repulsive force acts in the direction $\mathbf{d} = \mathbf{p} - \mathbf{q}$ and is inversely proportional to the particles' distance from each other. For example, we could use the expression

$$\mathbf{f} = -k_r \frac{\mathbf{d}}{|\mathbf{d}|^3}$$

for an inverse-square-law term. Changing the minus sign to a positive sign and re-placing k_r by $(m_a m_b)/g$ gives us the attractive force between two particles of mass m_a and m_b, where g is the gravitational constant.

In the general case, where each particle is subject to forces from all other particles, the computation of attractive and repulsive forces is $O(n^2)$. Unlike meshes of particles connected by springs, where we attempt to keep the particles in the same topological arrangement, particles subject to attractive and repulsive forces usually change their positions among themselves. Hence, strategies to avoid the $O(n^2)$ force calculation are more complex. One approach is to divide space into three-dimensional cells, each of which can contain multiple particles or even no particles, as shown in Figure 9.4.

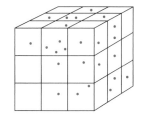

FIGURE 9.4 Division of space into cells.

For forces that are inversely proportional to distance, we can choose a cell size such that the forces on a particle from particles in other than its own or adjacent cells are negligible. If this partitioning is possible, then the $O(n^2)$ calculation is reduced to $O(n)$. However, there is a cost to partitioning, and particles can move from one cell to another. The difficulty of the first problem depends on the particular application, because we can often obtain an initial particle distribution with little effort, but at other times we might have to do a sort. We can solve the second problem by looking at the particle positions after each time step and redistributing the particles or, perhaps, changing the cells. We can use various data structures to store the particles and cell information.

One other approach that is often used is to replace interactions among particles by interactions between particles and a force field. For example, when we compute the gravitational force on a point mass on the surface of the earth, we use the value of the gravitational field rather than the point-to-point force between the point mass of the particle and a second large point mass at the center of the earth. If we were concerned with only the mass of the earth and our point on the surface, the two approaches would require about the same amount of work. However, if we were to also include the force from the moon, the situation would be more complex. If we used point masses, we would have two point-to-point forces to compute for our mass on the surface, but if we knew the gravitational field, the calculation would be the same as before. Of course, the calculation of the field is more complex when we consider the moon; for particle systems, however, we can often neglect distant particles, so the particle-field method may be more efficient. We can often compute the approximate field on a grid, then use the value at the nearest grid points to give the forces on each particle. After the new state of each particle has been computed, we can update the field. Both of these strategies can often reduce the $O(n^2)$ calculation of forces to $O(n \log n)$.

9.4 SOLVING PARTICLE SYSTEMS

Consider a particle system of n particles. If we restrict ourselves to the simple forces that we just described, the entire particle system can be described by $6n$ ordinary differential equations of the form

$$\dot{\mathbf{u}} = \mathbf{g}(\mathbf{u}, t),$$

where $\mathbf{u}$ is an array of the $6n$ position and velocity components of our n particles, and $\mathbf{g}$ includes any external forces applied to the particles. Thus, if we have two particles $\mathbf{a}$ and $\mathbf{b}$ connected by a spring without damping, we might have

$$\mathbf{u}^T = [\, u_0 \quad u_1 \quad u_2 \quad u_3 \quad u_4 \quad u_5 \quad u_6 \quad u_7 \quad u_8 \quad u_9 \quad u_{10} \quad u_{11} \,]$$
$$= [\, a_x \quad a_y \quad a_z \quad \dot{a}_x \quad \dot{a}_y \quad \dot{a}_z \quad b_x \quad b_y \quad b_z \quad \dot{b}_x \quad \dot{b}_y \quad \dot{b}_z \,].$$

Given the external forces and the state of the particle system $\mathbf{u}$ at any time t, we can evaluate

$$\mathbf{g}^T = \left[\, u_3 \quad u_4 \quad u_5 \quad -kd_x \quad -kd_y \quad -kd_z \quad u_9 \quad u_{10} \quad u_{11} \quad kd_x \quad kd_y \quad kd_z \,\right].$$

Here k is the spring constant and d_x, d_y, and d_z are the components of the normalized vector d between $\mathbf{a}$ and $\mathbf{b}$. Thus, we must first compute

$$\mathbf{d} = \frac{1}{\sqrt{(u_0 - u_5)^2 + (u_1 - u_6)^2 + (u_2 - u_7)^2}} \begin{bmatrix} u_0 - u_6 \\ u_1 - u_7 \\ u_2 - u_8 \end{bmatrix}.$$

Numerical ordinary differential equation solvers rely on our ability to evaluate $\mathbf{g}$ to approximate $\mathbf{u}$ at future times. We can develop a family of differential equation solvers based upon Taylor's theorem. The simplest is known as Euler's method. Suppose that we integrate the expression

$$\dot{\mathbf{u}} = \mathbf{g}(\mathbf{u}, t)$$

over a short time h:

$$\int_t^{t+h} \dot{\mathbf{u}} d\tau = \mathbf{u}(t+h) - \mathbf{u}(t) = \int_t^{t+h} \mathbf{g}(\mathbf{u}, \tau) d\tau.$$

If h is small, we can approximate the value of $\mathbf{g}$ over the interval $[t, t+h]$ by the value of $\mathbf{g}$ at t; thus,

$$\mathbf{u}(t+h) \approx \mathbf{u}(t) + h\mathbf{g}(\mathbf{u}(t), t).$$

This expression shows that we can use the value of the derivative at t to get us to an approximate value of $\mathbf{u}(t+h)$, as shown in Figure 9.5.

This expression matches the first two terms of the Taylor expansion; we can write it as

$$\mathbf{u}(t+h) = \mathbf{u}(t) + h\dot{\mathbf{u}}(t) + O(h^2) = \mathbf{u}(t) + h\mathbf{g}(\mathbf{u}(t), t) + O(h^2),$$

showing that the error we incur in making the approximation is proportional to the square of the step size.

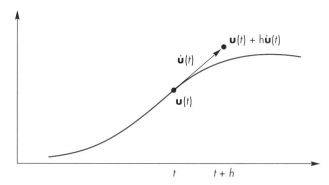

FIGURE 9.5   Approximation of the solution of a differential equation.

This method is particularly easy to implement. We evaluate the forces (both external and among particles) at time t, compute $\mathbf{g}$, multiply it by h, and add it to the present state. We can apply this method iteratively to compute further values at $t + 2h$, $t + 3h$, ... The work involved is one calculation of the forces for each time step.

There are two potential problems with Euler's method: accuracy and stability. Both are affected by the step size. The accuracy of Euler's method is proportional to the square of the step size. Consequently, to increase the accuracy we must cut the step size, thus increasing the time it takes to solve the system. A potentially more serious problem concerns stability. As we go from step to step, the per-step errors that we make come from two sources: the approximation error that we made by using the Taylor series approximation and the numerical errors that we make in computing the functions. These errors can either cancel themselves out as we compute further states, or they can accumulate and give us unacceptably large errors that mask the true solution. Such behavior is called **numerical instability**. Fortunately, for the standard types of forces that we have used, if we make the step size small enough, we can guarantee stability. Unfortunately, the required step size for stability may be so small that we cannot solve the equations numerically in a reasonable amount of time. This unstable behavior is most pronounced for spring-mass systems, where the spring constant determines the stiffness of the system and leads to what are called **stiff** sets of differential equations.

There are two general approaches to this problem. One is to seek another type of ordinary differential equation solver, called a stiff equation solver—a topic that is beyond the scope of this book. Another is to find other differential equation solvers similar in philosophy to Euler's method but with a higher per-step accuracy. We derive one such method because it gives us insight into the family of such methods. References to both approaches are given at the end of the chapter.

Suppose that we start as before by integrating the differential equations over a short time interval to obtain

$$\mathbf{u}(t+h) = \mathbf{u}(t) + \int_{t}^{t+h} \mathbf{g}(\mathbf{u}, \tau)d\tau.$$

This time, we approximate the integral by an average value over the interval $[t, t+h]$:

$$\int_{t}^{t+h} \mathbf{g}(\mathbf{u}, \tau)d\tau \approx \frac{h}{2}(\mathbf{g}(\mathbf{u}(t), t) + \mathbf{g}(\mathbf{u}(t+h), t+h)).$$

The problem now is we do not have $\mathbf{g}(\mathbf{u}(t+h), t+h)$; we have only $\mathbf{g}(\mathbf{u}(t), t)$. We can use Euler's method to approximate $\mathbf{g}(\mathbf{u}(t+h), t+h)$; that is, we can use

$$\mathbf{g}(\mathbf{u}(t+h), t+h) \approx \mathbf{g}(\mathbf{u}(t) + h\mathbf{g}(\mathbf{u}(t), t), t+h).$$

This method is known as the **improved Euler method** or the **Runge–Kutta method of order 2**. Note that to go from t to $t+h$, we must evaluate $\mathbf{g}$ twice. However, if we were to use Taylor's theorem to evaluate the per-step error, we would find that it is now $O(h^3)$. Thus, even though we are doing more work per step, we can use larger step sizes, and the method is stable for step sizes larger than those for which Euler's method was stable. In general, we can use increasingly more accurate per-step formulas and derive a set of methods called the Runge–Kutta formulas. The most popular is the fourth-order method that has a per-step error of $O(h^4)$ and requires four function evaluations per step. In practice, we can do even better with this number of function evaluations, achieving errors of $O(h^5)$. More important, good solvers adjust their own step size so as to ensure stability.

9.5   CONSTRAINTS

Simply allowing a group of particles to change state according to a set of differential equations often is insufficient to model real-world behavior such as collisions. Although the impact of an object hitting a wall is subject to Newton's laws, if we were to model the object as a collection of particles, the resulting system would be too complex for most purposes. Instead, we regard conditions such as the one in which two solid objects cannot penetrate each other as constraints that can be stated separately from the laws governing individual particle behavior.

There are two types of constraints that we can impose on particles. **Hard constraints** are those that must be adhered to exactly. For example, a ball must bounce off a wall; it cannot penetrate the wall and emerge from the other side. Nor can we allow the ball just to come close and then go off in another direction. **Soft constraints** are those that we need only come close to satisfying. For example, we might want two particles to be separated approximately by a specified distance, as in a particle mesh.

9.5.1 Collisions

Although, in general, hard constraints can be difficult to impose, there are a few situations that can be dealt with directly for ideal point particles. Consider the problem of collisions. We can separate the problem into two parts: detection and reaction.

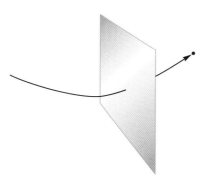

FIGURE 9.6   Particle penetrating a polygon.

Suppose that we have a collection of particles and other geometric objects and the particles repel one another. We therefore need to consider only collisions between each particle and the other objects. If there are n particles and m polygons that define the geometric objects, at each time step we can check whether any particle has gone through any of the polygons.

Suppose that one of the particles has penetrated a polygon, as shown in Figure 9.6. We can detect this collision by inserting the position of the particle into the equation of the plane of the polygon. If the time step of our differential equation solver is small, we can assume that the velocity between time steps is constant, and we can use linear interpolation to find the time at which the particle actually hit the polygon.

What happens to the particle after a collision is similar to what happens when light reflects from a surface. If there is an **inelastic collision**, the particle loses none of its energy, so its speed is unchanged. However, its direction after the collision is in the direction of a perfect reflection. Thus, given the normal at the point of collision P_c and the previous position of the particle P_0, we can compute the direction of a perfect reflection, as we did in Chapter 5, using the vector from the particle to the surface and the normal at the surface, as shown in Figure 9.7:

$$\mathbf{r} = 2(\mathbf{p}_0 - \mathbf{p}_c) \cdot \mathbf{n} \ \mathbf{n} - (\mathbf{P}_0 - \mathbf{P}_c).$$

The particle will be a distance along this reflector equal to the distance it would have penetrated the polygon in the absence of collision detection, as shown in Figure 9.8.

The velocity is changed to be along the direction of reflection, with the same magnitude. Equivalently, the tangential component of the velocity—the part in the plane of the polygon—is unchanged, whereas the direction of the normal component is reversed.

A slightly more complex calculation is required for an **elastic collision**, in which the particle loses some of its energy when it collides with another object. The **coefficient of restitution** of a particle is the fraction of the normal velocity retained after the collision. Thus, the angle of reflection is computed as for the inelastic collision,

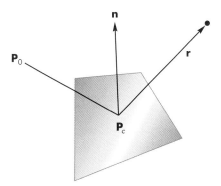

FIGURE 9.7 Particle reflection.

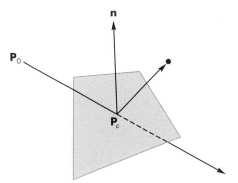

FIGURE 9.8 Position after collision.

and the normal component of the velocity is reduced by the coefficient of restitution. See Section 9.6.4 for an example.

The major cost of dealing with collisions is the complexity of detection. In applications such as games, approximate detection often is sufficient. In this case, we can replace complex objects consisting of many polygons by simple objects, such as their bounding volumes, for which collision detection is simpler.

Note that use of particles avoids the complex calculations necessary for objects with finite sizes. In many ways, solving the collision problem is similar to clipping arbitrary objects against each other; the calculation is conceptually simple but is in practice time-consuming and messy. In addition, if we have objects with finite size, we have to consider inertial forces, thereby increasing the dimension of the system of equations that we must solve. Consequently, in computer graphics, we are usually willing to accept an approximate solution using ideal point particles, and we obtain an acceptable rendering by placing objects at the location of the particle.

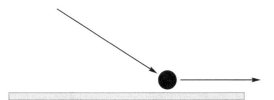

FIGURE 9.9   Contact force.

There is another case of hard constraints that arises often and can be handled correctly: contact forces. Suppose that we have a particle that is subject to a force pushing it along a surface, as shown in Figure 9.9. The particle cannot penetrate the surface, and it cannot bounce from the surface because of the force being applied to it. We can argue that the particle is subject to the tangential component of the applied force—that is, the part of the applied force along the surface. We can also apply frictional terms in this direction.

Note that collision detection, as opposed to how we deal with a collision once it has been detected, is often another $O(n^2)$ calculation. Consider, for example, a game such as pool, in which balls are moving around a table, or a simulation of molecules moving within a bounded volume. As any pair of particles can collide, a brute-force approach would be to check all pairs of particles at each time step. Faster approaches involve bounding-box methods and hardware support for collision detection.

9.5.2 Soft Constraints

Most hard constraints are difficult to enforce. For example, if we want to ensure that a particle's velocity is less than a maximum velocity or that all the particles have a constant amount of energy, then the resulting mathematics is far more difficult than what we have already seen, and such constraints do not always lead to a simple set of ordinary differential equations.

In many situations, we can work with soft constraints: constraints that we need to come only close to satisfying. For example, if we want a particle whose location is $\mathbf{p}$ to remain near the position $\mathbf{p}_0$, we can consider the **penalty function** $|\mathbf{p} - \mathbf{p}_0|^2$. The smaller this function is, the closer we are to obeying the constraint. This function is one example of an **energy function** whose value represents the amount of some type of energy stored in the system. In physics, such functions can represent quantities, such as the potential or kinetic energy in the system. Physical laws can be written either as differential equations, like those we used for our particles, or in terms of the minimization of expressions involving energy terms. One advantage of the latter form is that we can express constraints or desired behavior of a system directly in terms of potential or energy functions. Conversion of these expressions to force laws is a mechanical process, but its mathematical details are beyond the scope of this book.

9.6   A SIMPLE PARTICLE SYSTEM

We conclude this discussion by building a simple particle system that can be expanded to more complex behaviors. Our particles are all Newtonian so their state is described by their positions and velocities. In addition, each particle can have its own color index and mass. We start with the following structure:

```
typedef point4 vec4;

typedef struct particle
{
    int color;
    point4 position;
    vec4 velocity;
    float mass;
} particle;
```

Here we are using four-dimensional homogeneous coordinates for our positions and velocities. A particle system is an array of particles

```
particle particles[MAX_NUM_PARTICLES];
```

We can initialize the system with the particles in random locations inside a centered cube with side length 2.0 and with random velocities as follows:

```
int num_particles;

for(int i=0; i<num_particles; i++)
{
    particles[i].mass = 1.0;
    particles[i].color = i%NUM_COLORS;
    for(int j=0; j<3; j++)
    {
        particles[i].position[j] = 2.0*((float) rand()/RAND_MAX)-1.0;
        particles[i].velocity[j] = speed*2.0*((float)
                                          rand()/RAND_MAX)-1.0;
    }
     particles[i].position[3] = 1.0;
     particles[i].velocity[3] = 0.0;
}
```

9.6.1 Displaying the Particles

Given the position of a particle, we can display it using any set of primitives that we like. A simple starting point is to display each particle as a point. Here is a display callback that loops through the array of particles in which we have num_particles,

```
void display(void)
{
    glClear(GL_COLOR_BUFFER_BIT);
    for(i=0; i<num_particles; i++)
    {
        point_colors[i+24] = colors[particles[i].color];
        points[i+24] = particles[i].position;
    }
    glBindBuffer(GL_ARRAY_BUFFER, buffers[0]);
    glBufferData(GL_ARRAY_BUFFER, sizeof(points), +sizeof(colors)NULL,
                GL_DYNAMIC_DRAW);
    glBufferSubData(GL_ARRAY_BUFFER, 0, sizeofpoints,points);
    glBufferSubData(GL_ARRAY_BUFFER, sizeof(points), sizeof(colors),colors);
    glDrawArrays(GL_POINTS, 24, num_particles);
    glutSwapBuffers();
}
```

where the colors are stored in an array `colors`

```
typedef color4 vec4;

color4 colors[8] = {color4(0.0,0.0,0.0, 1.0), color4(1.0,0.0,0.0, 1.0),
                    color4(1.0,1.0,0.0, 1.0), color4(0.0,1.0,0.0, 1.0),
                    color4(0.0,0.0,1.0, 1.0), color4(1.0,0.0,1.0, 1.0),
                    color4(0.0,1.0,1.0, 1.0), color4(1.0,1.0,1.0, 1.0)};
```

9.6.2 Updating Particle Positions
We use the idle callback to update the particle positions using the elapsed time and Euler integration:

```
float last_time, present_time;

void idle(void)
{
    int i, j;
    float dt;
    present_time = glutGet(GLUT_ELAPSED_TIME); /* in milliseconds */
    dt = 0.001*(present_time - last_time); /* in seconds */
    for(i=0; i<num_particles; i++)
    {
        for(j=0; j<3; j++)
        {
            particles[i].position[j]+=dt*particles[i].velocity[j];
            particles[i].velocity[j]+=dt*forces(i,j)/particles[i].mass;
        }
```

```
            collision(i);
      }
      last_time = present_time;
      glutPostRedisplay();
}
```

The positions are updated using the velocity, and the velocity is updated by computing the forces on that particle. We have assumed that the time interval is short enough that we can compute the forces on each particle as we update its state. A more robust strategy would be to compute all the forces on all the particles first and put the results into an array that can be used to update the state.

We shall use the collision function to keep the particles inside a box. It could also be used to deal with collisions between particles.

9.6.3 Collisions

We use the collision function to keep the particles inside the initial axis-aligned box. Our strategy is to increment the position of each particle and then check if the particle has crossed one of the sides of the box. If it has crossed a side, then we can treat the bounce as a reflection. Thus, we need only change the sign of the velocity in the normal direction. If the coefficient of restitution is less than 1.0, the particles will slow down when they hit a side of the box.

```
float coef; /* coefficient of restitution */

void collision(int n)
{
   int i;
   for (i=0; i<3; i++)
   {
        if(particles[n].position[i]>=1.0)
        {
            particles[n].velocity[i] = -coef*particles[n].velocity[i];
            particles[n].position[i] = 1.0-coef*
                                    (particles[n].position[i]-1.0);
        }
        if(particles[n].position[i]<=-1.0)
        {
            particles[n].velocity[i] = -coef*particles[n].velocity[i];
            particles[n].position[i] = -1.0-coef*
                                    (particles[n].position[i]+1.0);
        }
   }
}
```

9.6.4 Forces

If the forces are set to zero, the particles will bounce around the box on linear paths continuously. If the coefficient is less than 1.0, eventually the particles will slow to a halt. The easiest force to add is gravity. For example, if all the particles have the same mass, we can add a gravitational term in the y-direction by

```
bool gravity =  TRUE;

float forces(int i, int j)
{
   if(!gravity) return(0.0);
     else if(j==1) return(-1.0);
      else return(0.0);
}
```

We can add repulsive or attractive forces (see Exercise 9.14) by computing the distances between all pairs of particles at the beginning of each iteration and then using any inverse square term. The exercises at the end of the chapter suggest some extensions to the system.

9.6.5 Flocking

Some of the most interesting applications of a particle system are for simulating complex behaviors among the particles. Perhaps a more accurate statement is that we can produce what appears to be complex behavior using some simple rules for how particles interact. A classic example is simulating the flocking behavior of birds. How does a large group of birds maintain a flock without each bird knowing the positions of all the other birds? We can investigate some possibilities by making some minor modifications to our particle system.

One possibility is to change the direction of each particle so the particle steers toward the center of the system. Thus, each time that we update the system, we compute the average position:

```
float cm[3];
for (k=0; k<3; k++)
{
   cm[k]=0;
   for(i=0;i<num_particles;i++) cm[k]+=particles[i].position[k];
   cm[k]/=num_particles;
}
```

We can now compute a new velocity direction that lies between the updated velocity vector `particles[i].velocity` and the vector from `particles[i].position` to the average position, as in Figure 9.10. See Exercise 9.20.

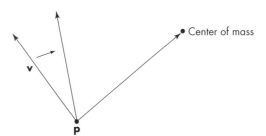

FIGURE 9.10   Changing a particle's direction.

9.7   LANGUAGE-BASED MODELS

Graphs, such as the trees and DAGs we introduced in Chapter 8, offer but one way of representing hierarchical relationships among objects. In this section, we look at language-based models for representing relationships. Not only do these methods provide an alternate way of showing relationships, but they also lead to procedural methods for describing objects, such as plants and terrain.

If we look at natural objects, such as plants, we see that although no two trees are identical, we may have no difficulty telling the difference between two species of trees. Various methods have been proposed that give different realizations each time the program is run but which have clear rules for defining the structure. We look at the use of tree data structures for generating objects that look like plants.

In computer science, tree data structures are used for describing the parsing of sentences into constituent parts, in both computer and natural languages. For computer programs, doing this parsing is part of compiling the statements in a computer program. For natural languages, we parse sentences to determine whether they are grammatically correct. The tree that results from the parsing of a correct sentence gives the structure or syntax of that sentence. The interpretation of the individual elements in the tree—the words—give the meaning or semantics of the sentence.

If we look at only the syntax of a language, there is a direct correlation between the rules of the language and the form of the trees that represent the sentences. We can extend this idea to hierarchical objects in graphics, relating a set of rules and a tree-structured model. These systems are known as **tree grammars**. A grammar can be defined by a set of symbols and a set of symbol-replacement rules, or **productions**, that specify how to replace a symbol by one or more symbols. Typical rules are written as

$A \rightarrow BC$,

$B \rightarrow ABA$.

Given a set of productions, we can generate an infinite number of strings. In general, there is more than one rule that we can apply to a given symbol at any time, and, if we select randomly which rule to apply, we can generate a different string each time the program is executed. Programs can be written that not only generate such strings

FIGURE 9.11   The Koch curve rule.

but also take strings as input and test whether the strings are valid members of the set of strings generated by a given set of rules. Thus, we might have a set of rules for generating a certain type of object, such as a tree or a bush, and a separate program that can identify objects in a scene based on which grammar generates the shape.

The interpretation of the symbols in a string converts the string to a graphical object. There are numerous ways to generate rules and to interpret the resulting strings as graphical objects. One approach starts with the **turtle graphics** (Exercise 2.4) system. In turtle graphics, we have three basic ways of manipulating a graphics cursor, or **turtle**. The turtle can move forward 1 unit, turn right, or turn left. Suppose that the angle by which the turtle can turn is fixed. We can then denote our three operations as F, R, and L. Any string of these operations has a simple graphical interpretation. For example, if the angle is 120 degrees, the string $FRFRFR$ generates an equilateral triangle. We use the special symbols [and] to denote pushing and popping the state of the turtle (its position and orientation) onto a stack (an operation equivalent to using parentheses). Consider the production rule

$$F \rightarrow FLFRRFLF,$$

with an angle of 60 degrees. The graphical interpretation of this rule is shown in Figure 9.11. If we apply the rule again, in parallel to all instances of F, we get the curve in Figure 9.12(a); if we apply it to a triangle, we get the closed curve in Figure 9.12(b). These curves are known as the **Koch curve** and **Koch snowflake**, respectively. If we scale the geometric interpretation of the curve each time that we execute the algorithm, so as to leave the original vertices in their original locations, we find we are generating a longer curve at each iteration, but this curve always fits inside the same box. In the limit, we have a curve that has infinite length, never crosses itself, but fits in a finite box. It also is continuous but has a discontinuous derivative everywhere.

Another classic example is the **Hilbert curve.** Hilbert curves are formed from four simple primitives we can call A_0, B_0, C_0, and D_0, shown in Figure 9.13. Each is a first-order Hilbert curve. The arrows are there to indicate we start drawing each in one corner. There are four Hilbert curves of each order N, which we can call A_N, B_N, C_N, and D_N. We form each from the order $N-1$ curves by combining the four types according to the following rules:

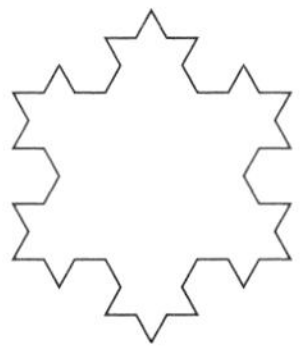

$$A_N = B_{N-1} \uparrow A_{N-1} \rightarrow A_{N-1} \downarrow C_{N-1},$$

$$B_N = A_{N-1} \rightarrow B_{N-1} \uparrow B_{N-1} \leftarrow D_{N-1},$$

$$C_N = D_{N-1} \leftarrow C_{N-1} \downarrow C_{N-1} \rightarrow A_{N-1},$$

$$D_N = C_{N-1} \downarrow D_{N-1} \leftarrow D_{N-1} \uparrow B_{N-1}.$$

(a)

(b)

FIGURE 9.12   Koch curves. (a) Curve. (b) Snowflake.

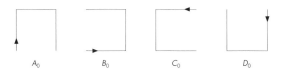

FIGURE 9.13 The zero order Hilbert patterns.

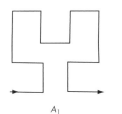

FIGURE 9.14 Hilbert rule for type A.

FIGURE 9.15 Second-order Hilbert curve.

FIGURE 9.16 The rule $F \rightarrow$ $F[RF]F[LF]F$.

FIGURE 9.17 Second iteration of the rule in Figure 9.16.

The interpretation of these rules is that the Nth pattern is formed by combining four patterns of order $N - 1$ in specified directions. We can see from Figure 9.14 for the first-order curve A_1 that **links** corresponding to the arrows in the formulas must be added to connect the patterns. Note also that each pattern starts in a different corner. When the curves are drawn, the arrows and links are left out, and we obtain curves such as in Figure 9.15.

If we scale the lengths of links as we go to higher-order curves, we can verify that, like the Koch curves, the Hilbert curves get longer and longer, never crossing themselves, but always fit in the same box. In the limit, the Hilbert curves fill every point in the box and are known as **space-filling curves**.

The push and pop operators allow us to develop side branches. Consider the rule

$$F \rightarrow F[RF]F[LF]F,$$

where the angle is 27 degrees (Figure 9.16). Note that we start at the bottom and the angle is measured as a right or left deviation from pointing forward.

If we start with a single line segment, the resulting object is that shown in Figure 9.16. We can proceed in a number of ways. One method is to apply the rule again to each F in the sequence, resulting in the object in Figure 9.17. We can also adjust the length corresponding to a forward movement of the turtle so that branches get smaller on successive iterations. The object resembles a bush and will look more like a bush if we iterate a few more times. However, having only one rule and applying it in parallel results in every bush looking the same.

A more interesting strategy is to apply the rule *randomly* to occurrences of F. If we do so, our single rule can generate both of the objects in Figure 9.18. Adding a few more productions and controlling the probability function that determines which rule is to be applied next allows the user to generate a variety of types of trees. With only slight modifications, we can also draw leaves at the ends of the branches.

One of the attractions of this strategy is that we have defined a class of objects based on only a handful of rules and a few parameters. Suppose that we wish to create a group of trees. The direct approach is to generate as many objects as needed, representing each one as a collection of geometric objects (lines, polygons, curves). In a complex scene, we might then be overwhelmed with the number of primitives generated. Depending on the viewing conditions, most of these primitives might not appear in the image, because they would be clipped out or would be too far from the viewer to be rendered at a visible size. In contrast, using our procedural method, we describe objects by simple algorithms and generate the geometric objects only when we need them and to only the level of detail that we need.

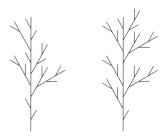

FIGURE 9.18 Results of random application of the rule from Figure 9.16.

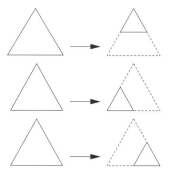

FIGURE 9.19 Three rules for the Sierpinski gasket.

We can also describe a grammar directly in terms of shapes and affine transformations, creating a **shape grammar**. Consider our old friend the Sierpinski gasket. We can define a subdivision step in terms of three affine transformations, each of which scales the original triangle to one-half of the size and places the small copy in a different position, as shown in Figure 9.19. We can apply these rules randomly, or we can apply all three in parallel. In either case, in the limit, we derive the gasket.

We now have three related procedural methods that can generate either models of natural objects or models of interesting mathematical objects. The examples of the Koch curve and the Sierpinski gasket introduce a new aspect to the generation process—a method that can be applied recursively and that, each time it is executed, generates detail similar in shape to the original object. Such phenomena can be explored through fractal geometry.

9.8 RECURSIVE METHODS AND FRACTALS

The language-based procedural models offer but one approach to generating complex objects with simple programs. Another approach, based on **fractal geometry**, uses the self-similarity of many real-world objects. Fractal geometry was developed by Mandelbrot, who was able to create a branch of mathematics that enables us to work with interesting phenomena with which we cannot deal using the tools of ordinary geometry. Workers in computer graphics have used the ideas of fractal geometry not only to create beautiful and complex objects but also to model many real-world entities that are not modeled easily by other methods. Graphical objects generated by fractals have been called **graftals.**

9.8.1 Rulers and Length

There are two pillars to fractal geometry: the dependence of geometry on scale and self-similarity. We can examine both through the exploration of one of the questions that led to fractal geometry: What is the length of a coastline? Say that we have a map of a coastline. Because a typical stretch of coastline is wavy and irregular, we can take a string, lay it over the image of the coastline, and then measure the length of the string, using the scale of the map to convert distances. However, if we get a second map that shows a closer view of the coastline, we see more detail. The added detail looks much like the view of the first map, but with additional inlets and protrusions visible. If we take our string and measure the length on the second map, taking into account the difference in scale between the two maps, we will measure a greater distance. We can continue this experiment by going to the coast and trying to measure with even greater precision. We find new detail, perhaps even to the level of measuring individual pebbles along the shore. In principle, we could continue this process down to the molecular level, each time seeing a similar picture with more detail and measuring a greater length.

If we want to get any useful information, or at least a measurement on which two people might agree, we must either limit the resolution of the map or, equivalently, pick the minimum unit that we can measure. In computer graphics, if we use perspective views, we have a similar problem, because what detail we see depends on how far we are from the object.

We can approach these problems mathematically by considering our recursion for the Koch snowflake in Section 9.7. Here, each line segment of length 1 was replaced by four line segments of length 1/3 (Figure 9.20). Hence, each time that we replace a segment, we span the distance between the same two endpoints with a curve four-thirds of the length of the original. If we consider the limit as we iterate an infinite number of times, the issue of dimension arises. The curve cannot be an ordinary one-dimensional curve, because, in the limit, it has infinite length and its first derivative is discontinuous everywhere. It is not a two-dimensional object, however, because it does not fill a two-dimensional region of the plane. We can resolve this problem by defining a fractional dimension.

FIGURE 9.20   Lengthening of the Koch curve.

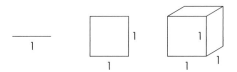

FIGURE 9.21   Line segment, square, and cube.

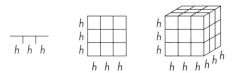

FIGURE 9.22   Subdivision of the objects for $h = \frac{1}{3}$.

9.8.2 Fractal Dimension

Consider a line segment of length 1, a unit square, and a unit cube, as shown in Figure 9.21. Under any reasonable definition of *dimension*, the line segment, square, and cube are one-, two-, and three-dimensional objects, respectively. Suppose that we have a ruler whose resolution is h, where $h = \frac{1}{n}$ is the smallest unit that we can measure. We assume that n is an integer. We can divide each of these objects into similar units in terms of h, as shown in Figure 9.22. We divide the line segment into $k = n$ identical segments, the square into $k = n^2$ small squares, and the cube into $k = n^3$ small cubes. In each case, we can say that we have created new objects by scaling the original object by a factor of h and replicating it k times. Suppose that d is the dimension of any one of these objects. What has remained constant in the subdivision is that the whole is the sum of the parts. Mathematically, for any of the objects, we have the equality

$$\frac{k}{n^d} = kn^{-d} = 1.$$

Solving for d, we can define the **fractal dimension** as

$$d = \frac{\ln k}{\ln n}.$$

In other words, the fractal dimension of an object is determined by how many similar objects we create by subdivision. Consider the Koch curve. We create four similar objects by the subdivision (scaling) of the original by a factor of 3. The corresponding fractal dimension is

$$d = \frac{\ln 4}{\ln 3} = 1.26186.$$

FIGURE 9.23 Subdivision of the Sierpinski gasket.

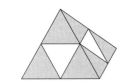

FIGURE 9.24 Solid gasket.

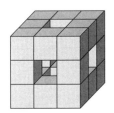

FIGURE 9.25 Subdivision of a cube.

Now consider the Sierpinski gasket. A scaling step is shown in Figure 9.23. Each time that we subdivide a side by a factor of 2, we keep three of the four triangles created, and

$$d = \frac{\ln 3}{\ln 2} = 1.58496.$$

In both examples, we can view the object created by the subdivision as occupying more space than a curve but less space than a filled area. We can create a solid version of the gasket in a three-dimensional space by starting with a tetrahedron and subdividing each of the faces, as shown in Figure 9.24. We keep the four tetrahedrons at the original vertices, discarding the region in the middle. The object that we create has a fractal dimension of

$$d = \frac{\ln 4}{\ln 2} = 2,$$

even though it does not lie in the plane. Also, note that although the volume is reduced by each subdivision, the surface area is increased. Suppose that we start with a cube and divide it into thirds, as shown in Figure 9.25. Next, we remove the center by pushing out the pieces in the middle of each face and the center, thus leaving 20 of the original 27 subcubes. This object has a fractal dimension of

$$d = \frac{\ln 20}{\ln 3} = 2.72683.$$

Although these constructions are interesting and are easy to generate graphically at any level of recursion, they are by themselves not useful for modeling the world. However, if we add randomness, we get a powerful modeling technique.

9.8.3 Midpoint Division and Brownian Motion

A fractal curve has dimension $1 \le d < 2$. Curves with lower fractal dimension appear smoother than curves with higher fractal dimension. A similar statement holds for surfaces that have fractal dimension $2 \le d < 3$. In computer graphics, there are many situations where we would like to create a curve or surface that appears random but that has a measurable amount of roughness. For example, the silhouette of a mountain range forms a curve that is rougher (has higher fractal dimension) than the skyline of the desert. Likewise, a surface model of mountain terrain should have a higher fractal dimension than the surface of farmland. We also often want to generate these objects in a resolution-dependent manner. For example, the detail that we generate for a terrain used in a speed-critical application, such as in a flight simulator, should be generated at high resolution for only those areas near the aircraft.

The random movement of particles in fluids is known as **Brownian motion**. Simulating such motion provides an interesting approach to generating natural curves and surfaces. Physicists have modeled Brownian motion by forming polylines in which each successive point on the polyline is displaced by a random distance and

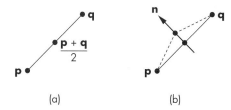

(a)   (b)

FIGURE 9.26   Midpoint displacement. (a) Original line segment. (b) Line segment after subdivision.

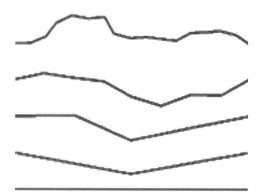

FIGURE 9.27   Fractal curves with 1, 2, 4, 8, and 16 segments.

in a random direction from its predecessor. True Brownian motion is based on a particular random-number distribution that generates paths that match physical particle paths. In computer graphics, we are more concerned with rapid computation, and with the ability to generate curves with a controllable amount of roughness; thus, we use the term *Brownian motion* in this broader sense.

Although we could attempt to generate Brownian motion through the direct generation of a polyline, a more efficient method is to use a simple recursive process. Consider the line segment in Figure 9.26(a). We find its midpoint; then, we displace the midpoint in the normal direction, by a random distance, as in Figure 9.26(b). We can repeat this process any number of times to produce curves like that in Figure 9.27. The variance of the random-number generator, or the average displacement, should be scaled by a factor, usually of 1/2, each time, because the line segments are shortened at each stage. We can also allow the midpoint to be displaced in a random direction, rather than only along the normal. If the random numbers are always positive, we can create skylines. If we use a zero-mean Gaussian random-number generator, with variance proportional to $l^{2(2-d)}$, where l is the length of the segment to be subdivided, then d is the fractal dimension of the resulting curve. The value $d = 1.5$ corresponds to true Brownian motion.

FIGURE 9.28   Midpoint subdivision of a tetrahedron facet.

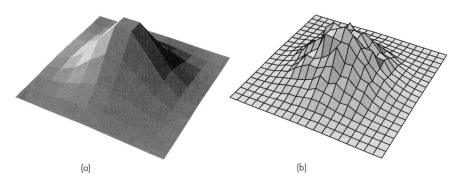

(a)   (b)

FIGURE 9.29   Fractal terrain. (a) Mesh. (b) Subdivided mesh with displaced vertices.

9.8.4 Fractal Mountains

The best-known uses of fractals in computer graphics have been to generate mountains and terrain. We can generate a mountain with our tetrahedron-subdivision process by adding in a midpoint displacement. Consider one facet of the tetrahedron, as shown in Figure 9.28. First, we find the midpoints of the sides; then, we displace each midpoint,[2] creating four new triangles. Once more, by controlling the variance of the random-number generator, we can control the roughness of the resulting object. Note that we must take great care in how the random numbers are generated if we are to create objects that are topologically correct and do not fold into themselves; see the suggested readings at the end of this chapter.

This algorithm can be applied equally well to any mesh. We can start with a flat mesh of rectangles in the x, z-plane, and subdivide each rectangle into four smaller rectangles, displacing all vertices upward (in the y-direction). Figure 9.29 shows one example of this process. Section 9.9 presents another approach that can be used for generating terrain.

---

2. We can also displace the original vertices.

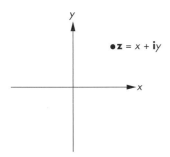

FIGURE 9.30   Complex plane.

9.8.5 The Mandelbrot Set

The famous Mandelbrot set is an interesting example of fractal geometry that can be generated easily with OpenGL's pixel drawing functionality. Although the Mandelbrot set is easy to generate, it shows infinite complexity in the patterns it generates. It also provides a good example of generating images and using color lookup tables. In this discussion, we assume that you have a basic familiarity with complex arithmetic.

We denote a point in the complex plane as

$$\mathbf{z} = x + \mathbf{i}y,$$

where x is the real part and y is the imaginary part of $\mathbf{z}$ (Figure 9.30). If $\mathbf{z}_1 = x_1 + \mathbf{i}y_1$ and $\mathbf{z}_2 = x_2 + \mathbf{i}y_2$ are two complex numbers, complex addition and multiplication are defined by

$$\mathbf{z}_1 + \mathbf{z}_2 = x_1 + x_2 + \mathbf{i}(y_1 + y_2),$$

$$\mathbf{z}_1\mathbf{z}_2 = x_1x_2 - y_1y_2 + \mathbf{i}(x_1y_2 + x_2y_1).$$

The pure imaginary number $\mathbf{i}$ has the property that $\mathbf{i}^2 = -1$. A complex number $\mathbf{z}$ has magnitude given by

$$|\mathbf{z}|^2 = x^2 + y^2.$$

In the complex plane, a function

$$\mathbf{w} = F(\mathbf{z})$$

maps complex points into complex points. We can use such a function to define a complex recurrence of the form

$$\mathbf{z}_{k+1} = F(\mathbf{z}_k),$$

where $\mathbf{z}_0 = \mathbf{c}$ is a given initial point. If we plot the locations of $\mathbf{z}_k$ for particular starting points, we can see several of the possibilities in Figure 9.31. For a particular

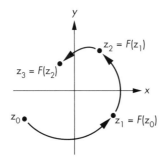

FIGURE 9.31   Paths from complex recurrence.

function F, some initial values generate sequences that go off to infinity. Others may repeat periodically, and still other sequences converge to points called **attractors**. For example, consider the function

$$\mathbf{z}_{k+1} = \mathbf{z}_k^2,$$

where $\mathbf{z}_0 = \mathbf{c}$. If $\mathbf{c}$ lies outside a unit circle, the sequence $\{\mathbf{z}_k\}$ diverges; if $\mathbf{c}$ is inside the unit circle, $\{\mathbf{z}_k\}$ converges to an attractor at the origin; if $|\mathbf{c}| = 1$, each $\mathbf{z}_k$ is on the unit circle. If we consider the points for which $|\mathbf{c}| = 1$, we can see that, depending on the value of $\mathbf{c}$, we can generate either a finite number of points or all the points on the unit circle.

A more interesting example is the function

$$\mathbf{z}_{k+1} = \mathbf{z}_k^2 + \mathbf{c},$$

with $\mathbf{z}_0 = 0 + \mathbf{i}0$. The point $\mathbf{c}$ is in the **Mandelbrot set** if and only if the points generated by this recurrence remain finite. Thus, we can break the complex plane into two groups of points: those that belong to the Mandelbrot set and those that do not. Graphically, we can take a rectangular region of the plane and color points black if they are in the set and white if they are not (Figure 9.32a). However, it is the regions on the edges of the set that show the most complexity, so we often want to magnify these regions.

The computation of the Mandelbrot set can be time-consuming; there are a few tricks to speed it up. The area centered at $\mathbf{c} = -0.5 + \mathbf{i}0.0$ is of the most interest, although we probably want to be able to change both the size and the center of our window.

We can usually tell after a few iterations whether a point will go off to infinity. For example, if $|\mathbf{z}_k| > 4$, successive values will be larger, and we can stop the iteration. It is more difficult to tell whether a point near the boundary will converge. Consequently, an approximation to the set is usually generated as follows. We fix a maximum number of iterations. If, for a given $\mathbf{c}$, we can determine that the point diverges, we color white the point corresponding to $\mathbf{c}$ in our image. If, after the maximum number of iterations, $|\mathbf{z}_k|$ is less than some threshold, we decide that it is in the set, and we color

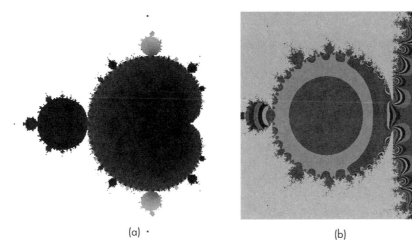

FIGURE 9.32 Mandelbrot set. (a) Black and white coloring. (b) Detail along edges.

it black. For other values of $|z_k|$, we assign a unique color to the point corresponding to **c**. These colors are usually based on the value of $|z_k|$ after the last iteration or, alternately, how rapidly the points converge or diverge.

The book's Web site contains a program that generates an approximation to the set. The user can set the size and center of the rectangle and the number of iterations to be carried out. The magnitudes of the numbers z_k are clamped to be in the range of 0.0 to 1.0. We generate an n × m 1-byte array `image` by looping over all pixels up to the maximum number of iterations.

We display the image as a texture mapped onto a square comprised of two triangles. Hence, the vertices and texture coordinates can be given using a unit cube as

```
point4 points[6] = {point4(0.0, 0.0, 0.0, 1.0), point4(0.0, 1.0, 0.0, 1.0),
                    point4(1.0, 1.0, 0.0, 1.0), point4(1.0, 1.0, 0.0, 1.0),
                    point4(1.0, 0.0, 0.0, 1.0), point4(0.0, 0.0, 0.0, 1.0)};

GLfloat tex_coord[6][2] = {{0.0, 0.0}, {0.0, 1.0}, {1.0, 1.0}, {1.0, 1.0},
                          {1.0, 0.0}, {0.0, 0.0}};
```

or if we use two-dimensional vertices, we can use the same array:

```
GLfloat points[6][2] = {{0.0, 0.0}, {0.0, 1.0}, {1.0, 1.0}, {1.0, 1.0},
                       {1.0, 0.0}, {0.0, 0.0}};
```

We set up a texture map just as in Chapter 7. We can create a texture image in many ways. The simplest is to construct a luminance image

```
GLfloat image[N][N];
```

from the values generated by the calculation of the set and then display it as usual:

```
void display()
{
    glClear(GL_COLOR_BUFFER_BIT);
    glDrawArrays(GL_TRIANGLES, 0, 6);
    glutSwapBuffers();
}
```

The image in Figure 9.32a was obtained in this manner. However, we can map the luminance values into colors in a manner that enhances the detail. Consider the RGB texture image

```
GLfloat image[N][M][3];
```

and the map from luminance values v generated by the iteration

```
            if(v>1.0) v=1.0; /* clamp if > 1 */
            image[i][j][0] = v;
            image[i][j][1] = 2.0*sin(v)-1.0;
            image[i][j][2] = 1.0 - v;
```

We specify an intensity-to-red map that assigns no red to black (0.0), assigns full red to white (1.0), and linearly interpolates between these values for the other intensities. For blue, we go from full blue for zero intensity to no blue for full intensity. We assign the intensity-to-green values sinusoidally. This green assignment enhances the detail in regions where there are slow changes in intensity (Figure 9.32b).

9.9 PROCEDURAL NOISE

We have used pseudorandom-number generators to generate the Sierpinski gasket and for fractal subdivision. The use of pseudorandom-number generators has many other uses in computer graphics ranging from generating textures to generating models of natural objects such as clouds and fluids. However, there are both practical and theoretical reasons that the simple random-number generator that we have used is not a good choice for our applications.

Let's start with the idea of **white noise**. White noise is what we get from thermal activity in electrical circuits or what we see on a television screen when we tune to a channel that has no signal. Ideal white noise has the property that if we look at a sequence of samples, we can find no correlation among the samples and thus we cannot predict the next sample from the previous samples. Mathematically, white noise has the property that its power spectrum—the average spectrum we would see in the frequency domain—is flat; all frequencies are present with equal strength.

Within the computer, we can generate pseudorandom sequences of numbers. These random-number generators, such as the function `rand` that we have used, produce uncorrelated sequences, but, because the sequences repeat after a long period, they are not truly random even though they work well enough for most applications. However, for many other applications white noise is not what we need. Often we want randomness but do not want successive samples to be totally uncorrelated. For example, suppose that we want to generate some terrain for an interactive game. We can use a polygonal mesh whose heights vary randomly. True white noise would give a very rough surface due to the high-frequency content in the noise. If we want a more realistic surface that might model a fairly smooth terrain, we would want adjacent vertices to be close to each other. Equivalently, we would like to remove high frequencies from the noise generator or at least alter or "color" the spectrum.

There is an additional problem with the high frequencies in white noise: aliasing. As we saw in Chapter 7, sampling will cause aliasing of frequencies about the Nyquist rate, which can lead to annoying visual artifacts in the image.

There are various possible solutions to these problems. Assume that we want to generate a sequence of random samples that are bandlimited and for which we know which frequencies we would like to be present. We could sample the sum of sinusoidal terms with low frequencies and random amplitudes and phases. This method of **Fourier synthesis** works in principle but requires expensive evaluations of trigonometric functions for each sample. Another class of methods is based on Figure 9.33. If the process is a digital filtering of the white noise, we can design the filter to include the frequencies we want at the desired magnitude and phase. Because this noise has a nonuniform spectrum, it is often called **colored noise**.

If we start with what we would like to see in a method, we can design a procedural approach that is based on Figure 9.33 but which is much more computationally feasible. Besides wanting to minimize the computation required, we want repeatability and locality. If we used a random method to form a pattern or a texture, we must be able to repeat it exactly as we regenerate an object. We also want to be able to generate our pattern or texture using only local data rather than global data.

Suppose that we generate a pseudorandom sequence on a one-, two-, or three-dimensional grid (or lattice) in which the grid points are integers. We can use the values at the grid points to generate points for noninteger values, that is, for points between the cells determined by adjacent grid values. For example, suppose that we want to generate a two-dimensional texture; we start by forming a rectangular array of pseudorandom numbers. We can use this array to generate values for any (s, t) texture coordinates by interpolation. A simple interpolation would be to find the cell corresponding to a given (s, t) pair and use bilinear interpolation on the values at the corners to get an interior value.

This method generates what is known as **value noise**. We can control the smoothness by selecting how large a part of the array we use. For example, suppose that we

FIGURE 9.33   Generating correlated random numbers.

generate a 256×256 array of pseudorandom numbers and use bilinear interpolation to form a 128×128 texture. We can use a single cell and interpolate the desired 128×128 values using only the four values at the corners of the cell. In this case, we would get a very smooth texture image. Alternately, we could use a larger part of the array. If we used a 4×4 part of the array, each of the 16 cells would be interpolated to provide 64 values of the texture. Since we would be using 16 of the pseudorandom numbers, this texture would show more variation than our first example. We could use a 128×128 part of the pseudorandom array. In this case, we would not need any interpolation and would have a completely uncorrelated texture.

The problem with this process is that bilinear interpolation over each cell will result in visible artifacts as we go from cell to cell forming our texture. We can get around this problem by using an interpolation formula that uses data from adjacent cells to give a smoother result. The most common methods use cubic polynomials of the type that we shall study in Chapter 10. Without going into detail on any particular type, we can note that a cubic polynomial has four coefficients, and thus we need four data points to specify it. For a two-dimensional process, we need the data at the eight adjacent cells, or 16 (4×4) data points, to determine values within that cell. In three dimensions, we need data at the 26 adjacent cells, or 64 data points. Although we would get a smoother result, in two or three dimensions the amount of computation and the required data manipulation make this method problematic.

The solution to this problem is to use **gradient noise**. Suppose that we model noise in three dimensions as a continuous function $n(x, y, z)$. Near a grid point (i, j, k) where i, j, and k are integers, we can approximate $n(x, y, z)$ by the first terms of the Taylor series

$$n(x, y, z) \approx n(i, j, k) + (x - i)\frac{\partial n}{\partial x} + (y - j)\frac{\partial n}{\partial y} + (z - k)\frac{\partial n}{\partial z}.$$

The vector

$$\mathbf{g} = \begin{bmatrix} g_x \\ g_y \\ g_z \end{bmatrix} = \begin{bmatrix} \frac{\partial n}{\partial x} \\ \frac{\partial n}{\partial y} \\ \frac{\partial n}{\partial z} \end{bmatrix}$$

is the gradient at (i, j, k). Note that $x - i$, $y - j$, and $z - k$ are the fractional parts of the position within a cell. To generate gradient noise, we first compute normalized pseudorandom gradient vectors at each grid point. We can get these vectors by generating a set of uniformly distributed random points on a unit sphere. We fix the values at the grid points to be zero ($n(i, j, k) = 0$). In three dimensions, within each cell, we have eight gradient vectors, one from each corner of the cell that we can use to approximate $n(x, y, z)$. The standard technique is to use a filtered (smoothed) interpolation of these gradients to generate noise at points inside the cell. Noise generated in this manner is often called **Perlin noise** after its original creator or just *noise*. This noise function is built into RenderMan and GLSL. The actual implementation of noise uses a hash table so that rather than finding random gradients for the entire grid only 256 or 512 pseudorandom numbers are needed. Figure 9.34 shows

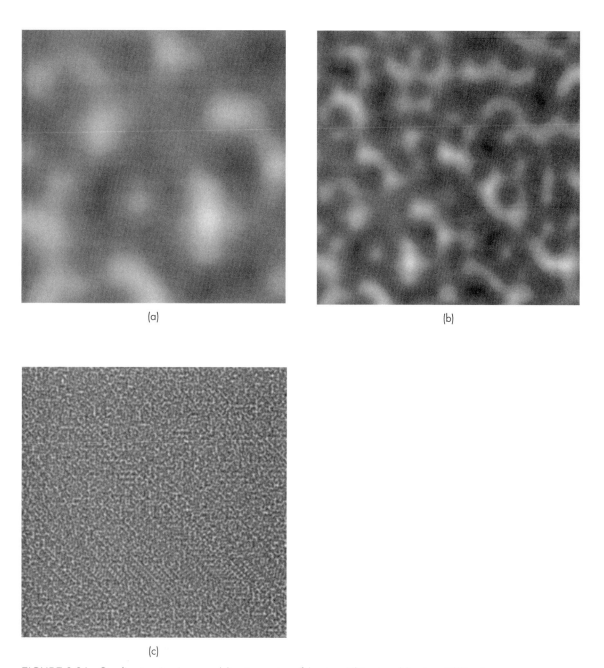

(a)   (b)

(c)

FIGURE 9.34   Gradient noise images (a) using noise, (b) using 50*noise, (c) using 100*noise.

two-dimensional gradient noise at three different frequencies. Each is a 256×256 luminance image that starts with the same array of pseudorandom numbers.

Procedural noise has been used in many ways. For example, adding a noise to the joint positions in our figure model can give a sense of realism to the model. Adding a nonlinearity such as taking the absolute value in the noise generator generates sequences that have been used to model turbulence in flows and to generate textures. Procedural noise is also used for modeling "fuzzy" objects such as simulated clouds.

SUMMARY AND NOTES

Procedural methods have advantages in that we can control how many primitives we produce and at which point in the process these primitives are generated. Equally important is that procedural graphics provides an object-oriented approach to building models—an approach that should be of increasing importance in the future.

Combining physics with computer graphics provides a set of techniques that has the promise of generating physically correct animations and of providing new modeling techniques. Recent examples, such as the use of physical modeling for the motion of 1000 balloons in Pixar Animation Studio's *Up*, show how the solution of complex systems of equations can provide the foundations of an animation.

Particle systems are but one example of physically based modeling, but they represent a technique that has wide applicability. One of the most interesting and informative exercises that you can undertake at this point is to build a particle system.

Particle methods are used routinely in commercial animations, both for simulation of physical phenomena, such as fire, clouds, and moving water, and in determining the positions of animated characters. Particle systems have also become a standard approach to simulating physical phenomena, often replace complex partial differential equation models, and are used even if a graphical result is not needed. In interactive games and simulations, each particle can be given complex behavioral rules. This merging of graphics and artificial intelligence is known as **agent-based modeling**.

Fractals provide another method for generating objects with simple algorithms and programs that produce images that appear to have great complexity. Procedural noise has been at the heart of almost all procedural-modeling methods, and its true power is often best demonstrated when it is combined with one or more of the other methods that we have presented.

As we look ahead, we see a further convergence of graphics methods with methods from physics, mathematics, and other sciences. Historically, given the available computing power, we were content to accept visuals that "looked OK" but were not especially close to the correct physics in applications such as simulation and interactive games. Even in applications in which we might spend days rendering a single frame, the true physics was still too complex to simulate well. However, with the continued advances in available computing power and the lowered cost of accessing such power, we expect to see more and more physically correct modeling in all applications of computer graphics.

SUGGESTED READINGS

Particle systems were introduced in computer graphics by Reeves [Ree83]. Since then, they have been used for a variety of phenomena, including flocking of birds [Rey87], fluid flow, fire, modeling of grass, and display of surfaces [Wit94a]. Particles are also used extensively in physics and mathematics and provide an alternative to solving complex systems of partial differential equations that characterize fluid flow and solid mechanics. See, for example, [Gre88]. Our approach follows Witkin [Wit94b]. Many examples of procedural modeling are in [Ebe02].

There is a wealth of literature on fractals and related methods. The paper by Fournier [Fou82] was the first to show the fractal mountain. For a deeper treatment of fractal mathematics, see the books by Mandelbrot [Man82] and Peitgen [Pei88]. The use of graph grammars has appeared in a number of forms [Pru90, Smi84, Lin68]. Both Hill [Hil07] and Prusinkiewicz [Pru90] present interesting space-filling curves and surfaces. Barnsley's iterated-function systems [Bar93] provide another approach to use of self-similarity; they have application in such areas as image compression.

Gradient noise is due to Perlin [Per85, Per89, Per02]. Many applications to texture and object generation are in [Ebe02], as is a discussion of value noise.

EXERCISES

9.1 What are the possible approaches to procedural modeling?

9.2 How could you model fireworks using computer graphics? How would you check the positions of the particles?

9.3 Start with the tetrahedron-subdivision program that we used in Chapter 5 to approximate a sphere. Convert this program into one that will generate a fractal mountain.

9.4 We can write a description of a binary tree, such as we might use for search, as a list of nodes with pointers to its children. Write an OpenGL program that will take such a description and display the tree graphically.

9.5 Write a program for a simple particle system of masses and springs. Render the particle system as a mesh of quadrilaterals. Include a form of interaction that allows a user to put particles in their initial positions.

9.6 Give a comparative study of the types of constraints that can be imposed on particles.

9.7 How is the flocking behavior of birds simulated? Explain with reference to simulating complex behaviors among particles.

9.8 Write a program that, given two polygons with the same number of vertices, will generate a sequence of images that converts one polygon into the other.

9.9 If we use the basic formula that we used for the Mandlebrot set but this time fix the value of the complex number c and find the set of initial points for which we get convergence, we have the Julia set for that c. Write a program to display Julia sets. Hint: Use values of c near the edges of the Mandelbrot set.

9.10   Write a particle system that simulates the sparks that are generated by welding or by fireworks.

9.11   How can the Koch curve and Koch snowflake be generated?

9.12   Describe the steps that would be used to generate some terrain for an interactive game.

9.13   Fractal geometry uses the self-similarity of many real-world objects. What are the two pillars to fractal geometry?

9.14   In the Lennard-Jones particle system, particles are attracted to each other by a force proportional to the inverse of the distance between them raised to the 12th power but are repelled by another force proportional to the inverse of the same distance raised to the 24th power. Simulate such a system in a box. To make the simulation easier, you can assume that a particle that leaves the box reenters the box from the opposite side.

9.15   Other than language-based procedural models, what other approach can be used to generate complex objects with simple programs?

9.16   In animations, particle systems are used to give the positions of the characters. Once the positions are determined, two-dimensional images of the characters can be texture-mapped onto polygons at these positions. Build such a system for moving characters subject to both external forces that move them in the desired direction and repulsive forces that keep them from colliding. How can you keep the polygons facing the camera?

9.17   Add particle lifetimes to the particle system. Reimplement the particle system using a linked list of particles rather than an array so that particles can be added or eliminated more easily.

9.18   A cloud is a "fuzzy" geometric object. How would you model simulated clouds? Explain your methodology.

9.19   A flag is a smooth surface which can be modeled using the concept of spring force. Describe how a flag blowing in the wind would be modeled.

9.20   Experiment with various flocking algorithms. For example, particles may update their velocities to move toward the center of mass of all particles. Another approach is to have each particle move toward a "friend" particle.

9.21   What is Brownian motion? Explain its use in computer graphics modeling.

9.22   Implement a fractal landscape using procedural noise. Include the capability to move the viewer and to zoom in and out.

CHAPTER 10

CURVES AND SURFACES

The world around us is full of objects of remarkable shapes. Nevertheless, in computer graphics, we continue to populate our virtual worlds with flat objects. We have a good reason for such persistence. Graphics systems can render flat three-dimensional polygons at high rates, including doing hidden-surface removal, shading, and texture mapping. We could take the approach that we took with our sphere model and define curved objects that are, in (virtual) reality, collections of flat polygons. Alternatively, and as we will do here, we can provide the application programmer with the means to work with curved objects in her program, leaving the eventual rendering of these objects to the implementation.

We introduce three ways to model curves and surfaces, paying most attention to the parametric polynomial forms. We also discuss how curves and surfaces can be rendered on current graphics systems, a process that usually involves subdividing the curved objects into collections of flat primitives. From the application programmer's perspective, this process is transparent because it is part of the implementation. It is important to understand the work involved, however, so that we can appreciate the practical limitations we face in using curves and surfaces.

10.1 REPRESENTATION OF CURVES AND SURFACES

Before proceeding to our development of parametric polynomial curves and surfaces, we pause to summarize our knowledge of the three major types of object representation—explicit, implicit, and parametric—and to observe the advantages and disadvantages of each form. We can illustrate the salient points using only lines, circles, planes, and spheres.

10.1.1 Explicit Representation

The **explicit form** of a curve in two dimensions gives the value of one variable, the **dependent variable**, in terms of the other, the **independent variable**. In x, y space, we might write

$$y = f(x),$$

or if we are fortunate, we might be able to invert the relationship and express x as a function of y:

$x = g(y)$.

There is no guarantee that either form exists for a given curve. For the line, we usually write the equation

$y = mx + h$,

in terms of its slope m and y-intercept h, even though we know that this equation does not hold for vertical lines. This problem is one of many coordinate-system–dependent effects that cause problems for graphics systems and, more generally, for all fields where we work with design and manipulation of curves and surfaces. Lines and circles exist independently of any representation, and any representation that fails for certain orientations, such as vertical lines, has serious deficiencies.

Circles provide an even more illustrative example. Consider a circle of radius r centered at the origin. A circle has constant **curvature**—a measure of how rapidly a curve is bending at a point. No closed two-dimensional curve can be more symmetric than the circle. However, the best we can do, using an explicit representation, is to write one equation for half of it,

$y = \sqrt{r^2 - x^2}$,

and a second equation,

$y = -\sqrt{r^2 - x^2}$,

for the other half. In addition, we must also specify that these equations hold only if

$0 \leq |x| \leq r$.

In three dimensions, the explicit representation of a curve requires two equations. For example, if x is again the independent variable, we have two dependent variables:

$y = f(x)$,
$z = g(x)$.

A surface requires two independent variables, and a representation might take the form

$z = f(x, y)$.

As is true in two dimensions, a curve or surface may not have an explicit representation. For example, the equations

$y = ax + b,$

$z = cx + d$

describe a line in three dimensions, but these equations cannot represent a line in a plane of constant x. Likewise, a surface represented by an equation of the form $z = f(x, y)$ cannot represent a sphere, because a given x and y can generate zero, one, or two points on the sphere.

10.1.2 Implicit Representations

Most of the curves and surfaces with which we work have implicit representations. In two dimensions, an **implicit curve** can be represented by the equation

$f(x, y) = 0.$

Our two examples—the line and the circle centered at the origin—have the respective representations

$ax + by + c = 0,$

$x^2 + y^2 - r^2 = 0.$

The function f, however, is really a testing, or **membership**, function that divides space into those points that belong to the curve and those that do not. It allows us to take an x, y pair and to evaluate f to determine whether this point lies on the curve. In general, however, it gives us no analytic way to find a value y on the curve that corresponds to a given x, or vice versa. The implicit form is less coordinate-system–dependent than is the explicit form, however, in that it does represent all lines and circles.

In three dimensions, the implicit form

$f(x, y, z) = 0$

describes a surface. For example, any plane can be written as

$ax + by + cz + d = 0$

for constants a, b, c, and d, and a sphere of radius r centered at the origin can be described by

$x^2 + y^2 + z^2 - r^2 = 0.$

Curves in three dimensions are not as easily represented in implicit form. We can represent a curve as the intersection, if it exists, of the two surfaces:

$f(x, y, z) = 0,$

$g(x, y, z) = 0.$

Thus, if we test a point (x, y, z) and it is on both surfaces, then it must lie on their intersection curve. In general, most of the curves and surfaces that arise in real applications have implicit representations. Their use is limited by the difficulty in obtaining points on them.

Algebraic surfaces are those for which the function $f(x, y, z)$ is the sum of polynomials in the three variables. Of particular importance are the **quadric** surfaces, where each term in f can have degree up to 2.[1] Quadrics are of interest not only because they include useful objects (such as spheres, disks, and cones) but also because when we intersect these objects with lines, at most two intersection points are generated. We will use this characteristic to render quadrics in Section 10.9 and for use in ray tracing in Chapter 11.

10.1.3 Parametric Form

The **parametric form** of a curve expresses the value of each spatial variable for points on the curve in terms of an independent variable, u, the **parameter**. In three dimensions, we have three explicit functions:

$$x = x(u),$$

$$y = y(u),$$

$$z = z(u).$$

One of the advantages of the parametric form is that it is the same in two and three dimensions. In the former case, we simply drop the equation for z. A useful interpretation of the parametric form is to visualize the locus of points $\mathbf{p}(u) = [\ x(u)\quad y(u)\quad z(u)\ ]^T$ being drawn as u varies, as shown in Figure 10.1. We can think of the derivative

$$\frac{d\mathbf{p}(u)}{du} = \begin{bmatrix} \frac{dx(u)}{du} \\ \frac{dy(u)}{du} \\ \frac{dz(u)}{du} \end{bmatrix}$$

as the velocity with which the curve is traced out and points in the direction tangent to the curve.

Parametric surfaces require two parameters. We can describe a surface by three equations of the form

$$x = x(u, v),$$

$$y = y(u, v),$$

$$z = z(u, v),$$

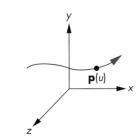

FIGURE 10.1 Parametric curve.

---

1. Degree is measured as the sum of the powers of the individual terms, so x, yz, or z^2 can be in a quadric, but xy^2 cannot.

or we can use the column matrix

$$\mathbf{p}(u, v) = \begin{bmatrix} x(u, v) \\ y(u, v) \\ z(u, v) \end{bmatrix}.$$

As u and v vary over some interval, we generate all the points $\mathbf{p}(u, v)$ on the surface. As we saw with our sphere example in Chapter 5, the vectors given by the column matrices

$$\frac{\partial \mathbf{p}}{\partial u} = \begin{bmatrix} \frac{\partial x(u, v)}{\partial u} \\ \frac{\partial y(u, v)}{\partial u} \\ \frac{\partial z(u, v)}{\partial u} \end{bmatrix}$$

and

$$\frac{\partial \mathbf{p}}{\partial v} = \begin{bmatrix} \frac{\partial x(u, v)}{\partial v} \\ \frac{\partial y(u, v)}{\partial v} \\ \frac{\partial z(u, v)}{\partial v} \end{bmatrix}$$

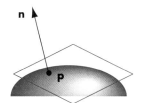

FIGURE 10.2 Tangent plane and normal at a point on a parametric surface.

determine the tangent plane at each point on the surface. In addition, as long as these vectors are not parallel, their cross product gives the normal (Figure 10.2) at each point; that is:

$$\mathbf{n} = \partial \mathbf{p}/\partial u \times \partial \mathbf{p}/\partial v.$$

The parametric form of curves and surfaces is the most flexible and robust for computer graphics. We could still argue that we have not fully removed all dependencies on a particular coordinate system or frame, because we are still using the x, y, and z for a particular representation. It is possible to develop a system solely on the basis of $\mathbf{p}(u)$ for curves and $\mathbf{p}(u, v)$ for surfaces. For example, the **Frenet frame** is often used for describing curves in three-dimensional space, and it is defined starting with the tangent and the normal at each point on the curve. As in our discussion of bump mapping in Chapter 7, we can compute a binormal for the third direction. However, this frame changes for each point on the curve. For our purposes, the parametric form for x, y, z within a particular frame is sufficiently robust.

10.1.4 Parametric Polynomial Curves

Parametric forms are not unique. A given curve or surface can be represented in many ways, but we will find that parametric forms in which the functions are polynomials in u for curves and polynomials in u and v for surfaces are of most use in computer graphics. Many of the reasons will be summarized in Section 10.2.

Consider a curve of the form[2]

$$\mathbf{p}(u) = \begin{bmatrix} x(u) \\ y(u) \\ z(u) \end{bmatrix}.$$

A polynomial parametric curve of degree[3] n is of the form

$$\mathbf{p}(u) = \sum_{k=0}^{n} u^k \mathbf{c}_k,$$

where each $\mathbf{c}_k$ has independent x, y, and z components; that is,

$$\mathbf{c}_k = \begin{bmatrix} c_{xk} \\ c_{yk} \\ c_{zk} \end{bmatrix}.$$

The $n + 1$ column matrices $\{\mathbf{c}_k\}$ are the coefficients of $\mathbf{p}$; they give us $3(n + 1)$ degrees of freedom in how we choose the coefficients of a particular $\mathbf{p}$. There is no coupling, however, among the x, y, and z components, so we can work with three independent equations, each of the form

$$p(u) = \sum_{k=0}^{n} u^k c_k,$$

where p is any one of x, y, or z. There are $n + 1$ degrees of freedom in $p(u)$. We can define our curves for any range interval of u:

$$u_{\min} \leq u \leq u_{\max};$$

however, with no loss of generality (see Exercise 10.3), we can assume that $0 \leq u \leq 1$. As the value of u varies over its range, we define a **curve segment**, as shown in Figure 10.3.

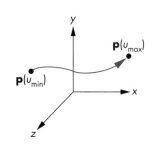

FIGURE 10.3   Curve segment.

10.1.5 Parametric Polynomial Surfaces

We can define a parametric polynomial surface as

$$\mathbf{p}(u, v) = \begin{bmatrix} x(u, v) \\ y(u, v) \\ z(u, v) \end{bmatrix} = \sum_{i=0}^{n} \sum_{j=0}^{m} \mathbf{c}_{ij} u^i v^j.$$

---

2. At this point there is no need to work in homogeneous coordinates; in Section 10.8 we shall work in them to derive NURBS curves.

3. OpenGL often uses the term *order* to mean one greater than the degree.

We must specify $3(n + 1)(m + 1)$ coefficients to determine a particular surface $\mathbf{p}(u, v)$. We will always take $n = m$ and let u and v vary over the rectangle $0 \leq u, v \leq 1$, defining a **surface patch**, as shown in Figure 10.4. Note that any surface patch can be viewed as the limit of a collection of curves that we generate by holding either u or v constant and varying the other. Our strategy will be to define parametric polynomial curves and to use the curves to generate surfaces with similar characteristics.

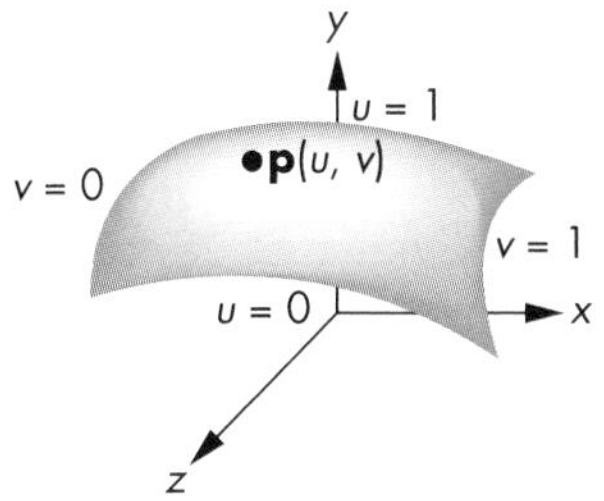

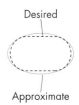

FIGURE 10.4   Surface patch.

10.2   DESIGN CRITERIA

The way curves and surfaces are used in computer graphics and computer-aided design is often different from the way they are used in other fields and from the way you may have seen them used previously. There are many considerations that determine why we prefer to use parametric polynomials of low degree, including:

- Local control of shape
- Smoothness and continuity
- Ability to evaluate derivatives
- Stability
- Ease of rendering

FIGURE 10.5   Model airplane.

We can understand these criteria with the aid of a simple example. Suppose that we want to build a model airplane, using flexible strips of wood for the structure. We can build the body of the model by constructing a set of cross sections and then connecting them with longer pieces, as shown in Figure 10.5. To design our cross sections, we might start with a picture of a real airplane or sketch a desired curve. One such cross section might be like that shown in Figure 10.6. We could try to get a single global description of this cross section, but that description probably would not be what we want. Each strip of wood can be bent to only a certain shape before breaking and can bend in only a smooth way. Hence, we can regard the curve in Figure 10.6 as only an approximation to what we actually build, which might be more like Figure 10.7. In practice, we probably will make our cross section out of a number of wood strips, each of which will become a curve segment for the cross section. Thus, not only will each segment have to be smooth, but we also want a degree of smoothness where the segments meet at **join points**.

FIGURE 10.6   Cross-section curve.

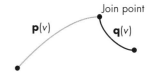

FIGURE 10.7   Approximation of cross-section curve.

Note that although we might be able to ensure that a curve segment is smooth, we have to be particularly careful at the join points. Figure 10.8 shows an example in which, although the two curve segments are smooth, at the join point the derivative is discontinuous. The usual definition of **smoothness** is given in terms of the derivatives along the curve. A curve with discontinuities is of little interest to us. Generally, a curve with a continuous first derivative is smoother than a curve whose first derivative has discontinuities (and so on for the higher derivatives). These notions become more precise in Section 10.3. For now, it should be clear that for a polynomial curve

FIGURE 10.8   Derivative discontinuity at join point.

$$\mathbf{p}(u) = \sum_{k=0}^{n} \mathbf{c}_k u^k,$$

all derivatives exist and can be computed analytically. Consequently, the only places where we can encounter continuity difficulties are at the join points.

We would like to design each segment individually, rather than designing all the segments by a single global calculation. One reason for this preference is that we would like to work interactively with the shape, carefully molding it to meet our specifications. When we make a change, this change will affect the shape in only the area where we are working. This sort of local control is but one aspect of a more general stability principle: *Small changes in the values of input parameters should cause only small changes in output variables.* Another statement of this principle is: *Small changes in independent variables should cause only small changes in dependent variables.*

Working with our piece of wood, we might be able to bend it to approximate the desired shape by comparing it to the entire curve. More likely, we would consider data at a small number of **control**, or **data**, **points** and would use only those data to design our shape. Figure 10.9 shows a possible curve segment and a collection of control points. Note that the curve passes through, or **interpolates**, some of the control points but only comes close to others. As we will see throughout this chapter, in computer graphics and CAD we are usually satisfied if the curve passes close to the control-point data, as long as it is smooth.

This example shows many of the reasons for working with polynomial parametric curves. In fact, the spline curves that we discuss in Sections 10.7 and 10.8 derive their name from a flexible wood or metal device that shipbuilders used to design the shape of hulls. Each spline was held in place by pegs, and the bending properties of the material gave the curve segment a polynomial shape.

Returning to computer graphics, remember that we need methods for rendering curves (and surfaces). A good mathematical representation may be of limited value if we cannot display the resulting curves and surfaces easily. We would like to display whatever curves and surfaces we choose with techniques similar to those used for flat objects, including color, shading, and texture mapping.

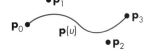

FIGURE 10.9   Curve segment and control points.

10.3   PARAMETRIC CUBIC POLYNOMIAL CURVES

Once we have decided to use parametric polynomial curves, we must choose the degree of the curve. On one hand, if we choose a high degree, we will have many parameters that we can set to form the desired shape, but evaluation of points on the curve will be costly. In addition, as the degree of a polynomial curve becomes higher, there is more danger that the curve will become rougher. On the other hand, if we pick too low a degree, we may not have enough parameters with which to work. However, if we design each curve segment over a short interval, we can achieve many of our purposes with low-degree curves. Although there may be only a few degrees of freedom, these few may be sufficient to allow us to produce the desired shape in a small region. For this reason, most designers, at least initially, work with cubic polynomial curves.

We can write a cubic parametric polynomial using a row and column matrix as

$$\mathbf{p}(u) = \mathbf{c}_0 + \mathbf{c}_1 u + \mathbf{c}_2 u^2 + \mathbf{c}_3 u^3 = \sum_{k=0}^{3} \mathbf{c}_k u^k = \mathbf{u}^T \mathbf{c},$$

where

$$\mathbf{c} = \begin{bmatrix} \mathbf{c}_0 \\ \mathbf{c}_1 \\ \mathbf{c}_2 \\ \mathbf{c}_3 \end{bmatrix}, \qquad \mathbf{u} = \begin{bmatrix} 1 \\ u \\ u^2 \\ u^3 \end{bmatrix}, \qquad \mathbf{c}_k = \begin{bmatrix} c_{kx} \\ c_{ky} \\ c_{kz} \end{bmatrix}.$$

Thus, $\mathbf{c}$ is a column matrix containing the coefficients of the polynomial; it is what we wish to determine from the control-point data. We will derive a number of types of cubic curves. The types will differ in how they use the control-point data. We seek to find 12 equations in 12 unknowns for each type, but because x, y, and z are independent, we can group these equations into three independent sets of four equations in four unknowns. When we discuss NURBS in Section 10.8.4, we will be working in homogeneous coordinates, so we will have to use the w coordinate and thus will have four sets of four equations in four unknowns.

The design of a particular type of cubic will be based on data given at some values of the parameter u. These data might take the form of interpolating conditions in which the polynomial must agree with the data at some points. The data may also require the polynomial to interpolate some derivatives at certain values of the parameter. We might also have smoothness conditions that enforce various continuity conditions at the join points that are shared by two curve segments. Finally, we may have conditions that are not as strict, requiring only that the curve pass close to several known data points. Each type of condition will define a different type of curve, and depending on how we use some given data, the same data can define more than a single curve.

10.4   INTERPOLATION

Our first example of a cubic parametric polynomial is the cubic **interpolating polynomial**. Although we rarely use interpolating polynomials in computer graphics, the derivation of this familiar polynomial illustrates the steps we must follow for our other types, and the analysis of the interpolating polynomial illustrates many of the important features by which we evaluate a particular curve or surface.

Suppose that we have four control points in three dimensions: $\mathbf{p}_0$, $\mathbf{p}_1$, $\mathbf{p}_2$, and $\mathbf{p}_3$. Each is of the form

$$\mathbf{p}_k = \begin{bmatrix} x_k \\ y_k \\ z_k \end{bmatrix}.$$

We seek the coefficients $\mathbf{c}$ such that the polynomial $\mathbf{p}(u) = \mathbf{u}^T\mathbf{c}$ passes through, or interpolates, the four control points. The derivation should be easy. We have four three-dimensional interpolating points; hence, we have 12 conditions and 12 unknowns. First, however, we have to decide at which values of the parameter u the interpolation takes place. Lacking any other information, we can take these values to be the equally spaced values $u = 0$, $\frac{1}{3}$, $\frac{2}{3}$, 1—remember that we have decided to let u always vary over the interval $[0, 1]$. The four conditions are thus

$$\mathbf{p}_0 = \mathbf{p}(0) = \mathbf{c}_0,$$

$$\mathbf{p}_1 = \mathbf{p}\left(\frac{1}{3}\right) = \mathbf{c}_0 + \frac{1}{3}\mathbf{c}_1 + \left(\frac{1}{3}\right)^2 \mathbf{c}_2 + \left(\frac{1}{3}\right)^3 \mathbf{c}_3,$$

$$\mathbf{p}_2 = \mathbf{p}\left(\frac{2}{3}\right) = \mathbf{c}_0 + \frac{2}{3}\mathbf{c}_1 + \left(\frac{2}{3}\right)^2 \mathbf{c}_2 + \left(\frac{2}{3}\right)^3 \mathbf{c}_3,$$

$$\mathbf{p}_3 = \mathbf{p}(1) = \mathbf{c}_0 + \mathbf{c}_1 + \mathbf{c}_2 + \mathbf{c}_3.$$

We can write these equations in matrix form as

$$\mathbf{p} = \mathbf{A}\mathbf{c},$$

where

$$\mathbf{p} = \begin{bmatrix} \mathbf{p}_0 \\ \mathbf{p}_1 \\ \mathbf{p}_2 \\ \mathbf{p}_3 \end{bmatrix}$$

and

$$\mathbf{A} = \begin{bmatrix} 1 & 0 & 0 & 0 \\ 1 & \frac{1}{3} & \left(\frac{1}{3}\right)^2 & \left(\frac{1}{3}\right)^3 \\ 1 & \frac{2}{3} & \left(\frac{2}{3}\right)^2 & \left(\frac{2}{3}\right)^3 \\ 1 & 1 & 1 & 1 \end{bmatrix}.$$

The matrix form here has to be interpreted carefully. If we interpret $\mathbf{p}$ and $\mathbf{c}$ as column matrices of 12 elements, the rules of matrix multiplication are violated. Instead, we view $\mathbf{p}$ and $\mathbf{c}$ each as a four-element column matrix whose elements are three-element row matrices. Hence, multiplication of an element of $\mathbf{A}$, a scalar, by an element of $\mathbf{c}$, a three-element column matrix, yields a three-element column matrix, which is the

FIGURE 10.10   Joining of interpolating segments.

same type as an element of $\mathbf{p}$.[4] We can show that $\mathbf{A}$ is nonsingular, and we can invert it to obtain the **interpolating geometry matrix**

$$\mathbf{M}_I = \mathbf{A}^{-1} = \begin{bmatrix} 1 & 0 & 0 & 0 \\ -5.5 & 9 & -4.5 & 1 \\ 9 & -22.5 & 18 & -4.5 \\ -4.5 & 13.5 & -13.5 & 4.5 \end{bmatrix}$$

and the desired coefficients

$$\mathbf{c} = \mathbf{M}_I \mathbf{p}.$$

Suppose that we have a sequence of control points $\mathbf{p}_0, \mathbf{p}_1, \ldots, \mathbf{p}_m$. Rather than deriving a single interpolating curve of degree m for all the points—a calculation we could do by following a similar derivation to the one for cubic polynomials—we can derive a set of cubic interpolating curves, each specified by a group of four control points, and each valid over a short interval in u. We can achieve continuity at the join points by using the control point that determines the right side of one segment as the first point for the next segment (Figure 10.10). Thus, we use $\mathbf{p}_0, \mathbf{p}_1, \mathbf{p}_2, \mathbf{p}_3$ to find the first segment, we use $\mathbf{p}_3, \mathbf{p}_4, \mathbf{p}_5, \mathbf{p}_6$ for the second, and so on. Note that if each segment is derived for the parameter u varying over the interval $(0, 1)$, then the matrix $\mathbf{M}_I$ is the same for each segment. Although we have achieved continuity for the sequence of segments, derivatives at the join points will not be continuous.

10.4.1 Blending Functions

We can obtain additional insights into the smoothness of the interpolating polynomial curves by rewriting our equations in a slightly different form. We can substitute the interpolating coefficients into our polynomial; we obtain

$$\mathbf{p}(u) = \mathbf{u}^T \mathbf{c} = \mathbf{u}^T \mathbf{M}_I \mathbf{p},$$

---

4. We could use row matrices for the elements of $\mathbf{p}$ and $\mathbf{c}$: In that case, ordinary matrix multiplications would work, because we would have a 4×4 matrix multiplying a 4×3 matrix. However, this method would fail for surfaces. The real difficulty is that we should be using *tensors* to carry out the mathematics—a topic beyond the scope of this book.

which we can write as

$$\mathbf{p}(u) = \mathbf{b}(u)^T \mathbf{p},$$

where

$$\mathbf{b}(u) = \mathbf{M}_I^T \mathbf{u}$$

is a column matrix of the four **blending polynomials**

$$\mathbf{b}(u) = \begin{bmatrix} b_0(u) \\ b_1(u) \\ b_2(u) \\ b_3(u) \end{bmatrix}.$$

Each blending polynomial is a cubic. If we express $\mathbf{p}(u)$ in terms of these blending polynomials as

$$\mathbf{p}(u) = b_0(u)\mathbf{p}_0 + b_1(u)\mathbf{p}_1 + b_2(u)\mathbf{p}_2 + b_3(u)\mathbf{p}_3 = \sum_{i=0}^{3} b_i(u)\mathbf{p}_i,$$

then we can see that the polynomials blend together the individual contributions of each control point and enable us to see the effect of a given control point on the entire curve. These blending functions for the cubic interpolating polynomial are shown in Figure 10.11 and are given by the equations

$$b_0(u) = -\frac{9}{2}\left(u - \frac{1}{3}\right)\left(u - \frac{2}{3}\right)(u - 1),$$

$$b_1(u) = \frac{27}{2}u\left(u - \frac{2}{3}\right)(u - 1),$$

$$b_2(u) = -\frac{27}{2}u\left(u - \frac{1}{3}\right)(u - 1),$$

$$b_3(u) = \frac{9}{2}u\left(u - \frac{1}{3}\right)\left(u - \frac{2}{3}\right).$$

Because all the zeros of the blending functions lie in the closed interval [0, 1], the blending functions must vary substantially over this interval and are not particularly smooth. This lack of smoothness is a consequence of the interpolating requirement that the curve must pass through the control points, rather than just come close to them. This characteristic is even more pronounced for interpolating polynomials of higher degree. This problem and the lack of derivative continuity at the join points account for limited use of the interpolating polynomial in computer graphics. However, the same derivation and analysis process will allow us to find smoother types of cubic curves.

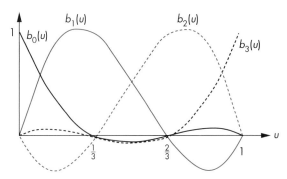

FIGURE 10.11   Blending polynomials for interpolation.

10.4.2 The Cubic Interpolating Patch

There is a natural extension of the interpolating curve to an interpolating patch. A **bicubic surface patch** can be written in the form

$$\mathbf{p}(u, v) = \sum_{i=0}^{3} \sum_{j=0}^{3} u^i v^j \mathbf{c}_{ij},$$

where $\mathbf{c}_{ij}$ is a three-element column matrix of the x, y, and z coefficients for the ijth term in the polynomial. If we define a 4×4 matrix whose elements are three-element column matrices,

$$\mathbf{C} = [\, \mathbf{c}_{ij} \,],$$

then we can write the surface patch as

$$\mathbf{p}(u, v) = \mathbf{u}^T \mathbf{C} \mathbf{v},$$

where

$$\mathbf{v} = \begin{bmatrix} 1 \\ v \\ v^2 \\ v^3 \end{bmatrix}.$$

A particular bicubic polynomial patch is defined by the 48 elements of $\mathbf{C}$—that is, 16 three-element vectors.

Suppose that we have 16 three-dimensional control points $\mathbf{p}_{ij}$, $i = 0, \ldots, 3$, $j = 0, \ldots, 3$. We can use these points to specify an interpolating surface patch, as shown in Figure 10.12. If we assume that these data are used for interpolation at the equally spaced values of both u and v of 0, $\frac{1}{3}$, $\frac{2}{3}$, and 1, then we get three sets of 16

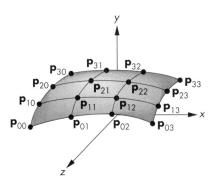

FIGURE 10.12   Interpolating surface patch.

equations in 16 unknowns. For example, for $u = v = 0$, we get the three independent equations

$$\mathbf{p}_{00} = [\,1 \quad 0 \quad 0 \quad 0\,]\,\mathbf{C} \begin{bmatrix} 1 \\ 0 \\ 0 \\ 0 \end{bmatrix} = \mathbf{c}_{00}.$$

Rather than writing down and solving all these equations, we can proceed in a more direct fashion. If we consider $v = 0$, we get a curve in u that must interpolate $\mathbf{p}_{00}$, $\mathbf{p}_{10}$, $\mathbf{p}_{20}$, and $\mathbf{p}_{30}$. Using our results on interpolating curves, we write this curve as

$$\mathbf{p}(u, 0) = \mathbf{u}^T \mathbf{M}_I \begin{bmatrix} \mathbf{p}_{00} \\ \mathbf{p}_{10} \\ \mathbf{p}_{20} \\ \mathbf{p}_{30} \end{bmatrix} = \mathbf{u}^T \mathbf{C} \begin{bmatrix} 1 \\ 0 \\ 0 \\ 0 \end{bmatrix}.$$

Likewise, the values of $v = \frac{1}{3}, \frac{2}{3}, 1$ define three other interpolating curves, each of which has a similar form. Putting these curves together, we can write all 16 equations as

$$\mathbf{u}^T \mathbf{M}_I \mathbf{P} = \mathbf{u}^T \mathbf{C} \mathbf{A}^T,$$

where $\mathbf{A}$ is the inverse of $\mathbf{M}_I$. We can solve this equation for the desired coefficient matrix

$$\mathbf{C} = \mathbf{M}_I \mathbf{P} \mathbf{M}_I^T,$$

and substituting into the equation for the surface, we have

$$\mathbf{p}(u, v) = \mathbf{u}^T \mathbf{M}_I \mathbf{P} \mathbf{M}_I^T \mathbf{v}.$$

We can interpret this result in several ways. First, the interpolating surface can be derived from our understanding of interpolating curves—a technique that will enable us to extend other types of curves to surfaces. Second, we can extend our use of blending polynomials to surfaces. By noting that $\mathbf{M}_I^T \mathbf{u}$ describes the interpolating blending functions, we can rewrite our surface patch as

$$\mathbf{p}(u, v) = \sum_{i=0}^{3} \sum_{j=0}^{3} b_i(u) b_j(v) \mathbf{p}_{ij}.$$

Each term $b_i(u) b_j(v)$ describes a **blending patch**. We form a surface by blending together 16 simple patches, each weighted by the data at a control point. The basic properties of the blending patches are determined by the same blending polynomials that arose for interpolating curves; thus, most of the characteristics of surfaces are similar to those of the curves. In particular, the blending patches are not particularly smooth, because the zeros of the functions $b_i(u) b_j(v)$ lie inside the unit square in u, v space. Surfaces formed from curves using this technique are known as **tensor-product surfaces**. Bicubic tensor-product surfaces are a subset of all surface patches that contain up to cubic terms in both parameters. They are an example of **separable surfaces**, which can be written as

$$\mathbf{p}(u, v) = \mathbf{f}(\mathbf{u})\mathbf{g}(v),$$

where $\mathbf{f}$ and $\mathbf{g}$ are suitably chosen row and column matrices, respectively. The advantage of such surfaces is that they allow us to work with functions in u and v independently.

10.5 HERMITE CURVES AND SURFACES

We can use the techniques that we developed for interpolating curves and surfaces to generate various other types of curves and surfaces. Each type is distinguished from the others by the way we use the data at control points.

10.5.1 The Hermite Form

Suppose that we start with only the control points $\mathbf{p}_0$ and $\mathbf{p}_3$,[5] and again, we insist that our curve interpolate these points at the parameter values $u = 0$ and $u = 1$, respectively. Using our previous notation, we have the two conditions

$$\mathbf{p}(0) = \mathbf{p}_0 = \mathbf{c}_0,$$

$$\mathbf{p}(1) = \mathbf{p}_3 = \mathbf{c}_0 + \mathbf{c}_1 + \mathbf{c}_2 + \mathbf{c}_3.$$

---

5. We use this numbering to be consistent with our interpolation notation, as well as with the numbering that we use for Bézier curves in Section 10.6.

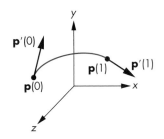

FIGURE 10.13 Definition of the Hermite cubic.

We can get two other conditions if we assume that we know the derivatives of the function at $u = 0$ and $u = 1$. The derivative of the polynomial is simply the parametric quadratic polynomial

$$\mathbf{p}'(u) = \begin{bmatrix} \frac{dx}{du} \\ \frac{dy}{du} \\ \frac{dz}{du} \end{bmatrix} = \mathbf{c}_1 + 2u\mathbf{c}_2 + 3u^2\mathbf{c}_3.$$

If we denote the given values of the two derivatives as $\mathbf{p}_0'$ and $\mathbf{p}_3'$, then our two additional conditions (Figure 10.13) are

$$\mathbf{p}_0' = \mathbf{p}'(0) = \mathbf{c}_1,$$

$$\mathbf{p}_3' = \mathbf{p}'(1) = \mathbf{c}_1 + 2\mathbf{c}_2 + 3\mathbf{c}_3.$$

We can write these equations in matrix form as

$$\begin{bmatrix} \mathbf{p}_0 \\ \mathbf{p}_3 \\ \mathbf{p}_0' \\ \mathbf{p}_3' \end{bmatrix} = \begin{bmatrix} 1 & 0 & 0 & 0 \\ 1 & 1 & 1 & 1 \\ 0 & 1 & 0 & 0 \\ 0 & 1 & 2 & 3 \end{bmatrix} \mathbf{c}.$$

Letting $\mathbf{q}$ denote the data matrix

$$\mathbf{q} = \begin{bmatrix} \mathbf{p}_0 \\ \mathbf{p}_3 \\ \mathbf{p}_0' \\ \mathbf{p}_3' \end{bmatrix},$$

we can solve the equations to find

$$\mathbf{c} = \mathbf{M}_H\mathbf{q},$$

where $\mathbf{M}_H$ is the **Hermite geometry** matrix

$$\mathbf{M}_H = \begin{bmatrix} 1 & 0 & 0 & 0 \\ 0 & 0 & 1 & 0 \\ -3 & 3 & -2 & -1 \\ 2 & -2 & 1 & 1 \end{bmatrix}.$$

The resulting polynomial is given by

$$\mathbf{p}(u) = \mathbf{u}^T\mathbf{M}_H\mathbf{q}.$$

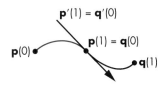

FIGURE 10.14 Hermite form at join point.

We use this method as shown in Figure 10.14, where both the interpolated value and the derivative are shared by the curve segments on the two sides of a join point, and thus both the resulting function and the first derivative are continuous over all segments.

We can get a more accurate idea of the increased smoothness of the Hermite form by rewriting the polynomial in the form

$$\mathbf{p}(u) = \mathbf{b}(u)^T \mathbf{q},$$

where the new blending functions are given by

$$\mathbf{b}(u) = \mathbf{M}_H^T \mathbf{u} = \begin{bmatrix} 2u^3 - 3u^2 + 1 \\ -2u^3 + 3u^2 \\ u^3 - 2u^2 + u \\ u^3 - u^2 \end{bmatrix}.$$

These four polynomials have none of their zeros inside the interval (0, 1) and are much smoother than are the interpolating polynomial blending functions (see Exercise 10.16).

We can go on and define a bicubic Hermite surface patch through these blending functions,

$$\mathbf{p}(u, v) = \sum_{i=0}^{3} \sum_{j=0}^{3} b_i(u) b_j(v) \mathbf{q}_{ij},$$

where $\mathbf{Q} = [\mathbf{q}_{ij}]$ is the extension of $\mathbf{q}$ to surface data. At this point, however, this equation is just a formal expression. It is not clear what the relationship is between the elements of $\mathbf{Q}$ and the derivatives of $\mathbf{p}(u, v)$. Four of the elements of $\mathbf{Q}$ are chosen to interpolate the corners of the patch, whereas the others are chosen to match certain derivatives at the corners of the patch. In most interactive applications, however, the user enters point data rather than derivative data; consequently, unless we have analytic formulations for the data, usually we do not have these derivatives. However, the approach we took with the Hermite curves and surfaces will lead to the Bézier forms that we introduce in Section 10.6.

10.5.2 Geometric and Parametric Continuity

Before we discuss the Bézier and spline forms, we examine a few issues concerning continuity and derivatives. Consider the join point in Figure 10.15. Suppose that the polynomial on the left is $\mathbf{p}(u)$ and the one on the right is $\mathbf{q}(u)$. We enforce various continuity conditions by matching the polynomials and their derivatives at $u = 1$ for $\mathbf{p}(u)$, with the corresponding values for $\mathbf{q}(u)$ at $u = 0$. If we want the function to be continuous, we must have

$$\mathbf{p}(1) = \begin{bmatrix} p_x(1) \\ p_y(1) \\ p_z(1) \end{bmatrix} = \mathbf{q}(0) = \begin{bmatrix} q_x(0) \\ q_y(0) \\ q_z(0) \end{bmatrix}.$$

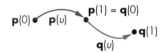

FIGURE 10.15 Continuity at the join point.

All three parametric components must be equal at the join point; we call this property C^0 **parametric continuity.**

When we consider derivatives, we can require, as we did with the Hermite curve, that

$$\mathbf{p}'(1) = \begin{bmatrix} p'_x(1) \\ p'_y(1) \\ p'_z(1) \end{bmatrix} = \mathbf{q}'(0) = \begin{bmatrix} q'_x(0) \\ q'_y(0) \\ q'_z(0) \end{bmatrix}.$$

If we match all three parametric equations and the first derivative, we have C^1 parametric continuity.

If we look at the geometry, however, we can take a different approach to continuity. In three dimensions, the derivative at a point on a curve defines the tangent line at that point. Suppose that instead of requiring matching of the derivatives for the two segments at the join point, we require only that their derivatives be proportional:

$$\mathbf{p}'(1) = \alpha \mathbf{q}'(0),$$

for some positive number α. If the tangents of the two curves are proportional, then they point in the same direction, but they may have different magnitudes. We call this type of continuity G^1 **geometric continuity.**[6] If the two tangent vectors need only to be proportional, we have only two conditions to enforce, rather than three, leaving 1 extra degree of freedom that we can potentially use to satisfy some other criterion. We can extend this idea to higher derivatives and can talk about both C^n and G^n continuity.

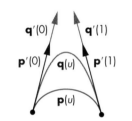

FIGURE 10.16 Change of magnitude in G^1 continuity.

Although two curves that have only G^1 continuity at the join points have a continuous tangent at the join points, the value of the constant of proportionality—or equivalently, the relative magnitudes of the tangents on the two sides of the join point—does matter. Curves with the same tangent direction but different magnitudes differ, as shown in Figure 10.16. The curves $\mathbf{p}(u)$ and $\mathbf{q}(u)$ share the same endpoints, and the tangents at the endpoints point in the same direction, but the curves are different. This result is exploited in many painting programs, where the user can interactively change the magnitude, leaving the tangent direction unchanged. However, in other applications, such as animation, where a sequence of curve segments describes the path of an object, G^1 continuity may be insufficient (see Exercise 10.11).

10.6 BÉZIER CURVES AND SURFACES

Comparing the Hermite form to the interpolating form is problematic; we are comparing forms with some similarities but with significant differences. Both are cubic polynomial curves, but the forms do not use the same data; thus, they cannot be compared on equal terms. We can use the same control-point data that we used to

---

6. G^0 continuity is the same as C^0 continuity.

derive the interpolating curves to approximate the derivatives in the Hermite curves. The resulting Bézier curves are excellent approximations to the Hermite curves and are comparable to the interpolating curves because they have been obtained using the same data. In addition, because these curves do not need derivative information, they are well suited for use in graphics and CAD.

10.6.1 Bézier Curves

Consider again the four control points: $\mathbf{p}_0$, $\mathbf{p}_1$, $\mathbf{p}_2$, and $\mathbf{p}_3$. Suppose that we still insist on interpolating known values at the endpoints with a cubic polynomial $\mathbf{p}(u)$:

$$\mathbf{p}_0 = \mathbf{p}(0),$$

$$\mathbf{p}_3 = \mathbf{p}(1).$$

Bézier proposed that rather than using the other two control points, $\mathbf{p}_2$ and $\mathbf{p}_3$, for interpolation, we use them to approximate the tangents at $u = 0$ and $u = 1$. In parameter space, we can use the linear approximations

$$\mathbf{p}'(0) \approx \frac{\mathbf{p}_1 - \mathbf{p}_0}{\frac{1}{3}} = 3(\mathbf{p}_1 - \mathbf{p}_0),$$

$$\mathbf{p}'(1) \approx \frac{\mathbf{p}_3 - \mathbf{p}_2}{\frac{1}{3}} = 3(\mathbf{p}_3 - \mathbf{p}_2),$$

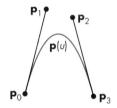

FIGURE 10.17 Approximating tangents.

as shown in Figure 10.17. Applying these approximations to the derivatives of our parametric polynomial, $\mathbf{p}(u) = \mathbf{u}^T\mathbf{c}$, at the two endpoints, we have the two conditions

$$3\mathbf{p}_1 - 3\mathbf{p}_0 = \mathbf{c}_1,$$
$$3\mathbf{p}_3 - 3\mathbf{p}_2 = \mathbf{c}_1 + 2\mathbf{c}_2 + 3\mathbf{c}_3$$

to add to our interpolation conditions

$$\mathbf{p}_0 = \mathbf{c}_0,$$

$$\mathbf{p}_3 = \mathbf{c}_0 + \mathbf{c}_1 + \mathbf{c}_2 + \mathbf{c}_3.$$

At this point, we again have three sets of four equations in four unknowns that we can solve, as before, to find

$$\mathbf{c} = \mathbf{M}_B\mathbf{p},$$

where $\mathbf{M}_B$ is the **Bézier geometry matrix**

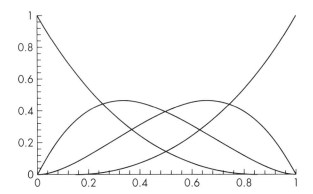

FIGURE 10.18   Blending polynomials for the Bézier cubic.

$$\mathbf{M}_B = \begin{bmatrix} 1 & 0 & 0 & 0 \\ -3 & 3 & 0 & 0 \\ 3 & -6 & 3 & 0 \\ -1 & 3 & -3 & 1 \end{bmatrix}.$$

The cubic Bézier polynomial is thus

$$\mathbf{p}(u) = \mathbf{u}^T \mathbf{M}_B \mathbf{p}.$$

We use this formula exactly as we did for the interpolating polynomial. If we have a set of control points, $\mathbf{p}_0, \ldots, \mathbf{p}_n$, we use $\mathbf{p}_0, \mathbf{p}_1, \mathbf{p}_2$, and $\mathbf{p}_3$ for the first curve; $\mathbf{p}_3, \mathbf{p}_4$, $\mathbf{p}_5$, and $\mathbf{p}_6$ for the second; and so on. It should be clear that we have C^0 continuity, but we have given up the C^1 continuity of the Hermite polynomial because we use different approximations on the left and right of a join point.

We can see important advantages to the Bézier curve by examining the blending functions in Figure 10.18. We write the curve as

$$\mathbf{p}(u) = \mathbf{b}(u)^T \mathbf{p},$$

where

$$\mathbf{b}(u) = \mathbf{M}_B^T \mathbf{u} = \begin{bmatrix} (1-u)^3 \\ 3u(1-u)^2 \\ 3u^2(1-u) \\ u^3 \end{bmatrix}.$$

These four polynomials are one case of the **Bernstein polynomials**,

$$b_{kd}(u) = \frac{d!}{k!(d-k)!} u^k (1-u)^{d-k},$$

which can be shown to have remarkable properties. First, all the zeros of the polynomials are either at $u = 0$ or at $u = 1$. Consequently, for each blending polynomial,

$$b_{id}(u) > 0,$$

for $1 > u > 0$. Without any zeros in the interval, each blending polynomial must be smooth. We can also show that, in this interval (see Exercise 10.5),

$$1 > b_{id}(u),$$

and

$$\sum_{i=0}^{d} b_{id}(u) = 1.$$

Under these conditions, the representation of our cubic Bézier polynomial in terms of its blending polynomials,

$$\mathbf{p}(u) = \sum_{i=0}^{3} b_i(u)\mathbf{p}_i,$$

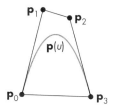

FIGURE 10.19 Convex hull and the Bézier polynomial.

is a convex sum. Consequently, $\mathbf{p}(u)$ must lie in the convex hull of the four control points, as shown in Figure 10.19. Thus, even though the Bézier polynomial does not interpolate all the control points, it cannot be far from them. These two properties, combined with the fact that we are using control-point data, make it easy to work interactively with Bézier curves. A user can enter the four control points to define an initial curve, and then can manipulate the points to control the shape.

10.6.2 Bézier Surface Patches

We can generate the **Bézier surface patches** through the blending functions. If $\mathbf{P}$ is a 4×4 array of control points,

$$\mathbf{P} = \left[\mathbf{p}_{ij} \right],$$

then the corresponding Bézier patch is

$$\mathbf{p}(u, v) = \sum_{i=0}^{3} \sum_{j=0}^{3} b_i(u)b_j(v)\mathbf{p}_{ij} = \mathbf{u}^T \mathbf{M}_B \mathbf{P} \mathbf{M}_B^T \mathbf{v}.$$

The patch is fully contained in the convex hull of the control points (Figure 10.20) and interpolates $\mathbf{p}_{00}$, $\mathbf{p}_{03}$, $\mathbf{p}_{30}$, and $\mathbf{p}_{33}$. We can interpret the other conditions as approximations to various derivatives at the corners of the patch.

Consider the corner for $u = v = 0$. We can evaluate $\mathbf{p}(u)$ and the first partial derivatives to find

$$\mathbf{p}(0, 0) = \mathbf{p}_{00},$$

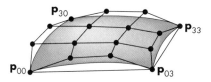

FIGURE 10.20   Bézier patch.

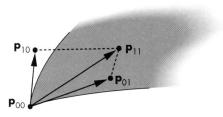

FIGURE 10.21   Twist at corner of Bézier patch.

$$\frac{\partial \mathbf{p}}{\partial u}(0, 0) = 3(\mathbf{p}_{10} - \mathbf{p}_{00}),$$

$$\frac{\partial \mathbf{p}}{\partial v}(0, 0) = 3(\mathbf{p}_{01} - \mathbf{p}_{00}),$$

$$\frac{\partial^2 \mathbf{p}}{\partial u \partial v}(0, 0) = 9(\mathbf{p}_{00} - \mathbf{p}_{01} + \mathbf{p}_{10} - \mathbf{p}_{11}).$$

The first three conditions are clearly extensions of our results for the Bézier curve. The fourth can be seen as a measure of the tendency of the patch to divert from being flat, or to **twist**, at the corner. If we consider the quadrilateral specified by these points (Figure 10.21), the points will lie in the same plane only if the twist is zero. Color Plate 25 uses Bézier patches to create a smooth surface from elevation data.

10.7   CUBIC B-SPLINES

In practice, the cubic Bézier curves and surface patches are widely used. They have one fundamental limitation: At the join points (or patch edges, for surfaces), we have only C^0 continuity. If, for example, we were to use these curves to design our model-airplane cross sections, as shown in Section 10.2, and then were to attempt to build those cross sections, we might be unhappy with the way that the pieces meet at the join points.

It might seem that we have reached the limit of what we can do with cubic parametric polynomials, and that if we need more flexibility, we have to either go to high-degree polynomials or shorten the interval and use more polynomial segments. Both of these tactics are possibilities—but there is another: We can use the same control-point data but not require the polynomial to interpolate any of these points. If we can come close to the control points and get more smoothness at the join points, we may be content with the result.

10.7.1 The Cubic B-Spline Curve

In this section, we illustrate a particular example of a B-spline curve and show how we can obtain C^2 continuity at the join points with a cubic. In Section 10.8, we give a short introduction to a more general approach to splines—an approach that is general enough to include the Bézier curves as a special case. Consider four control points in the middle of a sequence of control points: $\{\mathbf{p}_{i-2}, \mathbf{p}_{i-1}, \mathbf{p}_i, \mathbf{p}_{i+1}\}$. Our previous approach was to use these four points to define a cubic curve such that, as the parameter u varied from 0 to 1, the curve spanned the distance from $\mathbf{p}_{i-2}$ to $\mathbf{p}_{i+1}$, interpolating $\mathbf{p}_{i-2}$ and $\mathbf{p}_{i+1}$. Instead, suppose that as u goes from 0 to 1, we span only the distance between the middle two control points, as shown in Figure 10.22. Likewise, we use $\{\mathbf{p}_{i-3}, \mathbf{p}_{i-2}, \mathbf{p}_{i-1}, \mathbf{p}_i\}$ between $\mathbf{p}_{i-2}$ and $\mathbf{p}_{i-1}$, and $\{\mathbf{p}_{i-1}, \mathbf{p}_i, \mathbf{p}_{i+1}, \mathbf{p}_{i+2}\}$ between $\mathbf{p}_i$ and $\mathbf{p}_{i+1}$. Suppose that $\mathbf{p}(u)$ is the curve we use between $\mathbf{p}_{i-1}$ and $\mathbf{p}_i$, and $\mathbf{q}(u)$ is the curve to its left, used between $\mathbf{p}_{i-2}$ and $\mathbf{p}_{i-1}$. We can match conditions at $\mathbf{p}(0)$ with conditions at $\mathbf{q}(1)$. Using our standard formulation, we are looking for a matrix $\mathbf{M}$, such that the desired cubic polynomial is

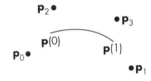

FIGURE 10.22 Four points that define a curve between the middle two points.

$$\mathbf{p}(u) = \mathbf{u}^T \mathbf{M} \mathbf{p},$$

where $\mathbf{p}$ is the matrix of control points

$$\mathbf{p} = \begin{bmatrix} \mathbf{p}_{i-2} \\ \mathbf{p}_{i-1} \\ \mathbf{p}_i \\ \mathbf{p}_{i+1} \end{bmatrix}.$$

We can use the same matrix to write $\mathbf{q}(u)$ as

$$\mathbf{q}(u) = \mathbf{u}^T \mathbf{M} \mathbf{q},$$

where

$$\mathbf{q} = \begin{bmatrix} \mathbf{p}_{i-3} \\ \mathbf{p}_{i-2} \\ \mathbf{p}_{i-1} \\ \mathbf{p}_i \end{bmatrix}.$$

In principle, we could write a set of conditions on $\mathbf{p}(0)$ that would match conditions for $\mathbf{q}(1)$, and we could write equivalent conditions matching various derivatives of $\mathbf{p}(1)$ with conditions for another polynomial that starts there. For example, the condition

$$\mathbf{p}(0) = \mathbf{q}(1)$$

requires continuity at the join point, without requiring interpolation of any data. Enforcing this condition gives one equation for the coefficients of $\mathbf{M}$. There are clearly many sets of conditions that we can use; each set can define a different matrix.

We can take a shortcut to deriving the most popular matrix, by noting that we must use symmetric approximations at the join point. Hence, any evaluation of conditions on $\mathbf{q}(1)$ cannot use $\mathbf{p}_{i-3}$, because this control point does not appear in the equation for $\mathbf{p}(u)$. Likewise, we cannot use $\mathbf{p}_{i+1}$ in any condition on $\mathbf{p}(0)$. Two conditions that satisfy this symmetry condition are

$$\mathbf{p}(0) = \mathbf{q}(1) = \frac{1}{6}(\mathbf{p}_{i-2} + 4\mathbf{p}_{i-1} + \mathbf{p}_i),$$

$$\mathbf{p}'(0) = \mathbf{q}'(1) = \frac{1}{2}(\mathbf{p}_i - \mathbf{p}_{i-2}).$$

If we write $\mathbf{p}(u)$ in terms of the coefficient array $\mathbf{c}$,

$$\mathbf{p}(u) = \mathbf{u}^T \mathbf{c},$$

these conditions are

$$\mathbf{c}_0 = \frac{1}{6}(\mathbf{p}_{i-2} + 4\mathbf{p}_{i-1} + \mathbf{p}_i),$$

$$\mathbf{c}_1 = \frac{1}{2}(\mathbf{p}_i - \mathbf{p}_{i-2}).$$

We can apply the symmetric conditions at $\mathbf{p}(1)$:

$$\mathbf{p}(1) = \mathbf{c}_0 + \mathbf{c}_1 + \mathbf{c}_2 + \mathbf{c}_3 = \frac{1}{6}(\mathbf{p}_{i-1} + 4\mathbf{p}_i + \mathbf{p}_{i+1}),$$

$$\mathbf{p}'(1) = \mathbf{c}_1 + 2\mathbf{c}_2 + 3\mathbf{c}_3 = \frac{1}{2}(\mathbf{p}_{i+1} - \mathbf{p}_{i-1}).$$

We now have four equations for the coefficients of $\mathbf{c}$, which we can solve for a matrix $\mathbf{M}_S$, the **B-spline geometry matrix**,

$$\mathbf{M}_S = \frac{1}{6} \begin{bmatrix} 1 & 4 & 1 & 0 \\ -3 & 0 & 3 & 0 \\ 3 & -6 & 3 & 0 \\ -1 & 3 & -3 & 1 \end{bmatrix}.$$

This particular matrix yields a polynomial that has several important properties. We can see these properties by again examining the blending polynomials:

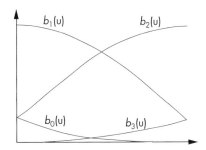

FIGURE 10.23   Spline-blending functions.

$$\mathbf{b}(u) = \mathbf{M}_S^T \mathbf{u} = \frac{1}{6} \begin{bmatrix} (1-u)^3 \\ 4 - 6u^2 + 3u^3 \\ 1 + 3u + 3u^2 - 3u^3 \\ u^3 \end{bmatrix}.$$

These polynomials are shown in Figure 10.23. We can show, as we did for the Bézier polynomials, that

$$\sum_{i=0}^{3} b_i(u) = 1,$$

and, in the interval $1 > u > 0$,

$$1 > b_i(u) > 0.$$

Thus, the curve must lie in the convex hull of the control points, as shown in Figure 10.24. Note that the curve is used for only part of the range of the convex hull. We defined the curve to have C^1 continuity; in fact, however, it has C^2 continuity,[7] as we can verify by computing $\mathbf{p}''(u)$ at $u = 0$ and $u = 1$ and seeing that the values are the same for the curves on the right and left. It is for this reason that spline curves are so important. From a physical point of view, metal will bend such that the second derivative is continuous. From a visual perspective, a curve made of cubic segments with C^2 continuity will be seen as smooth, even at the join points.

Although we have used the same control-point data as those we used for the Bézier cubic to derive a smoother cubic curve, we must be aware that we are doing three times the work that we would do for Bézier or interpolating cubics. The reason is that we are using the curve between only control point $i - 1$ and control point i. A Bézier curve using the same data would be used from control point $i - 2$ to control

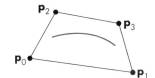

FIGURE 10.24   Convex hull for spline curve.

---

7. If we are concerned with only G^2, rather than with C^2, continuity, we can use the extra degrees of freedom to give additional flexibility in the design of the curves; see Barsky [Bar83].

point $i + 1$. Hence, each time we add a control point, a new spline curve must be computed, whereas for Bézier curves, we add the control points three at a time.

10.7.2 B-Splines and Basis

Instead of looking at the curve from the perspective of a single interval, we can gain additional insights by looking at the curve from the perspective of a single control point. Each control point contributes to the spline in four adjacent intervals. This property guarantees the locality of the spline; that is, if we change a single control point, we can affect the resulting curve in only four adjacent intervals. Consider the control point $\mathbf{p}_i$. In the interval between $u = 0$ and $u = 1$, it is multiplied by the blending polynomial $b_2(u)$. It also contributes to the interval on the left through $\mathbf{q}(u)$. In this interval, its contribution is $b_1(u + 1)$—we must shift the value of u by 1 to the left for this interval.

The total contribution of a single control point can be written as $B_i(u)\mathbf{p_i}$, where B_i is the function

$$
B_i(u) = \begin{cases}
0 & u < i - 2, \\
b_0(u + 2) & i - 2 \le u < i - 1, \\
b_1(u + 1) & i - 1 \le u < i, \\
b_2(u) & i \le u < i + 1, \\
b_3(u - 1) & i + 1 \le u < i + 2, \\
0 & u \ge i + 2.
\end{cases}
$$

This function is pictured in Figure 10.25. Given a set of control points $\mathbf{p}_0, \ldots, \mathbf{p}_m$, we can write the entire spline with the single expression[8]

$$
\mathbf{p}(u) = \sum_{i=1}^{m-1} B_i(u)\mathbf{p}_i.
$$

This expression shows that for the set of functions $B(u - i)$, each member is a shifted version of a single function, and the set forms a basis for all our cubic B-spline curves. Given a set of control points, we form a piecewise polynomial curve $\mathbf{p}(u)$ over the whole interval as a linear combination of basis functions. Figure 10.26 shows the function and the contributions from the individual basis functions. The general theory of splines that we develop in Section 10.8 expands this view by allowing higher-degree polynomials in the intervals and by allowing different polynomials in different intervals.

10.7.3 Spline Surfaces

B-spline surfaces can be defined in a similar way. If we start with the B-spline blending functions, the surface patch is given by

---

8. We determine the proper conditions for the beginning and end of the spline in Section 10.8.

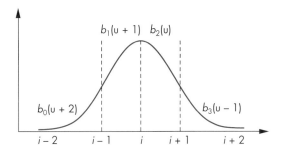

FIGURE 10.25   Spline basis function.

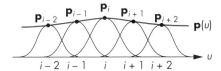

FIGURE 10.26   Approximating function over interval.

FIGURE 10.27   Spline surface patch.

$$\mathbf{p}(u, v) = \sum_{i=0}^{3} \sum_{j=0}^{3} b_i(u)b_j(v)\mathbf{p}_{ij}.$$

This expression is of the same form as are those for our other surface patches, but as we can see from Figure 10.27, we use the patch over only the central area, and we must do nine times the work that we would do with the Bézier patch. However, because of inheritance of the convex-hull property and the additional continuity at the edges from the B-spline curves, the B-spline patch is considerably smoother than a Bézier patch constructed from the same data would be.

10.8   GENERAL B-SPLINES

Suppose that we have a set of control points, $\mathbf{p}_0, \dots, \mathbf{p}_m$. The general approximation problem is to find a function $\mathbf{p}(u) = [\, x(u) \quad y(u) \quad z(u) \,]^T$, defined over an interval

$u_{max} \geq u \geq u_{min}$, that is smooth and is close, in some sense, to the control points. Suppose we have a set of values $\{u_k\}$, called **knots**, such that

$$u_{min} = u_0 \leq u_1 \leq \ldots \leq u_n = u_{max}.$$

We call the sequence $u_0, u_1, \ldots, u_n$ the **knot array**.[9] In splines, the function $\mathbf{p}(u)$ is a polynomial of degree d between the knots,

$$\mathbf{p}(u) = \sum_{j=0}^{d} \mathbf{c}_{jk} u^j, \quad u_k < u < u_{k+1}.$$

Thus, to specify a spline of degree d, we must specify the $n(d+1)$ three-dimensional coefficients $\mathbf{c}_{jk}$. We get the required conditions by applying various continuity requirements at the knots and interpolation requirements at control points.

For example, if $d = 3$, then we have a cubic polynomial in each interval, and, for a given n, we must specify $4n$ conditions. There are $n-1$ internal knots. If we want C^2 continuity at the knots, we have $3n-3$ conditions. If in addition we want to interpolate the $n+1$ control points, we have a total of $4n-2$ conditions. We can pick the other two conditions in various ways, such as by fixing the slope at the ends of the curve. However, this particular spline is global; we must solve a set of $4n$ equations in $4n$ unknowns, and each coefficient will depend on all the control points. Thus, although such a spline provides a smooth curve that interpolates the control points, it is not well suited to computer graphics and CAD.

10.8.1 Recursively Defined B-Splines

The approach taken in B-splines is to define the spline in terms of a set of basis, or blending, functions, each of which is nonzero over only the regions spanned by a few knots. Thus, we write the function $\mathbf{p}(u)$ as an expansion:

$$\mathbf{p}(u) = \sum_{i=0}^{m} B_{id}(u)\mathbf{p}_i,$$

where each function $B_{id}(u)$ is a polynomial of degree d, except at the knots, and is zero outside the interval $(u_{i_{min}}, u_{i_{max}})$. The name *B-splines* comes from the term *basis splines*, in recognition that the set of functions $\{B_{id}(u)\}$ forms a basis for the given knot sequence and degree. Although there are numerous ways to define basis splines, of particular importance is the set of splines defined by the **Cox-deBoor recursion**:[10]

$$B_{k0} = \begin{cases} 1, & u_k \leq u \leq u_{k+1}; \\ 0, & \text{otherwise} \end{cases}$$

---

9. Most researchers call this sequence the *knot vector*, but that terminology violates our decision to use *vector* for only directed line segments.

10. This formula is also known as the *deCasteljau recursion*.

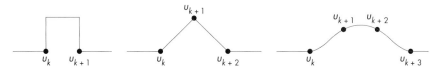

FIGURE 10.28   First three basis functions.

$$B_{kd} = \frac{u - u_k}{u_{k+d} - u_k} B_{k,d-1}(u) + \frac{u_{k+d} - u}{u_{k+d+1} - u_{k+1}} B_{k+1,\,d-1}(u).$$

Each of the first set of functions, B_{k0}, is constant over one interval and is zero everywhere else; each of the second, B_{k1}, is linear over each of two intervals and is zero elsewhere; each of the third, B_{k2}, is quadratic over each of three intervals; and so on (Figure 10.28). In general, B_{kd} is nonzero over the $d + 1$ intervals between u_k and u_{k+d+1}, and it is a polynomial of degree d in each of these intervals. At the knots, there is C^{d-1} continuity. The convex-hull property holds because

$$\sum_{i=0}^{m} B_{i,d}(u) = 1,$$

and

$$1 \geq B_{id}(u) \geq 0,$$

in the interval $u_{\max} \geq u \geq u_{\min}$.

However, because each B_{id} is nonzero in only $d + 1$ intervals, each control point can affect only $d + 1$ intervals, and each point on the resulting curve is within the convex hull defined by these $d + 1$ control points.

Note that careful examination of the Cox-deBoor formula shows that each step of the recursion is a linear interpolation of functions produced on the previous step. Linear interpolation of polynomials of degree k produces polynomials of degree $k + 1$.

A set of spline basis functions is defined by the desired degree and the knot array. Note that we need what appears to be $d - 1$ "extra" knot values to specify our spline because the recursion requires u_0 through u_{n+d} to specify splines from u_0 to u_{n+1}. These additional values are determined by conditions at the beginning and end of the whole spline.

Note that we have made no statement about the knot values other than that $u_k \leq u_{k+1}$. If we define any 0/0 term that arises in evaluating the recursion as equal to 1, then we can have repeated, or multiple, knots. If the knots are equally spaced, we have a **uniform spline**. However, we can achieve more flexibility by allowing not only nonuniform knot spacing but also repeated ($u_k = u_{k+1}$) knots. Let's examine a few of the possibilities.

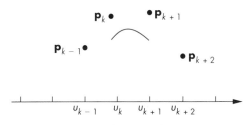

FIGURE 10.29   Uniform B-spline.

10.8.2 Uniform Splines

Consider the uniform knot sequence $\{0, 1, 2, \ldots, n\}$. The cubic B-spline we discussed in Section 10.7 could be derived from the Cox-deBoor formula with equally spaced knots. We use the numbering that we used there (which is shifted from the Cox-deBoor indexing); between knots k and $k + 1$, we use the control points $\mathbf{p}_{k-1}, \mathbf{p}_k,$ $\mathbf{p}_{k+1},$ and $\mathbf{p}_{k+2}$. Thus, we have a curve defined for only the interval $u = 1$ to $u = n - 1$. For the data shown in Figure 10.29, we define a curve that does not span the knots. In certain situations, such as that depicted in Figure 10.30, we can use the periodic nature of the control-point data to define the spline over the entire knot sequence. These **uniform periodic B-splines** have the property that each spline basis function is a shifted version of a single function.

FIGURE 10.30   Periodic uniform B-spline.

10.8.3 Nonuniform B-Splines

Repeated knots have the effect of pulling the spline closer to the control point associated with the knot. If a knot at the end has multiplicity $d + 1$, the B-spline of degree d must interpolate the point. Hence, one solution to the problem of the spline not having sufficient data to span the desired interval is to repeat knots at the ends, forcing interpolation at the endpoints, and using uniform knots everywhere else. Such splines are called **open splines**.

The knot sequence $\{0, 0, 0, 0, 1, 2, \ldots, n - 1, n, n, n, n\}$ is often used for cubic B-splines. The sequence $\{0, 0, 0, 0, 1, 1, 1, 1\}$ is of particular interest, because, in this case, the cubic B-spline becomes the cubic Bézier curve. In the general case, we can repeat internal knots, and we can have any desired spacing of knots.

10.8.4 NURBS

In our development of B-splines, we have assumed that $\mathbf{p}(u)$ is the array $[x(u)\ y(u)\ z(u)]^T$. In two dimensions, however, we could have replaced it with simply $[x(u)\ y(u)]^T$, and all our equations would be unchanged. Indeed, the equations remain unchanged if we go to four-dimensional B-splines. Consider a control point in three dimensions:

$$\mathbf{p}_i = [x_i \quad y_i \quad z_i].$$

The weighted homogeneous-coordinate representation of this point is

$$\mathbf{q}_i = w_i \begin{bmatrix} x_i \\ y_i \\ z_i \\ 1 \end{bmatrix}.$$

The idea is to use the weights w_i to increase or decrease the importance of a particular control point. We can use these weighted points to form a four-dimensional B-spline. The first three components of the resulting spline are simply the B-spline representation of the weighted points,

$$\mathbf{q}(u) = \begin{bmatrix} x(u) \\ y(u) \\ z(u) \end{bmatrix} = \sum_{i=0}^{n} B_{i,d}(u) w_i \mathbf{p}_i.$$

The w component is the scalar B-spline polynomial derived from the set of weights:

$$w(u) = \sum_{i=0}^{n} B_{i,d}(u) w_i.$$

In homogeneous coordinates, this representation has a w component that may not be equal to 1; thus, we must do a perspective division to derive the three-dimensional points:

$$\mathbf{p}(u) = \frac{1}{w(u)} \mathbf{q}(u) = \frac{\sum_{i=0}^{n} B_{i,d}(u) w_i \mathbf{p}_i}{\sum_{i=0}^{n} B_{i,d}(u) w_i}.$$

Each component of $\mathbf{p}(u)$ is now a rational function in u, and because we have not restricted the knots in any way, we have derived a **nonuniform rational B-spline (NURBS)** curve.

NURBS curves retain all the properties of our three-dimensional B-splines, such as the convex-hull and continuity properties. They have two other properties that make them of particular interest in computer graphics and CAD.

If we apply an affine transformation to a B-spline curve or surface, we get the same function as the B-spline derived from the transformed control points. Because perspective transformations are not affine, most splines will not be handled correctly in perspective viewing. However, the perspective division embedded in the construction of NURBS curves ensures that NURBS curves are handled correctly in perspective views.

Quadric surfaces are usually specified by algebraic implicit forms. If we are using nonrational splines, we can only approximate these surfaces. However, quadrics can be shown to be a special case of quadratic NURBS curves; thus, we can use a single modeling method, NURBS curves, for the most widely used curves and surfaces (see Exercises 10.14 and 10.15). Color Plate 5 shows the mesh generated by a NURBS modeling of the surfaces that make up the object in Color Plate 1. OpenGL ultimately renders this mesh with polygons.

10.8.5 Catmull-Rom Splines

If we relax the requirement that our curves and surfaces must lie within the convex hull of the data, we can use our data to form other types of splines. One of the most popular is the Catmull-Rom spline.

Consider again the four control points, $\mathbf{p}_0$, $\mathbf{p}_1$, $\mathbf{p}_2$, and $\mathbf{p}_3$, that we used in our derivation of the Bézier curve. Suppose that rather than deriving a cubic polynomial that interpolates $\mathbf{p}_0$ and $\mathbf{p}_1$, we interpolate the middle points $\mathbf{p}_1$ and $\mathbf{p}_2$:

$$\mathbf{p}(0) = \mathbf{p}_1,$$

$$\mathbf{p}(1) = \mathbf{p}_2.$$

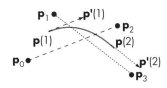

FIGURE 10.31 Constructing the Catmull-Rom spline.

Thus, like the B-spline, our polynomial will be defined over a shorter interval, and each time that we add a new control point, we find a new curve.

We use the points $\mathbf{p}_0$ and $\mathbf{p}_3$ to specify tangents at $\mathbf{p}_0$ and $\mathbf{p}_1$ (Figure 10.31):

$$\mathbf{p}'(0) \approx \frac{\mathbf{p}_2 - \mathbf{p}_0}{2},$$

$$\mathbf{p}'(1) \approx \frac{\mathbf{p}_3 - \mathbf{p}_1}{2}.$$

We now have four conditions on the curve

$$\mathbf{p}(u) = \mathbf{c}_0 + \mathbf{c}_1 u + \mathbf{c}_2 u^2 + \mathbf{c}_3 u^3,$$

which yield the equations

$$\mathbf{p}_1 = \mathbf{c}_0,$$

$$\mathbf{p}_2 = \mathbf{c}_0 + \mathbf{c}_1 + \mathbf{c}_2 + \mathbf{c}_3,$$

$$\frac{\mathbf{p}_2 - \mathbf{p}_0}{2} = \mathbf{c}_1,$$

$$\frac{\mathbf{p}_3 - \mathbf{p}_1}{2} = \mathbf{c}_1 + 2\mathbf{c}_2 + 3\mathbf{c}_3.$$

Note that because as u goes from 0 to 1, we only go from $\mathbf{p}_1$ to $\mathbf{p}_2$, so $\mathbf{p}_0$ and $\mathbf{p}_2$ are separated by 2 units in parameter space, as are $\mathbf{p}_1$ and $\mathbf{p}_3$. In addition, these four conditions ensure that the resulting curves are continuous and have continuous first derivatives at the control points, even though we do not have the convex hull property.

Solving the four equations yields

$$\mathbf{p}(u) = \mathbf{u}^T \mathbf{M}_R \mathbf{p},$$

where $\mathbf{M}_R$ is the Catmull-Rom geometry matrix

$$\mathbf{M}_R = \frac{1}{2} \begin{bmatrix} -1 & 3 & -3 & 0 \\ 2 & -5 & 4 & -1 \\ -1 & 0 & 1 & 0 \\ 0 & 2 & 0 & 0 \end{bmatrix}.$$

10.9 RENDERING CURVES AND SURFACES

Once we have specified a scene with curves and surfaces, we must find a way to render it. There are several approaches, depending on the type of representation. For explicit and parametric curves and surfaces, we can evaluate the curve or surface at a sufficient number of points that we can approximate it with our standard flat objects. We focus on this approach for parametric polynomial curves and surfaces.

For implicit surfaces, we can compute points on the object that are the intersection of rays from the center of projection through pixels with the object. We can then use these points to specify curve sections or meshes that can be rendered directly. However, except for quadrics (Section 10.11), the intersection calculation requires the solution of nonlinear equations of too high a degree to be practical for real-time computation.

Consider the cubic Bezier polynomial

$$\mathbf{b}(u) = (1 - u)^3 \mathbf{p}_0 + (1 - u)^2 u \mathbf{p}_1 + (1 - u) u^2 \mathbf{p}_0 + u^3 \mathbf{p}_3.$$

If we want to evaluate it at N equally spaced values of u and put the results into an array `points` as in our previous examples, the code for a two-dimensional example can be as simple as

```
float d = 1.0/(N-1.0);
float u, uu;
for(int i=0; i<N; i++)
{
    u = i*d;
    uu = 1.0 - u;
    for(int j=0; j<2; j++) points[i][j] = p[0][j]*uu*uu*uu
                                    + 3.0*p[1][j]*uu*uu*u
                                    + 3.0*p[2][j]*uu*u*u
                                    + p[3][j]*u*u*u;
}
```

where the control point data are in the array p.

10.9.1 Polynomial Evaluation Methods

Suppose that we have a representation over our standard interval

$$\mathbf{p}(u) = \sum_{i=0}^{n} \mathbf{c}_i u^i, \quad 0 \leq u \leq 1.$$

We can evaluate $\mathbf{p}(u)$ at some set of values $\{u_k\}$, and we can use a polyline (or GL_LINE_STRIP) to approximate the curve. Rather than evaluate each term u^k independently, we can group the terms as

$$\mathbf{p}(u) = \mathbf{c}_0 + u(\mathbf{c}_1 + u(\mathbf{c}_2 + u(\ldots + \mathbf{c}_n u))).$$

This grouping shows that we need only n multiplications to evaluate each $p(u_k)$; this algorithm is known as **Horner's method**. For our typical cubic $\mathbf{p}(u)$, the grouping becomes

$$\mathbf{p}(u) = \mathbf{c}_0 + u(\mathbf{c}_1 + u(\mathbf{c}_2 + u\mathbf{c}_3)).$$

If the points $\{u_i\}$ are spaced uniformly, we can use the method of **forward differences** to evaluate $\mathbf{p}(u_k)$ using $O(n)$ additions and no multiplications. The forward differences are defined iteratively by the formulas

$$\Delta^{(0)}\mathbf{p}(u_k) = \mathbf{p}(u_k),$$

$$\Delta^{(1)}\mathbf{p}(u_k) = \mathbf{p}(u_{k+1}) - \mathbf{p}(u_k),$$

$$\Delta^{(m+1)}\mathbf{p}(u_k) = \Delta^{(m)}\mathbf{p}(u_{k+1}) - \Delta^{(m)}\mathbf{p}(u_k).$$

If $u_{k+1} - u_k = h$ is constant, then we can show that if $\mathbf{p}(u)$ is a polynomial of degree n, then $\Delta^{(n)}\mathbf{p}(u_k)$ is constant for all k. This result suggests the strategy illustrated in Figure 10.32 for the scalar cubic polynomial

$$p(u) = 1 + 3u + 2u^2 + u^3.$$

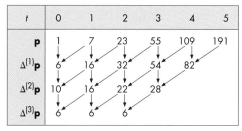

FIGURE 10.32   Construction of a forward-difference table.

t	0	1	2	3	4	5
p	1	7	23	55 → 109 → 191		
$\Delta^{(1)}$**p**	6	16	32 → 54 → 82			
$\Delta^{(2)}$**p**	10	16 → 22 → 28				
$\Delta^{(3)}$**p**	6 → 6 → 6					

FIGURE 10.33   Use of a forward-difference table.

We need the first $n + 1$ values of $p(u_k)$ to find $\Delta^{(n)}p(u_0)$. But once we have $\Delta^{(n)}p(u_0)$, we can copy this value across the table and work upward, as shown in Figure 10.33, to compute successive values of $p(u_k)$, using the rearranged recurrence

$$\Delta^{(m-1)}(p_{k+1}) = \Delta^{(m)}p(u_k) + \Delta^{(m-1)}p(u_k).$$

This method is efficient, but it is not without its faults: It applies only to a uniform grid, and it is prone to accumulation of numerical errors.

10.9.2 Recursive Subdivision of Bézier Polynomials

The most elegant rendering method performs recursive subdivision of the Bézier curve. The method is based on the use of the convex hull and never requires explicit evaluation of the polynomial. Suppose that we have a cubic Bézier polynomial (the method also applies to higher-degree Bézier curves). We know that the curve must lie within the convex hull of the control points. We can break the curve into two separate polynomials, $\mathbf{l}(u)$ and $\mathbf{r}(u)$, each valid over one-half of the original interval. Because the original polynomial is a cubic, each of these polynomials also is a cubic. Note that because each is to be used over one-half of the original interval, we must rescale the parameter u for $\mathbf{l}$ and $\mathbf{r}$ so that as u varies over the range $(0, 1)$, $\mathbf{l}(u)$ traces the left half of $\mathbf{p}(u)$, and $\mathbf{r}(u)$ traces the right half of $\mathbf{p}$. Each of our new polynomials has four control points that both specify the polynomial and form its convex hull. We denote these two sets of points by $\{\mathbf{l}_0, \mathbf{l}_1, \mathbf{l}_2, \mathbf{l}_3\}$ and $\{\mathbf{r}_0, \mathbf{r}_1, \mathbf{r}_2, \mathbf{r}_3\}$; the original control points for $\mathbf{p}(u)$ are $\{\mathbf{p}_0, \mathbf{p}_1, \mathbf{p}_2, \mathbf{p}_3\}$. These points and the two convex hulls are shown in Figure 10.34. Note that the convex hulls for $\mathbf{l}$ and $\mathbf{r}$ must lie inside the convex hull for p, a result known as the **variation-diminishing property** of the Bézier curve.

Consider the left polynomial. We can test the convex hull for flatness by measuring the deviation of $\mathbf{l}_1$ and $\mathbf{l}_2$ from the line segment connecting $\mathbf{l}_0$ and $\mathbf{l}_3$. If they are close, we can draw the line segment instead of the curve. If they are not close, we can divide $\mathbf{l}$ into two halves and test the two new convex hulls for flatness. Thus, we have a recursion that never requires us to evaluate points on a polynomial, but we have yet to discuss how to find $\{\mathbf{l}_0, \mathbf{l}_1, \mathbf{l}_2, \mathbf{l}_3\}$ and $\{\mathbf{r}_0, \mathbf{r}_1, \mathbf{r}_2, \mathbf{r}_3\}$. We will find the hull for $\mathbf{l}(u)$;

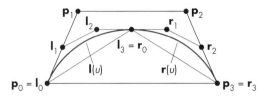

FIGURE 10.34   Convex hulls and control points.

the calculation for $\mathbf{r}(u)$ is symmetric. We can start with

$$\mathbf{p}(u) = \mathbf{u}^T \mathbf{M}_B \begin{bmatrix} \mathbf{p}_0 \\ \mathbf{p}_1 \\ \mathbf{p}_2 \\ \mathbf{p}_3 \end{bmatrix},$$

where

$$\mathbf{M}_B = \begin{bmatrix} 1 & 0 & 0 & 0 \\ -3 & 3 & 0 & 0 \\ 3 & -6 & 3 & 0 \\ -1 & 3 & -3 & -1 \end{bmatrix}.$$

The polynomial $\mathbf{l}(u)$ must interpolate $\mathbf{p}(0)$ and $\mathbf{p}\left(\frac{1}{2}\right)$; hence,

$$\mathbf{l}(0) = \mathbf{l}_0 = \mathbf{p}_0,$$

$$\mathbf{l}(1) = \mathbf{l}_3 = \mathbf{p}\left(\frac{1}{2}\right) = \frac{1}{8}(\mathbf{p}_0 + 3\mathbf{p}_1 + 3\mathbf{p}_2 + \mathbf{p}_3).$$

At $u = 0$, the slope of $\mathbf{l}$ must match the slope of $\mathbf{p}$, but, because the parameter for $\mathbf{p}$ covers only the range $(0, \frac{1}{2})$, while u varies over $(0, 1)$, implicitly we have made the substitution $\bar{u} = 2u$. Consequently, derivatives for $\mathbf{l}$ and $\mathbf{p}$ are related by $d\bar{u} = 2du$, and

$$\mathbf{l}'(0) = 3(\mathbf{l}_1 - \mathbf{l}_0) = \mathbf{p}'(0) = \frac{3}{2}(\mathbf{p}_1 - \mathbf{p}_0).$$

Likewise, at the midpoint,

$$\mathbf{l}'(1) = (\mathbf{l}_3 - \mathbf{l}_2) = \mathbf{p}'\left(\frac{1}{2}\right) = \frac{3}{8}(-\mathbf{p}_0 - \mathbf{p}_1 + \mathbf{p}_2 + \mathbf{p}_3).$$

These four equations can be solved algebraically. Alternatively, this solution can be expressed geometrically, with the aid of Figure 10.35. Here, we construct both the

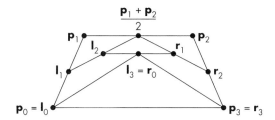

FIGURE 10.35   Construction of subdivision curves.

left and right sets of control points concurrently. First, we note that the interpolation condition requires that

$$\mathbf{l}_0 = \mathbf{p}_0,$$
$$\mathbf{r}_3 = \mathbf{p}_3.$$

We can verify by substitution in the four equations that the slopes on the left and right yield

$$\mathbf{l}_1 = \frac{1}{2}(\mathbf{p}_0 + \mathbf{p}_1),$$
$$\mathbf{r}_2 = \frac{1}{2}(\mathbf{p}_2 + \mathbf{p}_3).$$

The interior points are given by

$$\mathbf{l}_2 = \frac{1}{2}\left(\mathbf{l}_1 + \frac{1}{2}(\mathbf{p}_1 + \mathbf{p}_2)\right),$$
$$\mathbf{r}_1 = \frac{1}{2}\left(\mathbf{r}_2 + \frac{1}{2}(\mathbf{p}_1 + \mathbf{p}_2)\right).$$

Finally, the shared middle point is given by

$$\mathbf{l}_3 = \mathbf{r}_0 = \frac{1}{2}(\mathbf{l}_2 + \mathbf{r}_1).$$

The advantage of this formulation is that we can determine both sets of control points using only shifts (for the divisions by 2) and additions. However, one of the advantages of the subdivision approach is that it can be made adaptive, and only one of the sides may require subdivision at some point in the rendering. Also, note that because the rendering of the curve need not take place until the rasterization stage of the pipeline and can be done in screen or window coordinates, the limited resolution of the display places a limit on how many times the convex hull needs to be subdivided (Exercise 10.18).

10.9.3 Rendering Other Polynomial Curves by Subdivision

Just as any polynomial is a Bézier polynomial, it is also an interpolating polynomial, a B-spline polynomial, and any other type of polynomial for a properly selected set of control points. The efficiency of the Bézier subdivision algorithm is such that we usually are better off converting another curve form to Bézier form and then using the subdivision algorithm.[11] A conversion algorithm can be obtained directly from our curve formulations. Consider a cubic Bézier curve. We can write it in terms of the Bézier matrix $\mathbf{M}_B$ as

$$\mathbf{p}(u) = \mathbf{u}^T \mathbf{M}_B \mathbf{p},$$

where $\mathbf{p}$ is the **geometry matrix** of control points. The same polynomial can be written as

$$\mathbf{p}(u) = \mathbf{u}^T \mathbf{M} \mathbf{q},$$

where $\mathbf{M}$ is the matrix for some other type of polynomial and $\mathbf{q}$ is the matrix of control points for this type. We assume that both polynomials are specified over the same interval. The polynomials will be identical if we choose

$$\mathbf{q} = \mathbf{M}^{-1} \mathbf{M}_B \mathbf{p}.$$

For the conversion from interpolation to Bézier, the controlling matrix is

$$\mathbf{M}_B^{-1} \mathbf{M}_I = \begin{bmatrix} 1 & 0 & 0 & 0 \\ -\frac{5}{6} & 3 & -\frac{3}{2} & \frac{1}{3} \\ \frac{1}{3} & -\frac{3}{2} & 3 & -\frac{5}{6} \\ 0 & 0 & 0 & 1 \end{bmatrix}.$$

For the conversion between cubic B-splines and cubic Bézier curves, it is

$$\mathbf{M}_B^{-1} \mathbf{M}_S = \frac{1}{6} \begin{bmatrix} 1 & 4 & 1 & 0 \\ 0 & 4 & 2 & 0 \\ 0 & 2 & 4 & 0 \\ 0 & 1 & 4 & 1 \end{bmatrix}.$$

Figure 10.36 shows four control points and the cubic Bézier polynomial, interpolating polynomial, and spline polynomial. The interpolating and spline forms were generated as Bézier curves, from the new control points derived from the matrices

---

11. Even systems that do not render using subdivision are often optimized for rendering Bézier curves by other methods. Hence, we still might want to convert any type of polynomial curve or surface to a Bézier curve or surface.

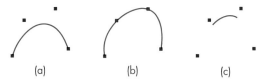

FIGURE 10.36 Cubic polynomials generated as Bézier curves by conversion of control points. (a) Bézier polynomial. (b) Interpolating polynomial. (c) B-spline polynomial.

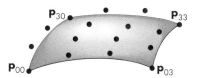

FIGURE 10.37 Cubic Bézier surface.

$\mathbf{M}_B^{-1}\mathbf{M}_I$ and $\mathbf{M}_B^{-1}\mathbf{M}_S$. All three curves were generated with using recursive subdivision of Bézier curves. Note that for the spline case, the resulting curve is generated between only the second and third of the original control points.

10.9.4 Subdivision of Bézier Surfaces

We can extend our subdivision algorithm to Bézier surfaces. Consider the cubic surface in Figure 10.37, with the 16 control points shown. Each four points in a row or column determine a Bézier curve that can be subdivided. However, our subdivision algorithm should split the patch into four patches, and we have no control points along the center of the patch. We can proceed in two steps.

First, we apply our curve-subdivision technique to the four curves determined by the 16 control points in the v direction. Thus, for each of $u = 0, \frac{1}{3}, \frac{2}{3}, 1$, we create two groups of four control points, with the middle point shared by each group. There are then seven different points along each original curve; these points are indicated in Figure 10.38 by circles. We see that there are three types of points: original control points that are kept after the subdivision (gray), original control points that are discarded after the subdivision (white), and new points created by the subdivision (black). We now subdivide in the u-direction using these points. Consider the rows of constant v, where v is one of $0, \frac{1}{3}, \frac{2}{3}, 1$. There are seven groups of four points. Each group defines a Bézier curve for a constant v. We can subdivide in the u-direction, each time creating two groups of four points, again with the middle point shared. These points are indicated in Figure 10.39. If we divide these points into four groups of 16, with points on the edges shared (Figure 10.40), each quadrant contains 16 points that are the control points for a subdivided Bézier surface.

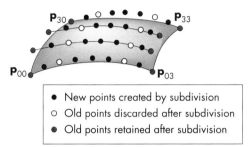

$\bullet$ New points created by subdivision
$\circ$ Old points discarded after subdivision
$\bullet$ Old points retained after subdivision

FIGURE 10.38   First subdivision of surface.

$\bullet$ New points created by subdivision
$\circ$ Old points discarded after subdivision
$\bullet$ Old points retained after subdivision

FIGURE 10.39   Points after second subdivision.

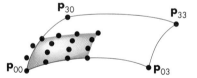

FIGURE 10.40   Subdivided quadrant.

Compared to the calculation for curves, the test for whether the new convex hull is flat enough to stop a subdivision process is more difficult. Many renderers use a fixed number of subdivisions, often letting the user pick the number. If a high-quality rendering is desired, we can let the subdivision continue until the projected size of the convex hull is less than the size of one pixel.

10.10 THE UTAH TEAPOT

We conclude our discussion of parametric surfaces with an example of recursive subdivision of a set of cubic Bézier patches. The object that we show has become known as the **Utah teapot**. The data for the teapot were created at the University of Utah by Mike Newell for testing of various rendering algorithms. These data have been used in the graphics community for more than 30 years. The teapot data consist of the control points for 32 bicubic Bézier patches. They are given in terms of 306 vertices. The first 12 patches define the body of the teapot; the next four define the handle; the next four define the spout; the following eight define the lid; and the final four define the bottom. These data are widely available.

For purposes of illustration, let's assume that we want to subdivide each patch n times and, after these subdivisions, we will render the final vertices using either line segments or polygons passing through the four corners of each patch. Thus, our final drawing can be done with the following function (for line segments), which adds the four corner points (which must interpolate the surface) to the array that will be rendered either with lines or filled triangles:

```
void draw_patch(point4 p[4][4])
{
    points[n] = p[0][0];
    n++;
    points[n] = p[3][0];
    n++;
    points[n] = p[3][3];
    n++;
    points[n] = p[0][3];
    n++;
}
```

We build our patch subdivider from the curve subdivider for a cubic curve c, using our `point4` type:

```
void divide_curve(point4 c[4], point4 r[4], point4 l[4])
{

/* division of convex hull of Bezier curve */

    int i;
    point4 t;
    for(i=0;i<3;i++)

        l[0][i]=c[0][i];
        r[3][i]=c[3][i];
        l[1][i]=(c[1][i]+c[0][i])/2;
        r[2][i]=(c[2][i]+c[3][i])/2;
        t[i]=(l[1][i]+r[2][i])/2;
        l[2][i]=(t[i]+l[1][i])/2;
        r[1][i]=(t[i]+r[2][i])/2;
        l[3][i]=r[0][i]=(l[2][i]+r[1][i])/2;

    for(i=0; i<4; i++) l[i][3] = r[i][3] = 1.0;
}
```

The patch subdivider is easier to write—but is slightly less efficient—if we assume that we have a matrix-transpose function `transpose4`. This code is then:

```
void divide_patch(point4 p[4][4], int n)
{
   point4 q[4][4], r[4][4], s[4][4], t[4][4];
   point4 a[4][4], b[4][4];
   int k;
   if(n==0) draw_patch(p); /* draw patch if recursion done */

/* subdivide curves in u direction, transpose results, divide
in u direction again (equivalent to subdivision in v) */

   else
       {
       for(k=0; k<4; k++) divide_curve(p[k], a[k], b[k]);
       transpose4(a);
       transpose4(b);
       for(k=0; k<4; k++)
           {
           divide_curve(a[k], q[k], r[k]);
           divide_curve(b[k], s[k], t[k]);
           }

/* recursive division of 4 resulting patches */

       divide_patch(q, n-1);
       divide_patch(r, n-1);
       divide_patch(s, n-1);
       divide_patch(t, n-1);
       }
}
```

A complete teapot-rendering program using shaded polygons is given in Appendix A. That program contains the teapot data.

Figure 10.41 shows the teapot as a wireframe and with constant shading. Note that the various patches have different curvatures and sizes; thus, carrying out all subdivisions to the same depth can create many unnecessarily small polygons.

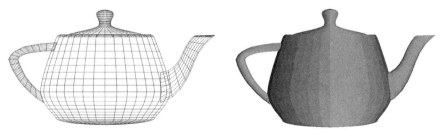

FIGURE 10.41   Rendered teapots.

10.11 ALGEBRAIC SURFACES

Although quadrics can be generated as a special case of NURBS curves, this class of algebraic objects is of such importance that it merits independent discussion. Quadrics are the most important case of the algebraic surfaces that we introduced in Section 10.1.

10.11.1 Quadrics

Quadric surfaces are described by implicit algebraic equations in which each term is a polynomial of the form $x^i y^j z^k$, with $i + j + k \leq 2$. Any quadric can be written in the form

$$q(x, y, z) = a_{11}x^2 + 2a_{12}xy + a_{22}y^2 + a_{33}z^2 + 2a_{23}yz + 2a_{13}xz$$
$$+ b_1 x + b_2 y + b_3 z + c = 0.$$

This class of surfaces includes ellipsoids, parabaloids, and hyperboloids. We can write the general equation in matrix form in terms of the three-dimensional column matrix $\mathbf{p} = [\, x \quad y \quad z \,]^T$ as the **quadratic form**

$$\mathbf{p}^T \mathbf{A} \mathbf{p} + \mathbf{b}^T \mathbf{p} + c = 0,$$

where

$$\mathbf{A} = \begin{bmatrix} a_{11} & a_{12} & a_{13} \\ a_{12} & a_{22} & a_{23} \\ a_{13} & a_{23} & a_{33} \end{bmatrix}, \qquad \mathbf{b} = \begin{bmatrix} b_1 \\ b_2 \\ b_3 \end{bmatrix}.$$

The 10 independent coefficients in $\mathbf{A}$, $\mathbf{b}$, and c determine a given quadric. However, for the purpose of classification, we can apply a sequence of rotations and translations that reduces a quadric to a standard form without changing the type of surface. In three dimensions, we can write such a transformation as

$$\mathbf{p}' = \mathbf{M}\mathbf{p} + \mathbf{d}.$$

This substitution creates another quadratic form with $\mathbf{A}$ replaced by the matrix $\mathbf{M}^T \mathbf{A} \mathbf{M}$. The matrix $\mathbf{M}$ can always be chosen to be a rotation matrix such that $\mathbf{D} = \mathbf{M}^T \mathbf{A} \mathbf{M}$ is a diagonal matrix. The diagonal elements of $\mathbf{D}$ can be used to determine the type of quadric. If, for example, the equation is that of an ellipsoid, the resulting quadratic form can be put in the form

$$a'_{11}x'^2 + a'_{22}y'^2 + a_{33}z'^2 - c' = 0,$$

where all the coefficients are positive. Note that because we can convert to a standard form by an affine transformation, quadrics are preserved by affine transformations and thus fit well with our other standard primitives.

10.11.2 Rendering of Surfaces by Ray Casting

Quadrics are easy to render because we can find the intersection of a quadric with a ray by solving a scalar quadratic equation. We represent the ray from $\mathbf{p}_0$ in the direction $\mathbf{d}$ parametrically as

$$\mathbf{p} = \mathbf{p}_0 + \alpha \mathbf{d}.$$

Substituting into the equation for the quadric, we obtain the scalar equation for α:

$$\alpha^2 \mathbf{d}^T \mathbf{A} \mathbf{d} + \alpha \mathbf{d}^T (\mathbf{b} + 2\mathbf{A}\mathbf{p}_0) + \mathbf{p}_0^T \mathbf{A}\mathbf{p}_0 + \mathbf{b}^T \mathbf{d} + c = 0.$$

As for any quadratic equation, we may find zero, one, or two real solutions. We can use this result to render a quadric into the frame buffer or as part of a ray-tracing calculation. In addition, we can apply our standard shading model at every point on a quadric because we can compute the normal by taking the derivatives

$$\mathbf{n} = \begin{bmatrix} \frac{\partial q}{\partial x} \\ \frac{\partial q}{\partial y} \\ \frac{\partial q}{\partial z} \end{bmatrix} = 2\mathbf{A}\mathbf{p} - \mathbf{b}.$$

This method of rendering can be extended to any algebraic surface. Suppose that we have an algebraic surface

$$q(\mathbf{p}) = q(x, y, z) = 0.$$

As part of the rendering pipeline, we cast a ray from the center of projection through each pixel. Each of these rays can be written in the parametric form

$$\mathbf{p}(\alpha) = \mathbf{p}_0 + \alpha \mathbf{d}.$$

Substituting this expression into q yields an implicit polynomial equation in α:

$$q(\mathbf{p}(\alpha)) = 0.$$

We can find the points of intersection by numerical methods, or for quadrics, by the quadratic formula. If we have terms up to $x^i y^j z^k$, we can have $i + j + k$ points of intersection, and the surface may require considerable time to render.

10.12   SUBDIVISION CURVES AND SURFACES

Let's reexamine our subdivision formula from Section 10.9.2 from a slightly different perspective. We start with four points—$\mathbf{p}_0$, $\mathbf{p}_1$, $\mathbf{p}_2$, $\mathbf{p}_3$—and end up with seven points. We can call these new points $\mathbf{s}_0, \ldots, \mathbf{s}_6$. We can view each of these sets of points as defining a piecewise-linear curve, as illustrated in Figure 10.42.

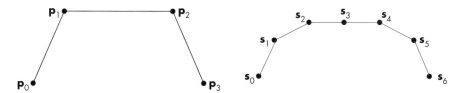

FIGURE 10.42   (a) Piecewise-linear curve determined by four points.
(b) Piecewise-linear curve after one subdivision step.

We can use our subdivision formulas to relate the two sets of points:

$$\mathbf{s}_0 = \mathbf{p}_0$$

$$\mathbf{s}_1 = \tfrac{1}{2}(\mathbf{p}_0 + \mathbf{p}_1),$$

$$\mathbf{s}_2 = \tfrac{1}{4}(\mathbf{p}_0 + 2\mathbf{p}_1 + \mathbf{p}_2),$$

$$\mathbf{s}_3 = \tfrac{1}{8}(\mathbf{p}_0 + 3\mathbf{p}_1 + 3\mathbf{p}_2 + \mathbf{p}_3),$$

$$\mathbf{s}_4 = \tfrac{1}{4}(\mathbf{p}_1 + 2\mathbf{p}_2 + \mathbf{p}_3),$$

$$\mathbf{s}_5 = \tfrac{1}{2}(\mathbf{p}_2 + \mathbf{p}_3),$$

$$\mathbf{s}_6 = \mathbf{p}_3.$$

The second curve is said to be a **refinement** of the first. As we saw in Section 10.9.2, we can continue the process iteratively and in the limit converge to the B-spline. However, in practice, we want to carry out only enough iterations so that the resulting piecewise-linear curve connecting the new points looks smooth. How many iterations we need to carry out depends on the size of the projected convex hull, which can be determined from the camera specifications. Thus, we have a method that allows us to render curves at different levels of detail.

These ideas and their benefits are not limited to B-splines. Over the past few years, a variety of methods for generating these **subdivision curves** have appeared. Some interpolate points—such as $\mathbf{p}_0$ and $\mathbf{p}_3$—while others do not interpolate any of the original points. But in all cases, the refined curves converge to a smooth curve.

10.12.1 Mesh Subdivision

The next issue we examine is how can we apply these ideas to surfaces. A theory of **subdivision surfaces** has emerged that deals with both the theoretical and practical aspects of these ideas. Rather than generating a general subdivision scheme, we will focus on meshes of triangles and meshes of quadrilaterals. In practice, many modeling programs produce one of these types of meshes or a mesh consisting of

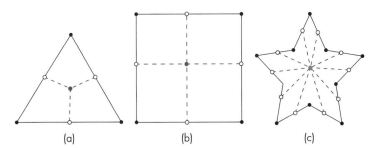

FIGURE 10.43   Polygon subdivision. (a) Triangle. (b) Rectangle. (c) Star-shaped polygon.

only triangles and quadrilaterals. If we start with a more general mesh, we can use tessellation to replace the original mesh with one consisting of only triangles or quadrilaterals.

We can form a quadrilateral mesh from an arbitrary mesh using the Catmull-Clark method. We divide each edge in half, creating a new vertex at the midpoint. We create an additional vertex at the **centroid** of each polygon, that is, the point that is the average of the vertices that form the polygon. We then form a quadrilateral mesh by connecting each original vertex to the new vertices on either side of it and connecting the two new vertices to the centroid. Figure 10.43 shows the subdivision for some simple polygons. Note that in each case the subdivision creates a quadrilateral mesh.

Once we have created the quadrilateral mesh, it is clear that successive subdivisions create a finer quadrilateral mesh. However, we have yet to do anything to create a smoother surface. In particular, we want to ensure as much continuity as possible at the vertices.

Consider the following procedure. First, we compute the average position of each polygon, its centroid. Then, we replace each vertex by the average of the centroids of all the polygons that contain the vertex. At this point, we have a smoother surface but one for which, at vertices not of valence 4, we can see sharp changes in smoothness. The Catmull-Clark scheme produces a smoother surface with one additional step. For each vertex not of valence 4, we replace it by

$$\mathbf{p} = \mathbf{p}_0 + \frac{4}{k}\mathbf{p}_1,$$

where $\mathbf{p}_0$ is the vertex position before the averaging step, $\mathbf{p}_1$ is its position after the averaging pass, and k is the valence of the vertex. The **valence** of a vertex is the number of polygons that share the vertex. This method tends to move edge vertices at corners more than other outer vertices. Figure 10.44 shows the sequence for a single rectangle. In Figure 10.44(a), the original vertices are black and the vertices at the midpoints of the edges are white. The centroid of the original polygon is the gray vertex at the center, and the centroids of the subdivided polygons are shown as colored vertices. Figure 10.44(b) shows the movement of the vertices by averaging,

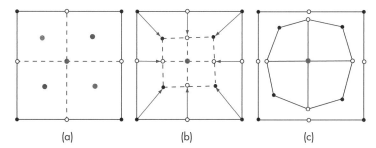

FIGURE 10.44   Catmull-Clark subdivision.

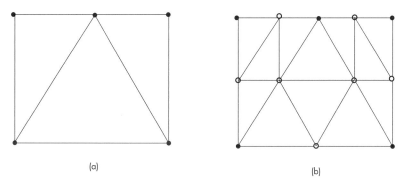

FIGURE 10.45   Loop subdivision. (a) Triangular mesh. (b) Triangles after one subdivision.

and Figure 10.44(c) shows the final Catmull-Clark subdivision after the correction factor has been applied.

This scheme does not work as well for meshes that start with all triangles, because the interior vertices have high valences that do not change with refinement. For triangular meshes, there is a simple method called *Loop subdivision* that we can describe as a variant of the general scheme. We start by doing a standard subdivision of each triangle by connecting the bisectors of the sides to create four triangles. We proceed as before but use a weighted centroid of the vertices with a weight of 1/4 for the vertex that is being moved and 3/8 for the other two vertices that form the triangle. We can get a smoother surface by taking a weighted average of the vertex positions before and after the averaging step, as we did for the Catmull-Clark scheme. Loop's method uses a weight of $\frac{5}{3} - \frac{8}{3}(\frac{3}{8} + \frac{1}{4}\cos(\frac{2\pi}{k}))^2$. Figure 10.45 shows a simple triangle mesh and the resulting mesh after the subdivision step.

The figures in Color Plate 29 were developed using subdivision surfaces. Figure 10.46 shows a sequence of meshes generated by a subdivision-surface algorithm and the rendered surface from the highest resolution mesh. Note that the original mesh contains polygons with different numbers of sides and vertices with different

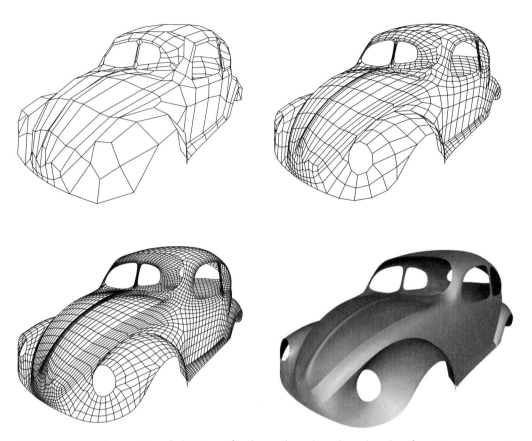

FIGURE 10.46   Successive subdivisions of polygonal mesh and rendered surface. (Images courtesy Caltech Multi-Res Modeling Group)

valences. Also, note that as the mesh is subdivided, each subdivision step yields a smoother surface.

We have not covered some tricky issues, such as the data structures needed to ensure that when we insert vertices we get consistent results for shared edges. The references in the Suggested Readings should help you get started.

10.13   MESH GENERATION FROM DATA

In all our examples, we have assumed that the positions for our data were given either at the nodes of a rectangular grid or possibly at the nodes of a general graph. In many circumstances, we are given a set of locations that we know are from a surface, but otherwise the locations are unstructured. Thus, we have a list of locations but no notion of which points are close to each other.

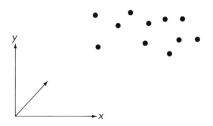

FIGURE 10.47   Height data.

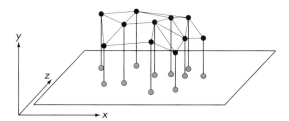

FIGURE 10.48   Height data projected onto plane $y = 0$.

10.13.1 Height Fields Revisited

One example of how such data arises is topography, where we might take measurements of the heights of random points on the ground from an airplane or satellite, such as the height fields we considered in Chapter 4, where they were based on these measurements being taken over a regular grid in which $y = 0$ represents the ground. Consequently, the height data were of the form y_{ij}, all of which could be stored in a matrix. Here, the data are obtained at random unstructured locations, so the starting point is a set of values $\{x_i, y_i, z_i\}$. The topography example has some structure in that we know all the points lie on a single surface and that no two points can have the same x_i and z_i. Figure 10.47 shows a set of points, all of which are above the plane $y = 0$. These points can be projected onto the plane $y = 0$, as in Figure 10.48. We seek an algorithm that connects these points into a triangular mesh, as shown in Figure 10.49. The mesh in the plane can then be projected back up to connect the original data with triangles. These three-dimensional triangles can be rendered to give an approximation to the surface that yielded the data. Figure 10.50 shows this mesh.

In the next section, we examine how we can obtain a triangular mesh from a set of points in the plane.

10.13.2 Delaunay Triangulation

Given a set of points in a plane, there are many ways to form a triangular mesh that uses all the points as vertices. Even four vertices that specify a convex quadrilateral can form a two-triangle mesh in two ways, depending on which way we draw a

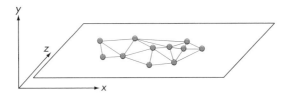

FIGURE 10.49   Triangular mesh.

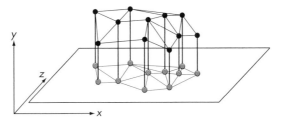

FIGURE 10.50   Three-dimensional mesh.

FIGURE 10.51   Two splits of a quadrilateral.

diagonal. For a mesh of n vertices, there will be $n - 2$ triangles in the mesh but many ways to triangulate the mesh. From the graphics perspective, not all the meshes from a given set of vertices are equivalent. Consider the two ways we can triangulate the four points in Figure 10.51. Because we always want a mesh in which no edges cross, the four edges colored in black must be in the mesh. Note that they form the convex hull of the four points. Hence, we only have a choice as to the diagonal. In Figure 10.51(a), the diagonal creates two long thin triangles whereas the diagonal in Figure 10.51(b) creates two more robust triangles. We prefer the second case because long, thin triangles tend to render badly, showing artifacts from the interpolation of vertex attributes.

In general, the closer a triangle is to an equilateral triangle, the better it is for rendering. In more mathematical terms, the best triangles have the largest minimum interior angle. If we compare two triangular meshes derived from the same set of points, we can say the better mesh is the one with the largest minimum interior angle of all the triangles in the mesh. Although it may appear that determining such a mesh for a large number of triangles is difficult, we can approach the problem in a manner that will yield the smallest minimum angle.

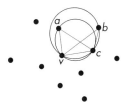

FIGURE 10.52   Circles determined by possible triangulations.

Consider some vertices in the plane that will be part of a mesh (Figure 10.52). Focusing on vertex v, it appears that one of the triangles a, v, c or v, c, b should be part of the mesh. Recall that three points in the plane determine a unique circle that interpolates them. Note that the circle formed by a, v, c does not include another point, whereas the circle formed by v, c, b does. Moreover, the triangle formed by a, v, c has a smaller minimum angle than the triangle formed by v, c, b. Because these two triangles share an edge, we can only use one of them in our mesh.

These observations suggest a strategy known as **Delaunay triangulation**. Given a set of n points in the plane, the Delaunay triangulation has the following properties, any one of which is sufficient to define the triangulation:

1. For any triangle in Delaunay triangulation, the circle passing through its three vertices has no other vertices in its interior.

2. For any edge in the Delaunay triangulation, there is no circle passing through the endpoints (vertices) of this edge that includes another vertex in its interior.

3. If we consider the set of angles of all the triangles in a triangulation, the Delaunay triangulation has the greatest minimum angle.

Proofs of these properties are in the Suggested Readings at the end of the chapter. The third property ensures that the triangulation is a good one for computer graphics. The first two properties follow from how we construct the triangulation.

We start by adding three vertices such that all the points in the set of vertices lie inside the triangle formed by these three vertices, as in Figure 10.53. These extra vertices and the edges connecting them to other vertices can be removed at the end. We next pick a vertex v from our data set at random and connect it to the three added vertices, thus creating three triangles, as shown in Figure 10.54. Note there is no way a circle determined by any three of the four vertices can include the other, so we need not do any testing yet.

We next pick a vertex u randomly from the remaining vertices. From Figure 10.55, we see that this vertex lies inside the triangle formed by a, v, and c and that the three triangles it forms do not present a problem. However, the edge between a and v is a diagonal for the quadrilateral formed by a, u, v, and b, and the circle that interpolates a, u, and v has b in its interior. Hence, if we use this edge, we will violate the criteria for a Delaunay triangulation. There is a simple solution to this

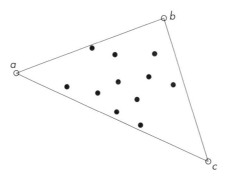

FIGURE 10.53   Starting a Delaunay triangulation.

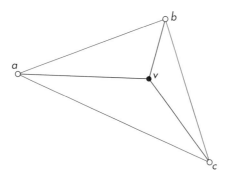

FIGURE 10.54   Triangulation after adding first data point.

problem. We can choose the other diagonal of the quadrilateral and replace the edge between a and v with an edge between u and b, an operation called **flipping**. The resulting partial mesh is shown in Figure 10.56. Now the circle passing through u, v, and b does not include any other vertices, nor do any of the other circles determined by any of the triangles. Thus, we have a Delaunay triangulation of a subset of the points.

We continue the process by adding another randomly chosen vertex from the original set of vertices, flipping as necessary. Note that it is not sufficient in general to flip only one edge corresponding to a just-added vertex. The act of flipping one edge can require the flipping of other edges, so the process is best described recursively. Because each flip gives an improvement, the process terminates for each added vertex, and once we have added all the vertices, we can remove the three vertices we added to get started and all the edges connected to them. On the average, the triangulation has a $O(n \log n)$ complexity.

There are some potential problems with our approach that arise because we create the mesh in a plane and project it back up to the data points. A triangle that has

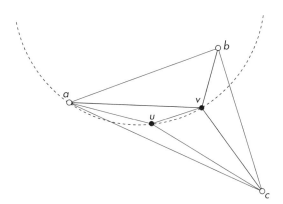

FIGURE 10.55 Adding a vertex requiring flipping.

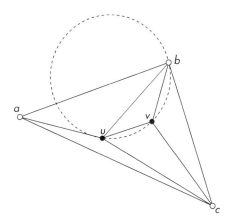

FIGURE 10.56 Mesh after flipping.

almost equal angles in the plane may not have such nice angles when the corresponding original vertices are connected to form a triangle in three dimensions. A potential solution would be to apply a similar strategy directly to the three-dimensional data rather than projecting them onto a plane. For each four points, we can determine a unique sphere that they interpolate. Thus, we can define a three-dimensional Delaunay triangulation as one in which no other data point lies in the sphere and we use the four points to specify a tetrahedron. Unfortunately, determining such a spatial division requires far more work than the Delaunay triangulation in the plane.

10.13.3 Point Clouds

Delaunay triangulation relied on the assumption that our data were $2\frac{1}{2}$ dimensional; that is, we knew they came from a single surface and could be recovered from their projections onto a plane. In many situations, we have data that are completely unstructured, and often these data sets are very large. For example, laser scans can output tens of millions of points in a short time. Such data sets are known as **point clouds**. Often, such data are displayed directly using point primitives. Because we can shade points in OpenGL as we would a surface, a high density of shaded points can show three-dimensional structure, especially if the camera can be moved interactively.

SUMMARY AND NOTES

Once again, we have only scratched the surface of a deep and important topic. Also once again, our focus has been on what we can do on a graphics system using a standard API such as OpenGL. From this perspective, there are huge advantages to using parametric Bézier curves and surfaces. The parametric form is robust and is easy to use interactively because the required data are points that can be entered and manipulated interactively. The subdivision algorithm for Bézier curves and surfaces gives us the ability to render the resulting objects to any desired degree of accuracy.

We have seen that although Bézier surfaces are easy to render, splines can provide additional smoothness and control. The texts in the Suggested Readings discuss many variants of splines that are used in the CAD community.

Quadric surfaces are used extensively with ray tracers, because solving for the points of intersection between a ray and a quadric requires the solution of only a scalar quadratic equation. Deciding whether the point of intersection between a ray and the plane determined by a flat polygon is inside the polygon can be more difficult than solving the intersection problem for quadric surfaces. Hence, many ray tracers allow only infinite planes, quadrics, and, perhaps, convex polygons.

Subdivision surfaces have become increasingly more important for two reasons. First, because commodity hardware can render polygons at such high rates, we can often achieve the desired smoothness using a large number of polygons that can be rendered faster than a smaller number of surface patches. However, future hardware may change this advantage if rendering of curved surfaces is built into the rasterizer. Second, because we can render a subdivision surface at any desired level of detail, we can often use subdivision very effectively by not rendering a highly subdivided surface when it projects to a small area on the screen.

SUGGESTED READINGS

The book by Farin [Far88] provides an excellent introduction to curves and surfaces. It also has an interesting preface in which Bézier discusses the almost simultaneous discovery by him and deCasteljau of the surfaces that bear Bézier's name. Unfortunately, deCasteljau's work was described in unpublished technical reports, so deCasteljau did not receive the credit he deserved for his work until recently. Books such as those by Rogers [Rog90], Foley [Fol90], Bartels [Bar87], and Watt [Wat00] discuss many other forms of splines. See Rogers [Rog00] for an introduction to NURBS. The Catmull-Rom splines were proposed in [Cat75].

The book by Faux [Fau80] discusses the coordinate-free approach to curves and surfaces and the Frenet frame.

Although the book edited by Glassner [Gla89] primarily explores ray tracing, the section by Haines has considerable material on working with quadrics and other algebraic surfaces.

There has been much recent activity on subdivision curves and surfaces. For some of the seminal work in the area, see [Che95], [Deb96], [Gor96], [Lev96], [Sei96], and [Tor96]. Our development follows [War04]. Catmull-Clark subdivision was proposed in [Cat78]. See also [War03] and [Sta03]. Delaunay triangulation is covered in most books on computational geometry. See [deB08].

EXERCISES

10.1 What is the parametric form of a curve? Explain how the curve is represented in terms of an independent variable, u. What are the advantages of the parametric form?

10.2 Consider the equation $f(x, y) = 0$. What type of curve does it describe?

10.3 Suppose that you have a polynomial $p(u) = \sum_{k=0}^{n} c_k u^k$. Find a polynomial $q(v) = \sum_{k=0}^{n} d_k v^k$ such that, for each point of p in the interval (a, b), there is a point v in the range $0 \le v \le 1$, such that $p(u) = q(v)$.

10.4 An important property of the cubic Bézier curve is that the curve must always lie completely within the convex hull of the four control points. What is a convex hull?

10.5 Show that in the interval $(0, 1)$, the Bernstein polynomials must be less than 1.

10.6 Verify the C^0 parametric continuity of curves.

10.7 In Section 10.9, we showed that we can write a cubic polynomial as a cubic Bézier polynomial by choosing a proper set of control points or, equivalently, the proper convex hull. Using this fact, show how to render an interpolating curve using the Bézier renderer provided by OpenGL.

10.8 How are quadric surfaces described?

10.9 Suppose that we render Bézier patches by adaptive subdivision so that each patch can be subdivided a different number of times. Do we maintain continuity along the edges of the patches? Explain your answer.

10.10 Write an OpenGL program that will take as input a set of control points and that will produce the interpolating, B-spline, and Bézier curves for these data.

10.11 Suppose that you use a set of spline curves to describe a path in time that an object will take as part of an animation. How might you notice the difference between G^1 and C^1 continuity in this situation?

10.12 Write a program to generate a cubic Bézier polynomial from an arbitrary number of points entered interactively. The user should be able to manipulate the control points interactively.

10.13 How can Bézier surface patches be generated?

10.14 Derive the open rational quadratic B-spline with the knots {0, 0, 0, 0, 1, 1, 1, 1} and the weights $w_0 = w_2 = 1$ and $w_1 = w$.

10.15 Using the result of Exercise 10.14, show that if $w = \frac{r}{1-r}$, for $0 \le r \le 1$, you get all the conic sections. *Hint*: Consider $r < \frac{1}{2}$ and $r > \frac{1}{2}$.

10.16 Define and derive G^1 geometric continuity.

10.17 What is the relationship between the control-point data for a Hermite patch and the derivatives at the corners of the patch?

10.18 For a 1024 × 1280 display screen, what is the maximum number of subdivisions that are needed to render a cubic polynomial surface?

10.19 Suppose you have three points, P_0, P_1, and P_2. First, connect successive points with parametric line segments where u ranges from 0 to 1 for each. Next, linearly interpolate between successive pairs of line segments by connecting points for the same value of u with a line segment and then using the same value of u to obtain a value along this new line segment. How can you describe the curve created by this process?

10.20 Extend Exercise 10.19 by considering four points. Linearly interpolate, first between the three curves constructed as in that exercise and, second, between the two curves thus created. Describe the final curve determined by the four points.

10.21 How are curves like the Bézier curve and the B-spline curve useful? Give an application where a curve can be used as a reference.

10.22 Suppose that we divide a Bézier surface patch, first along the u-direction. Then in v, we only subdivide one of the two patches we have created. Show how this process can create a gap in the resulting surface. Find a simple solution to this difficulty.

10.23 Write a program to carry out subdivision of triangular or quadrilateral meshes. When the subdivision is working correctly, add the averaging step to form a smoother surface.

10.24 Name a method that is based on the use of the convex hull and never requires explicit evaluation of the polynomial.

10.25 Name the properties of the NURBS curve that are similar to the three-dimensional B-splines curve.

CHAPTER 11

ADVANCED RENDERING

In this final chapter, we consider a variety of alternative approaches to the standard pipeline rendering strategy we have used for interactive applications. We have multiple motivations for introducing these other approaches. We want to be able to incorporate effects, such as global illumination, that usually are not possible to render in real time. We also want to produce high-quality images whose resolution is beyond that of standard computer displays. For example, a single frame of a digital movie may contain over 10 million pixels and take hours to render.

11.1 GOING BEYOND PIPELINE RENDERING

Almost everything we have done so far has led us to believe that given a scene description containing geometric objects, cameras, light sources, and attributes, we could render the scene in close to real time using available hardware and software. This view dictated that we would use a pipeline renderer of the type described by the OpenGL architecture and supported by graphics hardware. Although we have developed a reasonably large bag of tricks that enable us to handle most applications and get around many of the consequences of using the local lighting model supported by such renderers, there are still limitations on what we can do. For example, there are many global illumination situations that we cannot approximate well with a pipeline renderer. We would also like to generate images with higher resolution than on a standard workstation and that contain fewer aliasing artifacts. In many situations, we are willing either to render at slower speeds or to use multiple computers to achieve these goals. In this chapter, we introduce a variety of techniques, all of which are of current interest both to researchers and practitioners.

First, we examine other rendering strategies that are based on the physics of image formation. Our original discussion of image formation was based on following rays of light. That approach is built on a very simple physical model and led to the ray-tracing paradigm for rendering. We start by exploring this model in greater detail than in previous chapters and show how to get started writing your own ray tracer.

We can also take approaches to rendering, other than ray tracing, that are also based on physics. We will examine an approach based on energy conservation and consider an integral equation, the **rendering equation**, that describes a closed environment with light sources and reflective surfaces. Although this equation is not solvable in general, we can develop a rendering approach called **radiosity** that satisfies the rendering equation when all surfaces are perfectly diffuse reflectors.

We will also look at two approaches that are somewhere between physically correct renderers and real-time renderers. One is the approach taken in RenderMan. The other is an approach to rendering that starts with images. Although these methods are different from each other, both have become important in the animation industry.

We then turn to the problems of working with large data sets and high-resolution displays. These problems are related because large data sets contain detail that requires displays with a resolution beyond what we can get with standard commodity devices such as LCD panels. We will consider solutions that use parallelism making use of commodity components, both processors and graphics cards.

Finally, we introduce image-based rendering, in which we start with multiple two-dimensional images of a three-dimensional scene and try to use these images to obtain an image from another viewpoint.

11.2   RAY TRACING

In many ways, ray tracing is a logical extension to rendering with a local lighting model. It is based on our previous observation that of the light rays leaving a source, the only ones that contribute to our image are those that enter the lens of our synthetic camera, passing through the center of projection. Figure 11.1 shows several of the possible interactions with a single point source and perfectly specular surfaces. Rays can enter the lens of the camera directly from the source, from interactions with

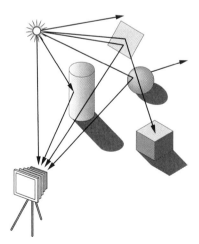

FIGURE 11.1   Rays leaving source.

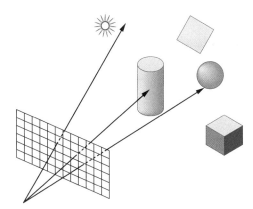

FIGURE 11.2   Ray-casting model.

a surface visible to the camera, after multiple reflections from surfaces, or after transmission through one or more surfaces.

Most of the rays that leave a source do not enter the lens and do not contribute to our image. Hence, attempting to follow all rays from a light source is a time-wasting endeavor. However, if we reverse the direction of the rays, and consider only those rays that start at the center of projection, we know that these **cast rays** must contribute to the image. Consequently, we start our ray tracer as shown in Figure 11.2. Here we have included the image plane, and we have ruled it into pixel-sized areas. Knowing that we must assign a color to every pixel, we must cast at least one ray through each pixel. Each cast ray either intersects a surface or a light source, or goes off to infinity without striking anything. Pixels corresponding to this latter case can be assigned a background color. Rays that strike surfaces—for now, we can assume that all surfaces are opaque—require us to calculate a shade for the point of intersection. If we were simply to compute the shade at the point of intersection, using the modified-Phong model, we would produce the same image as would our local renderer. However, we can do much more.

Note that the process that we have described thus far requires all the same steps as we use in our pipeline renderer: object modeling, projection, and visible-surface determination. However, as we saw in Chapter 6, the order in which the calculations are carried out is different. The pipeline renderer works on a vertex-by-vertex basis; the ray tracer works on a pixel-by-pixel basis.

In ray tracing, rather than immediately applying our reflection model, we first check whether the point of intersection between the cast ray and the surface is illuminated. We compute **shadow**, or **feeler**, **rays** from the point on the surface to each source. If a shadow ray intersects a surface before it meets the source, the light is blocked from reaching the point under consideration, and this point is in shadow, at least from this source. No lighting calculation needs to be done for sources that are blocked from a point on the surface. If all surfaces are opaque and we do not consider light scattered from surface to surface, we have an image that has shadows added to

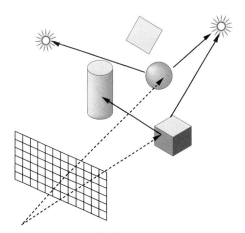

FIGURE 11.3   Shadow rays.

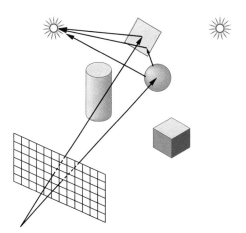

FIGURE 11.4   Ray tracing with a mirror.

what we have already done without ray tracing. The price we pay is the cost of doing a type of hidden-surface calculation for each point of intersection between a cast ray and a surface. Figure 11.3 shows the shadow rays (solid lines) for two cast rays (dashed lines) that hit the cube and sphere. A shadow ray from the cube intersects the cylinder. Hence, the point of intersection on the cube from the cast ray is illuminated by only one of the two sources.

    Suppose that some of our surfaces are highly reflective, like those shown in Figure 11.4. We can follow the shadow ray as it bounces from surface to surface, until it either goes off to infinity or intersects a source. Figure 11.4 shows just two of the paths. The left cast ray intersects the mirror, and the shadow ray to the light source on the left is not blocked, so if the mirror is in front of the second source, the point

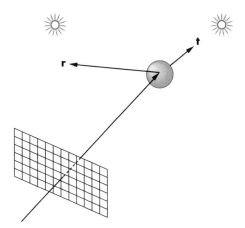

FIGURE 11.5   Ray tracing with reflection and transmission.

of intersection is illuminated by only one source. The cast ray on the right intersects the sphere, and in this case a shadow can reflect from the mirror to the source on the left and in addition the point of intersection is illuminated directly by the source on the left.

Such calculations are usually done recursively and take into account any absorption of light at surfaces.

Ray tracing is particularly good at handling surfaces that both reflect light and transmit light through refraction. Using our basic paradigm, we follow a cast ray to a surface (Figure 11.5) with the property that if a ray from a source strikes a point, then the light from the source is partially absorbed and some of this light contributes to the diffuse reflection term. The rest of the incoming light is divided between a transmitted ray and a reflected ray. From the perspective of the cast ray, if a light source is visible at the intersection point, then we need to do three tasks. First, we must compute the contribution from the light source at the point, using our standard reflection model. Second, we must cast a ray in the direction of a perfect reflection. Third, we must cast a ray in the direction of the transmitted ray. These two cast rays are treated just like the original cast ray; that is, they may intersect other surfaces, they can end at a source, or they can go off to infinity. At each surface that these rays intersect, additional rays may be generated by reflection and transmission of light. Figure 11.6 shows a single cast ray and the path it can follow through a simple environment. Figure 11.7 shows the **ray tree** generated. This tree shows which rays must be traced; it is constructed dynamically by the ray-tracing process.

Although our ray tracer uses the Blinn-Phong model to include a diffuse term at the point of intersection between a ray and a surface, the light that is scattered diffusely at this point is ignored. If we were to attempt to follow such light, we would have so many rays to deal with that the ray tracer might never complete execution. Thus, ray tracers are best suited for highly reflective environments. Color Plate 15 was rendered with a public-domain ray tracer. Although the scene contains only a few

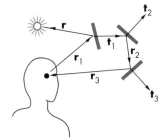

FIGURE 11.6   Simple ray-traced environments.

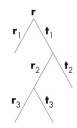

FIGURE 11.7   Ray tree corresponding to Figure 11.6.

objects, the reflective and transparent surfaces could not have been rendered realistically without the ray tracer. Also, note the complexity of the shadows in the scene, another effect created automatically by ray tracing. The image also demonstrates that ray tracers can incorporate texture mapping with no more difficulty than with our pipeline renderer.

11.3   BUILDING A SIMPLE RAY TRACER

The easiest way to describe a ray tracer is recursively, through a single function that traces a ray and calls itself for the reflected and transmitted rays. Most of the work in ray tracing goes into the calculation of intersections between rays and surfaces. One reason that it is difficult to implement a ray tracer that can handle a variety of objects is that as we add more complex objects, computing intersections becomes problematic. Consequently, most basic ray tracers support only flat and quadric surfaces.

We have seen the basic considerations that determine the ray-tracing process. Building a simple recursive ray tracer that can handle simple objects—quadrics and polyhedra—is quite easy. In this section, we will examine the basic structure and the functions that are required. Details can be found in the Suggested Readings at the end of the chapter.

We need two basic functions. The recursive function `raytrace` follows a ray, specified by a point and a direction, and returns the shade of the first surface that it intersects. It will use the function `intersect` to find the location of the closest surface that the specified ray intersects.

11.3.1 Recursive Ray Tracing

Let's consider the procedure `trace` in pseudocode. We give it a starting point `p` and a direction `d`, and it returns a color `c`. In order to stop the ray tracer from recursing forever, we can specify a maximum number of steps `max` that it can take. We will assume, for simplicity, that we have only a single light source whose properties, as well as the description of the objects and their surface properties, are all available globally. If there are additional light sources, we can add in their contributions in a manner similar to the way in which we deal with the single source:

```
color c = trace(point p, vector d, int step)
{

   color local, reflected, transmitted;
   point q;
   normal n;

   if (step > max) return(background_color);

   q = intersect(p, d, status);
```

```
if (status == light_source) return(light_source_color);
if (status == no_intersection) return(background_color);

n = normal(q);
r = reflect(q, n);
t = transmit(q, n);

local = phong(q, n, r);
reflected = trace(q, r, step+1);
transmitted = trace(q, t, step+1);

return(local + reflected + transmitted);
}
```

Note that the calculation of reflected and transmitted colors must take into account how much energy is absorbed at the surface before reflection and transmission. If we have exceeded the maximum number of steps, we return a specified background color. Otherwise, we use `intersect` to find the intersection of the given ray with the closest object. This function must have the entire database of objects available to it, and it must be able to find the intersections of rays with all types of objects supported. Consequently, most of the time spent in the ray tracer and the complexity of the code is hidden in this function. We examine some of the intersection issues in Section 11.3.2.

If the ray does not intersect any object, we can return a status variable from `intersect` and return the background color from `trace`. Likewise, if the ray intersects the light source, we return the color of the source. If an intersection is returned, there are three components to the color at this point: a local color that can be computed using the modified Phong (or any other) model, a reflected color, and, if the surface is translucent, a transmitted color. Before computing these colors, we must compute the normal at the point of intersection, as well as the direction of reflected and transmitted rays, as in Chapter 5. The complexity of computing the normal depends on the class of objects supported by the ray tracer, and this calculation can be part of the function `trace`.

The computation of the local color requires a check to see if the light source is visible from the point of closest intersection. Thus, we cast a feeler or shadow ray from this point toward the light source and check whether it intersects any objects. We can note that this process can also be recursive because the shadow ray might hit a reflective surface, such as a mirror, or a translucent surface, such as a piece of glass. In addition, if the shadow ray hits a surface that itself is illuminated, some of this light should contribute to the color at q. Generally, we ignore these possible contributions because they will slow the calculation significantly. Practical ray tracing requires that we make some compromises and is never quite physically correct.

Next, we have two recursive steps that compute the contributions from the reflected and transmitted rays starting at q using `trace`. It is these recursions that make this code a ray tracer rather than a simple ray-casting rendering in which we find the first intersection and apply a lighting model at that point. Finally, we add the three colors to obtain the color at p.

11.3.2 Calculating Intersections

Most of the time spent in a typical ray tracer is in the calculation of intersections in the function `intersect`. Hence, we must be very careful in limiting the objects to those for which we can find intersections easily. The general intersection problem can be expressed cleanly if we use an implicit representation of our objects. Thus, if an object is defined by the surface(s)

$$f(x, y, z) = f(\mathbf{p}) = 0,$$

and a ray from a point $\mathbf{p}_0$ in the direction $\mathbf{d}$ is represented by the parametric form

$$\mathbf{p}(t) = \mathbf{p}_0 + t\mathbf{d},$$

then the intersections are given for the values of t such that

$$f(\mathbf{p}_0 + t\mathbf{d}) = 0,$$

which is a scalar equation in t. If f is an algebraic surface, then f is a sum of polynomial terms of the form $x^i y^j z^k$ and $f(\mathbf{p}_0 + t\mathbf{d})$ is a polynomial in t. Finding the intersections reduces to finding all the roots of a polynomial. Unfortunately, there are only a few cases that do not require numerical methods.

One is quadrics. In Chapter 10, we saw that all quadrics could be written as the quadratic form

$$\mathbf{p}^T \mathbf{A} \mathbf{p} + \mathbf{b}^T \mathbf{p} + c = 0.$$

Substituting in the equation for a ray leaves us with a scalar quadratic equation to solve for the values of t that yield zero, one, or two intersections. Because the solution of the quadratic equation requires only the taking of a single square root, ray tracers can handle quadrics without difficulty. In addition, we can eliminate those rays that miss a quadric object and those that are tangent to it before taking the square root, further simplifying the calculation.

Consider, for example, a sphere centered at $\mathbf{p}_c$ with radius r, which can be written as

$$(\mathbf{p} - \mathbf{p}_c) \cdot (\mathbf{p} - \mathbf{p}_c) - r^2 = 0.$$

Substituting in the equation of the ray

$$\mathbf{p}(t) = \mathbf{p}_0 + t\mathbf{d},$$

we get the quadratic equation

$$\mathbf{d} \cdot \mathbf{d} t^2 + 2(\mathbf{p}_0 - \mathbf{p}_c) \cdot \mathbf{d} t + (\mathbf{p}_0 - \mathbf{p}_c) \cdot (\mathbf{p}_0 - \mathbf{p}_c) - r^2 = 0.$$

Planes are also simple. We can take the equation for the ray and substitute it into the equation of a plane

$$\mathbf{p} \cdot \mathbf{n} + c = 0,$$

which yields a scalar equation that requires only a single division to solve. Thus, for the ray

$$\mathbf{p} = \mathbf{p}_0 + t\mathbf{d},$$

we find

$$t = -\frac{\mathbf{p}_0 \cdot \mathbf{n} + c}{\mathbf{n} \cdot \mathbf{d}}.$$

However, planes by themselves have limited applicability in modeling scenes. We are usually interested either in the intersection of multiple planes that form convex objects (polyhedra) or a piece of a plane that defines a flat polygon. For polygons, we must decide whether the point of intersection lies inside or outside the polygon. The difficulty of such a test depends on whether the polygon is convex and, if not convex, whether it is simple. These issues are similar to the rendering issues that we discussed for polygons in Chapter 6. For convex polygons, there are very simple tests that are similar to the tests for ray intersections with polyhedra that we consider next.

Although we can define polyhedra by their faces, we can also define them as the convex objects that are formed by the intersection of planes. Thus, a parallelepiped is defined by six planes and a tetrahedron by four. For ray tracing, the advantage of this definition is that we can use the simple ray–plane intersection equation to derive a ray–polyhedron intersection test.

We develop the test as follows. Let's assume that all the planes defining our polyhedron have normals that are outward facing. Consider the ray in Figure 11.8 that intersects the polyhedron. It can enter and leave the polygon only once. It must enter through a plane that is facing the ray and leave through a plane that faces in the direction of the ray. However, this ray must also intersect all the planes that form the polyhedron (except those parallel to the ray).

Consider the intersections of the ray with all the front-facing planes—that is, those whose normals point toward the starting point of the ray. The entry point must be the intersection farthest along the ray. Likewise, the exit point is the nearest intersection point of all the planes facing away from the origin of the ray, and the entry point must be closer to the initial point than the exit point. If we consider a ray that misses the same polyhedron, as shown in Figure 11.9, we see that the farthest intersection with a front-facing plane is farther from the initial point than the closest intersection with a back-facing plane. Hence, our test is to find these possible entry and exit points by computing the ray–plane intersection points, in any order, and updating the possible entry and exit points as we find the intersections. The test can be halted if we ever find a possible exit point closer than the present entry point or a possible entry point farther than the present exit point.

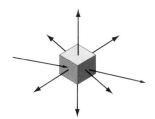

FIGURE 11.8 Ray intersecting a polyhedron with outward-facing normals shown.

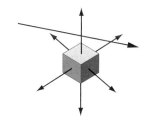

FIGURE 11.9 Ray missing a polyhedron with outward-facing normals shown.

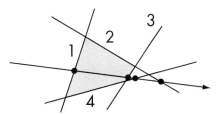

FIGURE 11.10   Ray intersecting a convex polygon.

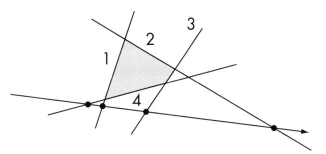

FIGURE 11.11   Ray missing a convex polygon.

Consider the two-dimensional example illustrated in Figure 11.10 that tests for a ray–convex polygon intersection in a plane. Here lines replace planes, but the logic is the same. Suppose that we do the intersections with the lines in the order 1, 2, 3, 4. Starting with line 1, we find that this line faces the initial point by looking at the sign of the dot product of the normal with the direction of the ray. The intersection with line 1 then yields a possible entry point. Line 2 faces away from the initial point and yields a possible exit point that is farther away than our present estimate of the entry point. Line 3 yields an even closer exit point but still one that is farther than the entry point. Line 4 yields a farther exit point that can be discarded. At this point, we have tested all the lines and conclude the ray passes through the polygon.

Figure 11.11 has the same lines and the same convex polygon but shows a ray that misses the polygon. The intersection with line 1 still yields a possible entry point. The intersections with lines 2 and 3 still yield possible exit points that are farther than the entry point. But the intersection with line 4 yields an exit point closer than the entry point, which indicates that the ray must miss the polygon.

11.3.3 Ray-Tracing Variations

Most ray tracers employ multiple methods for determining when to stop the recursive process. One method that is fairly simple to implement is to neglect all rays that go past some distance, assuming that such rays go off to infinity. We can implement this test by assuming that all objects lie inside a large sphere centered at the origin.

Thus, if we treat this sphere as an object colored with a specified background color, whenever the intersection calculation determines that this sphere is the closest object, we terminate the recursion for the ray and return the background color.

Another simple termination strategy is to look at the fraction of energy remaining in a ray. When a ray passes through a translucent material or reflects from a shiny surface, we can estimate the fraction of the incoming energy that is in these outgoing rays and how much has been absorbed at the surface. If we add an energy parameter to the ray tracer,

```
trace(point p, vector d, int steps, float energy);
```

then we need only to add a line of code to check if there is sufficient energy remaining to continue tracing a ray.

There are many improvements we can make to speed up a ray tracer or make it more accurate. For example, it is fairly simple to replace the recursion in the ray tracer with iteration. Much of the work in finding intersections often can be avoided by the use of bounding boxes or bounding spheres, because the intersection with these objects can be done very quickly. Often, bounding volumes can be used to group objects effectively, as can the BSP trees that we introduced in Chapter 8.

Because ray tracing is a sampling method, it is subject to aliasing errors. As we saw in Chapter 7, aliasing errors occur when we do not have enough samples. However, in our basic ray tracer, the amount of work is proportional to the number of rays. Many ray tracers use a stochastic sampling method in which the decision as to where to cast the next ray is based upon the results of rays cast thus far. Thus, if rays do not intersect any objects in a particular region, few additional rays will be cast toward it, while the opposite holds for rays that are cast in a direction where they intersect many objects. This strategy is also used in RenderMan (Section 11.6). Although we could argue that stochastic sampling only works in a probabilistic sense—as there may well be small objects in areas that are not well sampled—it has the advantage that images produced by stochastic sampling tend not to show the moiré patterns characteristic of images produced using uniform sampling.

Ray tracing is an inherently parallel process, as every ray can be cast independently of every other ray. However, the difficulty is that every ray can potentially intersect any object. Hence, every tracing of a ray needs access to all objects. In addition, when we follow reflected and transmitted rays, we tend to lose any locality that might have helped us avoid a lot of data movement. Consequently, parallel ray tracers are best suited for shared-memory parallel architectures. With the availability of multi-core processors with 64-bit addressing, commodity computers can support sufficient memory to make ray tracing a viable alternative in many applications.

11.4 THE RENDERING EQUATION

Most of the laws of physics can be expressed as conservation laws, such as the conservation of momentum and the conservation of energy. Because light is a form of

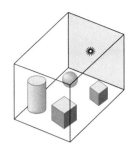

FIGURE 11.12   Closed environment with four objects and a light source.

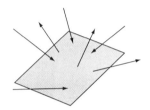

FIGURE 11.13   A simple surface.

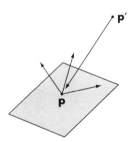

FIGURE 11.14   Light from $\mathbf{p}'$ arriving at $\mathbf{p}$.

energy, an energy-based approach can provide an alternative to ray tracing. Consider the closed environment shown in Figure 11.12. We see some surfaces that define the closed environment, some objects, and a light source inside. Physically, all these surfaces, including the surface of the light source, can be modeled in the same way. Although each one may have different parameters, each obeys the same physical laws. Any surface can absorb some light and reflect some light. Any surface can be an emitter of light. From the ray-tracing perspective, we can say that the shades that we see are the result of an infinite number of rays bouncing around the environment, starting with sources and not ending until all the energy has been absorbed. However, when we look at the scene, we see the steady state; that is, we see each surface having its own shades. We do not see how the rays have bounced around; we see only the end result. The energy approach allows us to solve for this steady state directly, thus avoiding tracing many rays through many reflections.

Let's consider just one surface, as shown in Figure 11.13. We see rays of light entering from many directions and other rays emerging, also possibly in all directions. The light leaving the surface can have two components. If the surface is a light source, then some fraction of the light leaving the surface is from emission. The rest of the light is the reflection of incoming light from other surfaces. Hence, the incoming light also consists of emissions and reflections from other surfaces.

We can simplify the analysis by considering two arbitrary points $\mathbf{p}$ and $\mathbf{p}'$, as shown in Figure 11.14. If we look at the light arriving at and leaving $\mathbf{p}$, the energy must balance. Thus, the emission of energy, if there is a source at $\mathbf{p}$, and the reflected light energy must equal the incoming light energy from all possible points $\mathbf{p}'$. Let $i(\mathbf{p}, \mathbf{p}')$ be the intensity of light leaving the point $\mathbf{p}'$ and arriving at the point $\mathbf{p}$.[1] The rendering equation

$$i(\mathbf{p}, \mathbf{p}') = v(\mathbf{p}, \mathbf{p}')(\epsilon(\mathbf{p}, \mathbf{p}') + \int \rho(\mathbf{p}, \mathbf{p}', \mathbf{p}'')i(\mathbf{p}', \mathbf{p}'')d\mathbf{p}''),$$

expresses this balance. The intensity leaving $\mathbf{p}'$ consists of two parts. If $\mathbf{p}'$ is an emitter of light (a source), there is a term $\epsilon(\mathbf{p}, \mathbf{p}')$ in the direction of $\mathbf{p}$. The second term is the contribution from reflections from every possible point ($\mathbf{p}''$) that are reflected at $\mathbf{p}'$ in the direction of $\mathbf{p}$. The reflection function $\rho(\mathbf{p}, \mathbf{p}', \mathbf{p}'')$ characterizes the material properties at $\mathbf{p}'$. The term $v(\mathbf{p}, \mathbf{p}')$ has two possible values. If there is an opaque surface between $\mathbf{p}$ and $\mathbf{p}'$, then the surface occludes $\mathbf{p}'$ from $\mathbf{p}$ and no light from $\mathbf{p}'$ reaches $\mathbf{p}$. In this case, $v(\mathbf{p}, \mathbf{p}') = 0$. Otherwise, we must account for the effect of the distance between $\mathbf{p}$ and $\mathbf{p}'$ and

$$v(\mathbf{p}, \mathbf{p}') = \frac{1}{r^2},$$

where r is the distance between the two points.

---

1. We are being careful to avoid introducing the units and terminology of radiometry. We see the intensity of light. Energy is the integral of intensity over time, but, if the light sources are unchanging, we are in the steady state, and this distinction does not matter. Most references work with the energy or intensity per unit area (the **energy flux**) rather than energy or intensity.

Although the form of the rendering equation is wonderfully simple, solving it is not an easy task. The main difficulty is the dimensionality. Because $\mathbf{p}$ and $\mathbf{p}'$ are points in three-dimensional space, $i(\mathbf{p}, \mathbf{p}')$ has six variables and ρ has nine. In addition, we have not included an additional variable for the wavelength of light, which would be necessary to work with color.

There have been some efforts to solve a general form of the rendering equation by numerical methods. Most of these have been Monte Carlo methods that are somewhat akin to stochastic sampling. Recently, **photon mapping** has become a viable approach. Photon mapping follows individual photons, the carriers of light energy, from when they are produced at the light sources to when they are finally absorbed by surfaces in the scene. Photons typically go through multiple reflections and transmissions from creation to final absorption. The potential advantage of this approach is that it can handle complex lighting of the sort that characterizes real-world scenes.

Although we argued when we discussed ray tracing that, because such a small percentage of light emitted from sources reaches the viewer, tracing rays from a source is inefficient, photon mapping uses many clever strategies to make the process computationally feasible. In particular, photon mapping uses a conservation of energy approach combined with Monte Carlo methods. For example, consider what happens when light strikes a diffuse surface. As we have seen, the reflected light is diffused in all directions. In photon mapping, when a photon strikes a diffuse surface, a photon can be reflected or absorbed. Whether the photon is absorbed or not—and the specified angle of reflection, if it is reflected—is determined stochastically in a manner that yields the correct results on the average. Thus, what happens to two photons that strike a surface at the same place and with the same angle of incidence can be very different. The more photons that are generated from sources, the greater the accuracy—but at the cost of tracing more photons.

There are special circumstances that simplify the rendering equation. For example, for perfectly specular surfaces, the reflection function is nonzero only when the angle of incidence equals the angle of reflection and the vectors lie in the same plane. Under these circumstances, ray tracing can be looked at as a method for solving the rendering equation.

The other special case that leads to a viable rendering method occurs when all surfaces are perfectly diffuse. In this case, the amount of light reflected is the same in all directions. Thus, the intensity function depends only on $\mathbf{p}$. We examine this case in the next section.

11.5 RADIOSITY

One way to simplify the rendering equation is to consider an environment in which all the surfaces are perfectly diffuse reflectors. Because a perfectly diffuse surface looks the same to all viewers, the corresponding BRDF is far simpler than the general cases considered by the rendering equation.

Note, however, that although a perfectly diffuse surface reflects light equally in all directions, even if the surface is flat, it can show variations in shading that are not shown when we render using the modified Phong lighting model. Suppose that

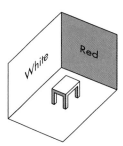

FIGURE 11.15   Simple scene with diffuse surfaces.

we have a simple scene, such as that shown in Figure 11.15, in which all the surfaces are perfectly diffuse. If we render this scene with a distant light source, each polygon surface is rendered as a single color. If this were a real scene, however, some of the diffuse reflections from the red wall would fall on the white wall, causing red light to be added to the white light reflected from those parts of the white wall that are near the red wall. Diffuse light reflected from the white wall would have a similar effect on the red wall. Our simple shading model has not considered these **diffuse–diffuse interactions**.

An ideal global renderer would capture these interactions. The radiosity method can approximate them very well using an energy approach that was originally used for solving problems in heat transfer.

The basic radiosity method breaks up the scene into small flat polygons, or **patches**, each of which can be assumed to be perfectly diffuse and renders in a constant shade. First we must find these shades. Once we have found them, we have effectively assigned a color to each patch that is independent of the viewer. Effectively, we have assigned colors to a set of polygon patches in a three-dimensional environment. We can now place the viewer wherever we wish and render the scene in a conventional manner, using a pipeline renderer.

11.5.1 The Radiosity Equation

Let's assume our scene consists of n patches numbered from 1 to n. The **radiosity** of patch i, b_i, is the light intensity (energy/unit time) per unit area leaving the patch. Typically, the radiosity would be measured in units such as *watts/meter²*. As we are measuring intensity at a fixed wavelength, we can think of a radiosity function $b_i(\lambda)$ that determines the color of patch i. Suppose that patch i has area a_i. Because we have assumed that each patch is a perfectly diffuse surface, the total intensity leaving patch i is $b_i a_i$. Following reasoning similar to that which we used to derive the rendering equation, the emitted intensity consists of an emissive component, also assumed to be constant across the patch, and a reflective component due to the intensities of all other patches whose light strikes patch i, and we obtain the equation

$$b_i a_i = e_i a_i + \rho_i \sum_{j=0}^{n} f_{ji} b_j a_j.$$

The term f_{ij} is called the **form factor** between patch i and patch j. It represents the fraction of the energy leaving patch i that reaches patch j. The form factor depends on how the two patches are oriented relative to each other, how far they are from each other, and whether any other patches occlude the light from patch j and prevent it from reaching patch i. We will discuss the calculation of these factors in the next subsection. The reflectivity of patch i is ρ_i.

There is a simple relationship between the factors f_{ij} and f_{ji} known as the **reciprocity equation**,

$$f_{ij}a_i = f_{ji}a_j.$$

Substituting into the equation for the equation for the patch intensities, we find

$$b_i a_i = e_i a_i + \rho_i \sum_{j=0}^{n} f_{ij} b_j a_i.$$

We can now divide by a_i, obtaining an equation for the patch radiosity:

$$b_i = e_i + \rho_i \sum_{j=0}^{n} f_{ij} b_j.$$

This result is called the **radiosity equation**.

Assuming that we have computed the form factors, we have a set of n linear equations in the n unknown radiosities. Comparing this equation to the rendering equation, we can see that if the patches were made smaller and smaller, in the limit we would have an infinite number of patches. The sum would become an integral, and the resulting radiosity equation would be a special case of the rendering equation in which all surfaces are perfectly diffuse reflectors.

We can put these equations in matrix form by defining the column matrix of radiosities

$$\mathbf{b} = [b_i],$$

a column matrix of the patch emissions

$$\mathbf{e} = [e_i],$$

a diagonal matrix from the reflection coefficients

$$\mathbf{R} = [\, r_{ij} \,], \qquad a_{ij} = \begin{cases} \rho_i & \text{if } i = j, \\ 0 & \text{otherwise}, \end{cases}$$

and a matrix of the form factors

$$\mathbf{F} = [f_{ij}].$$

Now the set of equations for the radiosities becomes

$$\mathbf{b} = \mathbf{e} + \mathbf{RFb}.$$

We can write the formal solution as

$$\mathbf{b} = [\mathbf{I} - \mathbf{RF}]^{-1}\mathbf{e}.$$

11.5.2 Solving the Radiosity Equation

Although it can be shown that the radiosity equation must have a solution, the real difficulties are practical. A typical scene will have thousands of patches, so that solving the equations by a direct method, such as Gaussian elimination, usually is not possible. Most methods rely on the fact that the matrix $\mathbf{F}$ is sparse. Most of its elements are effectively zero because most patches are sufficiently far from each other so that almost none of the light that a patch emits or reflects reaches most other patches.

Solution of sets of equations involving sparse matrices are based on iterative methods that require the multiplication of these sparse matrices, an efficient operation. Suppose that we use the equation for the patches to create the iterative equation

$$\mathbf{b}^{k+1} = \mathbf{e} + \mathbf{RFb}^{k}.$$

Each iteration of this equation requires the matrix multiplication $\mathbf{RFb}^k$, which, assuming $\mathbf{F}$ is sparse, requires $O(n)$ operations, rather than the $O(n^2)$ operations for the general case. In terms of the individual radiosities, we have

$$b_i^{k+1} = e_i + \sum_{j=1}^{n} \rho_i f_{ij} b_j^k.$$

This method, which is known as Jacobi's method, will converge for this problem regardless of the initial starting point $\mathbf{b}^0$.

In general, patches are not self-reflecting so that $f_{ij} = 0$. If we apply updates as soon as they are available, we obtain the Gauss-Seidel method:

$$b_i^{k+1} = e_i + \sum_{j=1}^{i-1} \rho_i f_{ij} b_j^{k+1} + \sum_{j=i+1}^{n} \rho_i f_{ij} b_j^k.$$

There is another possible iteration that provides additional physical insight. Consider the scalar formula

$$\frac{1}{1-x} = \sum_{i=0}^{\infty} x^i,$$

which holds if $|x| < 1$. The matrix form of this equation for **RF** is[2]

$$[\mathbf{I} - \mathbf{RF}]^{-1} = \sum_{i=0}^{\infty} (\mathbf{RF})^i.$$

Thus, we can write **b** as

$$\mathbf{b} = \sum_{i=0}^{\infty} (\mathbf{RF})^i \mathbf{e}$$

$$= \mathbf{e} + (\mathbf{RF})\mathbf{e} + (\mathbf{RF})^2\mathbf{e} + (\mathbf{RF})^3\mathbf{e} + \ldots.$$

We can use this expression, terminating it at some point, to approximate **b**. Each term has an interesting physical interpretation. The first term, **e**, is the direct light emitted from each patch so that an approximate solution with just this term will show only the sources. The second term, **(RF)e**, adds in the light that is the result of exactly one reflection of the sources onto other patches. The next term adds on the contribution from double reflections, and so on for the other terms.

11.5.3 Computing Form Factors

At this point, we have ways of solving for the patch radiosities that are reasonably efficient, but we have yet to discuss the calculation of the form factors. We start with a general derivation of an equation for the form factor between two patches, and then we will look at how we might find approximate form factors using the tools that we have available.

Consider two perfectly diffuse flat patches, P_i and P_j, as shown in Figure 11.16, which we have drawn without any other patches that might cause occlusion. Each patch has a normal that gives its orientation. Although each patch emits light equally in all directions, the amount of light leaving two different points on P_j that reaches any point on P_i is different because of the different distances between two points on P_j and a point on P_i. Thus, to collect all the light from P_j that falls on P_i, we must integrate over all points on P_j. The same reasoning applies to two points on P_i that receive light from a point on P_j; they will receive a different amount of light, and thus to determine the light falling on P_i, we must also integrate over all points on P_i.

We can derive the required integral based on our understanding of diffuse shading from Chapter 5. Consider a small area on each patch, da_i and da_j. Each can be considered to be an ideal diffuse reflector (Figure 11.17). They are a distance r apart, where r is the distance between two points, $\mathbf{p}_i$ and $\mathbf{p}_j$, at the center of the two small areas. The light leaving da_j goes in the direction $\mathbf{d} = \mathbf{p}_i - \mathbf{p}_j$. However, the intensity of this light is reduced or foreshortened by $\cos \phi_j$, where ϕ_j is the angle between the normal for patch j and the vector $\mathbf{d}$. Likewise, the light arriving at da_i is foreshortened

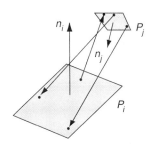

FIGURE 11.16   Two patches.

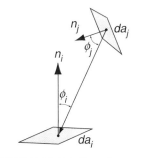

FIGURE 11.17   Foreshortening between two small patches.

---

2. The formula converges if the magnitudes of all the eigenvalues of **BF** are less than unity, a condition that must be true for the radiosity equation.

by $\cos\phi_i$, where ϕ_i is the angle between the normal for patch i and the vector $\mathbf{d}$. To obtain the desired form factor, f_{ij}, we must also account for the distance between the patches and the possibility of occlusion. We can do both by first defining the term

$$o_{ij} = \begin{cases} 1 & \text{if } \mathbf{p}_j \text{ is visible from } \mathbf{p}_i, \\ 0 & \text{otherwise.} \end{cases}$$

Then, by averaging over the total area of the patch, we obtain the form-factor equation

$$f_{ij} = \frac{1}{a_i} \int_{a_i} \int_{a_j} o_{ij} \frac{\cos\phi_i \cos\phi_j}{\pi r^2} da_i da_j.$$

Although the form of this integral is simple, there are only a few special cases for which it can be solved analytically. For real scenes, we need numerical methods. Because there are n^2 form factors, most methods are a compromise between accuracy and time.

We will sketch two approaches. The first method starts with the notion of two-step mappings that we used in our discussion of texture mapping in Chapter 7. Consider two patches again, this time with a hemisphere separating them, as shown in Figure 11.18. Suppose that we want to compute the light from P_i that reaches P_j at a point $\mathbf{p}_i$. We center the hemisphere at this point and orient the patch so that the normal is pointing up. We can now project P_j onto the hemisphere and observe that we can use the projected patch for our computation of the form factor rather than the original patch. If we convert to polar coordinates, the form factor equation becomes simpler for the projected patch. However, for each small area of P_i, we have to move the hemisphere and add the contribution from each area.

A simpler approach for most graphics applications is to use a hemicube rather than a hemisphere, as shown in Figure 11.19. The hemicube is centered like the hemisphere but its surface is divided into small squares called pixels. The light that strikes patch i is independent of the type of intermediate surface that we use. The advantage of the hemicube is that its surfaces are either parallel to or orthogonal

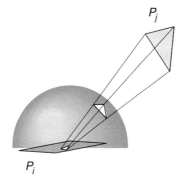

P_j

P_i

FIGURE 11.18   Projecting patch on a hemisphere.

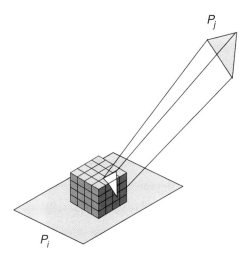

FIGURE 11.19   Projecting patch on a hemicube and onto another patch.

to P_i. Consequently, it is straightforward to project P_j onto the hemicube and to compute the contribution of each pixel on the hemicube to the light that reaches point $\mathbf{p}_i$. Thus, if the surface of the hemicube is divided into m pixels, numbered 1 to m, then we can compute the contribution of those pixels that are projections of P_j and are visible from $\mathbf{p}_i$ and add them to form the **delta form factor** Δf_{ij}, which is the contribution of P_j to the small area da_i at the center of the hemicube. We then get the desired form factor by adding the contributions of all the delta form factors. The contributions from each pixel can be computed analytically once we know whether P_j projects on it, a calculation that is similar to the ray-tracing calculation required to determine whether an object is visible from a light source. The details are included in the Suggested Readings at the end of the chapter.

Another approach to computing form factors exploits our ability to use a graphics system to compute simple renderings very rapidly. Suppose that we want to compute f_{ij}. If we illuminate P_i with a known amount of light only from P_j, we will have an experimental measurement of the desired form factor. We can approximate this measurement by placing point light sources on P_j and then rendering the scene with whatever renderer we have available. Because of the possibility that another patch obscures P_i from P_j, we must use a renderer that can handle shadows.

11.5.4 Carrying Out Radiosity

In practice, radiosity rendering has three major steps. First, we divide the scene into a mesh of patches, as shown in Figure 11.20. This step requires some skill, because more patches require the calculation of more form factors. However, it is the division of surfaces into patches that allows radiosity to yield images with subtle diffuse–diffuse interactions. The creation of the initial mesh often can be done interactively, allowing the placement of more patches in regions such as corners between surfaces

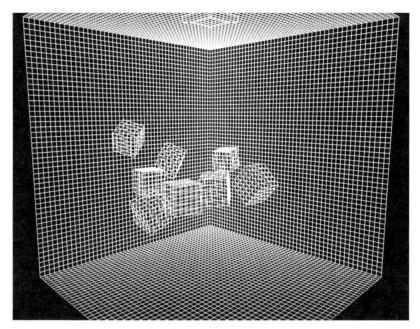

FIGURE 11.20   Division of surfaces into patches. (Courtesy of A. Van Pernis, K. Rasche, and R. Geist, Clemson University)

where we expect to see diffuse–diffuse interactions. Another approach is based on the observation that the radiosity of a large surface is equal to the area-weighted sum of the radiosities of any subdivision of it. Hence, we can start with a fairly rough mesh and refine it later (**progressive radiosity**). Once we have a mesh, we can compute the form factors, the most computationally intense part of the process.

Once we have the mesh and the form factors, we can solve the radiosity equation. We form the emission array **e** using the values for the light sources in the scene and assign colors to the surfaces, forming **R**. Now we can solve the radiosity equation to determine **b**.

The components of **b** act as the new colors of the patches. We can now place the viewer in the scene and render with a conventional renderer.

The image in Color Plate 16 was rendered using radiosity. It started with the initial mesh in Figure 11.20, which was then altered with a particle system to achieve a better set of patches. It shows the strength of radiosity for rendering interiors that are composed of diffuse reflectors.

11.6   RENDERMAN

There are other approaches to rendering that have arisen from the needs of the animation industry. Although interaction is required in the design of an animation, real-time rendering is not required when the final images are produced. Of greater importance is producing images free of rendering artifacts such as the jaggedness and moiré patterns that arise from aliasing. However, rendering the large number of frames required for a feature-length film cannot be done with ray tracers or radiosity renderers, even though animations are produced using large numbers of computers—**render farms**—whose sole task is to render scenes at the required resolution. In addition, neither ray tracers nor radiosity renderers alone produce images that have the desired artistic qualities.

The RenderMan interface is based on the use of the modeling–rendering paradigm that we introduced in Chapter 1. The design of a scene is done interactively, using simple renderers of the type that we discussed in Chapter 6. When the design is complete, the objects, lights, material properties, cameras, motion descriptions, and textures can be described in a file that can be sent to a high-quality renderer or to a render farm.

In principle, this off-line renderer could be any type of renderer. However, given the special needs of the animation industry, Pixar developed both the interface (RenderMan) and a renderer called Reyes that was designed to produce the types of images needed for commercial motion pictures. Like a ray tracer, Reyes was designed to work a pixel at a time. Unlike a ray tracer, it was not designed to incorporate global illumination effects. By working a pixel at a time, Reyes collects all the light from all objects at a resolution that avoids aliasing problems. Reyes divides (**dices**) objects—both polygonal and curved—into **micropolygons**, which are small quadrilaterals that project to a size of about half of a pixel. Because each micropolygon projects to such a small area, it can be flat-shaded, thereby simplifying its rendering. The smooth shading of surfaces is accomplished by coloring the micropolygons carefully during the dicing process.

Reyes incorporates many other interesting techniques. It uses random or stochastic sampling rather than point sampling to reduce visible aliasing effects. Generally, it works on small regions of the frame at one time to allow efficient use of textures. Note that even with its careful design, a single scene with many objects and complex lighting effects can take hours to render.

There are many renderers of this type available, some either public domain or shareware. Some renderers are capable of incorporating different rendering styles within one product. Thus, we might use ray tracing on a subset of the objects that have shiny surfaces. Likewise, we might want to use radiosity on some other subset of the surfaces. In general, these renderers support a large variety of effects and allow the user to balance rendering time against sophistication and image quality.

11.7 PARALLEL RENDERING

In many applications, particularly in the scientific visualization of large geometric data sets, we create images from data sets that might contain more than 500 million data points and generate more than 100 million polygons. This situation presents two immediate challenges. First, if we are to display this many polygons, how can we

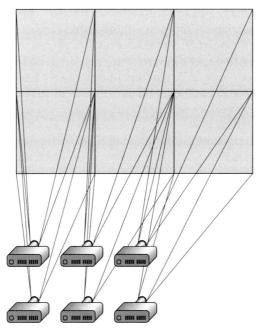

FIGURE 11.21   Power wall using six projectors.

do so when even the best commodity displays contain only about 2 million pixels? Second, if we have multiple frames to display, either from new data or because of transformations of the original data set, we need to be able to render this large amount of geometry faster than can be achieved even with high-end systems.

A popular solution to the display-resolution problem is to build a **power wall**, a large projection surface that is illuminated by an array of projectors (Figure 11.21), each with the resolution of 1024×1280, or 1920×1080 for HD projectors. Generally, the light output from the projectors is tapered at the edges, and the displays are overlapped slightly to created a seamless image. We can also create high-resolution displays from arrays of standard-size LCD panels, although at the cost of seeing small separations between panels, which can give the appearance of a window with multiple panes.

One approach to both these problems is to use clusters of standard computers connected with a high-speed network. Each computer might have a commodity graphics card. Note that such configurations are one aspect of a major revolution in high-performance computing. Formerly, supercomputers were composed of expensive, fast processors that usually incorporated a high degree of parallelism in their designs. These processors were custom designed and required special interfaces, peripheral systems, and environments that made them extremely expensive and thus affordable only by a few government laboratories and large corporations. Over the last few years, commodity processors have become extremely fast and inexpensive. In addition, the trend is toward incorporating multiple processors in the same CPU or GPU, thus creating the potential for various types of parallelism ranging from using a single CPU with multiple graphics cards, using many multicore CPUs, to GPUs with hundreds of programmable processors.

Consequently, there are multiple ways we can distribute the work that must be done to render a scene among the various processors. The simplest approach is to execute the same application program on each processor but have each use a different window that corresponds to where the processor's display is located in the output array. Given the speed of modern CPUs and GPUs and the large amount of memory available to them, this is often a viable approach.

We will examine three other possibilities. In this taxonomy, the key difference is where in the rendering process we assign, or sort, primitives to the correct areas of the display. Where we place this step leads to the designations **sort first**, **sort last**, and **sort middle**.

Suppose that we start with a large number of processors of two types: geometry processors and raster processors. This distinction corresponds to the two phases of the rendering pipeline that we discussed in Chapter 6. The geometry processors can handle front-end floating-point calculations, including transformations, clipping, and shading. The raster processors manipulate bits and handle operations such as scan conversion. Note that the present general-purpose processors and graphics processors can each do either of these tasks. Consequently, we can apply the following strategies to either the CPUs or the GPUs. We can achieve parallelism among distinct nodes, within a processor chip through multiple cores, or within the GPU. The use of the sorting paradigm will help us organize the architectural possibilities.

11.7.1 Sort-Middle Rendering

Consider a group of geometry processors (each labeled with a G) and raster processors (each labeled with an R) connected as shown in Figure 11.22. Suppose that we have an application that generates a large number of geometric primitives. It can use multiple geometry processors in two obvious ways. It can run on a single processor and send different parts of the geometry generated by the application to different geometry processors. Alternatively, we can run the application on multiple processors, each of which generates only part of the geometry. At this point, we need not worry about how the geometry gets to the geometry processors—as the best way is often application dependent—but on how to best employ the geometry processors that are available.

Assume that we can send any primitive to any of the geometry processors, each of which acts independently. When we use multiple processors in parallel, a major concern is **load balancing**, that is, having each of the processors do about the same amount of work, so that none is sitting idle for a significant amount of time, thus wasting resources. One obvious approach would be to divide the object-coordinate space equally among the processors. Unfortunately, this approach often leads to poor load balancing because in many applications the geometry is not uniformly distributed in object space. An alternative approach is to distribute the geometry

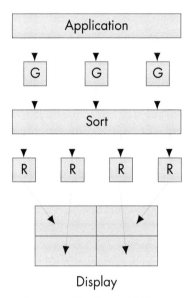

FIGURE 11.22   Sort-middle rendering.

uniformly among the processors as objects are generated, independently of where the geometric objects are located. Thus, with n processors, we might send the first geometric entity to the first processor, the second to the second processor, the nth to the nth processor, the $(n + 1)$-st to the first processor, and so on. Now consider the raster processors. We can assign each of these to a different region of the frame buffer or, equivalently, assign each to a different region of the display. Thus, each raster processor renders a fixed part of screen space.

Now the problem is how to assign the outputs of the geometry processors to the raster processors. Note that each geometry processor can process objects that could go anywhere on the display. Thus, we must sort their outputs and assign primitives that emerge from the geometry processors to the correct raster processors. Consequently, some sorting must be done before the raster stage. We refer to this architecture as *sort middle*.

This configuration was popular with high-end graphics workstations a few years ago, when special hardware was available for each task and there were fast internal buses to convey information through the sorting step. Recent GPUs contain multiple geometry processors and multiple fragment processors and so can be looked at as sort-middle processors.[3] For now, let's consider a graphics card with a single GPU as a combination of one geometry processor and one raster processor, thus aggregating the parallelism inside the GPU. Now the problem is how to use a group of commodity

---

3. Some GPUs now provide a large number of processors that can be used as either vertex or fragment processors.

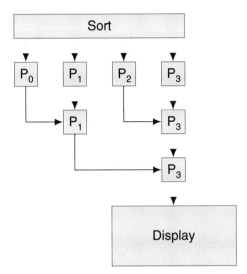

FIGURE 11.25   Binary-tree compositing.

to the closest point to the viewer.[4] Fortunately, if we are using our standard OpenGL pipeline, the necessary information is in the z buffer. For each pixel, we need only compare the depths in each of the z buffers and write the color in the frame buffer of the processor with the closest depth. The difficulty is determining how to do this comparison efficiently when the information is stored on many processors.

Conceptually, the simplest approach, sometimes called **binary-tree compositing**, is to have pairs of processors combine their information. Consider the example shown in Figure 11.25, where we have four geometry/raster pipelines, numbered 0–3. Processors 0 and 1 can combine their information to form a correct image for the geometry they have seen, while processors 2 and 3 do the same thing concurrently with their information. Let's assume that we form these new images on processors 1 and 3. Thus, processors 0 and 2 have to send *both* their color buffers *and* their z buffers to their neighbors (processors 1 and 3, respectively). We then repeat the process between processors 1 and 3, with the final image being formed in the frame buffer of processor 3. Note that the code is very simple. The geometry/raster pairs each do an ordinary rendering. The compositing step requires only reading pixels and some simple comparisons. However, in each successive step of the compositing process, only half the processors that were used in the previous step are still needed. In the end, the final image is prepared on a single processor.

There is another approach to the compositing step known as **binary-swap compositing** that avoids the idle-processor problem. In this technique, each processor is responsible for one part of the final image. Hence, for compositing to be correct, each

---

4. For simplicity, we are assuming that all the geometric objects are opaque.

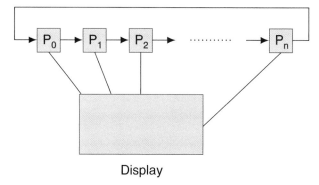

Display

FIGURE 11.26   Binary-swap compositing.

processor must see all the data. If we have n processors involved in the compositing, we can arrange them in a round-robin fashion, as shown in Figure 11.26. The compositing takes n steps (rather than the $\log n$ steps required by tree compositing). On the first step, processor 0 sends portion 0 of its frame buffer to processor 1 and receives portion n from processor n. The other processors do a similar send and receive of the portion of the color and depth buffers of their neighbors. At this point, each processor can update one area of the display that will be correct for the data from a pair of processors. For processor 0, this will be region n. On the second round, processor 0 will receive from processor n the data from region $n - 1$, which is correct for the data from processors n and $n - 1$. Processor 0 will also send the data from region n, as will the other processors for part of their frame buffers. All the processors will now have a region that is correct for the data from three processors. Inductively, it should be clear that after $n - 1$ steps, each processor has $1/n$ of the final image. Although we have taken more steps, far less data has been transferred than with tree compositing, and we have used all processors in each step.

11.7.3 Sort-First Rendering

One of the most appealing features of sort-last rendering is that we can pair geometric and raster processors and use standard computers with standard graphics cards. Suppose that we could decide first where each primitive lies on the final display. Then we could assign a separate portion of the display to each geometry/raster pair and avoid the necessity of a compositing network. The configuration might look as illustrated in Figure 11.27. Here we have included a processor at the front end to make the assignment as to which primitives go to which processors.

This front-end sort is the key to making this scheme work. In one sense, it might seem impossible, since we are implying that we know the solution—where primitives appear in the display—before we have solved the problem for which we need the geometric pipeline. But things are not hopeless. Many problems are structured so that we may know this information in advance. We also can get the information back from the pipeline using `glGetFloatv` to find the mapping from object coordinates

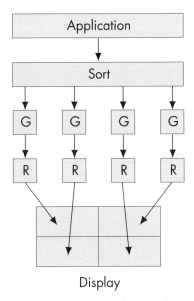

FIGURE 11.27   Sort-first rendering.

to screen coordinates. In addition, we need not always be correct. A primitive can be sent to multiple geometry processors if it straddles more than one region of the display. Even if we send a primitive to the wrong processor, that processor may be able to send it on to the correct processor. Because each geometry processor performs a clipping step, we are assured that the resulting image will be correct.

Sort-first rendering does not address the load-balancing issue, because if there are regions of the screen with very few primitives, the corresponding processors may not be very heavily loaded. However, sort-first rendering has one important advantage over sort-last rendering: It is ideally suited for generating high-resolution displays. Suppose that we want to display our output at a resolution much greater than we get with typical CRT or LCD displays that have a resolution in the range of 1–3 million pixels. Such displays are needed when we wish to examine high-resolution data that might contain more than 100 million geometric primitives.

One approach to this problem is to build a tiled display or power wall consisting of an array of standard displays (or tiles). The tiles can be CRTs, LCD panels, or the output of projectors. From the rendering perspective, we want to render an image whose resolution is the array of the entire display, which can exceed 4000 × 4000 pixels. Generally, these displays are driven by a cluster of PCs with commodity graphics cards. Hence, the candidate rendering strategies are sort first and sort last.

However, sort-last rendering cannot work in this setting, because each geometry/rasterizer processor must have a frame buffer the size of the final image, and for the compositing step, extremely large amounts of data must be exchanged between processors. Sort-first renderers do not have this problem. Each geometry/processor pair need only be responsible for a small part of the final image, typically an image the size of a standard frame buffer.

11.8   VOLUME RENDERING

Our development of computer graphics has focused on the display of surfaces. Hence, even though we can render an object so we see its three-dimensionality, we do so by modeling it as a set of two-dimensional surfaces within a three-dimensional space and then rendering these surfaces. This approach does not work well if we have a set of data in which each value represents a value at a point within a three-dimensional region.

Consider a function f that is defined over some region of three-dimensional space. Thus, at every point within this region, we have a scalar value $f(x, y, z)$ and we say that f defines a **scalar field**. For example, at each point f might be the density inside an object, or the absorption of X-rays in the human body as measured by a computed-tomography (CT) scan, or the translucency of a slab of glass. Visualization of scalar fields is more difficult than the problems that we have considered thus far for two reasons. First, three-dimensional problems have more data with which we must work. Consequently, operations that are routine for two-dimensional data, such as reading files and performing transformations, present practical difficulties. Second, when we had a problem with two independent variables, we were able to use the third dimension to visualize scalars. When we have three independent variables, we lack the extra dimension to use for display. Nevertheless, if we are careful, we can extend our previously developed methods to visualize three-dimensional scalar fields.

The field of **volume rendering** deals with these problems. Most of the methods for visualizing such volumetric data sets are extensions of the methods we have developed, and we will survey a few approaches in the next few sections. Further detail can be found in the Suggested Readings at the end of the chapter.

11.8.1 Volumetric Data Sets

We start with a discrete set of data that might have been obtained from a set of measurements of some physical process as with a medical data set from a CT scan. Alternately, we might obtain data by evaluating (or sampling) a function $f(x, y, z)$ at a set of points $\{x_i, y_i, z_i\}$, creating a **volumetric data set**.

Assume that our samples are taken at equally spaced points in x, y, and z, as shown in Figure 11.28—a simplifying but not necessary assumption. Thus,

$$x_i = x_0 + i\Delta x,$$

$$y_i = y_0 + j\Delta y,$$

$$z_i = z_0 + k\Delta z,$$

and we can define

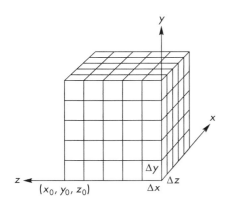

FIGURE 11.28 A volumetric data set.

$$f_{ijk} = f(x_i, y_j, z_k).$$

Each f_{ijk} can be thought of as the average value of the scalar field within a right parallelepiped of sides Δx, Δy, Δz centered at (x_i, y_j, z_k). We call this parallelepiped a volume element, or **voxel**.

The three-dimensional array of voxel values that corresponds to equally spaced samples is called a **structured data set**, because we do not need to store the information about where each sample is located in space. The terms *structured data set* and *set of voxels* often are used synonymously.

Scattered data require us to store this information in addition to the scalar values, and such data sets are called **unstructured**. Visualization of unstructured data sets is more complex but can be done with the same techniques that we use for structured data sets; consequently, we shall not pursue this topic.

Even more so than for two-dimensional data, there are multiple ways to display these data sets. However, there are two basic approaches: direct volume rendering and isosurfaces. **Direct volume rendering** makes use of every voxel in producing an image; isosurface methods use only a subset of the voxels. For a function $f(x, y, z)$, an **isosurface** is the surface defined by the implicit equation

$$f(x, y, z) = c.$$

The value of the constant c is the **isosurface value.** For the discrete problem where we start with a set of voxels, isosurface methods seek to find approximate isosurfaces.

11.8.2 Visualization of Implicit Functions

Isosurface visualization is the natural extension of contours to three dimensions and thus has a connection to visualization of implicit functions. Consider the implicit function in three dimensions

$$g(x, y, z) = 0,$$

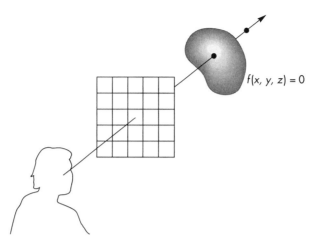

FIGURE 11.29   Ray casting of an implicit function.

where g is known analytically. If any points satisfy this equation, then this function describes one or more surfaces. Simple examples include spheres, planes, more general quadrics, and the torus of radius r and cross section a:

$$(x^2 + y^2 + z^2 - r^2 - a^2)^2 - 4a^2(r^2 - z^2) = 0.$$

As we discussed in Chapter 10, g is a membership function that allows us to test whether a particular point lies on the surface, but there is no general method for finding points on the surface. Thus, given a particular g, we need visualization methods to "see" the surface.

One way to attack this problem involves using a simple form of ray tracing sometimes referred to as **ray casting**. Figure 11.29 shows a function, a viewer, and a projection plane. Any projector can be written in the form of a parametric function:

$$\mathbf{p}(t) = \mathbf{p}_0 + t\mathbf{d}.$$

It also can be written in terms of the individual components:

$$x(t) = x_0 + td_x,$$

$$y(t) = y_0 + td_y,$$

$$z(t) = z_0 + td_z.$$

Substituting into the implicit equation, we obtain the *scalar* equation in t,

$$f(x_0 + td_x, y_0 + td_y, z_0 + td_z) = u(t) = 0.$$

The solutions of this equation correspond to the points where the projector (ray) enters or leaves the isosurface. If f is a simple function, such as a quadric or a torus, then $u(t)$ may be solvable directly, as we saw in our discussion of ray tracing in Section 11.3.

Once we have the intersections, we can apply a simple shading model to the surface. The required normal at the surface is given by the partial derivatives at the point of intersection:

$$
\mathbf{n} = \begin{bmatrix} \frac{\partial f(x,y,z)}{\partial x} \\ \frac{\partial f(x,y,z)}{\partial y} \\ \frac{\partial f(x,y,z)}{\partial z} \end{bmatrix}.
$$

Usually, we do not bother with global illumination considerations and thus do not compute either shadow rays (to determine whether the point of intersection is illuminated) or any reflected and traced rays. For scenes composed of simple objects, such as quadrics, ray casting not only is a display technique but also performs visible surface determination and often is used with CSG models. For functions more complex than quadrics, the amount of work required by the intersection calculations is prohibitive and we must consider alternate methods. First, we generalize the problem from one of viewing surfaces to one of viewing volumes.

Suppose that instead of the surface described by $g(x, y, z) = 0$, we consider a scalar field $f(x, y, z)$, which is specified at every point in some region of three-dimensional space. If we are interested in a single value c of f, then the visualization problem is that of displaying the isosurface:

$$
g(x, y, z) = f(x, y, z) - c = 0.
$$

Sometimes, displaying a single isosurface for a particular value of c is sufficient. For example, if we are working with CT data, we might pick c to correspond to the X-ray density of the tissues that we want to visualize. In other situations, we might display multiple isosurfaces.

Finding isosurfaces usually involves working with a discretized version of the problem, replacing the continuous function g by a set of samples taken over some grid. Our prime isosurface visualization method is called marching cubes, the three-dimensional version of marching squares.

11.9   ISOSURFACES AND MARCHING CUBES

Assume that we have data set $\{f_{ijk}\}$, where each voxel value is a sample of the scalar field $f(x, y, z)$, and, when the samples are taken on a regular grid, that the discrete data form a set of voxels. We seek an approximate isosurface using the sampled data to define a polygonal mesh. For any value of c, there may be no surface, one surface, or many surfaces that satisfy the equation for a given value of c. Given how well we can display three-dimensional triangles, we describe a method, called **marching cubes**,

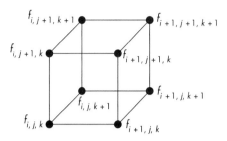

FIGURE 11.30   Voxel cell.

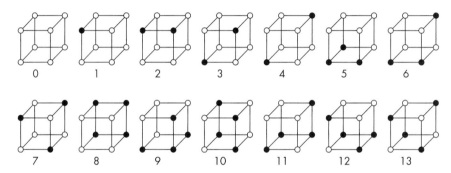

FIGURE 11.31   Vertex colorings.

that approximates a surface by generating a set of three-dimensional triangles, each of which is an approximation to a piece of the isosurface.

We have assumed that our voxel values $\{f_{ijk}\}$ are on a regular three-dimensional grid that passes through the centers of the voxels. If they are not, we can use an interpolation scheme to obtain values on such a grid. Eight adjacent grid points specify a three-dimensional cell, as shown in Figure 11.30. Vertex (i, j, k) of the cell is assigned the data value f_{ijk}. We can now look for parts of isosurfaces that pass through each of these cells, based on only the values at the vertices.

For a given isosurface value c, we can color the vertices of each cell black or white, depending on whether the value at the vertex is greater than or less than c. There are $256 = 2^8$ possible vertex colorings, but, once we account for symmetries, there are only the 14 unique cases shown in Figure 11.31.[5] Using the simplest interpretation of the data, we can generate the points of intersection between the surface and the edges of the cubes by linear interpolation between the values at the vertices. Finally, we can use the triangular polygons to tessellate these intersections, forming pieces of a tri-

---

5. The original paper by Lorensen and Cline [Lor87] and many of the subsequent papers refer to 15 cases, but 2 of those cases are symmetric.

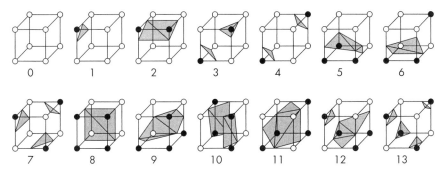

FIGURE 11.32 Tessellations for marching cubes.

angular mesh passing through the cell. These tessellations are shown in Figure 11.32. Note that not all these tessellations are unique.

Like the cells from our contour plots, each three-dimensional cell can be processed individually. In terms of the sampled data, each interior voxel value contributes to eight cells. We can go through the data, row by row, then plane by plane. As we do so, the location of the cell that we generate marches through the data set, giving the algorithm its name.

As each cell is processed, any triangles that it generates are sent off to be displayed through our graphics pipeline, where they can be lit, shaded, rotated, texture mapped, and rasterized. Because the algorithm is so easy to parallelize and, like the contour plot, can be table-driven, marching cubes is a popular way of displaying three-dimensional data.

Marching cubes is both a data-reduction algorithm and a modeling algorithm. Both simulations and imaging systems can generate data sets containing from 10^7 to 10^9 voxels. With data sets this large, simple operations (such as reading in the data, rescaling the values, or rotating the data set) are time-consuming, memory-intensive tasks. In many of these applications, however, after executing the algorithm, we might have only 10^3 to 10^4 three-dimensional triangles—a number of geometric objects handled easily by a graphics system. We can rotate, color, and shade the surfaces in real time to interpret the data. In general, few voxels contribute to a particular isosurface; consequently, the information in the unused voxels is not in the image.

There is an ambiguity problem in marching cubes. The problem can arise whenever we have different colors assigned to the diagonally opposite vertices of a side of a cell. Consider the cell coloring in Figure 11.33(a). Figures 11.33(b) and 11.33(c) show two ways to assign triangles to these data. If we compare two isosurfaces generated with the two different interpretations, areas where these cases arise will have completely different shapes and topologies. The wrong selection of an interpretation for a particular cell can leave a hole in an otherwise smooth surface. Researchers have attempted to deal with this problem; no approach works all the time. As we saw with

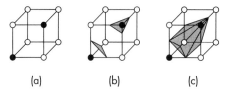

FIGURE 11.33 Ambiguity problem for marching cubes. (a) Cell. (b) One interpretation of cell. (c) Second interpretation.

contour plots, an always-correct solution requires more information than is present in the data.

11.10 MESH SIMPLIFICATION

We have looked at marching cubes as a method of generating small triangular pieces of an isosurface. Equivalently, we can view the output of the algorithm as one or more triangular meshes. These meshes are highly irregular even though they are composed of only triangles.

One of the disadvantages of marching cubes is that the algorithm can generate many more triangles than are really needed to display the isosurface. One reason for this phenomenon is that the number of triangles primarily depends on the resolution of the data set, rather than on the smoothness of the isosurface. Thus, we can often create a new mesh with far fewer triangles such that the rendered surfaces are visually indistinguishable. There are multiple approaches to this **mesh simplification** problem.

One popular approach, called **triangle decimation**, seeks to simplify the mesh by removing some edges and vertices. Consider the mesh in Figure 11.34. If we move vertex A to coincide with vertex B, we eliminate two triangles and obtain the simplified mesh in Figure 11.35. Decisions as to which triangles are to be removed can be made using criteria such as the local smoothness or the shape of the triangles. The latter criterion is important because long, thin triangles do not render well.

Other approaches are based on resampling the surface generated by the original mesh, thus creating a new set of points that lie on the surface. These points are

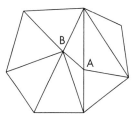

FIGURE 11.34 Original mesh.

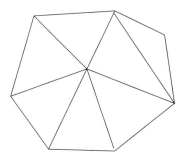

FIGURE 11.35   Mesh after simplification.

unstructured, lacking the connectivity in the original mesh. Thus, we are free to connect them in some optimal way. Probably the most popular technique is the Delaunay triangulation procedure from Chapter 10.

Another approach to resampling is to place points on the original mesh or select a subset of the vertices and then use a particle system to control the final placement of the points (particles). Repulsive forces among the particles cause the particles to move to positions that lead to a good mesh.

11.11   DIRECT VOLUME RENDERING

The weakness of isosurface rendering is that not all voxels contribute to the final image. Consequently, we could miss the most important part of the data by selecting the wrong isovalue. **Direct volume rendering** constructs images in which all voxels can make a contribution to the image. Usually these techniques are either extensions of the compositing methods we introduced in Chapter 7 or applications of ray tracing. Because the voxels typically are located on a rectangular grid, once the location of the viewer is known, there is an ordering by which we can do either front-to-back or back-to-front rendering.

Early methods for direct volume rendering treated each voxel as a small cube that was either transparent or completely opaque. If the image was rendered in a front-to-back manner, rays were traced until the first opaque voxel was encountered on each ray; then, the corresponding pixel in the image was colored black. If no opaque voxel was found along the ray, the corresponding pixel in the image was colored white. If the data set was rendered back to front, a painter's algorithm was used to paint only the opaque voxels. Both techniques produced images with serious aliasing artifacts due to treating each voxel as a cube that was projected to the screen. They also failed to display the information in all the voxels. With the use of color and opacity, we can avoid or mitigate these problems.

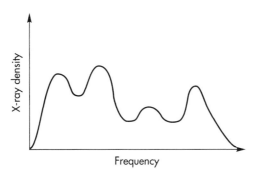

FIGURE 11.36   Histogram of CT data.

11.11.1 Assignment of Color and Opacity

We start by assigning a color and transparency to each voxel. For example, if the data are from a CT scan of a person's head, we might assign colors based on the X-ray density. Soft tissues (low densities) might be red, fatty tissues (medium densities) might be blue, hard tissues (high densities) might be white, and empty space might be black. Often, these color assignments can be based on looking at the distribution of voxel values—the **histogram** of the data. Figure 11.36 shows a histogram with four peaks. We can assign a color to each peak, and, if we use indexed color, we can assign red, green, and blue to the color indices through tables determined from curves such as those shown in Figure 11.37. If these data came from a CT scan, the skull might account for the low peak on the left and be assigned white, whereas empty space might correspond to the rightmost peak in the histogram and be colored black.

Opacities are assigned on the basis of which voxels we wish to emphasize in the image. If we want to show the brain but not the skull, we can assign zero opacity to the values corresponding to the skull. The assignment of colors and opacities is a pattern-recognition problem that we will not pursue. Often, a user interface allows the user to control these values interactively. Here, we are interested in how to construct a two-dimensional image after these assignments have been made.

11.11.2 Splatting

Once colors and opacities are assigned, we can assign a geometric shape to each voxel and apply the compositing techniques from Chapter 7. One method is to apply back-to-front painting. Consider the group of voxels in Figure 11.38. Here, the term *front* is defined relative to the viewer. For three-dimensional data sets, once we have positioned the viewer relative to the data set, *front* defines the order in which we process the array of voxels. As we saw in Chapter 8, octrees can provide an efficient mechanism for storing voxel data sets. Positioning the viewer determines an order for traversing the octree.

One particularly simple way to generate an image is known as **splatting**. Each voxel is assigned a simple shape, and this shape is projected onto the image plane. Figure 11.39 shows a spherical voxel and the associated splat, or **footprint**. Note that

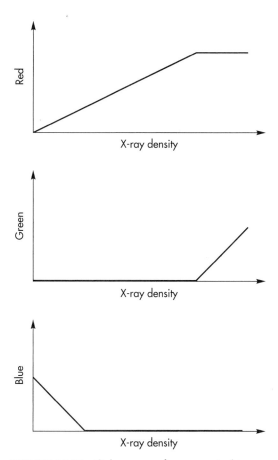

FIGURE 11.37 Color curves for computed-tomography data.

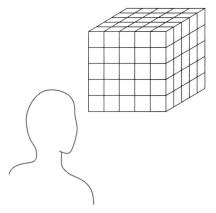

FIGURE 11.38 Volume of voxels.

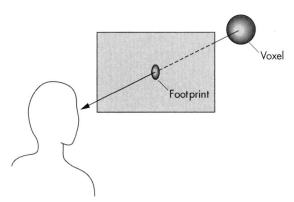

FIGURE 11.39   Splat, or footprint, of a voxel.

if we are using a parallel projection and each voxel is assigned the same shape, the splats differ in only color and opacity. Thus, we do not need to carry out a projection for each voxel, but rather can save the footprint as a bitmap that can be bitblt into the frame buffer.

The shape to assign each voxel is a sampling issue of the type we considered in Chapter 7. If the process that generated the data were ideal, each splat would be the projection of a three-dimensional sinc function. The use of hexagonal or elliptical splats is based on approximating a voxel with a parallelepiped or ellipsoid rather than using the reconstruction part of the sampling theorem. A better approximation is to use a Gaussian splat, which is the projection of a three-dimensional Gaussian approximation to the sinc function.

The key issue in creating a splatted image is how each splat is composited into the image. The data, being on a grid, are already sorted with respect to their distance from the viewer or the projection plane. We can go through the data back to front, adding the contributions of each voxel through its splat. We start with a background image and blend in successive splats.

11.11.3 Volume Ray Tracing

An alternative direct volume-rendering technique is front-to-back rendering by ray tracing (Figure 11.40). Using the same compositing formulas that we used for splatting along a ray, we determine when an opaque voxel is reached, and we stop tracing this ray immediately. The difficulty with this approach is that a given ray passes through many slices of the data, and thus we need to keep all the data available.

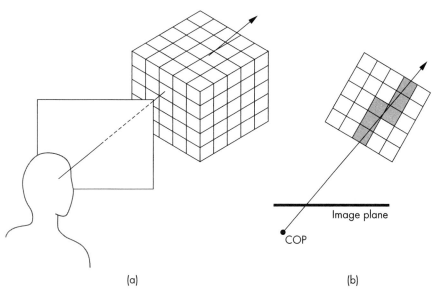

FIGURE 11.40   Volume ray casting. (a) Three-dimensional view. (b) Top view.

It should be clear that the issues that govern the choice between a back-to-front and a front-to-back renderer are similar to the issues that arise when we choose between an image-oriented renderer and an object-oriented renderer. We have merely added opacity to the process. Consequently, a volume ray tracer can produce images that have a three-dimensional appearance and can make use of all the data. However, the ray-traced image must be recomputed from scratch each time that the viewing conditions change or that we make a transformation on the data.

The approach used most often in volume ray tracing is often called **ray casting** because we generally display only the shading at the intersection of the ray with the voxels and do not bother with shadow rays. Recently, researchers have explored various strategies to use GPUs for much of the calculations.

11.11.4 Texture Mapping of Volumes

The hardware and software support for texture mapping is the basis for another approach to direct volume rendering using three-dimensional textures. Suppose that we have sufficient texture memory to hold our entire data set. We can now define a set of planes parallel to the viewer. We can map texture coordinates to world coordinates such that these planes cut through the texture memory, forming a set of parallel polygons, as shown in Figure 11.41. We now texture map the voxels to these polygons for display. Because we need only a few hundred polygons to be compatible with the number of data points that we have in most problems, we place little burden on our rendering hardware. Unlike all the other volume-rendering methods, this one is fast

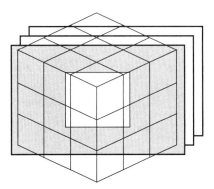

FIGURE 11.41   Slicing of three-dimensional texture memory with polygons.

enough that we can move the viewer in real time and do interactive visualization. There is, however, an aliasing problem with this technique that depends on the angle the polygons make with the texture array.

11.12   IMAGE-BASED RENDERING

Recently there has been a great deal of interest in starting with a set of two-dimensional images and either extracting three-dimensional information or forming new images from them. This problem has appeared in many forms over the years. Some of the most important examples in the past have included the following:

- Using aerial photographs to obtain terrain information
- Using a sequence of two-dimensional X-rays to obtain a three-dimensional image in computerized axial tomography (CT)
- Obtaining geometric models from cameras in robotics
- Warping one image into another (morphing)

Newer applications have focused on creating new images from a sequence of stored images that have been carefully collected. For example, suppose that we take a sequence of photographs of an object—a person, a building, or a CAD model—and want to see the object from a different viewpoint. If we had a three-dimensional model, we would simply move the viewer or the object and construct the new image. But what can we do if we have only two-dimensional information? These problems all fit under the broad heading **image-based rendering**. Techniques involve elements of computer graphics, image processing, and computer vision.

11.12.1 A Simple Example

We can get some idea of the issues involved by considering the problem shown in Figure 11.42. On the left is a perspective camera located at a point $\mathbf{p}_1$, and on the

FIGURE 11.42   Two cameras imaging the same point.

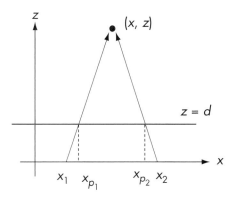

FIGURE 11.43   Top view of the two cameras.

right is a second camera located at $\mathbf{p}_2$. Consider a point $\mathbf{q}$ that is imaged by both cameras. Assuming that we know everything about these cameras—their locations, orientations, fields of view—can we determine $\mathbf{q}$ from the two images produced by the cameras? Figure 11.43 has a top view of a simplified version of the problem with the two cameras both located on the x-axis and with their image planes parallel at $z = d$. Using our standard equations for projections, we have the two relationships

$$\frac{x_1 - x_{p1}}{d} = \frac{x_1 - x}{z},$$

$$\frac{x_2 - x_{p2}}{d} = \frac{x_2 - x}{z}.$$

These are two linear equations in the unknowns x and z that we can solve, yielding

$$z = \frac{d\,\Delta x}{\Delta x - \Delta x_p},$$

$$x = \frac{x_{p1}\Delta x - x_1\Delta x_p}{\Delta x - \Delta x_p},$$

where $\Delta x = x_2 - x_1$ and $\Delta x_p = x_{p2} - x_{p1}$.

Thus, we have determined $\mathbf{q}$ from the two images. This result does not depend on where the cameras are located; moving them only makes the equations a little more complex. Once we have $\mathbf{q}$, we can obtain an image from any viewpoint.

On closer examination, we can see some practical problems. First, there are numerical problems. Any small errors in the measurement of the camera position can cause large errors in the estimate of $\mathbf{q}$. Such numerical issues have plagued many of the traditional applications, such as terrain measurement. One way around such

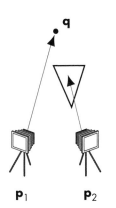

FIGURE 11.44   Imaging with occlusion.

problems is to use more than two measurements and then to determine a best estimate of the desired position.

There are other potentially serious problems. For example, how do we obtain the points $\mathbf{p}_1$ and $\mathbf{p}_2$? Given the images from the two cameras, we need a method of identifying corresponding points. This problem is one of the fundamental problems in computer vision and one for which there are no perfect solutions. Note that if there is occlusion, the same point may not even be present in the two images, as shown in Figure 11.44.

Many early techniques were purely image based, using statistical methods to find corresponding points. Other techniques were interactive, requiring the user to identify corresponding points. Recently, within the computer graphics community, there have been some novel approaches to the problem. We will mention a few of the more noteworthy ones. The details of each are referenced in the Suggested Readings at the end of the chapter.

One way around the difficulties in pure image-based approaches has been to use geometric models rather than points for the registration. For example, in a real environment, we might know that there are many objects that are composed of right parallelepipeds. This extra information can be used to derive very accurate position information.

One use of image-based techniques has been to generate new images for a single viewer from a sequence of images. Variations of this general problem have been used in the movie industry, in providing new images in virtual reality applications, such as Apple's QuickTime VR, and for viewing objects remotely.

Others have looked at the mathematical relationship between two-dimensional images and the light distribution in a three-dimensional environment. Each two-dimensional image is a sample of a four-dimensional light field. In a manner akin to how three-dimensional images are constructed from two-dimensional projections in computerized axial tomography, two-dimensional projections from multiple cameras can be used to reconstruct the three-dimensional world. Two of these techniques are known as the **lumigraph** and **light-field rendering**. Because all the information about a scene is contained in the light field, there is growing interest in measuring the light field, something that, given the large amount of data involved, was not possible until recently. One of the interesting applications of measuring the light field is in relighting a scene. In such applications, the lighting that was in the scene is removed and it is relit using the light field generated by sources at other locations.

SUMMARY AND NOTES

This chapter has illustrated that there are many approaches to rendering. The physical basis for rendering with global illumination is contained in the rendering equation. Unfortunately, it contains too many variables to be solvable, even by numerical methods, for the general case. Radiosity and ray tracing can handle some global effects, although they make opposite assumptions on the types of surfaces that are in the scene. As GPUs become more and more powerful, they can handle much of the computation required by alternate rendering methods. Consequently, we may see less of a distinction than presently exists between pipeline approaches and all other rendering methods for real-time applications.

Although the speed and cost of computers make it possible to ray-trace scenes and do radiosity calculations that were not possible a few years ago, these techniques alone are not the solution to all problems in computer graphics. If we look at what has been happening in the film, television, and game industries, it appears that we can create photorealistic imagery using a wealth of modeling methods and a variety of commercial and shareware renderers. However, there is a growing acceptance of the view that photorealism is not the ultimate goal. Hence, we see increasing interest in such areas as combining realistic rendering and computer modeling with traditional hand animation. The wide range of image-based methods fits in well with many of these applications.

Most of what we see on the consumer end of graphics is driven by computer games. It appears that no matter how fast and inexpensive processors are, the demands of consumers for more sophisticated computer games will continue to force developers to come up with faster processors with new capabilities. As high-definition television (HDTV) becomes more of a standard, we are seeing a greater variety of high-resolution displays available at reasonable prices.

On the scientific side, the replacement of traditional supercomputers by clusters of commodity computers will continue to have a large effect on scientific visualization. The enormous data sets generated by applications run on these clusters will drive application development on the graphics side. Not only will these applications need imagery generated for high-resolution displays, but the difficulties of storing these data sets will drive efforts to visualize these data as fast as they can be generated.

What is less clear is the future of computer architectures and how it will affect computer graphics. Commodity computers, such as the Apple MacPro, have multiple buses that support multiple graphics cards and multiple processors, each with multiple cores. Game boxes are starting to use alternate components, such the IBM cell processor that drives the Sony PlayStation 3. How we can best use these components is an open issue. What can be said with a great degree of certainty is that there is still much to be done in computer graphics.

SUGGESTED READINGS

Ray tracing was introduced by Appel [App68] and popularized by Whitted [Whi80]. Many of the early papers on ray tracing are included in a volume by Joy and colleagues [Joy88]. The book by Glassner [Gla89] is particularly helpful if you plan to write your own ray tracer. Many of the tests for intersections are described in Haines's chapter in [Gla89] and in the *Graphics Gems* series [Gra90, Gra91, Gra92, Gra94, Gra95]. See also [Suf07] and [Shi03]. There are many excellent ray tracers available (see, for example, [War94]).

The Rendering Equation is due to Kajiya [Kaj86]. Radiosity is based on a method first used in heat transfer [Sie81]. It was first applied in computer graphics by Goral and colleagues [Gor84]. Since its introduction, researchers have done a great deal of work on increasing its efficiency [Coh85, Coh88, Coh93] and incorporating specular terms [Sil89]. The method of using point light sources to find form factors appeared in [Kel97]. Photon mapping has been popularized by Jensen [Jen01].

The RenderMan Interface is described in [Ups89]. The Reyes rendering architecture was first presented in [Coo87]. Maya [Wat02] allows multiple types of renderers.

The sorting classification of parallel rendering was suggested by Molnar and colleagues [Mol94]. The advantages of sort-middle architectures were used in SGI's high-end workstations such as the Infinite Reality Graphics [Mon97]. The sort-last architecture was developed as part of the Pixel Flow architecture [Mol92]. Binary-swap compositing was suggested by [Ma94]. Software for sort-last renderings using clusters of commodity computers is discussed in [Hum01]. Power walls are described in [Her00, Che00].

The marching-squares method is a special case of the marching-cubes method popularized by Lorenson and Kline [Lor87]. The method has been rediscovered many times. The ambiguity problem is discussed in [Van94]. Early attempts to visualize volumes were reported by Herman [Her79] and by Fuchs [Fuc77]. Ray-tracing volumes was introduced by Levoy [Lev88]. Splatting is due to Westover [Wes90]. Particles can also be used for visualization [Wit94a, Cro97]. Many other visualization strategies are discussed in [Gal95, Nie97]. One approach to building visualization applications is to use an object-oriented toolkit [Schr06].

Image-based rendering by warping frames was part of Microsoft's Talisman hardware [Tor96]. Apple's Quicktime VR [Che95] was based on creating new views from a single viewpoint from a 360-degree panorama. Debevec and colleagues [Deb96] showed that by using a model-based approach, new images from multiple viewpoints could be constructed from a small number of images. Other warping methods were proposed in [Sei96]. Work on the lumigraph [Gor96] and light fields [Lev96] established the mathematical foundations for image-based techniques. Applications to image-based lighting are in [Rei05].

EXERCISES

11.1 What is ray tracing? How is ray casting different from ray tracing? Build and test a ray tracer.

11.2 Most ray tracers employ multiple methods for determining when to stop the recursive process. Explain two such methods.

11.3 Derive an implicit equation for a torus whose center is at the origin. You can derive the equation by noting that a plane that cuts through the torus reveals two circles of the same radius.

11.4 Explain the process of photon mapping.

11.5 Consider a ray passing through a sphere. Find the point on this ray closest to the center of the sphere. *Hint:* Consider a line from the center of the sphere that is normal to the ray. How can you use this result for intersection testing?

11.6 We can get increased accuracy from a ray tracer by using more rays. Suppose for each pixel, we cast a ray through the center of the pixel and through its four corners. How much more work does this approach require as compared to the one-ray-per-pixel ray tracer?

11.7 In the sort-middle approach to parallel rendering, what type of information must be conveyed between the geometry processors and raster processors?

11.8 How is ray tracing computed?

11.9 One way to classify parallel computers is by whether their memory is shared among the processors or distributed so that each processer has its own memory that is not accessible to other processors. How does this distinction affect the various rendering strategies that we have discussed?

11.10 The weakness of isosurface rendering is that not all voxels contribute to the final image. Which technique can be used to overcome this problem and how?

11.11 Why is the approach used most often in volume ray tracing often called ray casting? Build a simple ray caster. There are many interesting data sets available on the Internet with which to test your code.

11.12 Suppose that you have an algebraic function in which the highest term is $x^i y^j z^k$. What is the degree of the polynomial that we need to solve for the intersection of a ray with the surface defined by this function?

11.13 Which technique avoids the idle-processor problem in the parallel rendering process? Explain how it works.

11.14 For one or more OpenGL implementations, find how many triangles per second can be rendered. Determine what part of the rendering time is spent in hidden-surface removal, shading, texture mapping, and rasterization. If you are using a commodity graphics card, how does the performance that you measure compare with the specifications for the card?

11.15 Determine the pixel performance of your graphics card. Determine how many pixels per second can be read or written. Do the reading and writing of pixels occur at different rates? Is there a difference in writing texture maps?

11.16 Splatting is a simple way to generate an image. What is the difference between using a Gaussian splat and using hexagonal or elliptical splats?

11.17 Explain the advantage of sort-first rendering over sort-last rendering.

11.18 Consider a two-dimensional implicit function of the form $f(x, y) = c$. For each value of c, the resulting curves (if any) are **contours** of the function. We can display such contours using marching cubes, a three-dimensional version of marching squares. Consider a two-dimensional rectangular cell and a contour value. We color each corner of the cell black or white depending whether the value at the corner is greater or less than the contour value. How may cell colorings are there? Is there an ambiguity in how contours pass through the cells?

11.19 Give an example of the direct volume rendering technique.

APPENDIX A

SAMPLE PROGRAMS

This appendix contains the source code for many of the example programs that we developed in the text. These programs and others that are referred to in the text are also available at www.cs.unm.edu/~angel. Present there are the include files `Angel.h`, `matrix.h`, and `vector.h`, as well as a `Makefile` that should take care of the differences between architectures. Also there are additional sample programs and some implementation notes. Other examples, including those in the *OpenGL Programmer's Guide* and GLUT, can be found starting from the OpenGL Web site (www.opengl.org).

The drivers for particular graphics cards implement OpenGL using a combination of hardware and software. Thus, as long as the drivers are properly installed, using OpenGL is identical on all systems. Graphics cards differ in their performance and what extras they provide in the form of extensions. They also differ in how recent a version of OpenGL they support. You can find this information either at the manufacturer's Web site or under display properties on your computer.

OpenGL is standard on almost all workstations. For systems that use Microsoft Windows, the dynamic library for GL is in the system folder. The corresponding .lib files and include files are provided with language compilers such as Visual C++. The corresponding GLUT files (glut32.dll, glut32.lib, and glut.h) are available over the Web (see www.opengl.org). A more up-to-date choice is `freeglut`, which is also available on the Web. One of the advantages of `freeglut` is that you can check whether your code is is compatible with a particular version of OpenGL. We have included these functions in our examples but have commented them in the first couple of examples.

Most users will want to use the GLEW library so they won't have to deal with versions and extensions. At the time of this writing, OpenGL 3.0 and above are not part of Mac OS X. We expect to see such support soon as OpenGL is core to all graphics on Macs. You can run these examples on the Mac with only minor changes. Examples are on our Web site. Mac users should not need to use GLEW.

Most Linux distributions provide the Mesa distribution of OpenGL (www.mesa3D.org) and include GLUT. Although Mesa is a pure software implementation of OpenGL (and includes the source for those interested in implementation issues), increasingly manufacturers of commodity graphics cards are providing Linux drivers that allow Linux users to take advantage of the cards' capabilities.

The programs that follow use the GLUT library for interfacing with the window system. The naming of the functions follows the *OpenGL Programming Guide* and the *GLUT Users Guide*. These programs share much of the same code. You should find functions, such as the reshape callback, the initialization function, and the `main` function, almost identical across the programs. Consequently, only the first instance of each function contains extensive comments.

In all these programs, illustration of graphical principles, other than efficiency, was the most important design criterion. You should find numerous ways to extend these programs and to make them run more efficiently. In some instances, the same visual results can be generated in a completely different manner, using OpenGL capabilities other than the ones we used in the sample program.

The following programs include:

1. `InitShader` function
2. A program that generates 5000 points on the Sierpinski gasket (Chapter 2)
3. A version of the gasket program using recursion (Chapter 2)
4. Rotating-cube program sending rotation angles to GPU (Chapter 3)
5. Cube viewing with perspective (Chapter 4)
6. Rotating shaded cube (Chapter 5)
7. Shaded recursively generated sphere with per-fragment lighting (Chapter 5)
8. Rotating cube with texture (Chapter 7)
9. Tree-based figure program (Chapter 8)
10. Teapot renderer (Chapter 10)

A.1   SHADER INITIALIZATION FUNCTION

A.1.1 Application Code

```
#include "Angel.h" // Book header file

namespace Angel {

// Create a NULL-terminated string by reading the provided file
static char*
readShaderSource(const char* shaderFile)
{
    FILE* fp = fopen(shaderFile, "r");

    if ( fp == NULL ) { return NULL; }

    fseek(fp, 0L, SEEK_END);
    long size = ftell(fp);
```

```
        fseek(fp, 0L, SEEK_SET);
        char* buf = new char[size + 1];
        fread(buf, 1, size, fp);

        buf[size] = ' ';
        fclose(fp);

        return buf;
    }


    // Create a GLSL program object from vertex and fragment shader files

    GLuint
    InitShader(const char* vShaderFile, const char* fShaderFile)
    {
        struct Shader {
            const char*  filename;
            GLenum       type;
            GLchar*      source;
        } shaders[2] = {
            { vShaderFile, GL_VERTEX_SHADER, NULL },
            { fShaderFile, GL_FRAGMENT_SHADER, NULL }
        };

        GLuint program = glCreateProgram( void );

        for ( int i = 0; i < 2; ++i ) {
            Shader& s = shaders[i];
            s.source = readShaderSource( s.filename );
            if ( shaders[i].source == NULL ) {
                std::cerr << "Failed to read " << s.filename << std::endl;
                exit( EXIT_FAILURE );
            }

            GLuint shader = glCreateShader( s.type );
            glShaderSource( shader, 1, (const GLchar**) &s.source, NULL );
            glCompileShader( shader );

            GLint  compiled;
            glGetShaderiv( shader, GL_COMPILE_STATUS, &compiled );
            if ( !compiled ) {
                std::cerr << s.filename << " failed to compile:" << std::endl;
                GLint  logSize;
                glGetShaderiv( shader, GL_INFO_LOG_LENGTH, &logSize );
                char* logMsg = new char[logSize];
                glGetShaderInfoLog( shader, logSize, NULL, logMsg );
                std::cerr << logMsg << std::endl;
                delete [] logMsg;
```

```
                exit( EXIT_FAILURE );
            }

            delete [] s.source;

            glAttachShader( program, shader );
        }

        // link  and error check
        glLinkProgram(program);

        GLint  linked;
        glGetProgramiv( program, GL_LINK_STATUS, &linked );
        if ( !linked ) {
            std::cerr << "Shader program failed to link" << std::endl;
            GLint  logSize;
            glGetProgramiv( program, GL_INFO_LOG_LENGTH, &logSize);
            char* logMsg = new char[logSize];
            glGetProgramInfoLog( program, logSize, NULL, logMsg );
            std::cerr << logMsg << std::endl;
            delete [] logMsg;

            exit( EXIT_FAILURE );
        }

        // use program object
        glUseProgram(program);

        return program;
    }

}  // Close namespace Angel block
```

A.2   SIERPINSKI GASKET PROGRAM

A.2.1 Application Code

```
// Two-Dimensional Sierpinski Gasket
// Generated using randomly selected vertices and bisection

#include "Angel.h"
const int NumPoints = 5000;

void
init( void )
{
    vec2 points[NumPoints];
```

```
    // Specify the vertices for a triangle
    vec2 vertices[3] = {
        vec2( -1.0, -1.0 ), vec2( 0.0, 1.0 ), vec2( 1.0, -1.0 )
    };

    // Select an arbitrary initial point inside of the triangle
    points[0] = vec2( 0.25, 0.50 );

    // compute and store N-1 new points
    for ( int i = 1; i < NumPoints; ++i ) {
        int j = rand( void ) % 3;    // pick a vertex at random

        // Compute the point halfway between the selected vertex
        //    and the previous point
        points[i] = ( points[i - 1] + vertices[j] ) / 2.0;
    }

    // Load shaders and use the resulting shader program
    GLuint program = InitShader( "vshader21.glsl", "fshader21.glsl" );
    glUseProgram( program );

    // Create a vertex array object
    GLuint vao;
    glGenVertexArrays( 1, &vao );
    glBindVertexArray( vao );

    // Create and initialize a buffer object
    GLuint buffer;
    glGenBuffers( 1, &buffer );
    glBindBuffer( GL_ARRAY_BUFFER, buffer );
    glBufferData( GL_ARRAY_BUFFER, sizeof(points), points, GL_STATIC_DRAW );

    // Initialize the vertex position attribute from the vertex shader
    GLuint loc = glGetAttribLocation( program, "vPosition" );
    glEnableVertexAttribArray( loc );
    glVertexAttribPointer( loc, 2, GL_FLOAT, GL_FALSE, 0,
                           BUFFER_OFFSET(0) );

    glClearColor( 1.0, 1.0, 1.0, 1.0 ); // white background
}


//----------------------------------------------------------------------

void
display( void )
{
    glClear( GL_COLOR_BUFFER_BIT );     // clear the window
    glDrawArrays( GL_POINTS, 0, NumPoints );    // draw the points
```

```
        glFlush( void );
    }

    //----------------------------------------------------------------------

    int
    main( int argc, char **argv )
    {
        glutInit( &argc, argv );
        glutInitDisplayMode( GLUT_RGBA );
        glutInitWindowSize( 512, 512 );

        // If you are using freeglut, the next two lines will check if
        // the code is truly 3.2. Otherwise, comment them out

        glutInitContextVersion( 3, 2 );
        glutInitContextProfile( GLUT_CORE_PROFILE );

        glutCreateWindow( "Sierpinski Gasket" );

        glewInit( void );
        init( void );
        glutDisplayFunc( display );

        glutMainLoop( void );
        return 0;
    }
```

A.2.2 Vertex Shader

```
#version 150  //GLSL Version 1.5

in vec4 vPosition;

void main()
{
    gl_Position = vPosition;
}
```

A.2.3 Fragment Shader

```
#version 150

out vec4  fColor;

void main()
{
    fColor = vec4( 1.0, 0.0, 0.0, 1.0 );
}
```

A.3 RECURSIVE GENERATION OF SIERPINSKI GASKET

A.3.1 Application Code

```
// Recursive subdivision of triangle to form Sierpinski gasket
//   Number of recursive steps given on command line

#include "Angel.h"

using namespace Angel;

const int NumTimesToSubdivide = 5;
const int NumTriangles = 729;  // 3^5 triangles generated
const int NumVertices  = 3 * NumTriangles;

vec2 points[NumVertices];
int Index = 0;

//----------------------------------------------------------------

void
triangle( const vec2& a, const vec2& b, const vec2& c )
{
    points[Index++] = a;
    points[Index++] = b;
    points[Index++] = c;
}


//----------------------------------------------------------------

void
divide_triangle( const vec2& a, const vec2& b, const vec2& c, int count )
{
    if ( count > 0 ) {
    //compute midpoints of sides
        vec2 v0 = ( a + b ) / 2.0;
        vec2 v1 = ( a + c ) / 2.0;
        vec2 v2 = ( b + c ) / 2.0;
    //subdivide all but middle triangle
        divide_triangle( a, v0, v1, count - 1 );
        divide_triangle( c, v1, v2, count - 1 );
        divide_triangle( b, v2, v0, count - 1 );
    }
    else {
        triangle( a, b, c );    // draw triangle at end of recursion
    }
}
```

```
//----------------------------------------------------------------------

void
init( void )
{
    vec2 vertices[3] = {
        vec2( -1.0, -1.0 ), vec2( 0.0, 1.0 ), vec2( 1.0, -1.0 )
    };

    // Subdivide the original triangle
    divide_triangle( vertices[0], vertices[1], vertices[2],
                     NumTimesToSubdivide );

    // Load shaders and use the resulting shader program
    GLuint program = InitShader( "vshader22.glsl", "fshader22.glsl" );
    glUseProgram( program );

    // Create a vertex array object
    GLuint vao;
    glGenVertexArrays( 1, &vao );
    glBindVertexArray( vao );

    // Create and initialize a buffer object
    GLuint buffer;
    glGenBuffers( 1, &buffer );
    glBindBuffer( GL_ARRAY_BUFFER, buffer );
    glBufferData( GL_ARRAY_BUFFER, sizeof(points), points,
                  GL_STATIC_DRAW );

    // Initialize the vertex position attribute from the vertex shader
    GLuint loc = glGetAttribLocation( program, "vPosition" );
    glEnableVertexAttribArray( loc );
    glVertexAttribPointer( loc, 2, GL_FLOAT, GL_FALSE, 0,
                           BUFFER_OFFSET(0) );

    glClearColor( 1.0, 1.0, 1.0, 1.0 ); // white background
}

//----------------------------------------------------------------------

void
display( void )
{
    glClear( GL_COLOR_BUFFER_BIT );
    glDrawArrays( GL_TRIANGLES, 0, NumTriangles );
    glFlush( void );
}

//----------------------------------------------------------------------
```

```
int
main( int argc, char **argv )
{
    glutInit( &argc, argv );
    glutInitDisplayMode( GLUT_RGBA );
    glutInitWindowSize( 512, 512 );
    glutInitContextVersion( 3, 2 );
    glutInitContextProfile( GLUT_CORE_PROFILE );
    glutCreateWindow( "Sierpinski Gasket" );

    glewInit( void );

    init( void );

    glutDisplayFunc( display );

    glutMainLoop( void );
    return 0;
}
```

A.3.2 Vertex Shader

```
#version 150

in vec4 vPosition;

void main()
{
    gl_Position = vPosition;
}
```

A.3.3 Fragment Shader

```
#version 150

out vec4 fColor;

void main()
{
    fColor = vec4( 1.0, 0.0, 0.0, 1.0 );
}
```

A.4 ROTATING CUBE WITH ROTATION IN SHADER

A.4.1 Application Code

```
//
// Display a rotating color cube
```

```cpp
// In this version, idle function increments angles
// which are sent to vertex shader where rotation takes place

#include "Angel.h"

typedef Angel::vec4  color4;
typedef Angel::vec4  point4;

const int NumVertices = 36; //(6 faces)(2 triangles/face)
                            //(3 vertices/triangle)

point4 points[NumVertices];
color4 colors[NumVertices];

// Vertices of a unit cube centered at origin, sides aligned with axes
point4 vertices[8] = {
    point4( -0.5, -0.5,  0.5, 1.0 ),
    point4( -0.5,  0.5,  0.5, 1.0 ),
    point4(  0.5,  0.5,  0.5, 1.0 ),
    point4(  0.5, -0.5,  0.5, 1.0 ),
    point4( -0.5, -0.5, -0.5, 1.0 ),
    point4( -0.5,  0.5, -0.5, 1.0 ),
    point4(  0.5,  0.5, -0.5, 1.0 ),
    point4(  0.5, -0.5, -0.5, 1.0 )
};

// RGBA colors
color4 vertex_colors[8] = {
    color4( 0.0, 0.0, 0.0, 1.0 ),  // black
    color4( 1.0, 0.0, 0.0, 1.0 ),  // red
    color4( 1.0, 1.0, 0.0, 1.0 ),  // yellow
    color4( 0.0, 1.0, 0.0, 1.0 ),  // green
    color4( 0.0, 0.0, 1.0, 1.0 ),  // blue
    color4( 1.0, 0.0, 1.0, 1.0 ),  // magenta
    color4( 1.0, 1.0, 1.0, 1.0 ),  // white
    color4( 0.0, 1.0, 1.0, 1.0 )   // cyan
};

// Array of rotation angles (in degrees) for each coordinate axis
enum { Xaxis = 0, Yaxis = 1, Zaxis = 2, NumAxes = 3 };
int      Axis = Xaxis;
GLfloat  Theta[NumAxes] = { 0.0, 0.0, 0.0 };

GLuint  theta;  // The location of the "theta" shader uniform variable

//----------------------------------------------------------------

// quad generates two triangles for each face and assigns colors
//    to the vertices
```

```
int Index = 0;
void
quad( int a, int b, int c, int d )
{
    colors[Index] = vertex_colors[a]; points[Index] = vertices[a]; Index++;
    colors[Index] = vertex_colors[b]; points[Index] = vertices[b]; Index++;
    colors[Index] = vertex_colors[c]; points[Index] = vertices[c]; Index++;
    colors[Index] = vertex_colors[a]; points[Index] = vertices[a]; Index++;
    colors[Index] = vertex_colors[c]; points[Index] = vertices[c]; Index++;
    colors[Index] = vertex_colors[d]; points[Index] = vertices[d]; Index++;
}

//----------------------------------------------------------------------

// generate 12 triangles: 36 vertices and 36 colors
void
colorcube( void )
{
    quad( 1, 0, 3, 2 );
    quad( 2, 3, 7, 6 );
    quad( 3, 0, 4, 7 );
    quad( 6, 5, 1, 2 );
    quad( 4, 5, 6, 7 );
    quad( 5, 4, 0, 1 );
}

//----------------------------------------------------------------------

// OpenGL initialization
void
init( void )
{
    colorcube( void );

    // Load shaders and use the resulting shader program
    GLuint program = InitShader( "vshader36.glsl", "fshader36.glsl" );
    glUseProgram( program );

    // Create a vertex array object
    GLuint vao;
    glGenVertexArrays( 1, &vao );
    glBindVertexArray( vao );

    // Create and initialize a buffer object
    GLuint buffer;
    glGenBuffers( 1, &buffer );
    glBindBuffer( GL_ARRAY_BUFFER, buffer );
    glBufferData( GL_ARRAY_BUFFER, sizeof(points) + sizeof(colors),
        NULL, GL_STATIC_DRAW );
```

```
        glBufferSubData( GL_ARRAY_BUFFER, 0, sizeof(points), points );
        glBufferSubData( GL_ARRAY_BUFFER, sizeof(points),
                         sizeof(colors), colors );

        // set up vertex arrays
        GLuint vPosition = glGetAttribLocation( program, "vPosition" );
        glEnableVertexAttribArray( vPosition );
        glVertexAttribPointer( vPosition, 4, GL_FLOAT, GL_FALSE, 0,
                BUFFER_OFFSET(0) );

        GLuint vColor = glGetAttribLocation( program, "vColor" );
        glEnableVertexAttribArray( vColor );
        glVertexAttribPointer( vColor, 4, GL_FLOAT, GL_FALSE, 0,
                BUFFER_OFFSET(sizeof(points)) );

        theta = glGetUniformLocation( program, "theta" );

        glEnable( GL_DEPTH_TEST );
        glClearColor( 1.0, 1.0, 1.0, 1.0 );
    }

    //----------------------------------------------------------------------

    void
    display( void )
    {
        glClear( GL_COLOR_BUFFER_BIT | GL_DEPTH_BUFFER_BIT );

        glUniform3fv( theta, 1, Theta );
        glDrawArrays( GL_TRIANGLES, 0, NumVertices );

        glutSwapBuffers( void );
    }

    //----------------------------------------------------------------------

    void
    keyboard( unsigned char key, int x, int y )
    {
        switch( key ) {
            case 033: // Escape Key
            case 'q': case 'Q':
                exit( EXIT_SUCCESS );
                break;
        }
    }

    //----------------------------------------------------------------------
```

```
void
mouse( int button, int state, int x, int y )
{
    if ( state == GLUT_DOWN ) {
        switch( button ) {
            case GLUT_LEFT_BUTTON:    Axis = Xaxis;  break;
            case GLUT_MIDDLE_BUTTON:  Axis = Yaxis;  break;
            case GLUT_RIGHT_BUTTON:   Axis = Zaxis;  break;
        }
    }
}

//----------------------------------------------------------------------

void
idle( void )
{
    Theta[Axis] += 0.01;

    if ( Theta[Axis] > 360.0 ) {
        Theta[Axis] -= 360.0;
    }

    glutPostRedisplay( void );
}

//----------------------------------------------------------------------

int
main( int argc, char **argv )
{
    glutInit( &argc, argv );
    glutInitDisplayMode( GLUT_RGBA | GLUT_DOUBLE | GLUT_DEPTH );
    glutInitWindowSize( 512, 512 );
    glutCreateWindow( "Color Cube" );

    glewInit( void );

    init( void );

    glutDisplayFunc( display );
    glutKeyboardFunc( keyboard );
    glutMouseFunc( mouse );
    glutIdleFunc( idle );

    glutMainLoop( void );
    return 0;
}
```

A.4.2 Vertex Shader

```
#version 150

in  vec4 vPosition;
in  vec4 vColor;
out vec4 color;

uniform vec3 theta;

void main()
{
    // Compute the sines and cosines of theta for each of
    //   the three axes in one computation.
    vec3 angles = radians( theta );
    vec3 c = cos( angles );
    vec3 s = sin( angles );

    // Remember: these matrices are column-major
    mat4 rx = mat4( 1.0, 0.0,  0.0, 0.0,
                    0.0, c.x, -s.x, 0.0,
                    0.0, s.x,  c.x, 0.0,
                    0.0, 0.0,  0.0, 1.0 );

    mat4 ry = mat4(  c.y, 0.0, s.y, 0.0,
                     0.0, 1.0, 0.0, 0.0,
                    -s.y, 0.0, c.y, 0.0,
                     0.0, 0.0, 0.0, 1.0 );

    mat4 rz = mat4( c.z, -s.z, 0.0, 0.0,
                    s.z,  c.z, 0.0, 0.0,
                    0.0,  0.0, 1.0, 0.0,
                    0.0,  0.0, 0.0, 1.0 );

    color = vColor;
    gl_Position = rx * ry * rz * vPosition;
}
```

A.4.3 Fragment Shader

```
#version 150

in  vec4 color;
out vec4 fColor;

void main()
{
    fColor = color;
}
```

A.5 PERSPECTIVE PROJECTION

A.5.1 Application Code

```
// Perspective view of a color cube using LookAt( void ) and Frustum( void )

#include "Angel.h"

typedef Angel::vec4  color4;
typedef Angel::vec4  point4;

const int NumVertices = 36; //(6 faces)(2 triangles/face)(3 vertices/triangle)

point4 points[NumVertices];
color4 colors[NumVertices];

// Vertices of a unit cube centered at origin, sides aligned with axes
point4 vertices[8] ={
    point4( -0.5, -0.5,  0.5, 1.0 ),
    point4( -0.5,  0.5,  0.5, 1.0 ),
    point4(  0.5,  0.5,  0.5, 1.0 ),
    point4(  0.5, -0.5,  0.5, 1.0 ),
    point4( -0.5, -0.5, -0.5, 1.0 ),
    point4( -0.5,  0.5, -0.5, 1.0 ),
    point4(  0.5,  0.5, -0.5, 1.0 ),
    point4(  0.5, -0.5, -0.5, 1.0 )
};

// RGBA colors
color4 vertex_colors[8] ={
    color4( 0.0, 0.0, 0.0, 1.0 ),  // black
    color4( 1.0, 0.0, 0.0, 1.0 ),  // red
    color4( 1.0, 1.0, 0.0, 1.0 ),  // yellow
    color4( 0.0, 1.0, 0.0, 1.0 ),  // green
    color4( 0.0, 0.0, 1.0, 1.0 ),  // blue
    color4( 1.0, 0.0, 1.0, 1.0 ),  // magenta
    color4( 1.0, 1.0, 1.0, 1.0 ),  // white
    color4( 0.0, 1.0, 1.0, 1.0 )   // cyan
};

// Viewing transformation parameters

GLfloat radius = 1.0;
GLfloat theta = 0.0;
GLfloat phi = 0.0;

const GLfloat  dr = 5.0 * DegreesToRadians;

GLuint  model_view;  // model-view matrix uniform shader variable location
```

```
// Projection transformation parameters

GLfloat  left = -1.0, right = 1.0;
GLfloat  bottom = -1.0, top = 1.0;
GLfloat  zNear = 0.5, zFar = 3.0;

GLuint  projection; // projection matrix uniform shader variable location

//----------------------------------------------------------------------

// quad generates two triangles for each face and assigns colors
//    to the vertices

int Index = 0;

void
quad( int a, int b, int c, int d )
{
    colors[Index] = vertex_colors[a]; points[Index] = vertices[a];
                    Index++;
    colors[Index] = vertex_colors[b]; points[Index] = vertices[b];
                    Index++;
    colors[Index] = vertex_colors[c]; points[Index] = vertices[c];
                    Index++;
    colors[Index] = vertex_colors[a]; points[Index] = vertices[a];
                    Index++;
    colors[Index] = vertex_colors[c]; points[Index] = vertices[c];
                    Index++;
    colors[Index] = vertex_colors[d]; points[Index] = vertices[d];
                    Index++;
}

//----------------------------------------------------------------------

// generate 12 triangles: 36 vertices and 36 colors
void
colorcube( void )
{
    quad( 1, 0, 3, 2 );
    quad( 2, 3, 7, 6 );
    quad( 3, 0, 4, 7 );
    quad( 6, 5, 1, 2 );
    quad( 4, 5, 6, 7 );
    quad( 5, 4, 0, 1 );
}

//----------------------------------------------------------------------
```

```c
// OpenGL initialization
void
init( void )
{
    colorcube( void );

    // Load shaders and use the resulting shader program
    GLuint program = InitShader( "vshader42.glsl", "fshader42.glsl" );
    glUseProgram( program );

    // Create a vertex array object
    GLuint vao;
    glGenVertexArrays( 1, &vao );
    glBindVertexArray( vao );

    // Create and initialize a buffer object
    GLuint buffer;
    glGenBuffers( 1, &buffer );
    glBindBuffer( GL_ARRAY_BUFFER, buffer );
    glBufferData( GL_ARRAY_BUFFER, sizeof(points) + sizeof(colors),
        NULL, GL_STATIC_DRAW );
    glBufferSubData( GL_ARRAY_BUFFER, 0, sizeof(points), points );
    glBufferSubData( GL_ARRAY_BUFFER, sizeof(points), sizeof(colors), colors );

    // set up vertex arrays
    GLuint vPosition = glGetAttribLocation( program, "vPosition" );
    glEnableVertexAttribArray( vPosition );
    glVertexAttribPointer( vPosition, 4, GL_FLOAT, GL_FALSE, 0,
            BUFFER_OFFSET(0) );

    GLuint vColor = glGetAttribLocation( program, "vColor" );
    glEnableVertexAttribArray( vColor );
    glVertexAttribPointer( vColor, 4, GL_FLOAT, GL_FALSE, 0,
            BUFFER_OFFSET(sizeof(points)) );

    model_view = glGetUniformLocation( program, "model_view" );
    projection = glGetUniformLocation( program, "projection" );

    glEnable( GL_DEPTH_TEST );
    glClearColor( 1.0, 1.0, 1.0, 1.0 );
}

//----------------------------------------------------------------------

void
display( void )
{
    glClear( GL_COLOR_BUFFER_BIT | GL_DEPTH_BUFFER_BIT );
```

```
                    point4  eye( radius*sin(theta)*cos(phi),
                       radius*sin(theta)*sin(phi),
                       radius*cos(theta),
                       1.0 );
                    point4  at( 0.0, 0.0, 0.0, 1.0 );
                    vec4    up( 0.0, 1.0, 0.0, 0.0 );

                    mat4  mv = LookAt( eye, at, up );
                    glUniformMatrix4fv( model_view, 1, GL_TRUE, mv );

                    mat4  p = Frustum( left, right, bottom, top, zNear, zFar );
                    glUniformMatrix4fv( projection, 1, GL_TRUE, p );

                    glDrawArrays( GL_TRIANGLES, 0, NumVertices );

                    glutSwapBuffers( void );
                }

                //------------------------------------------------------------------

                void
                keyboard( unsigned char key, int x, int y )
                {
                    switch( key ) {
                        case 033: // Escape Key
                        case 'q': case 'Q':
                            exit( EXIT_SUCCESS );
                            break;

                        case 'x': left *= 1.1; right *= 1.1; break;
                        case 'X': left *= 0.9; right *= 0.9; break;
                        case 'y': bottom *= 1.1; top *= 1.1; break;
                        case 'Y': bottom *= 0.9; top *= 0.9; break;
                        case 'z': zNear  *= 1.1; zFar *= 1.1; break;
                        case 'Z': zNear  *= 0.9; zFar *= 0.9; break;
                        case 'r': radius *= 2.0; break;
                        case 'R': radius *= 0.5; break;
                        case 'o': theta += dr; break;
                        case 'O': theta -= dr; break;
                        case 'p': phi += dr; break;
                        case 'P': phi -= dr; break;

                        case ' ':  // reset values to their defaults
                            left = -1.0;
                            right = 1.0;
                            bottom = -1.0;
                            top = 1.0;
                            zNear = 0.5;
                            zFar = 3.0;
```

```
            radius = 1.0;
            theta  = 0.0;
            phi    = 0.0;
            break;
    }

    glutPostRedisplay( void );
}

//-------------------------------------------------------------------

void
reshape( int width, int height )
{
    glViewport( 0, 0, width, height );
}

//-------------------------------------------------------------------

int
main( int argc, char **argv )
{
    glutInit( &argc, argv );
    glutInitDisplayMode( GLUT_RGBA | GLUT_DOUBLE | GLUT_DEPTH );
    glutInitWindowSize( 512, 512 );
    glutCreateWindow( "Color Cube" );

    glewInit( void );

    init( void );

    glutDisplayFunc( display );
    glutKeyboardFunc( keyboard );
    glutReshapeFunc( reshape );

    glutMainLoop( void );
    return 0;
}
```

A.5.2 Vertex Shader

```
in  vec4 vPosition;
in  vec4 vColor;
out vec4 color;

uniform mat4 model_view;
uniform mat4 projection;
```

```
void main()
{
    gl_Position = projection*model_view*vPosition/vPosition.w;
    color = vColor;
}
```

A.5.3 Fragment Shader

```
#version 150

in  vec4 color;
out vec4 fColor;

void main()
{
    fColor = color;
}
```

A.6   ROTATING SHADED CUBE

A.6.1 Application Code

```
//  Display a rotating cube with lighting
//
//  Light and material properties are sent to the shader as uniform
//    variables.  Vertex positions and normals are sent after each
//    rotation.

#include "Angel.h"

typedef Angel::vec4  color4;
typedef Angel::vec4  point4;

const int NumVertices = 36; //(6 faces)(2 triangles/face)
                            (3 vertices/triangle)

point4 points[NumVertices];
vec3   normals[NumVertices];

// Vertices of a unit cube centered at origin, sides aligned with axes
point4 vertices[8] = {
    point4( -0.5, -0.5,  0.5, 1.0 ),
    point4( -0.5,  0.5,  0.5, 1.0 ),
    point4(  0.5,  0.5,  0.5, 1.0 ),
    point4(  0.5, -0.5,  0.5, 1.0 ),
    point4( -0.5, -0.5, -0.5, 1.0 ),
    point4( -0.5,  0.5, -0.5, 1.0 ),
    point4(  0.5,  0.5, -0.5, 1.0 ),
    point4(  0.5, -0.5, -0.5, 1.0 )
};
```

```
// Array of rotation angles (in degrees) for each coordinate axis
enum { Xaxis = 0, Yaxis = 1, Zaxis = 2, NumAxes = 3 };
int      Axis = Xaxis;
GLfloat  Theta[NumAxes] = { 0.0, 0.0, 0.0 };

// Model-view and projection matrices uniform location
GLuint  ModelView, Projection;

//----------------------------------------------------------------------

// quad generates two triangles for each face and assigns colors
//    to the vertices

int Index = 0;

void
quad( int a, int b, int c, int d )
{
    // Initialize temporary vectors along the quad's edge to
    //    compute its face normal
    vec4 u = vertices[b] - vertices[a];
    vec4 v = vertices[c] - vertices[b];

    vec3 normal = normalize( cross(u, v) );

    normals[Index] = normal; points[Index] = vertices[a]; Index++;
    normals[Index] = normal; points[Index] = vertices[b]; Index++;
    normals[Index] = normal; points[Index] = vertices[c]; Index++;
    normals[Index] = normal; points[Index] = vertices[a]; Index++;
    normals[Index] = normal; points[Index] = vertices[c]; Index++;
    normals[Index] = normal; points[Index] = vertices[d]; Index++;
}

//----------------------------------------------------------------------

// generate 12 triangles: 36 vertices and 36 colors
void
colorcube( void )
{
    quad( 1, 0, 3, 2 );
    quad( 2, 3, 7, 6 );
    quad( 3, 0, 4, 7 );
    quad( 6, 5, 1, 2 );
    quad( 4, 5, 6, 7 );
    quad( 5, 4, 0, 1 );
}

//----------------------------------------------------------------------

// OpenGL initialization
```

```
void
init( void )
{
    colorcube( void );

    // Create a vertex array object
    GLuint vao;
    glGenVertexArrays( 1, &vao );
    glBindVertexArray( vao );

    // Create and initialize a buffer object
    GLuint buffer;
    glGenBuffers( 1, &buffer );
    glBindBuffer( GL_ARRAY_BUFFER, buffer );
    glBufferData( GL_ARRAY_BUFFER, sizeof(points) + sizeof(normals),
        NULL, GL_STATIC_DRAW );
    glBufferSubData( GL_ARRAY_BUFFER, 0, sizeof(points), points );
    glBufferSubData( GL_ARRAY_BUFFER, sizeof(points),
            sizeof(normals), normals );

    // Load shaders and use the resulting shader program
    GLuint program = InitShader( "vshader53.glsl", "fshader53.glsl" );
    glUseProgram( program );

    // set up vertex arrays
    GLuint vPosition = glGetAttribLocation( program, "vPosition" );
    glEnableVertexAttribArray( vPosition );
    glVertexAttribPointer( vPosition, 4, GL_FLOAT, GL_FALSE, 0,
            BUFFER_OFFSET(0) );

    GLuint vNormal = glGetAttribLocation( program, "vNormal" );
    glEnableVertexAttribArray( vNormal );
    glVertexAttribPointer( vNormal, 3, GL_FLOAT, GL_FALSE, 0,
            BUFFER_OFFSET(sizeof(points)) );

    // Initialize shader lighting parameters
    point4 light_position( 0.0, 0.0, -1.0, 0.0 );
    color4 light_ambient( 0.2, 0.2, 0.2, 1.0 );
    color4 light_diffuse( 1.0, 1.0, 1.0, 1.0 );
    color4 light_specular( 1.0, 1.0, 1.0, 1.0 );

    color4 material_ambient( 1.0, 0.0, 1.0, 1.0 );
    color4 material_diffuse( 1.0, 0.8, 0.0, 1.0 );
    color4 material_specular( 1.0, 0.8, 0.0, 1.0 );
    float  material_shininess = 100.0;

    color4 ambient_product = light_ambient * material_ambient;
    color4 diffuse_product = light_diffuse * material_diffuse;
    color4 specular_product = light_specular * material_specular;
```

```
    glUniform4fv( glGetUniformLocation(program, "AmbientProduct"),
        1, ambient_product );
    glUniform4fv( glGetUniformLocation(program, "DiffuseProduct"),
        1, diffuse_product );
    glUniform4fv( glGetUniformLocation(program, "SpecularProduct"),
        1, specular_product );

    glUniform4fv( glGetUniformLocation(program, "LightPosition"),
        1, light_position );

    glUniform1f( glGetUniformLocation(program, "Shininess"),
        material_shininess );

    // Retrieve transformation uniform variable locations
    ModelView = glGetUniformLocation( program, "ModelView" );
    Projection = glGetUniformLocation( program, "Projection" );

    glEnable( GL_DEPTH_TEST );

    glShadeModel(GL_FLAT);

    glClearColor( 1.0, 1.0, 1.0, 1.0 );
}

//----------------------------------------------------------------------

void
display( void )
{
    glClear(GL_COLOR_BUFFER_BIT | GL_DEPTH_BUFFER_BIT);

    //  Generate the model-view matrix

    const vec3 viewer_pos( 0.0, 0.0, 2.0 );
    mat4  model_view = ( Translate( -viewer_pos ) *
        RotateX( Theta[Xaxis] ) *
        RotateY( Theta[Yaxis] ) *
        RotateZ( Theta[Zaxis] ) );

    glUniformMatrix4fv( ModelView, 1, GL_TRUE, model_view );

    glDrawArrays( GL_TRIANGLES, 0, NumVertices );
    glutSwapBuffers( void );
}

//----------------------------------------------------------------------

void
mouse( int button, int state, int x, int y )
```

```
{
    if ( state == GLUT_DOWN ) {
        switch( button ) {
            case GLUT_LEFT_BUTTON:    Axis = Xaxis;  break;
            case GLUT_MIDDLE_BUTTON:  Axis = Yaxis;  break;
            case GLUT_RIGHT_BUTTON:   Axis = Zaxis;  break;
        }
    }
}

//----------------------------------------------------------------------

void
idle( void )
{
    Theta[Axis] += 0.01;

    if ( Theta[Axis] > 360.0 ) {
        Theta[Axis] -= 360.0;
    }

    glutPostRedisplay( void );
}

//----------------------------------------------------------------------

void
keyboard( unsigned char key, int x, int y )
{
    switch( key ) {
        case 033: // Escape Key
        case 'q': case 'Q':
            exit( EXIT_SUCCESS );
            break;
    }
}

//----------------------------------------------------------------------

void
reshape( int width, int height )
{
    glViewport( 0, 0, width, height );

    GLfloat aspect = GLfloat(width)/height;
    mat4  projection = Perspective( 45.0, aspect, 0.5, 3.0 );

    glUniformMatrix4fv( Projection, 1, GL_TRUE, projection );
}
```

```
//----------------------------------------------------------------------

int
main( int argc, char **argv )
{
    glutInit( &argc, argv );
    glutInitDisplayMode( GLUT_RGBA | GLUT_DOUBLE | GLUT_DEPTH );
    glutInitWindowSize( 512, 512 );
    glutCreateWindow( "Color Cube" );

    glewInit( void );

    init( void );

    glutDisplayFunc( display );
    glutKeyboardFunc( keyboard );
    glutReshapeFunc( reshape );
    glutMouseFunc( mouse );
    glutIdleFunc( idle );

    glutMainLoop( void );
    return 0;
}
```

A.6.2 Vertex Shader

```
#version 150

in  vec4 vPosition;
in  vec3 vNormal;
out vec4 color;

uniform vec4 AmbientProduct, DiffuseProduct, SpecularProduct;
uniform mat4 ModelView;
uniform mat4 Projection;
uniform vec4 LightPosition;
uniform float Shininess;
void main()
{
    // Transform vertex  position into eye coordinates
    vec3 pos = (ModelView * vPosition).xyz;

    vec3 L = normalize( LightPosition.xyz - pos );
    vec3 E = normalize( -pos );
    vec3 H = normalize( L + E );

    // Transform vertex normal into eye coordinates
    vec3 N = normalize( ModelView*vec4(vNormal, 0.0) ).xyz;
```

```
                        // Compute terms in the illumination equation
                        vec4 ambient = AmbientProduct;

                        float Kd = max( dot(L, N), 0.0 );
                        vec4  diffuse = Kd*DiffuseProduct;

                        float Ks = pow( max(dot(N, H), 0.0), Shininess );
                        vec4  specular = Ks * SpecularProduct;

                        if( dot(L, N) < 0.0 ) specular = vec4(0.0, 0.0, 0.0, 1.0);

                        gl_Position = Projection * ModelView * vPosition;

                        color = ambient + diffuse + specular;
                        color.a = 1.0;
                    }
```

A.6.3 Fragment Shader

```
#version 150

in  vec4 color;
out vec4 fColor;

void main()
{
    fColor = color;
}
```

A.7   PER-FRAGMENT LIGHTING OF SPHERE MODEL

A.7.1 Application Code

```
// fragment shading of sphere model

#include "Angel.h"

const int NumTimesToSubdivide = 5;
const int NumTriangles        = 4096;
// (4 faces)^(NumTimesToSubdivide + 1)
const int NumVertices         = 3 * NumTriangles;

typedef Angel::vec4 point4;
typedef Angel::vec4 color4;

point4 points[NumVertices];
vec3   normals[NumVertices];

// Model-view and projection matrices uniform location
```

```
GLuint  ModelView, Projection;

//---------------------------------------------------------------------

int Index = 0;

void
triangle( const point4& a, const point4& b, const point4& c )
{
    vec3  normal = normalize( cross(b - a, c - b) );

    normals[Index] = normal;  points[Index] = a;  Index++;
    normals[Index] = normal;  points[Index] = b;  Index++;
    normals[Index] = normal;  points[Index] = c;  Index++;
}

//---------------------------------------------------------------------

point4
unit( const point4& p )
{
    float len = p.x*p.x + p.y*p.y + p.z*p.z;

    point4 t;
    if ( len > DivideByZeroTolerance ) {
        t = p / sqrt(len);
        t.w = 1.0;
    }

    return t;
}

void
divide_triangle( const point4& a, const point4& b,
        const point4& c, int count )
{
    if ( count > 0 ) {
        point4 v1 = unit( a + b );
        point4 v2 = unit( a + c );
        point4 v3 = unit( b + c );
        divide_triangle(  a, v1, v2, count - 1 );
        divide_triangle(  c, v2, v3, count - 1 );
        divide_triangle(  b, v3, v1, count - 1 );
        divide_triangle( v1, v3, v2, count - 1 );
    }
    else {
        triangle( a, b, c );
    }
}
```

```
void
tetrahedron( int count )
{
    point4 v[4] = {
        vec4( 0.0, 0.0, 1.0, 1.0 ),
        vec4( 0.0, 0.942809, -0.333333, 1.0 ),
        vec4( -0.816497, -0.471405, -0.333333, 1.0 ),
        vec4( 0.816497, -0.471405, -0.333333, 1.0 )
    };

    divide_triangle( v[0], v[1], v[2], count );
    divide_triangle( v[3], v[2], v[1], count );
    divide_triangle( v[0], v[3], v[1], count );
    divide_triangle( v[0], v[2], v[3], count );
}

//----------------------------------------------------------------------

// OpenGL initialization
void
init( void )
{
    // Subdivide a tetrahedron into a sphere
    tetrahedron( NumTimesToSubdivide );

    // Create a vertex array object
    GLuint vao;
    glGenVertexArrays( 1, &vao );
    glBindVertexArray( vao );

    // Create and initialize a buffer object
    GLuint buffer;
    glGenBuffers( 1, &buffer );
    glBindBuffer( GL_ARRAY_BUFFER, buffer );
    glBufferData( GL_ARRAY_BUFFER, sizeof(points) + sizeof(normals),
        NULL, GL_STATIC_DRAW );
    glBufferSubData( GL_ARRAY_BUFFER, 0, sizeof(points), points );
    glBufferSubData( GL_ARRAY_BUFFER, sizeof(points),
            sizeof(normals), normals );

    // Load shaders and use the resulting shader program
    GLuint program = InitShader( "vshader56.glsl", "fshader56.glsl" );
    glUseProgram( program );

    // set up vertex arrays
    GLuint vPosition = glGetAttribLocation( program, "vPosition" );
    glEnableVertexAttribArray( vPosition );
    glVertexAttribPointer( vPosition, 4, GL_FLOAT, GL_FALSE, 0,
            BUFFER_OFFSET(0) );
```

```
    GLuint vNormal = glGetAttribLocation( program, "vNormal" );
    glEnableVertexAttribArray( vNormal );
    glVertexAttribPointer( vNormal, 3, GL_FLOAT, GL_FALSE, 0,
            BUFFER_OFFSET(sizeof(points)) );

    // Initialize shader lighting parameters
    point4 light_position( 0.0, 0.0, 2.0, 0.0 );
    color4 light_ambient( 0.2, 0.2, 0.2, 1.0 );
    color4 light_diffuse( 1.0, 1.0, 1.0, 1.0 );
    color4 light_specular( 1.0, 1.0, 1.0, 1.0 );

    color4 material_ambient( 1.0, 0.0, 1.0, 1.0 );
    color4 material_diffuse( 1.0, 0.8, 0.0, 1.0 );
    color4 material_specular( 1.0, 0.0, 1.0, 1.0 );
    float  material_shininess = 5.0;

    color4 ambient_product = light_ambient * material_ambient;
    color4 diffuse_product = light_diffuse * material_diffuse;
    color4 specular_product = light_specular * material_specular;

    glUniform4fv( glGetUniformLocation(program, "AmbientProduct"),
        1, ambient_product );
    glUniform4fv( glGetUniformLocation(program, "DiffuseProduct"),
        1, diffuse_product );
    glUniform4fv( glGetUniformLocation(program, "SpecularProduct"),
        1, specular_product );

    glUniform4fv( glGetUniformLocation(program, "LightPosition"),
        1, light_position );

    glUniform1f( glGetUniformLocation(program, "Shininess"),
        material_shininess );

    // Retrieve transformation uniform variable locations
    ModelView = glGetUniformLocation( program, "ModelView" );
    Projection = glGetUniformLocation( program, "Projection" );

    glEnable( GL_DEPTH_TEST );

    glClearColor( 1.0, 1.0, 1.0, 1.0 ); // white background
}

//-------------------------------------------------------------------

void
display( void )
{
    glClear( GL_COLOR_BUFFER_BIT | GL_DEPTH_BUFFER_BIT );

    point4 at( 0.0, 0.0, 0.0, 1.0 );
```

```
    point4 eye( 0.0, 0.0, 2.0, 1.0 );
    vec4   up( 0.0, 1.0, 0.0, 0.0 );

    mat4 model_view = LookAt( eye, at, up );
    glUniformMatrix4fv( ModelView, 16, GL_TRUE, model_view );

    glDrawArrays( GL_TRIANGLES, 0, NumVertices );
    glutSwapBuffers( void );
}

//----------------------------------------------------------------------

void
keyboard( unsigned char key, int x, int y )
{
    switch( key ) {
        case 033: // Escape Key
        case 'q': case 'Q':
            exit( EXIT_SUCCESS );
            break;
    }
}

//----------------------------------------------------------------------

void
reshape( int width, int height )
{
    glViewport( 0, 0, width, height );

    GLfloat left = -2.0, right = 2.0;
    GLfloat top = 2.0, bottom = -2.0;
    GLfloat zNear = -20.0, zFar = 20.0;

    GLfloat aspect = GLfloat(width)/height;

    if ( aspect > 1.0 ) {
        left *= aspect;
        right *= aspect;
    }
    else {
        top /= aspect;
        bottom /= aspect;
    }

    mat4 projection = Ortho( left, right, bottom, top, zNear, zFar );
    glUniformMatrix4fv( Projection, 1, GL_TRUE, projection );
}

//----------------------------------------------------------------------
```

```
int
main( int argc, char **argv )
{
    glutInit( &argc, argv );
    glutInitDisplayMode( GLUT_RGBA | GLUT_DEPTH );
    glutInitWindowSize( 512, 512 );
    glutCreateWindow( "Sphere" );

    glewInit( void );

    init( void );

    glutDisplayFunc( display );
    glutReshapeFunc( reshape );
    glutKeyboardFunc( keyboard );

    glutMainLoop( void );
    return 0;
}
```

A.7.2 Vertex Shader

```
#version 150

in   vec4 vPosition;
in   vec3 vNormal;

// output values that will be interpolated per-fragment
out  vec3 fN;
out  vec3 fE;
out  vec3 fL;

uniform mat4 ModelView;
uniform vec4 LightPosition;
uniform mat4 Projection;

void main()
{
    fN = vNormal;
    fE = vPosition.xyz;
    fL = LightPosition.xyz;

    if( LightPosition.w != 0.0 ) {
        fL = LightPosition.xyz - vPosition.xyz;
    }

    gl_Position = Projection*ModelView*vPosition;
}
```

A.7.3 Fragment Shader

```glsl
#version 150

// per-fragment interpolated values from the vertex shader
in  vec3 fN;
in  vec3 fL;
in  vec3 fE;

out vec4 fColor;

uniform vec4 AmbientProduct, DiffuseProduct, SpecularProduct;
uniform mat4 ModelView;
uniform vec4 LightPosition;
uniform float Shininess;

void main()
{
    // Normalize the input lighting vectors
    vec3 N = normalize(fN);
    vec3 E = normalize(fE);
    vec3 L = normalize(fL);

    vec3 H = normalize( L + E );

    vec4 ambient = AmbientProduct;

    float Kd = max(dot(L, N), 0.0);
    vec4 diffuse = Kd*DiffuseProduct;

    float Ks = pow(max(dot(N, H), 0.0), Shininess);
    vec4 specular = Ks*SpecularProduct;

    // discard the specular highlight if the light's behind the vertex
    if( dot(L, N) < 0.0 ) {
        specular = vec4(0.0, 0.0, 0.0, 1.0);
    }

    fColor = ambient + diffuse + specular;
    fColor.a = 1.0;
}
```

A.8   ROTATING CUBE WITH TEXTURE

A.8.1 Application Code

```
// rotating cube with two texture objects
// change textures with 1 and 2 keys
```

```cpp
#include "Angel.h"

const int  NumTriangles = 12; // (6 faces)(2 triangles/face)
const int  NumVertices  = 3 * NumTriangles;
const int  TextureSize  = 64;

typedef Angel::vec4 point4;
typedef Angel::vec4 color4;

// Texture objects and storage for texture image
GLuint textures[2];

GLubyte image[TextureSize][TextureSize][3];
GLubyte image2[TextureSize][TextureSize][3];

// Vertex data arrays
point4  points[NumVertices];
color4  quad_colors[NumVertices];
vec2    tex_coords[NumVertices];

// Array of rotation angles (in degrees) for each coordinate axis
enum { Xaxis = 0, Yaxis = 1, Zaxis = 2, NumAxes = 3 };
int      Axis = Xaxis;
GLfloat  Theta[NumAxes] = { 0.0, 0.0, 0.0 };
GLuint   theta;

//----------------------------------------------------------------------

int Index = 0;

void
quad( int a, int b, int c, int d )
{
    point4 vertices[8] = {
        point4( -0.5, -0.5,  0.5, 1.0 ),
        point4( -0.5,  0.5,  0.5, 1.0 ),
        point4(  0.5,  0.5,  0.5, 1.0 ),
        point4(  0.5, -0.5,  0.5, 1.0 ),
        point4( -0.5, -0.5, -0.5, 1.0 ),
        point4( -0.5,  0.5, -0.5, 1.0 ),
        point4(  0.5,  0.5, -0.5, 1.0 ),
        point4(  0.5, -0.5, -0.5, 1.0 )
    };

    color4 colors[8] = {
        color4( 0.0, 0.0, 0.0, 1.0 ),  // black
        color4( 1.0, 0.0, 0.0, 1.0 ),  // red
        color4( 1.0, 1.0, 0.0, 1.0 ),  // yellow
        color4( 0.0, 1.0, 0.0, 1.0 ),  // green
```

```
            color4( 0.0, 0.0, 1.0, 1.0 ),  // blue
            color4( 1.0, 0.0, 1.0, 1.0 ),  // magenta
            color4( 0.0, 1.0, 1.0, 1.0 ),  // white
            color4( 1.0, 1.0, 1.0, 1.0 )   // cyan
        };

        quad_colors[Index] = colors[a];
        points[Index] = vertices[a];
        tex_coords[Index] = vec2( 0.0, 0.0 );
        Index++;

        quad_colors[Index] = colors[a];
        points[Index] = vertices[b];
        tex_coords[Index] = vec2( 0.0, 1.0 );
        Index++;

        quad_colors[Index] = colors[a];
        points[Index] = vertices[c];
        tex_coords[Index] = vec2( 1.0, 1.0 );
        Index++;

        quad_colors[Index] = colors[a];
        points[Index] = vertices[a];
        tex_coords[Index] = vec2( 0.0, 0.0 );
        Index++;

        quad_colors[Index] = colors[a];
        points[Index] = vertices[c];
        tex_coords[Index] = vec2( 1.0, 1.0 );
        Index++;

        quad_colors[Index] = colors[a];
        points[Index] = vertices[d];
        tex_coords[Index] = vec2( 1.0, 0.0 );
        Index++;
    }

    //----------------------------------------------------------------------

    void
    colorcube( void )
    {
        quad( 1, 0, 3, 2 );
        quad( 2, 3, 7, 6 );
        quad( 3, 0, 4, 7 );
        quad( 6, 5, 1, 2 );
        quad( 4, 5, 6, 7 );
        quad( 5, 4, 0, 1 );
    }
```

```
//----------------------------------------------------------------------

void
init( void )
{
    colorcube( void );

    // Create a checkerboard pattern
    for ( int i = 0; i < 64; i++ ) {
        for ( int j = 0; j < 64; j++ ) {
            GLubyte c = (((i & 0x8) == 0) ^ ((j & 0x8)  == 0)) * 255;
            image[i][j][0]  = c;
            image[i][j][1]  = c;
            image[i][j][2]  = c;
            image2[i][j][0] = c;
            image2[i][j][1] = 0;
            image2[i][j][2] = c;
        }
    }

    // Initialize texture objects
    glGenTextures( 2, textures );

    glBindTexture( GL_TEXTURE_2D, textures[0] );
    glTexImage2D( GL_TEXTURE_2D, 0, GL_RGB, TextureSize, TextureSize, 0,
                  GL_RGB, GL_UNSIGNED_BYTE, image );
    glTexParameterf( GL_TEXTURE_2D, GL_TEXTURE_WRAP_S, GL_REPEAT );
    glTexParameterf( GL_TEXTURE_2D, GL_TEXTURE_WRAP_T, GL_REPEAT );
    glTexParameterf( GL_TEXTURE_2D, GL_TEXTURE_MAG_FILTER, GL_NEAREST );
    glTexParameterf( GL_TEXTURE_2D, GL_TEXTURE_MIN_FILTER, GL_NEAREST );

    glBindTexture( GL_TEXTURE_2D, textures[1] );
    glTexImage2D( GL_TEXTURE_2D, 0, GL_RGB, TextureSize, TextureSize, 0,
                  GL_RGB, GL_UNSIGNED_BYTE, image2 );
    glTexParameterf( GL_TEXTURE_2D, GL_TEXTURE_WRAP_S, GL_REPEAT );
    glTexParameterf( GL_TEXTURE_2D, GL_TEXTURE_WRAP_T, GL_REPEAT );
    glTexParameterf( GL_TEXTURE_2D, GL_TEXTURE_MAG_FILTER, GL_NEAREST );
    glTexParameterf( GL_TEXTURE_2D, GL_TEXTURE_MIN_FILTER, GL_NEAREST );

    glActiveTexture( GL_TEXTURE0 );
    glBindTexture( GL_TEXTURE_2D, textures[0] );

    // Create a vertex array object
    GLuint vao;
    glGenVertexArrays( 1, &vao );
    glBindVertexArray( vao );

    // Create and initialize a buffer object
    GLuint buffer;
```

```
glGenBuffers( 1, &buffer );
glBindBuffer( GL_ARRAY_BUFFER, buffer );
glBufferData( GL_ARRAY_BUFFER,
              sizeof(points) + sizeof(quad_colors) +
              sizeof(tex_coords), NULL, GL_STATIC_DRAW );

// Specify an offset to keep track of where we're placing data in
//   our vertex array buffer.  We'll use the same technique when we
//   associate the offsets with vertex attribute pointers.
GLintptr offset = 0;
glBufferSubData( GL_ARRAY_BUFFER, offset, sizeof(points), points );
offset += sizeof(points);

glBufferSubData( GL_ARRAY_BUFFER, offset,
                 sizeof(quad_colors), quad_colors );
offset += sizeof(quad_colors);

glBufferSubData( GL_ARRAY_BUFFER, offset, sizeof(tex_coords),
                 tex_coords );

// Load shaders and use the resulting shader program
GLuint program = InitShader( "vshader71.glsl", "fshader71.glsl" );
glUseProgram( program );

// set up vertex arrays
offset = 0;
GLuint vPosition = glGetAttribLocation( program, "vPosition" );
glEnableVertexAttribArray( vPosition );
glVertexAttribPointer( vPosition, 4, GL_FLOAT, GL_FALSE, 0,
                       BUFFER_OFFSET(offset) );
offset += sizeof(points);

GLuint vColor = glGetAttribLocation( program, "vColor" );
glEnableVertexAttribArray( vColor );
glVertexAttribPointer( vColor, 4, GL_FLOAT, GL_FALSE, 0,
                       BUFFER_OFFSET(offset) );
offset += sizeof(quad_colors);

GLuint vTexCoord = glGetAttribLocation( program, "vTexCoord" );
glEnableVertexAttribArray( vTexCoord );
glVertexAttribPointer( vTexCoord, 2, GL_FLOAT, GL_FALSE, 0,
                       BUFFER_OFFSET(offset) );

// Set the value of the fragment shader texture sampler variable
//   ("texture") to the appropriate texture unit. In this case,
//   zero, for GL_TEXTURE0 which was previously set by calling
//   glActiveTexture( void ).
glUniform1i( glGetUniformLocation(program, "texture"), 0 );
```

```
    theta = glGetUniformLocation( program, "theta" );

    glEnable( GL_DEPTH_TEST );

    glClearColor( 1.0, 1.0, 1.0, 1.0 );
}

void
display( void )
{
    glClear( GL_COLOR_BUFFER_BIT | GL_DEPTH_BUFFER_BIT );
    glUniform3fv( theta, 1, Theta );
    glDrawArrays( GL_TRIANGLES, 0, NumVertices );
    glutSwapBuffers( void );
}

//----------------------------------------------------------------------

void
mouse( int button, int state, int x, int y )
{
    if ( state == GLUT_DOWN ) {
        switch( button ) {
            case GLUT_LEFT_BUTTON:    Axis = Xaxis;  break;
            case GLUT_MIDDLE_BUTTON:  Axis = Yaxis;  break;
            case GLUT_RIGHT_BUTTON:   Axis = Zaxis;  break;
        }
    }
}

//----------------------------------------------------------------------

void
idle( void )
{
    Theta[Axis] += 0.01;

    if ( Theta[Axis] > 360.0 ) {
        Theta[Axis] -= 360.0;
    }

    glutPostRedisplay( void );
}

//----------------------------------------------------------------------

void
keyboard( unsigned char key, int mousex, int mousey )
{
```

```
        switch( key ) {
            case 033: // Escape Key
            case 'q': case 'Q':
                exit( EXIT_SUCCESS );
                break;
            case '1':
                glBindTexture( GL_TEXTURE_2D, textures[0] );
                    break;

            case '2':
                glBindTexture( GL_TEXTURE_2D, textures[1] );
                break;
        }

    glutPostRedisplay( void );
}

//--------------------------------------------------------------------

int
main( int argc, char **argv )
{
    glutInit( &argc, argv );
    glutInitDisplayMode( GLUT_RGBA | GLUT_DOUBLE | GLUT_DEPTH );
    glutInitWindowSize( 512, 512 );
    glutInitContextVersion( 3, 2 );
    glutInitContextProfile( GLUT_CORE_PROFILE );
    glutCreateWindow( "Color Cube" );

    glewInit( void );

    init( void );

    glutDisplayFunc( display );
    glutKeyboardFunc( keyboard );
    glutMouseFunc( mouse );
    glutIdleFunc( idle );

    glutMainLoop( void );
    return 0;
}
```

A.8.2 Vertex Shader

```
#version 150

in  vec4 vPosition;
in  vec4 vColor;
in  vec2 vTexCoord;
```

```
out vec4 color;
out vec2 texCoord;

uniform vec3 theta;

void main()
{
    const float  DegreesToRadians = 3.14159265 / 180.0;

    vec3 c = cos( DegreesToRadians * theta );
    vec3 s = sin( DegreesToRadians * theta );

    mat4 rx = mat4( 1.0, 0.0,  0.0, 0.0,
          0.0, c.x, -s.x, 0.0,
          0.0, s.x,  c.x, 0.0,
          0.0, 0.0,  0.0, 1.0);

    mat4 ry = mat4(   c.y, 0.0, s.y, 0.0,
            0.0, 1.0, 0.0, 0.0,
           -s.y, 0.0, c.y, 0.0,
            0.0, 0.0, 0.0, 1.0 );

    mat4 rz = mat4( c.z, -s.z, 0.0, 0.0,
          s.z,  c.z, 0.0, 0.0,
          0.0,  0.0, 1.0, 0.0,
          0.0,  0.0, 0.0, 1.0 );

    color       = vColor;
    texCoord    = vTexCoord;
    gl_Position = rz * ry * rx * vPosition;
}
```

A.8.3 Fragment Shader

```
#version 150

in  vec4 color;
in  vec2 texCoord;

out vec4 fColor;

uniform sampler2D texture;

void main()
{
    fColor = color * texture2D( texture, texCoord );
}
```

A.9   FIGURE WITH TREE TRAVERSAL

A.9.1 Application Code

```
#include "Angel.h"
#include <assert.h>

typedef Angel::vec4 point4;
typedef Angel::vec4 color4;

const int NumVertices = 36; //(6 faces)(2 triangles/face)
                                (3 vertices/triangle)

point4 points[NumVertices];
color4 colors[NumVertices];

point4 vertices[8] = {
    point4( -0.5, -0.5, 0.5, 1.0 ),
    point4( -0.5, 0.5, 0.5, 1.0 ),
    point4( 0.5, 0.5, 0.5, 1.0 ),
    point4( 0.5, -0.5, 0.5, 1.0 ),
    point4( -0.5, -0.5, -0.5, 1.0 ),
    point4( -0.5, 0.5, -0.5, 1.0 ),
    point4( 0.5, 0.5, -0.5, 1.0 ),
    point4( 0.5, -0.5, -0.5, 1.0 )
};

// RGBA colors
color4 vertex_colors[8] = {
    color4( 0.0, 0.0, 0.0, 1.0 ),  // black
    color4( 1.0, 0.0, 0.0, 1.0 ),  // red
    color4( 1.0, 1.0, 0.0, 1.0 ),  // yellow
    color4( 0.0, 1.0, 0.0, 1.0 ),  // green
    color4( 0.0, 0.0, 1.0, 1.0 ),  // blue
    color4( 1.0, 0.0, 1.0, 1.0 ),  // magenta
    color4( 1.0, 1.0, 1.0, 1.0 ),  // white
    color4( 0.0, 1.0, 1.0, 1.0 )   // cyan
};

//-------------------------------------------------------------------

class MatrixStack {
    int    _index;
    int    _size;
    mat4*  _matrices;

  public:
    MatrixStack( int numMatrices = 32 ):_index(0), _size(numMatrices)
```

```cpp
        { _matrices = new mat4[numMatrices]; }

    ~MatrixStack( void )
        { delete[]_matrices; }

    mat4& push( const mat4& m ) {
        assert( _index + 1 < _size );
        _matrices[_index++] = m;
    }

    mat4& pop( void ) {
        assert( _index - 1 >= 0 );
        _index--;
        return _matrices[_index + 1];
    }
};

MatrixStack  mvstack;
mat4         model_view;
GLuint       ModelView, Projection;


//-----------------------------------------------------------------

#define TORSO_HEIGHT 5.0
#define TORSO_WIDTH 1.0
#define UPPER_ARM_HEIGHT 3.0
#define LOWER_ARM_HEIGHT 2.0
#define UPPER_LEG_WIDTH  0.5
#define LOWER_LEG_WIDTH  0.5
#define LOWER_LEG_HEIGHT 2.0
#define UPPER_LEG_HEIGHT 3.0
#define UPPER_LEG_WIDTH  0.5
#define UPPER_ARM_WIDTH  0.5
#define LOWER_ARM_WIDTH  0.5
#define HEAD_HEIGHT 1.5
#define HEAD_WIDTH 1.0

// Set up menu item indices, which we can also use with the joint angles
enum {
    Torso = 0,
    Head  = 1,
    Head1 = 1,
    Head2 = 2,
    LeftUpperArm = 3,
    LeftLowerArm = 4,
    RightUpperArm = 5,
    RightLowerArm = 6,
    LeftUpperLeg = 7,
```

```
                LeftLowerLeg = 8,
                RightUpperLeg = 9,
                RightLowerLeg = 10,
                NumNodes,
                Quit
        };

        // Joint angles with initial values
        GLfloat
        theta[NumNodes] = {
            0.0,     // Torso
            0.0,     // Head1
            0.0,     // Head2
            0.0,     // LeftUpperArm
            0.0,     // LeftLowerArm
            0.0,     // RightUpperArm
            0.0,     // RightLowerArm
            180.0,   // LeftUpperLeg
            0.0,      // LeftLowerLeg
            180.0,   // RightUpperLeg
            0.0      // RightLowerLeg
        };

        GLint angle = Head2;

        //----------------------------------------------------------------------

        struct Node {
            mat4  transform;
            void  (*render)( void );
            Node* sibling;
            Node* child;

            Node( void ) :
                render(NULL), sibling(NULL), child(NULL) {}

            Node( mat4& m, void (*render)( void ), Node* sibling, Node* child ) :
                transform(m), render(render), sibling(sibling), child(child) {}
        };

        Node  nodes[NumNodes];

        //----------------------------------------------------------------------

        int Index = 0;

        void
        quad( int a, int b, int c, int d )
```

```
{
    colors[Index] = vertex_colors[a]; points[Index] = vertices[a]; Index++;
    colors[Index] = vertex_colors[a]; points[Index] = vertices[b]; Index++;
    colors[Index] = vertex_colors[a]; points[Index] = vertices[c]; Index++;
    colors[Index] = vertex_colors[a]; points[Index] = vertices[a]; Index++;
    colors[Index] = vertex_colors[a]; points[Index] = vertices[c]; Index++;
    colors[Index] = vertex_colors[a]; points[Index] = vertices[d]; Index++;
}

void
colorcube( void )
{
    quad( 1, 0, 3, 2 );
    quad( 2, 3, 7, 6 );
    quad( 3, 0, 4, 7 );
    quad( 6, 5, 1, 2 );
    quad( 4, 5, 6, 7 );
    quad( 5, 4, 0, 1 );
}

//----------------------------------------------------------------------

void
traverse( Node* node )
{
    if ( node == NULL ) { return; }

    mvstack.push( model_view );

    model_view *= node->transform;
    node->render( void );

    if ( node->child ) { traverse( node->child ); }

    model_view = mvstack.pop( void );

    if ( node->sibling ) { traverse( node->sibling ); }
}

//----------------------------------------------------------------------

void
torso( void )
{
    mvstack.push( model_view );

    mat4 instance = ( Translate( 0.0, 0.5 * TORSO_HEIGHT, 0.0 ) *
                        Scale( TORSO_WIDTH, TORSO_HEIGHT, TORSO_WIDTH ) );
```

```
        glUniformMatrix4fv( ModelView, 1, GL_TRUE, model_view * instance );
        glDrawArrays( GL_TRIANGLES, 0, NumVertices );

        model_view = mvstack.pop( void );
    }

    void
    head( void )
    {
        mvstack.push( model_view );

        mat4 instance = (Translate( 0.0, 0.5 * HEAD_HEIGHT, 0.0 ) *
                         Scale( HEAD_WIDTH, HEAD_HEIGHT, HEAD_WIDTH ) );

        glUniformMatrix4fv( ModelView, 1, GL_TRUE, model_view * instance );
        glDrawArrays( GL_TRIANGLES, 0, NumVertices );

        model_view = mvstack.pop( void );
    }

    void
    left_upper_arm( void )
    {
        mvstack.push( model_view );

        mat4 instance = (Translate( 0.0, 0.5 * UPPER_ARM_HEIGHT, 0.0 ) *
                         Scale( UPPER_ARM_WIDTH,
                                UPPER_ARM_HEIGHT,
                                UPPER_ARM_WIDTH ) );

        glUniformMatrix4fv( ModelView, 1, GL_TRUE, model_view * instance );
        glDrawArrays( GL_TRIANGLES, 0, NumVertices );

        model_view = mvstack.pop( void );
    }

    void
    left_lower_arm( void )
    {
        mvstack.push( model_view );

        mat4 instance = ( Translate( 0.0, 0.5 * LOWER_ARM_HEIGHT, 0.0 ) *
                          Scale( LOWER_ARM_WIDTH,
                                 LOWER_ARM_HEIGHT,
                                 LOWER_ARM_WIDTH ) );

        glUniformMatrix4fv( ModelView, 1, GL_TRUE, model_view * instance );
        glDrawArrays( GL_TRIANGLES, 0, NumVertices );
```

```
    model_view = mvstack.pop( void );
}

void
right_upper_arm( void )
{
    mvstack.push( model_view );

    mat4 instance = (Translate( 0.0, 0.5 * UPPER_ARM_HEIGHT, 0.0 ) *
                     Scale( UPPER_ARM_WIDTH,
                            UPPER_ARM_HEIGHT,
                            UPPER_ARM_WIDTH ) );

    glUniformMatrix4fv( ModelView, 1, GL_TRUE, model_view * instance );
    glDrawArrays( GL_TRIANGLES, 0, NumVertices );

    model_view = mvstack.pop( void );
}

void
right_lower_arm( void )
{
    mvstack.push( model_view );

    mat4 instance = (Translate( 0.0, 0.5 * LOWER_ARM_HEIGHT, 0.0 ) *
                     Scale( LOWER_ARM_WIDTH,
                            LOWER_ARM_HEIGHT,
                            LOWER_ARM_WIDTH ) );

    glUniformMatrix4fv( ModelView, 1, GL_TRUE, model_view * instance );
    glDrawArrays( GL_TRIANGLES, 0, NumVertices );

    model_view = mvstack.pop( void );
}

void
left_upper_leg( void )
{
    mvstack.push( model_view );

    mat4 instance = ( Translate( 0.0, 0.5 * UPPER_LEG_HEIGHT, 0.0 ) *
                      Scale( UPPER_LEG_WIDTH,
                             UPPER_LEG_HEIGHT,
                             UPPER_LEG_WIDTH ) );

    glUniformMatrix4fv( ModelView, 1, GL_TRUE, model_view * instance );
    glDrawArrays( GL_TRIANGLES, 0, NumVertices );
```

```
    model_view = mvstack.pop( void );
}

void
left_lower_leg( void )
{
    mvstack.push( model_view );

    mat4 instance = (Translate( 0.0, 0.5 * LOWER_LEG_HEIGHT, 0.0 ) *
                      Scale( LOWER_LEG_WIDTH,
                             LOWER_LEG_HEIGHT,
                             LOWER_LEG_WIDTH ) );

    glUniformMatrix4fv( ModelView, 1, GL_TRUE, model_view * instance );
    glDrawArrays( GL_TRIANGLES, 0, NumVertices );

    model_view = mvstack.pop( void );
}

void
right_upper_leg( void )
{
    mvstack.push( model_view );

    mat4 instance = (Translate( 0.0, 0.5 * UPPER_LEG_HEIGHT, 0.0 ) *
                      Scale( UPPER_LEG_WIDTH,
                             UPPER_LEG_HEIGHT,
                             UPPER_LEG_WIDTH ) );

    glUniformMatrix4fv( ModelView, 1, GL_TRUE, model_view * instance );
    glDrawArrays( GL_TRIANGLES, 0, NumVertices );

    model_view = mvstack.pop( void );
}

void
right_lower_leg( void )
{
    mvstack.push( model_view );

    mat4 instance = ( Translate( 0.0, 0.5 * LOWER_LEG_HEIGHT, 0.0 ) *
                      Scale( LOWER_LEG_WIDTH,
                             LOWER_LEG_HEIGHT,
                             LOWER_LEG_WIDTH ) );

    glUniformMatrix4fv( ModelView, 1, GL_TRUE, model_view * instance );
    glDrawArrays( GL_TRIANGLES, 0, NumVertices );

    model_view = mvstack.pop( void );
}
```

```
//---------------------------------------------------------------------

void
display( void )
{
    glClear( GL_COLOR_BUFFER_BIT | GL_DEPTH_BUFFER_BIT );
    traverse( &nodes[Torso] );
    glutSwapBuffers( void );
}

//---------------------------------------------------------------------

void
mouse( int button, int state, int x, int y )
{
    if ( button == GLUT_LEFT_BUTTON && state == GLUT_DOWN ) {
        theta[angle] += 5.0;
        if ( theta[angle] > 360.0 ) { theta[angle] -= 360.0; }
    }

    if ( button == GLUT_RIGHT_BUTTON && state == GLUT_DOWN ) {
        theta[angle] -= 5.0;
        if ( theta[angle] < 0.0 ) { theta[angle] += 360.0; }
    }

    mvstack.push( model_view );

    switch( angle ) {
        case Torso:
            nodes[Torso].transform =
                RotateY( theta[Torso] );
            break;

        case Head1: case Head2:
            nodes[Head].transform =
                Translate(0.0, TORSO_HEIGHT+0.5*HEAD_HEIGHT, 0.0) *
                RotateX(theta[Head1]) *
                RotateY(theta[Head2]) *
                Translate(0.0, -0.5*HEAD_HEIGHT, 0.0);
            break;

        case LeftUpperArm:
            nodes[LeftUpperArm].transform =
                Translate(-(TORSO_WIDTH+UPPER_ARM_WIDTH),
                          0.9*TORSO_HEIGHT, 0.0) *
                RotateX(theta[LeftUpperArm]);
            break;

        case RightUpperArm:
            nodes[RightUpperArm].transform =
```

```
                         Translate(TORSO_WIDTH+UPPER_ARM_WIDTH,
                                 0.9*TORSO_HEIGHT, 0.0) *
                         RotateX(theta[RightUpperArm]);
                break;

            case RightUpperLeg:
                nodes[RightUpperLeg].transform =
                    Translate(TORSO_WIDTH+UPPER_LEG_WIDTH,
                                0.1*UPPER_LEG_HEIGHT, 0.0) *
                    RotateX(theta[RightUpperLeg]);
                break;

            case LeftUpperLeg:
                nodes[LeftUpperLeg].transform =
                    Translate(-(TORSO_WIDTH+UPPER_LEG_WIDTH),
                                0.1*UPPER_LEG_HEIGHT, 0.0) *
                    RotateX(theta[LeftUpperLeg]);
                break;

            case LeftLowerArm:
                nodes[LeftLowerArm].transform =
                    Translate(0.0, UPPER_ARM_HEIGHT, 0.0) *
                    RotateX(theta[LeftLowerArm]);
                break;

            case LeftLowerLeg:
                nodes[LeftLowerLeg].transform =
                    Translate(0.0, UPPER_LEG_HEIGHT, 0.0) *
                    RotateX(theta[LeftLowerLeg]);
                break;

            case RightLowerLeg:
                nodes[RightLowerLeg].transform =
                    Translate(0.0, UPPER_LEG_HEIGHT, 0.0) *
                    RotateX(theta[RightLowerLeg]);
                break;

            case RightLowerArm:
                nodes[RightLowerArm].transform =
                    Translate(0.0, UPPER_ARM_HEIGHT, 0.0) *
                    RotateX(theta[RightLowerArm]);
                break;
        }

    model_view = mvstack.pop( void );
    glutPostRedisplay( void );
}

//-----------------------------------------------------------------
```

```
void
menu( int option )
{
    if ( option == Quit ) {
        exit( EXIT_SUCCESS );
    }

    angle = option;
}

//----------------------------------------------------------------------

void
reshape( int width, int height )
{
    glViewport( 0, 0, width, height );

    GLfloat left = -10.0, right = 10.0;
    GLfloat bottom = -10.0, top = 10.0;
    GLfloat zNear = -10.0, zFar = 10.0;

    GLfloat aspect = GLfloat( width ) / height;

    if ( aspect > 1.0 ) {
        left *= aspect;
        right *= aspect;
    }
    else {
        bottom /= aspect;
        top /= aspect;
    }

    mat4 projection = Ortho( left, right, bottom, top, zNear, zFar );
    glUniformMatrix4fv( Projection, 1, GL_TRUE, projection );

    model_view = mat4( 1.0 );   // An Identity matrix
}

//----------------------------------------------------------------------

void
initNodes( void )
{
    mat4  m;

    m = RotateY( theta[Torso] );
    nodes[Torso] = Node( m, torso, NULL, &nodes[Head1] );

    m = Translate(0.0, TORSO_HEIGHT+0.5*HEAD_HEIGHT, 0.0) *
```

```
                        RotateX(theta[Head1]) *
                        RotateY(theta[Head2]);
                nodes[Head1] = Node( m, head, &nodes[LeftUpperArm], NULL );

                m = Translate(-(TORSO_WIDTH+UPPER_ARM_WIDTH), 0.9*TORSO_HEIGHT,
                    0.0) * RotateX(theta[LeftUpperArm]);
                nodes[LeftUpperArm] =
                    Node( m, left_upper_arm, &nodes[RightUpperArm],
                                            &nodes[LeftLowerArm] );

                m = Translate(TORSO_WIDTH+UPPER_ARM_WIDTH, 0.9*TORSO_HEIGHT, 0.0) *
                    RotateX(theta[RightUpperArm]);
                nodes[RightUpperArm] =
                    Node( m, right_upper_arm,
                        &nodes[LeftUpperLeg], &nodes[RightLowerArm] );

                m = Translate(-(TORSO_WIDTH+UPPER_LEG_WIDTH),
                    0.1*UPPER_LEG_HEIGHT, 0.0) *
                    RotateX(theta[LeftUpperLeg]);
                nodes[LeftUpperLeg] =
                    Node( m, left_upper_leg, &nodes[RightUpperLeg],
                                            &nodes[LeftLowerLeg] );

                m = Translate(TORSO_WIDTH+UPPER_LEG_WIDTH,
                    0.1*UPPER_LEG_HEIGHT, 0.0) * RotateX(theta[RightUpperLeg]);
                nodes[RightUpperLeg] =
                    Node( m, right_upper_leg, NULL, &nodes[RightLowerLeg] );

                m = Translate(0.0, UPPER_ARM_HEIGHT, 0.0) *
                    RotateX(theta[LeftLowerArm]);
                nodes[LeftLowerArm] = Node( m, left_lower_arm, NULL, NULL );

                m = Translate(0.0, UPPER_ARM_HEIGHT, 0.0) *
                    RotateX(theta[RightLowerArm]);
                nodes[RightLowerArm] = Node( m, right_lower_arm, NULL, NULL );

                m = Translate(0.0, UPPER_LEG_HEIGHT, 0.0) *
                    RotateX(theta[LeftLowerLeg]);
                nodes[LeftLowerLeg] = Node( m, left_lower_leg, NULL, NULL );

                m = Translate(0.0, UPPER_LEG_HEIGHT, 0.0) *
                    RotateX(theta[RightLowerLeg]);
                nodes[RightLowerLeg] = Node( m, right_lower_leg, NULL, NULL );
            }

            //-----------------------------------------------------------------

            void
            init( void )
```

```
{
    colorcube( void );

    // Initialize tree
    initNodes( void );

    // Create a vertex array object
    GLuint vao;
    glGenVertexArrays( 1, &vao );
    glBindVertexArray( vao );

    // Create and initialize a buffer object
    GLuint buffer;
    glGenBuffers( 1, &buffer );
    glBindBuffer( GL_ARRAY_BUFFER, buffer );
    glBufferData( GL_ARRAY_BUFFER, sizeof(points) + sizeof(colors),
                  NULL, GL_DYNAMIC_DRAW );
    glBufferSubData( GL_ARRAY_BUFFER, 0, sizeof(points), points );
    glBufferSubData( GL_ARRAY_BUFFER, sizeof(points), sizeof(colors),
                     colors );

    // Load shaders and use the resulting shader program
    GLuint program = InitShader( "vshader83.glsl", "fshader83.glsl" );
    glUseProgram( program );

    GLuint vPosition = glGetAttribLocation( program, "vPosition" );
    glEnableVertexAttribArray( vPosition );
    glVertexAttribPointer( vPosition, 4, GL_FLOAT, GL_FALSE, 0,
                           BUFFER_OFFSET(0) );

    GLuint vColor = glGetAttribLocation( program, "vColor" );
    glEnableVertexAttribArray( vColor );
    glVertexAttribPointer( vColor, 4, GL_FLOAT, GL_FALSE, 0,
                           BUFFER_OFFSET(points) );

    ModelView = glGetUniformLocation( program, "ModelView" );
    Projection = glGetUniformLocation( program, "Projection" );

    glEnable( GL_DEPTH_TEST );
    glPolygonMode( GL_FRONT_AND_BACK, GL_LINE );

    glClearColor( 1.0, 1.0, 1.0, 1.0 );

}

//----------------------------------------------------------------------

void
keyboard( unsigned char key, int x, int y )
```

```
{
    switch( key ) {
        case 033: // Escape Key
        case 'q': case 'Q':
            exit( EXIT_SUCCESS );
            break;
    }
}

//----------------------------------------------------------------------

int
main( int argc, char **argv )
{
    glutInit( &argc, argv );
    glutInitDisplayMode( GLUT_DOUBLE | GLUT_RGB | GLUT_DEPTH );
    glutInitWindowSize( 512, 512 );
    glutInitContextVersion( 3, 2 );
    glutInitContextProfile( GLUT_CORE_PROFILE );
    glutCreateWindow( "robot" );

    glewInit( void );

    init( void );

    glutDisplayFunc( display );
    glutReshapeFunc( reshape );
    glutKeyboardFunc( keyboard );
    glutMouseFunc( mouse );

    glutCreateMenu( menu );
    glutAddMenuEntry( "torso", Torso );
    glutAddMenuEntry( "head1", Head1 );
    glutAddMenuEntry( "head2", Head2 );
    glutAddMenuEntry( "right_upper_arm", RightUpperArm );
    glutAddMenuEntry( "right_lower_arm", RightLowerArm );
    glutAddMenuEntry( "left_upper_arm", LeftUpperArm );
    glutAddMenuEntry( "left_lower_arm", LeftLowerArm );
    glutAddMenuEntry( "right_upper_leg", RightUpperLeg );
    glutAddMenuEntry( "right_lower_leg", RightLowerLeg );
    glutAddMenuEntry( "left_upper_leg", LeftUpperLeg );
    glutAddMenuEntry( "left_lower_leg", LeftLowerLeg );
    glutAddMenuEntry( "quit", Quit );
    glutAttachMenu( GLUT_MIDDLE_BUTTON );

    glutMainLoop( void );
    return 0;
}
```

A.9.2 Vertex Shader

```
#version 150

in   vec4 vPosition;
in   vec4 vColor;
out vec4 color;

uniform mat4 ModelView;
uniform mat4 Projection;

void main()
{
    color = vColor;
    gl_Position = Projection*ModelView*vPosition;
}
```

A.9.3 Fragment Shader

```
#version 150

in   vec4 color;
out vec4 fColor;

void main()
{
    fColor = color;
}
```

A.10   TEAPOT RENDERER

A.10.1 Application Code

```
#include "Angel.h"

typedef Angel::vec4 point4;

// Define a convenient type for referencing patch control points, which
//   is used in the declaration of the vertices' array (used in "vertices.h")
typedef GLfloat     point3[3];
#include "vertices.h"
#include "patches.h"

const int NumTimesToSubdivide = 3;
const int PatchesPerSubdivision = 4;
const int NumQuadsPerPatch =
    (int) pow( PatchesPerSubdivision, NumTimesToSubdivide );
const int NumTriangles =
```

```
                ( NumTeapotPatches * NumQuadsPerPatch * 2 // triangles / quad );
const int NumVertices =
    ( NumTriangles * 3 // vertices / triangle );

int     Index = 0;
point4  points[NumVertices];

GLuint  Projection;

enum { X = 0, Y = 1, Z = 2 };

//----------------------------------------------------------------------

void
divide_curve( point4 c[4], point4 r[4], point4 l[4] )
{
    // Subdivide a Bezier curve into two equivalent Bezier curves:
    //    left (l) and right (r) sharing the midpoint of the middle
    //    control point
    point4  t, mid = ( c[1] + c[2] ) / 2;

    l[0] = c[0];
    l[1] = ( c[0] + c[1] ) / 2;
    l[2] = ( l[1] + mid ) / 2;

    r[3] = c[3];
    r[2] = ( c[2] + c[3] ) / 2;
    r[1] = ( mid + r[2] ) / 2;

    l[3] = r[0] = ( l[2] + r[1] ) / 2;

    for ( int i = 0; i < 4; ++i ) {
    l[i].w = 1.0;
    r[i].w = 1.0;
    }
}

//----------------------------------------------------------------------

void
draw_patch( point4 p[4][4] )
{
    // Draw the quad (as two triangles) bounded by the corners of the
    //    Bezier patch.
    points[Index++] = p[0][0];
    points[Index++] = p[3][0];
    points[Index++] = p[3][3];
    points[Index++] = p[0][0];
    points[Index++] = p[3][3];
```

```
        points[Index++] = p[0][3];
}

//------------------------------------------------------------------

inline void
transpose( point4 a[4][4] )
{
    for ( int i = 0; i < 4; i++ ) {
        for ( int j = i; j < 4; j++ ) {
            point4 t = a[i][j];
            a[i][j] = a[j][i];
            a[j][i] = t;
        }
    }
}

void
divide_patch( point4 p[4][4], int count )
{
    if ( count > 0 ) {
    point4 q[4][4], r[4][4], s[4][4], t[4][4];
    point4 a[4][4], b[4][4];

    // subdivide curves in u direction, transpose results, divide
    // in u direction again (equivalent to subdivision in v)
        for ( int k = 0; k < 4; ++k ) {
            divide_curve( p[k], a[k], b[k] );
        }

        transpose( a );
        transpose( b );

        for ( int k = 0; k < 4; ++k ) {
            divide_curve( a[k], q[k], r[k] );
            divide_curve( b[k], s[k], t[k] );
        }

    // recursive division of 4 resulting patches
        divide_patch( q, count - 1 );
        divide_patch( r, count - 1 );
        divide_patch( s, count - 1 );
        divide_patch( t, count - 1 );
    }
    else {
        draw_patch( p );
    }
}
```

```
//------------------------------------------------------------------

void
init( void )
{
    for ( int n = 0; n < NumTeapotPatches; n++ ) {
    point4  patch[4][4];

    // Initialize each patch's control point data
    for ( int i = 0; i < 4; ++i ) {
        for ( int j = 0; j < 4; ++j ) {
        point3& v = vertices[indices[n][i][j]];
        patch[i][j] = point4( v[X], v[Y], v[Z], 1.0 );
        }
    }

    // Subdivide the patch
        divide_patch( patch, NumTimesToSubdivide );
    }

    // Create a vertex array object
    GLuint vao;
    glGenVertexArrays( 1, &vao );
    glBindVertexArray( vao );

    // Create and initialize a buffer object
    GLuint buffer;
    glGenBuffers( 1, &buffer );
    glBindBuffer( GL_ARRAY_BUFFER, buffer );
    glBufferData( GL_ARRAY_BUFFER, sizeof(points), points,
                  GL_STATIC_DRAW );

    // Load shaders and use the resulting shader program
    GLuint program = InitShader( "vshader101.glsl", "fshader101.glsl" );
    glUseProgram( program );

    // set up vertex arrays
    GLuint vPosition = glGetAttribLocation( program, "vPosition" );
    glEnableVertexAttribArray( vPosition );
    glVertexAttribPointer( vPosition, 4, GL_FLOAT, GL_FALSE, 0,
                BUFFER_OFFSET(0) );

    Projection = glGetUniformLocation( program, "Projection" );

    glPolygonMode( GL_FRONT_AND_BACK, GL_LINE );

    glClearColor( 1.0, 1.0, 1.0, 1.0 );
}
```

```
//----------------------------------------------------------------------

void
display( void )
{
    glClear( GL_COLOR_BUFFER_BIT );
    glDrawArrays( GL_TRIANGLES, 0, NumVertices );
    glutSwapBuffers( void );
}

//----------------------------------------------------------------------

void
reshape( int width, int height )
{
    glViewport( 0, 0, width, height );

    GLfloat  left = -4.0, right = 4.0;
    GLfloat  bottom = -3.0, top = 5.0;
    GLfloat  zNear = -10.0, zFar = 10.0;

    GLfloat  aspect = GLfloat(width)/height;

    if ( aspect > 0 ) {
        left *= aspect;
        right *= aspect;
    }
    else {
        bottom /= aspect;
        top /= aspect;
    }

    mat4 projection = Ortho( left, right, bottom, top, zNear, zFar );
    glUniformMatrix4fv( Projection, 1, GL_TRUE, projection );
}

//----------------------------------------------------------------------

void
keyboard( unsigned char key, int x, int y )
{
    switch ( key ) {
    case 'q': case 'Q': case 033 // Escape key:
        exit( EXIT_SUCCESS );
        break;
    }
}

//----------------------------------------------------------------------
```

```
int
main( int argc, char *argv[] )
{
    glutInit( &argc, argv );
    glutInitDisplayMode( GLUT_RGBA | GLUT_DOUBLE );
    glutInitWindowSize( 512, 512 );
    glutInitContextVersion( 3, 2 );
    glutInitContextProfile( GLUT_CORE_PROFILE );
    glutCreateWindow( "teapot" );

    glewInit( void );

    init( void );

    glutDisplayFunc( display );
    glutReshapeFunc( reshape );
    glutKeyboardFunc( keyboard );

    glutMainLoop( void );
    return 0;
}
```

A.10.2 Vertex Shader

```
#version 150

in  vec4 vPosition;

uniform mat4 Projection;

void main()
{
    gl_Position = Projection * vPosition;
}
```

A.10.3 Fragment Shader

```
#version 150

out vec4 fColor;

void main()
{
    fColor = vec4( 0.0, 0.0, 0.0, 1.0 );
}
```

SPACES

Computer graphics is concerned with the representation and manipulation of sets of geometric elements, such as points and line segments. The necessary mathematics is found in the study of various types of abstract spaces. In this appendix, we review the rules governing three such spaces: the (linear) vector space, the affine space, and the Euclidean space. The **(linear) vector space** contains only two types of objects: scalars, such as real numbers, and vectors. The **affine space** adds a third element: the point. **Euclidean spaces** add the concept of distance.

The vectors of interest in computer graphics are directed line segments and the n-tuples of numbers that are used to represent them. In Appendix C, we discuss matrix algebra as a tool for manipulating n-tuples. In this appendix, we are concerned with the underlying concepts and rules. It is probably helpful to think of these entities (scalars, vectors, points) as abstract data types, and the axioms as defining the valid operations on them.

B.1 SCALARS

Ordinary real numbers and the operations on them are one example of a **scalar field**. Let S denote a set of elements called **scalars**, $\alpha, \beta, \ldots$. Scalars have two fundamental operations defined between pairs. These operations are often called addition and multiplication, and are symbolized by the operators $+$ and $\cdot$,[1] respectively. Hence, for $\forall \alpha, \beta \in S$, $\alpha + \beta \in S$, and $\alpha \cdot \beta \in S$. These operations are associative, commutative, and distributive, $\forall \alpha, \beta, \gamma \in S$:

$$\alpha + \beta = \beta + \alpha,$$

$$\alpha \cdot \beta = \beta \cdot \alpha,$$

$$\alpha + (\beta + \gamma) = (\alpha + \beta) + \gamma,$$

---

1. Often, if there is no ambiguity, we can write $\alpha\beta$ instead of $\alpha \cdot \beta$.

$$\alpha \cdot (\beta \cdot \gamma) = (\alpha \cdot \beta) \cdot \gamma,$$

$$\alpha \cdot (\beta + \gamma) = (\alpha \cdot \beta) + (\alpha \cdot \gamma).$$

There are two special scalars—the additive identity (0) and the multiplicative identity (1)—such that $\forall \alpha \in S$:

$$\alpha + 0 = 0 + \alpha = \alpha,$$

$$\alpha \cdot 1 = 1 \cdot \alpha = \alpha.$$

Each element α has an additive inverse, denoted $-\alpha$, and a multiplicative inverse, denoted $\alpha^{-1} \in S$, such that

$$\alpha + (-\alpha) = 0,$$

$$\alpha \cdot \alpha^{-1} = 1.$$

The real numbers using ordinary addition and multiplication form a scalar field, as do the complex numbers (under complex addition and multiplication) and rational functions (ratios of two polynomials).

B.2   VECTOR SPACES

A vector space, in addition to scalars, contains a second type of entity: **vectors**. Vectors have two operations defined: vector–vector addition and scalar–vector multiplication. Let u, v, w denote vectors in a vector space V. Vector addition is defined to be closed ($u + v \in V$, $\forall u, v \in V$), commutative ($u + v = v + u$), and associative ($u + (v + w) = (u + v) + w$). There is a special vector (the **zero vector**) **0** defined such that $\forall u \in V$:

$$u + \mathbf{0} = u.$$

Every vector u has an additive inverse denoted by $-u$ such that

$$u + (-u) = \mathbf{0}.$$

Scalar–vector multiplication is defined such that, for any scalar α and any vector u, αu is a vector in V. The scalar–vector operation is distributive. Hence,

$$\alpha(u + v) = \alpha u + \alpha v,$$

$$(\alpha + \beta)u = \alpha u + \beta u.$$

The two examples of vector spaces that we use are geometric vectors (directed line segments) and the n-tuples of real numbers. Consider a set of directed line segments that we can picture as shown in Figure B.1. If our scalars are real numbers,

FIGURE B.1   Directed line segments.

then scalar–vector multiplication changes the length of a vector, but not that vector's direction (Figure B.2).

Vector–vector addition can be defined by the **head-to-tail axiom**, which we can visualize easily for the example of directed line segments. We form the vector $u + v$ by connecting the head of u to the tail of v, as shown in Figure B.3. You should be able to verify that all the rules of a vector field are satisfied.

The second example of a vector space is n-tuples of scalars—usually, real or complex numbers. Hence, a vector can be written as

$$v = (v_1, v_2, \ldots, v_n).$$

Scalar–vector multiplication and vector–vector addition are given by

$$u + v = (u_1, u_2, \ldots, u_n) + (v_1, v_2, \ldots, v_n)$$
$$= (u_1 + v_1, u_2 + v_2, \ldots, u_n + v_n),$$
$$\alpha v = (\alpha v_1, \alpha v_2, \ldots, \alpha v_n).$$

This space is denoted $\mathbf{R}^n$ and is the vector space in which we can manipulate vectors using matrix algebra (Appendix C).

In a vector space, the concepts of linear independence and basis are crucial. A **linear combination** of n vectors $u_1, u_2, \ldots, u_n$ is a vector of the form

$$u = \alpha_1 u_1 + \alpha_2 u_2 + \ldots + \alpha_n u_n.$$

If the only set of scalars such that

$$\alpha_1 u_1 + \alpha_2 u_2 \ldots + \alpha_n u_n = 0$$

is

$$\alpha_1 = \alpha_2 = \ldots = \alpha_n = 0,$$

then the vectors are said to be **linearly independent**. The greatest number of linearly independent vectors that we can find in a space gives the **dimension** of the space. If a vector space has dimension n, any set of n linearly independent vectors form a **basis**. If $v_1, v_2, \ldots, v_n$ is a basis for V, any vector v can be expressed uniquely in terms of the basis vectors as

$$v = \beta_1 v_1 + \beta_2 v_2 + \ldots + \beta_n v_n.$$

The scalars $\{\beta_i\}$ give the **representation** of v with respect to the basis $v_1, v_2, \ldots, v_n$. If $v'_1, v'_2, \ldots, v'_n$ is some other basis (the number of vectors in a basis is constant), there is a representation of v with respect to this basis; that is,

$$v = \beta'_1 v'_1 + \beta'_2 v'_2 + \ldots + \beta'_n v'_n.$$

There exists an $n \times n$ matrix $\mathbf{M}$ such that

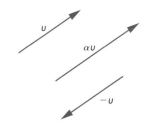

FIGURE B.2   Scalar–vector multiplication.

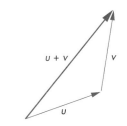

FIGURE B.3   Head-to-tail axiom for vectors.

$$\begin{bmatrix} \beta'_1 \\ \beta'_2 \\ \vdots \\ \beta'_N \end{bmatrix} = \mathbf{M} \begin{bmatrix} \beta_1 \\ \beta_2 \\ \vdots \\ \beta_N \end{bmatrix}.$$

We derive $\mathbf{M}$ in Appendix C. This matrix gives a way of changing representations through a simple linear transformation involving only scalar operations for carrying out matrix multiplication. More generally, once we have a basis for a vector space, we can work only with representations. If the scalars are real numbers, then we can work with n-tuples of reals and use matrix algebra, instead of doing operations in the original abstract vector space.

B.3 AFFINE SPACES

A vector space lacks any geometric concepts, such as location and distance. If we use the example of directed line segments as the natural vector space for our geometric problems, we get into difficulties because these vectors, just like the physicist's vectors, have magnitude and direction, but have no position. The vectors shown in Figure B.4 are identical.

If we think of this problem in terms of coordinate systems, we can express a vector in terms of a set of basis vectors that define a **coordinate system**. Figure B.5(a) shows three basis vectors emerging from a particular reference point, the **origin**. The location of the vectors in Figure B.5(b) is equally valid, however, because vectors have no position. In addition, we have no way to express this special point, because our vector space has only vectors and scalars as its members.

We can resolve this difficulty by introducing an affine space that adds a third type of entity—points—to a vector space. The points $(P, Q, R, \ldots)$ form a set. There is a

FIGURE B.4   Identical vectors.

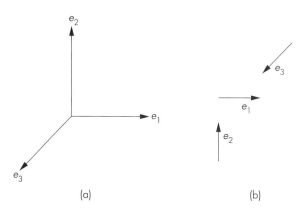

(a)   (b)

FIGURE B.5   Coordinate system. (a) Basis vectors located at the origin. (b) Arbitrary placement of basis vectors.

single new operation, **point–point subtraction**, that yields a vector. Hence, if P and Q are any two points, the subtraction

$$v = P - Q$$

always yields a vector in V. Conversely, for every v and every P, we can find a Q such that the preceding relation holds. We can thus write

$$Q = v + P,$$

defining a vector–point addition. A consequence of the head-to-tail axiom is that for any three points P, Q, R,

$$(P - Q) + (Q - R) = (P - R).$$

If we visualize the vector $P - Q$ as the line segment from the point Q to the point P, using an arrow to denote direction, the head-to-tail axiom can be drawn as shown in Figure B.6.

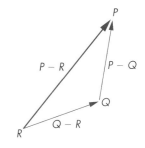

FIGURE B.6 Head-to-tail axiom for points.

Various properties follow from affine geometry. Perhaps the most important is that if we use a frame, rather than a coordinate system, we can specify both points and vectors in an affine space. A **frame** consists of a point P_0, and a set of vectors $v_1, v_2, \ldots, v_n$ that defines a basis for the vector space. Given a frame, an arbitrary vector can be written uniquely as

$$v = \alpha_1 v_1 + \alpha_2 v_2 + \ldots + \alpha_n v_n,$$

and an arbitrary point can be written uniquely as

$$P = P_0 + \beta_1 v_1 + \beta_2 v_2 + \ldots + \beta_n v_n.$$

The two sets of scalars, $\{\alpha_1, \ldots, \alpha_n\}$ and $\{\beta_1, \ldots, \beta_n\}$, give the representations of the vector and point, respectively, with each representation consisting of n scalars. We can regard the point P_0 as the origin of the frame; all points are defined from this reference point.

If the origin never changes, we can worry about only those changes of frames corresponding to changes in coordinate systems. In computer graphics, however, we usually have to deal with making changes in frames and with representing objects in different frames. For example, we usually define our objects within a physical frame. The viewer, or camera, can be expressed in terms of this frame, but, as part of the image-creation process, it is to our advantage to express object positions with respect to the camera frame—a frame whose origin usually is located at the center of projection.

B.4 EUCLIDEAN SPACES

Although affine spaces contain the necessary elements for building geometric models, there is no concept of how far apart two points are, or of what the length of a vector is. Euclidean spaces have such a concept. Strictly speaking, a Euclidean space contains only vectors and scalars.

Suppose that E is a Euclidean space. It is a vector space containing scalars ($\alpha, \beta, \gamma, \ldots$) and vectors ($u, v, w, \ldots$). We assume that the scalars are the ordinary real numbers. We add a new operation—the **inner (dot) product**—that combines two vectors to form a real. The inner product must satisfy the properties that, for any three vectors u, v, w and scalars α, β,

$$u \cdot v = v \cdot u,$$

$$(\alpha u + \beta v) \cdot w = \alpha u \cdot w + \beta v \cdot w,$$

$$v \cdot v > 0 \text{ if } v \neq 0,$$

$$\mathbf{0} \cdot \mathbf{0} = 0.$$

If

$$u \cdot v = 0,$$

then u and v are **orthogonal**. The magnitude (length) of a vector is usually measured as

$$|v| = \sqrt{v \cdot v}.$$

Once we add affine concepts, such as points, to the Euclidean space, we naturally get a measure of distance between points, because, for any two points P and Q, $P - Q$ is a vector, and hence

$$|P - Q| = \sqrt{(P - Q) \cdot (P - Q)}.$$

We can use the inner product to define a measure of the angle between two vectors:

$$u \cdot v = |u||v| \cos \theta.$$

It is easy to show that $\cos \theta$ as defined by this formula is 0 when the vectors are orthogonal, lies between −1 and +1, and has magnitude 1 if the vectors are parallel ($u = \alpha v$).

B.5   PROJECTIONS

We can derive several of the important geometric concepts from the use of orthogonality. The concept of **projection** arises from the problem of finding the shortest distance from a point to a line or plane. It is equivalent to the following problem. Given two vectors, we can take one of them and divide it into two parts, one parallel and one orthogonal to the other vector, as shown in Figure B.7 for directed line segments. Suppose that v is the first vector and w is the second. Then, w can be written as

$$w = \alpha v + u.$$

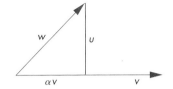

FIGURE B.7   Projection of one vector onto another.

The parallel part is αv, but, for u to be orthogonal to v, we must have

$$u \cdot v = 0.$$

Because u and v are defined to be orthogonal,

$$w \cdot v = \alpha v \cdot v + u \cdot v = \alpha v \cdot v,$$

allowing us to find

$$\alpha = \frac{w \cdot v}{v \cdot v}.$$

The vector αv is the projection of w onto v, and

$$u = w - \frac{w \cdot v}{v \cdot v} v.$$

We can extend this result to construct a set of orthogonal vectors from an arbitrary set of linearly independent vectors.

B.6   GRAM-SCHMIDT ORTHOGONALIZATION

Given a set of basis vectors, $a_1, a_2, \ldots, a_n$, in a space of dimension n, it is relatively straightforward to create another basis $b_1, b_2, \ldots, b_n$ that is **orthonormal**, that is, a basis in which each vector has unit length and is orthogonal to each other vector in the basis, or mathematically:

$$b_i \cdot b_j = \begin{cases} 1 & \text{if } i = j, \\ 0 & \text{otherwise.} \end{cases}$$

Hence, there is no real loss of generality in using orthogonal (Cartesian) coordinate systems.

We proceed iteratively. We look for a vector of the form

$$b_2 = a_2 + \alpha b_1,$$

which we can make orthogonal to b_1 by choosing α properly. Taking the dot product, we must have

$$b_2 \cdot b_1 = 0 = a_2 \cdot b_1 + \alpha b_1 \cdot b_1.$$

Solving, we have

$$\alpha = -\frac{a_2 \cdot b_1}{b_1 \cdot b_1}$$

and

$$b_2 = a_2 - \frac{a_2 \cdot b_1}{b_1 \cdot b_1} b_1.$$

We have constructed the orthogonal vector by removing the part parallel to b_1—that is, the projection of a_2 onto b_1.

The general iterative step is to find a

$$b_k = a_k + \sum_{i=1}^{k-1} \alpha_i b_i$$

that is orthogonal to $b_1, \ldots, b_{k-1}$. There are $k - 1$ orthogonality conditions that allow us to find

$$\alpha_i = -\frac{a_k \cdot b_i}{b_i \cdot b_i}.$$

We can normalize each vector, either at the end of the process, by replacing b_i by $b_i/|b_i|$, or, more efficiently, by normalizing each b_i as soon as possible.

SUGGESTED READINGS

There are many excellent books on linear algebra and vector spaces. For practitioners of computer graphics, the preferred approach is to start with vector-space ideas and to see linear algebra as a tool for working with general vector spaces. Unfortunately, most of the linear-algebra textbooks are concerned with only the Euclidean spaces of n-tuples, $\mathbf{R}^n$. See Bowyer and Woodwark [Bow83] and Banchoff and Werner [Ban83].

Affine spaces can be approached in a number of ways. See Foley [Fol90] for a more geometric development.

EXERCISES

B.1   Prove that the complex numbers form a scalar field. What are the additive and multiplicative identity elements?

B.2   Prove that the rational functions form a scalar field.

B.3   Prove that the rational functions with real coefficients form a vector space.

B.4   Prove that the number of elements in a basis is unique.

B.5   Consider a set of n real functions $\{f_i(x)\}$, $i = 1, \ldots, n$. Show how to form a vector space of functions with these elements. Define *basis* and *dimension* for this space.

B.6   Show that the set of polynomials of degree up to n form an n-dimensional vector space.

B.7   The most important Euclidean space is the space of n-tuples, $a_1, \ldots, a_n$: $\mathbf{R}^n$. Define the operations of vector addition and scalar-vector multiplication in this space. What is the dot product in $\mathbf{R}^n$?

B.8   Suppose that you are given three vectors in $\mathbf{R}^3$. How can you find whether they form a basis?

B.9   Consider the three vectors in $\mathbf{R}^3$: $(1, 0, 0)$, $(1, 1, 0)$, and $(1, 1, 1)$. Show that they are linearly independent. Derive an orthonormal basis from these vectors, starting with $(1, 0, 0)$.

APPENDIX C

MATRICES

In computer graphics, the major use of matrices is in the representation of changes in coordinate systems and frames. In the studies of vector analysis and linear algebra, the use of the term *vector* is somewhat different. Unfortunately, computer graphics relies on both these fields, and the interpretation of *vector* has caused confusion. To remedy this situation, we use the terms *row matrix* and *column matrix*, rather than the linear algebra terms of *row vector* and *column vector*. We reserve the *vector* to denote directed line segments, and occasionally, as in Appendix B, to denote the abstract-data-type vector that is an element of a vector space.

This appendix reviews the major results that you will need to manipulate matrices in computer graphics. We almost always use matrices that are 4 × 4. Hence, the parts of linear algebra that deal with manipulations of general matrices, such as the inversion of an arbitrary square matrix, are of limited interest. Most implementations, instead, implement inversion of 4 × 4 matrices directly in the hardware or software.

C.1 DEFINITIONS

A **matrix** is an $n \times m$ array of scalars, arranged conceptually as n rows and m columns. Often, n and m are referred to as the row and column **dimensions** of the matrix, and, if $m = n$, we say that the matrix is a **square matrix** of dimension n. We use real numbers for scalars, almost exclusively, although most results hold for complex numbers as well. The elements of a matrix $\mathbf{A}$ are the members of the set of scalars, $\{a_{ij}\}$, $i = 1, \ldots, n, j = 1, \ldots, m$. We write $\mathbf{A}$ in terms of its elements as

$$\mathbf{A} = [\, a_{ij} \,].$$

The **transpose** of an $n \times m$ matrix $\mathbf{A}$ is the $m \times n$ matrix that we obtain by interchanging the rows and columns of $\mathbf{A}$. We denote this matrix as $\mathbf{A}^T$, and it is given as

$$\mathbf{A}^T = [\, a_{ji} \,].$$

The special cases of matrices with one column ($n \times 1$ matrix) and one row ($1 \times m$ matrix) are called **column matrices** and **row matrices**. We denote column matrices with lowercase letters:

$$\mathbf{b} = [\, b_i \,].$$

The transpose of a row matrix is a column matrix; we write it as $\mathbf{b}^T$.

C.2   MATRIX OPERATIONS

There are three basic matrix operations: scalar–matrix multiplication, matrix–matrix addition, and matrix–matrix multiplication. You can assume that the scalars are real numbers, although all these operations are defined in the same way when the elements of the matrices and the scalar multipliers are of the same type.

Scalar–matrix multiplication is defined for any size matrix $\mathbf{A}$; it is simply the element-by-element multiplication of the elements of the matrix by a scalar α. The operation is written as

$$\alpha \mathbf{A} = [\, \alpha a_{ij} \,].$$

We define **matrix–matrix addition**, the sum of two matrices, by adding the corresponding elements of the two matrices. The sum makes sense only if the two matrices have the same dimensions. The sum of two matrices of the same dimensions is given by the matrix

$$\mathbf{C} = \mathbf{A} + \mathbf{B} = [\, a_{ij} + b_{ij} \,].$$

For **matrix–matrix multiplication**, the product of an $n \times l$ matrix $\mathbf{A}$ by an $l \times m$ matrix $\mathbf{B}$ is the $n \times m$ matrix

$$\mathbf{C} = \mathbf{AB} = [\, c_{ij} \,],$$

where

$$c_{ij} = \sum_{k=1}^{l} a_{ik} b_{kj}.$$

The matrix–matrix product is thus defined only if the number of columns of $\mathbf{A}$ is the same as the number of rows of $\mathbf{B}$. We say that $\mathbf{A}$ premultiplies $\mathbf{B}$, or that $\mathbf{B}$ postmultiplies $\mathbf{A}$.

Scalar–matrix multiplication obeys a number of simple rules that hold for any matrix $\mathbf{A}$, and for scalars α and β, such as

$$\alpha(\beta \mathbf{A}) = (\alpha \beta)\mathbf{A},$$

$$\alpha \beta \mathbf{A} = \beta \alpha \mathbf{A},$$

all of which follow from the fact that our matrix operations reduce to scalar multiplications on the scalar elements of a matrix. For matrix–matrix addition, we have the **commutative** property. For any $n \times m$ matrices **A** and **B**:

$$\mathbf{A} + \mathbf{B} = \mathbf{B} + \mathbf{A}.$$

We also have the **associative** property, which states that for any three $n \times m$ matrices **A**, **B**, and **C**:

$$\mathbf{A} + (\mathbf{B} + \mathbf{C}) = (\mathbf{A} + \mathbf{B}) + \mathbf{C}.$$

Matrix–matrix multiplication, although associative,

$$\mathbf{A}(\mathbf{B}\mathbf{C}) = (\mathbf{A}\mathbf{B})\mathbf{C},$$

is almost never commutative. So not only is it almost always the case that $\mathbf{AB} \neq \mathbf{BA}$, but also one product may not even be defined when the other is. In graphics applications, where matrices represent transformations such as translation and rotation, these results express that the order in which you carry out a sequence of transformations is important. A rotation followed by a translation is not the same as a translation followed by a rotation. However, if we do a rotation followed by a translation followed by a scaling, we get the same result if we first combine the scaling and translation, preserving the order, and then apply the rotation to the combined transformation.

The identity matrix **I** is a square matrix with 1s on the diagonal and 0s elsewhere:

$$\mathbf{I} = [\, a_{ij} \,], \qquad a_{ij} = \begin{cases} 1 & \text{if } i = j; \\ 0 & \text{otherwise.} \end{cases}$$

Assuming that the dimensions make sense,

$$\mathbf{AI} = \mathbf{A},$$

$$\mathbf{IB} = \mathbf{B}.$$

C.3 ROW AND COLUMN MATRICES

The $1 \times n$ and $n \times 1$ row and column matrices are of particular interest to us. We can represent either a vector or a point in three-dimensional space,[1] with respect to some frame, as the column matrix

$$\mathbf{p} = \begin{bmatrix} x \\ y \\ z \end{bmatrix}.$$

---

1. The homogeneous-coordinate representation introduced in Chapter 3 distinguishes between the representation of a point and the representation of a vector.

We use lowercase letters for column matrices. The transpose of $\mathbf{p}$ is the row matrix

$$\mathbf{p}^T = [\, x \quad y \quad z \,].$$

Because the product of an $n \times l$ and an $l \times m$ matrix is an $n \times m$ matrix, the product of a square matrix of dimension n and a column matrix of dimension n is a new column matrix of dimension n. Our standard mode of representing transformations of points is to use a column matrix of two, three, or four dimensions to represent a point (or vector), and a square matrix to represent a transformation of the point (or vector). Thus, the expression

$$\mathbf{p}' = \mathbf{A}\mathbf{p}$$

yields the representation of a transformed point (or vector), and expressions such as

$$\mathbf{p}' = \mathbf{ABC}\mathbf{p}$$

describe sequences, or **concatenations**, of transformations. Note that because the matrix–matrix product is associative, we do not need parentheses in this expression.

Many graphics books prefer to use row matrices to represent points. If we do so, using the fact that the transpose of a product can be written as

$$(\mathbf{AB})^T = \mathbf{B}^T \mathbf{A}^T,$$

then the concatenation of the three transformations can be written in row form as

$$\mathbf{p}'^T = \mathbf{p}^T \mathbf{C}^T \mathbf{B}^T \mathbf{A}^T.$$

The professed advantage of this form is that, in English, we read the transformations in the order in which they are performed; first $\mathbf{C}$, then $\mathbf{B}$, then $\mathbf{A}$. Almost all the scientific, mathematics, and engineering literature, however, uses column matrices rather than row matrices. Consequently, we prefer the column form. Although the choice is conceptually simple, in practice you have to be careful regarding which one your API is using, as not only is the order of transformations reversed, but also the transformation matrices themselves must be transposed.

C.4 RANK

In computer graphics, the primary use of matrices is as representations of points and of transformations. If a square matrix represents the transformation of a point or vector, we are often interested in whether or not the transformation is reversible or **invertible**. Thus, if

$$\mathbf{q} = \mathbf{A}\mathbf{p},$$

we want to know whether we can find a square matrix $\mathbf{B}$ such that

$\mathbf{p} = \mathbf{Bq}$.

Substituting for $\mathbf{q}$,

$\mathbf{p} = \mathbf{Bq} = \mathbf{BAp} = \mathbf{Ip} = \mathbf{p}$

and

$\mathbf{BA} = \mathbf{I}$.

If such a **B** exists, it is the **inverse** of **A**, and **A** is said to be **nonsingular**. A noninvertible matrix is **singular**. The inverse of **A** is written as $\mathbf{A}^{-1}$.

The fundamental result about inverses is as follows: *The inverse of a square matrix exists if and only if the determinant of the matrix is nonzero.* Although the determinant of **A** is a scalar, denoted by $|\mathbf{A}|$, its computation, for anything but low-dimensional matrices, requires almost as much work as does computation of the inverse. These calculations are $O(n^3)$ for an n-dimensional matrix. For the two-, three-, and four-dimensional matrices of interest in computer graphics, we can compute determinants by Cramer's rule and inverses using determinants, or we can use geometric reasoning. For example, the inverse of a translation is a translation back, and thus the inverse of a translation matrix must be a translation matrix. We pursue this course in Chapter 3.

For general nonsquare matrices, the concept of rank is important. We can regard a square matrix as a row matrix whose elements are column matrices or, equivalently, as a column matrix whose elements are row matrices. In terms of the vector-space concepts of Appendix B, the rows of an $n \times m$ matrix are elements of the Euclidean space $\mathbf{R}^m$, whereas the columns are elements of $\mathbf{R}^n$. We can determine how many rows (or columns) are **linearly independent**. The row (column) **rank** is the maximum number of linearly independent rows (columns), and thus *for an $n \times n$ matrix, the row rank and the column rank are the same and the matrix is nonsingular if and only if the rank is n.* Thus, a matrix is invertible if and only if its rows (and columns) are linearly independent.

C.5 CHANGE OF REPRESENTATION

We can use matrices to represent changes in bases for any set of vectors satisfying the rules of Appendix B. Suppose that we have a vector space of dimension n. Let $\{u_1, u_2, \ldots, u_n\}$ and $\{v_1, v_2, \ldots, v_n\}$ be two bases for the vector space. Hence, a given vector v can be expressed as either

$v = \alpha_1 u_1 + \alpha_2 u_2 + \ldots + \alpha_n u_n$

or

$v = \beta_1 v_1 + \beta_2 v_2 + \ldots + \beta_n v_n$.

Thus, $(\alpha_1, \alpha_2, \ldots, \alpha_n)$ and $(\beta_1, \beta_2, \ldots, \beta_n)$ are two different representations of v, and each can be expressed, equivalently, as a vector in the Euclidean space $\mathbf{R}^n$ or as a column matrix of dimension n. When we are working with representations, rather than with the vectors, we have to be careful to make sure that our notation reflects the difference. We write the representations of v as either

$$\mathbf{v} = [\, \alpha_1 \quad \alpha_2 \quad \ldots \quad \alpha_n \,]^T$$

or

$$\mathbf{v}' = [\, \beta_1 \quad \beta_2 \quad \ldots \quad \beta_n \,]^T,$$

depending on which basis we use.

We can now address the problem of how we convert from the representation $\mathbf{v}$ to the representation $\mathbf{v}'$. The basis vectors $\{v_1, v_2, \ldots, v_n\}$ can be expressed as vectors in the basis $\{u_1, u_2, \ldots, u_n\}$. Thus, there exists a set of scalars γ_{ij} such that

$$u_i = \gamma_{i1}v_1 + \gamma_{i2}v_2 + \ldots + \gamma_{in}v_n, \quad i = 1, \ldots, n.$$

We can write the expression in matrix form for all u_i as

$$\begin{bmatrix} u_1 \\ u_2 \\ \vdots \\ u_n \end{bmatrix} = \mathbf{A} \begin{bmatrix} v_1 \\ v_2 \\ \vdots \\ v_n \end{bmatrix},$$

where $\mathbf{A}$ is the $n \times n$ matrix:

$$\mathbf{A} = [\, \gamma_{ij} \,].$$

We can use column matrices to express both $\mathbf{v}$ and $\mathbf{v}'$ in terms of the vectors' representations as

$$\mathbf{v} = \mathbf{a}^T \begin{bmatrix} u_1 \\ u_2 \\ \vdots \\ u_n \end{bmatrix},$$

where

$$\mathbf{a} = [\, \alpha_i \,].$$

We can define $\mathbf{b}$ as

$$\mathbf{b} = [\, \beta_i \,],$$

and we can write $\mathbf{v}'$ as

$$\mathbf{v}' = \mathbf{b}^T \begin{bmatrix} v_1 \\ v_2 \\ \vdots \\ v_n \end{bmatrix}.$$

The matrix $\mathbf{A}$ relates the two bases, so we find by direct substitution that

$$\mathbf{b}^T = \mathbf{a}^T \mathbf{A}.$$

The matrix $\mathbf{A}$ is the **matrix representation** of the change between the two bases. It allows us to convert directly between the two representations. Equivalently, we can work with matrices of scalars rather than with abstract vectors. For geometric problems, although our vectors may be directed line segments, we can represent them by sets of scalars, and we can represent changes of bases or transformations by direct manipulation of these scalars.

C.6 THE CROSS PRODUCT

Given two nonparallel vectors, u and v, in a three-dimensional space, the cross product gives a third vector, w, that is orthogonal to both. Regardless of the representation, we must have

$$w \cdot u = w \cdot v = 0.$$

We can assign one component of w arbitrarily, because it is the direction of w, rather than the length, that is of importance, leaving us with three conditions for the three components of w. Within a particular coordinate system, if u has components $\alpha_1, \alpha_2, \alpha_3$, and v has components $\beta_1, \beta_2, \beta_3$, then, in this system, the **cross product** is defined as

$$\mathbf{w} = \mathbf{u} \times \mathbf{v} = \begin{bmatrix} \alpha_2\beta_3 - \alpha_3\beta_2 \\ \alpha_3\beta_1 - \alpha_1\beta_3 \\ \alpha_1\beta_2 - \alpha_2\beta_1 \end{bmatrix}.$$

Note that vector w is defined by u and v; we use their representation only when we wish to compute w in a particular coordinate system. The cross product gives a consistent orientation for $u \times v$. For example, consider the x-, y-, and z-axes as three vectors that determine the three coordinate directions of a right-handed coordinate system.[2] If we use the usual x- and y-axes, the cross product $x \times y$ points in the direction of the positive z-axis.

---

2. A right-handed coordinate system has positive directions determined by the thumb, index finger, and middle finger of the right hand used for the x-, y-, and z-axes, respectively. Equivalently, on a piece of paper, if positive x points left to right and positive y points bottom to top, then positive z points out of the page.

C.7 EIGENVALUES AND EIGENVECTORS

Square matrices are operators that transform column matrices into other column matrices of the same dimension. Because column matrices can represent points and vectors, we are interested in questions such as, When does a transformation leave a point or vector unchanged? For example, every rotation matrix leaves a particular point—the fixed point—unchanged. Let's consider a slightly more general problem. When does the matrix equation

$$\mathbf{Mu} = \lambda \mathbf{u}$$

have a nontrivial solution for some scalar λ, that is, a solution with $\mathbf{u}$ not being a matrix of zeros? If such a solution exists, then $\mathbf{M}$ transforms certain vectors $\mathbf{u}$—its **eigenvectors**—into scalar multiples of themselves. The values of λ for which this relationship holds are called the **eigenvalues** of the matrix. Eigenvalues and eigenvectors are also called **characteristic values** and **characteristic vectors**, respectively. These values characterize many properties of the matrix that are invariant under such operations as changes in representation.

We can find the eigenvalues by solving the equivalent matrix equation

$$\mathbf{Mu} - \lambda \mathbf{u} = \mathbf{Mu} - \lambda \mathbf{Iu} = (\mathbf{M} - \lambda \mathbf{I})\mathbf{u} = \mathbf{0}.$$

This equation can have a nontrivial solution if and only if the determinant[3]

$$|\mathbf{M} - \lambda \mathbf{I}| = 0.$$

If $\mathbf{M}$ is $n \times n$, then the determinant yields a polynomial of degree n in λ. Thus, there are n roots, some of which may be repeated or complex. For each distinct eigenvalue, we can then find a corresponding eigenvector. Note that every multiple of an eigenvector is itself an eigenvector, so that we can choose an eigenvector with unit magnitude. Eigenvectors corresponding to distinct eigenvalues are linearly independent. Thus, if all the eigenvalues are distinct, then any set of eigenvectors corresponding to the distinct eigenvalues form a basis for an n-dimensional vector space.

If there are repeated eigenvalues, the situation can be more complex. However, we need not worry about these cases for the matrices we will use in graphics. Thus, if $\mathbf{R}$ is a 3×3 rotation matrix and $\mathbf{p} = [\ x \quad y \quad z\ ]^T$ is the fixed point, then

$$\mathbf{Rp} = \mathbf{p}.$$

Thus, every rotation matrix must have an eigenvalue of 1. This result is the same whether we work in three dimensions or use the four-dimensional homogenous coordinate representation in Chapter 3.

---

3. The general statement, known as the Fredholm alternative, states that the n linear equations in n unknowns $\mathbf{Ax} = \mathbf{b}$ have a unique solution if and only if $|\mathbf{A}| \neq 0$. If $|\mathbf{A}| = 0$, there are multiple nontrivial solutions.

Suppose that $\mathbf{T}$ is a nonsingular matrix. Consider the matrix

$\mathbf{Q} = \mathbf{T}^{-1}\mathbf{MT}$.

Its eigenvalues and eigenvectors are solutions of the equation

$\mathbf{Qv} = \mathbf{T}^{-1}\mathbf{MTv} = \lambda\mathbf{v}$.

But if we multiply by $\mathbf{T}$, this equation becomes

$\mathbf{MTv} = \lambda\mathbf{Tv}$.

Thus, the eigenvalues of $\mathbf{Q}$ are the same as those of $\mathbf{M}$, and the eigenvectors are the transformations of the eigenvectors of $\mathbf{M}$. The matrices $\mathbf{M}$ and $\mathbf{Q}$ are said to be **similar**. Many of the transformations that arise in computer graphics involve similar matrices. One interpretation of this result is that changes of coordinate systems leave fundamental properties, such as the eigenvalues, unchanged. If we can find a similarity transformation that converts $\mathbf{M}$ to a diagonal matrix $\mathbf{Q}$, then the diagonal elements of $\mathbf{Q}$ are the eigenvalues of both matrices.

Eigenvalues and eigenvectors have a geometric interpretation. Consider an ellipsoid, centered at the origin, with its axes aligned with the coordinate axes. It can be written as

$$\lambda_1 x^2 + \lambda_2 y^2 + \lambda_3 z^2 = 1$$

for positive values of λ_1, λ_2, and λ_3, or in matrix form,

$$\begin{bmatrix} x & y & z \end{bmatrix} \begin{bmatrix} \lambda_1 & 0 & 0 \\ 0 & \lambda_2 & 0 \\ 0 & 0 & \lambda_3 \end{bmatrix} \begin{bmatrix} x \\ y \\ z \end{bmatrix} = 1.$$

Thus, λ_1, λ_2, and λ_3 are both the eigenvalues of the diagonal matrix and the inverses of the lengths of the major and minor axes of the ellipsoid. If we apply a change of coordinate system through a rotation matrix, we create a new ellipsoid that is no longer aligned with the coordinate axes. However, we have not changed the length of axes of the ellipse, a property that is invariant under coordinate system changes.

C.8   VECTOR AND MATRIX CLASSES

Although we have avoided using the term *vector* for matrices of one row or one column, much of the literature prefers to use *vector* for such matrices. More problematic for this book has been that GLSL uses *vector* this way. Consequently, we created separate vector and matrix C++ classes to use with our examples. These classes are defined in the files `vector.h` and `matrix.h` that are included by the file `Angel.h` used in all the examples.

The vector class defines separate vec2, vec3, and vec4 types for one-, two-, and three-dimensional vectors. It includes overloaded arithmetic operators for these types and the usual constructors to create them and work with multiple types in a single application. The classes are for general vectors of these dimensions and are not specialized for homogeneous coordinates. We also include the standard functions for normalization, cross products, dot products, and length.

The matrix class supports two-, three-, and four-dimensional square matrices (mat2, mat3, and mat4) and overloads the standard arithmetic operators to support their manipulation and operations between vectors and matrices. We also included many of the functions that were in earlier versions of OpenGL and the deprecated. These include most of the transformation and viewing functions. In most cases, we used the same names as did OpenGL, for example, Rotate, Scale, Translate, Ortho, Frustum, LookAt.

SUGGESTED READINGS

Some of the standard references on linear algebra and matrices include Strang [Str93] and Banchoff and Werner [Ban83]. See also Rogers and Adams [Rog90] and the *Graphics Gems* series [Gra90, Gra91, Gra92, Gra94, Gra95].

The issue of row versus column matrices is an old one. Early graphics books [New73] used row matrices. The trend now is to use column matrices [Fol90], although a few books still use row representations [Wat00]. Within the API, it may not be clear which is being used, because the elements of a square matrix can be represented as a simple array of n^2 elements. Certain APIs, such as OpenGL, allow only postmultiplication of an internal matrix by a user-defined matrix; others, such as PHIGS, support both pre- and postmultiplication.

EXERCISES

C.1   In $\mathbf{R}^3$, consider the two bases $\{(1, 0, 0), (1, 1, 0), (1, 1, 1)\}$ and $\{(1, 0, 0), (0, 1, 0), (0, 0, 1)\}$. Find the two matrices that convert representations between the two bases. Show that they are inverses of each other.

C.2   Consider the vector space of polynomials of degree up to 2. Show that the sets of polynomials $\{1, x, x^2\}$ and $\{1, 1 + x, 1 + x + x^2\}$ are bases. Give the representation of the polynomial $1 + 2x + 3x^2$ in each basis. Find the matrix that converts between representations in the two bases.

C.3   Suppose that $\mathbf{i}$, $\mathbf{j}$, and $\mathbf{k}$ represent the unit vectors in the x-, y-, and z-directions, respectively, in $\mathbf{R}^3$. Show that the cross product $u \times v$ is given by the matrix

$$u \times v = \begin{vmatrix} \mathbf{i} & \mathbf{j} & \mathbf{k} \\ u_1 & u_2 & u_3 \\ v_1 & v_2 & v_3 \end{vmatrix}.$$

C.4   Show that, in $\mathbf{R}^3$,

$$|u \times v| = |u||v|| \sin \theta|,$$

where θ is the angle between u and v.

C.5   Find the eigenvalues and eigenvectors of the two-dimensional rotation matrix

$$\mathbf{R} = \begin{bmatrix} \cos \theta & -\sin \theta \\ \sin \theta & \cos \theta \end{bmatrix}.$$

C.6   Find the eigenvalues and eigenvectors of the three-dimensional rotation matrix

$$\mathbf{R} = \begin{bmatrix} \cos \theta & -\sin \theta & 0 \\ \sin \theta & \cos \theta & 0 \\ 0 & 0 & 1 \end{bmatrix}.$$

SYNOPSIS OF OPENGL FUNCTIONS

D.1 INITIALIZATION AND WINDOW FUNCTIONS

```
void glutInit(int *argc, char **argv)
```

initializes GLUT. The arguments from main are passed in and can be used by the application.

```
void glewInit(void)
```

initializes GLEW if used by application.

```
int glutCreateWindow(char *title)
```

creates a window on the display. The string title can be used to label the window. The return value provides a reference to the window that can be used when there are multiple windows.

```
void glutInitDisplayMode(unsigned int mode)
```

requests a display with the properties in mode. The value of mode is determined by the logical OR of options including the color model (GLUT_RGB, GLUT_INDEX) and buffering (GLUT_SINGLE, GLUT_DOUBLE).

```
void glutInitWindowSize(int width, int height)
```

specifies the initial height and width of the window in pixels.

```
void glutInitWindowPosition(int x, int y)
```

specifies the initial position of the top-left corner of the window in pixels.

```
void glViewport(int x, int y, GLsizei width, GLsizei height)
```

specifies a `width` × `height` viewport in pixels whose lower-left corner is at (x, y) measured from the origin of the window.

```
void glutMainLoop()
```

causes the program to enter an event-processing loop. It should be the last statement in `main`.

```
void glutDisplayFunc(void (*func)(void))
```

registers the display function `func` that is executed when the window needs to be redrawn.

```
void glutPostRedisplay()
```

requests that the display callback be executed after the current callback returns.

```
void glutSwapBuffers()
```

swaps the front and back buffers.

```
void glFlush()
```

forces any buffered OpenGL commands to execute.

```
void glutSetWindow(int id)
```

sets the current window to the window with identifier `id`.

```
void glutContextVersion(int major_version, int minor_version)
```

sets the desired context, e.g., `glutContextVersion(3, 1)` for OpenGL 3.1. Only available in freeglut.

```
void glutContextProfile(init profile)
```

sets the desired context to either `GLUT_CORE_PROFILE` or `GLUT_COMPATIBILITY_PROFILE`. Compatibility profile allows backward compatibility. Only available with freeglut.

D.2 VERTEX BUFFER OBJECTS

```
void glGenVertexArrays(GLsizei n, GLuint *array)
```

generates `n` unused identifiers for vertex array objects in `array`.

```
void glBindVertexArray(GLuint id)
```

creates a new vertex array object with identifier `id`. Subsequent calls with the same identifier make that the active array.

```
void glGenBuffers(GLsizei n, GLuint *buffer)
```

generates `n` unused identifiers for buffer objects in `buffer`.

```
void glBindBuffer(GLenum target, GLint id)
```

creates a new buffer object with identifier `id`. Subsequent calls with the same identifier make that the active buffer object. The type of buffer object is given by `target`. Types include `GL_ARRAY_BUFFER` for vertex attribute data.

```
void glBufferData(GLenum target, GLsizeiptr size, const GLvoid *data,
                  GLenum usage)
```

allocates `size` units of server memory for vertex array objects of type `target` pointed to by `data`. Types include `GL_ARRAY_BUFFER`. The `usage` parameter specifies how the data will be read and includes `GL_STATIC_DRAW` and `GL_DYNAMIC_DRAW`.

```
void glBufferSubData(GLenum target, GLintiptr offset, GLsizeiptr size,
                     const GLvoid *data)
```

updates size bytes starting at offset in the current buffer object with data of type target starting at data.

```
void glVertexAttrib[1234][sfd](GLunit index, TYPE data);
void glVertexAttrib[1234][sfd]v(GLunit index, TYPE *data);
```

specifies values for vertex attributes with the given index.

```
void glVertexAttribPointer(GLuint index, GLint size, GLenum type,
   GLboolean normalized, GLsizei stride, const GLvoid* data)
```

points to data where vertex data of size components corresponding to index are stored. Data are one of the standard types such as GL_INT and GL_FLOAT. If normalized is set to GL_TRUE, the data will be normalized when stored. If stride is set to 0, the data are assumed to be contiguous.

```
void glEnableVertexAttribArray(GLuint index)
```

enables the vertex array with identifier index.

```
void glDrawArrays(GLenum mode, GLint first,  GLsizei count)
```

creates count elements of the standard OpenGL types mode, such as GL_TRIANGLES or GL_LINES starting at first.

D.3 INTERACTION

```
void glutMouseFunc(void *f(int button, int state, int x, int y))
```

registers the mouse callback function f. The callback function returns the button (GLUT_LEFT_BUTTON, GLUT_MIDDLE_BUTTON, GLUT_RIGHT_BUTTON), the state of the button after the event (GLUT_UP, GLUT_DOWN), and the position of the mouse relative to the top-left corner of the window.

```
void glutReshapeFunc(void *f(int width, int height))
```

registers the reshape callback function `f`. The callback returns the height and width of the new window. The reshape callback invokes a display callback.

```
void glutKeyboardFunc(void *f(char key, int width, int height))
```

registers the keyboard callback function `f`. The callback function returns the ASCII code of the key pressed and the position of the mouse.

```
void glutIdleFunc(void (*f)(void))
```

registers the display callback function `f` that is executed whenever there are no other events to be handled.

```
int glutCreateMenu(void (*f)(int value))
```

returns an identifier for a top-level menu and registers the callback function `f` that returns an integer `value` corresponding to the menu entry selected.

```
void glutSetMenu(int id)
```

sets the current menu to the menu with identifier `id`.

```
void glutAddMenuEntry(char *name, int value)
```

adds an entry with the string `name` displayed to the current menu. `value` is returned to the menu callback when the entry is selected.

```
void glutAttachMenu(int button)
```

attaches the current menu to the specified mouse `button`.

```
void glutAddSubMenu(char *name, int menu)
```

adds a submenu entry `name` to the current menu. The value of `menu` is the identifier returned when the submenu was created.

```
void glutTimerFunc(int delay, void (*f)(int v), int value)
```

registers the timer callback function f and delays the event loop by delay milliseconds. After the timer counts down, f is executed with the parameter v. value is available to f.

```
void glutMotionFunc(void (*f)(int x, int y))
```

registers the motion callback function f. The position of the mouse is returned by the callback when the mouse is moved at with least one of the mouse buttons pressed.

```
void glutPassiveMotionFunc(void (*f)(int x, int y))
```

registers the motion callback function f. The position of the mouse is returned by the callback when the mouse is moved.

D.4   SETTING ATTRIBUTES AND ENABLING FEATURES

```
void glEnable(GLenum feature)
```

enables an OpenGL feature. Features that can be enabled include GL_DEPTH_TEST, GL_TEXTURE_1D, GL_TEXTURE_2D, GL_TEXTURE_3D, GL_LINE_SMOOTH, GL_POLYGON_SMOOTH, GL_POINT_SMOOTH, GL_BLEND.

```
void glDisable(GLenum feature)
```

disables an OpenGL feature.

```
void glPolygonMode(glEnum faces, glEnum mode)
```

sets the desired mode for polygon rendering the faces (GL_FRONT_AND_BACK). mode can be GL_POINTS, GL_LINES, or GL_FILL.

```
void glClearColor(GLclampf r, GLclampf g, GLclampf b, GLclampf a)
```

sets the present RGBA clear color used when clearing the color buffer. Variables of type GLclampf are floating-point numbers between 0.0 and 1.0.

```
void glPointSize(GLfloat size)
```

sets the point size attribute in pixels.

```
void glPolygonOffset(GLfloat factor, GLfloat units)
```

offsets polygon depths by a linear combination of `factor` and `units`. The multiplicative constants in the computation depend on the slope of the polygon and the precision of the depth values.

```
glDepthMask(GLboolean flag)
```

sets `flag` to make the depth buffer read-only (GL_FALSE) or writable (GL_TRUE).

```
void glBlendFunc(GLenum source, GLenum destination)
```

sets the `source` and `destination` blending factors. Options include GL_ONE, GL_ZERO, GL_SRC_COLOR, GL_SRC_ALPHA, GL_ONE_MINUS_SRC_COLOR, GL_ONE_MINUS_SRC_ALPHA, GL_DST_COLOR, GL_ONE_MINUS_DST_COLOR, GL_DST_ALPHA, GL_ONE_MINUS_DST_ALPHA.

D.5 TEXTURE AND IMAGE FUNCTIONS

```
glTexImage2D[ui us f]v(GLenum target, GLint level, GLint iformat,
    GLsizei width, GLsizei height, GLint border, GLenum format,
    GLenum type, GLvoid *texels)
```

sets up a two-dimensional texture of `height` × `width` texels of `type` and `format`. The array `texels` is of format `iformat`. A `border` of 0 or 1 texels can be specified.

```
glTexParameter[if](GLenum target, GLenum param, TYPE value)
glTexParameter[if]v(GLenum target, GLenum param, TYPE *value)
```

sets the texture parameter `param` to `value` for texture of type `target` (GL_TEXTURE_1D, GL_TEXTURE_2D, or GL_TEXTURE_3D).

```
glGenTextures(GLsizei n, GLuint name)
```

returns in `name` the first integer of n unused integer for texture-object identifiers.

```
glBindTexture(GLenum target, GLuint name)
```

binds name to texture of type target (GL_TEXTURE_1D, GL_TEXTURE_2D, GL_TEXTURE_3D, GL_TEXTURE_CUBE_MAP).

```
glDeleteTextures(GLsizei n, GLuint *namearray)
```

deletes n texture objects from the array namearray that holds texture-object names.

D.6   STATE AND BUFFER MANIPULATION

```
void glDrawBuffer(GLenum buffer)
```

selects the color buffer buffer for rendering.

```
void glLogicOp(GLenum op)
```

selects one of the 16 logical writing modes if the feature GL_COLOR_LOGIC_OP is enabled. Modes include replacement (GL_COPY), the default, and exclusive or (GL_XOR).

```
glReadPixels(GLint x, GLint y, GLsizei width, GLsizei height,
         GLenum format, GLenum type, GLvoid *image)
```

reads a width × height rectangle of pixels from the present read buffer starting at x, y into the array image. The pixels are in the specified format in the read buffer and written as the specified data type.

```
glPixelStore[if](GLenum param, TYPE value)
```

sets the pixel store parameter param to value. Parameters include GL_UNPACK_SWAP_BYTES, GL_PACK_SWAP_BYTES, GL_PACK_ALIGNMENT, GL_UNPACK_ALIGNMENT.

D.7   QUERY FUNCTIONS

```
void glGetBooleanv(GLenum name, GLboolean *param)
void glGetIntegerv(GLenum name, GLinteger *param)
void glGetFloatv(GLenum name, GLfloat *param)
```

```
void glGetDoublev(GLenum name, GLdouble *param)
void glGetPointerv(GLenum name, GLvoid **param)
```

writes the present value of the parameter name into param.

```
int glutGet(GLenum state)
```

returns the current value of a GLUT state variable such as GLUT_WINDOW_WIDTH, GLUT_WINDOW_HEIGHT, GLUT_ELAPSED_TIME.

D.8 GLSL FUNCTIONS

```
GLuint glCreateProgram()
```

creates an empty program object and returns an identifier for it.

```
GLuint glCreateShader(GLenum type)
```

creates an empty shader object of type GL_VERTEX_SHADER or GL_FRAGMENT_ SHADER and returns an identifier for it.

```
void glShaderSource(GLuint shader, GLsizei nstrings, const GLchar
    **strings, const GLint *lengths)
```

identifies the source code for shader as coming from an array of nstrings strings of lengths characters. If the shader is a single null-terminated string, then nstrings is 1 and lengths is NULL.

```
void glCompileShader(GLuint shader)
```

compiles shader object shader.

```
void glAttachShader(GLunit program, GLuint shader)
```

attaches shader object shader to program object program.

```
void glLinkProgram(GLuint program)
```

links together the application and shaders in program object program.

```
void glUseProgram(GLuint program)
```

makes program the active program object.

```
GLint glGetAttribLocation(GLuint program, const GLchar *name)
```

returns the index of the attribute name from the linked program object name.

```
void glVertexAttrib[1234][sfd](GLuint index, TYPE value1,
    TYPE value2,...)
void glVertexAttrib[123][sfd]v(GLuint index, TYPE *value)
```

specifies the value of the vertex attribute with the specified index.

```
GLint glGetUniformLocation(GLuint program, const GLchar *name)
```

returns the index of uniform variable name from the linked program object program.

```
void glUniform1234[if](GLint index, TYPE value)
void glUniform1234[if]v(GLint index, GLsizei num, TYPE value)
void glUniformMatrix[234]f(GLint index, GLsizei num,
     GLboolean transpose, const GLfloat *value)
```

sets the value of a uniform variable, array, or matrix with the specified index. For the array and matrix, num is the number of elements to be changed.

```
void glGetProgram(GLuint program, GLenum pname, GLinit *param)
```

returns in param the value of parameter pname for program object program. Parameters include link status GL_LINK_STATUS, which returns GL_TRUE or GL_FALSE, and GL_INFO_LOG_LENGTH, which returns the number of characters in the information log.

```
void glGetShaderiv(GLuint shader, GLenum pname, GLint *param)
```

returns in param the value of parameter pname for shader object shader. Parameters include compile status GL_COMPILE_STATUS, which returns GL_TRUE or GL_FALSE, and GL_INFO_LOG_LENGTH, which returns the number of characters in the information log.

```
void getProgramInfoLog(GLuint program, GLsizei maxL, GLsizei *len,
    GLchar *infoLog)
```

returns the info log string for program object `program` into the array `infoLog` of lenth `maxL` and the length of the string in `len`.

```
void getShaderInfoLog(GLuint program, GLsizei maxL, GLsizei *len,
    GLchar *infoLog)
```

returns the info log string for shader object `program` into the array `infoLog` of length `maxL` and the length of the string in `len`.

REFERENCES

Ado85   Adobe Systems Incorporated, *PostScript Language Reference Manual*, Addison-Wesley, Reading, MA, 1985.

Ake88   Akeley, K., and T. Jermoluk, "High Performance Polygon Rendering," *Computer Graphics*, 22(4), 239–246, 1988.

Ake93   Akeley, K., "Reality Engine Graphics," *Computer Graphics*, 109–116, 1993.

Ang90   Angel, E., *Computer Graphics*, Addison-Wesley, Reading, MA, 1990.

Ang08   Angel, E., *OpenGL, A Primer,* Third Edition, Addison-Wesley, Reading, MA, 2008.

ANSI85   American National Standards Institute (ANSI), *American National Standard for Information Processing Systems—Computer Graphics—Graphical Kernel System (GKS) Functional Description,* ANSI, X3.124-1985, ANSI, New York, 1985.

ANSI88   American National Standards Institute (ANSI), *American National Standard for Information Processing Systems—Programmer's Hierarchical Interactive Graphics System (PHIGS),* ANSI, X3.144-1988, ANSI, New York, 1988.

App68   Appel, A., "Some Techniques for Shading Machine Renderings of Solids," *Spring Joint Computer Conference,* 37–45, 1968.

Arn96   Arnold, K., and J. Gosling, *The Java Programming Language,* Addison-Wesley, Reading, MA, 1996.

Ban83   Banchoff, T., and J. Werner, *Linear Algebra Through Geometry,* Springer-Verlag, New York, 1983.

Bar93   Barnsley, M., *Fractals Everywhere,* Second Edition, Academic Press, San Diego, CA, 1993.

Bar83   Barsky, B.A., and C. Beatty, "Local Control of Bias and Tension in Beta-Splines," *ACM Transactions on Graphics,* 2(2), 109–134, 1983.

Bar87   Bartels, R.H., C. Beatty, and B.A. Barsky, *An Introduction to Splines for Use in Computer Graphics and Geometric Modeling*, Morgan Kaufmann, Los Altos, CA, 1987.

Bli76   Blinn, J.F., and M.E. Newell, "Texture and Reflection in Computer Generated Images," *CACM,* 19(10), 542–547, 1976.

Bli77   Blinn, J.F., "Models of Light Reflection for Computer-Synthesized Pictures," *Computer Graphics*, 11(2), 192–198, 1977.

Bow83   Bowyer, A., and J. Woodwark, *A Programmer's Geometry*, Butterworth, London, 1983.

Bre65   Bresenham, J.E., "Algorithm for Computer Control of a Digital Plotter," *IBM Systems Journal*, January, 25–30, 1965.

Bre87   Bresenham, J.E., "Ambiguities in Incremental Line Rastering," *IEEE Computer Graphics and Applications*, May, 31–43, 1987.

Car78   Carlbom, I., and J. Paciorek, "Planar Geometric Projection and Viewing Transformations," *Computing Surveys*, 10(4), 465–502, 1978.

Cas96   Castleman, K.C., *Digital Image Processing*, Prentice-Hall, Englewood Cliffs, NJ, 1996.

Cat78a   Catmull, E., "A Hidden-Surface Algorithm with Antialiasing," *Computer Graphics*, 12(3), 6–11, 1978.

Cat78b   Catmull, E., and J. Clark, "Recursively Generated B-Spline Surfaces on Arbitrary Topological Meshes," *Proceedings of Computer-Aided Design, 10*, 350-355, 1978.

Cha98   Chan, P., and R. Lee, *The Java Class Libraries: Java.Applet, Java.Awt, Java.Beans* (Vol. 2), Addison-Wesley, Reading, MA, 1998.

Che95   Chen, S.E., "Quicktime VR: An Image-Based Approach to Virtual Environment Navigation," *Computer Graphics*, 29–38, 1995.

Che00   Chen, K.L. et al., "Building and Using a Scalable Display Wall System," *IEEE Computer Graphics and Applications*, 20(4), 29–37, 2000.

Cla82   Clark, J.E., "The Geometry Engine: A VLSI Geometry System for Graphics," *Computer Graphics*, 16, 127–133, 1982.

Coh85   Cohen, M.F., and D.P. Greenberg, "The Hemi-Cube: A Radiosity Solution for Complex Environments," *Computer Graphics*, 19(3), 31–40, 1985.

Coh88   Cohen, M.F., S.E. Chen, J.R. Wallace, and D.P. Greenberg, "A Progressive Refinement Approach to Fast Radiosity Image Generation," *Computer Graphics*, 22(4), 75–84, 1988.

Coh93   Cohen, M.F., and J.R. Wallace, *Radiosity and Realistic Image Synthesis*, Academic Press Professional, Boston, MA, 1993.

Coo82   Cook, R.L., and K.E. Torrance, "A Reflectance Model for Computer Graphics," *ACM Transactions on Graphics*, 1(1), 7–24, 1982.

Coo87   Cook, R.L., L. Carpenter, and E. Catmull, "The Reyes Image Rendering Architecture," *Computer Graphics*, 21(4), 95–102, July 1987.

Cro81   Crow, F.C., "A Comparison of Antialiasing Techniques," *IEEE Computer Graphics and Applications*, 1(1), 40–48, 1981.

Cro97   Crossno, P.J., and E. Angel, "Isosurface Extraction Using Particle Systems," *IEEE Visualization*, 1997.

Deb96   Debevec, P.E., C.J. Taylor, and J. Malik, "Modeling and Rendering Architecture from Photographs: A Hybrid Geometry- and Image-Based Approach," *Computer Graphics*, 11–20, 1996.

deB08   deBerg, M., C. Otfried, M. van Kreveld, and M. Overmars, *Computational Geometry, Third Edition,* Springer-Verlag, Berlin Heidelberg, 2008.

DeR88   DeRose, T.D., "A Coordinate-Free Approach to Geometric Programming," SIGGRAPH Course Notes, *SIGGRAPH*, 1988.

DeR89   DeRose, T.D., "A Coordinate-Free Approach to Geometric Programming," in *Theory and Practice of Geometric Modeling*, W. Strasser and H.P. Seidel (Eds.), Springer-Verlag, Berlin, 1989.

Dre88   Drebin, R.A., L. Carpenter, and P. Hanrahan, "Volume Rendering," *Computer Graphics*, 22(4), 65–74, 1988.

Ebe01   Eberly, D.H., *3D Game Engine Design,* Morgan Kaufmann, San Francisco, 2001.

Ebe02   Ebert, D., F.K. Musgrave, D. Peachey, K. Perlin, and S. Worley, *Texturing and Modeling, A Procedural Approach*, Third Edition, Morgan Kaufman, San Francisco, 2002.

End84   Enderle, G., K. Kansy, and G. Pfaff, *Computer Graphics Programming: GKS—The Graphics Standard*, Springer-Verlag, Berlin, 1984.

Far88   Farin, G., *Curves and Surfaces for Computer Aided Geometric Design,* Academic Press, New York, 1988.

Fau80   Faux, I.D., and M.J. Pratt, *Computational Geometry for Design and Manufacturing*, Halsted, Chichester, England, 1980.

Fern03   Fernando, R., and M.J. Kilgard, *The Cg Tutorial: The Definitive Guide to Programmable Real-Time Graphics*, Addison-Wesley, Reading, MA, 2003.

Fern04   Fernando, R., *GPU Gems: Programming Techniques, Tips, and Tricks for Real-Time Graphics*, Addison-Wesley, Reading, MA, 2004.

Fol90   Foley, J.D., A. van Dam, S.K. Feiner, and J.F. Hughes, *Computer Graphics,* Second Edition, Addison-Wesley, Reading, MA, 1990 (C Version 1996).

Fol94   Foley, J.D., A. van Dam, S.K. Feiner, J.F. Hughes, and R. Phillips, *Introduction to Computer Graphics,* Addison-Wesley, Reading, MA, 1994.

Fos97   Fosner, R., *OpenGL Programming for Windows 95 and Windows NT,* Addison-Wesley, Reading, MA, 1997.

Fou82   Fournier, A., D. Fussell, and L. Carpenter, "Computer Rendering of Stochastic Models," *CACM*, 25(6), 371–384, 1982.

Fuc77   Fuchs, H., J. Duran, and B. Johnson, "A System for Automatic Acquisition of Three-Dimensional Data," *Proceedings of the 1977 NCC*, AFIPS Press, 49–53, Montvale, NJ, 1977.

Fuc80   Fuchs, H., Z.M. Kedem, and B.F. Naylor, "On Visible Surface Generation by A Priori Tree Structures," *SIGGRAPH 80*, 124–133, 1980.

Gal95   Gallagar, R.S., *Computer Visualization: Graphics Techniques for Scientific and Engineering Analysis*, CRC Press, Boca Raton, FL, 1995.

Gla89   Glassner, A.S. (Ed.), *An Introduction to Ray Tracing,* Academic Press, New York, 1989.

Gla95   Glassner, A.S., *Principles of Digital Image Synthesis,* Morgan Kaufmann, San Francisco, 1995.

Gon08   Gonzalez, R., and R.E. Woods, *Digital Image Processing*, Third Edition, Addison-Wesley, Reading, MA, 2008.

Gor84   Goral, C.M., K.E. Torrance, D.P. Greenberg, and B. Battaile, "Modeling the Interaction of Light Between Diffuse Surfaces," *Computer Graphics (SIGGRAPH 84),* 18(3), 213–222, 1984.

Gor96   Gortler, S.J., R. Grzeszczuk, R. Szeliski, and M.F. Cohen, "The Lumigraph," *Computer Graphics,* 43–54, 1996.

Gou71   Gouraud, H., "Computer Display of Curved Surfaces," *IEEE Trans. Computers,* C-20, 623–628, 1971.

Gra90   *Graphics Gems I*, Glassner, A.S. (Ed.), Academic Press, San Diego, CA, 1990.

Gra91   *Graphics Gems II*, Arvo, J. (Ed.), Academic Press, San Diego, CA, 1991.

Gra92   *Graphics Gems III*, Kirk, D. (Ed.), Academic Press, San Diego, CA, 1992.

Gra94   *Graphics Gems IV*, Heckbert, P. (Ed.), Academic Press, San Diego, CA, 1994.

Gra95   *Graphics Gems V*, Paeth, A. (Ed.), Academic Press, San Diego, CA, 1995.

Gra03   Gray, K., *The Microsoft DirectX 9 Programmable Graphics Pipeline*, Microsoft Press, 2003.

Gre88   Greengard, L.F., *The Rapid Evolution of Potential Fields in Particle Systems,* MIT Press, Cambridge, MA, 1988.

Hal89   Hall, R., *Illumination and Color in Computer Generated Imagery,* Springer-Verlag, New York, 1989.

Har96   Hartman, J., and J. Wernecke, *The VRML 2.0 Handbook*, Addison-Wesley, Reading, MA, 1996.

Hea11   Hearn, D., M.P. Baker, and W.R. Carithers, *Computer Graphics*, Fourth Edition, Prentice-Hall, Englewood Cliffs, NJ, 2011.

Hec84   Heckbert, P.S., and P. Hanrahan, "Beam Tracing Polygonal Objects," *Computer Graphics,* 18(3), 119–127, 1984.

Hec86   Heckbert, P.S., "Survey of Texture Mapping," *IEEE Computer Graphics and Applications,* 6(11), 56–67, 1986.

Her79   Herman, G.T., and H.K. Liu, "Three-Dimensional Display of Human Organs from Computed Tomograms," *Computer Graphics and Image Processing,* 9, 1–21, 1979.

Her00   Hereld, M., I.R. Judson, and R.L. Stevens, "Tutorial: Introduction to Building Projection-Based Tiled Display Systems," *IEEE Computer Graphics and Applications,* 20(4), 22–26, 2000.

Hil07   Hill, F.S., Jr., and S.M. Kelley,, *Computer Graphics*, Third Edition, Prentice Hall, Upper Saddle River, NJ, 2007.

Hop83   Hopgood, F.R.A., D.A. Duce, J.A. Gallop, and D.C. Sutcliffe, *Introduction to the Graphical Kernel System: GKS*, Academic Press, London, 1983.

Hop91   Hopgood, F.R.A., and D.A. Duce, *A Primer for PHIGS*, John Wiley & Sons, Chichester, England, 1991.

Hum01   Humphreys, G., M. Elridge, I. Buck, G. Stoll, M. Everett, and P. Hanrahan, "WireGL: A Scalable Graphics System for Clusters," *SIGGRAPH 2001.*

ISO88   International Standards Organization, *International Standard Information Processing Systems—Computer Graphics—Graphical Kernel System for Three Dimensions (GKS-3D),* ISO Document Number 8805:1988(E), American National Standards Institute, New York, 1988.

Jar76   Jarvis, J.F., C.N. Judice, and W.H. Ninke, "A Survey of Techniques for the Image Display of Continuous Tone Pictures on Bilevel Displays," *Computer Graphics and Image Processing,* 5(1), 13–40, 1976.

Jen01   Jensen, H.W., "Realistic Image Synthesis Using Photon Mapping," A K Peters, 2001.

Joy88   Joy, K.I., C.W. Grant, N.L. Max, and L. Hatfield, *Computer Graphics: Image Synthesis*, Computer Society Press, Washington, DC, 1988.

Kaj86   Kajiya, J.T., "The Rendering Equation," *Computer Graphics,* 20(4), 143–150, 1986.

Kel97   Keller, H., "Instant Randiosity," *Computer Graphics*, 49–56, 1997.

Kil94a   Kilgard, M.J., "OpenGL and X, Part 3: Integrated OpenGL with Motif," *The X Journal*, SIGS Publications, July/August 1994.

Kil94b   Kilgard, M.J., "An OpenGL Toolkit," *The X Journal*, SIGS Publications, November/December 1994.

Kil96   Kilgard, M.J., *OpenGL Programming for the X Windows System*, Addison-Wesley, Reading, MA, 1996.

Knu87   Knuth, D.E., "Digital Halftones by Dot Diffusion," *ACM Transactions on Graphics,* 6(40), 245–273, 1987.

Kov97   Kovatch, P.J., *The Awesome Power of Direct3D/DirectX*, Manning Publications Company, Greenwich, CT, 1997.

Kue08   Kuehhne, R.P., and J.D. Sullivan, *OpenGL Programming on Mac OS X*, Addison-Wesley, Boston, MA, 2008.

Kui99   Kuipers, J.B., *Quaternions and Rotation Sequences*, Princeton University Press, Princeton, NJ, 1999.

Las87   Lasseter, J., "Principles of Traditional Animation Applied to 3D Computer Animation," *Computer Graphics*, 21(4), 33–44, 1987.

Lev88   Levoy, M., "Display of Surface from Volume Data," *IEEE Computer Graphics and Applications*, 8(3), 29–37, 1988.

Lev96   Levoy, M., and P. Hanrahan, "Light Field Rendering," *Computer Graphics*, 31–42, 1996.

Lia84   Liang, Y., and B. Barsky, "A New Concept and Method for Line Clipping," *ACM Transactions on Graphics*, 3(1), 1–22, 1984.

Lin68   Lindenmayer, A., "Mathematical Models for Cellular Interactions in Biology," *Journal of Theoretical Biology*, 18, 280–315, 1968.

Lin01   Linholm, E., M.J. Kilgard, and H. Morelton, "A User-Programmable Vertex Engine," *SIGGRAPH*, 2001.

Lor87   Lorensen, W.E., and H.E. Cline, "Marching Cubes: A High Resolution 3D Surface Construction Algorithm," *Computer Graphics*, 21(4), 163–169, 1987.

Ma94   Ma, K.L., J. Painter, C. Hansen, and M. Krogh, "Parallel Volume Rendering Using Binary-Swap Compositing," *IEEE Computer Graphics and Applications*, 14(4), 59–68, 1994.

Mag85   Magnenat-Thalmann, N., and D. Thalmann, *Computer Animation: Theory and Practice*, Springer-Verlag, Tokyo, 1985.

Man82   Mandelbrot, B., *The Fractal Geometry of Nature*, Freeman Press, New York, 1982.

Mat95   The MathWorks, *Student Edition of MatLab Version 4 Users Guide*, Prentice-Hall, Englewood Cliffs, NJ, 1995.

Mau06   Maurina, E., *The Game Programmer's Guide to Torque*, A K Peters, 2006.

Max51   Maxwell, E.A., *General Homogeneous Coordinates in Space of Three Dimensions*, Cambridge University Press, Cambridge, England, 1951.

Mia99   Miamo, J., *Compressed Image File Formats*, ACM Press, New York, 1999.

Mol92   Molnar, S., J. Eyles, and J. Poulton, "PixelFlow: High-Speed Rendering Using Image Composition," *Computer Graphics*, 26(2), 231–240, 1992.

Mol94   Molnar, S., M. Cox, D. Ellsworth, and H. Fuchs, "A Sorting Classification of Parallel Rendering," *IEEE Computer Graphics and Applications*, 26(2), 231–240, 1994.

Mol02   Möller, T., and E. Haines, *Real-Time Rendering*, Second, Edition, A K Peters, 2002.

Mon97   Montrym, J., D. Baum, D. Dignam, and C. Migdal, "InfiniteReality: A Real-Time Graphics System," *Computer Graphics*, 293–392, 1997.

Mur94   Murray, J.D., and W. Van Ryper, *Encyclopedia of Graphics File Formats*, O'Reilly and Associates, Sebastopol, CA, 1994.

New73   Newman, W.M., and R.F. Sproull, *Principles of Interactive Computer Graphics*, McGraw-Hill, New York, 1973.

Ngu07   Nguyen, H. (Ed), *GPU Gems 3*, Addison-Wesley Professional, Boston, MA, 2007.

Nie97   Nielson, G.M., H. Hagen, and H. Muller, *Scientific Visualization: Overviews, Methodologies, and Techniques*, IEEE Computer Society, Piscataway, NJ, 1997.

Ope05   OpenGL Architecture Review Board, *OpenGL Reference Manual*, Fourth Edition, Addison-Wesley, Reading, MA, 2005.

OSF89   Open Software Foundation, *OSF/Motif Style Guide,* Prentice-Hall, Englewood Cliffs, NJ, 1989.

Ost94   Osterhaut, J., *Tcl and the Tk Toolkit,* Addison-Wesley, Reading, MA, 1994.

Pap81   Papert, S., *LOGO: A Language for Learning*, Creative Computer Press, Middletown, NJ, 1981.

Pav95   Pavlidis, T., *Interactive Computer Graphics in X*, PWS Publishing, Boston, MA, 1995.

Per85   Perlin, K. "An Image Synthesizer," Computer Graphics, 19(3), 287–297, 1985.

Per89   Perlin, K., and E. Hoffert, "Hypertexture," *Computer Graphics*, 23(3), 253–262, 1989.

Per02   Perlon, K., "Improved Noise," Computer Graphics, 35(3), 2002.

Pei88   Peitgen, H.O., and S. Saupe (Eds.), *The Science of Fractal Images*, Springer-Verlag, New York, 1988.

Pha05   Pharr, M., and R. Fernando (Eds.), *GPU Gems 2: Programming Techniques for High-Performance Graphics and General-Purpose Computation*, Addison-Wesley Professional, Boston, MA, 2005.

PHI89   PHIGS+ Committee, "PHIGS+ Functional Description, Revision 3.0," *Computer Graphics,* 22(3), 125–218, July 1989.

Pho75   Phong, B.T., "Illumination for Computer Generated Scenes," *Communications of the ACM*, 18(6), 311–317, 1975.

Por84   Porter, T., and T. Duff, "Compositing Digital Images," *Computer Graphics*, 18(3), 253–259, 1984.

Pra78   Pratt, W.K., *Digital Image Processing*, Wiley, New York, 1978.

Pru90   Prusinkiewicz, P., and A. Lindenmayer, *The Algorithmic Beauty of Plants*, Springer-Verlag, Berlin, 1990.

Ree83   Reeves, W.T., "Particle Systems—A Technique for Modeling a Class of Fuzzy Objects," *Computer Graphics*, 17(3), 359–376, 1983.

Rei05   Reinhard, Erik, G. Ward, S. Pattanaik, and P. Debevec, *High Dynamic Range Imaging: Acquisition, Display, and Image-Based Lighting*, Morgan Kaufmann, San Francisco, 2005.

Rey87   Reynolds, C.W., "Flocks, Herds, and Schools: A Distributed Behavioral Model," *Computer Graphics*, 21(4), 25–34, 1987.

Rie81   Riesenfeld, R.F., "Homogeneous Coordinates and Projective Planes in Computer Graphics," *IEEE Computer Graphics and Applications*, 1(1), 50–56, 1981.

Rob63   Roberts, L.G., "Homogenous Matrix Representation and Manipulation of N-Dimensional Constructs," MS-1505. MIT Lincoln Laboratory, Lexington, MA, 1963.

Rog98   Rogers, D.F., *Procedural Elements for Computer Graphics,* Second Edition, McGraw-Hill, New York, 1998.

Rog90   Rogers, D.F., and J.A. Adams, *Mathematical Elements for Computer Graphics,* McGraw-Hill, New York, 1990.

Rog00   Rogers, D.F., *An Introduction to NURBS: With Historical Perspective,* Morgan Kaufmann, San Francisco, CA, 2000.

Ros09   Rost, R.J., B. Licea-Kane, D. Ginsberg, and J.M. Kessenich, *OpenGL Shading Language*, Third Edition, Addison-Wesley, Reading, MA, 2009.

Sch88   Schiefler, R.W., J. Gettys, and R. Newman, *X Window System,* Digital Press, Woburn, MA, 1988.

Schr06 Schroeder, W., K. Martin, and B. Lorensen, *The Visualization Toolkit: An Object-Oriented Approach to 3D Graphics,* Fourth Edition, Kitware, Clifton Park, NY, 2006.

Sei96   Seitz, S.M., and C.R. Dyer, "View Morphing," *Computer Graphics*, 21–30, 1996.

Seg92   Segal, M., and K. Akeley, *The OpenGL Graphics System: A Specification,* Version 1.0, Silicon Graphics, Mountain View, CA, 1992.

Shi03   Shirley, P., R.K. Morley, and K. Morley, *Realistic Ray Tracing*, Second Edition, A K Peters, 2003.

Shi05   Shirley, P., M. Ashikhmin, M. Gleicher, S. Marschner, E. Reinhard, K. Sung, W. Thompson, and P. Willemsen, *Fundamentals of Computer Graphics*, Second Edition, A K Peters, 2005.

Sho85   Shoemake, K., "Animating Rotation with Quaternion Curves," *Computer Graphics*, 19(3), 245–254, 1985.

Shr10   Shreiner, D., *OpenGL Programming Guide*, Seventh Edition, Addison-Wesley, Reading, MA, 2010.

Sie81   Siegel, R., and J. Howell, *Thermal Radiation Heat Transfer,* Hemisphere, Washington, DC, 1981.

Sil89   Sillion, F.X., and C. Puech, "A General Two-Pass Method Integrating Specular and Diffuse Reflection," *Computer Graphics,* 22(3), 335–344, 1989.

Smi84   Smith, A.R., "Plants, Fractals and Formal Languages," *Computer Graphics,* 18(3), 1–10, 1984.

Sta03   Stam, J., and C. Loop, "Quad/Triangle Subdivision," *Computer Graphics Forum, 22,* 1–7, 2003.

Str93   Strang, G., *Introduction to Linear Alegbra,* Wellesley-Cambridge Press, Wellesley, MA, 1993.

Suf07   Suffern, K., *Ray Tracing from the Ground Up,* A K Peters, 2007.

Sut63   Sutherland, I.E., *Sketchpad, A Man–Machine Graphical Communication System, SJCC*, 329, Spartan Books, Baltimore, MD, 1963.

Sut74a   Sutherland, I.E., and G.W. Hodgeman, "Reentrant Polygon Clipping," *Communications of the ACM*, 17, 32–42, 1974.

Sut74b   Sutherland, I.E., R.F. Sproull, and R.A. Schumacker, "A Characterization of Ten Hidden-Surface Algorithms," *Computer Surveys*, 6(1), 1–55, 1974.

Swo00   Swoizral, H., K. Rushforth, and M. Deering, *The Java 3D API Specification,* Second Edition, Addison-Wesley, Reading, MA, 2000.

Tor67   Torrance, K.E., and E.M. Sparrow, "Theory for Off–Specular Reflection from Roughened Surfaces," *Journal of the Optical Society of America,* 57(9), 1105–1114, 1967.

Tor96   Torborg, J., and J.T. Kajiya, "Talisman: Commodity Realtime 3D Graphics for the PC," *Computer Graphics*, 353–363, 1996.

Tuf83   Tufte, E.R., *The Visual Display of Quantitative Information*, Graphics Press, Cheshire, CT, 1983.

Tuf90   Tufte, E.R., *Envisioning Information*, Graphics Press, Cheshire, CT, 1990.

Tuf97   Tufte, E.R., *Visual Explanations*, Graphics Press, Cheshire, CT, 1997.

Ups89   Upstill, S., *The RenderMan Companion: A Programmer's Guide to Realistic Computer Graphics,* Addison-Wesley, Reading, MA, 1989.

Van94   Van Gelder, A., and J. Wilhelms, "Topological Considerations in Isosurface Generation," *ACM Transactions on Graphics,* 13(4), 337–375, 1994.

War94   Ward, G., "The RADIANCE Lighting Simulation and Rendering System," *Computer Graphics*, July 1994.

War03   Warren, J., and H. Weimer, *Subdivision Methods for Geometric Design,* Morgan Kaufmann, San Francisco, 2003.

War04   Warren, J., and S. Schaefer, "A Factored Approach to Subdivision Surfaces," *IEEE Computer Graphics and Applications*, 24(3), 74-81, 2004.

Wat92   Watt, A., and M. Watt, *Advanced Animation and Rendering Techniques,* Addison-Wesley, Wokingham, England, 1992.

Wat98   Watt, A., and F. Policarpo, *The Computer Image*, Addison-Wesley, Wokingham, England, 1998.

Wat00   Watt, A., *3D Computer Graphics*, Third Edition, Addison-Wesley, Wokingham, England, 2000.

Wat02   Watkins, A., *The Maya 4 Handbook*, Charles River Media, Hingham, MA, 2002.

Wer94   Wernecke, J., *The Inventor Mentor*, Addison-Wesley, Reading, MA, 1994.

Wes90   Westover, L., "Footprint Evaluation for Volume Rendering," *Computer Graphics*, 24(4), 367–376, 1990.

Whi80   Whitted, T., "An Improved Illumination Model for Shaded Display," *Communications of ACM*, 23(6), 343–348, 1980.

Wit94a   Witkin, A.P., and P.S. Heckbert, "Using Particles to Sample and Control Implicit Surfaces," *Computer Graphics,* 28(3), 269–277, 1994.

Wit94b   Witkin, A. (Ed.), *An Introduction to Physically Based Modeling,* Course Notes, *SIGGRAPH 94,* 1994.

Wol91   Wolfram, S., *Mathematica*, Addison-Wesley, Reading, MA, 1991.

Wri11   Wright, R.S., Jr., H. Haemel, G. Sellers, and B. Lipchak, *OpenGL Super-bible*, Fifth Edition, Addison-Wesley, Boston, MA, 2011.

Wys82   Wyszecki, G., and W.S. Stiles, *Color Science*, Wiley, New York, 1982.

OPENGL FUNCTION INDEX

This index includes the appearances of those OpenGL functions that are used in the text. A complete description of OpenGL functions is contained in the *OpenGL Programming Guide* and the GLUT documentation. The functions are grouped according to their inclusion in the GL or GLUT libraries. Functions with multiple forms, such as `glUniform`, are listed once. Appendix D contains a synopsis of these functions.

SUBJECT INDEX

Color Plate 1 Image of sun object created using NURBS surfaces and rendered with bump mapping.

(Courtesy of Fulldome Project, University of New Mexico.)

Color Plate 2 Wire-frame representation of sun object surfaces.

(Courtesy of Fulldome Project, University of New Mexico.)

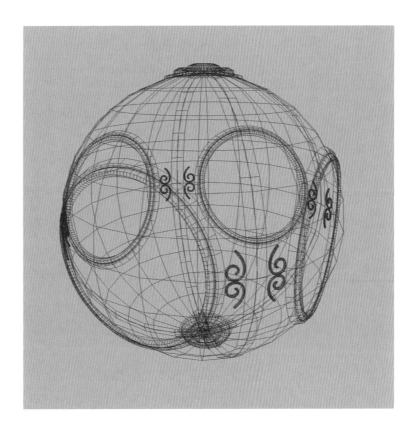

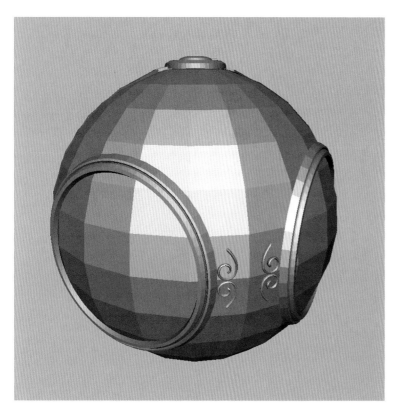

Color Plate 3 Flat-shaded polygonal rendering of sun object.

(Courtesy of Fulldome Project, University of New Mexico.)

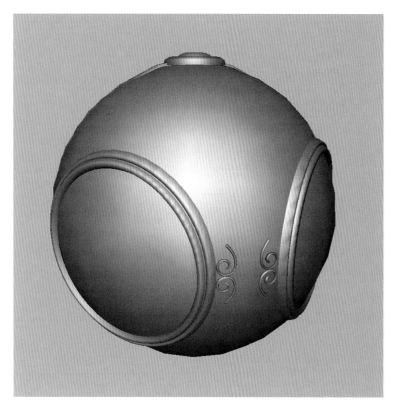

Color Plate 4 Smooth-shaded polygonal rendering of sun object.

(Courtesy of Fulldome Project, University of New Mexico.)

Color Plate 5 Wire-frame of NURBS representation of sun object showing the high number of polygons used in rendering the NURBS surfaces.

(Courtesy of Fulldome Project, University of New Mexico.)

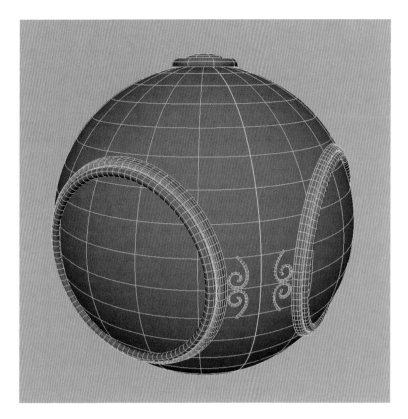

Color Plate 6 Rendering of sun object showing bump map.

(Courtesy of Fulldome Project, University of New Mexico.)

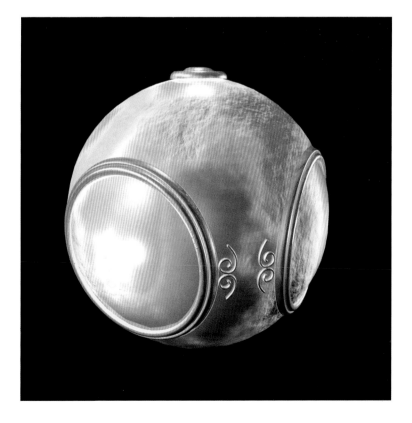

Color Plate 7 Rendering of sun object with an environment map.

(Courtesy of Fulldome Project, University of New Mexico.)

Color Plate 8 Rendering of a small part of the sun object with an environment map. (Courtesy of Fulldome Project, University of New Mexico.)

(a) Without antialiasing

(b) With antialiasing

Color Plate 9 Axonometric view from outside of temple.

(Courtesy of Richard Nordhaus, Architect, Albuquerque, NM.)

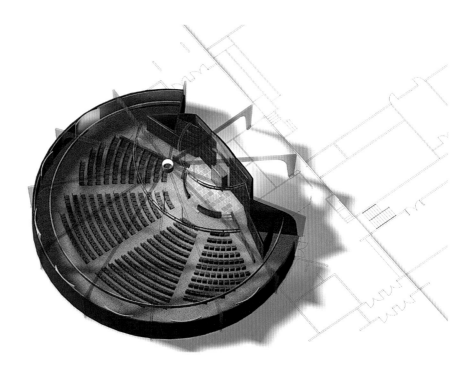

Color Plate 10 Perspective view of interior of temple.

(Courtesy of Richard Nordhaus, Architect, Albuquerque, NM.)

Color Plate 11 Cartoon-shaded teapot.

(Courtesy of Ed Angel, University of New Mexico.)

Color Plate 12 Reflection map from a color cube on teapot.

(Courtesy of Ed Angel, University of New Mexico.)

Color Plate 13 Interface for animation using Maya.

(Courtesy of Hue Walker, ARTS Lab, University of New Mexico.)

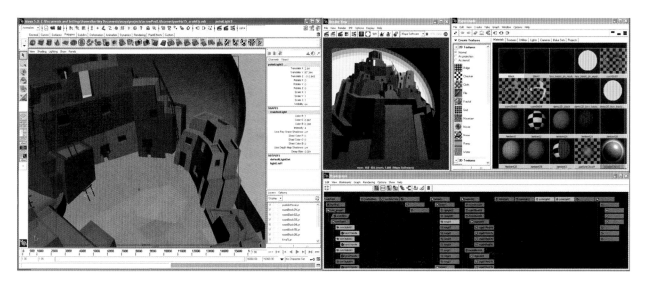

Color Plate 14 (a) Wire-frame model of a wave.

(Courtesy of Sony Pictures Entertainment.)

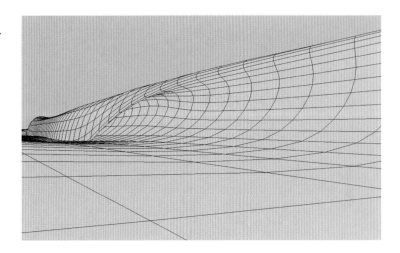

Color Plate 14 (b) White water and spray created by particle system.

(Courtesy of Sony Pictures Entertainment.)

Color Plate 14 (c) Final composited image from "Surf's Up."

(Courtesy of Sony Pictures Entertainment.)

Color Plate 15 Rendering using ray tracer.

(Courtesy of Patrick McCormick.)

Color Plate 16 Radiosity rendering showing soft shadows and diffuse–diffuse reflections.

(Courtesy of A. Van Pernis, K. Rasche, R. Geist, Clemson University.)

Color Plate 17 Array of Utah teapots with different material properties.

(Courtesy of SGI.)

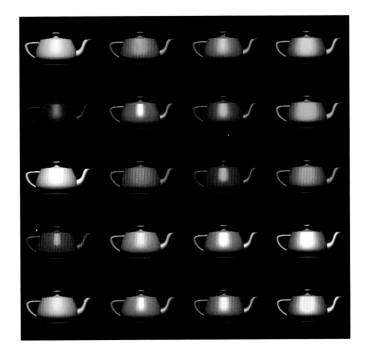

Color Plate 18 Phong-Blinn shaded teapots.   (Courtesy of Ed Angel, University of New Mexico.)

(a) Using per-vertex lighting

(b) Using per-fragment lighting

(c) Area near highlight

(d) Area near highlight

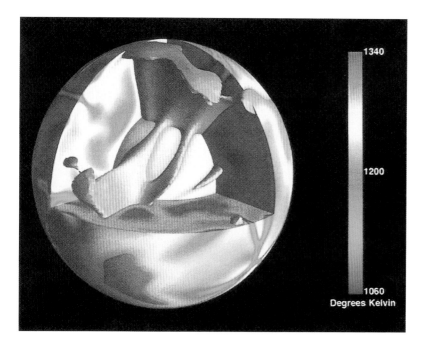

Color Plate 19 Fluid dynamics of the mantle of the Earth. Pseudocolor mapping of temperatures and isotemperature surface.

(Courtesy of James Painter, Los Alamos National Laboratory.)

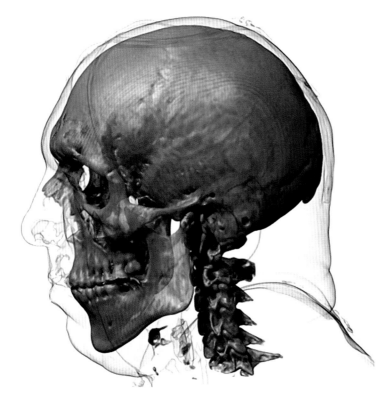

Color Plate 20 Volume rendering of CT data.

(Courtesy of J. Kniss, G. Kindlmann, C. Hansen, Scientific Computing and Imaging Institute, University of Utah.)

Color Plate 21 RGB color cube.

(Courtesy of University of New Mexico.)

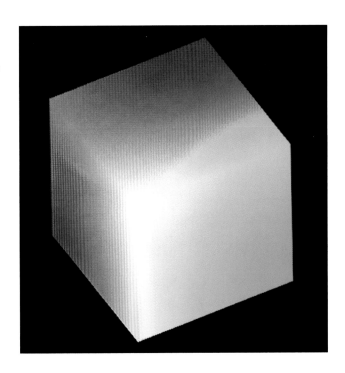

Color Plate 22 Avatar representing a patient who is being diagnosed and treated by a remotely located health professional (inset).

(Courtesy of Tom Caudell, Visualization Laboratory, Albuquerque High Performance Computing Center, University of New Mexico.)

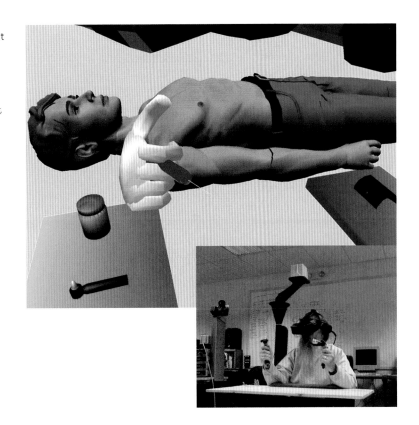

Color Plate 23 One frame from Pixar's "Geri's Game" showing refraction through reflections on Geri's glasses.

(Courtesy of Pixar Animation Studios.)

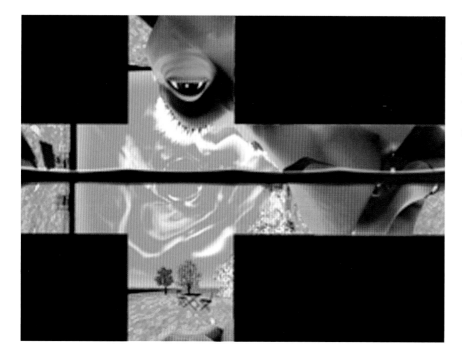

Color Plate 24 Reflection map from environment computed from the center of the lens on Geri's glasses. The reflection map is then mapped to the glasses as part of the rendering process.

(Courtesy of Pixar Animation Studios.)

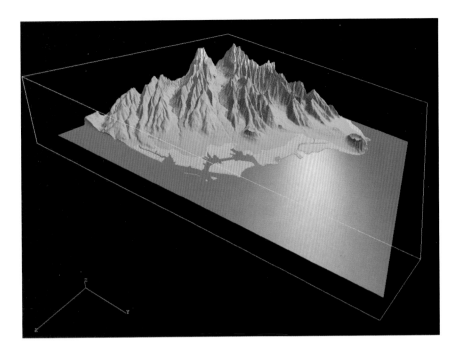

Color Plate 25 Elevation data for Honolulu, Hawaii, displayed using a quadmesh to define control points for a Bezier surface.

(Courtesy of Brian Wylie, University of New Mexico and Sandia National Laboratories.)

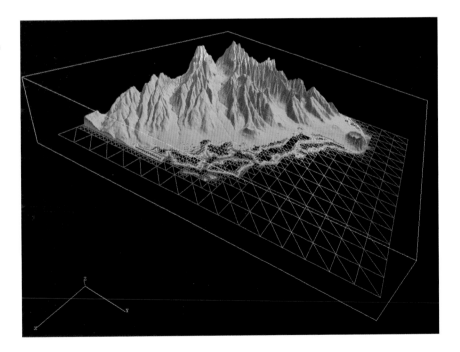

Color Plate 26 Wire frame of the quadmesh showing lower resolution in flat areas.

(Courtesy of Brian Wylie, University of New Mexico and Sandia National Laboratories.)

Color Plate 27 Rendering of hierarchical robot figure.

(Courtesy of University of New Mexico.)

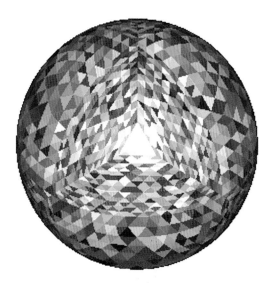

Color Plate 28 Sphere computed by recursive subdivision of tetrahedrons; triangle colors assigned randomly.

(Courtesy of University of New Mexico.)

Color Plate 29 Shadows from a cube onto ground. Computed by two passes over the data with viewpoint shifted between viewer and light source.

(Courtesy of University of New Mexico.)

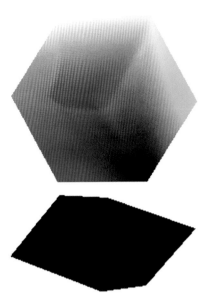

Color Plate 30 Visualization of thermohaline flows in the Carribean Sea using streamtubes colored by water temperature.

(Courtesy of David Munich, High Performance Computing Center, University of New Mexico.)

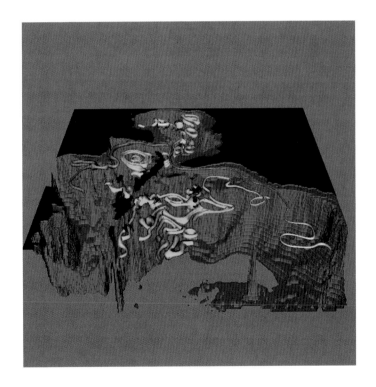

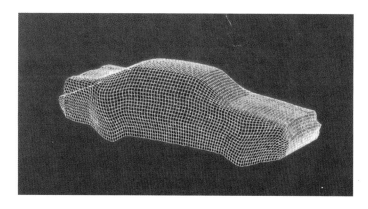

(a) Mesh of particles

b) Model of Lexus with surface

(c) Wind blowing mesh off Lexus

(d) Mesh blown away from Lexus